Contents

Preface

Digital logic is concerned with the interconnection among digital components and modules and is a term used to denote the design and analysis of digital systems. The best known example of a digital system is the general purpose digital computer. This book presents the basic concepts used in the design and analysis of digital systems and introduces the principles of digital computer organization and design. It provides various methods and techniques suitable for a variety of digital system design applications. It covers all aspects of digital systems from the electronic gate circuits to the complex structure of microcomputer systems.

Chapters 1 through 6 present digital logic design techniques from the *classical* point of view. Boolean algebra and truth tables are used for the analysis and design of combinational circuits and state transition techniques for the analysis and design of sequential circuits. Chapters 7 through 12 present digital system design methods from the *register-transfer* point of view. The digital system is decomposed into register subunits and the system is specified with a list of register-transfer statements that describe the operational transfers among the information stored in registers. The register-transfer method is used for the analysis and design of processor units, control units, a computer central processor, and for describing the internal operations of microprocessors and microcomputers. Chapter 13 deals with the electronics of digital circuits and presents the most common integrated circuit digital logic families.

The components used to construct digital systems are manufactured in integrated circuit form. Integrated circuits contain a large amount of interconnected digital circuits within a single small package. Medium scale integration (MSI) devices provide digital functions and large scale integration (LSI) devices provide complete computer modules. It is very important for the logic designer to be familiar with the various digital components encountered in integrated circuit form. For this reason, many MSI and LSI circuits are introduced throughout the book and their logical function fully explained. The use of integrated circuits in the design of digital systems is illustrated by means of examples in the text and in problems at the end of the chapters.

This book was originally planned as a second edition to the author's *Computer Logic Design* (Prentice-Hall, 1972). Because of the amount of new material added and the extensive revisions that have taken place, it seems more appropriate to adopt a new title for the present text. About one third of the text is material that appears in the previous book. The other two thirds constitutes new or revised information. The underlying factors for the revisions and additions arise from developments in the digital electronics technology. Great emphasis is given to MSI and LSI circuits and to design methods using integrated circuits. The book covers various LSI components of the bit-slice and microcomputer variety. It presents applications of the read only memory (ROM) and programmable logic array (PLA). Moreover, further developments in the register transfer method of design mandated a complete rewriting of the second half of the book.

Chapter 1 presents various binary systems suitable for representing information in digital components. The binary number system is explained and binary codes are illustrated to show the representation of decimal and alphanumeric information. Binary logic is introduced from an intuitive point of view before proceeding with a formal definition of Boolean algebra.

The basic postulates and theorems of Boolean algebra are found in Chapter 2. The correlation between a Boolean expression and its equivalent interconnection of gates is emphasized. All possible logic operations for two variables are investigated and from that, the most useful logic gates are derived. The characteristics of digital gates available in integrated circuit form are presented early in this chapter but a more detailed analysis describing the internal construction of the gates is left for the last chapter.

Chapter 3 supplies the map and tabulation methods for simplifying Boolean functions. The map method is used to simplify digital circuits constructed with AND, OR, NAND, NOR, and wired-logic gates. The various simplification procedures are summarized in tabular form for easy reference.

Design and analysis procedures for combinational circuits are provided in Chapter 4. Some basic components used in the design of digital systems, such as adders and code converters, are introduced as design or analysis examples. The chapter investigates possible implementations using multilevel NAND and NOR combinational circuits.

Chapter 5 deals with combinational logic MSI and LSI components. Often used functions such as parallel adders, decoders, and multiplexers are explained, and their use in the design of combinational circuits is illustrated with examples. The read only memory (ROM) and programmable logic array (PLA) are introduced and their usefulness in the design of complex combinational circuits is demonstrated.

Chapter 6 outlines various methods for the design and analysis of clocked sequential circuits. The chapter starts by presenting various types of flip-flops and the way they are triggered. The state diagram, state table, and state equations are shown to be convenient tools for analyzing sequential circuits. The design methods presented transform the sequential circuit to a set of Boolean functions that specify the input logic to the circuit flip-flops. The input Boolean functions are derived from the excitation table and are simplified by means of maps.

In Chapter 7, a variety of registers, shift-registers, and counters similar to those available in integrated circuit packages is presented. The operation of the random access memory (RAM) is also explained. The digital functions introduced in this chapter are the basic building blocks from which more complex digital systems are constructed.

Chapter 8 introduces the register-transfer method for describing digital systems. It shows how to express in symbolic form the operation sequence among the registers of a digital system. Symbols are defined for interregister transfer, arithmetic, logic, and shift microoperations. The different data types that are stored in computer registers are covered in detail. Some typical examples are used to show how computer instructions are represented in binary coded form and how the operations specified by instructions can be expressed with register-transfer statements. The chapter concludes with the design of a very simple computer to demonstrate the register-transfer method of digital system design.

Chapter 9 is concerned with the processor unit of digital computers. It discusses alternatives for organizing a processor unit with buses or scratchpad memory. A typical arithmetic logic unit (ALU) is presented and a procedure is developed for the design of any other ALU configuration. Other components commonly found in processors, such as shifters and status registers, are also presented. The design of a general purpose accumulator register is undertaken, starting from a specified set of register-transfer operations and culminating in a logic diagram.

Four methods of control logic design are introduced in Chapter 10. Two of the methods constitute a hard-wired control. The other two introduce the concept of microprogramming and how to design a controller with the programmable logic array (PLA). The four methods are demonstrated by means of examples that show the development of design algorithms and the procedure for obtaining the control circuits for the system. The last section introduces an LSI microprogram sequencer and shows how it can be used to design a microprogram control unit.

Chapter 11 is devoted to the design of a small digital computer. The registers in the computer are defined and a set of computer instructions is specified. The computer description is formalized with register-transfer statements that specify the microoperations among the registers as well as the control functions that initiate these microoperations. It is then shown that the set of microoperations can be used to design the data processor part of the computer. The control functions in the list of register-transfer statements supply the information for the design of the control unit. The control unit for the computer is designed by three different methods: hard-wired control, PLA control, and microprogram control.

Chapter 12 focuses on various LSI components that form a microcomputer system. The organization of a typical microprocessor is described and its internal operation explained. A typical set of instructions for the microprocessor is presented and various addressing modes are explained. The operation of a stack and the handling of subroutines and interrupts is covered from the hardware point of view. The chapter also illustrates the connection of memory chips to a micro-processor bus system and the operation of various interface units that communicate with input-output devices. It concludes with a description of the direct memory access mode of transfer.

Chapter 13 details the electronic circuits of the basic gate in seven integrated circuit logic families. This final chapter should be considered as an appendix and can be omitted if desired. Chapter 13 assumes prior knowledge of basic electronics, but there is no specific prerequisite for the rest of the book.

Every chapter includes a set of problems and a list of references. Answers to selected problems appear in the Appendix to provide an aid for the student and to help the independent reader. A *solutions manual* is available for the instructor from the publisher.

The book is suitable for a course in digital logic and computer design in an electrical or computer engineering department. It can also be used in a computer science department for a course in computer organization. Parts of the book can be used in a variety of ways. (1) As a first course in digital logic or switching circuits by covering Chapters 1 through 7 and possibly Chapter 13; (2) As a second course in digital computer logic with a prerequisite of a course in basic switching circuits by covering Chapter 5 and Chapters 7 through 12; (3) As an introduction to the hardware of microprocessors and microcomputers by covering Chapters 8 through 12.

In conclusion, I would like to explain the philosophy underlying the material presented in this book. The classical method has been predominant in the past for describing the operations of digital circuits. With the advent of integrated circuits, and especially the introduction of microcomputer LSI components, the classical method seems to be far removed from practical applications. Although the classical method for describing complex digital systems is not directly applicable, the basic concepts of Boolean algebra, combinational logic, and sequential logic procedures, are still important for understanding the internal construction of many digital functions. On the other hand, the register-transfer method provides a better representation for describing the operations among the various modules in digital systems. It is concerned with the transfer of bit strings in parallel and may be considered to be one level higher in the hierarchy of digital system representation. The transition from the classical to the register-transfer method is made in the book by way of integrated circuit MSI functions. Chapters 5 and 7 cover many digital functions which are available in integrated circuits. Their operation is explained in terms of gates and flip-flops that make up the particular digital circuit. Each MSI circuit is considered as a functional unit that performs a particular operation. This operation is then described in the register-transfer method of notation. Thus, the analysis and design of registers and other digital functions is done by means of the classical method but the use of these functions in describing the operations of a digital system is specified by means of register-transfer state-ments. The register-transfer method is then used to define computer instructions, to express digital operations in concise form, to demonstrate the organization of digital computers, and to specify the hardware components for the design of digital systems.

I wish to express my thanks to Dr. John L. Fike for reviewing the original manuscript and to Professor Victor Payse for pointing out corrections while teaching a course using the manuscript. Most of the typing was done by Mrs. Lucy Albert and her skilled help is gratefully appreciated. My greatest thanks go to my wife for all the suggestions she made for improving the readability of the text and for her encouragement and support during the preparation of this book.

M. MORRIS MANO

Binary
Systems

1

1-1 DIGITAL COMPUTERS AND DIGITAL SYSTEMS

Digital computers have made possible many scientific, industrial, and commercial advances that would have been unattainable otherwise. Our space program would have been impossible without real-time, continuous computer monitoring, and many business enterprises function efficiently only with the aid of automatic data processing. Computers are used in scientific calculations, commercial and business data processing, air traffic control, space guidance, the educational field, and many other areas. The most striking property of a digital computer is its generality. It can follow a sequence of instructions, called a *program*, that operates on given data. The user can specify and change programs and/or data according to the specific need. As a result of this flexibility, general-purpose digital computers can perform a wide variety of information-processing tasks.

The general-purpose digital computer is the best-known example of a digital system. Other examples include telephone switching exchanges, digital voltmeters, frequency counters, calculating machines, and teletype machines. Characteristic of a digital system is its manipulation of *discrete elements* of information. Such discrete elements may be electric impulses, the decimal digits, the letters of an alphabet, arithmetic operations, punctuation marks, or any other set of meaningful symbols. The juxtaposition of discrete elements of information represents a quantity of information. For example, the letters *d*, *o*, and *g* form the word *dog*. The digits 237 form a number. Thus, a sequence of discrete elements forms a language, that is, a discipline that conveys information. Early digital computers were used mostly for numerical computations. In this case the discrete elements used are the digits. From this application, the term *digital computer* has emerged. A more appropriate name for a digital computer would be a "discrete information processing system."

Discrete elements of information are represented in a digital system by physical quantities called *signals*. Electrical signals such as voltages and currents

1

are the most common. The signals in all present-day electronic digital systems have only two discrete values and are said to be *binary*. The digital-system designer is restricted to the use of binary signals because of the lower reliability of many-valued electronic circuits. In other words, a circuit with ten states, using one discrete voltage value for each state, can be designed, but it would possess a very low reliability of operation. In contrast, a transistor circuit that is either on or off has two possible signal values and can be constructed to be extremely reliable. Because of this physical restriction of components, and because human logic tends to be binary, digital systems that are constrained to take discrete values are further constrained to take binary values.

Discrete quantities of information emerge either from the nature of the process or may be purposely quantized from a continuous process. For example, a payroll schedule is an inherently discrete process that contains employee names, social security numbers, weekly salaries, income taxes, etc. An employee's paycheck is processed using discrete data values such as letters of the alphabet (names), digits (salary), and special symbols such as $. On the other hand, a research scientist may observe a continous process but record only specific quantities in tabular form. The scientist is thus quantizing his continuous data. Each number in his table is a discrete element of information.

Many physical systems can be described mathematically by differential equations whose solutions as a function of time give the complete mathematical behavior of the process. An *analog computer* performs a direct *simulation* of a physical system. Each section of the computer is the analog of some particular portion of the process under study. The variables in the analog computer are represented by continous signals, usually electric voltages that vary with time. The signal variables are considered analogous to those of the process and behave in the same manner. Thus measurements of the analog voltage can be substituted for variables of the process. The term *analog signal* is sometimes substituted for *continuous signal* because "analog computer" has come to mean a computer that manipulates continuous variables.

To simulate a physical process in a digital computer, the quantities must be quantized. When the variables of the process are presented by real-time continuous signals, the latter are quantized by an analog-to-digital conversion device. A physical system whose behavior is described by mathematical equations is simulated in a digital computer by means of numerical methods. When the problem to be processed is inherently discrete, as in commercial applications, the digital computer manipulates the variables in their natural form.

A block diagram of the digital computer is shown in Fig. 1-1. The memory unit stores programs as well as input, output, and intermediate data. The processor unit performs arithmetic and other data-processing tasks as specified by a program. The control unit supervises the flow of information between the various units. The control unit retrieves the instructions, one by one, from the program which is stored in memory. For each instruction, the control unit informs the processor to execute the operation specified by the instruction. Both program and data are

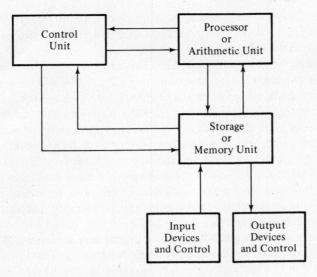

Figure 1-1 Block diagram of a digital computer

stored in memory. The control unit supervises the program instructions, and the processor manipulates the data as specified by the program.

The program and data prepared by the user are transferred into the memory unit by means of an input device such as punch-card reader or a teletypewriter. An output device, such as a printer, receives the result of the computations and the printed results are presented to the user. The input and output devices are special digital systems driven by electromechanical parts and controlled by electronic digital circuits.

An electronic calculator is a digital system similar to a digital computer, with the input device being a keyboard and the output device a numerical display. Instructions are entered in the calculator by means of the function keys, such as plus and minus. Data are entered through the numeric keys. Results are displayed directly in numeric form. Some calculators come close to resembling a digital computer by having printing capabilities and programmable facilities. A digital computer, however, is a more powerful device than a calculator. A digital computer can accommodate many other input and output devices; it can perform not only arithmetic computations but logical operations as well and can be programmed to make decisions based on internal and external conditions.

A digital computer is an interconnection of digital modules. To understand the operation of each digital module, it is necessary to have a basic knowledge of digital systems and their general behavior. The first half of this book deals with digital systems in general to provide the background necessary for their design. The second half of the book discusses the various modules of the digital computer, their operation and design. The operational characteristics of the memory unit are explained in Chapter 7. The organization and design of the processor unit is undertaken in Chapter 9. Various methods for designing the control unit are introduced in Chapter 10. The organization and design of a small, complete digital computer is presented in Chapter 11.

A processor, when combined with the control unit, forms a component referred to as a *central processor unit* or CPU. A CPU enclosed in small integrated-circuit package is called a *microprocessor*. The memory unit, as well as the part that controls the interface between the microprocessor and the input and output devices, may be enclosed within the microprocessor package or may be available in other small integrated-circuit packages. A CPU combined with memory and interface control to form a small-size computer is called a *microcomputer*. The availability of microcomputer components has revolutionized the digital system design technology, giving the designer the freedom to create structures that were previously uneconomical. The various components of a microcomputer system are presented in Chapter 12.

It has already been mentioned that a digital computer manipulates discrete elements of information and that these elements are represented in the binary form. Operands used for calculations may be expressed in the binary number system. Other discrete elements, including the decimal digits, are represented in binary codes. Data processing is carried out by means of binary logic elements using binary signals. Quantities are stored in binary storage elements. The purpose of this chapter is to introduce the various binary concepts as a frame of reference for further detailed study in the suceeding chapters.

1-2   BINARY NUMBERS

A decimal number such as 7392 represents a quantity equal to 7 thousands plus 3 hundreds, plus 9 tens, plus 2 units. The thousands, hundreds, etc., are powers of 10 implied by the position of the coefficients. To be more exact, 7392 should be written as:

$$7 \times 10^3 + 3 \times 10^2 + 9 \times 10^1 + 2 \times 10^0$$

However, the convention is to write only the coefficients and from their position deduce the necessary powers of 10. In general, a number with a decimal point is represented by a series of coefficients as follows:

$$a_5 a_4 a_3 a_2 a_1 a_0 \cdot a_{-1} a_{-2} a_{-3}$$

The a_j coefficients are one of the ten digits (0, 1, 2, . . . , 9), and the subscript value j gives the place value and, hence, the power of 10 by which the coefficient must be multiplied.

$$10^5 a_5 + 10^4 a_4 + 10^3 a_3 + 10^2 a_2 + 10^1 a_1 + 10^0 a_0 + 10^{-1} a_{-1}$$
$$+ 10^{-2} a_{-2} + 10^{-3} a_{-3}$$

The decimal number system is said to be of *base*, or *radix*, 10 because it uses ten digits and the coefficients are multiplied by powers of 10. The *binary* system is a different number system. The coefficients of the binary numbers system have two possible values: 0 and 1. Each coefficient a_j is multiplied by 2^j. For example, the decimal equivalent of the binary number 11010.11 is 26.75, as shown from the multiplication of the coefficients by powers of 2:

$$1 \times 2^4 + 1 \times 2^3 + 0 \times 2^2 + 1 \times 2^1 + 0 \times 2^0 + 1 \times 2^{-1}$$
$$+ 1 \times 2^{-2} = 26.75$$

In general, a number expressed in base-r system has coefficients multiplied by powers of r:

$$a_n \cdot r^n + a_{n-1} \cdot r^{n-1} + \cdots + a_2 \cdot r^2 + a_1 \cdot r + a_0$$
$$+ a_{-1} \cdot r^{-1} + a_{-2} \cdot r^{-2} + \cdots + a_{-m} \cdot r^{-m}$$

The coefficients a_j range in value from 0 to $r - 1$. To distinguish between numbers of different bases, we enclose the coefficients in parentheses and write a subscript equal to the base used (except sometimes for decimal numbers, where the content makes it obvious that it is decimal). An example of a base-5 number is:

$$(4021.2)_5 = 4 \times 5^3 + 0 \times 5^2 + 2 \times 5^1 + 1 \times 5^0 + 2 \times 5^{-1} = (511.4)_{10}$$

Note that coefficient values for base 5 can be only 0, 1, 2, 3, and 4.

It is customary to borrow the needed r digits for the coefficients from the decimal system when the base of the number is less than 10. The letters of the alphabet are used to supplement the ten decimal digits when the base of the number is greater than 10. For example, in the *hexadecimal* (base 16) number system, the first ten digits are borrowed from the decimal system. The letters A, B, C, D, E, and F are used for digits 10, 11, 12, 13, 14, and 15, respectively. An example of a hexadecimal number is:

$$(B65F)_{16} = 11 \times 16^3 + 6 \times 16^2 + 5 \times 16 + 15 = (46687)_{10}$$

The first 16 numbers in the decimal, binary, octal, and hexadecimal systems are listed in Table 1-1.

Arithmetic operations with numbers in base r follow the same rules as for decimal numbers. When other than the familiar base 10 is used, one must be careful to use only the r allowable digits. Examples of addition, subtraction, and multiplication of two binary numbers are shown below:

augend:	101101	minuend:	101101	multiplicand:	1011
addend:	+100111	subtrahend:	−100111	multiplier:	× 101
sum:	1010100	difference:	000110		1011
					0000
					1011
				product:	110111

TABLE 1-1 Numbers with different bases

Decimal (base 10)	Binary (base 2)	Octal (base 8)	Hexadecimal (base 16)
00	0000	00	0
01	0001	01	1
02	0010	02	2
03	0011	03	3
04	0100	04	4
05	0101	05	5
06	0110	06	6
07	0111	07	7
08	1000	10	8
09	1001	11	9
10	1010	12	A
11	1011	13	B
12	1100	14	C
13	1101	15	D
14	1110	16	E
15	1111	17	F

The sum of two binary numbers is calculated by the same rules as in decimal, except that the digits of the sum in any significant position can be only 0 or 1. Any "carry" obtained in a given significant position is used by the pair of digits one significant position higher. The subtraction is slightly more complicated. The rules are still the same as in decimal, except that the "borrow" in a given significant position adds 2 to a minuend digit. (A borrow in the decimal system adds 10 to a minuend digit.) Multiplication is very simple. The multiplier digits are always 1 or 0. Therefore, the partial products are equal either to the multiplicand or to 0.

1-3 NUMBER BASE CONVERSIONS

A binary number can be converted to decimal by forming the sum of the powers of 2 of those coefficients whose value is 1. For example:

$$(1010.011)_2 = 2^3 + 2^1 + 2^{-2} + 2^{-3} = (10.375)_{10}$$

The binary number has four 1's and the decimal equivalent is found from the sum of four powers of 2. Similarly, a number expressed in base r can be converted to its decimal equivalent by multiplying each coefficient with the corresponding power of r and adding. The following is an example of octal-to-decimal conversion:

$$(630.4)_8 = 6 \times 8^2 + 3 \times 8 + 4 \times 8^{-1} = (408.5)_{10}$$

The conversion from decimal to binary or to any other base-r system is more convenient if the number is separated into an *integer part* and a *fraction part* and the conversion of each part done separately. The conversion of an *integer* from decimal to binary is best explained by example.

EXAMPLE 1-1: Convert decimal 41 to binary. First, 41 is divided by 2 to give an integer quotient of 20 and a remainder of $\frac{1}{2}$. The quotient is again divided by 2 to give a new quotient and remainder. This process is continued until the integer quotient becomes 0. The *coefficients* of the desired binary number are obtained from the *remainders* as follows:

integer quotient		*remainder*	*coefficient*
$\dfrac{41}{2} = 20$	$+$	$\dfrac{1}{2}$	$a_0 = 1$
$\dfrac{20}{2} = 10$	$+$	0	$a_1 = 0$
$\dfrac{10}{2} = 5$	$+$	0	$a_2 = 0$
$\dfrac{5}{2} = 2$	$+$	$\dfrac{1}{2}$	$a_3 = 1$
$\dfrac{2}{2} = 1$	$+$	0	$a_4 = 0$
$\dfrac{1}{2} = 0$	$+$	$\dfrac{1}{2}$	$a_5 = 1$

answer: $(41)_{10} = (a_5 a_4 a_3 a_2 a_1 a_0)_2 = (101001)_2$

The arithmetic process can be manipulated more conveniently as follows:

integer	*remainder*
41	
20	1
10	0
5	0
2	1
1	0
0	1

$101001 = $ answer

The conversion from decimal integers to any base-r system is similar to the above example, except that division is done by r instead of 2.

EXAMPLE 1-2: Convert decimal 153 to octal. The required base r is 8. First, 153 is divided by 8 to give an integer quotient of 19 and a remainder of 1. Then 19 is divided by 8 to give an integer quotient of 2 and a remainder of 3. Finally, 2 is divided by 8 to give a quotient of 0 and a remainder of 2. This process can be conveniently manipulated as follows:

$$
\begin{array}{c|l}
153 & \\
19 & 1 \\
2 & 3 \\
0 & 2 \quad = (231)_8
\end{array}
$$

The conversion of a decimal *fraction* to binary is accomplished by a method similar to that used for integers. However, multiplication is used instead of division, and integers are accumulated instead of remainders. Again, the method is best explained by example.

EXAMPLE 1-3: Convert $(0.6875)_{10}$ to binary. First, 0.6875 is multiplied by 2 to give an integer and a fraction. The new fraction is multiplied by 2 to give a new integer and a new fraction. This process is continued until the fraction becomes 0 or until the number of digits have sufficient accuracy. The coefficients of the binary number are obtained from the integers as follows:

	integer		*fraction*	*coefficient*
$0.6875 \times 2 =$	1	+	0.3750	$a_{-1} = 1$
$0.3750 \times 2 =$	0	+	0.7500	$a_{-2} = 0$
$0.7500 \times 2 =$	1	+	0.5000	$a_{-3} = 1$
$0.5000 \times 2 =$	1	+	0.0000	$a_{-4} = 1$

answer: $(0.6875)_{10} = (0.a_{-1}a_{-2}a_{-3}a_{-4})_2 = (0.1011)_2$

To convert a decimal fraction to a number expressed in base r, a similar procedure is used. Multiplication is by r instead of 2, and the coefficients found from the integers may range in value from 0 to $r - 1$ instead of 0 and 1.

EXAMPLE 1-4: Convert $(0.513)_{10}$ to octal.

$$
\begin{aligned}
0.513 \times 8 &= 4.104 \\
0.104 \times 8 &= 0.832 \\
0.832 \times 8 &= 6.656 \\
0.656 \times 8 &= 5.248 \\
0.248 \times 8 &= 1.984 \\
0.984 \times 8 &= 7.872
\end{aligned}
$$

The answer, to seven significant figures, is obtained from the integer part of the products:

$$(0.513)_{10} = (0.406517 \ldots)_8$$

The conversion of decimal numbers with both integer and fraction parts is done by converting the integer and fraction separately and then combining the two answers together. Using the results of Examples 1-1 and 1-3, we obtain:

$$(41.6875)_{10} = (101001.1011)_2$$

From Examples 1-2 and 1-4, we have:

$$(153.513)_{10} = (231.406517)_8$$

1-4 OCTAL AND HEXADECIMAL NUMBERS

The conversion from and to binary, octal, and hexadecimal plays an important part in digital computers. Since $2^3 = 8$ and $2^4 = 16$, each octal digit corresponds to three binary digits and each hexadecimal digit corresponds to four binary digits. The conversion from binary to octal is easily accomplished by partitioning the binary number into groups of three digits each, starting from the binary point and proceeding to the left and to the right. The corresponding octal digit is then assigned to each group. The following example illustrates the procedure:

$$(\underbrace{10}_{2} \ \underbrace{110}_{6} \ \underbrace{001}_{1} \ \underbrace{101}_{5} \ \underbrace{011}_{3} \cdot \underbrace{111}_{7} \ \underbrace{100}_{4} \ \underbrace{000}_{0} \ \underbrace{110}_{6})_2 = (26153.7406)_8$$

Conversion from binary to hexadecimal is similar, except that the binary number is divided into groups of four digits:

$$(\underbrace{10}_{2} \ \underbrace{1100}_{C} \ \underbrace{0110}_{6} \ \underbrace{1011}_{B} \cdot \underbrace{1111}_{F} \ \underbrace{0010}_{2})_2 = (2C6B.F2)_{16}$$

The corresponding hexadecimal (or octal) digit for each group of binary digits is easily remembered after studying the values listed in Table 1-1.

Conversion from octal or hexadecimal to binary is done by a procedure reverse to the above. Each octal digit is converted to its three-digit binary equivalent. Similarly, each hexadecimal digit is converted to its four-digit binary equivalent. This is illustrated in the following examples:

$$(673.124)_8 = (\underbrace{110}_{6} \ \underbrace{111}_{7} \ \underbrace{011}_{3} \cdot \underbrace{001}_{1} \ \underbrace{010}_{2} \ \underbrace{100}_{4})_2$$

$$(306.D)_{16} = (\underbrace{0011}_{3} \ \underbrace{0000}_{0} \ \underbrace{0110}_{6} \cdot \underbrace{1101}_{D})_2$$

Binary numbers are difficult to work with because they require three or four times as many digits as their decimal equivalent. For example, the binary number 111111111111 is equivalent to decimal 4095. However, digital computers use binary numbers and it is sometimes necessary for the human operator or user to communicate directly with the machine by means of binary numbers. One scheme that retains the binary system in the computer but reduces the number of digits the human must consider utilizes the relationship between the binary number system and the octal or hexadecimal system. By this method, the human thinks in terms of octal or hexadecimal numbers and performs the required conversion by inspection when direct communication with the machine is necessary. Thus the binary number 111111111111 has 12 digits and is expressed in octal as 7777 (four digits) or in hexadecimal as FFF (three digits). During communication between people (about binary numbers in the computer), the octal or hexadecimal representation is more desirable because it can be expressed more compactly with a third or a quarter of the number of digits required for the equivalent binary number. When the human communicates with the machine (through console switches or indicator lights or by means of programs written in *machine language*), the conversion from octal or hexadecimal to binary and vice versa is done by inspection by the human user.

1-5   COMPLEMENTS

Complements are used in digital computers for simplifying the subtraction operation and for logical manipulations. There are two types of complements for each base-r system: (1) the r's complement and (2) the $(r - 1)$'s complement. When the value of the base is substituted, the two types receive the names 2's and 1's complement for binary numbers, or 10's and 9's complement for decimal numbers.

The r's Complement

Given a positive number N in base r with an integer part of n digits, the r's complement of N is defined as $r^n - N$ for $N \neq 0$ and 0 for $N = 0$. The following numerical example will help clarify the definition.

The 10's complement of $(52520)_{10}$ is $10^5 - 52520 = 47480$.

The number of digits in the number is $n = 5$.

The 10's complement of $(0.3267)_{10}$ is $1 - 0.3267 = 0.6733$.

No integer part, so $10^n = 10^0 = 1$.

The 10's complement of $(25.639)_{10}$ is $10^2 - 25.639 = 74.361$.

The 2's complement of $(101100)_2$ is $(2^6)_{10} - (101100)_2 = (1000000 - 101100)_2$
    $= 010100$.

The 2's complement of $(0.0110)_2$ is $(1 - 0.0110)_2 = 0.1010$.

From the definition and the examples, it is clear that the 10's complement of a decimal number can be formed by leaving all least significant zeros unchanged, subtracting the first nonzero least significant digit from 10, and then subtracting all other higher significant digits from 9. The 2's complement can be formed by leaving all least significant zeros and the first nonzero digit unchanged, and then replacing 1's by 0's and 0's by 1's in all other higher significant digits. A third, simpler method for obtaining the r's complement is given after the definition of the $(r - 1)$'s complement.

The r's complement of a number exists for any base r (r greater than but not equal to 1) and may be obtained from the definition given above. The examples listed here use numbers with $r = 10$ (decimal) and $r = 2$ (binary) because these are the two bases of most interest to us. The name of the complement is related to the base of the number used. For example, the $(r - 1)$'s complement of a number in base 11 is named the 10's complement, since $r - 1 = 10$ for $r = 11$.

The ($r - 1$)'s Complement

Given a positive number N in base r with an integer part of n digits and a fraction part of m digits, the $(r - 1)$'s complement of N is defined as $r^n - r^{-m} - N$. Some numerical examples follow:

The 9's complement of $(52520)_{10}$ is $(10^5 - 1 - 52520) = 99999 - 52520 = 47479$.

No fraction part, so $10^{-m} = 10^0 = 1$.

The 9's complement of $(0.3267)_{10}$ is $(1 - 10^{-4} - 0.3267) = 0.9999 - 0.3267 = 0.6732$.

No integer part, so $10^n = 10^0 = 1$.

The 9's complement of $(25.639)_{10}$ is $(10^2 - 10^{-3} - 25.639) = 99.999 - 25.639 = 74.360$.

The 1's complement of $(101100)_2$ is $(2^6 - 1) - (101100) = (111111 - 101100)_2 = 010011$.

The 1's complement of $(0.0110)_2$ is $(1 - 2^{-4})_{10} - (0.0110)_2 = (0.1111 - 0.0110)_2 = 0.1001$.

From the examples, we see that the 9's complement of a decimal number is formed simply by subtracting every digit from 9. The 1's complement of a binary number is even simpler to form: the 1's are changed to 0's and the 0's to 1's. Since the $(r - 1)$'s complement is very easily obtained, it is sometimes convenient to use it when the r's complement is desired. From the definitions and from a comparison of the results obtained in the examples, it follows that the r's complement can be obtained from the $(r - 1)$'s complement after the addition of r^{-m} to the least significant digit. For example, the 2's complement of 10110100 is obtained from the 1's complement 01001011 by adding 1 to give 01001100.

It is worth mentioning that the complement of the complement restores the number to its original value. The r's complement of N is $r^n - N$ and the complement of $(r^n - N)$ is $r^n - (r^n - N) = N$; and similarly for the 1's complement.

Subtraction with r's Complements

The direct method of subtraction taught in elementary schools uses the borrow concept. In this method, we borrow a 1 from a higher significant position when the minuend digit is smaller than the corresponding subtrahend digit. This seems to be easiest when people perform subtraction with paper and pencil. When subtraction is implemented by means of digital components, this method is found to be less efficient than the method that uses complements and addition as stated below.

The subtraction of two positive numbers $(M - N)$, both of base r, may be done as follows:

1. Add the minuend M to the r's complement of the subtrahend N.

2. Inspect the result obtained in step 1 for an end carry:
   (a) If an end carry occurs, discard it.
   (b) If an end carry does not occur, take the r's complement of the number obtained in step 1 and place a negative sign in front.

The following examples illustrate the procedure:

> **EXAMPLE 1-5:** Using 10's complement, subtract $72532 - 3250$.

$$M = 72532 \qquad\qquad 72532$$
$$N = 03250$$

$$\text{10's complement of } N = 96750 \qquad\qquad \overset{+}{96750}$$
$$\text{end carry} \rightarrow 1 \diagup 69282$$

answer: 69282

> **EXAMPLE 1-6:** Subtract: $(3250 - 72532)_{10}$.

$$M = 03250 \qquad\qquad 03250$$
$$N = 72532$$

$$\text{10's complement of } N = 27468 \qquad\qquad \overset{+}{27468}$$
$$\text{no carry} \diagup 30718$$

answer: $-69282 = -$ (10's complement of 30718)

EXAMPLE 1-7: Use 2's complement to perform $M - N$ with the given binary numbers.

(a) $M = 1010100$ 1010100
                 $N = 1000100$

                                                                      $+$
2's complement of $N = 0111100$ 0111100

                              end carry $\rightarrow 1$ $\diagup \overline{0010000}$

answer: 10000

(b) $M = 1000100$ 1000100
                 $N = 1010100$

                                                                      $+$
2's complement of $N = 0101100$ 0101100

                              no carry $\diagup 1110000$

answer: $-10000 = -$ (2's complement of 1110000)

The proof of the procedure is: The addition of M to the r's complement of N gives $(M + r^n - N)$. For numbers having an integer part of n digits, r^n is equal to a 1 in the $(n + 1)$th position (what has been called the "end carry"). Since both M and N are assumed to be positive, then:

(a) $(M + r^n - N) \geqslant r^n$ if $M \geqslant N$, or
(b) $(M + r^n - N) < r^n$ if $M < N$

In case (a) the answer is positive and equal to $M - N$, which is directly obtained by discarding the end carry r^n. In case (b) the answer is negative and equal to $-(N - M)$. This case is detected from the absence of an end carry. The answer is obtained by taking a second complement and adding a negative sign:

$$-[r^n - (M + r^n - N)] = -(N - M).$$

Subtraction with $(r - 1)$'s Complement

The procedure for subtraction with the $(r - 1)$'s complement is exactly the same as the one used with the r's complement except for one variation, called "end-around carry," as shown below. The subtraction of $M - N$, both positive numbers in base r, may be calculated in the following manner:

1. Add the minuend M to the $(r - 1)$'s complement of the subtrahend N.

2. Inspect the result obtained in step 1 for an end carry.
   (a) If an end carry occurs, add 1 to the least significant digit (end-around carry).

(b) If an end carry does not occur, take the $(r - 1)$'s complement of the number obtained in step 1 and place a negative sign in front.

The proof of this procedure is very similar to the one given for the r's complement case and is left as an exercise. The following examples illustrate the procedure.

EXAMPLE 1-8: Repeat Examples 1-5 and 1-6 using 9's complements.

(a) $M = 72532$ 72532
                             $N = 03250$
9's complement of $N = 96749$ +   96749

                                                        -1 $\overline{\Big/\,69281}$

                    end-around carry   +

                                                                    $\rightarrow 1$
                                                              $\overline{69282}$

answer: 69282

(b) $M = 03250$ 03250
                             $N = 72532$
9's complement of $N = 27467$ +   27467

                                  no carry $\overline{\Big/\,30717}$

answer: $-69282 = -$ (9's complement of 30717)

EXAMPLE 1-9: Repeat Example 1-7 using 1's complement.

(a) $M = 1010100$ 1010100
                             $N = 1000100$
1's complement of $N = 0111011$ +   0111011

                                                        -1 $\overline{\Big/\,0001111}$

                    end-around carry   +

                                                                    $\rightarrow 1$
                                                              $\overline{0010000}$

answer: 10000

(b) $M = 1000100$ 1000100

                      $N = 1010100$ $+$

1's complement of $N = 0101011$ 0101011

                                  no carry $\diagup\overline{1101111}$

answer: $-10000 = -$ (1's complement of 1101111)

Comparison between 1's and 2's Complements

A comparison between 1's and 2's complements reveals the advantages and disadvantages of each. The 1's complement has the advantage of being easier to implement by digital components since the only thing that must be done is to change 0's into 1's and 1's into 0's. The implementation of the 2's complement may be obtained in two ways: (1) by adding 1 to the least significant digit of the 1's complement, and (2) by leaving all leading 0's in the least significant positions and the first 1 unchanged, and only then changing all 1's into 0's and all 0's into 1's. During subtraction of two numbers by complements, the 2's complement is advantageous in that only one arithmetic addition operation is required. The 1's complement requires two arithmetic additions when an end-around carry occurs. The 1's complement has the additional disadvantage of possessing two arithmetic zeros: one with all 0's and one with all 1's. To illustrate this fact, consider the subtraction of the two equal binary numbers $1100 - 1100 = 0$.

Using 1's complement:

$$+\quad \frac{\begin{array}{r}1100 \\ 0011\end{array}}{}$$
$$+\quad \overline{1111}$$

Complement again to obtain -0000.

Using 2's complement:

$$+\quad \frac{\begin{array}{r}1100 \\ 0100\end{array}}{}$$
$$+\quad \overline{0000}$$

While the 2's complement has only one arithmetic zero, the 1's complement zero can be positive or negative, which may complicate matters.

Complements, very useful for arithmetic manipulations in digital computers, are discussed more in Chapters 8 and 9. However, the 1's complement is also useful in logical manipulations (as will be shown later), since the change of 1's to

0's and vice versa is equivalent to a logical inversion operation. The 2's complement is used only in conjunction with arithmetic applications. Consequently, it is convenient to adopt the following convention: When the word *complement*, without mention of the type, is used in conjunction with a nonarithmetic application, the type is assumed to be the 1's complement.

1-6   BINARY CODES

Electronic digital systems use signals that have two distinct values and circuit elements that have two stable states. There is a direct analogy among binary signals, binary circuit elements, and binary digits. A binary number of n digits, for example, may be represented by n binary circuit elements, each having an output signal equivalent to a 0 or a 1. Digital systems represent and manipulate not only binary numbers, but also many other discrete elements of information. Any discrete element of information distinct among a group of quantities can be represented by a binary code. For example, *red* is one distinct color of the spectrum. The letter A is one distinct letter of the alphabet.

A *bit*, by definition, is a binary digit. When used in conjunction with a binary code, it is better to think of it as denoting a binary quantity equal to 0 or 1. To represent a group of 2^n distinct elements in a binary code requires a minimum of n bits. This is because it is possible to arrange n bits in 2^n distinct ways. For example, a group of four distinct quantities can be represented by a two-bit code, with each quantity assigned one of the following bit combinations: 00, 01, 10, 11. A group of eight elements requires a three-bit code, with each element assigned to one and only one of the following: 000, 001, 010, 011, 100, 101, 110, 111. The examples show that the distinct bit combinations of an n-bit code can be found by counting in binary from 0 to $(2^n - 1)$. Some bit combinations are unassigned when the number of elements of the group to be coded is not a multiple of the power of 2. The ten decimal digits 0, 1, 2, . . . , 9 are an example of such a group. A binary code that distinguishes among ten elements must contain at least four bits; three bits can distinguish a maximum of eight elements. Four bits can form 16 distinct combinations, but since only ten digits are coded, the remaining six combinations are unassigned and not used.

Although the *minimum* number of bits required to code 2^n distinct quantities is n, there is no *maximum* number of bits that may be used for a binary code. For example, the ten decimal digits can be coded with ten bits, and each decimal digit assigned a bit combination of nine 0's and a 1. In this particular binary code, the digit 6 is assigned the bit combination 0001000000.

Decimal Codes

Binary codes for decimal digits require a minimum of four bits. Numerous different codes can be obtained by arranging four or more bits in ten distinct possible combinations. A few possibilities are shown in Table 1-2.

TABLE 1-2   Binary codes for the decimal digits

Decimal digit	(BCD) 8421	Excess-3	84-2-1	2421	(Biquinary) 5043210
0	0000	0011	0000	0000	0100001
1	0001	0100	0111	0001	0100010
2	0010	0101	0110	0010	0100100
3	0011	0110	0101	0011	0101000
4	0100	0111	0100	0100	0110000
5	0101	1000	1011	1011	1000001
6	0110	1001	1010	1100	1000010
7	0111	1010	1001	1101	1000100
8	1000	1011	1000	1110	1001000
9	1001	1100	1111	1111	1010000

The BCD (binary-coded decimal) is a straight assignment of the binary equivalent. It is possible to assign weights to the binary bits according to their positions. The weights in the BCD code are 8, 4, 2, 1. The bit assignment 0110, for example, can be interpreted by the weights to represent the decimal digit 6 because $0 \times 8 + 1 \times 4 + 1 \times 2 + 0 \times 1 = 6$. It is also possible to assign negative weights to a decimal code, as shown by the 8, 4, -2, -1 code. In this case the bit combination 0110 is interpreted as the decimal digit 2, as obtained from $0 \times 8 + 1 \times 4 + 1 \times (-2) + 0 \times (-1) = 2$. Two other weighted codes shown in the table are the 2421 and the 5043210. A decimal code that has been used in some old computers is the excess-3 code. This is an unweighted code; its code assignment is obtained from the corresponding value of BCD after the addition of 3.

Numbers are represented in digital computers either in binary or in decimal through a binary code. When specifying data, the user likes to give the data in decimal form. The input decimal numbers are stored internally in the computer by means of a decimal code. Each decimal digit requires at least four binary storage elements. The decimal numbers are converted to binary when arithmetic operations are done internally with numbers represented in binary. It is also possible to perform the arithmetic operations directly in decimal with all numbers left in a coded form throughout. For example, the decimal number 395, when converted to binary, is equal to 110001011 and consists of nine binary digits. The same number, when represented internally in the BCD code, occupies four bits for each decimal digit, for a total of 12 bits: 001110010101. The first four bits represent a 3, the next four a 9, and the last four a 5.

It is very important to understand the difference between *conversion* of a decimal number to binary and the binary *coding* of a decimal number. In each case the final result is a series of bits. The bits obtained from conversion are binary digits. Bits obtained from coding are combinations of 1's and 0's arranged according to the rules of the code used. Therefore, it is extremely important to realize that a series of 1's and 0's in a digital system may sometimes represent a binary number and at other times represent some other discrete quantity of information as specified by a given binary code. The BCD code, for example, has been chosen to be both a code and a direct binary conversion, as long as the decimal numbers are integers from 0 to 9. For numbers greater than 9, the conversion and the coding are completely different. This concept is so important that it is worth repeating with another example. The binary conversion of decimal 13 is 1101; the coding of decimal 13 with BCD is 00010011.

From the five binary codes listed in Table 1-2, the BCD seems the most natural to use and is indeed the one most commonly encountered. The other four-bit codes listed have one characteristic in common that is not found in BCD. The excess-3, the 2, 4, 2, 1, and the 8, 4, $-$ 2, $-$ 1 are self-complementary codes, that is, the 9's complement of the decimal number is easily obtained by changing 1's to 0's and 0's to 1's. For example, the decimal 395 is represented in the 2, 4, 2, 1 code by 001111111011. Its 9's complement 604 is represented by 110000000100, which is easily obtained from the replacement of 1's by 0's and 0's by 1's. This property is useful when arithmetic operations are internally done with decimal numbers (in a binary code) and subtraction is calculated by means of 9's complement.

The biquinary code shown in Table 1-2 is an example of a seven-bit code with error-detection properties. Each decimal digit consists of five 0's and two 1's placed in the corresponding weighted columns. The error-detection property of this code may be understood if one realizes that digital systems represent binary 1 by one distinct signal and binary 0 by a second distinct signal. During transmission of signals from one location to another, an error may occur. One or more bits may change value. A circuit in the receiving side can detect the presence of more (or less) than two 1's and, if the received combination of bits does not agree with the allowable combination, an error is detected.

Error-Detection Codes

Binary information, be it pulse-modulated signals or digital computer input or output, may be transmitted through some form of communication medium such as wires or radio waves. Any external noise introduced into a physical communication medium changes bit values from 0 to 1 or vice versa. An error-detection code can be used to detect errors during transmission. The detected error cannot be corrected, but its presence is indicated. The usual procedure is to observe the frequency of errors. If errors occur only once in a while, at random, and without a pronounced effect on the overall information transmitted, then either nothing is done or the particular erroneous message is transmitted again. If errors occur so often as to distort the meaning of the received information, the system is checked for malfunction.

A *parity* bit is an extra bit included with a message to make the total number of 1's either odd or even. A message of four bits and a parity bit, P, are shown in Table 1-3. In (a), P is chosen so that the sum of all 1's is odd (in all five bits). In (b), P is chosen so that the sum of all 1's is even. During transfer of information

TABLE 1-3 Parity-bit generation

(a) Message	P (odd)	(b) Message	P (even)
0000	1	0000	0
0001	0	0001	1
0010	0	0010	1
0011	1	0011	0
0100	0	0100	1
0101	1	0101	0
0110	1	0110	0
0111	0	0111	1
1000	0	1000	1
1001	1	1001	0
1010	1	1010	0
1011	0	1011	1
1100	1	1100	0
1101	0	1101	1
1110	0	1110	1
1111	1	1111	0

from one location to another, the parity bit is handled as follows. In the sending end, the message (in this case the first four bits) is applied to a "parity-generation" network where the required P bit is generated. The message, including the parity bit, is transferred to its destination. In the receiving end, all the incoming bits (in this case five) are applied to a "parity-check" network to check the proper parity adopted. An error is detected if the checked parity does not correspond to the adopted one. The parity method detects the presence of one, three, or any odd combination of errors. An even combination of errors is undetectable. Further discussion of parity generation and checking can be found in Sec. 4-9.

The Reflected Code

Digital systems can be designed to process data in discrete form only. Many physical systems supply continous output data. These data must be converted into digital or discrete form before they are applied to a digital system. Continuous or analog information is converted into digital form by means of an analog-to-digital converter. It is sometimes convenient to use the reflected code shown in Table 1-4 to represent the digital data converted from the analog data. The advantage of the reflected code over pure binary numbers is that a number in the reflected code changes by only one bit as it proceeds from one number to the next. A typical application of the reflected code occurs when the analog data are represented by a continouous change of a shaft position. The shaft is partitioned into segments, and each segment is assigned a number. If adjacent segments are made to correspond to adjacent reflected-code numbers, ambiguity is reduced when detection is sensed

TABLE 1-4 Four-bit reflected code

Reflected code	Decimal equivalent
0000	0
0001	1
0011	2
0010	3
0110	4
0111	5
0101	6
0100	7
1100	8
1101	9
1111	10
1110	11
1010	12
1011	13
1001	14
1000	15

in the line that separates any two segments. The reflected code shown in Table 1-4 is only one of many possible such codes. To obtain a different reflected code, one can start with any bit combination and proceed to obtain the next bit combination by changing only one bit from 0 to 1 or 1 to 0 in any desired random fashion, as long as two numbers do not have identical code assignments. The reflected code is also known as the *Gray* code.

Alphanumeric Codes

Many applications of digital computers require the handling of data that consist not only of numbers, but also of letters. For instance, an insurance company with millions of policy holders may use a digital computer to process its files. To represent the policy holder's name in binary form, it is necessary to have a binary code for the alphabet. In addition, the same binary code must represent decimal numbers and some other special characters. An alphanumeric (sometimes abbreviated *alphameric*) code is a binary code of a group of elements consisting of the ten decimal digits, the 26 letters of the alphabet, and a certain number of special symbols such as $. The total number of elements in an alphanumeric group is greater than 36. Therefore, it must be coded with a minimum of six bits ($2^6 = 64$, but $2^5 = 32$ is insufficient).

One possible arrangement of a six-bit alphanumeric code is shown in Table 1-5 under the name "internal code." With a few variations, it is used in many computers to represent alphanumeric characters internally. The need to represent more than 64 characters (the lowercase letters and special control characters for the

TABLE 1-5 Alphanumeric character codes

Character	6-Bit internal code		7-Bit ASCII code		8-Bit EBCDIC code		12-Bit card code
A	010	001	100	0001	1100	0001	12,1
B	010	010	100	0010	1100	0010	12,2
C	010	011	100	0011	1100	0011	12,3
D	010	100	100	0100	1100	0100	12,4
E	010	101	100	0101	1100	0101	12,5
F	010	110	100	0110	1100	0110	12,6
G	010	111	100	0111	1100	0111	12,7
H	011	000	100	1000	1100	1000	12,8
I	011	001	100	1001	1100	1001	12,9
J	100	001	100	1010	1101	0001	11,1
K	100	010	100	1011	1101	0010	11,2
L	100	011	100	1100	1101	0011	11,3
M	100	100	100	1101	1101	0100	11,4
N	100	101	100	1110	1101	0101	11,5
O	100	110	100	1111	1101	0110	11,6
P	100	111	101	0000	1101	0111	11,7
Q	101	000	101	0001	1101	1000	11,8
R	101	001	101	0010	1101	1001	11,9
S	110	010	101	0011	1110	0010	0,2
T	110	011	101	0100	1110	0011	0,3
U	110	100	101	0101	1110	0100	0,4
V	110	101	101	0110	1110	0101	0,5
W	110	110	101	0111	1110	0110	0,6
X	110	111	101	1000	1110	0111	0,7
Y	111	000	101	1001	1110	1000	0,8
Z	111	001	101	1010	1110	1001	0,9
0	000	000	011	0000	1111	0000	0
1	000	001	011	0001	1111	0001	1
2	000	010	011	0010	1111	0010	2
3	000	011	011	0011	1111	0011	3
4	000	100	011	0100	1111	0100	4
5	000	101	011	0101	1111	0101	5
6	000	110	011	0110	1111	0110	6
7	000	111	011	0111	1111	0111	7
8	001	000	011	1000	1111	1000	8
9	001	001	011	1001	1111	1001	9
blank	110	000	010	0000	0100	0000	no punch
.	011	011	010	1110	0100	1011	12,8,3
(	111	100	010	1000	0100	1101	12,8,5
+	010	000	010	1011	0100	1110	12,8,6
$	101	011	010	0100	0101	1011	11,8,3
*	101	100	010	1010	0101	1100	11,8,4
)	011	100	010	1001	0101	1101	11,8,5
−	100	000	010	1101	0110	0000	11
/	110	001	010	1111	0110	0001	0,1
,	111	011	010	1100	0110	1011	0,8,3
=	001	011	011	1101	0111	1110	8,6

transmission of digital information) gave rise to seven- and eight-bit alphanumeric codes. One such code is known as ASCII (American Standard Code for Information Interchange); another is known as EBCDIC (Extended BCD Interchange Code). The ASCII code listed in Table 1-5 consists of seven bits but is, for all practical purposes, an eight-bit code because an eighth bit is invariably added for parity. When discrete information is transferred through punch cards, the alphanumeric characters use a 12-bit binary code. A punch card consists of 80 columns and 12 rows. In each column, an alphanumeric character is represented by holes punched in the appropriate rows. A hole is sensed as a 1 and the absence of a hole is sensed as a 0. The 12 rows are marked, starting from the top, as the 12, 11, 0, 1, 2,..., 9 punch. The first three are called the *zone* punch and the last nine are called the *numeric* punch. The 12-bit card code shown in Table 1-5 lists the rows where a hole is punched (giving the 1's). The remaining unlisted rows are assumed to be 0's. The 12-bit card code is inefficient with respect to the number of bits used. Most computers translate the input code into an internal six-bit code. As an example, the internal code representation of the name "John Doe" is:

100001	100110	011000	100101	110000	010100	100110	010101
J	O	H	N	blank	D	O	E

1-7 BINARY STORAGE AND REGISTERS

The discrete elements of information in a digital computer must have a physical existence in some information storage medium. Furthermore, when discrete elements of information are represented in binary form, the information storage medium must contain binary storage elements for storing individual bits. A *binary cell* is a device that possesses two stable states and is capable of storing one bit of information. The input to the cell receives excitation signals that set it to one of the two states. The output of the cell is a physical quantity that distinguishes between the two states. The information stored in a cell is a 1 when it is in one stable state and a 0 when in the other stable state. Examples of binary cells are electronic flip-flop circuits, ferrite cores used in memories, and positions punched with a hole or not punched in a card.

Registers

A *register* is a group of binary cells. Since a cell stores one bit of information, it follows that a register with n cells can store any discrete quantity of information that contains n bits. The *state* of a register is an n-tuple number of 1's and 0's, with each bit designating the state of one cell in the register. The *content* of a register is a function of the interpretation given to the information stored in it. Consider, for example, the following 16-cell register:

1	1	0	0	0	0	1	1	1	1	0	0	1	0	0	1
1	2	3	4	5	6	7	8	9	10	11	12	13	14	15	16

Physically, one may think of the register as composed of 16 binary cells, with each cell storing either a 1 or a 0. Suppose that the bit configuration stored in the register is as shown. The state of the register is the 16-tuple number 1100001111001001. Clearly, a register with n cells can be in one of 2^n possible states. Now, if one assumes that the content of the register represents a binary integer, then obviously the register can store any binary number from 0 to $2^{16} - 1$. For the particular example shown, the content of the register is the binary equivalent of the decimal number 50121. If it is assumed that the register stores alphanumeric characters of an eight-bit code, the content of the register is any two meaningful characters (unassigned bit combinations do not represent meaningful information). In the EBCDIC code, the above example represents the two characters C (left eight bits) and I (right eight bits). On the other hand, if one interprets the content of the register to be four decimal digits represented by a four-bit code, the content of the register is a four-digit decimal number. In the excess-3 code, the above example is the decimal number 9096. The content of the register is meaningless in BCD since the bit combination 1100 is not assigned to any decimal digit. From this example, it is clear that a register can store one or more discrete elements of information and that the same bit configuration may be interpreted differently for different types of elements of information. It is important that the user store meaningful information in registers and that the computer be programmed to process this information according to the *type* of information stored.

Register Transfer

A digital computer is characterized by its registers. The memory unit (Fig. 1-1) is merely a collection of thousands of registers for storing digital information. The processor unit is composed of various registers that store operands upon which operations are performed. The control unit uses registers to keep track of various computer sequences, and every input or output device must have at least one register to store the information transferred to or from the device. An *inter-register transfer* operation, a basic operation in digital systems, consists of a transfer of the information stored in one register into another. Figure 1-2 illustrates the transfer of information among registers and demonstrates pictorially the transfer of binary information from a teletype keyboard into a register in the memory unit. The input teletype unit is assumed to have a keyboard, a control circuit, and an input register. Each time a key is struck, the control enters into the input register an equivalent eight-bit alphanumeric character code. We shall assume that the code used is the ASCII code with an odd-parity eighth bit. The information from the input register

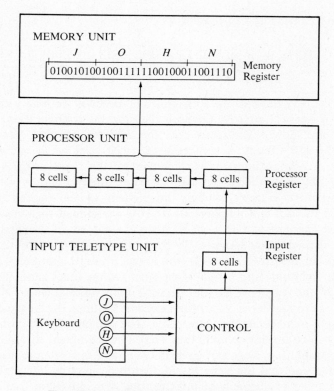

Figure 1-2 Transfer of information with registers

is transferred into the eight least significant cells of a processor register. After every transfer, the input register is cleared to enable the control to insert a new eight-bit code when the keyboard is struck again. Each eight-bit character transferred to the processor register is preceded by a shift of the previous character to the next eight cells on its left. When a transfer of four characters is completed, the processor register is full, and its contents are transferred into a memory register. The content stored in the memory register shown in Fig. 1-2 came from the transfer of the characters JOHN after the four appropirate keys were struck.

To process discrete quantities of information in binary form, a computer must be provided with (1) devices that hold the data to be processed and (2) circuit elements that manipulate individual bits of information. The device most commonly used for holding data is a register. Manipulation of binary variables is done by means of digital logic circuits. Figure 1-3 illustrates the process of adding two 10-bit binary numbers. The memory unit, which normally consists of thousands of registers, is shown in the diagram with only three of its registers. The part of the processor unit shown consists of three registers, R1, R2, and R3, together with digital logic circuits that manipulate the bits of R1 and R2 and transfer into R3 a binary number equal to their arithmetic sum. Memory registers store information and are incapable of processing the two operands. However, the information stored in memory can be transferred to processor registers. Results obtained in

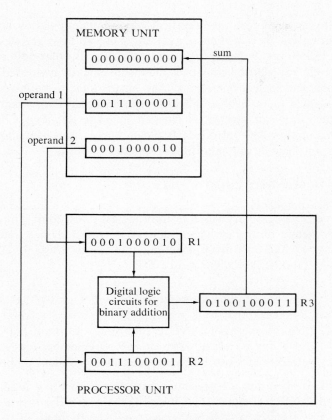

Figure 1-3 Example of binary information processing

processor registers can be transferred back into a memory register for storage until needed again. The diagram shows the contents of two operands transferred from two memory registers into R1 and R2. The digital logic circuits produce the sum, which is transferred to register R3. The contents of R3 can now be transferred back to one of the memory registers.

The last two examples demonstrated the information flow capabilities of a digital system in a very simple manner. The registers of the system are the basic elements for storing and holding the binary information. The digital logic circuits process the information. Digital logic circuits and their manipulative capabilities are introduced in the next section. The subject of registers and register transfer operations is taken up again in Chapter 8.

1-8 BINARY LOGIC

Binary logic deals with variables that take on two discrete values and with operations that assume logical meaning. The two values the variables take may be called by different names (e.g., *true* and *false*, *yes* and *no*, etc.), but for our purpose it is convenient to think in terms of bits and assign the values of 1 and 0. Binary logic is used to describe, in a mathematical way, the manipulation and processing of binary information. It is particularly suited for the analysis and design of digital systems. For example, the digital logic circuits of Fig. 1-3 that perform the binary arithmetic are circuits whose behavior is most conveniently expressed by means of binary variables and logical operations. The binary logic to be introduced in this section is equivalent to an algebra called Boolean algebra. The formal presentation of a two-valued Boolean algebra is covered in more detail in Chapter 2. The purpose of this section is to introduce Boolean algebra in a heuristic manner and relate it to digital logic circuits and binary signals.

Definition of Binary Logic

Binary logic consists of binary variables and logical operations. The variables are designated by letters of the alphabet such as A, B, C, x, y, z, etc., with each variable having two and only two distinct possible values: 1 and 0. There are three basic logical operations: AND, OR, and NOT.

1. AND: This operation is represented by a dot or by the absence of an operator. For example, $x \cdot y = z$ or $xy = z$ is read "x AND y is equal to z." The logical operation AND is interpreted to mean that $z = 1$ if and only if $x = 1$ *and* $y = 1$; otherwise $z = 0$. (Remember that x, y, and z are binary variables and can be equal either to 1 or 0, and nothing else.)

2. OR: This operation is represented by a plus sign. For example, $x + y = z$ is read "x OR y is equal to z," meaning that $z = 1$ if $x = 1$ *or* if $y = 1$ *or* if both $x = 1$ and $y = 1$. If both $x = 0$ and $y = 0$, then $z = 0$.

3. NOT: This operation is represented by a prime (sometimes by a bar). For example, $x' = z$ (or $\bar{x} = z$) is read "x not is equal to z," meaining that z is what x is not. In other words, if $x = 1$, then $z = 0$; but if $x = 0$, then $z = 1$.

Binary logic resembles binary arithmetic, and the operations AND and OR have some similarities to multiplication and addition, respectively. In fact, the symbols used for AND and OR are the same as those used for multiplication and addition. However, binary logic should not be confused with binary arithmetic. One should realize that an arithmetic variable designates a number that may consist of many digits. A logic variable is always either a 1 or a 0. For example, in binary arithmetic we have $1 + 1 = 10$ (read: "one plus one is equal to 2"), while in binary logic we have $1 + 1 = 1$ (read: "one OR one is equal to one").

For each combination of the values of x and y, there is a value of z specified by the definition of the logical operation. These definitions may be listed in a compact form using *truth tables*. A truth table is a table of all possible combinations of the variables showing the relation between the values that the variables may take and the result of the operation. For example, the truth tables for the

TABLE 1-6 Truth tables of logical operations

AND			OR			NOT	
x y	$x \cdot y$		x y	$x + y$		x	x'
0 0	0		0 0	0		0	1
0 1	0		0 1	1		1	0
1 0	0		1 0	1			
1 1	1		1 1	1			

operations AND and OR with variables x and y are obtained by listing all possible values that the variables may have when combined in pairs. The result of the operation for each combination is then listed in a separate row. The truth tables for AND, OR, and NOT are listed in Table 1-6. These tables clearly demonstrate the definitions of the operations.

Switching Circuits and Binary Signals

The use of binary variables and the application of binary logic are demonstrated by the simple switching circuits of Fig. 1-4. Let the manual switches A and B represent two binary variables with values equal to 0 when the switch is open and 1 when the switch is closed. Similarly, let the lamp L represent a third binary variable equal to 1 when the light is on and 0 when off. For the switches in series, the light turns on if A *and* B are closed. For the switches in parallel, the light turns on if A *or* B is closed. It is obvious that the two circuits can be expressed by means of binary logic with the AND and OR operations, respectively:

$$L = A \cdot B \quad \text{for the circuit of Fig. 1-4(a)}$$
$$L = A + B \quad \text{for the circuit of Fig. 1-4(b)}$$

Electronic digital circuits are sometimes called *switching circuits* because they behave like a switch, with the active element such as a transistor either conducting (switch closed) or not conducting (switch open). Instead of changing the switch manually, an electronic switching circuit uses binary signals to control the conduction or nonconduction state of the active element. Electrical signals such as

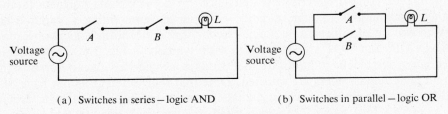

(a) Switches in series – logic AND   (b) Switches in parallel – logic OR

Figure 1-4 Switching circuits that demonstrate binary logic

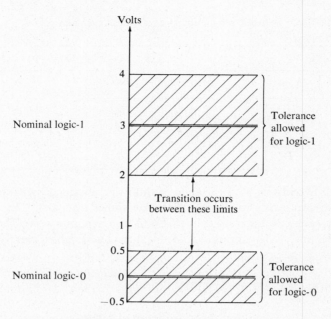

Figure 1-5 Example of binary signals

voltages or currents exist throughout a digital system in either one of two recognizable values (except during transition). Voltage-operated circuits, for example, respond to two separate voltage levels which represent a binary variable equal to logic-1 or logic-0. For example, a particular digital system may define logic-1 as a signal with a nominal value of 3 volts, and logic-0 as a signal with a nominal value of 0 volt. As shown in Fig. 1-5, each voltage level has an acceptable deviation from the nominal. The intermediate region between the allowed regions is crossed only during state transitions. The input terminals of digital circuits accept binary signals within the allowable tolerances and respond at the output terminal with binary signals that fall within the specified tolerances.

Logic Gates

Electronic digital circuits are also called *logic circuits* because, with the proper input, they establish logical manipulation paths. Any desired information for computing or control can be operated upon by passing binary signals through various combinations of logic circuits, each signal representing a variable and carrying one bit of information. Logic circuits that perform the logical operations of AND, OR, and NOT are shown with their symbols in Fig. 1-6. These circuits, called *gates*, are blocks of hardware that produce a logic-1 or logic-0 output signal if input logic requirements are satisfied. Note that four different names have been used for the same type of circuits: digital circuits, switching circuits, logic circuits, and gates. All four names are widely used, but we shall refer to the circuits as

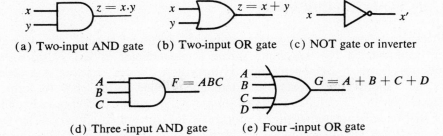

(a) Two-input AND gate   (b) Two-input OR gate   (c) NOT gate or inverter

(d) Three-input AND gate   (e) Four-input OR gate

Figure 1-6 Symbols for digital logic circuits

AND, OR, and NOT gates. The NOT gate is sometimes called an *inverter circuit* since it inverts a binary signal.

The input signals x and y in the two-input gates of Fig. 1-6 may exist in one of four possible states: 00, 10, 11, or 01. These input signals are shown in Fig. 1-7, together with the output signals for the AND and OR gates. The timing diagrams in Fig. 1-7 illustrate the response of each circuit to each of the four possible input binary combinations. The reason for the name "inverter" for the NOT gate is apparent from a comparison of the signal x (input of inverter) and that of x' (output of inverter).

AND and OR gates may have more than two inputs. An AND gate with three inputs and an OR gate with four inputs are shown in Fig. 1-6. The three-input AND gate responds with a logic-1 output if all three input signals are logic-1. The output produces a logic-0 signal if any input is logic 0. The four input OR gate responds with a logic-1 when any input is a logic-1. Its output becomes logic-0 if all input signals are logic-0.

The mathematical system of binary logic is better known as Boolean, or switching, algebra. This algebra is conveniently used to describe the operation of complex networks of digital circuits. Designers of digital systems use Boolean algebra to transform circuit diagrams to algebraic expressions and vice versa. Chapters 2 and 3 are devoted to the study of Boolean algebra, its properties, and manipulative capabilities. Chapter 4 shows how Boolean algebra may be used to express mathematically the interconnections among networks of gates.

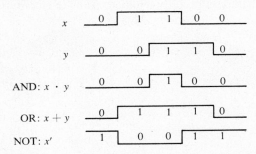

Figure 1-7 Input-output signals for gates (a), (b), and (c) of Fig. 1-6

1-9 INTEGRATED CIRCUITS

Digital circuits are invariably constructed with integrated circuits. An integrated circuit (abbreviated IC) is a small silicon semiconductor crystal, called a *chip*, containing electrical components such as transistors, diodes, resistors, and capacitors. The various components are interconnected inside the chip to form an electronic circuit. The chip is mounted on a metal or plastic package, and connections are welded to external pins to form the IC. Integrated circuits differ from other electronic circuits composed of detachable components in that individual components in the IC cannot be separated or disconnected and the circuit inside the package is accessible only through the external pins.

Integrated circuits come in two types of packages, the *flat* package and the *dual-in-line* (DIP) package, as shown in Fig. 1-8. The dual-in-line package is the most widely used type because of the low price and easy installation on circuit boards. The envelope of the IC package is made of plastic or ceramic. Most packages have standard sizes, and the number of pins ranges from 8 to 64. Each IC has a numeric designation printed on the surface of the package for identification. Each vendor publishes a data book or catalog that provides the necessary information concerning the various products.

The size of IC packages is very small. For example, four AND gates are enclosed inside a 14-pin dual-in-line package with dimensions of $20 \times 8 \times 3$ millimeters. An entire microprocessor is enclosed within a 40-pin dual-in-line package with dimensions of $50 \times 15 \times 4$ millimeters.

Besides a substantial reduction in size, ICs offer other advantages and benefits compared to electronic circuits with discrete components. The cost of ICs is very low, which makes them economical to use. Their reduced power consumption makes the digital system more economical to operate. They have a high reliability against failure, so the digital system needs less repairs. The operating speed is higher, which makes them suitable for high-speed operations. The use of ICs reduces the number of external wiring connections because many of the connections are internal to the package. Because of all these advantages, digital systems are always constructed with integrated circuits.

Integrated circuits are classified in two general categories, *linear* and *digital*. Linear ICs operate with continuous signals to provide electronic functions such as

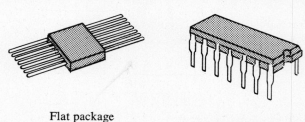

Flat package

Dual-in-line package

Figure 1-8   Integrated-circuit packages

amplifiers and voltage comparators. Digital integrated circuits operate with binary signals and are made up of interconnected digital gates. Here we are concerned only with digital integrated circuits.

As the technology of ICs has improved, the number of gates that can be put on a single silicon chip has increased considerably. The differentiation between those ICs that have a few internal gates and those having tens or hundreds of gates is made by a customary reference to a package as being either a small-, medium-, or large-scale integration device. Several logic gates in a single package make it a small-scale integration (SSI) device. To qualify as a medium-scale integration (MSI) device, the IC must perform a complete logic function and have a complexity of 10 to 100 gates. A large-scale integration (LSI) device performs a logic function with more than 100 gates. There are also very-large-scale integration (VLSI) devices that contain thousands of gates in a single chip.

Many diagrams of digital circuits considered throughout this book are shown in detail up to the individual gates and their interconnections. Such diagrams are useful for demonstrating the logical construction of a particular function. However, it must be realized that, in practice, the function may be obtained from an MSI or LSI device, and the user has access only to external inputs and outputs but not to inputs and outputs of intermediate gates. For example, a designer who wants to incorporate a register in his system is more likely to choose such a function from an available MSI circuit instead of designing it with individual digital circuits as may be shown in a diagram.

REFERENCES

1. Richard, R. K., *Arithmetic Operations in Digital Computers*. New York: Van Nostrand Co., 1955.

2. Flores, I., *The Logic of Computer Arithmetic*. Englewood Cliffs, N. J.: Prentice-Hall, Inc., 1963.

3. Chu, Y., *Digital Computer Design Fundamentals*. New York: McGraw-Hill Book Co., 1962, Chaps. 1 and 2.

4. Kostopoulos, G. K., *Digital Engineering*. New York: John Wiley & Sons, Inc., 1975, Chap. 1.

5. Rhyne, V. T., *Fundamentals of Digital Systems Design*. Englewood Cliffs, N. J.: Prentice-Hall, Inc., 1973, Chap. 1.

PROBLEMS

1-1.   Write the first 20 decimal digits in base 3.

1-2.   Add and multiply the following numbers in the given base without converting to decimal.

(a) $(1230)_4$ and $(23)_4$

(b) $(135.4)_6$ and $(43.2)_6$

(c) $(367)_8$ and $(715)_8$

(d) $(296)_{12}$ and $(57)_{12}$

1-3. Convert the decimal number 250.5 to base 3, base 4, base 7, base 8, and base 16.

1-4. Convert the following decimal numbers to binary: 12.0625, 10^4, 673.23, and 1998.

1-5. Convert the following binary numbers to decimal: 10.10001, 101110.0101, 1110101.110, 1101101.111.

1-6. Convert the following numbers from the given base to the bases indicated:

(a) decimal 225.225 to binary, octal, and hexadecimal

(b) binary 11010111.110 to decimal, octal, and hexadecimal

(c) octal 623.77 to decimal, binary, and hexadecimal

(d) hexadecimal 2AC5.D to decimal, octal, and binary

1-7. Convert the following numbers to decimal:

(a) $(1001001.011)_2$ (e) $(0.342)_6$

(b) $(12121)_3$ (f) $(50)_7$

(c) $(1032.2)_4$ (g) $(8.3)_9$

(d) $(4310)_5$ (h) $(198)_{12}$

1-8. Obtain the 1's and 2's complement of the following binary numbers: 1010101, 0111000, 0000001, 10000, 00000.

1-9. Obtain the 9's and 10's complement of the following decimal numbers: 13579, 09900, 90090, 10000, 00000.

1-10. Find the 10's complement of $(935)_{11}$.

1-11. Perform the subtraction with the following decimal numbers using (1) 10's complement and (2) 9's complement. Check the answer by straight subtraction.

(a) $5250 - 321$ (c) $753 - 864$

(b) $3570 - 2100$ (d) $20 - 1000$

1-12. Perform the subtraction with the following binary numbers using (1) 2's complement and (2) 1's complement. Check the answer by straight subtraction.

(a) $11010 - 1101$ (c) $10010 - 10011$

(b) $11010 - 10000$ (d) $100 - 110000$

1-13. Prove the procedure stated in Sec. 1-5 for the subtraction of two numbers with $(r - 1)$'s complement.

1-14. For the weighted codes (a) 3, 3, 2, 1 and (b) 4, 4, 3, $- 2$ for the decimal digits, determine all possible tables so that the 9's complement of each decimal digit is obtained by changing 1's to 0's and 0's to 1's.

1-15. Represent the decimal number 8620 (a) in BCD, (b) in excess-3 code, (c) in 2, 4, 2, 1 code, and (d) as a binary number.

1-16.   A binary code uses ten bits to represent each of the ten decimal digits. Each digit is assigned a code of nine 0's and a 1. The code for digit 6, for example, is 0001000000. Determine the binary code for the remaining decimal digits.

1-17.   Obtain the weighted binary code for the base-12 digits using weights of 5421.

1-18.   Determine the odd-parity bit generated when the message consists of the ten decimal digits in the 8, 4, $-$ 2, $-$ 1 code.

1-19.   Determine two other combinations for a reflected code other than the one shown in Table 1-4.

1-20.   Obtain a binary code to represent all base-6 digits so that the 5's complement is obtained by replacing 1's by 0's and 0's by 1's in the bits of the code.

1-21.   Assign a binary code in some orderly manner to the 52 playing cards. Use the minimum number of bits.

1-22.   Write your first name, middle initial, and last name in an eight-bit code made up of the seven ASCII bits of Table 1-5 and an even parity bit in the most significant position. Include blanks between names and a period after the middle initial.

1-23.   Show the bit configuration of a 24-cell register when its content represents (a) the number $(295)_{10}$ in binary, (b) the decimal number 295 in BCD, and (c) the characters XY5 in EBCDIC.

1-24.   The state of a 12-cell register is 010110010111. What is its content if it represents (a) three decimal digits in BCD, (b) three decimal digits in excess-3 code, (c) three decimal digits in 2, 4, 2, 1 code, and (d) two characters in the internal code of Table 1-5?

1-25.   Show the contents of all registers in Fig. 1-3 if the two binary numbers added have the decimal equivalent of 257 and 1050. (Assume registers with 11 cells.)

1-26.   Express the following switching circuit in binary logic notation.

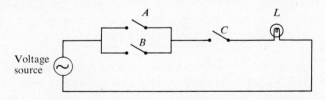

1-27.   Show the signals (by means of a diagram similar to Fig. 1-7) of the outputs F and G in Fig. 1-6. Use arbitrary binary signals for the inputs A, B, C, and D.

Boolean Algebra and Logic Gates

2-1 BASIC DEFINITIONS

Boolean algebra, like any other deductive mathematical system, may be defined with a set of elements, a set of operators, and a number of unproved axioms or postulates. A *set* of elements is any collection of objects having a common property. If S is a set, and x and y are certain objects, then $x \in S$ denotes that x is a member of the set S, and $y \notin S$ denotes that y is not an element of S. A set with a denumerable number of elements is specified by braces: A = {1, 2, 3, 4}, i.e., the elements of set A are the numbers 1, 2, 3, and 4. A *binary operator* defined on a set S of elements is a rule that assigns to each pair of elements from S a unique element from S. As an example, consider the relation $a*b = c$. We say that $*$ is a binary operator if it specifies a rule for finding c from the pair (a, b) and also if a, b, $c \in S$. However, $*$ is not a binary operator if a, $b \in S$, while the rule finds $c \notin S$.

The postulates of a mathematical system form the basic assumptions from which it is possible to deduce the rules, theorems, and properties of the system. The most common postulates used to formulate various algebraic structures are:

1. *Closure*. A set S is closed with respect to a binary operator if, for every pair of elements of S, the binary operator specifies a rule for obtaining a unique element of S. For example, the set of natural numbers N = {1, 2, 3, 4, . . . } is closed with respect to the binary operator plus (+) by the rules of arithmetic addition, since for any a, $b \in N$ we obtain a unique $c \in N$ by the operation $a + b = c$. The set of natural numbers is not closed with respect to the binary operator minus (−) by the rules of arithmetic subtraction because $2 - 3 = -1$ and 2, 3 ∈ N, while (−1) ∉ N.

2. *Associative law*. A binary operator $*$ on a set S is said to be associative whenever:

$$(x*y)*z = x*(y*z) \qquad \text{for all } x, y, z \in S$$

3. *Commutative law*. A binary operator $*$ on a set S is said to be commutative whenever:

$$x*y = y*x \qquad \text{for all } x, y \in S$$

4. *Identity element*. A set S is said to have an identity element with respect to a binary operation $*$ on S if there exists an element $e \in S$ with the property:

$$e*x = x*e = x \qquad \text{for every } x \in S$$

Example: The element 0 is an identity element with respect to operation $+$ on the set of integers $I = \{ \ldots, -3, -2, -1, 0, 1, 2, 3, \ldots \}$ since:

$$x + 0 = 0 + x = x \qquad \text{for any } x \in I$$

The set of natural numbers N has no identity element since 0 is excluded from the set.

5. *Inverse*. A set S having the identity element e with respect to a binary operator $*$ is said to have an inverse whenever, for every $x \in S$, there exists an element $y \in S$ such that:

$$x*y = e$$

Example: In the set of integers I with $e = 0$, the inverse of an element a is $(-a)$ since $a + (-a) = 0$.

6. *Distributive law*. If $*$ and $\cdot$ are two binary operators on a set S, $*$ is said to be distributive over $\cdot$ whenever:

$$x*(y \cdot z) = (x*y) \cdot (x*z)$$

An example of an algebraic structure is a *field*. A field is a set of elements, together with two binary operators, each having properties 1 to 5 and both operators combined to give property 6. The set of real numbers together with the binary operators $+$ and $\cdot$ form the field of real numbers. The field of real numbers is the basis for arithmetic and ordinary algebra. The operators and postulates have the following meanings:

The binary operator $+$ defines addition.

The additive identity is 0.

The additive inverse defines subtraction.

The binary operator $\cdot$ defines multiplication.

The multiplicative identity is 1.

The multiplicative inverse of $a = 1/a$ defines division, i.e., $a \cdot 1/a = 1$.

The only distributive law applicable is that of $\cdot$ over $+$:

$$a \cdot (b + c) = (a \cdot b) + (a \cdot c)$$

2-2 AXIOMATIC DEFINITION
OF BOOLEAN ALGEBRA

In 1854 George Boole (1) introduced a systematic treatment of logic and developed for this purpose an algebraic system now called *Boolean algebra*. In 1938 C. E. Shannon (2) introduced a two-valued Boolean algebra called *switching algebra*, in which he demonstrated that the properties of bistable electrical switching circuits can be represented by this algebra. For the formal definition of Boolean algebra, we shall employ the postulates formulated by E. V. Huntington (3) in 1904. These postulates or axioms are not unique for defining Boolean algebra. Other sets of postulates have been used.* Boolean algebra is an algebraic structure defined on a set of elements B together with two binary operators $+$ and $\cdot$ provided the following (Huntington) postulates are satisfied:

1. (a) Closure with respect to the operator $+$.
   (b) Closure with respect to the operator $\cdot$.

2. (a) An identity element with respect to $+$, designated by 0: $x + 0 = 0 + x = x$.
   (b) An identity element with respect to $\cdot$, designated by 1: $x \cdot 1 = 1 \cdot x = x$.

3. (a) Commutative with respect to $+$: $x + y = y + x$.
   (b) Commutative with respect to $\cdot$: $x \cdot y = y \cdot x$.

4. (a) $\cdot$ is distributive over $+$: $x \cdot (y + z) = (x \cdot y) + (x \cdot z)$.
   (b) $+$ is distributive over $\cdot$: $x + (y \cdot z) = (x + y) \cdot (x + z)$.

5. For every element $x \in B$, there exists an element $x' \in B$ (called the complement of x) such that: (a) $x + x' = 1$ and (b) $x \cdot x' = 0$.

6. There exists at least two elements $x, y \in B$ such that $x \neq y$.

Comparing Boolean algebra with arithmetic and ordinary algebra (the field of real numbers), we note the following differences:

1. Huntington postulates do not include the associative law. However, this law holds for Boolean algebra and can be derived (for both operators) from the other postulates.

---

*See, for example, Birkoff and Bartee (4), Chapter 5.

2. The distributive law of $+$ over $\cdot$, i.e., $x + (y \cdot z) = (x + y) \cdot (x + z)$, is valid for Boolean algebra, but not for ordinary algebra.

3. Boolean algebra does not have additive or multiplicative inverses; therefore, there are no subtraction or division operations.

4. Postulate 5 defines an operator called *complement* which is not available in ordinary algebra.

5. Ordinary algebra deals with the real numbers, which constitute an infinite set of elements. Boolean algebra deals with the as yet undefined set of elements B, but in the two-valued Boolean algebra defined below (and of interest in our subsequent use of this algebra), B is defined as a set with only two elements, 0 and 1.

Boolean algebra resembles ordinary algebra in some respects. The choice of symbols $+$ and $\cdot$ is intentional to facilitate Boolean algebraic manipulations by persons already familiar with ordinary algebra. Although one can use some knowledge from ordinary algebra to deal with Boolean algebra, the beginner must be careful not to substitute the rules of ordinary algebra where they are not applicable.

It is important to distinguish between the elements of the set of an algebraic structure and the variables of an algebraic system. For example, the elements of the field of real numbers are numbers, whereas variables such as a, b, c, etc., used in ordinary algebra, are symbols that stand for real numbers. Similarly in Boolean algebra, one defines the elements of the set B, and variables such as x, y, z are merely symbols that represent the elements. At this point, it is important to realize that in order to have a Boolean algebra, one must show:

1. the elements of the set B,

2. the rules of operation for the two binary operators, and

3. that the set of elements B, together with the two operators, satisfies the six Huntington postulates.

One can formulate many Boolean algebras, depending on the choice of elements of B and the rules of operation.* In our subsequent work, we deal only with a two-valued Boolean algebra, i.e., one with only two elements. Two-valued Boolean algebra has applications in set theory (the algebra of classes) and in propositional logic. Our interest here is with the application of Boolean algebra to gate-type circuits.

Two-Valued Boolean Algebra

A two-valued Boolean algebra is defined on a set of two elements, $B = \{0, 1\}$, with rules for the two binary operators $+$ and $\cdot$ as shown in the following operator tables (the rule for the complement operator is for verification of postulate 5):

*See, for example, Hohn (6), Whitesitt (7), or Birkhoff and Bartee (4).

x y	$x \cdot y$
0 0	0
0 1	0
1 0	0
1 1	1

x y	$x + y$
0 0	0
0 1	1
1 0	1
1 1	1

x	x'
0	1
1	0

These rules are exactly the same as the AND, OR, and NOT operations, respectively, defined in Table 1-6. We must now show that the Huntington postulates are valid for the set $B = \{0, 1\}$ and the two binary operators defined above.

1. *Closure* is obvious from the tables since the result of each operation is either 1 or 0 and 1, $0 \in B$.

2. From the tables we see that:

   (a) $0 + 0 = 0$ $0 + 1 = 1 + 0 = 1$
   (b) $1 \cdot 1 = 1$ $1 \cdot 0 = 0 \cdot 1 = 0$

   which establishes the two *identity elements* 0 for $+$ and 1 for $\cdot$ as defined by postulate 2.

3. The *commutative* laws are obvious from the symmetry of the binary operator tables.

4. (a) The *distributive* law $x \cdot (y + z) = (x \cdot y) + (x \cdot z)$ can be shown to hold true from the operator tables by forming a truth table of all possible values of x, y, and z. For each combination, we derive $x \cdot (y + z)$ and show that the value is the same as $(x \cdot y) + (x \cdot z)$.

x y z	$y + z$	$x \cdot (y + z)$	$x \cdot y$	$x \cdot z$	$(x \cdot y) + (x \cdot z)$
0 0 0	0	0	0	0	0
0 0 1	1	0	0	0	0
0 1 0	1	0	0	0	0
0 1 1	1	0	0	0	0
1 0 0	0	0	0	0	0
1 0 1	1	1	0	1	1
1 1 0	1	1	1	0	1
1 1 1	1	1	1	1	1

   (b) The *distributive* law of $+$ over $\cdot$ can be shown to hold true by means of a truth table similar to the one above.

5. From the complement table it is easily shown that:

   (a) $x + x' = 1$, since $0 + 0' = 0 + 1 = 1$ and $1 + 1' = 1 + 0 = 1$
   (b) $x \cdot x' = 0$, since $0 \cdot 0' = 0 \cdot 1 = 0$ and $1 \cdot 1' = 1 \cdot 0 = 0$ which verifies postulate 5.

6. Postulate 6 is satisfied because the two-valued Boolean algebra has two distinct elements 1 and 0 with $1 \neq 0$.

We have just established a two-valued Boolean algebra having a set of two elements, 1 and 0, two binary operators with operation rules equivalent to the AND and OR operations, and a complement operator equivalent to the NOT operator. Thus, Boolean algebra has been defined in a formal mathematical manner and has been shown to be equivalent to the binary logic presented heuristically in Section 1-8. The heuristic presentation is helpful in understanding the application of Boolean algebra to gate-type circuits. The formal presentation is necessary for developing the theorems and properties of the algebraic system. The two-valued Boolean algebra defined in this section is also called "switching algebra" by engineers. To emphasize the similarities between two-valued Boolean algebra and other binary systems, this algebra was called "binary logic" in Section 1-8. From here on, we shall drop the adjective "two-valued" from Boolean algebra in subsequent discussions.

2-3 BASIC THEOREMS AND PROPERTIES OF BOOLEAN ALGEBRA

Duality

The Huntington postulates have been listed in pairs and designated by part (a) and part (b). One part may be obtained from the other if the binary operators and the identity elements are interchanged. This important property of Boolean algebra is called the *duality principle*. It states that every algebraic expression deducible from the postulates of Boolean algebra remains valid if the operators and identity elements are interchanged. In a two-valued Boolean algebra, the identity elements and the elements of the set B are the same: 1 and 0. The duality principle has many applications. If the *dual* of an algebraic expression is desired, we simply interchange OR and AND operators and replace 1's by 0's and 0's by 1's.

Basic Theorems

Table 2-1 lists six theorems of Boolean algebra and four of its postulates. The notation is simplified by omitting the $\cdot$ whenever this does not lead to confusion. The theorems and postulates listed are the most basic relationships in Boolean algebra. The reader is advised to become familiar with them as soon as possible. The theorems, like the postulates, are listed in pairs; each relation is the dual of the one paired with it. The postulates are basic axioms of the algebraic structure and need no proof. The theorems must be proven from the postulates. The proofs of the theorems with one variable are presented below. At the right is listed the number of the postulate which justifies each step of the proof.

TABLE 2-1 Postulates and theorems of Boolean algebra

Postulate 2	(a) $x + 0 = x$	(b) $x \cdot 1 = x$
Postulate 5	(a) $x + x' = 1$	(b) $x \cdot x' = 0$
Theorem 1	(a) $x + x = x$	(b) $x \cdot x = x$
Theorem 2	(a) $x + 1 = 1$	(b) $x \cdot 0 = 0$
Theorem 3, involution	$(x')' = x$	
Postulate 3, commutative	(a) $x + y = y + x$	(b) $xy = yx$
Theorem 4, associative	(a) $x + (y + z) = (x + y) + z$	(b) $x(yz) = (xy)z$
Postulate 4, distributive	(a) $x(y + z) = xy + xz$	(b) $x + yz = (x + y)(x + z)$
Theorem 5, DeMorgan	(a) $(x + y)' = x'y'$	(b) $(xy)' = x' + y'$
Theorem 6, absorption	(a) $x + xy = x$	(b) $x(x + y) = x$

THEOREM 1(a): $x + x = x$.

$$
\begin{aligned}
x + x &= (x + x) \cdot 1 && \text{by postulate: 2(b)} \\
&= (x + x)(x + x') && 5(a) \\
&= x + xx' && 4(b) \\
&= x + 0 && 5(b) \\
&= x && 2(a)
\end{aligned}
$$

THEOREM 1(b): $x \cdot x = x$.

$$
\begin{aligned}
x \cdot x &= xx + 0 && \text{by postulate: 2(a)} \\
&= xx + xx' && 5(b) \\
&= x(x + x') && 4(a) \\
&= x \cdot 1 && 5(a) \\
&= x && 2(b)
\end{aligned}
$$

Note that theorem 1(b) is the dual of theorem 1(a) and that each step of the proof in part (b) is the dual of part (a). Any dual theorem can be similarly derived from the proof of its corresponding pair.

THEOREM 2(a): $x + 1 = 1$.

$$
\begin{aligned}
x + 1 &= 1 \cdot (x + 1) && \text{by postulate: 2(b)} \\
&= (x + x')(x + 1) && 5(a) \\
&= x + x' \cdot 1 && 4(b) \\
&= x + x' && 2(b) \\
&= 1 && 5(a)
\end{aligned}
$$

THEOREM 2(b): $x \cdot 0 = 0$ by duality.

THEOREM 3: $(x')' = x$. From postulate 5, we have $x + x' = 1$ and $x \cdot x' = 0$, which defines the complement of x. The complement of x' is x and is also $(x')'$. Therefore, since the complement is unique, we have that $(x')' = x$.

The theorems involving two or three variables may be proven algebraically from the postulates and the theorems which have already been proven. Take, for example, the absorption theorem.

THEOREM 6(a): $x + xy = x$.

$$\begin{aligned}
x + xy &= x \cdot 1 + xy && \text{by postulate 2(b)} \\
&= x(1 + y) && \text{by postulate 4(a)} \\
&= x(y + 1) && \text{by postulate 3(a)} \\
&= x \cdot 1 && \text{by theorem 2(a)} \\
&= x && \text{by postulate 2(b)}
\end{aligned}$$

THEOREM 6(b): $x(x + y) = x$ by duality.

The theorems of Boolean algebra can be shown to hold true by means of truth tables. In truth tables, both sides of the relation are checked to yield identical results for all possible combinations of variables involved. The following truth table verifies the first absorption theorem.

x	y	xy	$x + xy$
0	0	0	0
0	1	0	0
1	0	0	1
1	1	1	1

The algebraic proofs of the associative law and De Morgan's theorem are long and will not be shown here. However, their validity is easily shown with truth tables. For example, the truth table for the first De Morgan's theorem $(x + y)' = x'y'$ is shown below.

x	y	$x + y$	$(x + y)'$	x'	y'	$x'y'$
0	0	0	1	1	1	1
0	1	1	0	1	0	0
1	0	1	0	0	1	0
1	1	1	0	0	0	0

Operator Precedence

The operator precedence for evaluating Boolean expressions is (1) parentheses, (2) NOT, (3) AND, and (4) OR. In other words, the expression inside the parentheses must be evaluated before all other operations. The next operation that holds precedence is the complement, then follows the AND, and finally the OR. As an example, consider the truth table for De Morgan's theorem. The left side of the expression is $(x + y)'$. Therefore, the expression inside the parentheses is evaluated first and the result then complemented. The right side of the expression is $x'y'$. Therefore, the complement of x and the complement of y are both evaluated first and the result is then ANDed. Note that in ordinary arithmetic the same precedence holds (except for the complement) when multiplication and addition are replaced by AND and OR, respectively.

Venn Diagram

A helpful illustration that may be used to visualize the relationships among the variables of a Boolean expression is the *Venn diagram*. This diagram consists of a rectangle such as shown in Fig. 2-1, inside of which are drawn overlapping circles, one for each variable. Each circle is labeled by a variable. We designate all points inside a circle as belonging to the named variable and all points outside a circle as not belonging to the variable. Take, for example, the circle labeled x. If we are inside the circle, we say that $x = 1$; when outside, we say $x = 0$. Now, with two overlapping circles, there are four distinct areas inside the rectangle: the area not belonging to either x or y $(x'y')$, the area inside circle y but outside x $(x'y)$, the area inside circle x but outside y (xy'), and the area inside both circles (xy).

Venn diagrams may be used to illustrate the postulates of Boolean algebra or to show the validity of theorems. Figure 2-2, for example, illustrates that the area belonging to xy is inside the circle x and therefore $x + xy = x$. Figure 2-3 illustrates the distributive law $x(y + z) = xy + xz$. In this diagram we have three overlapping circles, one for each of the variables x, y, and z. It is possible to distinguish eight distinct areas in a three-variable Venn diagram. For this particular example, the distributive law is demonstrated by noting that the area intersecting the circle x with the area enclosing y or z is the same area belonging to xy or xz.

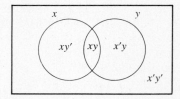

Figure 2-1   Venn diagram for two variables

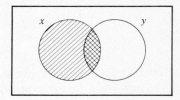

Figure 2-2   Venn diagram illustration $x = xy + x$

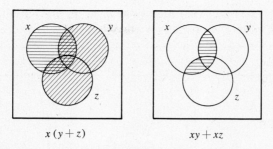

$$x(y+z) \qquad\qquad xy+xz$$

Figure 2-3   Venn diagram illustration of the distributive law

2-4   BOOLEAN FUNCTIONS

A binary variable can take the value of 0 or 1. A Boolean function is an expression formed with binary variables, the two binary operators OR and AND, the unary operator NOT, parentheses, and equal sign. For a given value of the variables, the function can be either 0 or 1. Consider, for example, the Boolean function:

$$F_1 = xyz'$$

The function F_1 is equal to 1 if $x = 1$ *and* $y = 1$ *and* $z' = 1$; otherwise $F_1 = 0$. The above is an example of a Boolean function represented as an algebraic expression. A Boolean function may also be represented in a truth table. To represent a function in a truth table, we need a list of the 2^n combinations of 1's and 0's of the n binary variables, and a column showing the combinations for which the function is equal to 1 or 0. As shown in Table 2-2, there are eight possible distinct combinations for assigning bits to three variables. The column labeled F_1 contains either a 0 or a 1 for each of these combinations. The table shows that the function F_1 is equal to 1 only when $x = 1$, $y = 1$, and $z = 0$. It is equal to 0 otherwise. (Note that the statement $z' = 1$ is equivalent to saying that $z = 0$.) Consider now the function:

$$F_2 = x + y'z$$

$F_2 = 1$ if $x = 1$ or if $y = 0$, while $z = 1$. In Table 2-2, $x = 1$ in the last four rows and $yz = 01$ in rows 001 and 101. The latter combination applies also for $x = 1$. Therefore, there are five combinations that make $F_2 = 1$. As a third example, consider the function:

$$F_3 = x'y'z + x'yz + xy'$$

This is shown in Table 2-2 with four 1's and four 0's. F_4 is the same as F_3 and is considered below.

TABLE 2-2 Truth tables for $F_1 = xyz'$, $F_2 = x + y'z$, $F_3 = x'y'z + x'yz + xy'$, and $F_4 = xy' + x'z$

x	y	z	F_1	F_2	F_3	F_4
0	0	0	0	0	0	0
0	0	1	0	1	1	1
0	1	0	0	0	0	0
0	1	1	0	0	1	1
1	0	0	0	1	1	1
1	0	1	0	1	1	1
1	1	0	1	1	0	0
1	1	1	0	1	0	0

Any Boolean function can be represented in a truth table. The number of rows in the table is 2^n, where n is the number of binary variables in the function. The 1's and 0's combinations for each row is easily obtained from the binary numbers by counting from 0 to $2^n - 1$. For each row of the table, there is a value for the function equal to either 1 or 0. The question now arises, Is an algebraic expression of a given Boolean function unique? In other words, Is it possible to find two algebraic expressions that specify the same function? The answer to this question is yes. As a matter of fact, the manipulation of Boolean algebra is applied mostly to the problem of finding simpler expressions for the same function. Consider, for example, the function:

$$F_4 = xy' + x'z$$

From Table 2-2, we find that F_4 is the same as F_3, since both have identical 1's and 0's for each combination of values of the three binary variables. In general, two functions of n binary variables are said to be equal if they have the same value for all possible 2^n combinations of the n variables.

A Boolean function may be transformed from an algebraic expression into a logic diagram composed of AND, OR, and NOT gates. The implementation of the four functions introduced in the previous discussion is shown in Fig. 2-4. The logic diagram includes an inverter circuit for every variable present in its complement form. (The inverter is unnecessary if the complement of the variable is available.) There is an AND gate for each term in the expression, and an OR gate is used to combine two or more terms. From the diagrams, it is obvious that the implementation of F_4 requires fewer gates and fewer inputs than F_3. Since F_4 and F_3 are equal Boolean functions, it is more economical to implement the F_4 form than the F_3 form. To find simpler circuits, one must know how to manipulate Boolean functions to obtain equal and simpler expressions. What constitutes the best form of a Boolean function depends on the particular application. In this section, consideration is given to the criterion of equipment minimization.

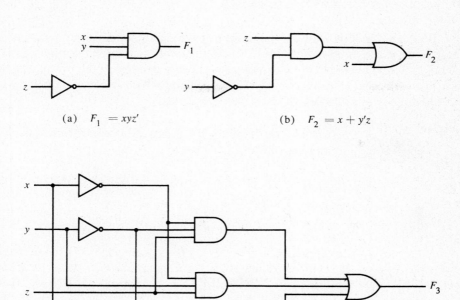

(a) $F_1 = xyz'$

(b) $F_2 = x + y'z$

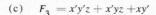

(c) $F_3 = x'y'z + x'yz + xy'$

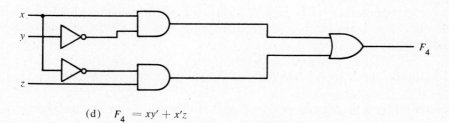

(d) $F_4 = xy' + x'z$

Figure 2-4 Implementation of Boolean functions with gates

Algebraic Manipulation

A *literal* is a primed or unprimed variable. When a Boolean function is implemented with logic gates, each literal in the function designates an input to a gate, and each term is implemented with a gate. The minimization of the number of literals and the number of terms results in a circuit with less equipment. It is not always possible to minimize both simultaneously; usually, further criteria must be available. At the moment, we shall narrow the minimization criterion to literal minimization. We shall discuss other criteria in Chapter 5. The number of literals in a Boolean function can be minimized by algebraic manipulations. Unfortunately, there are no specific rules to follow that will guarantee the final answer. The only method available is a cut-and-try procedure employing the postulates, the basic theorems, and any other manipulation method which becomes familiar with use. The following examples illustrate this procedure.

EXAMPLE 2-1: Simplify the following Boolean functions to a minimum number of literals.

1. $x + x'y = (x + x')(x + y) = 1 \cdot (x + y) = x + y$

2. $x(x' + y) = xx' + xy = 0 + xy = xy$

3. $x'y'z + x'yz + xy' = x'z(y' + y) + xy' = x'z + xy'$

4. $xy + x'z + yz = xy + x'z + yz(x + x')$
$$= xy + x'z + xyz + x'yz$$
$$= xy(1 + z) + x'z(1 + y)$$
$$= xy + x'z$$

5. $(x + y)(x' + z)(y + z) = (x + y)(x' + z)$ by duality from function 4.

Functions 1 and 2 are the duals of each other and use dual expressions in corresponding steps. Function 3 shows the equality of the functions F_3 and F_4 discussed previously. The fourth illustrates the fact that an increase in the number of literals sometimes leads to a final simpler expression. Function 5 is not minimized directly but can be derived from the dual of the steps used to derive function 4.

Complement of a Function

The complement of a function F is F' and is obtained from an interchange of 0's for 1's and 1's for 0's in the value of F. The complement of a function may be derived algebraically through De Morgan's theorem. This pair of theorems is listed in Table 2-1 for two variables. De Morgan's theorems can be extended to three or more variables. The three-variable form of the first De Morgan's theorem is derived below. The postulates and theorems are those listed in Table 2-1.

$$(A + B + C)' = (A + X)' \qquad \text{let } B + C = X$$
$$= A'X' \qquad \text{by theorem 5(a) (De Morgan)}$$
$$= A' \cdot (B + C)' \qquad \text{substitute } B + C = X$$
$$= A' \cdot (B'C') \qquad \text{by theorem 5(a) (De Morgan)}$$
$$= A'B'C' \qquad \text{by theorem 4(b) (associative)}$$

De Morgan's theorems for any number of variables resemble in form the two-variable case and can be derived by successive substitutions similar to the method used in the above derivation. These theorems can be generalized as follows:

$$(A + B + C + D + \cdots + F)' = A'B'C'D' \ldots F'$$
$$(ABCD \cdots F)' = A' + B' + C' + D' + \ldots + F'$$

The generalized form of De Morgan's theorem states that the complement of a function is obtained by interchanging AND and OR operators and complementing each literal.

> **EXAMPLE 2-2:** Find the complement of the functions $F_1 = x'yz' + x'y'z$ and $F_2 = x(y'z' + yz)$. Applying De Morgan's theorem as many times as necessary, the complements are obtained as follows:
>
> $$F_1' = (x'yz' + x'y'z)' = (x'yz')'(x'y'z)' = (x + y' + z)(x + y + z')$$
> $$F_2' = [x(y'z' + yz)]' = x' + (y'z' + yz)' = x' + (y'z')' \cdot (yz)'$$
> $$= x' + (y + z)(y' + z')$$

A simpler procedure for deriving the complement of a function is to take the dual of the function and complement each literal. This method follows from the generalized De Morgan's theorem. Remember that the dual of a function is obtained from the interchange of AND and OR operators and 1's and 0's.

> **EXAMPLE 2-3:** Find the complement of the functions F_1 and F_2 of Example 2-2 by taking their duals and complementing each literal.
>
> 1. $F_1 = x'yz' + x'y'z$.
>   The dual of F_1 is $(x' + y + z')(x' + y' + z)$.
>   Complement each literal: $(x + y' + z)(x + y + z') = F_1'$.
>
> 2. $F_2 = x(y'z' + yz)$.
>   The dual of F_2 is $x + (y' + z')(y + z)$.
>   Complement each literal: $x' + (y + z)(y' + z') = F_2'$.

2-5 CANONICAL AND STANDARD FORMS

Minterms and Maxterms

A binary variable may appear either in its normal form (x) or in its complement form (x'). Now consider two binary variables x and y combined with an AND operation. Since each variable may appear in either form, there are four possible

TABLE 2-3 Minterms and maxterms for three binary variables

x y z	Minterms		Maxterms	
	Term	Designation	Term	Designation
0 0 0	$x'y'z'$	m_0	$x + y + z$	M_0
0 0 1	$x'y'z$	m_1	$x + y + z'$	M_1
0 1 0	$x'yz'$	m_2	$x + y' + z$	M_2
0 1 1	$x'yz$	m_3	$x + y' + z'$	M_3
1 0 0	$xy'z'$	m_4	$x' + y + z$	M_4
1 0 1	$xy'z$	m_5	$x' + y + z'$	M_5
1 1 0	xyz'	m_6	$x' + y' + z$	M_6
1 1 1	xyz	m_7	$x' + y' + z'$	M_7

combinations: $x'y'$, $x'y$, xy', and xy. Each of these four AND terms represents one of the distinct areas in the Venn diagram of Fig. 2-1 and is called a *minterm* or a *standard product*. In a similar manner, n variables can be combined to form 2^n minterms. The 2^n different minterms may be determined by a method similar to the one shown in Table 2-3 for three variables. The binary numbers from 0 to $2^n - 1$ are listed under the n variables. Each minterm is obtained from an AND term of the n variables, with each variable being primed if the corresponding bit of the binary number is a 0 and unprimed if a 1. A symbol for each minterm is also shown in the table and is of the form m_j, where j denotes the decimal equivalent of the binary number of the minterm designated.

In a similar fashion, n variables forming an OR term, with each variable being primed or unprimed, provide 2^n possible combinations, called *maxterms* or *standard sums*. The eight maxterms for three variables, together with their symbolic designation, are listed in Table 2-3. Any 2^n maxterms for n variables may be determined similarly. Each maxterm is obtained from an OR term of the n variables, with each variable being unprimed if the corresponding bit is a 0 and primed if a 1.* Note that each maxterm is the complement of its corresponding minterm, and vice versa.

A Boolean function may be expressed algebraically from a given truth table by forming a minterm for each combination of the variables which produces a 1 in the function, and then taking the OR of all those terms. For example, the function f_1 in Table 2-4 is determined by expressing the combinations 001, 100, and 111 as $x'y'z$, $xy'z'$, and xyz, respectively. Since each one of these minterms results in $f_1 = 1$, we should have:

$$f_1 = x'y'z + xy'z' + xyz = m_1 + m_4 + m_7$$

*Some books define a maxterm as an OR term of the n variables, with each variable being unprimed if the bit is a 1 and primed if a 0. The definition adopted in this book is preferable as it leads to simpler conversions between maxterm- and minterm-type functions.

TABLE 2-4   Functions of three variables

x	y	z	Function f_1	Function f_2
0	0	0	0	0
0	0	1	1	0
0	1	0	0	0
0	1	1	0	1
1	0	0	1	0
1	0	1	0	1
1	1	0	0	1
1	1	1	1	1

Similarly, it may be easily verified that:

$$f_2 = x'yz + xy'z + xyz' + xyz = m_3 + m_5 + m_6 + m_7$$

These examples demonstrate an important property of Boolean algebra: Any Boolean function can be expressed as a sum of minterms (by "sum" is meant the ORing of terms).

Now consider the complement of a Boolean function. It may be read from the truth table by forming a minterm for each combination that produces a 0 in the function and then ORing those terms. The complement of f_1 is read as:

$$f_1' = x'y'z' + x'yz' + x'yz + xy'z + xyz'$$

If we take the complement of f_1', we obtain the function f_1:

$$f_1 = (x + y + z)(x + y' + z)(x + y' + z')(x' + y + z')(x' + y' + z)$$
$$= M_0 \cdot M_2 \cdot M_3 \cdot M_5 \cdot M_6$$

Similarly, it is possible to read the expression for f_2 from the table:

$$f_2 = (x + y + z)(x + y + z')(x + y' + z)(x' + y + z)$$
$$= M_0 M_1 M_2 M_4$$

These examples demonstrate a second important property of Boolean algebra: Any Boolean function can be expressed as a product of maxterms (by "product" is meant the ANDing of terms). The procedure for obtaining the product of maxterms directly from the truth table is as follows. Form a maxterm for each combination of the variables which produces a 0 in the function, and then form the AND of all those maxterms. Boolean functions expressed as a sum of minterms or product of maxterms are said to be in *canonical form*.

Sum of Minterms

It was previously stated that for n binary variables, one can obtain 2^n distinct minterms, and that any Boolean function can be expressed as a sum of minterms. The minterms whose sum defines the Boolean function are those that give the 1's of the function in a truth table. Since the function can be either 1 or 0 for each minterm, and since there are 2^n minterms, one can calculate the possible functions that can be formed with n variables to be 2^{2^n}. It is sometimes convenient to express the Boolean function in its sum-of-minterms form. If not in this form, it can be made so by first expanding the expression into a sum of AND terms. Each term is then inspected to see if it contains all the variables. If it misses one or more variables, it is ANDed with an expression such as $x + x'$, where x is one of the missing variables. The following example clarifies this procedure.

EXAMPLE 2-4: Express the Boolean function $F = A + B'C$ in a sum of minterms. The function has three variables A, B, and C. The first term A is missing two variables; therefore:

$$A = A(B + B') = AB + AB'$$

This is still missing one variable:

$$A = AB(C + C') + AB'(C + C')$$
$$= ABC + ABC' + AB'C + AB'C'$$

The second term $B'C$ is missing one variable:

$$B'C = B'C(A + A') = AB'C + A'B'C$$

Combining all terms, we have:

$$F = A + B'C$$
$$= ABC + ABC' + AB'C + AB'C' + AB'C + A'B'C$$

But $AB'C$ appears twice, and according to theorem 1 $(x + x = x)$, it is possible to remove one of them. Rearranging the minterms in ascending order, we finally obtain:

$$F = A'B'C + AB'C' + AB'C + ABC' + ABC$$
$$= m_1 + m_4 + m_5 + m_6 + m_7$$

It is sometimes convenient to express the Boolean function, when in its sum of minterms, in the following short notation:

$$F(A, B, C) = \Sigma\,(1, 4, 5, 6, 7)$$

The summation symbol Σ stands for the ORing of terms; the numbers following it are the minterms of the function. The letters in parentheses following F form a list of the variables in the order taken when the minterm is converted to an AND term.

Product of Maxterms

Each of the 2^{2^n} functions of n binary variables can be also expressed as a product of maxterms. To express the Boolean function as a product of maxterms, it must first be brought into a form of OR terms. This may be done by using the distributive law $x + yz = (x + y)(x + z)$. Then any missing variable x in each OR term is ORed with xx'. This procedure is clarified by the following example.

> **EXAMPLE 2-5:** Express the Boolean function $F = xy + x'z$ in a product of maxterm form. First convert the function into OR terms using the distributive law:
>
> $$F = xy + x'z = (xy + x')(xy + z)$$
> $$= (x + x')(y + x')(x + z)(y + z)$$
> $$= (x' + y)(x + z)(y + z)$$
>
> The function has three variables: x, y, and z. Each OR term is missing one variable; therefore:
>
> $$x' + y = x' + y + zz' = (x' + y + z)(x' + y + z')$$
> $$x + z = x + z + yy' = (x + y + z)(x + y' + z)$$
> $$y + z = y + z + xx' = (x + y + z)(x' + y + z)$$
>
> Combining all the terms and removing those that appear more than once, we finally obtain:
>
> $$F = (x + y + z)(x + y' + z)(x' + y + z)(x' + y + z')$$
> $$= M_0 M_2 M_4 M_5$$
>
> A convenient way to express this function is as follows:
>
> $$F(x, y, z) = \Pi(0, 2, 4, 5)$$

The product symbol, Π, denotes the ANDing of maxterms; the numbers are the maxterms of the function.

Conversion between Canonical Forms

The complement of a function expressed as the sum of minterms equals the sum of minterms missing from the original function. This is because the original function is expressed by those minterms that make the function equal to 1, while its complement is a 1 for those minterms that the function is a 0. As an example, consider the function:

$$F(A, B, C) = \Sigma(1, 4, 5, 6, 7)$$

This has a complement that can be expressed as:

$$F'(A, B, C) = \Sigma(0, 2, 3) = m_0 + m_2 + m_3$$

Now, if we take the complement of F' by De Morgan's theorem, we obtain F in a different form:

$$F = (m_0 + m_2 + m_3)' = m_0' \cdot m_2' \cdot m_3' = M_0 M_2 M_3 = \Pi(0, 2, 3)$$

The last conversion follows from the definition of minterms and maxterms as shown in Table 2-3. From the table, it is clear that the following relation holds true:

$$m_j' = M_j$$

That is, the maxterm with subscript j is a complement of the minterm with the same subscript j, and vice versa.

The last example demonstrates the conversion between a function expressed in sum of minterms and its equivalent in product of maxterms. A similar argument will show that the conversion between the product of maxterms and the sum of minterms is similar. We now state a general conversion procedure. To convert from one canonical form to another, interchange the symbols Σ and Π and list those numbers missing from the original form. As another example, the function:

$$F(x, y, z) = \Pi(0, 2, 4, 5)$$

is expressed in the product of maxterm form. Its conversion to sum of minterms is:

$$F(x, y, z) = \Sigma(1, 3, 6, 7)$$

Note that, in order to find the missing terms, one must realize that the total number of minterms or maxterms is 2^n, where n is the number of binary variables in the function.

Standard Forms

The two canonical forms of Boolean algebra are basic forms that one obtains from reading a function from the truth table. These forms are very seldom the ones with the least number of literals, because each minterm or maxterm must contain, by definition, *all* the variables either complemented or uncomplemented.

Another way to express Boolean functions is in *standard* form. In this configuration, the terms that form the function may contain one, two or any number of literals. There are two types of standard forms: the sum of products and product of sums.

The *sum of products* is a Boolean expression containing AND terms, called *product terms*, of one or more literals each. The *sum* denotes the ORing of these terms. An example of a function expressed in sum of products is:

$$F_1 = y' + xy + x'yz'$$

The expression has three product terms of one, two, and three literals each, respectively. Their sum is in effect an OR operation.

A *product of sums* is a Boolean expression containing OR terms, called *sum terms*. Each term may have any number of literals. The *product* denotes the ANDing of these terms. An example of a function expressed in product of sums is:

$$F_2 = x(y' + z)(x' + y + z' + w)$$

This expression has three sum terms of one, two, and four literals each. The product is an AND operation. The use of the words *product* and *sum* stems from the similarity of the AND operation to the arithmetic product (multiplication) and the similarity of the OR operation to the arithmetic sum (addition).

A Boolean function may be expressed in a nonstandard form. For example, the function:

$$F_3 = (AB + CD)(A'B' + C'D')$$

is neither in sum of products nor in product of sums. It can be changed to a standard form by using the distributive law to remove the parentheses:

$$F_3 = A'B'CD + ABC'D'$$

2-6　OTHER LOGIC OPERATIONS

When the binary operators AND and OR are placed between two variables x and y, they form two Boolean functions $x \cdot y$ and $x + y$, respectively. It was stated previously that there are 2^{2^n} functions for n binary variables. For two variables, $n = 2$ and the number of possible Boolean functions is 16. Therefore, the AND and OR functions are only two of a total of 16 possible functions formed with two binary variables. It would be instructive to find the other 14 functions and investigate their properties.

The truth tables for the 16 functions formed with two binary variables x and y are listed in Table 2-5. In this table, each of the 16 columns F_0 to F_{15} represents a truth table of one possible function for the two given variables x and y. Note that the functions are determined from the 16 binary combinations that can be assigned to F. Some of the functions are shown with an operator symbol. For example, F_1

TABLE 2-5 Truth tables for the 16 functions of two binary variables

x	y	F_0	F_1	F_2	F_3	F_4	F_5	F_6	F_7	F_8	F_9	F_{10}	F_{11}	F_{12}	F_{13}	F_{14}	F_{15}
0	0	0	0	0	0	0	0	0	0	1	1	1	1	1	1	1	1
0	1	0	0	0	0	1	1	1	1	0	0	0	0	1	1	1	1
1	0	0	0	1	1	0	0	1	1	0	0	1	1	0	0	1	1
1	1	0	1	0	1	0	1	0	1	0	1	0	1	0	1	0	1
Operator Symbol			$\cdot$	/		/		$\oplus$	$+$	$\downarrow$	$\odot$	$'$	$\subset$	$'$	$\supset$	$\uparrow$	

represents the truth table for AND and F_7 represents the truth table for OR. The operator symbols for these functions are $(\cdot)$ and $(+)$, respectively.

The 16 functions listed in truth table form can be expressed algebraically by means of Boolean expressions. This is shown in the first column of Table 2-6. The Boolean expressions listed are simplified to their minimum number of literals.

Although each function can be expressed in terms of the Boolean operators AND, OR, and NOT, there is no reason one cannot assign special operator symbols for expressing the other functions. Such operator symbols are listed in the

TABLE 2-6 Boolean expressions for the 16 functions of two variables

Boolean functions	Operator symbol	Name	Comments
$F_0 = 0$		Null	Binary constant 0
$F_1 = xy$	$x \cdot y$	AND	x and y
$F_2 = xy'$	x/y	Inhibition	x but not y
$F_3 = x$		Transfer	x
$F_4 = x'y$	y/x	Inhibition	y but not x
$F_5 = y$		Transfer	y
$F_6 = xy' + x'y$	$x \oplus y$	Exclusive-OR	x or y but not both
$F_7 = x + y$	$x + y$	OR	x or y
$F_8 = (x + y)'$	$x \downarrow y$	NOR	Not-OR
$F_9 = xy + x'y'$	$x \odot y$	Equivalence*	x equals y
$F_{10} = y'$	y'	Complement	Not y
$F_{11} = x + y'$	$x \subset y$	Implication	If y then x
$F_{12} = x'$	x'	Complement	Not x
$F_{13} = x' + y$	$x \supset y$	Implication	If x then y
$F_{14} = (xy)'$	$x \uparrow y$	NAND	Not-AND
$F_{15} = 1$		Identity	Binary constant 1

Equivalence is also known as *equality*, *coincidence*, and *exclusive-NOR*.

second column of Table 2-6. However, all the new symbols shown, except for the exclusive-OR symbol ⊕, are not in common use by digital designers.

Each of the functions in Table 2-6 is listed with an accompanying name and a comment that explains the function in some way. The 16 functions listed can be subdivided into three categories:

1. Two functions that produce a constant 0 or 1.

2. Four functions with unary operations complement and transfer.

3. Ten functions with binary operators that define eight different operations AND, OR, NAND, NOR, exclusive - OR, equivalence, inhibition, and implication.

Any function can be equal to a constant, but a binary function can be equal to only 1 or 0. The complement function produces the complement of each of the binary variables. A function which is equal to an input variable has been given the name *transfer*, because the variable x or y is transferred through the gate that forms the function without changing its value. Of the eight binary operators, two (inhibition and implication) are used by logicians but are seldom used in computer logic. The AND and OR operators have been mentioned in conjunction with Boolean algebra. The other four functions are extensively used in the design of digital systems.

The NOR function is the complement of the OR function and its name is an abbreviation of *not-OR*. Similarly, NAND is the complement of AND and is an abbreviation of *not-AND*. The exclusive-OR, abbreviated XOR or EOR, is similar to OR but excludes the combination of *both* x and y being equal to 1. The equivalence is a function that is 1 when the two binary variables are equal, i.e., when both are 0 or both are 1. The exclusive-OR and equivalence functions are the complements of each other. This can be easily verified by inspecting Table 2-5. The truth table for the exclusive-OR is F_6 and for the equivalence is F_9, and these two functions are the complements of each other. For this reason, the equivalence function is often called exclusive-NOR, i.e., exclusive-OR-NOT.

Boolean algebra, as defined in Sections 2-2, has two binary operators, which we have called AND and OR, and a unary operator, NOT (complement). From the definitions, we have deduced a number of properties of these operators and now have defined other binary operators in terms of them. There is nothing unique about this procedure. We could have just as well started with the operator NOR (↓), for example, and later defined AND, OR, and NOT in terms of it. There are, nevertheless, good reasons for introducing Boolean algebra in the way it has been introduced. The concepts of "and," "or," and "not" are familiar and are used by people to express everyday logical ideas. Moreover, the Huntington postulates reflect the dual nature of the algebra, emphasizing the symmetry of + and · with respect to each other.

2-7 DIGITAL LOGIC GATES

Since Boolean functions are expressed in terms of AND, OR, and NOT operations, it is easier to implement a Boolean function with these types of gates. The possibility of constructing gates for the other logic operations is of practical interest. Factors to be weighed when considering the construction of other types of logic gates are (1) the feasibility and economy of producing the gate with physical components, (2) the possibility of extending the gate to more than two inputs, (3) the basic properties of the binary operator such as commutativity and associativity, and (4) the ability of the gate to implement Boolean functions alone or in conjuction with other gates.

Of the 16 functions defined in Table 2-6, two are equal to a constant and four others are repeated twice. There are only ten functions left to be considered as candidates for logic gates. Two, inhibition and implication, are not commutative or associative and thus are impractical to use as standard logic gates. The other eight: complement, transfer, AND, OR, NAND, NOR, exclusive-OR, and equivalence, are used as standard gates in digital design.

The graphic symbols and truth tables of the eight gates are shown in Fig. 2-5. Each gate has one or two binary input variables designated by x and y and one binary output variable designated by F. The AND, OR, and inverter circuits were defined in Fig. 1-6. The inverter circuit inverts the logic sense of a binary variable. It produces the NOT, or complement, function. The small circle in the output of the graphic symbol of an inverter designates the logic complement. The triangle symbol by itself designates a buffer circuit. A buffer produces the *transfer* function but does not produce any particular logic operation, since the binary value of the output is equal to the binary value of the input. This circuit is used merely for power amplification of the signal and is equivalent to two inverters connected in cascade.

The NAND function is the complement of the AND function, as indicated by a graphic symbol which consists of an AND graphic symbol followed by a small circle. The NOR function is the complement of the OR function and uses an OR graphic symbol followed by a small circle. The NAND and NOR gates are extensively used as standard logic gates and are in fact far more popular than the AND and OR gates. This is because NAND and NOR gates are easily constructed with transistor circuits and because Boolean functions can be easily implemented with them.

The exclusive-OR gate has a graphic symbol similar to that of the OR gate, except for the additional curved line on the input side. The equivalence, or exclusive-NOR, gate is the complement of the exclusive-OR, as indicated by the small circle on the output side of the graphic symbol.

Extension to Multiple Inputs

The gates shown in Fig. 2-5, except for the inverter and buffer, can be extended to have more than two inputs. A gate can be extended to have multiple inputs if the

Name	Graphic symbol	Algebraic function	Truth table		
			x	y	F
AND		$F = xy$	0	0	0
			0	1	0
			1	0	0
			1	1	1
			x	y	F
OR		$F = x + y$	0	0	0
			0	1	1
			1	0	1
			1	1	1
			x		F
Inverter		$F = x'$	0		1
			1		0
			x		F
Buffer		$F = x$	0		0
			1		1
			x	y	F
NAND		$F = (xy)'$	0	0	1
			0	1	1
			1	0	1
			1	1	0
			x	y	F
NOR		$F = (x + y)'$	0	0	1
			0	1	0
			1	0	0
			1	1	0
			x	y	F
Exclusive-OR (XOR)		$F = xy' + x'y$ $= x \oplus y$	0	0	0
			0	1	1
			1	0	1
			1	1	0
			x	y	F
Exclusive-NOR or equivalence		$F = xy + x'y'$ $= x \odot y$	0	0	1
			0	1	0
			1	0	0
			1	1	1

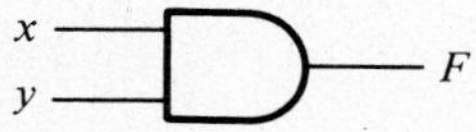

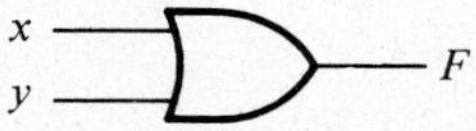

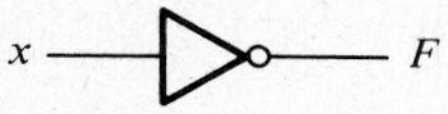

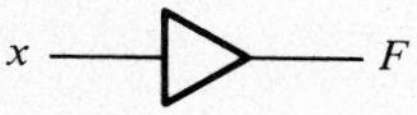

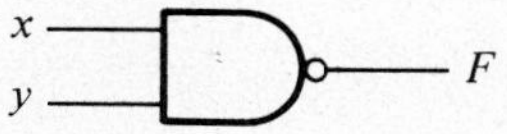

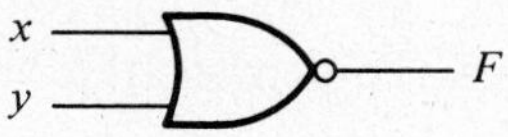

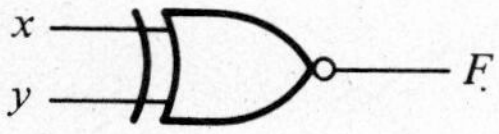

Figure 2-5 Digital logic gates

binary operation it represents is commutative and associative. The AND and OR operations, defined in Boolean algebra, possess these two properties. For the OR function we have:

$$x + y = y + x \qquad \text{commutative}$$

and

$$(x + y) + z = x + (y + z) = x + y + z \qquad \text{associative}$$

which indicates that the gate inputs can be interchanged and that the OR function can be extended to three or more variables.

The NAND and NOR functions are commutative and their gates can be extended to have more than two inputs, provided the definition of the operation is slightly modified. The difficulty is that the NAND and NOR operators are not associative, i.e., $(x{\downarrow}y){\downarrow}z \neq x{\downarrow}(y{\downarrow}z)$, as shown in Fig. 2-6 and below:

$$(x{\downarrow}y){\downarrow}z = [(x + y)' + z]' = (x + y)z' = xz' + yz'$$
$$x{\downarrow}(y{\downarrow}z) = [x + (y + z)']' = x'(y + z) = x'y + x'z$$

To overcome this difficulty, we define the multiple NOR (or NAND) gate as a complemented OR (or AND) gate. Thus, by definition, we have:

$$x{\downarrow}y{\downarrow}z = (x + y + z)'$$
$$x{\uparrow}y{\uparrow}z = (xyz)'$$

The graphic symbols for the three-input gates are shown in Fig. 2-7. In writing cascaded NOR and NAND operations, one must use the correct parentheses to signify the proper sequence of the gates. To demonstrate this, consider the circuit

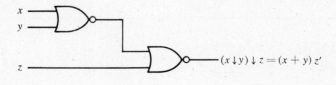

$$(x{\downarrow}y){\downarrow}z = (x + y)z'$$

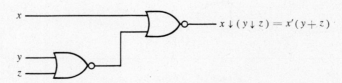

$$x{\downarrow}(y{\downarrow}z) = x'(y + z)$$

Figure 2-6 Demonstrating the nonassociativity of the NOR operator; $(x{\downarrow}y){\downarrow}z \neq x(y{\downarrow}z)$

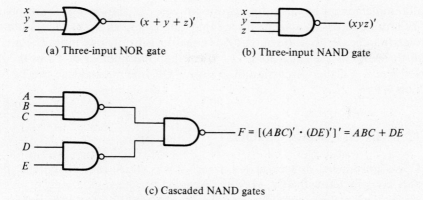

(a) Three-input NOR gate   (b) Three-input NAND gate

(c) Cascaded NAND gates

Figure 2-7   Multiple-input and cascaded NOR and NAND gates

of Fig. 2-7(c). The Boolean function for the circuit must be written as:

$$F = [(ABC)'(DE)']' = ABC + DE$$

The second expression is obtained from De Morgan's theorem. It also shows that an expression in sum of products can be implemented with NAND gates. Further discussion of NAND and NOR gates can be found in Sections 3-6, 4-7, and 4-8.

The exclusive-OR and equivalence gates are both commutative and associative and can be extended to more than two inputs. However, multiple-input exclusive-OR gates are uncommon from the hardware standpoint. In fact, even a two-input function is usually constructed with other types of gates. Moreover, the definition of these functions must be modified when extended to more than two variables. The exclusive-OR is an *odd* function, i.e., it is equal to 1 if the input variables have an odd number of 1's. The equivalence function is an *even* function, i.e., it is equal to 1 if the input variables have an even number of 0's. The construction of a three-input exclusive-OR function is shown in Fig. 2-8. It is

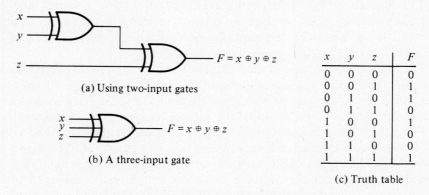

(a) Using two-input gates

(b) A three-input gate

x	y	z	F
0	0	0	0
0	0	1	1
0	1	0	1
0	1	1	0
1	0	0	1
1	0	1	0
1	1	0	0
1	1	1	1

(c) Truth table

Figure 2-8   Three-input exclusive-OR gate

normally implemented by cascading two-input gates as shown in (a). Graphically, it can be represented with a single three-input gate as shown in (b). The truth table in (c) clearly indicates that the output F is equal to 1 if only one input is equal to 1 or if all three inputs are equal to 1, i.e., when the total number of 1's in the input variables is *odd*. Further discussion of exclusive-OR and equivalence can be found in Section 4-9.

2-8 IC DIGITAL LOGIC FAMILIES

The IC was introduced in Section 1-9, where it was stated that digital circuits are invariably constructed with ICs. Having discussed various digital logic gates in the previous section, we are now in a position to present IC gates and discuss their general properties.

Digital IC gates are classified not only by their logic operation, but also by the specific logic-circuit family to which they belong. Each logic family has its own basic electronic circuit upon which more complex digital circuits and functions are developed. The basic circuit in each family is either a NAND or a NOR gate. The electronic components employed in the construction of the basic circuit are usually used to name the logic family. Many different logic families of digital ICs have been introduced commercially. The ones that have achieved widespread popularity are listed below.

TTL	Transistor-transistor logic
ECL	Emitter-coupled logic
MOS	Metal-oxide semiconductor
CMOS	Complementary metal-oxide semiconductor
I^2L	Integrated-injection logic

TTL has an extensive list of digital functions and is currently the most popular logic family. ECL is used in systems requiring high-speed operations. MOS and I^2L are used in circuits requiring high component density, and CMOS is used in systems requiring low power consumption.

The analysis of the basic electronic circuit in each logic family is presented in Chapter 13. The reader familiar with basic electronics can refer to Chapter 13 at this time to become acquainted with these electronic circuits. Here we restrict the discussion to the general properties of the various IC gates available commercially.

Because of the high density with which transistors can be fabricated in MOS and I^2L, these two families are mostly used for LSI functions. The other three families, TTL, ECL, and CMOS, have LSI devices and also a large number of MSI and SSI devices. SSI devices are those that come with a small number of gates or flip-flops (presented in Section 6-2) in one IC package. The limit on the number of circuits in SSI devices is the number of pins in the package. A 14-pin package, for example, can accommodate only four two-input gates, because each gate requires three external pins—two each for inputs and one each for output, for a total of 12 pins. The remaining two pins are needed for supplying power to the circuits.

Some typical SSI circuits are shown in Fig. 2-9. Each IC is enclosed within a 14- or 16-pin package. The pins are numbered along the two sides of the package and specify the connections that can be made. The gates drawn inside the ICs are for information only and cannot be seen because the actual IC package appears as shown in Fig. 1-8.

TTL ICs are usually distinguished by numerical designation as the 5400 and 7400 series. The former has a wide operating-temperature range, suitable for military use, and the latter has a narrower temperature range, suitable for industrial use. The numeric designation of the 7400 series means that IC packages are numbered as 7400, 7401, 7402, etc. Some vendors make available TTL ICs with different numerical designations, such as the 9000 or the 8000 series.

Figure 2-9(a) shows two TTL SSI circuits. The 7404 provides six (hex) inverters in a package. The 7400 provides four (quadruple) 2-input NAND gates. The terminals marked V_{CC} and GND are the power supply pins which require a voltage of 5 volts for proper operation.

The most common ECL type is designated as the 10,000 series. Figure 2-9(b) shows two ECL circuits. The 10102 provides four 2-input NOR gates. Note that an ECL gate may have two outputs, one for the NOR function and another for the OR function (pin 9 of the 10102 IC). The 10107 IC provides three exclusive-OR gates. Here again there are two outputs from each gate; the other output gives the exclusive-NOR function or equivalence. ECL gates have three terminals for power supply. V_{CC1} and V_{CC2} are usually connected to ground, and V_{EE} to a -5.2-volt supply.

CMOS circuits of the 4000 series are shown in Fig. 2-9(c). Only two 4-input NOR gates can be accommodated in the 4002 because of pin limitation. The 4050 type provides six buffer gates. Both ICs have two unused terminals marked NC (no connection). The terminal marked V_{DD} requires a power supply voltage from 3 to 15 volts, while V_{SS} is usually connected to ground.

Positive and Negative Logic

The binary signal at the inputs or output of any gate can have one of two values, except during transition. One signal value represents logic-1 and the other, logic-0. Since two signal values are assigned to two logic values, there exist two different assignments of signals to logic. Because of the principle of duality of Boolean algebra, an interchange of signal-value assignment results in a dual-function implementation.

Consider the two values of a binary signal as shown in Fig. 2-10. One value must be higher than the other since the two values must be different in order to distinguish between them. We designate the higher level by H and the lower level

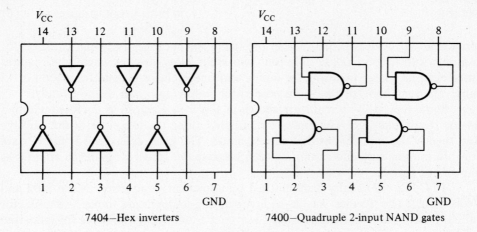

7404–Hex inverters

7400–Quadruple 2-input NAND gates

(a) TTL gates.

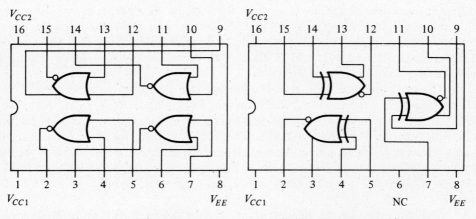

10102–Quadruple 2-input NOR gates

10107–Triple exclusive-OR/NOR gates

(b) ECL gates.

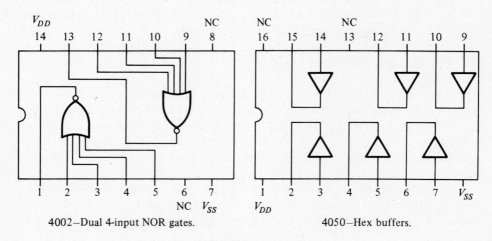

4002–Dual 4-input NOR gates.

4050–Hex buffers.

(c) CMOS gates.

Figure 2-9 Some typical integrated-circuit gates

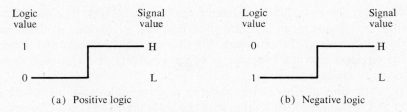

	Positive logic		Negative logic

(a) Positive logic   (b) Negative logic

Figure 2-10   Signal-amplitude assignment and type of logic

by L. There are two choices for logic-value assignment. Choosing the high-level H to represent logic-1, as shown in Fig. 2-10(a), defines a *positive-logic* system. Choosing the low-level L to represent logic-1, as shown in Fig. 2-10(b), defines a *negative-logic* system. The terms *positive* and *negative* are somewhat misleading since both signal values may be positive or both may be negative. It is not signal polarity that determines the type of logic, but rather the assignment of logic values according to the relative amplitudes of the signals.

Integrated-circuit data sheets define digital functions not in terms of logic-1 or logic-0, but rather in terms of H and L levels. It is up to the user to decide on a positive or negative logic assignment. The high-level and low-level voltages for the three IC digital logic families are listed in Table 2-7. In each family, there is a range of voltage values that the circuit will recognize as a high or low level. The typical value is the most commonly encountered. The table also lists the voltage-supply requirements for each family as a reference.

TTL has typical values of $H = 3.5$ volts and $L = 0.2$ volt. ECL has two negative values, with $H = -0.8$ volt and $L = -1.8$ volt. Note that even though both levels are negative, the higher one is -0.8. CMOS gates can use a supply voltage V_{DD} anywhere from 3 to 15 volts; typically, either 5 or 10 volts is used. The signal values in CMOS are a function of the supply voltage with $H = V_{DD}$ and $L = 0$ volt. The polarity assignments for positive and negative logic are also indicated in the table.

In light of this discussion, it would be necessary to justify the logic symbols used for the ICs listed in Fig. 2-9. Take, for example, one of the gates of the 7400

TABLE 2-7   H and L levels in IC logic families

IC family type	Voltage supply (V)	High-level voltage (V)		Low-level voltage (V)	
		Range	Typical	Range	Typical
TTL	$V_{CC} = 5$	2.4–5	3.5	0–0.4	0.2
ECL	$V_{EE} = -5.2$	$-0.95 - -0.7$	-0.8	$-1.9 - -1.6$	-1.8
CMOS	$V_{DD} = 3-10$	V_{DD}	V_{DD}	0–0.5	0
Positive logic:			logic-1		logic-0
Negative logic:			logic-0		logic-1

IC. This gate is shown in block diagram form in Fig. 2-11(b). The manufacturer's truth table for this gate given in a data sheet is shown in Fig. 2-11(a). This specifies the physical behavior of the gate, with H being typically 3.5 volts and L being 0.2 volt. This physical gate can function as either a NAND or NOR gate, depending on the polarity assignment.

The truth table of Fig. 2-11(c) assumes positive-logic assignment with $H = 1$ and $L = 0$. Checking this truth table with the truth tables in Fig. 2-5, we recognize it as a NAND gate. The graphic symbol for a positive-logic NAND gate is shown in Fig. 2-11(d) and is similar to the one adopted previously.

Now consider the negative-logic assignment for this physical gate with $L = 1$ and $H = 0$. The result is the truth table shown in Fig. 2-11(e). This table can be recognized to represent the NOR function even though its entries are listed backwards. The graphic symbol for a negative-logic NOR gate is shown in Fig. 2-11(f). The small triangle in the input and output wires designates a *polarity indicator*. The presence of this polarity indicator along a terminal indicates that negative logic is assigned to the terminal. Thus, the same physical gate can function either as a positive-logic NAND or as a negative-logic NOR. The one

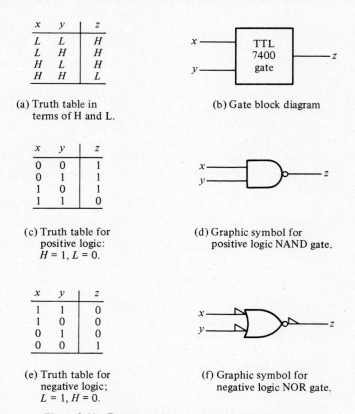

x	y	z
L	L	H
L	H	H
H	L	H
H	H	L

(a) Truth table in terms of H and L.

(b) Gate block diagram

x	y	z
0	0	1
0	1	1
1	0	1
1	1	0

(c) Truth table for positive logic: $H = 1, L = 0$.

(d) Graphic symbol for positive logic NAND gate.

x	y	z
1	1	0
1	0	0
0	1	0
0	0	1

(e) Truth table for negative logic; $L = 1, H = 0$.

(f) Graphic symbol for negative logic NOR gate.

Figure 2-11   Demonstration of positive and negative logic

drawn in the diagram is completely dependent on the polarity assignment that the designer wishes to employ.

In a similar manner, it is possible to show that a positive-logic NOR is the same physical gate as a negative-logic NAND. The same relation holds between AND and OR gates or between exclusive-OR and equivalence gates. In any case, if negative logic is assumed in any input or output terminal, it is necessary to include the polarity indicator triangle symbol along the terminal. Some digital designers use this convention to facilitate the design of digital circuits when NAND or NOR gates are used exclusively. We will not use this symbology in this book but will resort to other methods for designing with NAND and NOR gates. Note that the ICs presented in Fig. 2-9 are shown with their positive-logic graphic symbols. They could have been shown with their negative-logic symbols if one wished to do so.

The conversion from positive logic to negative logic, and vice versa, is essentially an operation that changes 1's to 0's and 0's to 1's in both inputs and output of a gate. Since this operation produces the dual of a function, the change of all terminals from one polarity to the other results in taking the dual of the function. The result of this conversion is that all AND operations are converted to OR operations (or graphic symbols) and vice versa. In addition, one must not forget to include the polarity indicator in graphic symbols when negative logic is assumed.

The small triangle that represents a polarity indicator and the small circle that represents a complementation have similar effects but different meanings. Therefore, one can be replaced by the other, but the interpretation is different. A circle followed by a triangle, as in Fig. 2-11(f), represents a complementation followed by a negative-logic polarity indicator. The two cancel each other and both can be removed. But if both are removed, then the inputs and output of the gate will represent different polarities.

Special Characteristics

The characteristics of IC digital logic families are usually compared by analyzing the circuit of the basic gate in each family. The most important parameters that are evaluated and compared are fan-out, power dissipation, propagation delay, and noise margin. We first explain the properties of these parameters and then use them to compare the IC logic families.

Fan-out specifies the number of standard loads that the output of a gate can drive without impairing its normal operation. A standard load is usually defined as the amount of current needed by an input of another gate in the same IC family. Sometimes the term *loading* is used instead of fan-out. This term is derived from the fact that the output of a gate can supply a limited amount of current, above which it ceases to operate properly and is said to be overloaded. The output of a gate is usually connected to the inputs of other similar gates. Each input consumes a certain amount of power from the gate input, so that each additional connection adds to the load of the gate. "Loading rules" are usually listed for a family of standard digital circuits. These rules specify the maximum amount of loading allowed for each output of each circuit. Exceeding the specified maximum load may cause a malfunction because the circuit cannot supply the power demanded from it. The fan-out is the maximum number of inputs that can be connected to the output of a gate, and it is expressed by a number.

The fan-out capabilities of a gate must be considered when simplifying Boolean functions. Care must be taken not to develop expressions that result in an overloaded gate. Noninverting amplifiers or buffers are sometimes employed to provide additional driving capabilities for heavy loads.

Power dissipation is the supplied power required to operate the gate. This parameter is expressed in milliwatts (mW) and represents the actual power dissipated in the gate. The number that represents this parameter does not include the power delivered from another gate; rather, it represents the power delivered to the gate from the power supply. An IC with four gates will require, from its power supply, four times the power dissipated in each gate. In a given system, there may be many ICs, and the power required by each IC must be considered. The total power dissipation in a system is the sum total of the power dissipated in all ICs.

Propagation delay is the average transition delay time for a signal to propagate from input to output when the binary signals change in value. The signals through a gate take a certain amount of time to propagate from the inputs to the output. This interval of time is defined as the propagation delay of the gate. Propagation delay is expressed in nanoseconds (ns), and 1 ns is equal to 10^{-9} of a second.

The signals that travel from the inputs of a digital circuit to its outputs pass through a series of gates. The sum of the propagation delays through the gates is the total propagation delay of the circuit. When speed of operation is important, each gate must have a small propagation delay and the digital circuit must have a minimum number of series gates between inputs and outputs.

The input signals in most digital circuits are applied simultaneously to more than one gate. All those gates that receive their inputs exclusively from external inputs constitute the first logic level of the circuit. Gates that receive at least one input from an output of a first-logic-level gate are considered to be in the second logic level, and similarly for third and higher levels. The total propagation delay of the circuit is equal to the propagation delay of a gate times the number of logic levels in the circuit. Thus, a reduction in the number of logic levels results in a reduction of signal delay and faster circuits. The reduction of the propagation delay in circuits may be more important than the reduction in the total number of gates if speed of operation is a major factor.

Noise margin is the maximum noise voltage added to the input signal of a digital circuit that does not cause an undesirable change in the circuit output. There are two types of noise to be considered. DC noise is caused by a drift in the voltage levels of a signal. AC noise is a random pulse that may be created by other switching signals. Thus, noise is a term used to denote an undesirable signal that is superimposed upon the normal operating signal. The ability of circuits to operate reliably in a noise environment is important in many applications. Noise margin is expressed in volts (V) and represents the maximum noise signal that can be tolerated by the gate.

Characteristics of IC Logic Families

The basic circuit of the TTL logic family is the NAND gate. There are many versions of TTL, and three of them are listed in Table 2-8. This table gives the general characteristics of the IC logic families. Values listed are representative on a comparison basis. For any one family or version, the values may vary somewhat.

TABLE 2-8   Typical characteristics of IC logic families

IC logic family	Fan-out	Power dissipation (mW)	Propagation delay (ns)	Noise margin (V)
Standard TTL	10	10	10	0.4
Schottky TTL	10	22	3	0.4
Low-power Schottky TTL	20	2	10	0.4
ECL	25	25	2	0.2
CMOS	50	0.1	25	3

The standard TTL gate was the first version of the TTL family. Additional improvements were added as the technology progressed. The Schottky TTL is a later improvement that reduces the propagation delay but results in an increase in power dissipation. The low-power Schottky TTL version sacrifices some speed for reduced power dissipation. It has the same propagation delay as the standard TTL, but the power dissipation is reduced considerably. The fan-out of the standard TTL is 10 but the low-power Schottky version has a fan-out of 20. Under certain conditions the other versions may also have a fan-out of 20. The noise margin is better than 0.4 V, with a typical value of 1 V.

The basic circuit of the ECL family is the NOR gate. The special advantage of ECL gates is their low propagation delay. Some ECL versions may have a propagation delay as low as 0.5 ns. The power dissipation in ECL gates is comparatively high and the noise margin low. These two parameters impose a disadvantage when choosing ECL over other logic families. However, because of its low propagation delay, ECL offers the highest speed of any family and is the ultimate choice for very fast systems.

The basic circuit of CMOS is the inverter from which both NAND and NOR gates can be constructed. The special advantage of CMOS is its extremely low power dissipation. Under static conditions, the CMOS gate power dissipation is negligible and averages about 10 nW. When the gate signal changes state, there is a dynamic power dissipation which is proportional to the frequency at which the circuit is exercised. The number listed in the table is a typical value of dynamic power dissipation in CMOS gates.

The one major disadvantage of CMOS is its high propagation delay. This means that it is not practical for use in systems requiring high-speed operations. The characteristic parameters for the CMOS gate depend on the power supply voltage V_{DD} that is used. The power dissipation increases with increase in voltage supply. The propagation delay decreases with increase in voltage supply, and the noise margin is estimated to be about 40% of the voltage supply value.

REFERENCES

1. Boole, G., *An Investigation of the Laws of Thought*. New York: Dover Pub., 1954.

2. Shannon, C. E., "A Symbolic Analysis of Relay and Switching Circuits." *Trans. of the AIEE*, Vol. 57 (1938), 713-23.

3. Huntington, E. V., "Sets of Independent Postulates for the Algebra of Logic." *Trans. Am. Math. Soc.*, Vol. 5 (1904), 288-309.

4. Birkhoff, G., and T. C. Bartee, *Modern Applied Algebra*. New York: McGraw-Hill Book Co., 1970.

5. Birkhoff, G., and S. Maclane, *A Survey of Modern Algebra*, 3rd ed. New York: The Macmillan Co., 1965.

6. Hohn, F. E., *Applied Boolean Algebra*, 2nd ed. New York: The Macmillan Co., 1966.

7. Whitesitt, J. E., *Boolean Algebra and its Applications*. Reading, Mass.: Addison-Wesley Pub. Co., 1961.

8. *The TTL Data Book for Design Engineers*. Dallas, Texas: Texas Instruments Inc., 1976.

9. *MECL Integrated Circuits Data Book*. Phoenix, Ariz.: Motorola Semiconductor Products, Inc., 1972.

10. *RCA Solid State Data Book Series*: *COS/MOS Digital Integrated Circuits*. Somerville, N. J.: RCA Solid State Div., 1974.

PROBLEMS

2-1. Which of the six basic laws (closure, associative, commutative, identity, inverse, and distributive) are satisfied for the pair of binary operators listed below?

+	0	1	2		·	0	1	2
0	0	0	0		0	0	1	2
1	0	1	1		1	1	1	2
2	0	1	2		2	2	2	2

2-2. Show that the set of three elements {0, 1, 2} and the two binary operators + and · as defined by the above table is not a Boolean algebra. State which of the Huntington postulates is not satisfied.

2-3. Demonstrate by means of truth tables the validity of the following theorems of Boolean algebra.

(a) The associative laws.

(b) De Morgan's theorems for three variables.

(c) The distributive law of + over ·.

2-4. Repeat problem 2-3 using Venn diagrams.

2-5. Simplify the following Boolean functions to a minimum number of literals.

(a) $xy + xy'$

(b) $(x + y)(x + y')$

(c) $xyz + x'y + xyz'$

(d) $zx + zx'y$

(e) $(A + B)'(A' + B')'$

(f) $y(wz' + wz) + xy$

2-6. Reduce the following Boolean expressions to the required number of literals.

(a) $ABC + A'B'C + A'BC + ABC' + A'B'C'$ — to five literals

(b) $BC + AC' + AB + BCD$ — to four literals

(c) $[(CD)' + A]' + A + CD + AB$ — to three literals

(d) $(A + C + D)(A + C + D')(A + C' + D)(A + B')$ — to four literals

2-7. Find the complement of the following Boolean functions and reduce them to a minimum number of literals.

(a) $(BC' + A'D)(AB' + CD')$

(b) $B'D + A'BC' + ACD + A'BC$

(c) $[(AB)'A][(AB)'B]$

(d) $AB' + C'D'$

2-8. Given two Boolean functions F_1 and F_2:

(a) Show that the Boolean function $E = F_1 + F_2$, obtained by ORing the two functions, contains the sum of all the minterms in F_1 and F_2.

(b) Show that the Boolean function $G = F_1F_2$, obtained from ANDing the two functions, contains those minterms common to both F_1 and F_2.

2-9. Obtain the truth table of the function:

$$F = xy + xy' + y'z$$

2-10. Implement the simplified Boolean functions from problem 2-6 with logic gates.

2-11. Given the Boolean function:

$$F = xy + x'y' + y'z$$

(a) Implement it with AND, OR, and NOT gates.

(b) Implement it with *only* OR and NOT gates.

(c) Implement it with *only* AND and NOT gates.

2-12. Simplify the functions T_1 and T_2 to a minimum number of literals.

A	B	C	T_1	T_2
0	0	0	1	0
0	0	1	1	0
0	1	0	1	0
0	1	1	0	1
1	0	0	0	1
1	0	1	0	1
1	1	0	0	1
1	1	1	0	1

2-13. Express the following functions in a sum of minterms and a product of maxterms.
(a) $F(A, B, C, D) = D(A' + B) + B'D$
(b) $F(w, x, y, z) = y'z + wxy' + wxz' + w'x'z$
(c) $F(A, B, C, D) = (A + B' + C)(A + B')(A + C' + D')$
$(A' + B + C + D')(B + C' + D')$
(d) $F(A, B, C) = (A' + B)(B' + C)$
(e) $F(x, y, z) = 1$
(f) $F(x, y, z) = (xy + z)(y + xz)$

2-14. Convert the following to the other canonical form.
(a) $F(x, y, z) = \Sigma(1, 3, 7)$
(b) $F(A, B, C, D) = \Sigma(0, 2, 6, 11, 13, 14)$
(c) $F(x, y, z) = \Pi(0, 3, 6, 7)$
(d) $F(A, B, C, D) = \Pi(0, 1, 2, 3, 4, 6, 12)$

2-15. What is the difference between canonical form and standard form? Which form is preferable when implementing a Boolean function with gates? Which form is obtained when reading a function from a truth table?

2-16. The sum of all minterms of a Boolean function of n variables is 1.
(a) Prove the above statement for $n = 3$.
(b) Suggest a procedure for a general proof.

2-17. The product of all maxterms of a Boolean function of n variables is 0.
(a) Prove the above statement for $n = 3$.
(b) Suggest a procedure for a general proof. Can we use the duality principle after proving (b) of problem 2-16?

2-18. Show that the dual of the exclusive-OR is equal to its complement.

2-19. By substituting the Boolean function equivalent of the binary operations as defined in Table 2-6, show that:
(a) The inhibition and implication operators are neither commutative nor associative.
(b) The exclusive-OR and equivalence operators are commutative and associative.

(c) The NAND operator is not associative.

(d) The NOR and NAND operators are not distributive.

2-20. A *majority* gate is a digital circuit whose output is equal to 1 if the majority of the inputs are 1's. The output is 0 otherwise. By means of a truth table, find the Boolean function implemented by a 3-input majority gate. Simplify the function.

2-21. Verify the truth table for the 3-input exclusive-OR gate listed in Fig. 2-8(c). List all eight combinations of x, y, and z; evaluate $A = x \oplus y$; then evaluate $F = A \oplus z = x \oplus y \oplus z$.

2-22. TTL SSI come mostly in 14-pin packages. Two pins are reserved for power supply and the other pins are used for input and output terminals. How many gates are enclosed in one such package if it contains the following types of gates:

(a) 2-input exclusive-OR gates.

(b) 3-input AND gates.

(c) 4-input NAND gates.

(d) 5-input NOR gates.

(e) 8-input NAND gates.

2-23. Show that a positive-logic AND gate is a negative-logic OR gate, and vice versa.

2-24. An IC logic family has NAND gates with fan-out of 5 and buffer gates with fan-out of 10. Show how the output signal of a single NAND gate can be applied to 50 other gate inputs.

Simplification of
Boolean Functions

3

3-1 THE MAP METHOD

The complexity of the digital logic gates that implement a Boolean function is directly related to the complexity of the algebraic expression from which the function is implemented. Although the truth table representation of a function is unique, expressed algebraically, it can appear in many different forms. Boolean functions may be simplified by algebraic means as discussed in Section 2-4. However, this procedure of minimization is awkward because it lacks specific rules to predict each succeeding step in the manipulative process. The map method provides a simple straightforward procedure for minimizing Boolean functions. This method may be regarded either as a pictorial form of a truth table or as an extension of the Venn diagram. The map method, first proposed by Veitch (1) and slightly modified by Karnaugh (2), is also known as the "Veitch diagram" or the "Karnaugh map."

The map is a diagram made up of squares. Each square represents one minterm. Since any Boolean function can be expressed as a sum of minterms, it follows that a Boolean function is recognized graphically in the map from the area enclosed by those squares whose minterms are included in the function. In fact, the map presents a visual diagram of all possible ways a function may be expressed in a standard form. By recognizing various patterns, the user can derive alternative algebraic expressions for the same function, from which he can select the simplest one. We shall assume that the simplest algebraic expression is any one in a sum of products or product of sums that has a minimum number of literals. (This expression is not necessarily unique.)

3-2 TWO- AND THREE-VARIABLE MAPS

A two-variable map is shown in Fig. 3-1. There are four minterms for two variables; hence the map consists of four squares, one for each minterm. The map is redrawn in (b) to show the relationship between the squares and the two

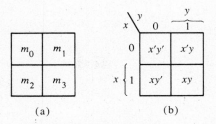

(a)   (b)

Figure 3-1   Two-variable map

variables. The 0's and 1's marked for each row and each column designate the values of variables x and y, respectively. Notice that x appears primed in row 0 and unprimed in row 1. Similarly, y appears primed in column 0 and unprimed in column 1.

If we mark the squares whose minterms belong to a given function, the two-variable map becomes another useful way to represent any one of the 16 Boolean functions of two variables. As an example, the function xy is shown in Fig. 3-2(a). Since xy is equal to m_3, a 1 is placed inside the square that belongs to m_3. Similarly, the function $x + y$ is represented in the map of Fig. 3-2(b) by three squares marked with 1's. These squares are found from the minterms of the function:

$$x + y = x'y + xy' + xy = m_1 + m_2 + m_3$$

The three squares could have also been determined from the intersection of variable x in the second row and variable y in the second column, which encloses the area belonging to x or y.

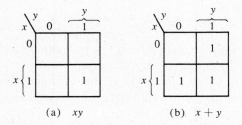

(a) xy (b) $x + y$

Figure 3-2   Representation of functions in the map

A three-variable map is shown in Fig. 3-3. There are eight minterms for three binary variables. Therefore, a map consists of eight squares. Note that the minterms are arranged, not in a binary sequence, but in a sequence similar to the reflected code listed in Table 1-4. The characteristic of this sequence is that only one bit changes from 1 to 0 or from 0 to 1 in the listing sequence. The map drawn in part (b) is marked with numbers in each row and each column to show the relationship between the squares and the three variables. For example, the square assigned to m_5 corresponds to row 1 and column 01. When these two numbers are concatenated, they give the binary number 101, whose decimal equivalent is 5.

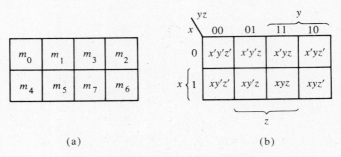

(a)   (b)

Figure 3-3 Three-variable map

Another way of looking at square $m_5 = xy'z$ is to consider it to be in the row marked x and the column belonging to $y'z$ (column 01). Note that there are four squares where each variable is equal to 1 and four where each is equal to 0. The variable appears unprimed in those four squares where it is equal to 1 and primed in those squares where it is equal to 0. For convenience, we write the variable with its letter symbol under the four squares where it is unprimed.

To understand the usefulness of the map for simplifying Boolean functions, we must recognize the basic property possessed by adjacent squares. Any two adjacent squares in the map differ by only one variable which is primed in one square and unprimed in the other. For example, m_5 and m_7 lie in two adjacent squares. Variable y is primed in m_5 and unprimed in m_7, while the other two variables are the same in both squares. From the postulates of Boolean algebra, it follows that the sum of two minterms in adjacent squares can be simplified to a single AND term consisting of only two literals. To clarify this, consider the sum of two adjacent squares such as m_5 and m_7:

$$m_5 + m_7 = xy'z + xyz = xz(y' + y) = xz$$

Here the two squares differ by the variable y, which can be removed when the sum of the two minterms is formed. Thus, any two minterms in adjacent squares that are ORed together will cause a removal of the different variable. The following example explains the procedure for minimizing a Boolean function with a map.

EXAMPLE 3-1: Simplify the Boolean function:

$$F = x'yz + x'yz' + xy'z' + xy'z$$

First, a 1 is marked in each square as needed to represent the function as shown in Fig. 3-4. This can be accomplished in two ways: either by converting each minterm to a binary number and then marking a 1 in the corresponding square, or by obtaining the coincidence of the variables in each term. For example, the term $x'yz$ has the corresponding binary number 011 and represents minterm m_3 in square 011. The second way to recognize the square is by the coincidence of variables x', y, and z, which is found in the map by

74

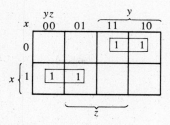

Figure 3-4 Map for Example 3-1; $x'yz + x'yz' + xy'z' + xy'z = x'y + xy'$

observing that x' belongs to the four squares in the first row, y belongs to the four squares in the two right columns, and z belongs to the four squares in the two middle columns. The area that belongs to all three literals is the single square in the first row and third column. In a similar manner, the other three squares belonging to the function F are marked by 1's in the map. The function is thus represented by an area containing four squares, each marked with a 1, as shown in Fig. 3-4. The next step is to subdivide the given area into adjacent squares. These are indicated in the map by two rectangles, each enclosing two 1's. The upper right rectangle represents the area enclosed by $x'y$; the lower left, the area enclosed by xy'. The sum of these two terms gives the answer:

$$F = x'y + xy'$$

Next consider the two squares labeled m_0 and m_2 in Fig. 3-3(a) or $x'y'z'$ and $x'yz'$ in Fig. 3-3(b). These two minterms also differ by one variable y, and their sum can be simplified to a two-literal expression:

$$x'y'z' + x'yz' = x'z'$$

Consequently, we must modify the definition of adjacent squares to include this and other similar cases. This is done by considering the map as being drawn on a surface where the right and left edges touch each other to form adjacent squares.

EXAMPLE 3-2: Simplify the Boolean function:

$$F = x'yz + xy'z' + xyz + xyz'$$

The map for this function is shown in Fig. 3-5. There are four squares marked with 1's, one for each minterm of the function. Two adjacent squares are combined in the third column to give a two-literal term yz. The remaining two squares with 1's are also adjacent by the new definition and are shown in the diagram enclosed by half rectangles. These two squares, when combined, give the two-literal term xz'. The simplified function becomes:

$$F = yz + xz'$$

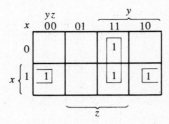

Figure 3-5 Map for Example 3-2; $x'yz + xy'z' + xyz + xyz' = yz + xz'$

Consider now any combination of four adjacent squares in the three-variable map. Any such combination represents the ORing of four adjacent minterms and results in an expression of only one literal. As an example, the sum of the four adjacent minterms m_0, m_2, m_4, and m_6 reduces to the single literal z' as shown:

$$x'y'z' + x'yz' + xy'z' + xyz' = x'z'(y' + y) + xz'(y' + y)$$
$$= x'z' + xz' = z'(x' + x) = z'$$

EXAMPLE 3-3: Simplify the Boolean function:

$$F = A'C + A'B + AB'C + BC$$

The map to simplify this function is shown in Fig. 3-6. Some of the terms in the function have less than three literals and are represented in the map by more than one square. For example, to find the squares corresponding to $A'C$, we form the coincidence of A' (first row) and C (two middle columns) and obtain squares 001 and 011. Note that when marking 1's in the squares, it is possible to find a 1 already placed there by a preceding term. In this example, the second term $A'B$ has 1's in squares 011 and 010, but square 011 is common to the first term $A'C$ and only one 1 is marked in it. The function in this example has five minterms, as indicated by the five squares marked with 1's. It is simplified by combining four squares in the center to give the literal C. The remaining single square marked with a 1 in 010 is combined with an adjacent square that has already been used once. This is permissible and even desirable since

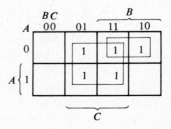

Figure 3-6 Map for Example 3-3; $A'C + A'B + AB'C + BC = C + A'B$

76

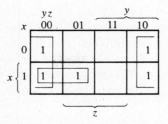

Figure 3-7 $f(x, y, z) = \Sigma(0, 2, 4, 5, 6) = z' + xy'$

the combination of the two squares gives the term $A'B$ while the single minterm represented by the square gives the three-variable term $A'BC'$. The simplified function is:

$$F = C + A'B$$

EXAMPLE 3-4: Simplify the Boolean function:

$$F(x, y, z) = \Sigma(0, 2, 4, 5, 6)$$

Here we are given the minterms by their decimal numbers. The corresponding squares are marked by 1's as shown in Fig. 3-7. From the map we obtain the simplified function:

$$F = z' + xy'$$

3-3 FOUR-VARIABLE MAP

The map for Boolean functions of four binary variables is shown in Fig. 3-8. In (a) are listed the 16 minterms and the squares assigned to each. In (b) the map is redrawn to show the relationship with the four variables. The rows and columns

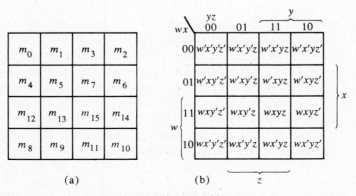

(a)   (b)

Figure 3-8 Four-variable map

are numbered in a reflected-code sequence, with only one digit changing value between two adjacent rows or columns. The minterm corresponding to each square can be obtained from the concatenation of the row number with the column number. For example, the numbers of the third row (11) and the second column (01), when concatenated, give the binary number 1101, the binary equivalent of decimal 13. Thus, the square in the third row and second column represents minterm m_{13}.

The map minimization of four-variable Boolean functions is similar to the method used to minimize three-variable functions. Adjacent squares are defined to be squares next to each other. In addition, the map is considered to lie on a surface with the top and bottom edges, as well as the right and left edges, touching each other to form adjacent squares. For example, m_0 and m_2 form adjacent squares, as do m_3 and m_{11}. The combination of adjacent squares that is useful during the simplification process is easily determined from inspection of the four-variable map:

One square represents one minterm, giving a term of four literals.

Two adjacent squares represent a term of three literals.

Four adjacent squares represent a term of two literals.

Eight adjacent squares represent a term of one literal.

Sixteen adjacent squares represent the function equal to 1.

No other combination of squares can simplify the function. The following two examples show the procedure used to simplify four-variable Boolean functions.

EXAMPLE 3-5: Simplify the Boolean function:

$$F(w, x, y, z) = \Sigma(0, 1, 2, 4, 5, 6, 8, 9, 12, 13, 14)$$

Since the function has four variables, a four-variable map must be used. The minterms listed in the sum are marked by 1's in the map of Fig. 3-9. Eight adjacent squares marked with 1's can be combined to form the one literal term y'. The remaining three 1's on the right cannot be combined together to give a simplified term. They must be combined as two or four adjacent squares. The larger the number of squares combined, the less the number of literals in the term. In this example, the top two 1's on the right are combined with the top two 1's on the left to give the term $w'z'$. Note that it is permissible to use the same square more than once. We are now left with a square marked by 1 in the third row and fourth column (square 1110). Instead of taking this square alone (which will give a term of four literals), we combine it with squares already used to form an area of

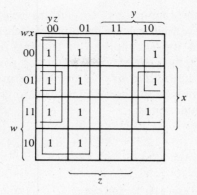

Figure 3-9 Map for Example 3-5; $F(w, x, y, z) =$
$\Sigma(0, 1, 2, 4, 5, 6, 8, 9, 12, 13, 14) = y' + w'z' + xz'$

four adjacent squares. These squares comprise the two middle rows and the two end columns, giving the term xz'. The simplified function is:

$$F = y' + w'z' + xz'$$

EXAMPLE 3-6: Simplify the Boolean function:

$$F = A'B'C' + B'CD' + A'BCD' + AB'C'$$

The area in the map covered by this function consists of the squares marked with 1's in Fig. 3-10. This function has four variables and, as expressed, consists of three terms, each with three literals, and one term of four literals. Each term of three literals is represented in the map by two squares. For example, $A'B'C'$ is represented in squares 0000 and 0001. The function can be simplified in the map by taking

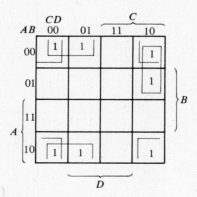

Figure 3-10 Map for Example 3-6; $A'B'C' + B'CD' + A'BCD' + AB'C'$
$= B'D' + B'C' + A'CD'$

the 1's in the four corners to give the term $B'D'$. This is possible because these four squares are adjacent when the map is drawn in a surface with top and bottom or left and right edges touching one another. The two left-hand 1's in the top row are combined with the two 1's in the bottom row to give the term $B'C'$. The remaining 1 may be combined in a two-square area to give the term $A'CD'$. The simplified function is:

$$F = B'D' + B'C' + A'CD'$$

3-4 FIVE- AND SIX-VARIABLE MAPS

Maps of more than four variables are not as simple to use. The number of squares becomes excessively large and the geometry for combining adjacent squares becomes more involved. The number of squares is always equal to the number of minterms. For five-variable maps, we need 32 squares; for six-variable maps, we need 64 squares. Maps with seven or more variables need too many squares. They are impractical to use. The five- and six-variable maps are shown in Figs. 3-11 and 3-12, respectively. The rows and columns are numbered in a reflected-code sequence; the minterm assigned to each square is read from these numbers. In this way, the square in the third row (11) and second column (001), in the five-variable map, is number 11001, the equivalent of decimal 25. Therefore, this square represents minterm m_{25}. The letter symbol of each variable is marked along those squares where the corresponding bit value of the reflected-code number is a 1. For example, in the five-variable map, the variable A is a 1 in the last two rows; B is a 1 in the middle two rows. The reflected numbers in the columns show variable C with a 1 in the rightmost four columns, variable D with a 1 in the middle four

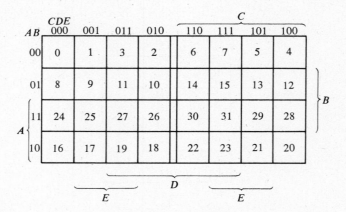

Figure 3-11 Five-variable map

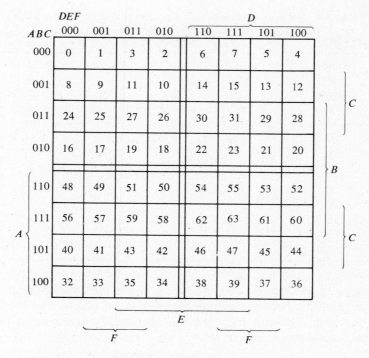

Figure 3-12 Six-variable map

columns, and the 1's for variable E not physically adjacent but split in two parts. The variable assignment in the six-variable map is determined similarly.

The definition of adjacent squares for the maps of Figs. 3-11 and 3-12 must be modified again to take into account the fact that some variables are split into two parts. The five-variable map must be thought to consist of two four-variable maps, and the six-variable map to consist of four four-variable maps. Each of these four-variable maps is recognized from the double lines in the center of the map; each retains the previously defined adjacency when taken individually. In addition, the center double line must be considered as the center of a book, with each half of the map being a page. When the book is closed, two adjacent squares will fall one on the other. In other words, the center double line is like a mirror with each square being adjacent, not only to its four neighboring squares, but also to its mirror image. For example, minterm 31 in the five-variable map is adjacent to minterms 30, 15, 29, 23, *and* 27. The same minterm in the six-variable map is adjacent to all these minterms plus minterm 63.

From inspection, and taking into account the new definition of adjacent squares, it is possible to show that any 2^k adjacent squares, for $k = 0, 1, 2, \ldots, n$, in an n-variable map, will represent an area that gives a term of $n - k$ literals. For the above statement to have any meaning, n must be larger than k. When $n = k$,

TABLE 3-1 The relationship between the number of adjacent squares and the number of literals in the term

k	2^k	Number of literals in a term in an n-variable map					
		$n = 2$	$n = 3$	$n = 4$	$n = 5$	$n = 6$	$n = 7$
0	1	2	3	4	5	6	7
1	2	1	2	3	4	5	6
2	4	0	1	2	3	4	5
3	8		0	1	2	3	4
4	16			0	1	2	3
5	32				0	1	2
6	64					0	1

the entire area of the map is combined to give the identity function. Table 3-1 shows the relationship between the number of adjacent squares and the number of literals in the term. For example, eight adjacent squares combine an area in the five-variable map to give a term of two literals.

EXAMPLE 3-7: Simplify the Boolean function:

$$F(A, B, C, D, E) = \Sigma(0, 2, 4, 6, 9, 11, 13, 15, 17, 21, 25, 27, 29, 31)$$

The five-variable map of this function is shown in Fig. 3-13. Each minterm is converted to its equivalent binary number and the

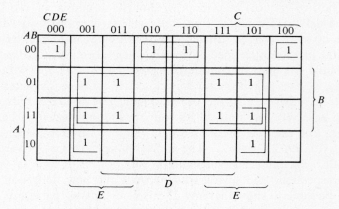

Figure 3-13 Map for Example 3-7; $F(A, B, C, D, E) =$
$\Sigma(0, 2, 4, 6, 9, 11, 13, 15, 17, 21, 25, 27, 29, 31)$
$= BE + AD'E + A'B'E'$

1's are marked in their corresponding squares. It is now necessary to find combinations of adjacent squares that will result in the largest possible area. The four squares in the center of the right-half map are reflected across the double line and are combined with the four squares in the center of the left-half map to give eight allowable adjacent squares equivalent to the term BE. The two 1's in the bottom row are the reflection of each other about the center double line. By combining them with the other two adjacent squares, we obtain the term $AD'E$. The four 1's in the top row are all adjacent and can be combined to give the term $A'B'E'$. All the 1's are now included. The simplified function is:

$$F = BE + AD'E + A'B'E'$$

3-5 PRODUCT OF SUMS SIMPLIFICATION

The minimized Boolean functions derived from the map in all previous examples were expressed in the sum of products form. With a minor modification, the product of sums form can be obtained.

The procedure for obtaining a minimized function in product of sums follows from the basic properties of Boolean functions. The 1's placed in the squares of the map represent the minterms of the function. The minterms not included in the function denote the complement of the function. From this we see that the complement of a function is represented in the map by the squares not marked by 1's. If we mark the empty squares by 0's and combine them into valid adjacent squares, we obtain a simplified expression of the complement of the function, i.e., of F'. The complement of F' gives us back the function F. Because of the generalized DeMorgan's theorem, the function so obtained is automatically in the product of sums form. The best way to show this is by example.

EXAMPLE 3-8: Simplify the following Boolean function in (a) sum of products and (b) product of sums.

$$F(A, B, C, D) = \Sigma(0, 1, 2, 5, 8, 9, 10)$$

The 1's marked in the map of Fig. 3-14 represent all the minterms of the function. The squares marked with 0's represent the minterms not included in F and therefore denote the complement of F. Combining the squares with 1's gives the simplified function in sum of products:

(a) $F = B'D' + B'C' + A'C'D$

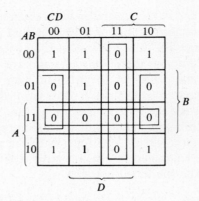

Figure 3-14 Map for Example 3-8; $F(A, B, C, D) =$
$\Sigma(0, 1, 2, 5, 8, 9, 10) = B'D' + B'C' + A'C'D$
$= (A' + B')(C' + D')(B' + D)$

If the squares marked with 0's are combined, as shown in the diagram, we obtain the simplified complemented function:

$$F' = AB + CD + BD'$$

Applying DeMorgan's theorem (by taking the dual and complementing each literal as described in Section 2-4), we obtain the simplified function in product of sums:

$$\text{(b)} \quad F = (A' + B')(C' + D')(B' + D)$$

The implementation of the simplified expressions obtained in Example 3-8 is shown in Fig. 3-15. The sum of products expression is implemented in (a) with a group of AND gates, one for each AND term. The outputs of the AND gates are connected to the inputs of a single OR gate. The same function is implemented in (b) in its product of sums form with a group of OR gates, one for each OR term. The outputs of the OR gates are connected to the inputs of a single AND gate. In each case, it is assumed that the input variables are directly available in their complement, so inverters are not needed. The configuration pattern established in Fig. 3-15 is the general form by which any Boolean function is implemented when expressed in one of the standard forms. AND gates are connected to a single OR gate when in sum of products; OR gates are connected to a single AND gate when in product of sums. Either configuration forms two levels of gates. Thus, the implementation of a function in a standard form is said to be a two-level implementation.

Example 3-8 showed the procedure for obtaining the product of sums simplification when the function is originally expressed in the sum of minterms canonical form. The procedure is also valid when the function is originally expressed in the product of maxterm canonical form. Consider, for example, the

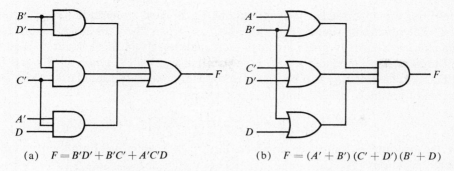

(a) $F = B'D' + B'C' + A'C'D$ (b) $F = (A' + B')(C' + D')(B' + D)$

Figure 3-15   Gate implementation of the function of Example 3-8

TABLE 3-2   Truth table of function F

x	y	z	F
0	0	0	0
0	0	1	1
0	1	0	0
0	1	1	1
1	0	0	1
1	0	1	0
1	1	0	1
1	1	1	0

truth table that defines the function F in Table 3-2. In sum of minterms, this function is expressed as:

$$F(x, y, z) = \Sigma(1, 3, 4, 6)$$

In product of maxterms, it is expressed as:

$$F(x, y, z) = \Pi(0, 2, 5, 7)$$

In other words, the 1's of the function represent the minterms, and the 0's represent the maxterms. The map for this function is drawn in Fig. 3-16. One can start

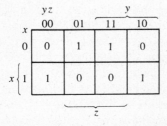

Figure 3-16   Map for the function of Table 3-2

simplifying this function by first marking the 1's for each minterm that the function is a 1. The remaining squares are marked by 0's. If, on the other hand, the product of maxterms is initially given, one can start marking 0's in those squares listed in the function; the remaining squares are then marked by 1's. Once the 1's and 0's are marked, the function can be simplified in either one of the standard forms. For the sum of products, we combine the 1's to obtain:

$$F = x'z + xz'$$

For the product of sums, we combine the 0's to obtain the simplified complemented function:

$$F' = xz + x'z'$$

which shows that the exclusive-OR function is the complement of the equivalence function (Section 2-6). Taking the complement of F', we obtain the simplified function in product of sums:

$$F = (x' + z')(x + z)$$

To enter a function expressed in product of sums in the map, take the complement of the function and from it find the squares to be marked by 0's. For example, the function:

$$F = (A' + B' + C)(B + D)$$

can be entered in the map by first taking its complement:

$$F' = ABC' + B'D'$$

and then marking 0's in the squares representing the minterms of F'. The remaining squares are marked with 1's.

3-6   NAND AND NOR IMPLEMENTATION

Digital circuits are more frequently constructed with NAND or NOR gates than with AND and OR gates. NAND and NOR gates are easier to fabricate with electronic components and are the basic gates used in all IC digital logic families. Because of the prominence of NAND and NOR gates in the design of digital circuits, rules and procedures have been developed for the conversion from Boolean functions given in terms of AND, OR, and NOT into equivalent NAND or NOR logic diagrams. The procedure for two-level implementation is presented in this section. Multilevel implementation is discussed in Section 4-7.

To facilitate the conversion to NAND and NOR logic, it is convenient to define two other graphic symbols for these gates. Two equivalent symbols for the NAND gate are shown in Fig. 3-17(a). The AND-invert symbol has been defined

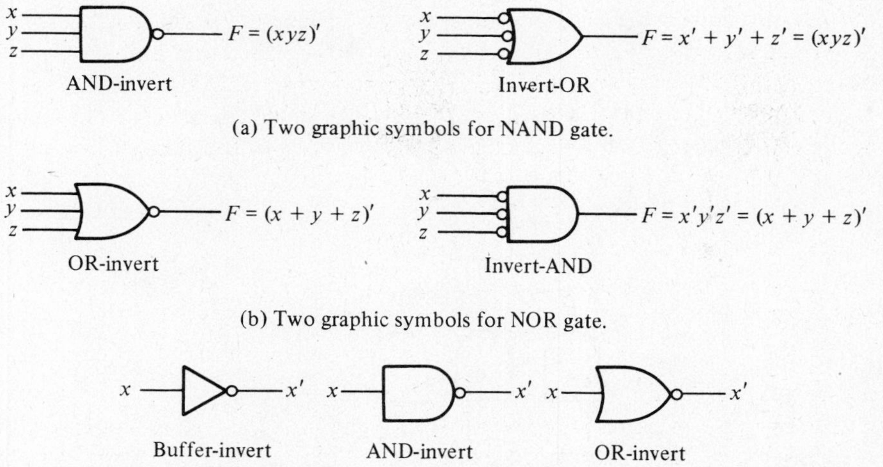

(a) Two graphic symbols for NAND gate.

(b) Two graphic symbols for NOR gate.

(c) Three graphic symbols for inverter.

Figure 3-17 Graphic symbols for NAND and NOR gates

previously and consists of an AND graphic symbol followed by a small circle. Instead, it is possible to represent a NAND gate by an OR graphic symbol preceded by small circles in all the inputs. The invert-OR symbol for the NAND gate follows from DeMorgan's theorem and from the convention that small circles denote complementation.

Similarly, there are two graphic symbols for the NOR gate as shown in Fig. 3-17(b). The OR-invert is the conventional symbol. The invert-AND is a convenient alternative that utilizes DeMorgan's theorem and the convention that small circles in the inputs denote complementation.

A one-input NAND or NOR gate behaves like an inverter. As a consequence, an inverter gate can be drawn in three different ways as shown in Fig. 3-17(c). The small circles in all inverter symbols can be transferred to the input terminal without changing the logic of the gate.

It should be pointed out that the alternate symbols for the NAND and NOR gates could be drawn with small triangles in all input terminals instead of the circles. A small triangle is a negative-logic polarity indicator (see Section 2-8 and Fig. 2-11). With small triangles in the input terminals, the graphic symbol denotes a negative-logic polarity for the inputs, but the output of the gate (not having a triangle) would have a positive-logic assignment. In this book, we prefer to stay with positive logic throughout and employ small circles when necessary to denote complementation.

NAND Implementation

The implementation of a Boolean function with NAND gates requires that the function be simplified in the sum of products form. To see the relationship between a sum of products expression and its equivalent NAND implementation,

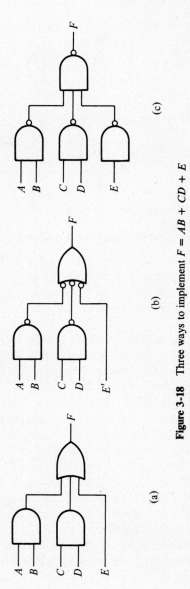

(a)

(b)

(c)

Figure 3-18 Three ways to implement $F = AB + CD + E$

consider the logic diagrams drawn in Fig. 3-18. All three diagrams are equivalent and implement the function:

$$F = AB + CD + E$$

The function is implemented in Fig. 3-18(a) in sum of products form with AND and OR gates. In (b) the AND gates are replaced by NAND gates and the OR gate is replaced by a NAND gate with an invert-OR symbol. The single variable E is complemented and applied to the second-level invert-OR gate. Remember that a small circle denotes complementation. Therefore, two circles on the same line represent double complementation and both can be removed. The complement of E goes through a small circle which complements the variable again to produce the normal value of E. Removing the small circles in the gates of Fig. 3-18(b) produces the circuit in (a). Therefore, the two diagrams implement the same function and are equivalent.

In Fig. 3-18(c), the output NAND gate is redrawn with the conventional symbol. The one-input NAND gate complements variable E. It is possible to remove this inverter and apply E' directly to the input of the second-level NAND gate. The diagram in (c) is equivalent to the one in (b), which in turn is equivalent to the diagram in (a). Note the similarity between the diagrams in (a) and (c). The AND and OR gates have been changed to NAND gates, but an additional NAND gate has been included with the single variable E. When drawing NAND logic diagrams, the circuit shown in either (b) or (c) is acceptable. The one in (b), however, represents a more direct relationship to the Boolean expression it implements.

The NAND implementation in Fig. 3-18(c) can be verified algebraically. The NAND function it implements can be easily converted to a sum of products form by using DeMorgan's theorem:

$$F = \left[(AB)' \cdot (CD)' \cdot E' \right]' = AB + CD + E$$

From the transformation shown in Fig. 3-18, we conclude that a Boolean function can be implemented with two levels of NAND gates. The rule for obtaining the NAND logic diagram from a Boolean function is as follows:

1. Simplify the function and express it in sum of products.

2. Draw a NAND gate for each product term of the function that has at least two literals. The inputs to each NAND gate are the literals of the term. This constitutes a group of first-level gates.

3. Draw a single NAND gate (using the AND-invert or invert-OR graphic symbol) in the second level, with inputs coming from outputs of first-level gates.

4. A term with a single literal requires an inverter in the first level or may be complemented and applied as an input to the second-level NAND gate.

Before applying these rules to a specific example, it should be mentioned that there is a second way to implement a Boolean function with NAND gates. Remember that if we combine the 0's in a map, we obtain the simplified expression of the *complement* of the function in sum of products. The complement of the function can then be implemented with two levels of NAND gates using the rules stated above. If the normal output is desired, it would be necessary to insert a one-input NAND or inverter gate to generate the true value of the output variable. There are occasions where the designer may want to generate the complement of the function; so this second method may be preferable.

EXAMPLE 3-9: Implement the following function with NAND gates:

$$F(x, y, z) = \Sigma(0, 6)$$

The first step is to simplify the function in sum of products form. This is attempted with the map shown in Fig. 3-19(a). There are only two 1's in the map, and they cannot be combined. The simplified function in sum of products for this example is:

$$F = x'y'z' + xyz'$$

The two-level NAND implementation is shown in Fig. 3-19(b). Next we try to simplify the complement of the function in sum of products. This is done by combining the 0's in the map:

$$F' = x'y + xy' + z$$

The two-level NAND gate for generating F' is shown in Fig. 3-19(c). If output F is required, it is necessary to add a one-input NAND gate to invert the function. This gives a three-level implementation. In each case, it is assumed that the input variables are available in both the normal and complement forms. If they were available in only one form, it would be necessary to insert inverters in the inputs, which would add another level to the circuits. The one-input NAND gate associated with the single variable z can be removed provided the input is changed to z'.

NOR Implementation

The NOR function is the dual of the NAND function. For this reason, all procedures and rules for NOR logic are the dual of the corresponding procedures and rules developed for NAND logic.

The implementation of a Boolean function with NOR gates requires that the function be simplified in product of sums form. A product of sums expression

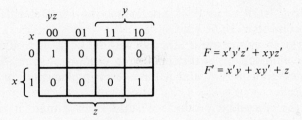

$$F = x'y'z' + xyz'$$
$$F' = x'y + xy' + z$$

(a) Map simplification in sum of products.

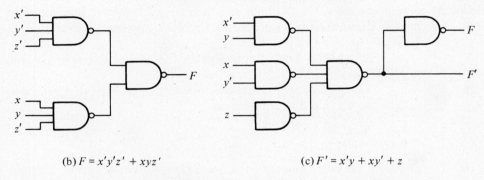

(b) $F = x'y'z' + xyz'$

(c) $F' = x'y + xy' + z$

Figure 3-19 Implementation of the function of Example 3-9 with NAND gates

specifies a group of OR gates for the sum terms, followed by an AND gate to produce the product. The transformation from the OR-AND to the NOR-NOR diagram is depicted in Fig. 3-20. It is similar to the NAND transformation discussed previously, except that now we use the product of sums expression:

$$F = (A + B)(C + D)E$$

The rule for obtaining the NOR logic diagram from a Boolean function can be derived from this transformation. It is similar to the three-step NAND rule, except that the simplified expression must be in the product of sums and the terms for the first-level NOR gates are the sum terms. A term with a single literal

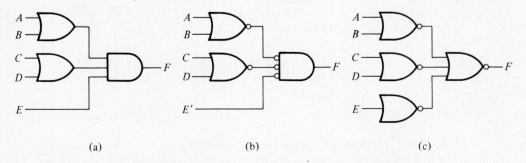

(a)

(b)

(c)

Figure 3-20 Three ways to implement $F = (A + B)(C + D)E$

requires a one-input NOR or inverter gate or may be complemented and applied directly to the second-level NOR gate.

A second way to implement a function with NOR gates would be to use the expression for the complement of the function in product of sums. This will give a two-level implementation for F' and a three-level implementation if the normal output F is required.

To obtain the simplified product of sums from a map, it is necessary to combine the 0's in the map and then complement the function. To obtain the simplified product of sums expression for the complement of the function, it is necessary to combine the 1's in the map and then complement the function. The following example demonstrates the procedure for NOR implementation.

EXAMPLE 3-10: Implement the function of Example 3-9 with NOR gates.

The map of this function is drawn in Fig. 3-19(a). First, combine the 0's in the map to obtain:

$$F' = x'y + xy' + z$$

This is the complement of the function in sum of products. Complement F' to obtain the simplified function in product of sums as required for NOR implementation:

$$F = (x + y')(x' + y)z'$$

The two-level implementation with NOR gates is shown in Fig. 3-21(a). The term with a single literal z' requires a one-input NOR or inverter gate. This gate can be removed and input z applied directly to the input of the second-level NOR gate.

A second implementation is possible from the complement of

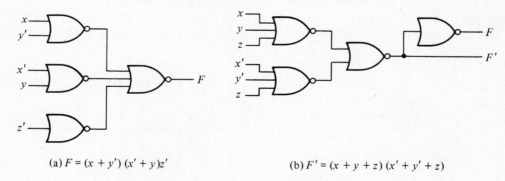

(a) $F = (x + y')(x' + y)z'$ (b) $F' = (x + y + z)(x' + y' + z)$

Figure 3-21   Implementation with NOR gates

TABLE 3-3 Rules for NAND and NOR implementation

Case	Function to simplify	Standard form to use	How to derive	Implement with	Number of levels to F
(a)	F	Sum of products	Combine 1's in map	NAND	2
(b)	F'	Sum of products	Combine 0's in map	NAND	3
(c)	F	Product of sums	Complement F' in (b)	NOR	2
(d)	F'	Product of sums	Complement F in (a)	NOR	3

the function in product of sums. For this case, first combine the 1's in the map to obtain:

$$F = x'y'z' + xyz'$$

This is the simplified expression in sum of products. Complement this function to obtain the complement of the function in product of sums as required for NOR implementation:

$$F' = (x + y + z)(x' + y' + z)$$

The two-level implementation for F' is shown in Fig. 3-21(b). If output F is desired, it can be generated with an inverter in the third level.

Table 3-3 summarizes the procedures for NAND or NOR implementation. One should not forget to always simplify the function in order to reduce the number of gates in the implementation. The standard forms obtained from the map simplification procedures apply directly and are very useful when dealing with NAND or NOR logic.

3-7 OTHER TWO-LEVEL IMPLEMENTATIONS

The types of gates most often found in integrated circuits are NAND and NOR. For this reason, NAND and NOR logic implementations are the most important from a practical point of view. Some NAND or NOR gates (but not all) allow the possibility of a wire connection between the outputs of two gates to provide a specific logic function. This type of logic is called *wired logic*. For example, open-collector TTL NAND gates, when tied together, perform the wired-AND logic. (The open-collector TTL gate is shown in Chapter 13, Fig. 13-11). The wired-AND logic performed with two NAND gates is depicted in Fig. 3-22(a). The

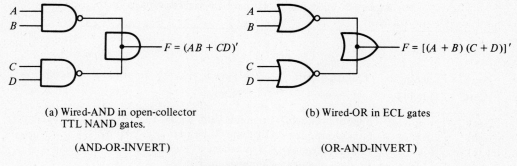

(a) Wired-AND in open-collector
TTL NAND gates.

(b) Wired-OR in ECL gates

(AND-OR-INVERT)

(OR-AND-INVERT)

Figure 3-22 Wired logic

AND gate is drawn with the lines going through the center of the gate to distinguish it from a conventional gate. The wired-AND gate is not a physical gate but only a symbol to designate the function obtained from the indicated wired connection. The logic function implemented by the circuit of Fig. 3-22(a) is:

$$F = (AB)' \cdot (CD)' = (AB + CD)'$$

and is called an AND-OR-INVERT function.

Similarly, the NOR output of ECL gates can be tied together to perform a wired-OR function. The logic function implemented by the circuit of Fig. 3-22(b) is:

$$F = (A + B)' + (C + D)' = [(A + B)(C + D)]'$$

and is called an OR-AND-INVERT function.

A wired-logic gate does not produce a physical second-level gate since it is just a wire connection. Nevertheless, for discussion purposes, we will consider the circuits of Fig. 3-22 as two-level implementations. The first level consists of NAND (or NOR) gates and the second level has a single AND (or OR) gate. The wired connection in the graphic symbol will be omitted in subsequent discussions.

Nondegenerate Forms

It will be instructive from a theoretical point of view to find out how many two-level combinations of gates are possible. We consider four types of gates: AND, OR, NAND, and NOR. If we assign one type of gate for the first level and one type for the second level, we find that there are 16 possible combinations of two-level forms. (The same type of gate can be in the first and second levels, as in NAND-NAND implementation.) Eight of these combinations are said to be *degenerate* forms because they degenerate to a single operation. This can be seen from a circuit with AND gates in the first level and an AND gate in the second level. The output of the circuit is merely the AND function of all input variables.

The other eight *nondegenerate* forms produce an implementation in sum of products or product of sums. The eight nondegenerate forms are:

AND-OR	OR-AND
NAND-NAND	NOR-NOR
NOR-OR	NAND-AND
OR-NAND	AND-NOR

The first gate listed in each of the forms constitutes a first level in the implementation. The second gate listed is a single gate placed in the second level. Note that any two forms listed in the same line are the duals of each other.

The AND-OR and OR-AND forms are the basic two-level forms discussed in Section 3-5. The NAND-NAND and NOR-NOR were introduced in Section 3-6. The remaining four forms are investigated in this section.

AND-OR-INVERT Implementation

The two forms NAND-AND and AND-NOR are equivalent forms and can be treated together. Both perform the AND-OR-INVERT function, as shown in Fig. 3-23. The AND-NOR form resembles the AND-OR form with an inversion done by the small circle in the output of the NOR gate. It implements the function:

$$F = (AB + CD + E)'$$

By using the alternate graphic symbol for the NOR gate, we obtain the diagram of Fig. 3-23(b). Note that the single variable E is *not* complemented because the only change made is in the graphic symbol of the NOR gate. Now we move the circles from the input terminal of the second-level gate to the output terminals of the first-level gates. An inverter is needed for the single variable to maintain the circle. Alternatively, the inverter can be removed provided input E is complemented. The circuit of Fig. 3-23(c) is a NAND-AND form and was shown in Fig. 3-22 to implement the AND-OR-INVERT function.

An AND-OR implementation requires an expression in sum of products. The AND-OR-INVERT implementation is similar except for the inversion. Therefore, if the *complement* of the function is simplified in sum of products (by combining the 0's in the map), it will be possible to implement F' with the AND-OR part of the function. When F' passes through the always present output inversion (the INVERT part), it will generate the output F of the function. An example for the AND-OR-INVERT implementation will be shown subsequently.

OR-AND-INVERT Implementation

The OR-NAND and NOR-OR forms perform the OR-AND-INVERT function. This is shown in Fig. 3-24. The OR-NAND form resembles the OR-AND form,

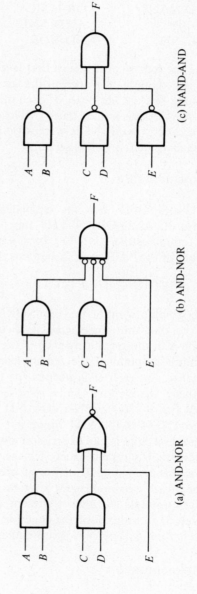

(a) AND-NOR

(b) AND-NOR

(c) NAND-AND

Figure 3-23 AND-OR-INVERT circuits; $F = (AB + CD + E)'$

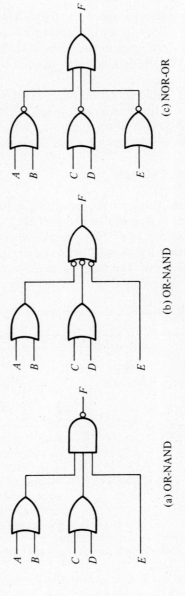

(a) OR-NAND

(b) OR-NAND

(c) NOR-OR

Figure 3-24 OR-AND-INVERT circuits; $F = [(A + B)(C + D)E]'$

except for the inversion done by the circle in the NAND gate. It implements the function:

$$F = [(A + B)(C + D)E]'$$

By using the alternate graphic symbol for the NAND gate, we obtain the diagram of Fig. 3-24(b). The circuit in (c) is obtained by moving the small circles from the inputs of the second-level gate to the outputs of the first-level gates. The circuit of Fig. 3-24(c) is a NOR-OR form and was shown in Fig. 3-22 to implement the OR-AND-INVERT function.

The OR-AND-INVERT implementation requires an expression in product of sums. If the complement of the function is simplified in product of sums, we can implement F' with the OR-AND part of the function. When F' passes through the INVERT part, we obtain the complement of F', or F, in the output.

Tabular Summary and Example

Table 3-4 summarizes the procedures for implementing a Boolean function in any one of the four two-level forms. Because of the INVERT part in each case, it is convenient to use the simplification of F' (the complement) of the function. When F' is implemented in one of these forms, we obtain the complement of the function in the AND-OR or OR-AND form. The four two-level forms invert this function, giving an output which is the complement of F'. This is the normal output F.

TABLE 3-4   Implementation with other two-level forms

Equivalent nondegenerate form		Implements the function	Simplify F' in	To get an output of
(a)	(b)*			
AND-NOR	NAND-AND	AND-OR-INVERT	Sum of products by combining 0's in the map	F
OR-NAND	NOR-OR	OR-AND-INVERT	Product of sums by combining 1's in the map and then complementing	F

*Form (b) requires a one-input NAND or NOR (inverter) gate for a single literal term.

EXAMPLE 3-11: Implement the function of Fig. 3-19(a) with the four two-level forms listed in Table 3-4. The complement of the function is simplified in sum of products by combining the 0's in the map:

$$F' = x'y + xy' + z$$

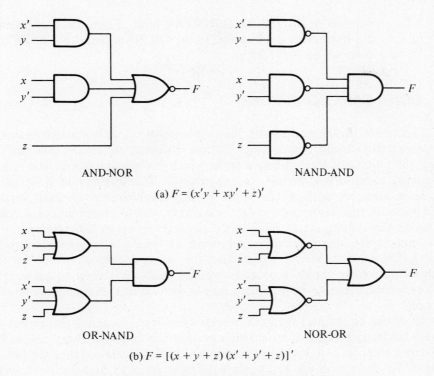

AND-NOR   NAND-AND

(a) $F = (x'y + xy' + z)'$

OR-NAND   NOR-OR

(b) $F = [(x + y + z)(x' + y' + z)]'$

Figure 3-25   Other two-level implementations

The normal output for this function can be expressed as

$$F = (x'y + xy' + z)'$$

which is in the AND-OR-INVERT form. The AND-NOR and NAND-AND implementations are shown in Fig. 3-25(a). Note that a one-input NAND or inverter gate is needed in the NAND-AND implementation, but not in the AND-NOR case. The inverter can be removed if we apply the input variable z' instead of z.

The OR-AND-INVERT forms require a simplified expression of the complement of the function in product of sums. To obtain this expression, we must first combine the 1's in the map:

$$F = x'y'z' + xyz'$$

Then we take the complement of the function:

$$F' = (x + y + z)(x' + y' + z)$$

The normal output F can now be expressed in the form:

$$F = [(x + y + z)(x' + y' + z)]'$$

which is in the OR-AND-INVERT form. From this expression we can implement the function in the OR-NAND and NOR-OR forms as shown in Fig. 3-25(b).

3-8 DON'T-CARE CONDITIONS

The 1's and 0's in the map signify the combination of variables that makes the function equal to 1 or 0, respectively. The combinations are usually obtained from a truth table that lists the conditions under which the function is a 1. The function is assumed equal to 0 under all other conditions. This assumption is not always true since there are applications where certain combinations of input variables never occur. A four-bit decimal code, for example, has six combinations which are not used. Any digital circuit using this code operates under the assumption that these unused combinations will never occur as long as the system is working properly. As a result, we don't care what the function output is to be for these combinations of the variables because they are guaranteed never to occur. These don't-care conditions can be used on a map to provide further simplification of the function.

It should be realized that a don't-care combination cannot be marked with a 1 on the map because it would require that the function always be a 1 for such input combination. Likewise, putting a 0 in the square requires the function to be 0. To distinguish the don't-care conditions from 1's and 0's, an X will be used.

When choosing adjacent squares to simplify the function in the map, the X's may be assumed to be either 0 or 1, whichever gives the simplest expression. In addition, an X need not be used at all if it does not contribute to covering a larger area. In each case, the choice depends only on the simplification that can be achieved.

EXAMPLE 3-12: Simplify the Boolean function:

$$F(w, x, y, z) = \Sigma(1, 3, 7, 11, 15)$$

and the don't-care conditions:

$$d(w, x, y, z) = \Sigma(0, 2, 5)$$

The minterms of F are the variable combinations that make the function equal to 1. The minterms of d are the don't-care combinations known never to occur. The minimization is shown in Fig. 3-26. The minterms of F are marked by 1's, those of d are marked by X's, and the remaining squares are filled with 0's. In (a), the 1's and X's are combined in any convenient manner so as to enclose the maximum number of adjacent squares. It is not necessary to include all or any of the X's, but only those useful for simplifying a term. One

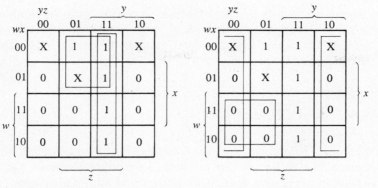

(a) Combining 1's and X's $F = w'z + yz$ (b) Combining 0's and X's $F = z(w' + y)$

Figure 3-26   Example with don't-care conditions

combination that gives a minimum function encloses one X and leaves two out. This results in a simplified sum-of-products function:

$$F = w'z + yz$$

In (b), the 0's are combined with any X's convenient to simplify the complement of the function. The best results are obtained if we enclose the two X's as shown. The complement function is simplified to:

$$F' = z' + wy'$$

Complementing again, we obtain a simplified product of sums function:

$$F = z(w' + y)$$

The two expressions obtained in Example 3-12 give two functions which can be shown to be algebraically equal. This is not always the case when don't-care conditions are involved. As a matter of fact, if an X is used as a 1 when combining the 1's and again as a 0 when combining the 0's, the two resulting functions will not yield algebraically equal answers. The selection of the don't-care condition as a 1 in the first case and as a 0 in the second results in different minterm expressions and thus different functions. This can be seen from Example 3-12. In the solution of this example, the X chosen to be a 1 was not chosen to be a 0. Now, if in Fig. 3-26(a) we choose the term $w'x'$ instead of $w'z$, we still obtain a minimized function:

$$F \doteq w'x' + yz$$

But it is not algebraically equal to the one obtained in product of sums because the same X's are used as 1's in the first minimization and as 0's in the second.

This example also demonstrates that an expression with the minimum number of literals is not necessarily unique. Sometimes the designer is confronted with a choice between two terms with an equal number of literals, with either choice resulting in a minimized expression.

3-9   THE TABULATION METHOD

The map method of simplification is convenient as long as the number of variables does not exceed five or six. As the number of variables increases, the excessive number of squares prevents a reasonable selection of adjacent squares. The obvious disadvantage of the map is that it is essentially a trial-and-error procedure which relies on the ability of the human user to recognize certain patterns. For functions of six or more variables, it is difficult to be sure that the best selection has been made.

The tabulation method overcomes this difficulty. It is a specific step-by-step procedure that is guaranteed to produce a simplified standard-form expression for a function. It can be applied to problems with many variables and has the advantage of being suitable for machine computation. However, it is quite tedious for human use and is prone to mistakes because of its routine, monotonous process. The tabulation method was first formulated by Quine (3) and later improved by McCluskey (4). It is also known as the Quine-McCluskey method.

The tabular method of simplification consists of two parts. The first is to find by an exhaustive search all the terms that are candidates for inclusion in the simplified function. These terms are called *prime-implicants*. The second operation is to choose among the prime-implicants those that give an expression with the least number of literals.

3-10   DETERMINATION OF PRIME-IMPLICANTS*

The starting point of the tabulation method is the list of minterms that specify the function. The first tabular operation is to find the prime-implicants by using a matching process. This process compares each minterm with every other minterm. If two minterms differ in only one variable, that variable is removed and a term with one less literal is found. This process is repeated for every minterm until the exhaustive search is completed. The matching-process cycle is repeated for those new terms just found. Third and further cycles are continued until a single pass through a cycle yields no further elimination of literals. The remaining terms and all the terms that did not match during the process comprise the prime-implicants. This tabulation method is illustrated by the following example.

*This section and the next may be omitted without loss of continuity.

EXAMPLE 3-13: Simplify the following Boolean function by using the tabulation method:

$$F = \Sigma(0, 1, 2, 8, 10, 11, 14, 15)$$

Step 1: Group binary representation of the minterms according to the number of 1's contained, as shown in Table 3-5, column (a). This is done by grouping the minterms into five sections separated by horizontal lines. The first section contains the number with no 1's in it. The second section contains those numbers that have only one 1. The third, fourth, and fifth sections contain those binary numbers with two, three, and four 1's, respectively. The decimal equivalents of the minterms are also carried along for identification.

Step 2: Any two minterms which differ from each other by only one variable can be combined, and the unmatched variable removed. Two minterm numbers fit into this category if they both have the same bit value in all positions except one. The minterms in one section are compared with those of the next section down only, because two terms differing by more than one bit cannot match. The minterm in the first section is compared with each of the three minterms in the second section. If any two numbers are the same in every position but one, a check is placed to the right of both minterms to show that they have been used. The resulting term,

TABLE 3-5 Determination of prime-implicants for Example 3-13

(a)		(b)		(c)	
$w\ x\ y\ z$		$w\ x\ y\ z$		$w\ x\ y\ z$	
0	0 0 0 0 √	0, 1	0 0 0 –	0, 2, 8, 10	– 0 – 0
		0, 2	0 0 – 0 √	0, 8, 2, 10	– 0 – 0
1	0 0 0 1 √	0, 8	– 0 0 0 √	10, 11, 14, 15	1 – 1 –
2	0 0 1 0 √			10, 14, 11, 15	1 – 1 –
8	1 0 0 0 √	2, 10	– 0 1 0 √		
		8, 10	1 0 – 0 √		
10	1 0 1 0 √				
		10, 11	1 0 1 – √		
11	1 0 1 1 √	10, 14	1 – 1 0 √		
14	1 1 1 0 √				
		11, 15	1 – 1 1 √		
15	1 1 1 1 √	14, 15	1 1 1 – √		

together with the decimal equivalents, is listed in column (b) of the table. The variable eliminated during the matching is denoted by a dash in its original position. In this case m_0 (0000) combines with m_1 (0001) to form (000 −). This combination is equivalent to the algebraic operation:

$$m_0 + m_1 = w'x'y'z' + w'x'y'z = w'x'y'$$

Minterm m_0 also combines with m_2 to form (00-0) and with m_8 to form (-000). The result of this comparison is entered into the first section of column (b). The minterms of sections two and three of column (a) are next compared to produce the terms listed in the second section of column (b). All other sections of (a) are similarly compared and subsequent sections formed in (b). This exhaustive comparing process results in the four sections of (b).

Step 3: The terms of column (b) have only three variables. A 1 under the variable means it is unprimed, a 0 means it is primed, and a dash means the variable is not included in the term. The searching and comparing process is repeated for the terms in column (b) to form the two-variable terms of column (c). Again, terms in each section need to be compared only if they have dashes in the same position. Note that the term (000-) does not match with any other term. Therefore, it has no check mark at its right. The decimal equivalents are written on the left-hand side of each entry for identification purposes. The comparing process should be carried out again in column (c) and in subsequent columns as long as proper matching is encountered. In the present example, the operation stops at the third column.

Step 4: The unchecked terms in the table form the prime-implicants. In this example we have the term $w'x'y'$ (000-) in column (b), and the terms $x'z'$(-0-0) and wy (1-1-) in column (c). Note that each term in column (c) appears twice in the table, and as long as the term forms a prime-implicant, it is unnecessary to use the same term twice. The sum of the prime-implicants gives a simplified expression for the function. This is because each checked term in the table has been taken into account by an entry of a simpler term in a subsequent column. Therefore, the unchecked entries (prime-implicants) are the terms left to formulate the function. For the present example, the sum of prime-implicants gives the minimized function in sum of products:

$$F = w'x'y' + x'z' + wy$$

It is worth comparing this answer with that obtained by the map method. Figure 3-27 shows the map simplification of this function. The combinations of

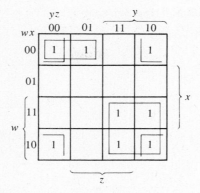

Figure 3-27 Map for the function of Example 3-13; $F = w'x'y' + x'z' + wy$

adjacent squares give the three prime-implicants of the function. The sum of these three terms is the simplified expression in sum of products.

It is important to point out that Example 3-13 was purposely chosen to give the simplified function from the sum of prime-implicants. In most other cases, the sum of prime-implicants does not necessarily form the expression with the minimum number of terms. This is demonstrated in Example 3-14.

The tedious manipulation that one must undergo when using the tabulation method is reduced if the comparing is done with decimal numbers instead of binary. A method will now be shown that uses subtraction of decimal numbers instead of the comparing and matching of binary numbers. We note that each 1 in a binary number represents the coefficient multiplied by a power of 2. When two minterms are the same in every position except one, the minterm with the extra 1 must be larger than the number of the other minterm by a power of 2. Therefore, two minterms can be combined if the number of the first minterm differs by a power of 2 from a second larger number in the next section down the table. We shall illustrate this procedure by repeating Example 3-13.

As shown in Table 3-6, column (a), the minterms are arranged in sections as before, except that now only the decimal equivalents of the minterms are listed. The process of comparing minterms is as follows: Inspect every two decimal numbers in adjacent sections of the table. If the number in the section below is *greater* than the number in the section above by a power of 2 (i.e., 1, 2, 4, 8, 16, etc.), check both numbers to show that they have been used, and write them down in column (b). The pair of numbers transferred to column (b) includes a third number in parentheses that designates the power of 2 by which the numbers differ. The number in parentheses tells us the position of the dash in the binary notation. The result of all comparisons of column (a) is shown in column (b).

The comparison between adjacent sections in column (b) is carried out in a similar fashion, except that only those terms with the same number in parentheses are compared. The pair of numbers in one section must differ by a power of 2 from the pair of numbers in the next section. And the numbers in the next section

TABLE 3-6 Determination of prime-implicants of Example 3-13 with decimal notation

(a)	(b)	(c)
0 √	0, 1 (1)	0, 2, 8, 10 (2, 8)
	0, 2 (2) √	0, 2, 8, 10 (2, 8)
1 √	0, 8 (8) √	
2 √		10, 11, 14, 15 (1, 4)
8 √	2, 10 (8) √	10, 11, 14, 15 (1, 4)
	8, 10 (2) √	
10 √		
	10, 11 (1) √	
11 √	10, 14 (4) √	
14 √		
	11, 15 (4) √	
15 √	14, 15 (1) √	

below must be *greater* for the combination to take place. In column (c), write all four decimal numbers with the two numbers in parentheses designating the positions of the dashes. A comparison of Tables 3-5 and 3-6 may be helpful in understanding the derivations in Table 3-6.

The prime-implicants are those terms not checked in the table. These are the same as before, except that they are given in decimal notation. To convert from decimal notation to binary, convert all decimal numbers in the term to binary and then insert a dash in those positions designated by the numbers in parentheses. Thus 0, 1 (1) is converted to binary as 0000, 0001; a dash in the first position of either number results in (000-). Similarly, 0, 2, 8, 10 (2, 8) is converted to the binary notation from 0000, 0010, 1000, and 1010, and a dash inserted in positions 2 and 8, to result in (-0-0)

EXAMPLE 3-14: Determine the prime-implicants of the function:

$$F(w, x, y, z) = \Sigma(1, 4, 6, 7, 8, 9, 10, 11, 15)$$

The minterm numbers are grouped in sections as shown in Table 3-7, column (a). The binary equivalent of the minterm is included for the purpose of counting the number of 1's. The binary numbers in the first section have only one 1; in the second section, two 1's; etc. The minterm numbers are compared by the decimal method and a match is found if the number in the section below is greater than that in the section above. If the number in the section below is smaller than the

TABLE 3-7   Determination of prime-implicants for Example 3-14

(a)			(b)			(c)
0001	1	√	1, 9	(8)		8, 9, 10, 11 (1, 2)
0100	4	√	4, 6	(2)		8, 9, 10, 11 (1, 2)
1000	8	√	8, 9	(1)	√	
			8, 10	(2)	√	
0110	6	√				
1001	9	√	6, 7	(1)		
1010	10	√	9, 11	(2)	√	
			10, 11	(1)	√	
0111	7	√				
1011	11	√	7, 15	(8)		
			11, 15	(4)		
1111	15	√				

Prime-implicants

Decimal	Binary $w \ x \ y \ z$	Term
1, 9 (8)	$- \ 0 \ 0 \ 1$	$x'y'z$
4, 6 (2)	$0 \ 1 \ - \ 0$	$w'xz'$
6, 7 (1)	$0 \ 1 \ 1 \ -$	$w'xy$
7, 15 (8)	$- \ 1 \ 1 \ 1$	xyz
11, 15 (4)	$1 \ - \ 1 \ 1$	wyz
8, 9, 10, 11 (1, 2)	$1 \ 0 \ - \ -$	wx'

one above, a match is not recorded even if the two numbers differ by a power of 2. The exhaustive search in column (a) results in the terms of column (b), with all minterms in column (a) being checked. There are only two matches of terms in column (b). Each gives the same two-literal term recorded in column (c). The prime-implicants consist of all the unchecked terms in the table. The conversion from the decimal to the binary notation is shown at the bottom of the table. The prime-implicants are found to be $x'y'z$, $w'xz'$, $w'xy$, xyz, wyz, and wx'.

The sum of the prime-implicants gives a valid algebraic expression for the function. However, this expression is not necessarily the one with the minimum number of terms. This can be demonstrated from inspection of the map for the

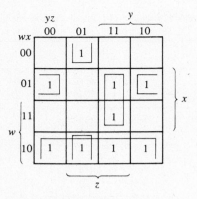

Figure 3-28 Map for the function of Example 3-14; $F = x'y'z + w'xz' + xyz + wx'$

function of Example 3-14. As shown in Fig. 3-28, the minimized function is recognized to be:

$$F = x'y'z + w'xz' + xyz + wx'$$

which consists of the sum of four of the six prime-implicants derived in Example 3-14. The tabular procedure for selecting the prime-implicants that give the minimized function is the subject of the next section.

3-11 SELECTION OF PRIME-IMPLICANTS

The selection of prime-implicants that form the minimized function is made from a prime-implicant table. In this table, each prime-implicant is represented in a row and each minterm in a column. Crosses are placed in each row to show the composition of minterms that make the prime-implicants. A minimum set of prime-implicants is then chosen that covers all the minterms in the function. This procedure is illustrated in Example 3-15.

> **EXAMPLE 3-15:** Minimize the function of Example 3-14. The prime-implicant table for this example is shown in Table 3-8. There are six rows, one for each prime-implicant (derived in Example 3-14), and nine columns, each representing one minterm of the function. Crosses are placed in each row to indicate the minterms contained in the prime-implicant of that row. For example, the two crosses in the first row indicate that minterms 1 and 9 are contained in the prime-implicant $x'y'z$. It is advisable to include the decimal equivalent of the prime-implicant in each row, as it conveniently gives the minterms contained in it. After all the crosses have been marked, we proceed to select a minimum number of prime-implicants.
>
> The completed prime-implicant table is inspected for columns

TABLE 3-8 Prime-implicant table for Example 3-15

		1	4	6	7	8	9	10	11	15
√ $x'y'z$	1, 9	X					X			
√ $w'xz'$	4, 6		X	X						
$w'xy$	6, 7			X	X					
xyz	7, 15				X					X
wyz	11, 15								X	X
√ wx'	8, 9, 10, 11					X	X	X	X	
		√	√	√		√	√	√	√	

containing only a single cross. In this example, there are four minterms whose columns have a single cross: 1, 4, 8, and 10. Minterm 1 is covered by prime-implicant $x'y'z$, i.e., the selection of prime-implicant $x'y'z$ guarantees that minterm 1 is included in the function. Similarly, minterm 4 is covered by prime-implicant $w'xz'$, and minterms 8 and 10, by prime-implicant wx'. Prime-implicants that cover minterms with a single cross in their column are called *essential prime-implicants*. To enable the final simplified expression to contain all the minterms, we have no alternative but to include essential prime-implicants. A check mark is placed in the table next to the essential prime-implicants to indicate that they have been selected.

Next we check each column whose minterm is covered by the selected essential prime-implicants. For example, the selected prime-implicant $x'y'z$ covers minterms 1 and 9. A check is inserted in the bottom of the columns. Similarly, prime-implicant $w'xz'$ covers minterms 4 and 6, and wx' covers minterms 8, 9, 10, and 11. Inspection of the prime-implicant table shows that the selection of the essential prime-implicants covers all the minterms of the function except 7 and 15. These two minterms must be included by the selection of one or more prime-implicants. In this example, it is clear that prime-implicant xyz covers both minterms and is therefore the one to be selected. We have thus found the minimum set of prime-implicants whose sum gives the required minimized function:

$$F = x'y'z + w'xz' + wx' + xyz$$

The simplified expressions derived in the preceding examples were all in the sum of products form. The tabulation method can be adapted to give a simplified expression in product of sums. As in the map method, we have to start with the complement of the function by taking the 0's as the initial list of minterms. This list contains those minterms not included in the original function which are numerically equal to the maxterms of the function. The tabulation process is carried out with the 0's of the function and terminates with a simplified expression in sum of products of the complement of the function. By taking the complement again, we obtain the simplified product of sums expression.

A function with don't-care conditions can be simplified by the tabulation method after a slight modification. The don't-care terms are included in the list of minterms when the prime-implicants are determined. This allows the derivation of prime-implicants with the least number of literals. The don't-care terms are not included in the list of minterms when the prime-implicant table is set up, because don't-care terms do not have to be covered by the selected prime-implicants.

3-12 CONCLUDING REMARKS

Two methods of Boolean function simplification were introduced in this chapter. The criterion for simplification was taken to be the minimization of the number of literals in sum of products or product of sums expressions. Both the map and the tabulation methods are restricted in their capabilities since they are useful for simplifying only Boolean functions expressed in the standard forms. Although this is a disadvantage of the methods, it is not very critical. Most applications prefer the standard forms over any other form. We have seen from Fig. 3-15 that the gate implementation of expressions in standard form consists of no more than two levels of gates. Expressions not in the standard form are implemented with more than two levels. Humphrey (5) shows an extension of the map method that produces simplified multilevel expressions.

One should recognize that the reflected-code sequence chosen for the maps is not unique. It is possible to draw a map and assign a binary reflected-code sequence to the rows and columns different from the sequence employed here. As long as the binary sequence chosen produces a change in only one bit between adjacent squares, it will produce a valid and useful map.

Two alternate versions of the three-variable maps which are often found in the digital logic literature are shown in Fig. 3-29. The minterm numbers are written

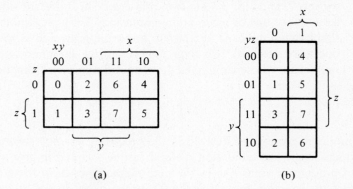

Figure 3-29 Variations of the three-variable map

in each square for reference. In (a), the assignment of the variables to the rows and columns is different from the one used in this book. In (b), the map has been rotated in a vertical position. The minterm number assignment in all maps remains in the order xyz. For example, the square for minterm 6 is found by assigning to the ordered variables the binary number $xyz = 110$. The square for this minterm is found in (a) from the column marked $xy = 11$ and the row with $z = 0$. The corresponding square in (b) belongs in the column marked with $x = 1$ and the row with $yz = 10$. The simplification procedure with these maps is exactly the same as described in this chapter except, of course, for the variations in minterm and variable assignment.

Two other versions of the four-variable map are shown in Fig. 3-30. The map in (a) is very popular and is used quite often in the literature. Here again, the difference is slight and is manifested by a mere interchange of variable assignment from rows to columns and vice versa. The map in (b) is the original Veitch diagram (1) which Karnaugh (2) modified to the one shown in (a). Again, the simplification procedures do not change when these maps are used instead of the one employed in this book. There are also variations of the five- and six-variable maps. In any case, any map that looks different from the one used in this book, or is called by a different name, should be recognized merely as a variation of minterm assignment to the squares in the map.

As is evident from Examples 3-13 and 3-14, the tabularion method has the drawback that errors inevitably occur in trying to compare numbers over long lists. The map method would seem to be preferable, but for more than five variables, we cannot be certain that the best simplified expression has been found. The real advantage of the tabulation method lies in the fact that it consists of specific step-by-step procedures that guarantee an answer. Moreover, this formal procedure is suitable for computer mechanization.

It was stated in Section 3-9 that the tabulation method always starts with the minterm list of the function. If the function is not in this form, it must be converted. In most applications, the function to be simplified comes from a truth

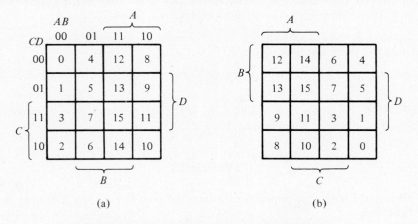

Figure 3-30 Variations of the four-variable map

table, from which the minterm list is readily available. Otherwise, the conversion to minterms adds considerable manipulative work to the problem. However, an extension of the tabulation method exists for finding prime-implicants from arbitrary sum of products expressions. See, for example, McCluskey (7).

In this chapter, we have considered the simplification of functions with many input variables and a single output variable. However, some digital circuits have more than one output. Such circuits are described by a set of Boolean functions, one for each output variable. A circuit with multiple outputs may sometimes have common terms among the various functions which can be utilized to form common gates during the implementation. This results in further simplification not taken into consideration when each function is simplified separately. There exists an extension of the tabulation method for multiple-output circuits (6, 7). However, this method is too specialized and very tedious for human manipulation. It is of practical importance only if a computer program based on this method is available to the user.

REFERENCES

1. Veitch, E. W., "A Chart Method for Simplifying Truth Functions." *Proc. of the ACM* (*May* 1952), 127–33.

2. Karnaugh, M., "A Map Method for Synthesis of Combinational Logic Circuits." *Trans. AIEE, Comm. and Electronics*, Vol. 72, Part I (November 1953), 593–99.

3. Quine, W. V., "The Problem of Simplifying Truth Functions." *Am. Math. Monthly*, Vol. 59, No. 8 (October 1952), 521–31.

4. McCluskey, E. J., Jr., "Minimization of Boolean Functions." *Bell System Tech. J.*, Vol. 35, No. 6 (November 1956), 1417–44.

5. Humphrey, W. S., Jr., *Switching Circuits with Computer Applications*. New York: McGraw-Hill Book Co., 1958, Chap. 4.

6. Hill, F. J., and G. R. Peterson, *Introduction to Switching Theory and Logical Design*, 2nd ed. New York: John Wiley & Sons, Inc., 1974, Chaps. 6 and 7.

7. McCluskey, E. J., Jr., *Introduction to the Theory of Switching Circuits*. New York: McGraw-Hill Book Co., 1965, Chap. 4.

8. Kohavi, Z., *Switching and Finite Automata Theory*. New York: McGraw-Hill Book Co., 1970.

9. Nagle, H. T. Jr., B. D. Carrol, and J. D. Irwin, *An Introduction to Computer Logic*. Englewood Cliffs, N.J.: Prentice-Hall, Inc., 1975.

PROBLEMS

3-1.   Obtain the simplified expressions in sum of products for the following Boolean functions:

   (a) $F(x, y, z) = \Sigma(2, 3, 6, 7)$

(b) $F(A, B, C, D) = \Sigma(7, 13, 14, 15)$

(c) $F(A, B, C, D) = \Sigma(4, 6, 7, 15)$

(d) $F(w, x, y, z) = \Sigma(2, 3, 12, 13, 14, 15)$

3-2. Obtain the simplified expressions in sum of products for the following Boolean functions:

(a) $xy + x'y'z' + x'yz'$

(b) $A'B + BC' + B'C'$

(c) $a'b' + bc + a'bc'$

(d) $xy'z + xyz' + x'yz + xyz$

3-3. Obtain the simplified expressions in sum of products for the following Boolean functions:

(a) $D(A' + B) + B'(C + AD)$

(b) $ABD + A'C'D' + A'B + A'CD' + AB'D'$

(c) $k'lm' + k'm'n + klm'n' + lmn'$

(d) $A'B'C'D' + AC'D' + B'CD' + A'BCD + BC'D$

(e) $x'z + w'xy' + w(x'y + xy')$

3-4. Obtain the simplified expressions in sum of products for the following Boolean functions:

(a) $F(A, B, C, D, E) = \Sigma(0, 1, 4, 5, 16, 17, 21, 25, 29)$

(b) $BDE + B'C'D + CDE + A'B'CE + A'B'C + B'C'D'E'$

(c) $A'B'CE' + A'B'C'D' + B'D'E' + B'CD' + CDE' + BDE'$

3-5. Given the following truth table:

x	y	z	F_1	F_2
0	0	0	0	0
0	0	1	1	0
0	1	0	1	0
0	1	1	0	1
1	0	0	1	0
1	0	1	0	1
1	1	0	0	1
1	1	1	1	1

(a) Express F_1 and F_2 in product of maxterms.

(b) Obtain the simplified functions in sum of products.

(c) Obtain the simplified functions in product of sums.

3-6. Obtain the simplified expressions in product of sums:

(a) $F(x, y, z) = \Pi(0, 1, 4, 5)$

(b) $F(A, B, C, D) = \Pi(0, 1, 2, 3, 4, 10, 11)$

(c) $F(w, x, y, z) = \Pi(1, 3, 5, 7, 13, 15)$

3-7. Obtain the simplified expressions in (1) sum of products and (2) product of sums:

(a) $x'z' + y'z' + yz' + xyz$

(b) $(A + B' + D)(A' + B + D)(C + D)(C' + D')$

(c) $(A' + B' + D')(A + B' + C')(A' + B + D')(B + C' + D')$

(d) $(A' + B' + D)(A' + D')(A + B + D')(A + B' + C + D)$

(e) $w'yz' + vw'z' + vw'x + v'wz + v'w'y'z'$

3-8.   Draw the gate implementation of the simplified Boolean functions obtained in problem 3-7 using AND and OR gates.

3-9.   Simplify each of the following functions and implement them with NAND gates. Give two alternatives.

(a) $F_1 = AC' + ACE + ACE' + A'CD' + A'D'E'$

(b) $F_2 = (B' + D')(A' + C' + D)(A + B' + C' + D)(A' + B + C' + D')$

3-10. Repeat problem 3-9 for NOR implementations.

3-11. Implement the following functions with NAND gates. Assume that both the normal and complement inputs are available.

(a) $BD + BCD + AB'C'D' + A'B'CD'$ with no more than six gates, each having three inputs.

(b) $(AB + A'B')(CD' + C'D)$ with two-input gates.

3-12. Implement the following functions with NOR gates. Assume that both the normal and complement inputs are available.

(a) $AB' + C'D' + A'CD' + DC'(AB + A'B') + DB(AC' + A'C)$

(b) $AB'CD' + A'BCD' + AB'C'D + A'BC'D$

3-13. List the eight degenerate two-level forms and show that they reduce to a single operation. Explain how the degenerate two-level forms can be used to extend the fan-in of gates.

3-14. Implement the functions of problem 3-9 with the following two-level forms: NOR-OR, NAND-AND, OR-NAND, and AND-NOR.

3-15. Simplify the Boolean function F in sum of products using the don't-care conditions d:

(a) $F = y' + x'z'$
    $d = yz + xy$

(b) $F = B'C'D' + BCD' + ABCD'$
    $d = B'CD' + A'BC'D$

3-16. Simplify the Boolean function F using the don't-care conditions d, in (1) sum of products and (2) product of sums:

(a) $F = A'B'D' + A'CD + A'BC$
    $d = A'BC'D + ACD + AB'D$

(b) $F = w'(x'y + x'y' + xyz) + x'z'(y + w)$
    $d = w'x(y'z + yz') + wyz$

(c) $F = ACE + A'CD'E' + A'C'DE$
    $d = DE' + A'D'E + AD'E'$

(d) $F = B'DE' + A'BE + B'C'E' + A'BC'D'$
    $d = BDE' + CD'E'$

3-17.   Implement the following functions using the don't-care conditions. Assume that both the normal and complement inputs are available.

(a) $F = A'B'C' + AB'D + A'B'CD'$ with no more than two NOR gates.
$d = ABC + AB'D'$

(b) $F = (A + D)(A' + B)(A' + C')$ with no more than three NAND gates.

(c) $F = B'D + B'C + ABCD$ with NAND gates.
$d = A'BD + AB'C'D'$

3-18.   Implement the following function with either NAND or NOR gates. Use only four gates. Only the normal inputs are available.

$$F = w'xz + w'yz + x'yz' + wxy'z$$
$$d = wyz$$

3-19.   The following Boolean expression:

$$BE + B'DE'$$

is a simplified version of the expression:

$$A'BE + BCDE + BC'D'E + A'B'DE' + B'C'DE'$$

Are there any don't-care conditions? If so, what are they?

3-20.   Give three possible ways to express the function:

$$F = A'B'D' + AB'CD' + A'BD + ABC'D$$

with eight or less literals.

3-21.   With the use of maps, find the simplest form in sum of products of the function $F = fg$, where f and g are given by:

$$f = wxy' + y'z + w'yz' + x'yz'$$
$$g = (w + x + y' + z')(x' + y' + z)(w' + y + z')$$

Hint: See problem 2-8(b).

3-22.   Simplify the Boolean function of problem 3-2(a) using the map defined in Fig. 3-29(a). Repeat with the map of Fig. 3-29(b).

3-23.   Simplify the Boolean function of problem 3-3(a) using the map defined in Fig. 3-30(a). Repeat with the map of Fig. 3-30(b).

3-24.   Simplify the following Boolean functions by means of the tabulation method.

(a) $F(A, B, C, D, E, F, G) = \Sigma(20, 28, 52, 60)$

(b) $F(A, B, C, D, E, F, G) = \Sigma(20, 28, 38, 39, 52, 60, 102, 103, 127)$

(c) $F(A, B, C, D, E, F) \quad = \Sigma(6, 9, 13, 18, 19, 25, 27, 29, 41, 45, 57, 61)$

3-25.   Repeat problem 3-6 using the tabulation method.

3-26.   Repeat problem 3-16(c) and (d) using the tabulation method.

Combinational Logic

4

4-1 INTRODUCTION

Logic circuits for digital systems may be combinational or sequential. A combinational circuit consists of logic gates whose outputs at any time are determined directly from the present combination of inputs without regard to previous inputs. A combinational circuit performs a specific information-processing operation fully specified logically by a set of Boolean functions. Sequential circuits employ memory elements (binary cells) in addition to logic gates. Their outputs are a function of the inputs and the state of the memory elements. The state of memory elements, in turn, is a function of previous inputs. As a consequence, the outputs of a sequential circuit depend not only on present inputs, but also on past inputs, and the circuit behavior must be specified by a time sequence of inputs and internal states. Sequential circuits are discussed in Chapter 6.

In Chapter 1 we learned to recognize binary numbers and binary codes that represent discrete quantities of information. These binary variables are represented by electric voltages or by some other signal. The signals can be manipulated in digital logic gates to perform required functions. In Chapter 2 we introduced Boolean algebra as a way to express logic functions algebraically. In Chapter 3 we learned how to simplify Boolean functions to achieve economical gate implementations. The purpose of this chapter is to use the knowledge acquired in previous chapters and formulate various systematic design and analysis procedures of combinational circuits. The solution of some typical examples will provide a useful catalog of elementary functions important for the understanding of digital computers and systems.

A combinational circuit consists of input variables, logic gates, and output variables. The logic gates accept signals from the inputs and generate signals to the outputs. This process transforms binary information from the given input data to the required output data. Obviously, both input and output data are represented by binary signals, i.e., they exist in two possible values, one representing logic-1

Figure 4-1 Block diagram of a combinational circuit

and the other logic-0. A block diagram of a combinational circuit is shown in Fig. 4-1. The n input binary variables come from an external source; the m output variables go to an external destination. In many applications, the source and/or destination are storage registers (Section 1-7) located either in the vicinity of the combinational circuit or in a remote external device. By definition, an external register does not influence the behavior of the combinational circuit because, if it does, the total system becomes a sequential circuit.

For n input variables, there are 2^n possible combinations of binary input values. For each possible input combination, there is one and only one possible output combination. A combinational circuit can be described by m Boolean functions, one for each output variable. Each output function is expressed in terms of the n input variables.

Each input variable to a combinational circuit may have one or two wires. When only one wire is available, it may represent the variable either in the normal form (unprimed) or in the complement form (primed). Since a variable in a Boolean expression may appear primed and/or unprimed, it is necessary to provide an inverter for each literal not available in the input wire. On the other hand, an input variable may appear in two wires, supplying both the normal and complement forms to the input of the circuit. If so, it is unnecessary to include inverters for the inputs. The type of binary cells used in most digital systems are flip-flop circuits (Chapter 6) that have outputs for both the normal and complement values of the stored binary variable. In our subsequent work, we shall assume that each input variable appears in two wires, supplying both the normal and complement values simultaneously. We must also realize that an inverter circuit can always supply the complement of the variable if only one wire is available.

4-2 DESIGN PROCEDURE

The design of combinational circuits starts from the verbal outline of the problem and ends in a logic circuit diagram, or a set of Boolean functions from which the logic diagram can be easily obtained. The procedure involves the following steps:

1. The problem is stated.

2. The number of available input variables and required output variables is determined.

3. The input and output variables are assigned letter symbols.

4. The truth table that defines the required relationships between inputs and outputs is derived.

5. The simplified Boolean function for each output is obtained.

6. The logic diagram is drawn.

A truth table for a combinational circuit consists of input columns and output columns. The 1's and 0's in the input columns are obtained from the 2^n binary combinations available for n input variables. The binary values for the outputs are determined from examination of the stated problem. An output can be equal to either 0 or 1 for every valid input combination. However, the specifications may indicate that some input combinations will not occur. These combinations become don't-care conditions.

The output functions specified in the truth table give the exact definition of the combinational circuit. It is important that the verbal specifications be interpreted correctly into a truth table. Sometimes the designer must use his intuition and experience to arrive at the correct interpretation. Word specifications are very seldom complete and exact. Any wrong interpretation which results in an incorrect truth table produces a combinational circuit that will not fulfill the stated requirements.

The output Boolean functions from the truth table are simplified by any available method, such as algebraic manipulation, the map method, or the tabulation procedure. Usually there will be a variety of simplified expressions from which to choose. However, in any particular application, certain restrictions, limitations, and criteria will serve as a guide in the process of choosing a particular algebraic expression. A practical design method would have to consider such constraints as (1) minimum number of gates, (2) minimum number of inputs to a gate, (3) minimum propagation time of the signal through the circuit, (4) minimum number of interconnections, and (5) limitations of the driving capabilities of each gate. Since all these criteria cannot be satisfied simultaneously, and since the importance of each constraint is dictated by the particular application, it is difficult to make a general statement as to what constitutes an acceptable simplification. In most cases the simplification begins by satisfying an elementary objective, such as producing a simplified Boolean function in a standard form, and from that proceeds to meet any other performance criteria.

In practice, designers tend to go from the Boolean functions to a wiring list that shows the interconnections among various standard logic gates. In that case the design need not go any further than the required simplified output Boolean functions. However, a logic diagram is helpful for visualizing the gate implementation of the expressions.

4-3 ADDERS

Digital computers perform a variety of information-processing tasks. Among the basic functions encountered are the various arithmetic operations. The most basic arithmetic operation, no doubt, is the addition of two binary digits. This simple addition consists of four possible elementary operations, namely, $0 + 0 = 0$, $0 + 1 = 1$, $1 + 0 = 1$, and $1 + 1 = 10$. The first three operations produce a sum whose length is one digit, but when both augend and addend bits are equal to 1, the binary sum consists of two digits. The higher significant bit of this result is called a *carry*. When the augend and addend numbers contain more significant digits, the carry obtained from the addition of two bits is added to the next higher-order pair of significant bits. A combinational circuit that performs the addition of two bits is called a *half-adder*. One that performs the addition of three bits (two significant bits and a previous carry) is a *full-adder*. The name of the former stems from the fact that two half-adders can be employed to implement a full-adder. The two adder circuits are the first combinational circuits we shall design.

Half-Adder

From the verbal explanation of a half-adder, we find that this circuit needs two binary inputs and two binary outputs. The input variables designate the augend and addend bits; the output variables produce the sum and carry. It is necessary to specify two output variables because the result may consist of two binary digits. We arbitrarily assign symbols x and y to the two inputs and S (for sum) and C (for carry) to the outputs.

Now that we have established the number and names of the input and output variables, we are ready to formulate a truth table to identify exactly the function of the half-adder. This truth table is shown below:

x	y	C	S
0	0	0	0
0	1	0	1
1	0	0	1
1	1	1	0

The carry output is 0 unless both inputs are 1. The S output represents the least significant bit of the sum.

The simplified Boolean functions for the two outputs can be obtained directly from the truth table. The simplified sum of products expressions are:

$$S = x'y + xy'$$
$$C = xy$$

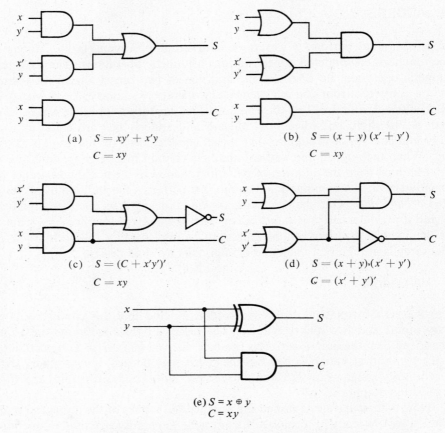

(a) $S = xy' + x'y$
$C = xy$

(b) $S = (x + y)(x' + y')$
$C = xy$

(c) $S = (C + x'y')'$
$C = xy$

(d) $S = (x + y) \cdot (x' + y')$
$C = (x' + y')'$

(e) $S = x \oplus y$
$C = xy$

Figure 4-2 Various implementations of a half-adder

The logic diagram for this implementation is shown in Fig. 4-2(a), as are four other implementations for a half-adder. They all achieve the same result as far as the input-output behavior is concerned. They illustrate the flexibility available to the designer when implementing even a simple combinational logic function such as this.

Figure 4-2(a), as mentioned above, is the implementation of the half-adder in sum of products. Figure 4-2(b) shows the implementation in product of sums:

$$S = (x + y)(x' + y')$$
$$C = xy$$

To obtain the implementation of Fig. 4-2(c), we note that S is the exclusive-OR of x and y. The complement of S is the equivalence of x and y (Section 2-6):

$$S' = xy + x'y'$$

120

but $C = xy$, and therefore we have:

$$S = (C + x'y')'$$

In Fig. 4-2(d) we use the product of sums implementation with C derived as follows:

$$C = xy = (x' + y')'$$

The half-adder can be implemented with an exclusive-OR and an AND gate as shown in Fig. 4-2(e). This form is used later to show that two half-adder circuits are needed to construct a full-adder circuit.

Full-Adder

A full-adder is a combinational circuit that forms the arithmetic sum of three input bits. It consists of three inputs and two outputs. Two of the input variables, denoted by x and y, represent the two significant bits to be added. The third input, z, represents the carry from the previous lower significant position. Two outputs are necessary because the arithmetic sum of three binary digits ranges in value from 0 to 3, and binary 2 or 3 needs two digits. The two outputs are designated by the symbols S for sum and C for carry. The binary variable S gives the value of the least significant bit of the sum. The binary variable C gives the output carry. The truth table of the full-adder is as follows:

x	y	z	C	S
0	0	0	0	0
0	0	1	0	1
0	1	0	0	1
0	1	1	1	0
1	0	0	0	1
1	0	1	1	0
1	1	0	1	0
1	1	1	1	1

The eight rows under the input variables designate all possible combinations of 1's and 0's that these variables may have. The 1's and 0's for the output variables are determined from the arithmetic sum of the input bits. When all input bits are 0's, the output is 0. The S output is equal to 1 when only one input is equal to 1 or when all three inputs are equal to 1. The C output has a carry of 1 if two or three inputs are equal to 1.

The input and output bits of the combinational circuit have different interpretations at various stages of the problem. Physically, the binary signals of the input wires are considered binary digits added arithmetically to form a two-digit sum at

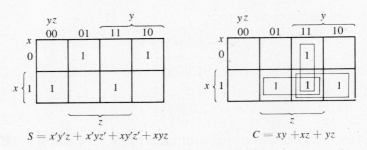

$$S = x'y'z + x'yz' + xy'z' + xyz \qquad C = xy + xz + yz$$

Figure 4-3 Maps for full-adder

the output wires. On the other hand, the same binary values are considered variables of Boolean functions when expressed in the truth table or when the circuit is implemented with logic gates. It is important to realize that two different interpretations are given to the values of the bits encountered in this circuit.

The input-output logical relationship of the full-adder circuit may be expressed in two Boolean functions, one for each output variable. Each output Boolean function requires a unique map for its simplification. Each map must have eight squares, since each output is a function of three input variables. The maps of Fig. 4-3 are used for simplifying the two output functions. The 1's in the squares for the maps of S and C are determined directly from the truth table. The squares with 1's for the S output do not combine in adjacent squares to give a simplified expression in sum of products. The C output can be simplified to a six-literal expression. The logic diagram for the full-adder implemented in sum of products is shown in Fig. 4-4. This implementation uses the following Boolean expressions:

$$S = x'y'z + x'yz' + xy'z' + xyz$$
$$C = xy + xz + yz$$

Other configurations for a full-adder may be developed. The product-of-sums implementation requires the same number of gates as in Fig. 4-4, with the

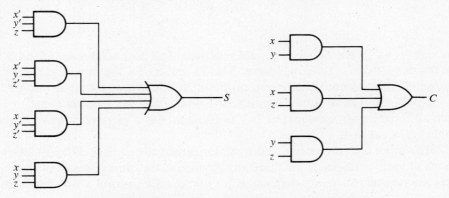

Figure 4-4 Implementation of full-adder in sum of products

122

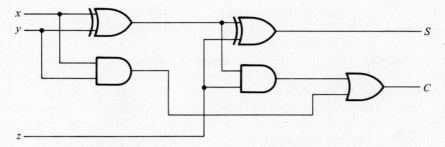

Figure 4-5 Implementation of a full-adder with two half-adders and an OR gate

number of AND and OR gates interchanged. A full-adder can be implemented with two half-adders and one OR gate, as shown in Fig. 4-5. The S output from the second half-adder is the exclusive-OR of z and the output of the first half-adder, giving:

$$
\begin{aligned}
S &= z \oplus (x \oplus y) \\
&= z'(xy' + x'y) + z(xy' + x'y)' \\
&= z'(xy' + x'y) + z(xy + x'y') \\
&= xy'z' + x'yz' + xyz + x'y'z
\end{aligned}
$$

and the carry output is:

$$
C = z(xy' + x'y) + xy = xy'z + x'yz + xy
$$

4-4 SUBTRACTORS

The subtraction of two binary numbers may be accomplished by taking the complement of the subtrahend and adding it to the minuend (Section 1-5). By this method, the subtraction operation becomes an addition operation requiring full-adders for its machine implementation. It is possible to implement subtraction with logic circuits in a direct manner, as done with paper and pencil. By this method, each subtrahend bit of the number is subtracted from its corresponding significant minuend bit to form a difference bit. If the minuend bit is smaller than the subtrahend bit, a 1 is borrowed from the next significant position. The fact that a 1 has been borrowed must be conveyed to the next higher pair of bits by means of a binary signal coming out (output) of a given stage and going into (input) the next higher stage. Just as there are half- and full-adders, there are half- and full-subtractors.

Half-Subtractor

A half-subtractor is a combinational circuit that subtracts two bits and produces their difference. It also has an output to specify if a 1 has been borrowed. Designate the minuend bit by x and the subtrahend bit by y. To perform $x - y$,

123

we have to check the relative magnitudes of x and y. If $x \geqslant y$, we have three possibilities: $0 - 0 = 0$, $1 - 0 = 1$, and $1 - 1 = 0$. The result is called the *difference bit*. If $x < y$, we have $0 - 1$, and it is necessary to borrow a 1 from the next higher stage. The 1 borrowed from the next higher stage adds 2 to the minuend bit, just as in the decimal system a borrow adds 10 to a minuend digit. With the minuend equal to 2, the difference becomes $2 - 1 = 1$. The half-subtractor needs two outputs. One output generates the difference and will be designated by the symbol D. The second output, designated B for borrow, generates the binary signal that informs the next stage that a 1 has been borrowed. The truth table for the input-output relationships of a half-subtractor can now be derived as follows:

x	y	B	D
0	0	0	0
0	1	1	1
1	0	0	1
1	1	0	0

The output borrow B is a 0 as long as $x \geqslant y$. It is a 1 for $x = 0$ and $y = 1$. The D output is the result of the arithmetic operation $2B + x - y$.

The Boolean functions for the two outputs of the half-subtractor are derived directly from the truth table:

$$D = x'y + xy'$$
$$B = x'y$$

It is interesting to note that the logic for D is exactly the same as the logic for output S in the half-adder.

Full-Subtractor

A full-subtractor is a combinational circuit that performs a subtraction between two bits, taking into account that a 1 may have been borrowed by a lower significant stage. This circuit has three inputs and two outputs. The three inputs, x, y, and z, denote the minuend, subtrahend, and previous borrow, respectively. The two outputs, D and B, represent the difference and output borrow, respectively. The truth table for the circuit is as follows:

x	y	z	B	D
0	0	0	0	0
0	0	1	1	1
0	1	0	1	1
0	1	1	1	0
1	0	0	0	1
1	0	1	0	0
1	1	0	0	0
1	1	1	1	1

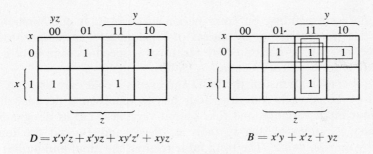

$$D = x'y'z + x'yz + xy'z' + xyz$$

$$B = x'y + x'z + yz$$

Figure 4-6 Maps for full-subtractor

The eight rows under the input variables designate all possible combinations of 1's and 0's that the binary variables may take. The 1's and 0's for the output variables are determined from the subtraction of $x - y - z$. The combinations having input borrow $z = 0$ reduce to the same four conditions of the half-adder. For $x = 0$, $y = 0$, and $z = 1$, we have to borrow a 1 from the next stage, which makes $B = 1$ and adds 2 to x. Since $2 - 0 - 1 = 1$, $D = 1$. For $x = 0$ and $yz = 11$, we need to borrow again, making $B = 1$ and $x = 2$. Since $2 - 1 - 1 = 0$, $D = 0$. For $x = 1$ and $yz = 01$, we have $x - y - z = 0$, which makes $B = 0$ and $D = 0$. Finally, for $x = 1, y = 1, z = 1$, we have to borrow 1, making $B = 1$ and $x = 3$, and $3 - 1 - 1 = 1$, making $D = 1$.

The simplified Boolean functions for the two outputs of the full-subtractor are derived in the maps of Fig. 4-6. The simplified sum of products output functions are:

$$D = x'y'z + x'yz' + xy'z' + xyz$$
$$B = x'y + x'z + yz$$

Again we note that the logic function for output D in the full-subtractor is exactly the same as output S in the full-adder. Moreover, the output B resembles the function for C in the full-adder, except that the input variable x is complemented. Because of these similarities, it is possible to convert a full-adder into a full-subtractor by merely complementing input x prior to its application to the gates that form the carry output.

4-5 CODE CONVERSION

The availability of a large variety of codes for the same discrete elements of information results in the use of different codes by different digital systems. It is sometimes necessary to use the output of one system as the input to another. A conversion circuit must be inserted between the two systems if each uses different codes for the same information. Thus, a code converter is a circuit that makes the two systems compatible even though each uses a different binary code.

To convert from binary code A to binary code B, the input lines must supply the bit combination of elements as specified by code A and the output lines must generate the corresponding bit combination of code B. A combinational circuit performs this transformation by means of logic gates. The design procedure of code converters will be illustrated by means of a specific example of conversion from the BCD to the excess-3 code.

The bit combinations for the BCD and excess-3 codes are listed in Table 1-2 (Section 1-6). Since each code uses four bits to represent a decimal digit, there must be four input variables and four output variables. Let us designate the four input binary variables by the symbols A, B, C, and D, and the four output variables by w, x, y, and z. The truth table relating the input and output variables is shown in Table 4-1. The bit combinations for the inputs and their corresponding outputs are obtained directly from Table 1-2. We note that four binary variables may have 16 bit combinations, only 10 of which are listed in the truth table. The six bit combinations not listed for the *input* variables are don't-care combinations. Since they will never occur, we are at liberty to assign to the output variables either a 1 or a 0, whichever gives a simpler circuit.

TABLE 4-1   Truth table for code-conversion example

Input BCD				Output Excess-3 code			
A	B	C	D	w	x	y	z
0	0	0	0	0	0	1	1
0	0	0	1	0	1	0	0
0	0	1	0	0	1	0	1
0	0	1	1	0	1	1	0
0	1	0	0	0	1	1	1
0	1	0	1	1	0	0	0
0	1	1	0	1	0	0	1
0	1	1	1	1	0	1	0
1	0	0	0	1	0	1	1
1	0	0	1	1	1	0	0

The maps in Fig. 4-7 are drawn to obtain a simplified Boolean function for each output. Each of the four maps of Fig. 4-7 represents one of the four outputs of this circuit as a function of the four input variables. The 1's marked inside the squares are obtained from the minterms that make the output equal to 1. The 1's are obtained from the truth table by going over the output columns one at a time. For example, the column under output z has five 1's; therefore, the map for z must have five 1's, each being in a square corresponding to the minterm that makes z equal to 1. The six don't-care combinations are marked by X's. One possible way to simplify the functions in sum of products is listed under the map of each variable.

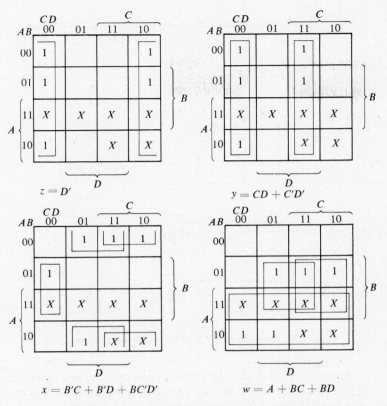

Figure 4-7 Maps for BCD-to-excess-3 code converter

A two-level logic diagram may be obtained directly from the Boolean expressions derived by the maps. There are various other possibilities for a logic diagram that implements this circuit. The expressions obtained in Fig. 4-7 may be manipulated algebraically for the purpose of using common gates for two or more outputs. This manipulation, shown below, illustrates the flexibility obtained with multiple-output systems when implemented with three or more levels of gates.

$$z = D'$$
$$y = CD + C'D' = CD + (C + D)'$$
$$x = B'C + B'D + BC'D' = B'(C + D) + BC'D'$$
$$\quad = B'(C + D) + B(C + D)'$$
$$w = A + BC + BD = A + B(C + D)$$

The logic diagram that implements the above expressions is shown in Fig. 4-8. In it we see that the OR gate whose output is $C + D$ has been used to implement partially each of three outputs.

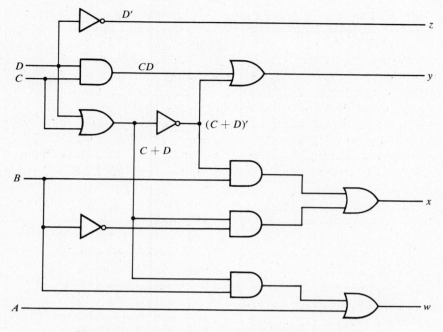

Figure 4-8 Logic diagram for BCD-to-excess-3 code converter

Not counting input inverters, the implementation in sum of products requires seven AND gates and three OR gates. The implementation of Fig. 4-8 requires four AND gates, four OR gates, and one inverter. If only the normal inputs are available, the first implementation will require inverters for variables B, C, and D, whereas the second implementation requires inverters for variables B and D.

4-6 ANALYSIS PROCEDURE

The design of a combinational circuit starts from the verbal specifications of a required function and culminates with a set of output Boolean functions or a logic diagram. The *analysis* of a combinational circuit is somewhat the reverse process. It starts with a given logic diagram and culminates with a set of Boolean functions, a truth table, or a verbal explanation of the circuit operation. If the logic diagram to be analyzed is accompanied by a function name or an explanation of what it is assumed to accomplish, then the analysis problem reduces to a verification of the stated function.

The first step in the analysis is to make sure that the given circuit is combinational and not sequential. The diagram of a combinational circuit has logic gates with no feedback paths or memory elements. A feedback path is a connection from the output of one gate to the input of a second gate that forms part of the input to the first gate. Feedback paths or memory elements in a digital circuit define a sequential circuit and must be analyzed according to procedures outlined in Chapter 6.

Once the logic diagram is verified as a combinational circuit, one can proceed to obtain the output Boolean functions and/or the truth table. If the circuit is accompanied by a verbal explanation of its function, then the Boolean functions or the truth table is sufficient for verification. If the function of the circuit is under investigation, then it is necessary to interpret the operation of the circuit from the derived truth table. The success of such investigation is enhanced if one has previous experience and familiarity with a wide variety of digital circuits. The ability to correlate a truth table with an information-processing task is an art one acquires with experience.

To obtain the output Boolean functions from a logic diagram, proceed as follows:

1. Label with arbitrary symbols all gate outputs that are a function of the input variables. Obtain the Boolean functions for each gate.

2. Label with other arbitrary symbols those gates which are a function of input variables and/or previously labeled gates. Find the Boolean functions for these gates.

3. Repeat the process outlined in step 2 until the outputs of the circuit are obtained.

4. By repeated substitution of previously defined functions, obtain the output Boolean functions in terms of input variables only.

Analysis of the combinational circuit in Fig. 4-9 illustrates the proposed procedure. We note that the circuit has three binary inputs, A, B, and C, and two binary outputs, F_1 and F_2. The outputs of various gates are labeled with intermediate symbols. The outputs of gates that are a function of input variables only are F_2, T_1, and T_2. The Boolean functions for these three outputs are:

$$F_2 = AB + AC + BC$$
$$T_1 = A + B + C$$
$$T_2 = ABC$$

Next we consider outputs of gates which are a function of already defined symbols:

$$T_3 = F_2' T_1$$
$$F_1 = T_3 + T_2$$

The output Boolean function F_2 expressed above is already given as a function of the inputs only. To obtain F_1 as a function of A, B, and C, form a series of

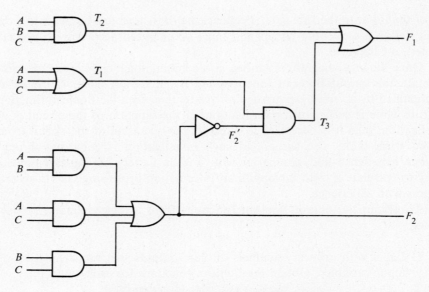

Figure 4-9 Logic diagram for analysis example

substitutions as follows:

$$F_1 = T_3 + T_2 = F_2'T_1 + ABC = (AB + AC + BC)'(A + B + C) + ABC$$

$$= (A' + B')(A' + C')(B' + C')(A + B + C) + ABC$$

$$= (A' + B'C')(AB' + AC' + BC' + B'C) + ABC$$

$$= A'BC' + A'B'C + AB'C' + ABC$$

If we want to pursue the investigation and determine the information-transformation task achieved by this circuit, we can derive the truth table directly from the Boolean functions and try to recognize a familiar operation. For this example, we note that the circuit is a full-adder, with F_1 being the sum output and F_2 the carry output. A, B, and C are the three inputs added arithmetically.

The derivation of the truth table for the circuit is a straightforward process once the output Boolean functions are known. To obtain the truth table directly from the logic diagram without going through the derivations of the Boolean functions, proceed as follows:

1. Determine the number of input variables to the circuit. For n inputs, form the 2^n possible input combinations of 1's and 0's by listing the binary numbers from 0 to $2^n - 1$.

2. Label the outputs of selected gates with arbitrary symbols.

3. Obtain the truth table for the outputs of those gates that are a function of the input variables only.

4. Proceed to obtain the truth table for the outputs of those gates that are a function of previously defined values until the columns for all outputs are determined.

This process can be illustrated using the circuit of Fig. 4-9. In Table 4-2, we form the eight possible combinations for the three input variables. The truth table for F_2 is determined directly from the values of A, B, and C, with F_2 equal to 1 for any combination that has two or three inputs equal to 1. The truth table for F_2' is the complement of F_2. The truth tables for T_1 and T_2 are the OR and AND functions of the input variables, respectively. The values for T_3 are derived from T_1 and F_2': T_3 is equal to 1 when both T_1 and F_2' are equal to 1, and to 0 otherwise. Finally, F_1 is equal to 1 for those combinations in which either T_2 or T_3 or both are equal to 1. Inspection of the truth table combinations for A, B, C, F_1, and F_2 of Table 4-2 shows that it is identical to the truth table of the full-adder given in Section 4-3 for x, y, z, S, and C, respectively.

TABLE 4-2   Truth table for logic diagram of Fig. 4-9

A	B	C	F_2	F_2'	T_1	T_2	T_3	F_1
0	0	0	0	1	0	0	0	0
0	0	1	0	1	1	0	1	1
0	1	0	0	1	1	0	1	1
0	1	1	1	0	1	0	0	0
1	0	0	0	1	1	0	1	1
1	0	1	1	0	1	0	0	0
1	1	0	1	0	1	0	0	0
1	1	1	1	0	1	1	0	1

Consider now a combinational circuit that has don't-care input combinations. When such a circuit is designed, the don't-care combinations are marked by X's in the map and assigned an output of either 1 or 0, whichever is more convenient for the simplification of the output Boolean function. When a circuit with don't-care combinations is being analyzed, the situation is entirely different. Even though we assume that the don't-care input combinations will never occur, the fact of the matter is that if any one of these combinations is applied to the inputs (intentionally or in error), a binary output will be present. The value of the output will depend on the choice for the X's taken during the design. Part of the analysis of such a circuit may involve the determination of the output values for the don't-care input combinations. As an example, consider the BCD-to-excess-3 code converter designed in Section 4-5. The outputs obtained when the six unused combinations of the BCD code are applied to the inputs are:

Unused BCD inputs				Outputs			
A	B	C	D	w	x	y	z
1	0	1	0	1	1	0	1
1	0	1	1	1	1	1	0
1	1	0	0	1	1	1	1
1	1	0	1	1	0	0	0
1	1	1	0	1	0	0	1
1	1	1	1	1	0	1	0

These outputs may be derived by means of the truth table analysis method as outlined in this section. In this particular case, the outputs may be obtained directly from the maps of Fig. 4-7. From inspection of the maps, we determine whether the X's in the corresponding minterm squares for each output have been included with the 1's or the 0's. For example, the square for minterm m_{10} (1010) has been included with the 1's for outputs w, x, and z, but not for y. Therefore, the outputs for m_{10} are $wxyz = 1101$, as listed in the above table. We also note that the first three outputs in the table have no meaning in the excess-3 code, and the last three outputs correspond to decimal 5, 6, and 7, respectively. This coincidence is entirely a function of the choice for the X's taken during the design.

4-7 MULTILEVEL NAND CIRCUITS

Combinational circuits are more frequently constructed with NAND or NOR gates rather than AND and OR gates. NAND and NOR gates are more common from the hardware point of view because they are readily available in integrated-circuit form. Because of the prominence of NAND and NOR gates in the design of combinational circuits, it is important to be able to recognize the relationships that exist between circuits constructed with AND-OR gates and their equivalent NAND or NOR diagrams.

The implementation of two-level NAND and NOR logic diagrams was presented in Section 3-6. Here we consider the more general case of multilevel circuits. The procedure for obtaining NAND circuits is presented in this section, and for NOR circuits in the next section.

Universal Gate

The NAND gate is said to be a universal gate because any digital system can be implemented with it. Combinational circuits and sequential circuits as well can be constructed with this gate because the flip-flop circuit (the memory element most frequently used in sequential circuits) can be constructed from two NAND gates connected back to back, as shown in Section 6-2.

To show that any Boolean function can be implemented with NAND gates, we need only show that the logical operations AND, OR, and NOT can be

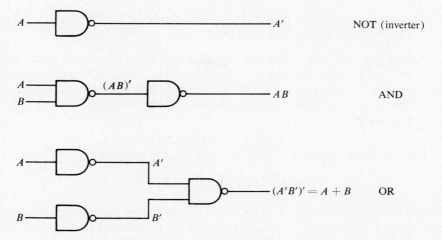

Figure 4-10 Implementation of NOT, AND, or OR by NAND gates

implemented with NAND gates. The implementation of the AND, OR, and NOT operations with NAND gates is shown in Fig. 4-10. The NOT operation is obtained from a one-input NAND gate, actually another symbol for an inverter circuit. The AND operation requires two NAND gates. The first produces the inverted AND and the second acts as an inverter to produce the normal output. The OR operation is achieved through a NAND gate with additional inverters in each input.

A convenient way to implement a combinational circuit with NAND gates is to obtain the simplified Boolean functions in terms of AND, OR, and NOT and convert the functions to NAND logic. The conversion of the algebraic expression from AND, OR, and NOT operations to NAND operations is usually quite complicated because it involves a large number of applications of De Morgan's theorem. This difficulty is avoided by the use of simple circuit manipulations and simple rules as outlined below.

Boolean Function Implementation— Block Diagram Method

The implementation of Boolean functions with NAND gates may be obtained by means of a simple block diagram manipulation technique. This method requires that two other logic diagrams be drawn prior to obtaining the NAND logic diagram. Nevertheless, the procedure is very simple and straightforward:

1. From the given algebraic expression, draw the logic diagram with AND, OR, and NOT gates. Assume that both the normal and complement inputs are available.

2. Draw a second logic diagram with the equivalent NAND logic, as given in Fig. 4-10, substituted for each AND, OR, and NOT gate.

3. Remove any two cascaded inverters from the diagram, since double inversion does not perform a logic function. Remove inverters connected to single external inputs and complement the corresponding input variable. The new logic diagram obtained is the required NAND gate implementation.

This procedure is illustrated in Fig. 4-11 for the function:

$$F = A(B + CD) + BC'$$

The AND-OR implementation of this function is shown in the logic diagram of Fig. 4-11(a). For each AND gate, we substitute a NAND gate followed by an inverter; for each OR gate, we substitute input inverters followed by a NAND gate. This substitution follows directly from the logic equivalences of Fig. 4-10 and is shown in the diagram of Fig. 4-11(b). This diagram has seven inverters and five two-input NAND gates listed with numbers inside the gate symbol. Pairs of inverters connected in cascade (from each AND box to each OR box) are removed since they form double inversion. The inverter connected to input B is removed and the input variable is designated by B'. The result is the NAND logic diagram shown in Fig. 4-11(c), with the number inside each symbol identifying the gate from Fig. 4-11(b).

This example demonstrates that the number of NAND gates required to implement the Boolean function is equal to the number of AND-OR gates, provided both the normal and the complement inputs are available. If only the normal inputs are available, inverters must be used to generate any required complemented inputs.

A second example of NAND implementation is shown in Fig. 4-12. The Boolean function to be implemented is:

$$F = (A + B')(CD + E)$$

The AND-OR implementation is shown in Fig. 4-12(a), and its NAND logic substitution, in Fig. 4-12(b). One pair of cascaded inverters may be removed. The three external inputs E, A, and B', which go directly to inverters, are complemented and the corresponding inverters removed. The final NAND gate implementation is in Fig. 4-12(c).

The number of NAND gates for the second example is equal to the number of AND-OR gates plus an additional inverter in the output (NAND gate 5). In general, the number of NAND gates required to implement a function equals the number of AND-OR gates, except for an occasional inverter. This is true provided both normal and complement inputs are available, because the conversion forces certain input variables to be complemented.

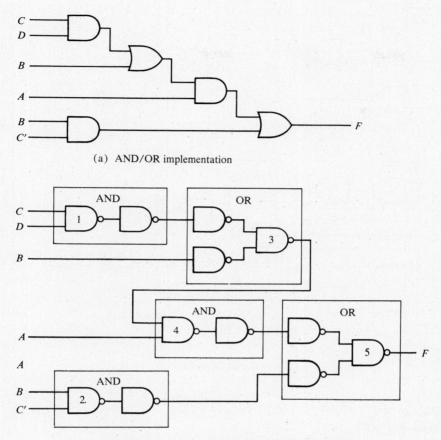

(a) AND/OR implementation

(b) Substituting equivalent NAND functions from Fig. 5-8

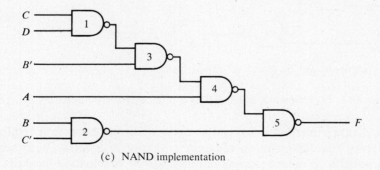

(c) NAND implementation

Figure 4-11 Implementation of $F = A(B + CD) + BC'$ with NAND gates

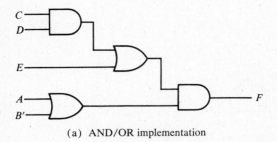

(a) AND/OR implementation

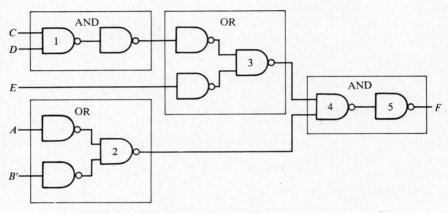

(b) Substituting equivalent NAND functions

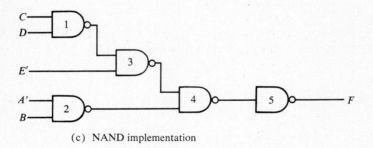

(c) NAND implementation

Figure 4-12 Implementation of $(A + B')(CD + E)$ with NAND gates

The block diagram method is somewhat tiresome to use because it requires the drawing of two logic diagrams to obtain the answer in a third. With some experience, it is possible to reduce the amount of labor by anticipating the pairs of cascaded inverters and the inverters in the inputs. Starting from the procedure just outlined, it is not too difficult to derive general rules for implementing Boolean functions with NAND gates directly from an algebraic expression.

Analysis Procedure

The foregoing procedure considered the problem of deriving a NAND logic diagram from a given Boolean function. The reverse process is the analysis problem which starts with a given NAND logic diagram and culminates with a Boolean expression or a truth table. The analysis of NAND logic diagrams follows the same procedures presented in Section 4-6 for the analysis of combinational circuits. The only difference is that NAND logic requires a repeated application of De Morgan's theorem. We shall now demonstrate the derivation of the Boolean function from a logic diagram. Then we will show the derivation of the truth table directly from the NAND logic diagram. Finally, a method will be presented for converting a NAND logic diagram to AND-OR logic diagram by means of block diagram manipulation.

Derivation of the Boolean Function
by Algebraic Manipulation

The procedure for deriving the Boolean function from a logic diagram is outlined in Section 4-6. This procedure is demonstrated for the NAND logic diagram shown in Fig. 4-13, which is the same as that in Fig. 4-11(c). First, all gate outputs are labeled with arbitrary symbols. Second, the Boolean functions for the outputs of gates that receive only external inputs are derived:

$$T_1 = (CD)' = C' + D'$$
$$T_2 = (BC')' = B' + C$$

The second form follows directly from De Morgan's theorem and may, at times, be more convenient to use. Third, Boolean functions of gates which have inputs from

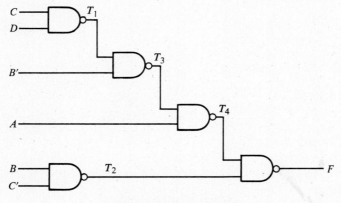

Figure 4-13   Analysis example

previously derived functions are determined in consecutive order until the output is expressed in terms of input variables:

$$T_3 = (B'T_1)' = (B'C' + B'D')'$$
$$= (B + C)(B + D) = B + CD$$
$$T_4 = (AT_3)' = [A(B + CD)]'$$
$$F = (T_2T_4)' = \{(BC')'[A(B + CD)]'\}'$$
$$= BC' + A(B + CD)$$

Derivation of the Truth Table

The procedure for obtaining the truth table directly from a logic diagram is also outlined in Section 4-6. This procedure is demonstrated for the NAND logic diagram of Fig. 4-13. First, the four input variables, together with their 16 combinations of 1's and 0's, are listed as in Table 4-3. Second, the outputs of all gates are labeled with arbitrary symbols as in Fig. 4-13. Third, we obtain the truth table for the outputs of those gates that are a function of the input variables only. These are T_1 and T_2. $T_1 = (CD)'$; so we mark 0's in those rows where both C and D are equal to 1 and fill the rest of the rows of T_1 with 1's. Also, $T_2 = (BC')'$; so we mark 0's in those rows where $B = 1$ and $C = 0$, and fill the rest of the rows of T_2 with 1's. We then proceed to obtain the truth table for the outputs of those gates that are a function of previously defined outputs until the column for the output F is determined. It is now possible to obtain an algebraic expression for the

TABLE 4-3   Truth table for the circuit of Figure 4-13

A	B	C	D	T_1	T_2	T_3	T_4	F
0	0	0	0	1	1	0	1	0
0	0	0	1	1	1	0	1	0
0	0	1	0	1	1	0	1	0
0	0	1	1	0	1	1	1	0
0	1	0	0	1	0	1	1	1
0	1	0	1	1	0	1	1	1
0	1	1	0	1	1	1	1	0
0	1	1	1	0	1	1	1	0
1	0	0	0	1	1	0	1	0
1	0	0	1	1	1	0	1	0
1	0	1	0	1	1	0	1	0
1	0	1	1	0	1	1	0	1
1	1	0	0	1	0	1	0	1
1	1	0	1	1	0	1	0	1
1	1	1	0	1	1	1	0	1
1	1	1	1	0	1	1	0	1

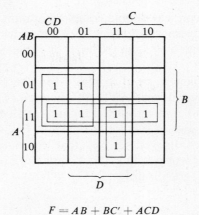

$$F = AB + BC' + ACD$$

Figure 4-14 Derivation of F from Table 4-3

output from the derived truth table. The map shown in Fig. 4-14 is obtained directly from Table 4-3 and has 1's in the squares of those minterms for which F is equal to 1. The simplified expression obtained from the map is:

$$F = AB + ACD + BC' = A(B + CD) + BC'$$

This is the same as the expression of Fig. 4-11, thus verifying the correct answer.

Block Diagram Transformation

It is sometimes convenient to convert a NAND logic diagram to its equivalent AND-OR logic diagram to facilitate the analysis procedure. By doing so, the Boolean function can be derived more easily without employing De Morgan's theorem. The conversion of logic diagrams is accomplished through a process reverse from that used for implementation. In Section 3-6, we showed two alternate graphic symbols for the NAND gate. These symbols are repeated in Fig. 4-15 for convenience. By judicious use of both symbols, it is possible to convert a NAND diagram to an equivalent AND-OR form.

The conversion of a NAND logic diagram to an AND-OR diagram is· achieved through a change in symbols from AND-invert to invert-OR in *alternate* levels of gates. The first level to be changed to an invert-OR symbol should be the last level. These changes produce pairs of circles along the same line, and these can

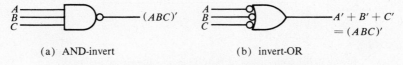

(a) AND-invert   (b) invert-OR

Figure 4-15 Two symbols for NAND gate

139

be removed since they represent double complementation. Moreover, a one-input AND or OR gate can be removed since it does not perform a logical function. A one-input AND or OR with a circle in the input or output is changed to an inverter circuit.

This procedure is demonstrated in Fig. 4-16. The NAND logic diagram of Fig. 4-16(a) is to be converted to an AND-OR diagram. The symbol of the gate in the last level is changed to an invert-OR. Looking for alternate levels, we find one more gate requiring a change of symbol as shown in Fig. 4-16(b). Any two circles along the same line are removed. Circles that go to external inputs are also removed, provided the corresponding input variable is complemented. The required AND-OR logic diagram is drawn in Fig. 4-16(c).

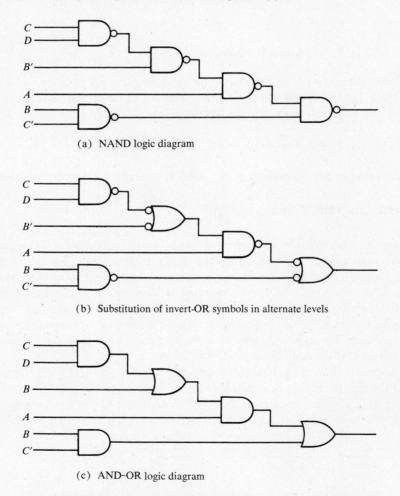

(a) NAND logic diagram

(b) Substitution of invert-OR symbols in alternate levels

(c) AND-OR logic diagram

Figure 4-16 Conversion of NAND logic diagram to AND-OR

4-8 MULTILEVEL NOR CIRCUITS

The NOR function is the dual of the NAND function. For this reason, all procedures and rules for NOR logic form a dual of the corresponding procedures and rules developed for NAND logic. This section enumerates various methods for NOR logic implementation and analysis by following the same list of topics used for NAND logic. However, less detailed explanation is included so as to avoid excessive repetition of the material in Section 4-7.

Universal Gate

The NOR gate is universal because any Boolean function can be implemented with it, including a flip-flop circuit as shown in Section 6-2. The conversion of AND, OR, and NOT to NOR is shown in Fig. 4-17. The NOT operation is obtained from a one-input NOR gate, yet another symbol for an inverter circuit. The OR operation requires two NOR gates. The first produces the inverted-OR and the second acts as an inverter to obtain the normal output. The AND operation is achieved through a NOR gate with additional inverters at each input.

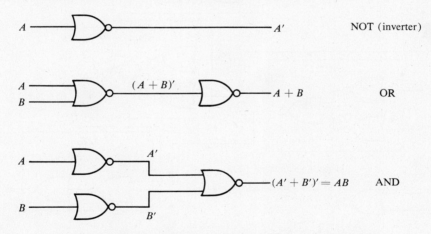

Figure 4-17 Implementation of NOT, OR, and AND by NOR gates

Boolean Function Implementation— Block Diagram Method

The block diagram procedure for implementing Boolean functions with NOR gates is similar to the procedure outlined in the previous section for NAND gates.

1. Draw the AND-OR logic diagram from the given algebraic expression. Assume that both the normal and the complement inputs are available.

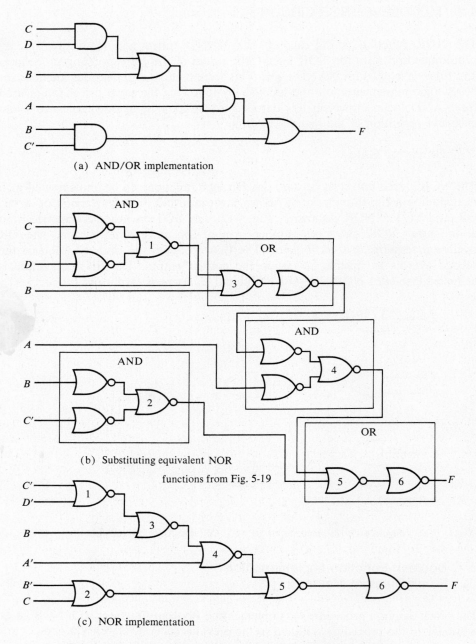

(a) AND/OR implementation

(b) Substituting equivalent NOR functions from Fig. 5-19

(c) NOR implementation

Figure 4-18 Implementation of $F = A(B + CD) + BC'$ with NOR gates

2. Draw a second logic diagram with equivalent NOR logic, as given in Fig. 4-17, substituted for each AND, OR, and NOT gate.

3. Remove pairs of cascaded inverters from the diagram. Remove inverters connected to single external inputs and complement the corresponding input variable.

The procedure is illustrated in Fig. 4-18 for the function:

$$F = A(B + CD) + BC'$$

The AND-OR implementation of the function is shown in the logic diagram of Fig. 4-18(a). For each OR gate, we substitute a NOR gate followed by an inverter. For each AND gate, we substitute input inverters followed by a NOR gate. The pair of cascaded inverters from the OR box to the AND box is removed. The four inverters connected to external inputs are removed and the input variables complemented. The result is the NOR logic diagram shown in Fig. 4-18(c). The number of NOR gates in this example equals the number of AND-OR gates plus an additional inverter in the output (NOR gate 6). In general, the number of NOR gates required to implement a Boolean function equals the number of AND-OR gates, except for an occasional inverter. This is true provided both normal and complement inputs are available, because the conversion forces certain input variables to be complemented.

Analysis Procedure

The analysis of NOR logic diagrams follows the same procedures presented in Section 4-6 for the analysis of combinational circuits. To derive the Boolean function from a logic diagram, we mark the outputs of various gates with arbitrary symbols. By repetitive substitutions, we obtain the output variable as a function of the input variables. To obtain the truth table from a logic diagram without first deriving the Boolean function, we form a table listing the n input variables with 2^n rows of 1's and 0's. The truth table of various NOR gate outputs is derived in succession until the output truth table is obtained. The output function of a typical NOR gate is of the form $T = (A + B' + C)'$; so the truth table for T is marked with a 0 for those combinations where $A = 1$ or $B = 0$ or $C = 1$. The rest of the rows are filled with 1's.

Block Diagram Transformation

To convert a NOR logic diagram to its equivalent AND-OR logic diagram, we use the two symbols for NOR gates shown in Fig. 4-19. The OR-invert is the normal symbol for a NOR gate and the invert-AND is a convenient alternative that utilizes De Morgan's theorem and the convention that small circles at the inputs denote complementation.

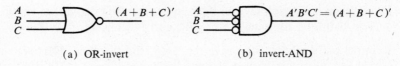

(a) OR-invert   (b) invert-AND

Figure 4-19 Two symbols for NOR gate

The conversion of a NOR logic diagram to an AND-OR diagram is achieved through a change in symbols from OR-invert to invert-AND starting from the last level and in alternate levels. Pairs of small circles along the same line are removed. A one-input AND or OR gate is removed, but if it has a small circle at the input or output, it is converted to an inverter.

This procedure is demonstrated in Fig. 4-20, where the NOR logic diagram in (a) is converted to an AND-OR diagram. The symbol of the gate in the last level

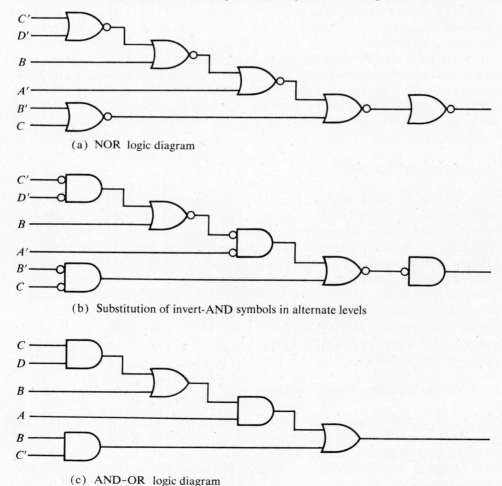

(a) NOR logic diagram

(b) Substitution of invert-AND symbols in alternate levels

(c) AND-OR logic diagram

Figure 4-20 Conversion of NOR logic diagram to AND-OR

(5) is changed to an invert-AND. Looking for alternate levels, we find one gate in level 3 and two in level 1. These three gates undergo a symbol change as shown in (b). Any two circles along the same line are removed. Circles that go to external inputs are also removed, provided the corresponding input variable is complemented. The gate in level 5 becomes a one-input AND gate and is removed. The required AND-OR logic diagram is drawn in Fig. 4-20(c).

4-9 EXCLUSIVE-OR AND EQUIVALENCE FUNCTIONS

Exclusive-OR and equivalence, denoted by $\oplus$ and $\odot$, respectively, are binary operations that perform the following Boolean functions:

$$x \oplus y = xy' + x'y$$
$$x \odot y = xy + x'y'$$

The two operations are the complements of each other. Each is commutative and associative. Because of these two properties, a function of three or more variables can be expressed without parentheses as follows:

$$(A \oplus B) \oplus C = A \oplus (B \oplus C) = A \oplus B \oplus C$$

This would imply the possibility of using exclusive-OR (or equivalence) gates with three or more inputs. However, multiple-input exclusive-OR gates are very uneconomical from a hardware standpoint. In fact, even a two-input function is usually constructed with other types of gates. For example, Fig. 4-21(a) shows the implementation of a two-input exclusive-OR function with AND, OR, and NOT gates. Figure 4-21(b) shows it with NAND gates.

Only a limited number of Boolean functions can be expressed exclusively in terms of exclusive-OR or equivalence operations. Nevertheless, these functions emerge quite often during the design of digital systems. The two functions are particularly useful in arithmetic operations and in error detection and correction.

An n-variable exclusive-OR expression is equal to the Boolean function with $2^n/2$ minterms whose equivalent binary numbers have an odd number of 1's. This is demonstrated in the map of Fig. 4-22(a) for the four-variable case. There are 16 minterms for four variables. Half the minterms have a numerical value with an odd number of 1's; the other half have a numerical value with an even number of 1's. The numerical value of a minterm is determined from the row and column numbers of the square that represents the minterm. The map of Fig. 4-22(a) has 1's in the squares whose minterm numbers have an odd number of 1's. The function can be expressed in terms of the exclusive-OR operations on the four variables. This is justified by the following algebraic manipulation:

$$A \oplus B \oplus C \oplus D = (AB' + A'B) \oplus (CD' + C'D)$$
$$= (AB' + A'B)(CD + C'D') + (AB + A'B')(CD' + C'D)$$
$$= \Sigma(1, 2, 4, 7, 8, 11, 13, 14)$$

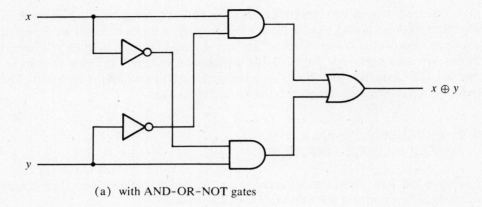

(a) with AND−OR−NOT gates

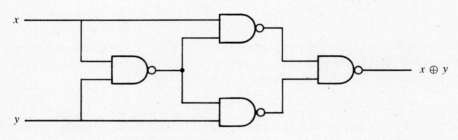

(b) with NAND gates

Figure 4-21 Exclusive-OR implementations

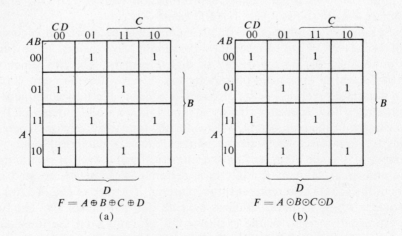

$$F = A \oplus B \oplus C \oplus D$$

(a)

$$F = A \odot B \odot C \odot D$$

(b)

Figure 4-22 Map for a four-variable (a) exclusive-OR function and (b) equivalence function

An n-variable equivalence expression is equal to the Boolean function with $2^n/2$ minterms, whose equivalent binary numbers have an even number of 0's. This is demonstrated in the map of Fig. 4-22(b) for the four-variable case. The squares with 1's represent the eight minterms with an even number of 0's, and the function can be expressed in terms of the equivalence operations on the four variables.

When the number of variables in a function is odd, the minterms with an even number of 0's are the same as the minterms with an odd number of 1's. This is demonstrated in the three-variable map of Fig. 4-23(a). Therefore, an exclusive-OR expression is equal to an equivalence expression when both have the same odd number of variables. However, they form the complements of each other when the number of variables is even, as demonstrated in the two maps of Fig. 4-22(a) and (b).

When the minterms of a function with an odd number of variables have an even number of 1's (or equivalently, an odd number of 0's), the function can be expressed as the complement of either an exclusive-OR or an equivalence expression. For example, the three-variable function shown in the map of Fig. 4-23(b) can be expressed as follows:

$$(A \oplus B \oplus C)' = A \oplus B \odot C$$

or

$$(A \odot B \odot C)' = A \odot B \oplus C$$

The S output of a full-adder and the D output of a full-subtractor (Section 4-3) can be implemented with exclusive-OR functions because each function consists of four minterms with numerical values having an odd number of 1's. The exclusive-OR function is extensively used in the implementation of digital arithmetic operations because the latter are usually implemented through procedures that require a repetitive addition or subtraction operation.

Exclusive-OR and equivalence functions are very useful in systems requiring error-detection and error-correction codes. As discussed in Section 1-6, a parity bit is a scheme for detecting errors during transmission of binary information. A

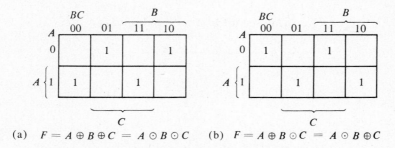

(a) $F = A \oplus B \oplus C = A \odot B \odot C$ (b) $F = A \oplus B \odot C = A \odot B \oplus C$

Figure 4-23 Map for three-variable functions

parity bit is an extra bit included with a binary message to make the number of 1's either odd or even. The message, including the parity bit, is transmitted and then checked at the receiving end for errors. An error is detected if the checked parity does not correspond to the one transmitted. The circuit that generates the parity bit in the transmitter is called a *parity generator*; the circuit that checks the parity in the receiver is called a *parity checker*.

As an example, consider a three-bit message to be transmitted with an odd-parity bit. Table 4-4 shows the truth table for the parity generator. The three bits x, y, and z constitute the message and are the inputs to the circuit. The parity bit P is the output. For odd parity, the bit P is generated so as to make the total number of 1's odd (including P). From the truth table, we see that $P = 1$ when the number of 1's in x, y, and z is even. This corresponds to the map of Fig. 4-23(b); so the function for P can be expressed as follows:

$$P = x \oplus y \odot z$$

The logic diagram for the parity generator is shown in Fig. 4-24(a). It consists of one two-input exclusive-OR gate and one two-input equivalence gate. The two gates can be interchanged and still produce the same function, since P is also equal to:

$$P = x \odot y \oplus z$$

The three-bit message and the parity bit are transmitted to their destination, where they are applied to a parity-checker circuit. An error occurs during transmission if the parity of the four bits received is even, since the binary information transmitted was originally odd. The output C of the parity checker should be a 1 when an error occurs, i.e., when the number of 1's in the four inputs is even. Table 4-5 is the truth table for the odd-parity checker circuit. From it we see that the function for C consists of the eight minterms with numerical values having an even number of 0's. This corresponds to the map of Fig. 4-22(b); so the function can be

TABLE 4-4   Odd-parity generation

Three-bit message			Parity bit generated
x	y	z	P
0	0	0	1
0	0	1	0
0	1	0	0
0	1	1	1
1	0	0	0
1	0	1	1
1	1	0	1
1	1	1	0

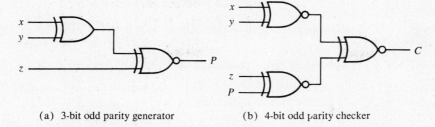

(a) 3-bit odd parity generator   (b) 4-bit odd parity checker

Figure 4-24 Logic diagrams for parity generation and checking

expressed with equivalence operators as follows:

$$C = x \odot y \odot z \odot P$$

The logic diagram for the parity checker is shown in Fig. 4-24(b) and consists of three two-input equivalence gates.

It is worth noting that the parity generator can be implemented with the circuit of Fig. 4-24(b) if the input P is permanently held at logic-0 and the output is marked P, the advantage being that the same circuit can be used for both parity generation and checking.

It is obvious from the foregoing example that parity generation and checking circuits always have an output function that includes half of the minterms whose numerical values have either an even or odd number of 1's. As a consequence, they can be implemented with equivalence and/or exclusive-OR gates.

TABLE 4-5 Odd-parity check

| Four-bits received | | | | Parity-error check |
x	y	z	P	C
0	0	0	0	1
0	0	0	1	0
0	0	1	0	0
0	0	1	1	1
0	1	0	0	0
0	1	0	1	1
0	1	1	0	1
0	1	1	1	0
1	0	0	0	0
1	0	0	1	1
1	0	1	0	1
1	0	1	1	0
1	1	0	0	1
1	1	0	1	0
1	1	1	0	0
1	1	1	1	1

REFERENCES

1. Rhyne, V. T., *Fundamentals of Digital Systems Design*. Englewood Cliffs, N.J.: Prentice-Hall, Inc., 1973.

2. Peatman, J. P., *The Design of Digital Systems*. New York: McGraw-Hill Book Co., 1972.

3. Nagle, H. T. Jr., B. D. Carrol, and J. D. Irwin, *An Introduction to Computer Logic*. Englewood Cliffs, N. J.: Prentice-Hall, Inc., 1975.

4 Hill, F. J., and G. R. Peterson, *Introduction to Switching Theory and Logical Design*, 2nd ed. New York: John Wiley & Sons, Inc., 1974.

5. Maley, G. A., and J. Earle, *The Logic Design of Transistor Digital Computers*. Englewood Cliffs, N. J.: Prentice-Hall, Inc., 1963.

6. Friedman, A. D., and P. R. Menon, *Theory and Design of Switching Circuits*. Woodland Hills, Calif.: Computer Science Press, Inc., 1975.

PROBLEMS

4-1 A combinational circuit has four inputs and one output. The output is equal to 1 when (1) all the inputs are equal to 1 or (2) none of the inputs are equal to 1 or (3) an odd number of inputs are equal to 1.

(a) Obtain the truth table.

(b) Find the simplified output function in sum of products.

(c) Find the simplified output function in product of sums.

(d) Draw the two logic diagrams.

4-2 Design a combinational circuit that accepts a three-bit number and generates an output binary number equal to the square of the input number.

4-3. It is necessary to multiply two binary numbers, each two bits long, in order to form their product in binary. Let the two numbers be represented by a_1, a_0 and b_1, b_0, where subscript 0 denotes the least significant bit.

(a) Determine the number of output lines required.

(b) Find the simplified Boolean expressions for each output.

4-4. Repeat problem 4-3 to form the sum (instead of the product) of the two binary numbers.

4-5. Design a combinational circuit with four input lines that represent a decimal digit in BCD and four output lines that generate the 9's complement of the input digit.

4-6. Design a combinational circuit whose input is a four-bit number and whose output is the 2's complement of the input number.

4-7. Design a combinational circuit that multiplies by 5 an input decimal digit represented in BCD. The output is also in BCD. Show that the outputs can be obtained from the input lines without using any logic gates.

4-8. Design a combinational circuit that detects an error in the representation of a decimal digit in BCD. In other words, obtain a logic diagram whose output is logic-1 when the inputs contain an unused combination in the code.

4-9.   Implement a full-subtractor with two half-subtractors and an OR gate.

4-10. Show how a full-adder can be converted to a full-subtractor with the addition of one inverter circuit.

4-11. Design a combinational circuit that converts a decimal digit from the $8,4,-2,-1$ code to BCD.

4-12. Design a combinational circuit that converts a decimal digit from the $2,4,2,1$ code to the $8,4,-2,-1$ code.

4-13. Obtain the logic diagram that converts a four-digit binary number to a decimal number in BCD. Note that two decimal digits are needed since the binary numbers range from 0 to 15.

4-14. A BCD-to-seven-segment decoder is a combinational circuit that accepts a decimal digit in BCD and generates the appropriate outputs for selection of segments in a display indicator used for displaying the decimal digit. The seven outputs of the decoder (a, b, c, d, e, f, g) select the corresponding segments in the display as shown in Fig. P4-14(a). The numeric designation chosen to represent the decimal digit is shown in Fig. P4-14(b). Design the BCD-to-seven-segment decoder circuit.

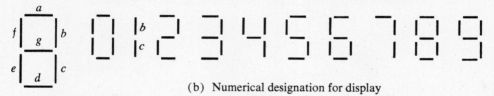

(b) Numerical designation for display

(a) Segment designation

Figure P4-14

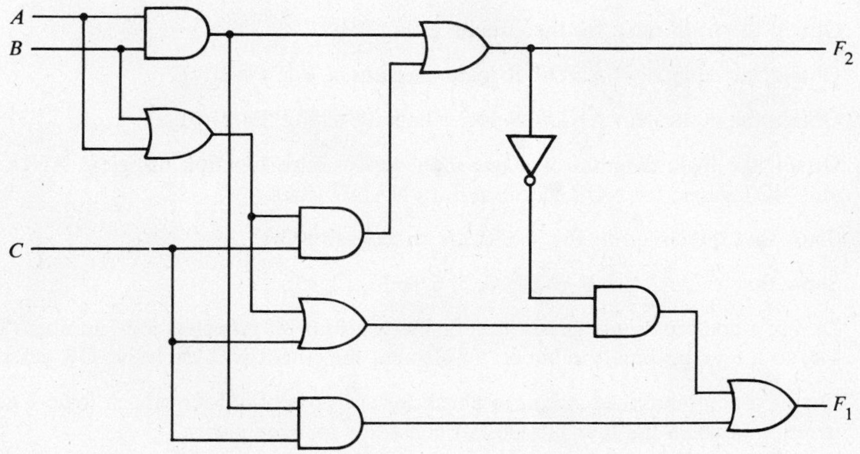

Figure P4-15

4-15. Analyze the two-output combinational circuits shown in Fig. P4-15. Obtain the Boolean functions for the two outputs and explain the circuit operation.

4-16. Derive the truth table of the circuit shown in Fig. P4-15.

4-17. Using the block diagram method, convert the logic diagram of Fig. 4-8 to a NAND implementation.

4-18. Repeat problem 4-17 for NOR implementation.

4-19. Obtain the NAND logic diagram of a full-adder from the Boolean functions:

$$C = xy + xz + yz$$
$$S = C'(x + y + z) + xyz$$

4-20. Determine the Boolean function for the output F of the circuit in Fig. P4-20. Obtain an equivalent circuit with fewer NOR gates.

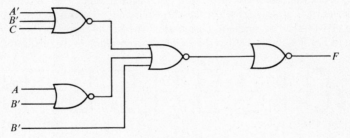

Figure P4-20

4-21. Determine the output Boolean functions of the circuits in Fig. P4-21.

4-22. Obtain the truth table for the circuits in Fig. P4-21.

4-23. Obtain the equivalent AND-OR logic diagram of Fig. P4-21(a).

4-24. Obtain the equivalent AND-OR logic diagram of Fig. P4-21(b).

4-25. Obtain the logic diagram of a two-input equivalence function using (a) AND, OR, and NOT gates; (b) NOR gates; and (c) NAND gates.

4-26. Show that the circuit in Fig. 4-21(b) is an exclusive-OR.

4-27. Show that $A \odot B \odot C \odot D = \Sigma(0, 3, 5, 6, 9, 10, 12, 15)$.

4-28. Design a combinational circuit that converts a four-bit reflected-code number (Table 1-4) to a four-bit binary number. Implement the circuit with exclusive-OR gates.

4-29. Design a combinational circuit to check for even parity of four bits. A logic-1 output is required when the four bits do not constitute an even parity.

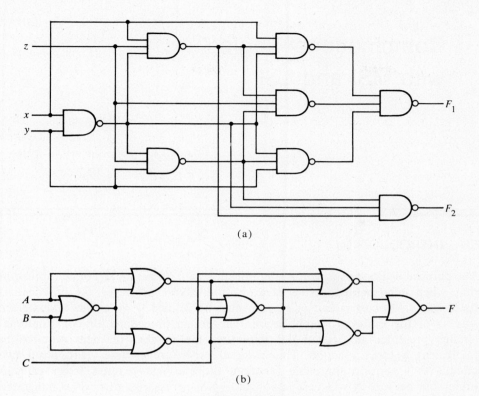

(a)

(b)

Figure P4-21

4-30. Implement the four Boolean functions listed using three half-adder circuits (Fig. 4-2e).

$$D = A \oplus B \oplus C$$
$$E = A'BC + AB'C$$
$$F = ABC' + (A' + B')C$$
$$G = ABC$$

4-31. Implement the Boolean function:

$$F = AB'CD' + A'BCD' + AB'C'D + A'BC'D$$

with exclusive-OR and AND gates.

Combinational Logic
with MSI and LSI

5

5-1 INTRODUCTION

The purpose of Boolean function simplification is to obtain an algebraic expression that, when implemented, results in a low-cost circuit. However, the criteria that determine a low-cost circuit or system must be defined if we are to evaluate the success of the achieved simplification. The design procedure for combinational circuits presented in Section 4-2 minimizes the number of gates required to implement a given function. This classical procedure assumes that, given two circuits that perform the same function, the one that requires fewer gates is preferable because it will cost less. This is not necessarily true when integrated circuits are used.

Since several logic gates are included in a single IC package, it becomes economical to use as many of the gates from an already used package even if, by doing so, we increase the total number of gates. Moreover, some of the interconnections among gates in many ICs are internal to the chip and it is more economical to use as many internal interconnections as possible in order to minimize the number of wires between external pins. With integrated circuits, it is not the count of gates that determines the cost but the number and type of ICs employed and the number of external interconnections needed to implement the given function.

There are numerous occasions where the classical method of Section 4-2 will not produce the best combinational circuit for implementing a given function. Moreover, the truth table and the simplification procedure in this method become too cumbersome if the number of input variables is excessively large. The final circuit obtained dictates that it be implemented with a random connection of SSI gates, which may require a relatively large number of ICs and interconnecting wires. In many cases the application of an alternate design procedure can produce a combinational circuit for a given function which is far better than the one obtained by following the classical design method. The possibility of an alternate design procedure depends on the particular problem and the ingenuity of the designer. The classical method constitutes a general procedure that, if followed, guarantees to produce a result. However, before applying the classical method, it is always wise to investigate the possibility of an alternate method which may be more efficient for the particular problem at hand.

The first question that must be answered before going through a detailed design of a combinational circuit is whether the function is already available in an IC package. Numerous MSI devices are available commercially. These devices perform specific digital functions commonly employed in the design of digital computer systems. If an MSI device cannot be found to produce exactly the function needed, a resourceful designer may be able to formulate a method so as to incorporate an MSI device in his circuit. The selection of MSI components in preference to SSI gates is extremely important, since it would invariably result in a considerable reduction of IC packages and interconnecting wires.

The first half of this chapter presents examples of combinational circuits designed by methods other than the classical procedure. All of the examples demonstrate the internal construction of existing MSI functions. Thus we present new design tools and at the same time acquaint the reader with existing MSI functions. Familiarity with available MSI functions is very important not only in the design of combinational circuits, but also in the design of more complicated digital computer systems.

Occasionally one finds MSI and LSI circuits that can be applied directly to the design and implementation of any combinational circuit. Four techniques of combinational logic design by means of MSI and LSI are introduced in the second half of the chapter. These techniques make use of the general properties of decoders, multiplexers, read-only memories (ROM), and programmable logic arrays (PLA). These four IC components have a large number of applications. Their use in implementing combinational circuits as described here is just one of many other applications.

5-2 BINARY PARALLEL ADDER

The full-adder introduced in Section 4-3 forms the sum of two bits and a previous carry. Two binary numbers of n bits each can be added by means of this circuit. To demonstrate with a specific example, consider two binary numbers, $A = 1011$ and $B = 0011$, whose sum is $S = 1110$. When a pair of bits are added through a full-adder, the circuit produces a carry to be used with the pair of bits one significant position higher. This is shown in the following table:

Subscript i	4 3 2 1		Full-adder of Fig. 4-5
Input carry	0 1 1 0	C_i	z
Augend	1 0 1 1	A_i	x
Addend	0 0 1 1	B_i	y
Sum	1 1 1 0	S_i	S
Output carry	0 0 1 1	C_{i+1}	C

The bits are added with full-adders, starting from the least significant position (subscript 1), to form the sum bit and carry bit. The inputs and outputs of the full-adder circuit of Fig. 4-5 are also indicated above. The input carry C_1 in the least significant position must be 0. The value of C_{i+1} in a given significant position is the output carry of the full-adder. This value is transferred into the input carry of the full-adder that adds the bits one higher significant position to the left. The sum bits are thus generated starting from the rightmost position and are available as soon as the corresponding previous carry bit is generated.

The sum of two n-bit binary numbers, A and B, can be generated in two ways: either in a serial fashion or in parallel. The serial addition method uses only one full-adder circuit and a storage device to hold the generated output carry. The pair of bits in A and B are transferred serially, one at a time, through the single full-adder to produce a string of output bits for the sum. The stored output carry from one pair of bits is used as an input carry for the next pair of bits. The parallel method uses n full-adder circuits, and all bits of A and B are applied simultaneously. The output carry from one full-adder is connected to the input carry of the full-adder one position to its left. As soon as the carries are generated, the correct sum bits emerge from the sum outputs of all full-adders.

A *binary parallel adder* is a digital function that produces the arithmetic sum of two binary numbers in parallel. It consists of full-adders connected in cascade, with the output carry from one full-adder connected to the input carry of the next full-adder.

Figure 5-1 shows the interconnection of four full-adder (FA) circuits to provide a 4-bit binary parallel adder. The augend bits of A and the addend bits of B are designated by subscript numbers from right to left, with subscript 1 denoting the low-order bit. The carries are connected in a chain through the full-adders. The input carry to the adder is C_1 and the output carry is C_5. The S outputs generate the required sum bits. When the 4-bit full-adder circuit is enclosed within an IC package, it has four terminals for the augend bits, four terminals for the addend bits, four terminals for the sum bits, and two terminals for the input and output carries.*

An n-bit parallel adder requires n full-adders. It can be constructed from 4-bit, 2-bit, and 1-bit full-adders ICs by cascading several packages. The output carry from one package must be connected to the input carry of the one with the next higher-order bits.

The 4-bit full-adders is a typical example of an MSI function. It can be used in many applications involving arithmetic operations. Observe that the design of this circuit by the classical method would require a truth table with $2^9 = 512$ entries, since there are nine inputs to the circuit. By using an iterative method of cascading an already known function, we were able to obtain a simple and well-organized implementation.

The application of this MSI function to the design of a combinational circuit is demonstrated in the following example.

*An example of a 4-bit full-adders is the TTL type 74283 IC.

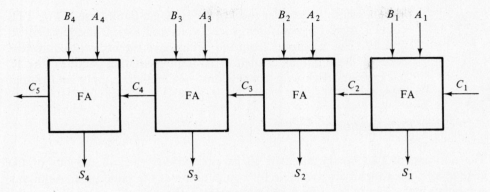

Figure 5-1 4-bit full-adders

EXAMPLE 5-1: Design a BCD-to-excess-3 code converter.

This circuit was designed in Section 4-5 by the classical method. The circuit obtained from this design is shown in Fig. 4-8 and requires 11 gates. When implemented with SSI gates, it requires 3 IC packages and 14 internal wire connections (not including input and output connections). Inspection of the truth table immediately reveals that the excess-3 equivalent code can be obtained from the BCD code by the addition of binary 0011. This addition can be easily implemented by means of a 4-bit full-adders MSI circuit, as shown in Fig. 5-2. The BCD digit is applied to inputs A. Inputs B are set to a constant 0011. This is done by applying logic-1 to B_1 and B_2 and logic-0 to B_3, B_4, and C_1. Logic-1 and logic-0 are physical

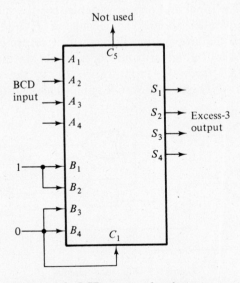

Figure 5-2 BCD-to-excess-3 code converter

157

signals whose values depend on the IC logic family used. For TTL circuits, logic-1 is equivalent to 3.5 volts and logic-0 is equivalent to ground. The S outputs from the circuit give the excess-3 equivalent code of the input BCD digit. This implementation requires one IC package and five wire connections, not including input and output wiring.

Carry Propagation

The addition of two binary numbers in parallel implies that all the bits of the augend and the addend are available for computation at the same time. As in any combinational circuit, the signal must propagate through the gates before the correct output sum is available in the output terminals. The total propagation time is equal to the propagation delay of a typical gate times the number of gate levels in the circuit. The longest propagation delay time in a parallel adder is the time it takes the carry to propagate through the full-adders. Since each bit of the sum output depends on the value of the input carry, the value of S_i in any given stage in the adder will be in its steady-state final value only after the input carry to that stage has been propagated. Consider output S_4 in Fig. 5-1. Inputs A_4 and B_4 reach a steady value as soon as input signals are applied to the adder. But input carry C_4 does not settle to its final steady-state value until C_3 is available in its steady-state value. Similarly, C_3 has to wait for C_2, and so on down to C_1. Thus only after the carry propagates through all stages will the last output S_4 and carry C_5 settle to their final steady-state value.

The number of gate levels for the carry propagation can be found from the circuit of the full-adder. This circuit was derived in Fig. 4-5 and is redrawn in Fig. 5-3 for convenience. The input and output variables use the subscript i to denote a typical stage in the parallel adder. The signals at P_i and G_i settle to their steady-state value after the propagation through their respective gates. These two signals are common to all full-adders and depend only on the input augend and addend bits. The signal from the input carry, C_i, to the output carry, C_{i+1}, propagates through an AND gate and an OR gate, which constitute two gate levels.

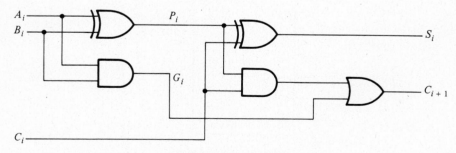

Figure 5-3   Full-adder circuit

If there are four full-adders in the parallel adder, the output carry C_5 would have $2 \times 4 = 8$ gate levels from C_1 to C_5. The total propagation time in the adder would be the propagation time in one half-adder plus eight gate levels. For an n-bit parallel adder, there are $2n$ gate levels for the carry to propagate through.

The carry propagation time is a limiting factor on the speed with which two numbers are added in parallel. Although a parallel adder, or any combinational circuit, will always have some value at its output terminals, the outputs will not be correct unless the signals are given enough time to propagate through the gates connected from the inputs to the outputs. Since all other arithmetic operations are implemented by successive additions, the time consumed during the addition process is very critical. An obvious solution for reducing the carry propagation delay time is to employ faster gates with reduced delays. But physical circuits have a limit to their capability. Another solution is to increase the equipment complexity in such a way that the carry delay time is reduced. There are several techniques for reducing the carry propagation time in a parallel adder. The most widely used technique employs the principle of *look-ahead* carry and is described below.

Consider the circuit of the full-adder shown in Fig. 5-3. If we define two new binary variables:

$$P_i = A_i \oplus B_i$$
$$G_i = A_i B_i$$

the output sum and carry can be expressed as:

$$S_i = P_i \oplus C_i$$
$$C_{i+1} = G_i + P_i C_i$$

G_i is called a *carry generate* and it produces an output carry when both A_i and B_i are one, regardless of the input carry. P_i is called a *carry propagate* because it is the term associated with the propagation of the carry from C_i to C_{i+1}.

We now write the Boolean function for the carry output of each stage and substitute for each C_i its value from the previous equations:

$$C_2 = G_1 + P_1 C_1$$
$$C_3 = G_2 + P_2 C_2 = G_2 + P_2(G_1 + P_1 C_1) = G_2 + P_2 G_1 + P_2 P_1 C_1$$
$$C_4 = G_3 + P_3 C_3 = G_3 + P_3 G_2 + P_3 P_2 G_1 + P_3 P_2 P_1 C_1$$

Since the Boolean function for each output carry is expressed in sum of products, each function can be implemented with one level of AND gates followed by an OR gate (or by a two-level NAND). The three Boolean functions for C_2, C_3, and C_4 are implemented in the look-ahead carry generator shown in Fig. 5-4. Note that C_4

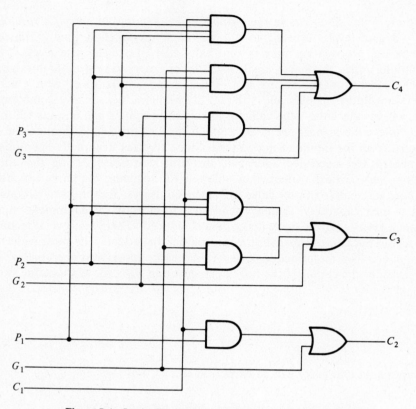

Figure 5-4 Logic diagram of a look-ahead carry generator

does not have to wait for C_3 and C_2 to propagate; in fact, C_4 is propagated at the same time as C_2 and C_3.*

The construction of a 4-bit parallel adder with a look-ahead carry scheme is shown in Fig. 5-5. Each sum output requires two exclusive-OR gates. The output of the first exclusive-OR gate generate the P_i variable, and the AND gate generates the G_i variable. All the P's and G's are generated in two gate levels. The carries are propagated through the look-ahead carry generator (similar to that in Fig. 5-4) and applied as inputs to the second exclusive-OR gate. After the P and G signals settle into their steady-state values, all output carries are generated after a delay of two levels of gates. Thus, outputs S_2 through S_4 have equal propagation delay times. The two-level circuit for the output carry C_5 is not shown in Fig. 5-4. This circuit can be easily derived by the equation-substitution method as done above (see Problem 5-4).

*A typical look-ahead carry generator is the IC type 74182. It is implemented with AND-OR-INVERT gates. It also has two outputs, G and P, to generate $C_5 = G + PC_1$.

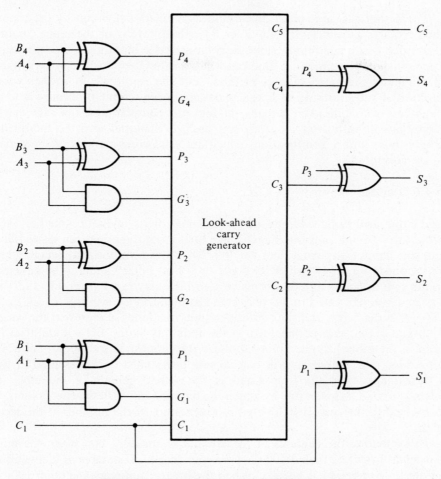

Figure 5-5 4-bit full-adders with look-ahead carry

5-3 DECIMAL ADDER

Computers or calculators that perform arithmetic operations directly in the decimal number system represent decimal numbers in binary-coded form. An adder for such a computer must employ arithmetic circuits that accept coded decimal numbers and present results in the accepted code. For binary addition, it was sufficient to consider a pair of significant bits at a time, together with a previous carry. A decimal adder requires a minimum of nine inputs and five outputs, since four bits are required to code each decimal digit and the circuit must have an input carry and output carry. Of course, there is a wide variety of possible decimal adder circuits, dependent upon the code used to represent the decimal digits.

The design of a nine-input, five-output combinational circuit by the classical method requires a truth table with $2^9 = 512$ entries. Many of the input combinations are don't-care conditions, since each binary code input has six combinations that are invalid. The simplified Boolean functions for the circuit may be obtained by a computer-generated tabular method, and the result would probably be a connection of gates forming an irregular pattern. An alternate procedure is to add the numbers with full-adder circuits, taking into consideration the fact that six combinations in each 4-bit input are not used. The output must be modified so that only those binary combinations which are valid combinations of the decimal code are generated.

BCD adder

Consider the arithmetic addition of two decimal digits in BCD, together with a possible carry from a previous stage. Since each input digit does not exceed 9, the output sum cannot be greater than $9 + 9 + 1 = 19$, the 1 in the sum being an input carry. Suppose we apply two BCD digits to a 4-bit binary adder. The adder will form the sum in *binary* and produce a result which may range from 0 to 19. These binary numbers are listed in Table 5-1 and are labeled by symbols K, Z_8, Z_4, Z_2, and Z_1. K is the carry, and the subscripts under the letter Z represent the weights 8, 4, 2, and 1 that can be assigned to the four bits in the BCD code. The first column in the table lists the binary sums as they appear in the outputs of a 4-bit *binary* adder. The output sum of two *decimal digits* must be represented in BCD and should appear in the form listed in the second column of the table. The problem is to find a simple rule by which the binary number in the first column can be converted to the correct BCD-digit representation of the number in the second column.

In examining the contents of the table, it is apparent that when the binary sum is equal to or less than 1001, the corresponding BCD number is identical, and therefore no conversion is needed. When the binary sum is greater than 1001, we obtain a nonvalid BCD representation. The addition of binary 6 (0110) to the binary sum converts it to the correct BCD representation and also produces an output carry as required.

The logic circuit that detects the necessary correction can be derived from the table entries. It is obvious that a correction is needed when the binary sum has an output carry $K = 1$. The other six combinations from 1010 to 1111 that need a correction have a 1 in position Z_8. To distinguish them from binary 1000 and 1001 which also have a 1 in position Z_8, we specify further that either Z_4 or Z_2 must have a 1. The condition for a correction and an output carry can be expressed by the Boolean function:

$$C = K + Z_8 Z_4 + Z_8 Z_2$$

when $C = 1$, it is necessary to add 0110 to the binary sum and provide an output carry for the next stage.

TABLE 5-1   Derivation of a BCD adder

Binary sum					BCD sum					Decimal
K	Z_8	Z_4	Z_2	Z_1	C	S_8	S_4	S_2	S_1	
0	0	0	0	0	0	0	0	0	0	0
0	0	0	0	1	0	0	0	0	1	1
0	0	0	1	0	0	0	0	1	0	2
0	0	0	1	1	0	0	0	1	1	3
0	0	1	0	0	0	0	1	0	0	4
0	0	1	0	1	0	0	1	0	1	5
0	0	1	1	0	0	0	1	1	0	6
0	0	1	1	1	0	0	1	1	1	7
0	1	0	0	0	0	1	0	0	0	8
0	1	0	0	1	0	1	0	0	1	9
0	1	0	1	0	1	0	0	0	0	10
0	1	0	1	1	1	0	0	0	1	11
0	1	1	0	0	1	0	0	1	0	12
0	1	1	0	1	1	0	0	1	1	13
0	1	1	1	0	1	0	1	0	0	14
0	1	1	1	1	1	0	1	0	1	15
1	0	0	0	0	1	0	1	1	0	16
1	0	0	0	1	1	0	1	1	1	17
1	0	0	1	0	1	1	0	0	0	18
1	0	0	1	1	1	1	0	0	1	19

A *BCD adder* is a circuit that adds two BCD digits in parallel and produces a sum digit also in BCD. A BCD adder must include the correction logic in its internal construction. To add 0110 to the binary sum, we use a second 4-bit binary adder as shown in Fig. 5-6. The two decimal digits, together with the input carry, are first added in the top 4-bit binary adder to produce the binary sum. When the output carry is equal to zero, nothing is added to the binary sum. When it is equal to one, binary 0110 is added to the binary sum through the bottom 4-bit binary adder. The output carry generated from the bottom binary adder can be ignored, since it supplies information already available at the output-carry terminal.

The BCD adder can be constructed with three IC packages. Each of the 4-bit adders is an MSI function and the three gates for the correction logic need one SSI package. However, the BCD adder is available in one MSI circuit.* To achieve shorter propagation delays, an MSI BCD adder includes the necessary circuits for look-ahead carries. The adder circuit for the correction does not need all four full-adders, and this circuit can be optimized within the IC package.

*TTL IC type 82S83 is a BCD adder.

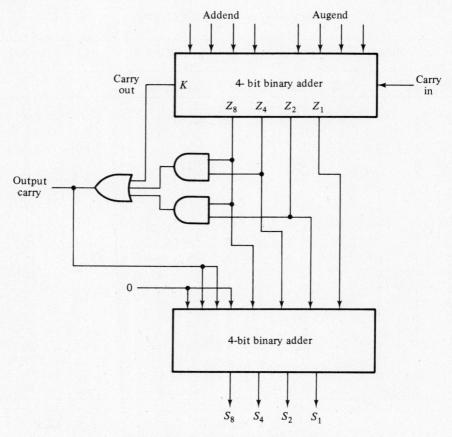

Figure 5-6 Block diagram of a BCD adder

A decimal parallel adder that adds n decimal digits needs n BCD adder stages. The output carry from one stage must be connected to the input carry of the next higher-order stage.

5-4 MAGNITUDE COMPARATOR

The comparison of two numbers is an operation that determines if one number is greater than, less than, or equal to the other number. A *magnitude comparator* is a combinational circuit that compares two numbers, A and B, and determines their relative magnitudes. The outcome of the comparison is specified by three binary variables that indicate whether $A > B$, $A = B$, or $A < B$.

The circuit for comparing two n-bit numbers has 2^{2n} entries in the truth table and becomes too cumbersome even with $n = 3$. On the other hand, as one may suspect, a comparator circuit possesses a certain amount of regularity. Digital functions which possess an inherent well-defined regularity can usually be designed by means of an algorithmic procedure if one is found to exist. An *algorithm* is a procedure that specifies a finite set of steps which, if followed, give the solution to a problem. We illustrate this method here by deriving an algorithm for the design of a 4-bit magnitude comparator.

The algorithm is a direct application of the procedure a person uses to compare the relative magnitudes of two numbers. Consider two numbers, A and B, with four digits each. Write the coefficients of the numbers with descending significance as follows:

$$A = A_3 A_2 A_1 A_0$$
$$B = B_3 B_2 B_1 B_0$$

where each subscripted letter represents one of the digits in the number. The two numbers are equal if all pairs of significant digits are equal i.e., if $A_3 = B_3$ and $A_2 = B_2$ and $A_1 = B_1$ and $A_0 = B_0$. When the numbers are binary, the digits are either 1 or 0 and the equality relation of each pair of bits can be expressed logically with an equivalence function:

$$x_i = A_i B_i + A'_i B'_i \qquad i = 0, 1, 2, 3$$

where $x_i = 1$ only if the pair of bits in position i are equal, i.e., if both are 1's or both are 0's.

The equality of the two numbers, A and B, is displayed in a combinational circuit by an output binary variable which we designate by the symbol $(A = B)$. This binary variable is equal to 1 if the input numbers, A and B, are equal, and it is equal to 0 otherwise. For the equality condition to exist, all x_i variables must be equal to 1. This dictates an AND operation of all variables:

$$(A = B) = x_3 x_2 x_1 x_0$$

the *binary* variable $(A = B)$ is equal to 1 only if all pairs of digits of the two numbers are equal.

To determine if A is greater than or less than B, we inspect the relative magnitudes of pairs of significant digits starting from the most significant position. If the two digits are equal, we compare the next lower significant pair of digits. This comparison continues until a pair of unequal digits is reached. If the corresponding digit of A is 1 and that of B is 0, we conclude that $A > B$. If the corresponding digit of A is 0 and that of B is 1, we have that $A < B$. The sequential comparison can be expressed logically by the following two Boolean functions:

$$(A > B) = A_3 B'_3 + x_3 A_2 B'_2 + x_3 x_2 A_1 B'_1 + x_3 x_2 x_1 A_0 B'_0$$
$$(A < B) = A'_3 B_3 + x_3 A'_2 B_2 + x_3 x_2 A'_1 B_1 + x_3 x_2 x_1 A'_0 B_0$$

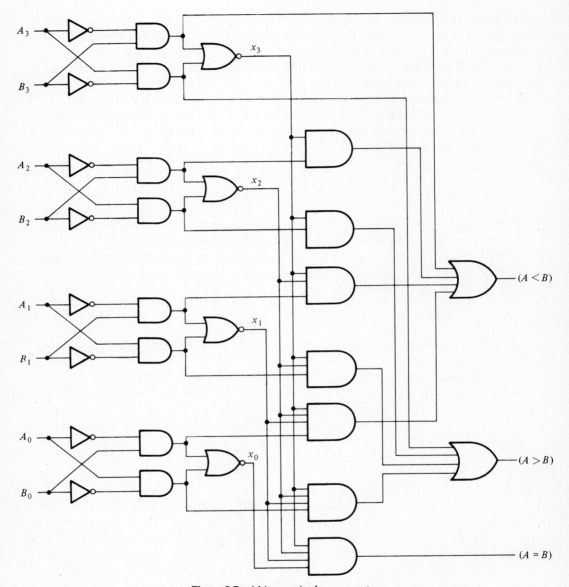

Figure 5-7 4-bit magnitude comparator

the symbols $(A > B)$ and $(A < B)$ are *binary* output variables which are equal to 1 when $A > B$ or $A < B$, respectively.

The gate implementation of the three output variables just derived is simpler than it seems because it involves a certain amount of repetition. The "unequal" outputs can use the same gates that are needed to generate the "equal" output. The logic diagram of the 4-bit magnitude comparator is shown in Fig. 5-7.* The four x

*TTL type 7485 is a 4-bit magnitude comparator. It has three more inputs for connecting comparators in cascade (see Problem 5-14).

outputs are generated with equivalence (exclusive-NOR) circuits and applied to an AND gate to give the output binary variable ($A = B$). The other two outputs use the x variables to generate the Boolean functions listed above. This is a multilevel implementation and, as clearly seen, it has a regular pattern. The procedure for obtaining magnitude comparator circuits for binary numbers with more than four bits should be obvious from this example. The same circuit can be used to compare the relative magnitudes of two BCD digits.

5-5   DECODERS

Discrete quantities of information are represented in digital systems with binary codes. A binary code of n bits is capable of representing up to 2^n distinct elements of the coded information. A *decoder* is a combinational circuit that converts binary information from n input lines to a maximum of 2^n unique output lines. If the n-bit decoded information has unused or don't-care combinations, the decoder output will have less than 2^n outputs.

The decoders presented here are called n-to-m line decoders where $m \leqslant 2^n$. Their purpose is to generate the 2^n (or less) minterms of n input variables. The

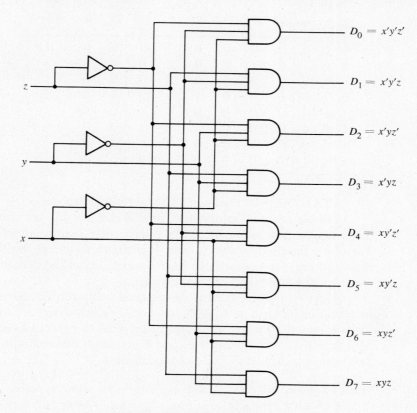

Figure 5-8   A 3-to-8 line decoder

name *decoder* is also used in conjunction with some code converters such as a BCD-to-seven-segment decoder (see Problem 4-14).

As an example, consider the 3-to-8 line decoder circuit of Fig. 5-8. The three inputs are decoded into eight outputs, each output representing one of the minterms of the 3-input variables. The three inverters provide the complement of the inputs, and each one of the eight AND gates generates one of the minterms. A particular application of this decoder would be a binary-to-octal conversion. The input variables may represent a binary number, and the outputs will then represent the eight digits in the octal number system. However, a 3-to-8 line decoder can be used for decoding any 3-bit code to provide eight outputs, one for each element of the code.

The operation of the decoder may be further clarified from its input-output relationships, listed in Table 5-2. Observe that the output variables are mutually exclusive because only one output can be equal to 1 at any one time. The output line whose value is equal to 1 represents the minterm equivalent of the binary number presently available in the input lines.*

TABLE 5-2   Truth table of a 3-to-8 line decoder

Inputs			Outputs							
x	y	z	D_0	D_1	D_2	D_3	D_4	D_5	D_6	D_7
0	0	0	1	0	0	0	0	0	0	0
0	0	1	0	1	0	0	0	0	0	0
0	1	0	0	0	1	0	0	0	0	0
0	1	1	0	0	0	1	0	0	0	0
1	0	0	0	0	0	0	1	0	0	0
1	0	1	0	0	0	0	0	1	0	0
1	1	0	0	0	0	0	0	0	1	0
1	1	1	0	0	0	0	0	0	0	1

EXAMPLE 5-2: Design a BCD-to-decimal decoder.

The elements of information in this case are the ten decimal digits represented by the BCD code. The code itself has four bits. Therefore, the decoder should have four inputs to accept the coded digit and ten outputs, one for each decimal digit. This will give a 4-line to 10-line BCD-to-decimal decoder.

There is really no need to design such a decoder because it can be found in IC form as an MSI function. We will design it anyway for two reasons. First, it gives insight on what to expect in such an MSI function. Second, this is a good example for demonstrating the practical consquences of don't-care conditions.

*IC type 74138 is a 3-to-8 line decoder. It is constructed with NAND gates. The outputs are the complements of the values shown in Table 5-2.

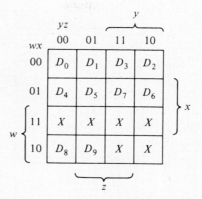

Figure 5-9 Map for simplifying a BCD-to-decimal decoder

Since the circuit has ten outputs, it would be necessary to draw ten maps to simplify each one of the output functions. There are six don't-care conditions here, and they must be taken into consideration when we simplify each of the output functions. Instead of drawing ten maps, we will draw only one map and write each of the output variables, D_0 to D_9, inside its corresponding minterm square as shown in Fig. 5-9. Six input combinations will never occur, so we mark their corresponding minterm squares with X's.

It is the designer's responsibility to decide on how to treat the don't-care conditions. Assume that it is decided to use them in such a way as to simplify the functions to the minimum number of literals. D_0 and D_1 cannot be combined with any don't-care minterms. D_2 can be combined with the don't care minterm m_{10} to give:

$$D_2 = x'yz'$$

The square with D_9 can be combined with three other don't-care squares to give:

$$D_9 = wz$$

Using the don't-care terms for the other outputs, we obtain the circuit shown in Fig. 5-10. Thus the don't-care terms cause a reduction in the number of inputs in most of the AND gates.

A careful designer should investigate the effect of the above minimization. Although it is true that under normal operating conditions the invalid six combinations will never occur, what if there is a malfunction and they do occur? An analysis of the circuit of Fig. 5-10 shows that the six invalid input combinations will produce outputs as listed in Table 5-3. The reader can look at the table and decide whether this is a good or bad design.

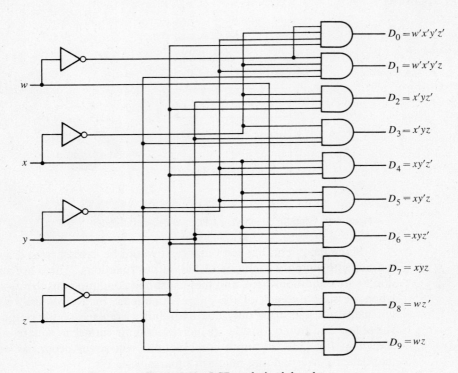

Figure 5-10 BCD-to-decimal decoder

TABLE 5-3 Partial truth table for the circuit of Fig. 5-10

Inputs				Outputs									
w	x	y	z	D_0	D_1	D_2	D_3	D_4	D_5	D_6	D_7	D_8	D_9
1	0	1	0	0	0	1	0	0	0	0	0	1	0
1	0	1	1	0	0	0	1	0	0	0	0	0	1
1	1	0	0	0	0	0	0	1	0	0	0	1	0
1	1	0	1	0	0	0	0	0	1	0	0	0	1
1	1	1	0	0	0	0	0	0	0	1	0	1	0
1	1	1	1	0	0	0	0	0	0	0	1	0	1

Another reasonable design decision would be to make all outputs equal to 0 when an invalid input combination occurs.* This would require ten 4-input AND gates. Other possibilities may be considered. In any case, one should not treat don't-care conditions indiscriminately but should try to investigate their effect once the circuit is in operation.

*IC type 7442 is a BCD-to-decimal decoder. The selected outputs are in the 0 state, and all the invalid combinations give an output of all 1's.

Combinational Logic Implementation

A decoder provides the 2^n minterm of n input variables. Since any Boolean function can be expressed in sum of minterms canonical form, one can use a decoder to generate the minterms and an external OR gate to form the sum. In this way, any combinational circuit with n inputs and m outputs can be implemented with an n-to-2^n line decoder and m OR gates.

The procedure for implementing a combinational circuit by means of a decoder and OR gates requires that the Boolean functions for the circuit be expressed in sum of minterms. This form can be easily obtained from the truth table or by expanding the functions to their sum of minterms (see Section 2-5). A decoder is then chosen which generates all the minterms of the n input variables. The inputs to each OR gate are selected from the decoder outputs according to the minterm list in each function.

EXAMPLE 5-3: Implement a full-adder circuit with a decoder and two OR gates.

From the truth table of the full-adder (Section 4-3), we obtain the functions for this combinational circuit in sum of minterms:

$$S(x, y, z) = \Sigma(1, 2, 4, 7)$$
$$C(x, y, z,) = \Sigma(3, 5, 6, 7)$$

Since there are three inputs and a total of eight minterms, we need a 3-to-8 line decoder. The implementation is shown in Fig. 5-11. The decoder generates the eight minterms for x, y, z. The OR gate for output S forms the sum of minterms 1, 2, 4, and 7. The OR gate for output C forms the sum of minterms 3, 5, 6, and 7.

A function with a long list of minterms requires an OR gate with a large number of inputs. A function F having a list of k minterms can be expressed in its

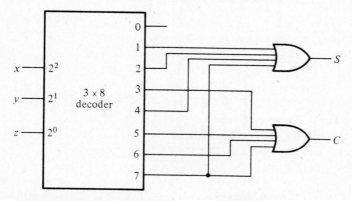

Figure 5-11 Implementation of a full-adder with a decoder

complemented form F' with $2^n - k$ minterms. If the number of minterms in a function is greater than $2^n/2$, then F' can be expressed with fewer minterms than required for F. In such a case, it is advantageous to use a NOR gate to sum the minterms of F'. The output of the NOR gate will generate the normal output F.

The decoder method can be used to implement any combinational circuit. However, its implementation must be compared with all other possible implementations to determine the best solution. In some cases this method may provide the best implementation, especially if the combinational circuit has many outputs and if each output function (or its complement) is expressed with a small number of minterms.

Demultiplexers

Some IC decoders are constructed with NAND gates. Since a NAND gate produces the AND operation with an inverted output, it becomes more economical to generate the decoder minterms in their complemented form. Most, if not all, IC decoders include one or more *enable* inputs to control the circuit operation. A 2-to-4 line decoder with an enable input constructed with NAND gates is shown in Fig. 5-12. All outputs are equal to 1 if enable input E is 1, regardless of the values of inputs A and B. When the enable input is 0, the circuit operates as a decoder with complemented outputs. The truth table lists these conditions. The X's under A and B are don't-care conditions. Normal decoder operation occurs only with $E = 0$, and the outputs are selected when they are in the 0 state.

The block diagram of the decoder is shown in Fig. 5-13(a). The small circle at input E indicates that the decoder is enabled when $E = 0$. The small circles at the outputs indicate that all outputs are complemented.

A decoder with an enable input can function as a demultiplexer. A *demultiplexer* is a circuit that receives information on a single line and transmits this information on one of 2^n possible output lines. The selection of a specific output

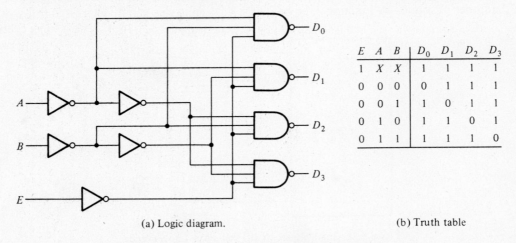

E	A	B	D_0	D_1	D_2	D_3
1	X	X	1	1	1	1
0	0	0	0	1	1	1
0	0	1	1	0	1	1
0	1	0	1	1	0	1
0	1	1	1	1	1	0

(a) Logic diagram.   (b) Truth table

Figure 5-12   A 2-to-4 line decoder with enable (E) input

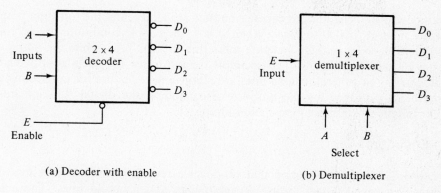

(a) Decoder with enable   (b) Demultiplexer

Figure 5-13 Block diagrams for the circuit of Fig. 5-12

line is controlled by the bit values of n selection lines. The decoder of Fig. 5-12 can function as a demultiplexer if the E line is taken as a data input line and lines A and B are taken as the selection lines. This is shown in Fig. 5-13(b). The single input variable E has a path to all four outputs, but the input information is directed to only one of the output lines, as specified by the binary value of the two selection lines A and B. This can be verified from the truth table of this circuit, shown in Fig. 5-12(b). For example, if the selection lines $AB = 10$, output D_2 will be the same as the input value E, while all other outputs are maintained at 1. Because decoder and demultiplexer operations are obtained from the same circuit, a decoder with an enable input is referred to as a *decoder/demultiplexer*. It is the enable input that makes the circuit a demultiplexer; the decoder itself can use AND, NAND, or NOR gates.

     Decoder/demultiplexer circuits can be connected together to form a larger decoder circuit. Figure 5-14 shows two 3×8 decoders with enable inputs connected to form a 4×16 decoder. When $w = 0$, the top decoder is enabled and the

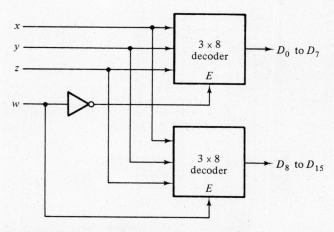

Figure 5-14 A 4×16 decoder constructed with two 3×8 decoders

other is disabled. The bottom decoder outputs are all 0's, and the top eight outputs generate minterms 0000 to 0111. When $w = 1$, the enable conditions are reversed; the bottom decoder outputs generate minterms 1000 to 1111, while the outputs of the top decoder are all 0's. This example demonstrates the usefulness of enable inputs in ICs. In general, enable lines are a convenient feature for connecting two or more IC packages for the purpose of expanding the digital function into a similar function with more inputs and outputs.

Encoders

An *encoder* is a digital function that produces a reverse operation from that of a decoder. An encoder has 2^n (or less) input lines and n output lines. The output lines generate the binary code for the 2^n input variables. An example of an encoder is shown in Fig. 5-15. The octal-to-binary encoder consists of eight inputs, one for each of the eight digits, and three outputs that generate the corresponding binary number. It is constructed with OR gates whose inputs can be determined from the truth table given in Table 5-4. The low-order output bit z is 1 if the input octal digit is odd. Output y is 1 for octal digits 2, 3, 6, or 7. Output x is a 1 for octal digits 4, 5, 6, or 7. Note that D_0 is not connected to any OR gate; the binary output must be all 0's in this case. An all 0's output is also obtained when all inputs are all 0's. This discrepancy can be resolved by providing one more output to indicate the fact that all inputs are not 0's.

The encoder in Fig. 5-15 assumes that only one input line can be equal to 1 at any time; otherwise the circuit has no meaning. Note that the circuit has eight inputs and could have $2^8 = 256$ possible input combinations. Only eight of these combinations have any meaning. The other input combinations are don't-care conditions.

Encoders of this type (Fig. 5-15) are not available in IC packages, since they can be easily constructed with OR gates. The type of encoder available in IC form

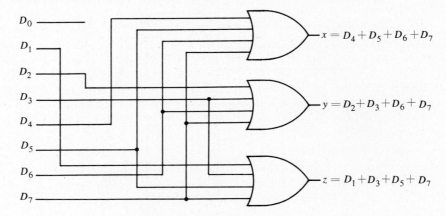

Figure 5-15   Octal-to-binary encoder

TABLE 5-4 Truth table of octal-to-binary encoder

Inputs								Outputs		
D_0	D_1	D_2	D_3	D_4	D_5	D_6	D_7	x	y	z
1	0	0	0	0	0	0	0	0	0	0
0	1	0	0	0	0	0	0	0	0	1
0	0	1	0	0	0	0	0	0	1	0
0	0	0	1	0	0	0	0	0	1	1
0	0	0	0	1	0	0	0	1	0	0
0	0	0	0	0	1	0	0	1	0	1
0	0	0	0	0	0	1	0	1	1	0
0	0	0	0	0	0	0	1	1	1	1

is called a *priority encoder*.* These encoders establish an input priority to ensure that only the highest-priority input line is encoded. Thus, in Table 5-4, if priority is given to an input with a higher subscript number over one with a lower subscript number, then if both D_2 and D_5 are logic-1 simultaneously, the output will be 101 because D_5 has a higher priority over D_2. Of course, the truth table of a priority encoder is different from the one in Table 5-4 (see Problem 5-21).

5-6 MULTIPLEXERS

Multiplexing means transmitting a large number of information units over a smaller number of channels or lines. A *digital multiplexer* is a combinational circuit that selects binary information from one of many input lines and directs it to a single output line The selection of a particular input line is controlled by a set of selection lines. Normally, there are 2^n input lines and n selection lines whose bit combinations determine which input is selected.

A 4-line to 1-line multiplexer is shown in Fig. 5-16. Each of the four input lines, I_0 to I_3, is applied to one input of an AND gate. Selection lines s_1 and s_0 are decoded to select a particular AND gate. The function table in the figure lists the input-to-output path for each possible bit combination of the selection lines. When this MSI function is used in the design of a digital system, it is represented in block diagram form as shown in Fig. 5-16(c). To demonstrate the circuit operation, consider the case when $s_1 s_0 = 10$. The AND gate associated with input I_2 has two of its inputs equal to 1 and the third input connected to I_2. The other three AND gates have at least one input equal to 0, which makes their output equal to 0. The OR-gate output is now equal to the value of I_2, thus providing a path from the selected input to the output. A multiplexer is also called a *data selector*, since it selects one of many inputs and steers the binary information to the output line.

*For example, IC type 74148.

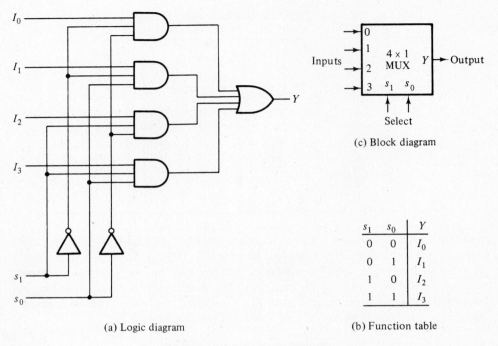

(c) Block diagram

(a) Logic diagram

(b) Function table

$$
\begin{array}{cc|c}
s_1 & s_0 & Y \\
\hline
0 & 0 & I_0 \\
0 & 1 & I_1 \\
1 & 0 & I_2 \\
1 & 1 & I_3 \\
\end{array}
$$

Figure 5-16 A 4-to-1 line multiplexer

The AND gates and inverters in the multiplexer resemble a decoder circuit and, indeed, they decode the input selection lines. In general, a 2^n-to-1 line multiplexer is constructed from an n-to-2^n decoder by adding to it 2^n input lines, one to each AND gate. The outputs of the AND gates are applied to a single OR gate to provide the 1-line output. The size of a multiplexer is specified by the number 2^n of its input lines and the single output line. It is then implied that it also contains n selection lines. A multiplexer is often abbreviated as MUX.

As in decoders, multiplexer ICs may have an *enable* input to control the operation of the unit. When the enable input is in a given binary state, the outputs are disabled, and when it is in the other state (the enable state), the circuit functions as a normal multiplexer. The enable input (sometimes called *strobe*) can be used to expand two or more multiplexer ICs to a digital multiplexer with a larger number of inputs.

In some cases two or more multiplexers are enclosed within one IC package. The selection and enable inputs in multiple-unit ICs may be common to all multiplexers. As an illustration, a quadruple 2-line to 1-line multiplexer IC is shown in Fig. 5-17.* It has four multiplexers, each capable of selecting one of two input lines. Output Y_1 can be selected to be equal to either A_1 or B_1. Similarly, output Y_2 may have the value of A_2 or B_2, and so on. One input selection line, S,

*This is similar to IC type 74157.

176

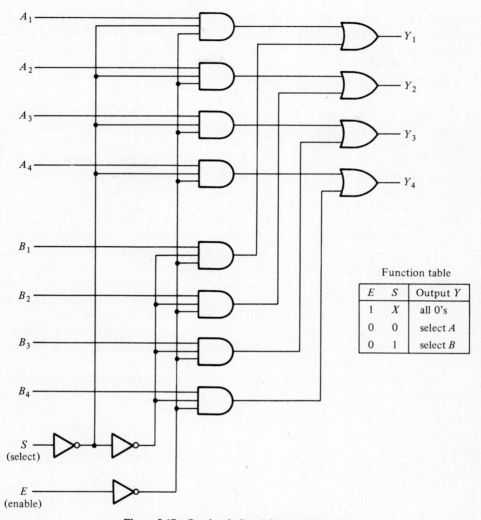

Figure 5-17 Quadruple 2-to-1 line multiplexers

Function table

E	S	Output Y
1	X	all 0's
0	0	select A
0	1	select B

suffices to select one of two lines in all four multiplexers. The control input E enables the multiplexers in the 0 state and disables them in the 1 state. Although the circuit contains four multiplexers, we may think of it as a circuit that selects one in a pair of 4-input lines. As shown in the function table, the unit is selected when $E = 0$. Then, if $S = 0$, the four A inputs have a path to the outputs. On the other hand, if $S = 1$, the four B inputs are selected. The outputs have all 0's when $E = 1$, regardless of the value of S.

The multiplexer is a very useful MSI function and has a multitude of applications. It is used for connecting two or more sources to a single destination among computer units, and it is useful for constructing a common bus system.

These and other uses of the multiplexer are discussed in later chapters in conjunction with their particular applications. Here we demonstrate the general properties of this device and show that it can be used to implement any Boolean function.

Boolean Function Implementation

It was shown in the previous section that a decoder can be used to implement a Boolean function by employing an external OR gate. A quick reference to the multiplexer of Fig. 5-16 reveals that it is essentially a decoder with the OR gate already available. The minterms out of the decoder to be chosen can be controlled with the input lines. The minterms to be included with the function being implemented are chosen by making their corresponding input lines equal to 1, those minterms not included in the function are disabled by making their input lines equal to 0. This gives a method for implementing any Boolean function of n variables with a 2^n-to-1 multiplexer. However, it is possible to do better than that.

If we have a Boolean function of $n + 1$ variables, we take n of these variables and connect them to the selection lines of a multiplexer. The remaining single variable of the function is used for the inputs of the multiplexer. If A is this single variable, the inputs of the multiplexer are chosen to be either A or A' or 1 or 0. By judicious use of these four values for the inputs and by connecting the other variables to the selection lines, one can implement any Boolean function with a multiplexer. In this way it is possible to generate any function of $n + 1$ variables with a 2^n-to-1 multiplexer.

To demonstrate this procedure with a concrete example, consider the function of three variables:

$$F(A, B, C) = \Sigma(1, 3, 5, 6)$$

The function can be implemented with a 4-to-1 multiplexer as shown in Fig. 5-18. Two of the variables, B and C are applied to the selection lines in that order, i.e., B is connected to s_1 and C to s_0. The inputs of the multiplexer are 0, 1, A, and A'. When $BC = 00$, output $F = 0$ since $I_0 = 0$. Therefore, both minterms $m_0 = A'B'C'$ and $m_4 = AB'C'$ produce a 0 output, since the output is 0 when $BC = 00$ regardless of the value of A. When $BC = 01$, output $F = 1$, since $I_1 = 1$. Therefore, both minterms $m_1 = A'B'C$ and $m_5 = AB'C$ produce a 1 output, since the output is 1 when $BC = 01$ regardless of the value of A. When $BC = 10$, input I_2 is selected. Since A is connected to this input, the output will be equal to 1 only for minterm $m_6 = ABC'$, but not for minterm $m_2 = A'BC'$, because when $A' = 1$, then $A = 0$, and since $I_2 = 0$, we have $F = 0$. Finally, when $BC = 11$, input I_3 is selected. Since A' is connected to this input, the output will be equal to 1 only for minterm $m_3 = A'BC$, but not for $m_7 = ABC$. This information is summarized in Fig. 5-18(b), which is the truth table of the function we want to implement.

The above discussion shows by analysis that the multiplexer implements the required function. We now present a general procedure for implementing any Boolean function of n variables with a 2^{n-1}-to-1 multiplexer.

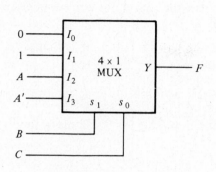

Minterm	A	B	C	F
0	0	0	0	0
1	0	0	1	1
2	0	1	0	0
3	0	1	1	1
4	1	0	0	0
5	1	0	1	1
6	1	1	0	1
7	1	1	1	0

(a) Multiplexer implementation   (b) Truth table

	I_0	I_1	I_2	I_3
A'	0	①	2	③
A	4	⑤	⑥	7
	0	1	A	A'

(c) Implementation table

Figure 5-18   Implementing $F(A, B, C) = \Sigma(1, 3, 5, 6)$ with a multiplexer

First, express the function in its sum of minterms form. Assume that the ordered sequence of variables chosen for the minterms is $ABCD \ldots$, where A is the leftmost variable in the ordered sequence of n variables and $BCD \ldots$ are the remaining $n - 1$ variables. Connect the $n - 1$ variables to the selection lines of the multiplexer with B connected to the high-order selection line, C to the next lower selection line, and so on down to the last variable, which is connected to the lowest-order selection line s_0. Consider now the single variable A. Since this variable is in the highest-order position in the sequence of variables, it will be complemented in minterms 0 to $(2^n/2) - 1$ which comprise the first half in the list of minterms. The second half of the minterms will have their A variable uncomplemented. For a three-variable function, A, B, C, we have eight minterms. Variable A is complemented in minterms 0 to 3 and uncomplemented in minterms 4 to 7.

List the inputs of the multiplexer and under them list all the minterms in two rows. The first row lists all those minterms where A is complemented, and the second row all the minterms with A uncomplemented, as shown in Fig. 5-18(c). Circle all the minterms of the function and inspect each column separately.

If the two minterms in a column are not circled, apply 0 to the corresponding multiplexer input.

If the two minterms are circled, apply 1 to the corresponding multiplexer input.

If the bottom minterm is circled and the top is not circled, apply A to the corresponding multiplexer input.

If the top minterm is circled and the bottom is not circled, apply A' to the corresponding multiplexer input.

This procedure follows from the conditions established during the previous analysis.

Figure 5-18(c) shows the implementation table for the Boolean function:

$$F(A, B, C) = \Sigma(1, 3, 5, 6)$$

from which we obtain the multiplexer connections of Fig. 5-18(a). Note that B must be connected to s_1 and C to s_0.

It is not necessary to choose the leftmost variable in the ordered sequence of a variable list for the inputs to the multiplexer. In fact, we can choose any one of the variables for the inputs of the multiplexer, provided we modify the multiplexer implementation table. Suppose we want to implement the same function with a multiplexer, but using variables A and B for selection lines s_1 and s_0, and variable C for the inputs of the multiplexer. Variable C is complemented in the even-numbered minterms and uncomplemented in the odd-numbered minterms, since it is the last variable in the sequence of listed variables. The arrangement of the two minterm rows in this case must be as shown in Fig. 5-19(a). By circling the minterms of the function and using the rules stated above, we obtain the multiplexer connection for implementing the function as in Fig. 5-19(b).

In a similar fashion, it is possible to use any single variable of the function for use in the multiplexer inputs. One can formulate various combinations for implementing a Boolean function with multiplexers. In any case, all the input variables, except one, are applied to the selection lines. The remaining single variable , or its complement, or 0 or 1, are then applied to the inputs of the multiplexer.

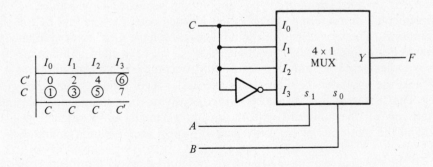

(a) Implementation table   (b) Multiplexer connection

Figure 5-19   Alternate implementation for $F(A, B, C) = \Sigma(1, 3, 5, 6)$

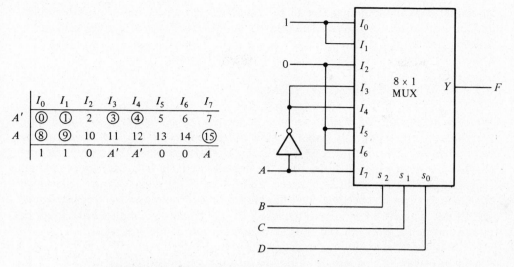

	I_0	I_1	I_2	I_3	I_4	I_5	I_6	I_7
A'	⓪	①	2	③	④	5	6	7
A	⑧	⑨	10	11	12	13	14	⑮
	1	1	0	A'	A'	0	0	A

Figure 5-20   Implementing $F(A, B, C\,D) = \Sigma(0, 1, 3, 4, 8, 9, 15)$

EXAMPLE 5-4: Implement the following function with a multiplexer:

$$F(A, B, C, D) = \Sigma(0, 1, 3, 4, 8, 9, 15)$$

This is a four-variable function and therefore we need a multiplexer with three selection lines and eight inputs. We choose to apply variables B, C, and D to the selection lines. The implementation table is then as shown in Fig. 5-20. The first half of the minterms are associated with A' and the second half with A. By circling the minterms of the function and applying the rules for finding values for the multiplexer inputs, we obtain the implementation shown.

Let us now compare the multiplexer method with the decoder method for implementing combinational circuits. The decoder method requires an OR gate for each output function, but only one decoder is needed to generate all minterms. The multiplexer method uses smaller-size units but requires one multiplexer for each output function. It would seem reasonable to assume that combinational circuits with a small number of outputs should be implemented with multiplexers. Combinational circuits with many output functions would probably use fewer ICs with the decoder method.

Although multiplexers and decoders may be used in the implementation of combinational circuits, it must be realized that decoders are mostly used for decoding binary information and multiplexers are mostly used to form a selected path between multiple sources and a single destination. They should be considered when designing small, special combinational circuits which are not otherwise available as MSI functions. For large combinational circuits with multiple inputs and outputs, there is a more suitable IC component, and it is presented in the following section.

5-7 READ-ONLY MEMORY (ROM)

We saw in Section 5-5 that a decoder generates the 2^n minterms of the n input variables. By inserting OR gates to sum the minterms of Boolean functions, we were able to generate any desired combinational circuit. A read-only memory (ROM) is a device that includes both the decoder and the OR gates within a single IC package. The connections between the outputs of the decoder and the inputs of the OR gates can be specified for each particular configuration by "programming" the ROM. The ROM is very often used to implement a complex combinational circuit in one IC package and thus eliminate all interconnecting wires.

A ROM is essentially a memory (or storage) device in which a fixed set of binary information is stored. The binary information must first be specified by the user and is then embedded in the unit to form the required interconnection pattern. ROMs come with special internal links that can be fused or broken. The desired interconnection for a particular application requires that certain links be fused to form the required circuit paths. Once a pattern is established for a ROM, it remains fixed even when power is turned off and then on again.

A block diagram of a ROM is shown in Fig. 5-21. It consists of n input lines and m output lines. Each bit combination of the input variables is called an *address*. Each bit combination that comes out of the output lines is called a *word*. The number of bits per word is equal to the number of output lines m. An address is essentially a binary number that denotes one of the minterms of n variables. The number of distinct addresses possible with n input variables is 2^n. An output word can be selected by a unique address, and since there are 2^n distinct addresses in a ROM, there are 2^n distinct words which are said to be stored in the unit. The word available on the output lines at any given time depends on the address value applied to the input lines. A ROM is characterized by the number of words 2^n and

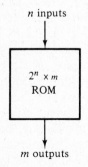

Figure 5-21   ROM block diagram

the number of bits per word m. This terminology is used because of the similarity between the read-only memory and the read-write memory which is presented in Section 7-7.

Consider a 32×8 ROM. The unit consists of 32 words of 8 bits each. This means that there are eight output lines and that there are 32 distinct words stored in the unit, each of which may be applied to the output lines. The particular word selected that is presently available on the output lines is determined from the five input lines. There are only five inputs in a 32×8 ROM because $2^5 = 32$, and with five variables we can specify 32 addresses or minterms. For each address input, there is a unique selected word. Thus, if the input address is 00000, word number 0 is selected and it appears on the output lines. If the input address is 11111, word number 31 is selected and applied to the output lines. In between, there are 30 other addresses that can select the other 30 words.

The number of addressed words in a ROM is determined from the fact that n input lines are needed to specify 2^n words. A ROM is sometimes specified by the total number of bits it contains, which is $2^n \times m$. For example, a 2048-bit ROM may be organized as 512 words of 4 bits each. This means that the unit has 4 output lines and 9 input lines to specify $2^9 = 512$ words. The total number of bits stored in the unit is $512 \times 4 = 2048$.

Internally, the ROM is a combinational circuit with AND gates connected as a decoder and a number of OR gates equal to the number of outputs in the unit. Figure 5-22 shows the internal logic construction of a 32×4 ROM. The five input

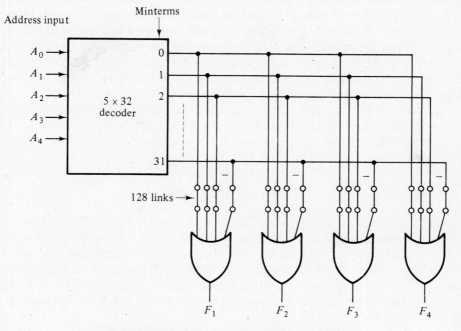

Figure 5-22   Logic construction of a 32×4 ROM

variables are decoded into 32 lines by means of 32 AND gates and 5 inverters. Each output of the decoder represents one of the minterms of a function of five variables. Each one of the 32 addresses selects one and only one output from the decoder. The address is a 5-bit number applied to the inputs, and the selected minterm out of the decoder is the one marked with the equivalent decimal number. The 32 outputs of the decoder are connected through *links* to each OR gate. Only four of these links are shown in the diagram, but actually each OR gate has 32 inputs and each input goes through a link that can be broken as desired.

The ROM is a two-level implementation in sum of minterms form. It does not have to be an AND-OR implementation, but it can be any other possible two-level minterm implementation. The second level is usually a wired-logic connection (see Section 3-7) to facilitate the fusing of links.

ROMs have many important applications in the design of digital computer systems. Their use for implementing complex combinational circuits is just one of these applications. Other uses of ROMs are presented in other parts of the book in conjunction with their particular applications.

Combinational Logic Implementation

From the logic diagram of the ROM, it is clear that each output provides the sum of all the minterms of the n input variables. Remember that any Boolean function can be expressed in sum-of-minterms form. By breaking the links of those minterms not included in the function, each ROM output can be made to represent the Boolean function of one of the output variables in the combinational circuit. For an n-input, m-output combinational circuit, we need a $2^n \times m$ ROM. The opening of the links is referred to as *programming* the ROM. The designer need only specify a ROM program table that gives the information for the required paths in the ROM. The actual programming is a hardware procedure which follows the specifications listed in the program table.

Let us clarify the process with a specific example. The truth table in Fig. 5-23(a) specifies a combinational circuit with two inputs and two outputs. The Boolean functions can be expressed in sum of minterms:

$$F_1(A_1, A_0) = \Sigma(1, 2, 3)$$
$$F_2(A_1, A_0) = \Sigma(0, 2)$$

When a combinational circuit is implemented by means of a ROM, the functions must be expressed in sum of minterms or, better yet, by a truth table. If the output functions are simplified, we find that the circuit needs only one OR gate and an inverter. Obviously, this is too simple a combinational circuit to be implemented with a ROM. The advantage of a ROM is in complex combinational circuits. This example merely demonstrates the procedure and should not be considered in a practical situation.

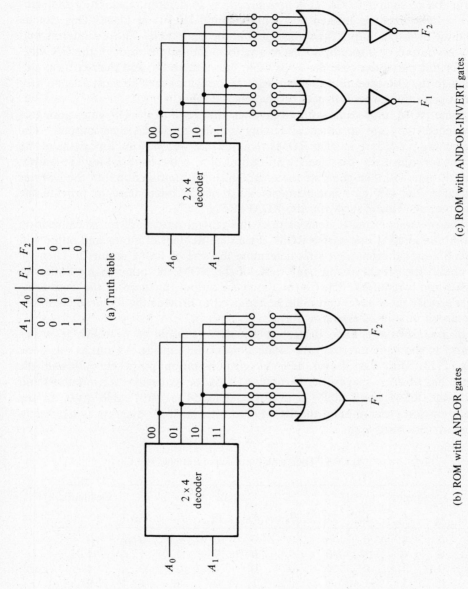

A_1	A_0	F_1	F_2
0	0	0	1
0	1	0	0
1	0	1	0
1	1	1	0

(a) Truth table

(b) ROM with AND-OR gates

(c) ROM with AND-OR-INVERT gates

Figure 5-23 Combinational-circuit implementation with a 4×2 ROM

The ROM that implements the combinational circuit must have two inputs and two outputs; so its size must be 4×2. Figure 5-23(b) shows the internal construction of such a ROM. It is now necessary to determine which of the eight available links must be broken and which should be left in place. This can be easily done from the output functions listed in the truth table. Those minterms that specify an output of 0 should not have a path to the output through the OR gate. Thus, for this particular case the truth table shows three 0's, and their corresponding links to the OR gates must be removed. It is obvious that we must assume here that an open input to an OR gate behaves as a 0 input.

Some ROM units come with an inverter after each of the OR gates and, as a consequence, they are specified as having initially all 0's at their outputs. The programming procedure in such ROMs requires that we open the link paths of the minterms (or addresses) that specify an output of 1 in the truth table. The output of the OR gate will then generate the complement of the function, but the inverter placed after the OR gate complements the function once more to provide the normal output. This is shown in the ROM of Fig. 5-23(c).

The previous example demonstrates the general procedure for implementing any combinational circuit with a ROM. From the number of inputs and outputs in the combinational circuit, we first determine the size of ROM required. Then we must obtain the programming truth table of the ROM; no other manipulation or simplification is required. The 0's (or 1's) in the output functions of the truth table directly specify those links that must be removed to provide the required combinational circuit in sum of minterms form.

In practice, when one designs a circuit by means of a ROM, it is not necessary to show the internal gate connections of links inside the unit as was done in Fig. 5-23. This was shown here for demonstration purposes only. All the designer has to do is specify the particular ROM (or its designation number) and provide the ROM truth table as in Fig. 5-23(a). The truth table gives all the information for programming the ROM. No internal logic diagram is needed to accompany the truth table.

TABLE 5-5 Truth table for circuit of Example 5-5

Inputs			Outputs						Decimal
A_2	A_1	A_0	B_5	B_4	B_3	B_2	B_1	B_0	
0	0	0	0	0	0	0	0	0	0
0	0	1	0	0	0	0	0	1	1
0	1	0	0	0	0	1	0	0	4
0	1	1	0	0	1	0	0	1	9
1	0	0	0	1	0	0	0	0	16
1	0	1	0	1	1	0	0	1	25
1	1	0	1	0	0	1	0	0	36
1	1	1	1	1	0	0	0	1	49

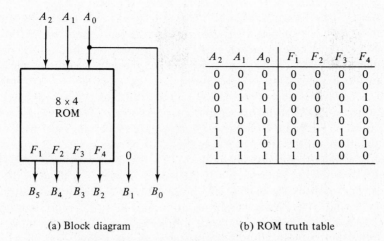

A_2	A_1	A_0	F_1	F_2	F_3	F_4
0	0	0	0	0	0	0
0	0	1	0	0	0	0
0	1	0	0	0	0	1
0	1	1	0	0	1	0
1	0	0	0	1	0	0
1	0	1	0	1	1	0
1	1	0	1	0	0	1
1	1	1	1	1	0	0

(a) Block diagram   (b) ROM truth table

Figure 5-24 ROM implementation of Example 5-5

EXAMPLE 5-5: Design a combinational circuit using a ROM. The circuit accepts a 3-bit number and generates an output binary number equal to the square of the input number.

The first step is to derive the truth table for the combinational circuit. In most cases this is all that is needed. In some cases we can fit a smaller truth table for the ROM by using certain properties in the truth table of the combinational circuit. Table 5-5 is the truth table for the combinational circuit. Three inputs and six outputs are needed to accommodate all possible numbers. We note that output B_0 is always equal to input A_0; so there is no need to generate B_0 with a ROM since it is equal to an input variable. Moreover, output B_1 is always 0, so this output is always known. We actually need to generate only four outputs with the ROM; the other two are easily obtained. The minimum size ROM needed must have three inputs and four outputs. Three inputs specify eight words, so the ROM size must be 8 $\times$ 4. The ROM implementation is shown in Fig. 5-24. The three inputs specify eight words of four bits each. The other two outputs of the combinational circuit are equal to 0 and A_0. The truth table in Fig. 5-24 specifies all the information needed for programming the ROM, and the block diagram shows the required connections.

Types of ROMs

The required paths in a ROM may be programmed in two different ways. The first is called *mask programming* and is done by the manufacturer during the last fabrication process of the unit. The procedure for fabricating a ROM requires that the customer fill out the truth table he wishes the ROM to satisfy. The truth table may be submitted on a special form provided by the manufacturer. More often, it is submitted on paper tape or punch cards in the format specified on the data sheet of the particular ROM. The manufacturer makes the corresponding mask for the paths to produce the 1's and 0's according to the customer's truth table. This procedure is costly because the vendor charges the customer a special fee for custom masking a ROM. For this reason, mask programming is economical only if large quantities of the same ROM configuration are to be manufactured.

For small quantities, it is more economical to use a second type of ROM called a *programmable read-only memory* or PROM. When ordered, PROM units contain all 0's (or all 1's) in every bit of the stored words. The links in the PROM are broken by application of current pulses through the output terminals. A broken link defines one binary state and an unbroken link represents the other state. This allows the user to program the unit in his own laboratory to achieve the desired relationship between input addresses and stored words. Special units called *PROM programmers* are available commercially to facilitate this procedure. In any case, all procedures for programming ROMs are *hardware* procedures even though the word *programming* is used.

The hardware procedure for programming ROMs or PROMs is irreversible and, once programmed the fixed pattern is permanent and cannot be altered. Once a bit pattern has been established, the unit must be discarded if the bit pattern is to be changed. A third type of unit available is called *erasable PROM* or EPROM. EPROMs can be restructured to the initial value (all 0's or all 1's) even though they have been changed previously. When an EPROM is placed under a special ultraviolet light for a given period of time, the short-wave radiation discharges the internal gates that serve as contacts. After erasure, the ROM returns to its initial state and can be reprogrammed. Certain ROMs can be erased with electrical signals instead of ultraviolet light, and these are sometimes called *electrically alterable ROMs* or EAROMs.

The function of a ROM can be interpreted in two different ways. The first interpretation is of a unit that implements any combinational circuit. From this point of view, each output terminal is considered separately as the output of a Boolean function expressed in sum of minterms. The second interpretation considers the ROM to be a storage unit having a fixed pattern of bit strings called *words*. From this point of view, the inputs specify an *address* to a specific stored word which is then applied to the outputs. For example, the ROM of Fig. 5-24 has three address lines which specify eight stored words as given by the truth table. Each word is four bits long. This is the reason why the unit is given the name *read-only memory*. *Memory* is commonly used to designate a storage unit. *Read* is commonly used to signify that the contents of a word specified by an address in a storage unit is placed at the output terminals. Thus, a ROM is a memory unit with a fixed word pattern that can be read out upon application of a given address. The bit pattern in the ROM is permanent and cannot be changed during normal operation.

ROMs are widely used to implement complex combinational circuits directly from their truth tables. They are useful for converting from one binary code to another (such as ASCII to EBCDIC and vice versa), for arithmetic functions such as multipliers, for display of characters in a cathode-ray tube, and in many other applications requiring a large number of inputs and outputs. They are also employed in the design of control units of digital systems. As such, they are used to store fixed bit patterns that represent the sequence of control variables needed to enable the various operations in the system. A control unit that utilizes a ROM to store binary control information is called a *microprogrammed control unit*. Chapter 10 deals with this subject in more detail.

5-8 PROGRAMMABLE LOGIC ARRAY (PLA)

A combinational circuit may occasionally have don't-care conditions. When implemented with a ROM, a don't-care condition becomes an address input that will never occur. The words at the don't-care addresses need not be programmed and may be left in their original state (all 0's or all 1's). The result is that not all the bit patterns available in the ROM are used, which may be considered a waste of available equipment.

Consider, for example, a combinational circuit that converts a 12-bit card code to a 6-bit internal alphanumeric code as listed in Table 1-5. The input card code consists of 12 lines designated by 0, 1, 2, . . . , 9, 11, 12. The size of the ROM for implementing the code converter must be 4096×6, since there are 12 inputs and 6 outputs. There are only 47 valid entries for the card code; all other input combinations are don't-care conditions. Thus only 47 words of the 4096 available are used. The remaining 4049 words of ROM are not used and are thus wasted.

For cases where the number of don't-care conditions is excessive, it is more economical to use a second type of LSI component called *programmable logic array* or PLA. A PLA is similar to a ROM in concept; however, the PLA does not provide full decoding of the variables and does not generate all the minterms as in the ROM. In the PLA, the decoder is replaced by a group of AND gates, each of which can be programmed to generate a product term of the input variables. The AND and OR gates inside the PLA are initially fabricated with links among them. The specific Boolean functions are implemented in sum of products form by opening appropriate links and leaving the desired connections.

A block diagram of the PLA is shown in Fig. 5-25. It consists of n inputs, m outputs, k product terms, and m sum terms. The product terms constitute a group of k AND gates and the sum terms constitute a group of m OR gates. Links are inserted between all n inputs and their complement values to each of the AND gates. Links are also provided between the outputs of the AND gates and the inputs of the OR gates. Another set of links in the output inverters allows the

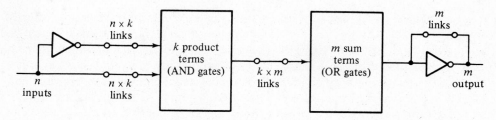

Figure 5-25 PLA block diagram

output function to be generated either in the AND-OR form or in the AND-OR-INVERT form. With the inverter link in place, the inverter is bypassed, giving an AND-OR implementation. With the link broken, the inverter becomes part of the circuit and the function is implemented in the AND-OR-INVERT form.

The size of the PLA is specified by the number of inputs, the number of product terms, and the number of outputs (the number of sum terms is equal to the number of outputs). A typical PLA has 16 inputs, 48 product terms, and 8 outputs.* The number of programmed links is $2n \times k + k \times m + m$, whereas that of a ROM is $2^n \times m$.

Figure 5-26 shows the internal construction of a specific PLA. It has three inputs, three product terms, and two outputs. Such a PLA is too small to be available commerically; it is presented here merely for demonstration purposes. Each input and its complement are connected through links to the inputs of all AND gates. The outputs of the AND gates are connected through links to each input of the OR gates. Two more links are provided with the output inverters. By breaking selected links and leaving others in place, it is possible to implement Boolean functions in their sum of products form.

As with a ROM, the PLA may be mask-programmable or field programmable. With a mask-programmable PLA, the customer must submit a PLA program table to the manufacturer. This table is used by the vendor to produce a custom-made PLA that has the required internal paths between inputs and outputs. A second type of PLA available is called a *field programmable logic array* or FPLA. The FPLA can be programmed by the user by means of certain recommended procedures. Commercial hardware programmer units are available for use in conjunction with certain FPLAs.

PLA Program Table

The use of a PLA must be considered for combinational circuits that have a large number of inputs and outputs. It is superior to a ROM for circuits that have a large number of don't-care conditions. The example presented below demonstrates

*TTL IC type 82S100.

190

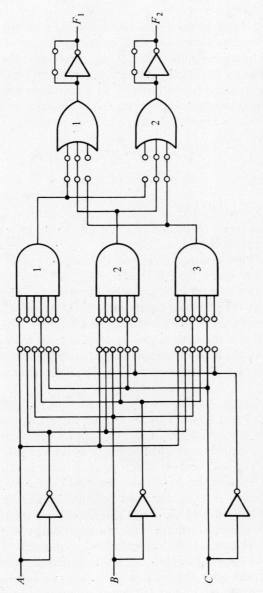

Figure 5-26 PLA with 3 inputs. 3 product terms, and 2 outputs; it implements the combinational circuit specified in Fig. 5-27

191

how a PLA is programmed. Bear in mind when going through the example that such a simple circuit will not require a PLA because it can be implemented more economically with SSI gates.

Consider the truth table of the combinational circuit, shown in Fig. 5-27(a). Although a ROM implements a combinational circuit in its sum of minterms form, a PLA implements the functions in their sum of products form. Each product term in the expression requires an AND gate. Since the number of AND gates in a PLA is finite, it is necessary to simplify the function to a minimum number of product terms in order to minimize the number of AND gates used. The simplified functions in sum of products are obtained from the maps of Fig. 5-27(b):

$$F_1 = AB' + AC$$

$$F_2 = AC + BC$$

There are three distinct product terms in this combinational circuit: AB', AC, and BC. The circuit has three inputs and two outputs; so the PLA of Fig. 5-26 can be used to implement this combinational circuit.

Programming the PLA means that we specify the paths in its AND-OR-NOT pattern. A typical PLA program table is shown in Fig. 5-27(c). It consists of three columns. The first column lists the product terms numerically. The second column specifies the required paths between inputs and AND gates. The third column specifies the paths between the AND gates and the OR gates. Under each output variable, we write a T (for true) if the output inverter is to be bypassed, and C (for complement) if the function is to be complemented with the output inverter. The Boolean terms listed at the left are not part of the table; they are included for reference only.

For each product term, the inputs are marked with 1, 0, or – (dash). If a variable in the product term appears in its normal form (unprimed), the corresponding input variable is marked with a 1. If it appears complemented (primed), the corresponding input variable is marked with a 0. If the variable is absent in the product term, it is marked with a dash. Each product term is associated with an AND gate. The paths between the inputs and the AND gates are specified under the column heading *inputs*. A 1 in the input column specifies a path from the corresponding input to the input of the AND gate that forms the product term. A 0 in the input column specifies a path from the corresponding complemented input to the input of the AND gate. A dash specifies no connection. The appropriate links are broken, and the ones left in place form the desired paths, as shown in Fig. 5-26. It is assumed that the open terminals in the AND gate behave like a 1 input.

The paths between the AND and OR gates are specified under the column heading *outputs*. The output variables are marked with 1's for all those product terms that formulate the function. In the example of Fig. 5-27, we have:

$$F_1 = AB' + AC$$

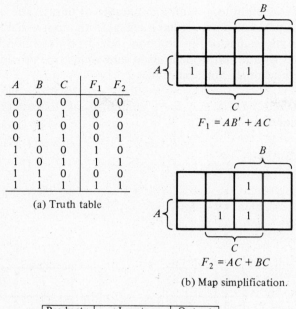

A	B	C	F_1	F_2
0	0	0	0	0
0	0	1	0	0
0	1	0	0	0
0	1	1	0	1
1	0	0	1	0
1	0	1	1	1
1	1	0	0	0
1	1	1	1	1

(a) Truth table

$F_1 = AB' + AC$

$F_2 = AC + BC$

(b) Map simplification.

	Product term	Inputs			Outputs	
		A	B	C	F_1	F_2
AB'	1	1	0	—	1	—
AC	2	1	—	1	1	1
BC	3	—	1	1	—	1
					T	T T/C

(c) PLA program table.

Figure 5-27 Steps required in PLA implementation

so F_1 is marked with 1's for product terms 1 and 2 and with a dash for product term 3. Each product term that has a 1 in the output column requires a path from the corresponding AND gate to the output OR gate. Those marked with a dash specify no connection. Finally, a T (true) output dictates that the link across the output inverter remains in place, and a C (complement) specifies that the corresponding link be broken. The internal paths of the PLA for this circuit are shown in Fig. 5-26. It is assumed that an open terminal in an OR gate behaves like a 0, and that a short circuit across the output inverter does not damage the circuit.

When designing a digital system with a PLA, there is no need to show the internal connections of the unit as was done in Fig. 5-26. All that is needed is a PLA program table from which the PLA can be programmed to supply the appropriate paths.

When implementing a combinational circuit with PLA, careful investigation must be undertaken in order to reduce the total number of distinct product terms, since a given PLA would have a finite number of AND terms. This can be done by simplifying each function to a minimum number of terms. The number of literals in a term is not important since we have available all input variables. Both the true value and the complement of the function should be simplified to see which one can be expressed with fewer product terms and which one provides product terms that are common to other functions.

EXAMPLE 5-6: A combinational circuit is defined by the functions:

$$F_1(A, B, C) = \Sigma(3, 5, 6, 7)$$
$$F_2(A, B, C) = \Sigma(0, 2, 4, 7)$$

Implement the circuit with a PLA having three inputs, four product terms, and two outputs.

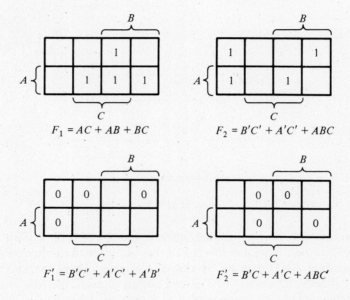

PLA program table

	Product term	Inputs			Output	
		A	B	C	F_1	F_2
$B'C'$	1	—	0	0	1	1
$A'C'$	2	0	—	0	1	1
$A'B'$	3	0	0	—	1	—
ABC	4	1	1	1	—	1
					C	T	T/C

Figure 5-28 Solution to Example 5-6

The two functions are simplified in the maps of Fig. 5-28. Both the true values and the complements of the functions are simplified. The combinations that gives a minimum number of product terms are:

$$F_1 = (B'C' + A'C' + A'B')'$$
$$F_2 = B'C' + A'C' + ABC$$

This gives only four distinct product terms: $B'C'$, $A'C'$, $A'B'$, and ABC. The PLA program table for this combination is shown in Fig. 5-28. Note that output F_1 is the normal (or true) output even though a C is marked under it. This is because F_1' is generated *prior to* the output inverter. The inverter complements the function to produce F_1 in the output.

The combinational circuit for this example is too small for practical implementation with a PLA. It was presented here merely for demonstration purposes. A typical commercial PLA would have over 10 inputs and about 50 product terms. The simplification of Boolean functions with so many variables should be carried out by means of a tabulation method or other computer-assisted simplification method. This is where a computer program may aid in the design of complex digital systems. The computer program should simplify each function of the combinational circuit and its complement to a minimum number of terms. The program then selects a minimum number of distinct terms that cover all functions in their true or complement form.

5-9 CONCLUDING REMARKS

This chapter presented a variety of design methods for combinational circuits. It also presented and explained a number of MSI and LSI circuits that can be used when designing more complicated digital systems. The emphasis here was on combinational logic MSI and LSI functions. Sequential logic MSI functions are discussed in Chapter 7. Processor and control MSI and LSI functions are presented in Chapters 9 and 10. Microcomputer LSI components are introduced in Chapter 12.

The MSI functions presented here and others available commercially are described in data books or catalogs. IC data books contain exact descriptions of many MSI and other integrated circuits. Some of these data books are listed in the following References.

MSI and LSI circuits can be used in a variety of applications. Some of these applications were discussed throughout the chapter, some are included in Problems, and others will be found in succeeding chapters in conjunction with their particular applications. Resourceful designers may find many other applications to suit their particular needs. Manufacturers of integrated circuits publish numerous *application notes* to suggest possible utilization of their products. A list of available application notes can be obtained by writing to manufacturers directly or by inquiring of their local representatives.

REFERENCES

1. Mano, M. M., *Computer System Architecture*. Englewood Cliffs, N. J.: Prentice-Hall, Inc., 1976.

2. Morris, R. L., and J. R. Miller, eds., *Designing with TTL Integrated Circuits*. New York: McGraw-Hill Book Co., 1971.

3. Blakeslee, T. R., *Digital Design with Standard MSI and LSI*. New York: John Wiley & Sons, 1975.

4. Barna A., and D. I. Porat, *Integrated Circuits in Digital Electronics*. New York: John Wiley & Sons, 1973.

5. Lee, S. C., *Digital Circuits and Logic Design*, Englewood Cliffs, N. J.: Prentice-Hall, Inc., 1976.

6. Semiconductor Manufacturers Data Books (Consult latest edition):
   (a) *The TTL Data Book for Design Engineers*. Dallas, Texas: Texas Instruments, Inc.
   (b) *The Fairchild Semiconductor TTL Data Book*. Mountain View, Calif.: Fairchild Semiconductor.
   (c) *Digital Integrated Circuits*. Santa Clara, Calif.: National Semiconductor Corp.
   (d) *Signetics Digital, Linear, MOS*. Sunnyvale, Calif.: Signetics.
   (e) *MECL Integrated Circuits Data Book*. Phoenix, Ariz.: Motorola Semiconductor Products, Inc.
   (f) *RCA Solid State Data Book Series*. Somerville, N. J.: RCA Solid State Div.

PROBLEMS

5-1. Design an excess-3-to-BCD code converter using a 4-bit full-adders MSI circuit.

5-2. Using four MSI circuits, construct a binary parallel adder to add two 16-bit binary numbers. Label all carries between the MSI circuits.

5-3. Using 4 exclusive-OR gates and a 4-bit full-adders MSI circuit, construct a 4-bit parallel adder/subtractor. Use an input select variable V so that when $V = 0$, the circuit adds and when $V = 1$, the circuit subtracts. (*Hint*: Use 2's complement subtraction.)

5-4. Derive the two-level equation for the output carry C_5 shown in the look-ahead carry generator of Fig. 5-5.

5-5. (a) Using the AND-OR-INVERT implementation procedure described in Section

3-7, show that the output carry in a full-adder circuit can be expressed as:

$$C_{i+1} = G_i + P_iC_i = (G_i'P_i' + G_i'C_i')'$$

(b) IC type 74182 is a look-ahead carry generator MSI circuit that generates the carries with AND-OR-INVERT gates. The MSI circuit assumes that the input terminals have the complements of the G's, the P's, and of C_1. Derive the Boolean functions for the look-ahead carries C_2, C_3, and C_4 in this IC. (*Hint*: Use the equation-substitution method to derive the carries in terms of C_1'.)

5-6. (a) Redefine the carry propagate and carry generate as follows:

$$P_i = A_i + B_i$$
$$G_i = A_iB_i$$

Show that the output carry and output sum of a full-adder becomes:

$$C_{i+1} = (C_i'G_i' + P_i')' = G_i + P_iC_i$$
$$S_i = (P_iG_i') \oplus C_i$$

(b) The logic diagram of the first stage of a 4-bit parallel adder as implemented in IC type 74283 is shown in Fig. P5-6. Identify the P_i' and G_i' terminals as defined in (a) and show that the circuit implements a full-adder circuit.

(c) Obtain the output carries C_3 and C_4 as a function of P_1', P_2', P_3', G_1', G_2', G_3', and C_1' in AND-OR-INVERT form, and draw the two-level look-ahead circuit for this IC. [*Hint*: Use the equation-substitution method as done in the text when deriving Fig. 5-4, but use the AND-OR-INVERT function given in (a) for C_{i+1}.]

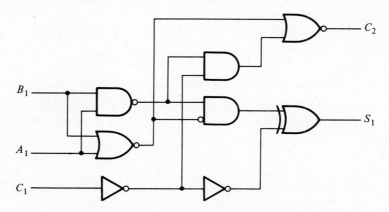

Figure P5-6 First stage of a parallel adder

5-7. (a) Assume that the exclusive-OR gate has a propagation delay of 20 ns and that the AND or OR gates have a propagation delay of 10 ns. What is the total propagation delay time in the 4-bit adder of Fig. 5-5?

(b) Assume that C_5 is propagated in the box of Fig. 5-5 at the same time as the other carries (see problem 5-4). What will be the propagation delay time of the 16-bit adder of problem 5-2?

5-8. Design a binary multiplier that multiplies a 4-bit number $B = b_3b_2b_1b_0$ by a 3-bit number $A = a_2a_1a_0$ to form the product $C = c_6c_5c_4c_3c_2c_1c_0$. This can be done with 12 gates and two 4-bit parallel adders. The AND gates are used to form the products of pairs of bits. For example, the product of a_0 and b_0 can be generated by ANDing a_0 with b_0. The partial products formed by the AND gates are summed with the parallel adders.

5-9. How many don't-care inputs are there in a BCD adder?

5-10. Design a combinational circuit that generates the 9's complement of a BCD digit.

5-11. Design a decimal arithmetic unit with two selection variables, V_1 and V_0, and two BCD digits, A and B. The unit should have four arithmetic operations which depend on the values of the selection variables as shown below.

V_1	V_0	Output function
0	0	A + 9's complement of B
0	1	$A + B$
1	0	A + 10's complement of B
1	1	$A + 1$ (add 1 to A)

Use MSI functions in the design and the 9's complementer of problem 5-10.

5-12. It is necessary to design a decimal adder for two digits represented in the excess-3 code (Table 1-2). Show that the correction after adding the two digits with a 4-bit binary adder is as follows:

(a) The output carry is equal to the carry out of the binary adder.

(b) If output carry = 1, add 0011.

(c) If output carry = 0, add 1101.

Construct the adder with two 4-bit binary adders and an inverter.

5-13. Design a circuit that compares two 4-bit numbers, A and B, to check if they are equal. The circuit has one output x, so that $x = 1$ if $A = B$, and $x = 0$ if $A \neq B$.

5-14. The 74L85 IC is a 4-bit magnitude comparator similar to that in Fig. 5-7, except that it has three more inputs and internal circuits that perform the equivalent logic as shown in Fig. P5-14. With these ICs, numbers of greater length may be compared by connecting comparators in cascade. The $A < B$, $A > B$, and $A = B$ outputs of a stage handling less-significant bits are connected to the corresponding $A < B$, $A > B$, and $A = B$ inputs of the next stage handling more-significant bits. The stage that handles the least-significant bits must be a circuit as shown in Fig. 5-7. If the 74L85 IC is used, a 1 must be applied to the $A = B$ input and a 0 to the $A < B$ and $A > B$ inputs in the IC that handles the four least-significant bits. Using one circuit as in Fig. 5-7 and one 74L85 IC, obtain a circuit to compare two 8-bit numbers. Justify the circuit operation.

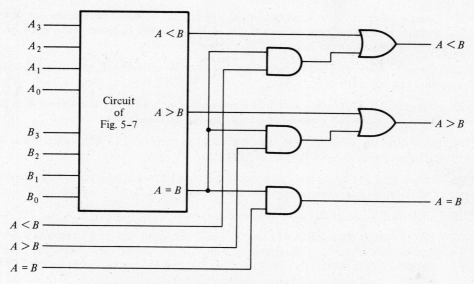

Figure P5-14 Logically equivalent circuit of IC type 74L85

5-15. Modify the BCD-to-decimal decoder of Fig. 5-10 to give an output of all 0's when any invalid input combination occurs.

5-16. Design a BCD-to-excess-3 code converter with a BCD-to-decimal decoder and four OR gates.

5-17. A combinational circuit is defined by the following three functions:

$$F_1 = x'y' + xyz'$$
$$F_2 = x' + y$$
$$F_3 = xy + x'y'$$

Design the circuit with a decoder and external gates.

5-18. A combinational circuit is defined by the following two functions:

$$F_1(x, y) = \Sigma(0, 3)$$
$$F_2(x, y) = \Sigma(1, 2, 3)$$

Implement the combinational circuit by means of the decoder shown in Fig. 5-12 and external NAND gates.

5-19. Construct a 5×32 decoder with four 3×8 decoder/demultiplexers and a 2×4 decoder. Use a block diagram construction as in Fig. 5-14.

5-20. Draw the logic diagram of a 2-line to 4-line decoder/demultiplexer using NOR gates only.

5-21.   Specify the truth table of an octal-to-binary priority encoder. Provide an output to indicate if at least one of the inputs is a 1. The table can be listed with 9 rows, and some of the inputs will have don't-care values.

5-22.   Design a 4-line to 2-line priority encoder. Include an output E to indicate that at least one input is a 1.

5-23.   Implement the Boolean function of Example 5-4 with an 8×1 multiplexer with A, B, and D connected to selection lines s_2, s_1, and s_0, respectively.

5-24.   Implement the combinational circuit specified in problem 5-17 with a dual 4-line to 1-line multiplexers, an OR gate, and inverter.

5-25.   Obtain an 8×1 multiplexer with a dual 4-line to 1-line multiplexers having separate enable inputs but common selection lines. Use a block diagram construction.

5-26.   Implement a full-adder circuit with multiplexers.

5-27.   The 32×6 ROM together with the 2^0 line as shown in Fig. P5-27 converts a 6-bit binary number to its corresponding 2-digit BCD number. For example, binary 100001 converts to BCD 011 0011 (decimal 33). Specify the truth table for the ROM.

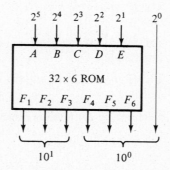

Figure P5-27   Binary-to-decimal converter

5-28.   Prove that a 32×8 ROM can be used to implement a circuit that generates the binary square of an input 5-bit number with $B_0 = A_0$ and $B_1 = 0$ as in Fig. 5-24(a). Draw a block diagram of the circuit and list the first four and the last four entries of the ROM truth table.

5-29.   What size ROM would it take to implement:
   (a) A BCD adder/subtractor with a control input to select between the addition and subtraction.
   (b) A binary multiplier that multiplies two 4-bit numbers.
   (c) Dual 4-line to 1-line multiplexers with common selection inputs.

5-30.   Each output inverter in the PLA of Fig. 5-26 is replaced by an exclusive-OR gate. Each exclusive-OR gate has two inputs. One input is connected to the output of the

OR gate, and the other input is connected through links to a signal equivalent to either 0 or 1. Show how to select the true/complement output in this configuration.

5-31.   Derive the PLA program table for a combinational circuit that squares a 3-bit number. Minimize the number of product terms. (See Fig. 5-24 for the equivalent ROM implementation.)

5-32.   List the PLA program table for the BCD-to-excess-3 code converter defined in Section 4-5.

Sequential
Logic

6

The digital circuits considered thus far have been combinational, i.e., the outputs at any instant of time are entirely dependent upon the inputs present at that time. Although every digital system is likely to have combinational circuits, most systems encountered in practice also include memory elements, which require that the system be described in terms of *sequential logic*.

A block diagram of a sequential circuit is shown in Fig. 6-1. It consists of a combinational circuit to which memory elements are connected to form a feedback path. The memory elements are devices capable of storing binary information within them. The binary information stored in the memory elements at any given time defines the *state* of the sequential circuit. The sequential circuit receives binary information from external inputs. These inputs, together with the present state of the memory elements, determine the binary value at the output terminals. They also determine the condition for changing the state in the memory elements. The block diagram demonstrates that the external outputs in a sequential circuit are a function not only of external inputs but also of the present state of the memory elements. The next state of the memory elements is also a function of external inputs and the present state. Thus, a sequential circuit is specified by a time sequence of inputs, outputs, and internal states.

There are two main types of sequential circuits. Their classification depends on the timing of their signals. A *synchronous* sequential circuit is a system whose behavior can be defined from the knowledge of its signals at discrete instants of time. The behavior of an *asynchronous* sequential circuit depends upon the order in which its input signals change and can be affected at any instant of time. The memory elements commonly used in asynchronous sequential circuits are time-delay devices. The memory capability of a time-delay device is due to the fact that it takes a finite time for the signal to propagate through the device. In practice, the internal propagation delay of logic gates is of sufficient duration to produce the

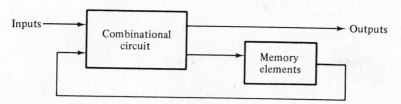

Figure 6-1 Block diagram of a sequential circuit

needed delay, so that physical time-delay units may be unnecessary. In gate-type asynchronous systems, the memory elements of Fig. 6-1 consist of logic gates whose propagation delays constitute the required memory. Thus, an asynchronous sequential circuit may be regarded as a combinational circuit with feedback. Because of the feedback among logic gates, an asynchronous sequential circuit may, at times, become unstable. The instability problem imposes many difficulties on the designer. Hence they are not as commonly used as synchronous systems.

A synchronous sequential logic system, by definition, must employ signals that affect the memory elements only at discrete instants of time. One way of achieving this goal is to use pulses of limited duration throughout the system so that one pulse amplitude represents logic-1 and another pulse amplitude (or the absence of a pulse) represents logic-0. The difficulty with a system of pulses is that any two pulses arriving from separate independent sources to the inputs of the same gate will exhibit unpredictable delays, will separate the pulses slightly, and will result in unreliable operation.

Practical synchronous sequential logic systems use fixed amplitudes such as voltage levels for the binary signals. Synchronization is achieved by a timing device called a *master-clock generator* which generates a periodic train of *clock pulses*. The clock pulses are distributed throughout the system in such a way that memory elements are affected only with the arrival of the synchronization pulse. In practice, the clock pulses are applied into AND gates together with the signals that specify the required change in memory elements. The AND gate outputs can transmit signals only at instants which coincide with the arrival of clock pulses. Synchronous sequential circuits that use clock pulses in the inputs of memory elements are called *clocked sequential circuits*. Clocked sequential circuits are the type encountered most frequently. They do not manifest instability problems and their timing is easily broken down into independent discrete steps, each of which is considered separately. The sequential circuits discussed in this book are exclusively of the clocked type.

The memory elements used in clocked sequential circuits are called *flip-flops*. These circuits are binary cells capable of storing one bit of information. A flip-flop circuit has two outputs, one for the normal value and one for the complement value of the bit stored in it. Binary information can enter a flip-flop in a variety of ways, a fact which gives rise to different types of flip-flops. In the next section we examine the various types of flip-flops and define their logical properties.

6-2 FLIP-FLOPS

A flip-flop circuit can maintain a binary state indefinitely (as long as power is delivered to the circuit) until directed by an input signal to switch states. The major differences among various types of flip-flops are in the number of inputs they possess and in the manner in which the inputs affect the binary state. The most common types of flip-flops are discussed below.

Basic Flip-Flop Circuit

It was mentioned in Sections 4-7 and 4-8 that a flip-flop circuit can be constructed from two NAND gates or two NOR gates. These constructions are shown in the logic diagrams of Figs. 6-2 and 6-3. Each circuit forms a basic flip-flop upon which other more complicated types can be built. The cross-coupled connection from the output of one gate to the input of the other gate constitutes a feedback path. For this reason, the circuits are classified as asynchronous sequential circuits. Each flip-flop has two outputs, Q and Q', and two inputs, *set* and *reset*. This type of flip-flop is sometimes called a *direct-coupled RS* flip-flop or *SR latch*. The R and S are the first letters of the two input names.

  To analyze the operation of the circuit of Fig. 6-2, we must remember that the output of a NOR gate is 0 if any input is 1, and that the output is 1 only when all inputs are 0. As a starting point, assume that the set input is 1 and the reset input is 0. Since gate 2 has an input of 1, its output Q' must be 0, which puts both inputs of gate 1 at 0, so that output Q is 1. When the set input is returned to 0, the outputs remain the same, because output Q remains a 1, leaving one input of gate 2 at 1. That causes output Q' to stay at 0, which leaves both inputs of gate number 1 at 0, so that output Q is a 1. In the same manner it is possible to show that a 1 in the reset input changes output Q to 0 and Q' to 1. When the reset input returns to 0, the outputs do not change.

  When a 1 is applied to both the set and the reset inputs, both Q and Q' outputs go to 0. This condition violates the fact that outputs Q and Q' are the complements of each other. In normal operation this condition must be avoided by making sure that 1's are not applied to both inputs simultaneously.

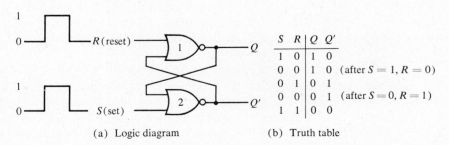

(a) Logic diagram

(b) Truth table

S	R	Q	Q'	
1	0	1	0	
0	0	1	0	(after $S = 1, R = 0$)
0	1	0	1	
0	0	0	1	(after $S = 0, R = 1$)
1	1	0	0	

Figure 6-2 Basic flip-flop circuit with NOR gates

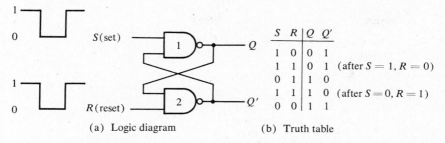

S	R	Q	Q'	
1	0	0	1	
1	1	0	1	(after $S = 1, R = 0$)
0	1	1	0	
1	1	1	0	(after $S = 0, R = 1$)
0	0	1	1	

(a) Logic diagram   (b) Truth table

Figure 6-3   Basic flip-flop circuit with NAND gates

A flip-flop has two useful states. When $Q = 1$ and $Q' = 0$, it is in the *set state* (or 1-state). When $Q = 0$ and $Q' = 1$, it is in the *clear state* (or 0-state). The outputs Q and Q' are complements of each other and are referred to as the normal and complement outputs, respectively. The binary state of the flip-flop is taken to be the value of the normal output.

Under normal operation, both inputs remain at 0 unless the state of the flip-flop has to be changed. The application of a momentary 1 to the set input causes the flip-flop to go to the set state. The set input must go back to 0 before a 1 is applied to the reset input. A momentary 1 applied to the reset input causes the flip-flop to go the clear state. When both inputs are initially 0, a 1 applied to the set input while the flip-flop is in the set state or a 1 applied to the reset input while the flip-flop is in the clear state leaves the outputs unchanged. When a 1 is applied to both the set and the reset inputs, both outputs go to 0. This state is undefined and is usually avoided. If both inputs now go to 0, the state of the flip-flop is indeterminate and depends on which input remains a 1 longer before the transition to 0.

The NAND basic flip-flop circuit of Fig. 6-3 operates with both inputs normally at 1 unless the state of the flip-flop has to be changed. The application of a momentary 0 to the set input causes output Q to go to 1 and Q' to go to 0, thus putting the flip-flop into the set state. After the set input returns to 1, a momentary 0 to the reset input causes a transition to the clear state. When both inputs go to 0, both outputs go to 1—a condition avoided in normal flip-flop operation.

Clocked *RS* Flip-Flop

The basic flip-flop as it stands is an asynchronous sequential circuit. By adding gates to the inputs of the basic circuit, the flip-flop can be made to respond to input levels during the occurrence of a clock pulse. The clocked *RS* flip-flop shown in Fig. 6-4(a) consists of a basic NOR flip-flop and two AND gates. The outputs of the two AND gates remain at 0 as long as the clock pulse (abbreviated *CP*) is 0, regardless of the *S* and *R* input values. When the clock pulse goes to 1, information from the *S* and *R* inputs is allowed to reach the basic flip-flop. The set state is reached with $S = 1$, $R = 0$, and $CP = 1$. To change to the clear state, the

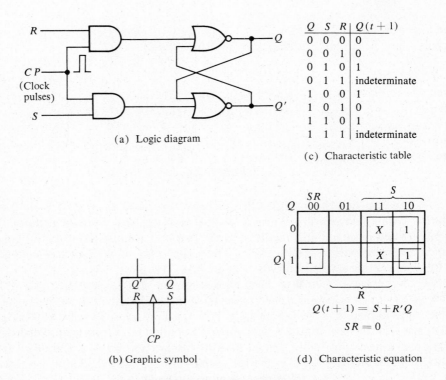

Q	S	R	Q(t+1)
0	0	0	0
0	0	1	0
0	1	0	1
0	1	1	indeterminate
1	0	0	1
1	0	1	0
1	1	0	1
1	1	1	indeterminate

(c) Characteristic table

(a) Logic diagram

(b) Graphic symbol

$$Q(t+1) = S + R'Q$$
$$SR = 0$$

(d) Characteristic equation

Figure 6-4 Clocked *RS* flip-flop

inputs must be $S = 0$, $R = 1$, and $CP = 1$. With both $S = 1$ and $R = 1$, the occurrence of a clock pulse causes both outputs to momentarily go to 0. When the pulse is removed, the state of the flip-flop is indeterminate, i.e., either state may result, depending on whether the set or the reset input of the basic flip-flop remains a 1 longer before the transition to 0 at the end of the pulse.

The graphic symbol for the clocked *RS* flip-flop is shown in Fig. 6-4(b). It has three inputs: *S*, *R*, and *CP*. The *CP* input is not written within the box because it is recognized from the marked small triangle. The triangle is a symbol for a *dynamic indicator* and denotes the fact that the flip-flop responds to an input clock *transition* from a low-level (binary 0) to a high-level (binary 1) signal. The outputs of the flip-flop are marked with *Q* and *Q' within* the box. The flip-flop can be assigned a different variable name even though *Q* is written inside the box. In that case the letter chosen for the flip-flop variable is marked *outside* the box along the output line. The state of the flip-flop is determined from the value of its normal output *Q*. If one wishes to obtain the complement of the normal output, it is not necessary to insert an inverter, because the complemented value is available directly from output *Q'*.

The characteristic table for the flip-flop is shown in Fig. 6-4(c). This table summarizes the operation of the flip-flop in a tabular form. *Q* is the binary state of the flip-flop at a given time (referred to as *present state*), the *S* and *R* columns give the possible values of the inputs, and $Q(t + 1)$ is the state of the flip-flop after the occurrence of a clock pulse (referred to as *next state*).

The characteristic equation of the flip-flop is derived in the map of Fig. 6-4(d). This equation specifies the value of the next state as a function of the present state and the inputs. The characteristic equation is an algebraic expression for the binary information of the characteristic table. The two indeterminate states are marked by X's in the map, since they may result in either a 1 or a 0. However, the relation $SR = 0$ must be included as part of the characteristic equation to specify that both S and R cannot equal 1 simultaneously.

D Flip-Flop

The D flip-flop shown in Fig. 6-5 is a modification of the clocked RS flip-flop. NAND gates 1 and 2 form a basic flip-flop and gates 3 and 4 modify it into a clocked RS flip-flop. The D input goes directly to the S input, and its complement, through gate 5, is applied to the R input. As long as the clock pulse input is at 0, gates 3 and 4 have a 1 in their outputs, regardless of the value of the other inputs. This conforms to the requirement that the two inputs of a basic NAND flip-flop (Fig. 6-3) remain initially at the 1 level. The D input is sampled during the occurrence of a clock pulse. If it is 1, the output of gate 3 goes to 0, switching the flip-flop to the set state (unless it was already set). If it is 0, the output of gate 4 goes to 0, switching the flip-flop to the clear state.

The D flip-flop receives the designation from its ability to transfer "data" into a flip-flop. It is basically an RS flip-flop with an inverter in the R input. The

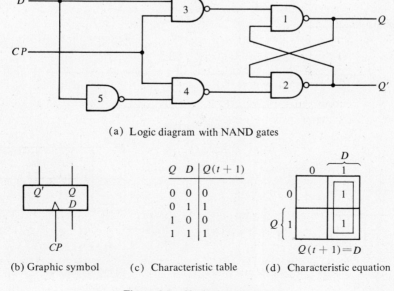

(a) Logic diagram with NAND gates

Q	D	$Q(t+1)$
0	0	0
0	1	1
1	0	0
1	1	1

(b) Graphic symbol   (c) Characteristic table   (d) Characteristic equation

$$Q(t+1) = D$$

Figure 6-5   Clocked D flip-flop

added inverter reduces the number of inputs from two to one. This type of flip-flop is sometimes called a *gated D-latch*. The *CP* input is often given the variable designation *G* (for *gate*) to indicate that this input enables the gated latch to make possible the data entry into the flip-flop.

The symbol for a clocked *D* flip-flop is shown in Fig. 6-5(b). The characteristic table is listed in part (c) and the characteristic equation is derived in part (d). The characteristic equation shows that the next state of the flip-flop is the same as the *D* input and is independent of the value of the present state.

JK Flip-Flop

A *JK* flip-flop is a refinement of the *RS* flip-flop in that the indeterminate state of the *RS* type is defined in the *JK* type. Inputs *J* and *K* behave like inputs *S* and *R* to set and clear the flip-flop (note that in a *JK* flip-flop, the letter *J* is for *set* and the letter *K* is for *clear*). When inputs are applied to both *J* and *K* simultaneously, the flip-flop switches to its complement state, that is, if $Q = 1$, it switches to $Q = 0$, and vice versa.

A clocked *JK* flip-flop is shown in Fig. 6-6(a). Output *Q* is ANDed with *K* and *CP* inputs so that the flip-flop is cleared during a clock pulse only if *Q* was previously 1. Similarly, output Q' is ANDed with *J* and *CP* inputs so that the flip-flop is set with a clock pulse only if Q' was previously 1.

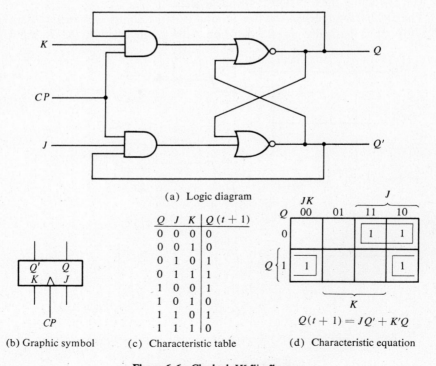

(a) Logic diagram

Characteristic table:

Q	J	K	Q(t+1)
0	0	0	0
0	0	1	0
0	1	0	1
0	1	1	1
1	0	0	1
1	0	1	0
1	1	0	1
1	1	1	0

$$Q(t+1) = JQ' + K'Q$$

(b) Graphic symbol   (c) Characteristic table   (d) Characteristic equation

Figure 6-6   Clocked *JK* flip-flop

As shown in the characteristic table in Fig. 6-6(c), the *JK* flip-flop behaves like an *RS* flip-flop, except when both *J* and *K* are equal to 1. When both *J* and *K* are 1, the clock pulse is transmitted through one AND gate only—the one whose input is connected to the flip-flop output which is presently equal to 1. Thus, if $Q = 1$, the output of the upper AND gate becomes 1 upon application of a clock pulse, and the flip-flop is cleared. If $Q' = 1$, the output of the lower AND gate becomes a 1 and the flip-flop is set. In either case, the output state of the flip-flop is complemented.

The inputs in the graphic symbol for the *JK* flip-flop must be marked with a *J* (under *Q*) and *K* (under *Q'*). The characteristic equation is given in Fig. 6-4(d) and is derived from the map of the characteristic table.

Note that because of the feedback connection in the *JK* flip-flop, a *CP* signal which remains a 1 (while $J = K = 1$) after the outputs have been complemented once will cause repeated and continuous transitions of the outputs. To avoid this undesirable operation, the clock pulses must have a time duration which is shorter than the propagation delay through the flip-flop. This is a restrictive requirement, since the operation of the circuit depends on the width of the pulses. For this reason, *JK* flip-flops are never constructed as shown in Fig. 6-6(a). The restriction on the pulse width can be eliminated with a master-slave or edge-triggered construction, as discussed in the next section. The same reasoning applies to the *T* flip-flop presented below.

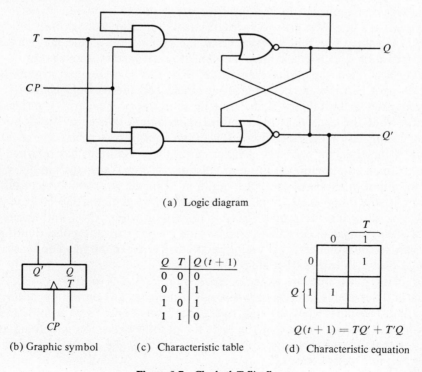

(a) Logic diagram

(b) Graphic symbol

Q	T	Q(t + 1)
0	0	0
0	1	1
1	0	1
1	1	0

(c) Characteristic table

$$Q(t + 1) = TQ' + T'Q$$

(d) Characteristic equation

Figure 6-7 Clocked *T* flip-flop

T Flip-Flop

The T flip-flop is a single-input version of the JK flip-flop. As shown in Fig. 6-7(a), the T flip-flop is obtained from a JK type if both inputs are tied together. The designation T comes from the ability of the flip-flop to "toggle," or change state. Regardless of the present state of the flip-flop, it assumes the complement state when the clock pulse occurs while input T is logic-1. The symbol, characteristic table, and characteristic equation of the T flip-flop are shown in Fig. 6-7, parts (b), (c), and (d), respectively.

The flip-flops introduced in this section are the most common types available commercially. The analysis and design procedures developed in this chapter are applicable for any clocked flip-flop once its characteristic table is defined.

6-3 TRIGGERING OF FLIP-FLOPS

The state of a flip-flop is switched by a momentary change in the input signal. This momentary change is called a *trigger* and the transition it causes is said to trigger the flip-flop. Asynchronous flip-flops, such as the basic circuits of Figs. 6-2 and 6-3, require an input trigger defined by a change of signal *level*. This level must be returned to its initial value (0 in the NOR and 1 in the NAND flip-flop) before a second trigger is applied. Clocked flip-flops are triggered by *pulses*. A pulse starts from an initial value of 0, goes momentarily to 1, and after a short time, returns to its initial 0 value. The time interval from the application of the pulse until the output transition occurs is a critical factor that needs further investigation.

As seen from the block diagram of Fig. 6-1, a sequential circuit has a feedback path between the combinational circuit and the memory elements. This path can produce instability if the outputs of memory elements (flip-flops) are changing while the outputs of the combinational circuit that go to flip-flop inputs are being sampled by the clock pulse. This timing problem can be prevented if the outputs of flip-flops do not start changing until the pulse input has returned to 0. To ensure such an operation, a flip-flop must have a signal propagation delay from input to output in excess of the pulse duration. This delay is usually very difficult to control if the designer depends entirely on the propagation delay of logic gates. One way of ensuring the proper delay is to include within the flip-flop circuit a physical delay unit having a delay equal to or greater than the pulse duration. A better way to solve the feedback timing problem is to make the flip-flop sensitive to the pulse *transition* rather than the pulse duration.

A clock pulse may be either positive or negative. A positive clock source remains at 0 during the interval between pulses and goes to 1 during the occurrence of a pulse. The pulse goes through two signal transitions: from 0 to 1 and the return from 1 to 0. As shown in Fig. 6-8, the positive transition is defined as the *positive edge* and the negative transition as the *negative edge*. This definition applies also to negative pulses.

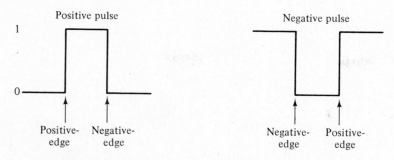

Figure 6-8 Definition of clock pulse transition

The clocked flip-flops introduced in Section 6-2 are triggered during the positive edge of the pulse, and the state transition starts as soon as the pulse reaches the logic-1 level. The new state of the flip-flop may appear at the output terminals while the input pulse is still 1. If the other inputs of the flip-flop change while the clock is still 1, the flip-flop will start responding to these new values and a new output state may occur. When this happens, the output of one flip-flop cannot be applied to the inputs of another flip-flop when both are triggered by the same clock pulse. However, if we can make the flip-flop respond to the positive (or negative) edge transition *only*, instead of the entire pulse duration, then the multiple-transition problem can be eliminated.

One way to make the flip-flop respond only to a pulse transition is to use capacitive coupling. In this configuration, an *RC* (resistor-capacitor) circuit is inserted in the clock input of the flip-flop. This circuit generates a spike in response to a momentary change of input signal. A positive edge emerges from such a circuit with a positive spike, and a negative edge emerges with a negative spike. Edge triggering is achieved by designing the flip-flop to neglect one spike and trigger on the occurrence of the other spike. Another way to achieve edge triggering is to use a master-slave or edge-triggered flip-flop as discussed below.

Master-Slave Flip-Flop

A master-slave flip-flop is constructed from two separate flip-flops. One circuit serves as a master and the other as a slave, and the overall circuit is referred to as a *master-slave flip-flop*. The logic diagram of an *RS* master-slave flip-flop is shown in Fig. 6-9. It consists of a master flip-flop, a slave flip-flop, and an inverter. When clock pulse *CP* is 0, the output of the inverter is 1. Since the clock input of the slave is 1, the flip-flop is enabled and output Q is equal to Y, while Q' is equal to Y'. The master flip-flop is disabled because $CP = 0$. When the pulse becomes 1, the information then at the external R and S inputs is transmitted to the master flip-flop. The slave flip-flop, however, is isolated as long as the pulse is at its 1 level, because the output of the inverter is 0. When the pulse returns to 0, the master flip-flop is isolated, which prevents the external inputs from affecting it. The slave flip-flop then goes to the same state as the master flip-flop.

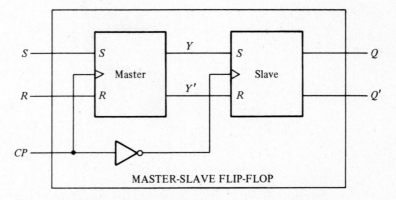

Figure 6-9 Logic diagram of master-slave flip-flop

The timing relationships shown in Fig. 6-10 illustrate the sequence of events that occur in a master-slave flip-flop. Assume that the flip-flop is in the clear state prior to the occurrence of a pulse, so that $Y = 0$ and $Q = 0$. The input conditions are $S = 1$, $R = 0$, and the next clock pulse should change the flip-flop to the set state with $Q = 1$. During the pulse transition from 0 to 1, the master flip-flop is set and changes Y to 1. The slave flip-flop is not affected because its CP input is 0. Since the master flip-flop is an internal circuit, its change of state is not noticeable in the outputs Q and Q'. When the pulse returns to 0, the information from the master is allowed to pass through to the slave, making the external output $Q = 1$. Note that the external S input can be changed at the same time that the pulse goes through its negative edge transition. This is because, once the CP reaches 0, the master is disabled and its R and S inputs have no influence until the next clock pulse occurs. Thus, in a master-slave flip-flop, it is possible to switch the output of the flip-flop and its input information with the same clock pulse. It must be realized that the S input could come from the output of another master-slave flip-flop that was switched with the same clock pulse.

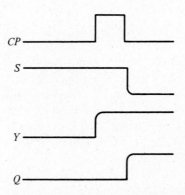

Figure 6-10 Timing relationships in a master-slave flip-flop

The behavior of the master-slave flip-flop just described dictates that the state changes in all flip-flops coincide with the negative edge transition of the pulse. However, some IC master-slave flip-flops change output states in the positive edge transition of clock pulses. This happens in flip-flops that have an additional inverter between the *CP* terminal and the input of the master. Such flip-flops are triggered with negative pulses (see Fig. 6-8), so that the negative edge of the pulse affects the master and the positive edge affects the slave and the output terminals.

The master-slave combination can be constructed for any type of flip-flop by adding a clocked *RS* flip-flop with an inverted clock to form the slave. An example of a master-slave *JK* flip-flop constructed with NAND gates is shown in Fig. 6-11. It consists of two flip-flops; gates 1 through 4 form the master flip-flop, and gates 5 through 8 form the slave flip-flop. The information present at the *J* and *K* inputs is transmitted to the master flip-flop on the positive edge of a clock pulse and is held there until the negative edge of the clock pulse occurs, after which it is allowed to pass through to the slave flip-flop. The clock input is normally 0, which keeps the outputs of gates 1 and 2 at the 1 level. This prevents the *J* and *K* inputs from affecting the master flip-flop. The slave flip-flop is a clocked *RS* type, with the master flip-flop supplying the inputs and the clock input being inverted by gate 9. When the clock is 0, the output of gate 9 is 1, so that output *Q* is equal to *Y*, and *Q'* is equal to *Y'*. When the positive edge of a clock pulse occurs, the master flip-flop is affected and may switch states. The slave flip-flop is isolated as long as the clock is at the 1 level, because the output of gate 9 provides a 1 to both inputs of the NAND basic flip-flop of gates 7 and 8. When the clock input returns to 0, the master flip-flop is isolated from the *J* and *K* inputs and the slave flip-flop goes to the same state as the master flip-flop.

Now consider a digital system containing many master-slave flip-flops, with the outputs of some flip-flops going to the inputs of other flip-flops. Assume that clock pulse inputs to all flip-flops are synchronized (occur at the same time). At the beginning of each clock pulse, some of the master elements change state, but all

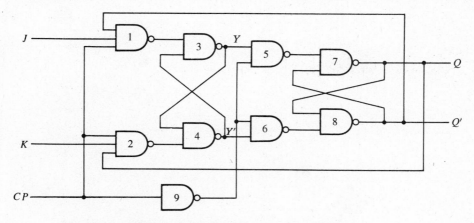

Figure 6-11 Clocked master-slave *JK* flip-flop

flip-flop outputs remain at their previous values. After the clock pulse returns to 0, some of the outputs change state, but none of these new states have an effect on any of the master elements until the next clock pulse. Thus the states of flip-flops in the system can be changed simultaneously during the same clock pulse, even though outputs of flip-flops are connected to inputs of flip-flops. This is possible because the new state appears at the output terminals only after the clock pulse has returned to 0. Therefore, the binary content of one flip-flop can be transferred to a second flip-flop and the content of the second transferred to the first, and both transfers can occur during the same clock pulse.

Edge-Triggered Flip-Flop

Another type of flip-flop that synchronizes the state changes during a clock pulse transition is the *edge-triggered* flip-flop. In this type of flip-flop, output transitions occur at a specific level of the clock pulse. When the pulse input level exceeds this threshold level, the inputs are locked out and the flip-flop is therefore unresponsive to further changes in inputs until the clock pulse returns to 0 and another pulse occurs. Some edge-triggered flip-flops cause a transition on the positive edge of the pulse, and others cause a transition on the negative edge of the pulse.

The logic diagram of a D-type positive-edge-triggered flip-flop is shown in Fig. 6-12. It consists of three basic flip-flops of the type shown in Fig. 6-3. NAND gates 1 and 2 make up one basic flip-flop and gates 3 and 4 another. The third basic flip-flop comprising gates 5 and 6 provides the outputs to the circuit. Inputs S and R of the third basic flip-flop must be maintained at logic-1 for the outputs to remain in their steady-state values. When $S = 0$ and $R = 1$, the output goes to the set state with $Q = 1$. When $S = 1$ and $R = 0$, the output goes to the clear state

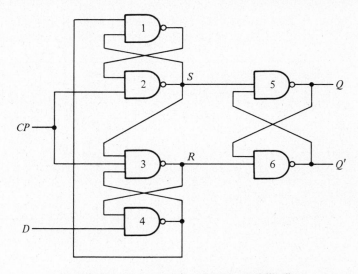

Figure 6-12 D-type positive-edge-triggered flip-flop

with $Q = 0$. Inputs S and R are determined from the states of the other two basic flip-flops. These two basic flip-flops respond to the external inputs D (data) and CP (clock pulse).

The operation of the circuit is explained in Fig. 6-13, where gates 1–4 are redrawn to show all possible transitions. Outputs S and R from gates 2 and 3 go to gates 5 and 6, as shown in Fig. 6-12, to provide the actual outputs of the flip-flop. Figure 6-13(a) shows the binary values at the outputs of the four gates when $CP = 0$. Input D may be equal to 0 or 1. In either case, a CP of 0 causes the outputs of gates 2 and 3 to go to 1, thus making $S = R = 1$, which is the condition for a steady-state output. When $D = 0$, gate 4 has a 1 output, which causes the

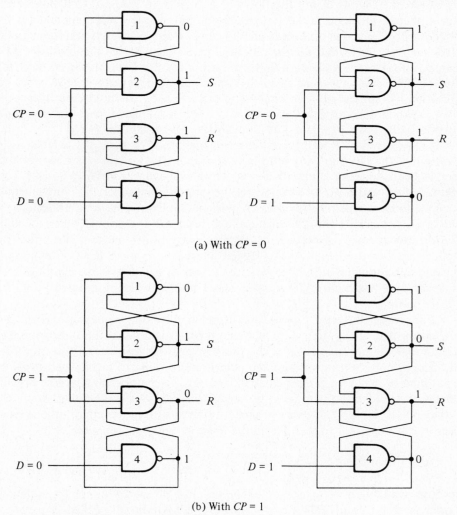

(a) With $CP = 0$

(b) With $CP = 1$

Figure 6-13 Operation of the D-type edge-triggered flip-flop

output of gate 1 to go to 0. When $D = 1$, gate 4 goes to 0, which causes the output of gate 1 to go to 1. These are the two possible conditions when the CP terminal, being 0, disables any changes at the outputs of the flip-flop, no matter what the value of D happens to be.

There is a definite time, called the *setup* time, in which the D input must be maintained at a constant value prior to the application of the pulse. The setup time is equal to the propagation delay through gates 4 and 1 since a change in D causes a change in the outputs of these two gates. Assume now that D does not change during the setup time and that input CP becomes 1. This situation is depicted in Fig. 6-13(b). If $D = 0$ when CP becomes 1, then S remains 1 but R changes to 0. This causes the output of the flip-flop Q to go to 0 (in Fig. 6-12). If now, while $CP = 1$, there is a change in the D input, the output of gate 4 will remain at 1 (even if D goes to 1), since one of the gate inputs comes from R which is maintained at 0. Only when CP returns to 0 can the output of gate 4 change; but then both R and S become 1, disabling any changes in the output of the flip-flop. However, there is a definite time, called the *hold time*, that the D input must not change after the application of the positive-going transition of the pulse. The hold time is equal to the propagation delay of gate 3, since it must be ensured that R becomes 0 in order to maintain the output of gate 4 at 1, regardless of the value of D.

If $D = 1$ when $CP = 1$, then S changes to 0 but R remains at 1, which causes the output of the flip-flop Q to go to 1. A change in D while $CP = 1$ does not alter S and R because gate 1 is maintained at 1 by the 0 signal from S. When CP goes to zero, both S and R go to 1 to prevent the output from undergoing any changes.

In summary, when the input clock pulse makes a positive-going transition, the value of D is transferred to Q. Changes in D when CP is maintained at a steady 1 value do not affect Q. Moreover, a negative pulse transition does not affect the output, nor does it when $CP = 0$. Hence, the edge-triggered flip-flop eliminates any feedback problems in sequential circuits just as a master-slave flip-flop does. The setup time and hold time must be taken into consideration when using this type of flip-flop.

When using different types of flip-flops in the same sequential circuit, one must ensure that all flip-flop outputs make their transitions at the same time, i.e., during either the negative edge or the positive edge of the pulse. Those flip-flops that behave opposite from the adopted polarity transition can be changed easily by the addition of inverters in their clock inputs. An alternate procedure is to provide both positive and negative pulses (by means of an inverter), and then apply the positive pulses to flip-flops that trigger during the negative edge and negative pulses to flip-flops that trigger during the positive edge, or vice versa.

Direct Inputs

Flip-flops available in IC packages sometimes provide special inputs for setting or clearing the flip-flop asynchronously. These inputs are usually called *direct preset* and *direct clear*. They affect the flip-flop on a positive (or negative) value of the

Function table

Inputs				Outputs	
Clear	Clock	J	K	Q	Q'
0	X	X	X	0	1
1	↓	0	0	No change	
1	↓	0	1	0	1
1	↓	1	0	1	0
1	↓	1	1	Toggle	

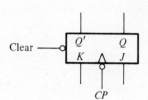

Figure 6-14 *JK* flip-flop with direct clear

input signal without the need for a clock pulse. These inputs are useful for bringing all flip-flops to an initial state prior to their clocked operation. For example, after power is turned on in a digital system, the states of its flip-flops are indeterminate. A *clear* switch clears all the flip-flops to an initial cleared state and a *start* switch begins the system's clocked operation. The clear switch must clear all flip-flops asynchronously without the need for a pulse.

The graphic symbol of a master-slave flip-flop with direct clear is shown in Fig. 6-14. The clock or *CP* input has a circle under the small triangle to indicate that the outputs change during the negative transition of the pulse. (The absence of the small circle would indicate a positive-edge-triggered flip-flop.) The direct clear input also has a small circle to indicate that, normally, this input must be maintained at 1. If the clear input is maintained at 0, the flip-flop remains cleared, regardless of the other inputs or the clock pulse. The function table specifies the circuit operation. The *X*'s are don't-care conditions which indicate that a 0 in the direct clear input disables all other inputs. Only when the clear input is 1 would a negative transition of the clock have an effect on the outputs. The outputs do not change if $J = K = 0$. The flip-flop toggles or complements when $J = K = 1$. Some flip-flops may also have a direct preset input which sets the output Q to 1 (and Q' to 0) asynchronously.

When direct asynchronous inputs are available in a master-slave flip-flop, they must connect to both the master and the slave in order to override the other inputs and the clock. A direct clear in the *JK* master-slave flip-flop of Fig. 6-10 is connected to the inputs of gates 1, 4, and 8. A direct clear in the *D* edge-triggered flip-flop of Fig. 6-12 is connected to the inputs of gates 2 and 6.

6-4 ANALYSIS OF CLOCKED SEQUENTIAL CIRCUITS

The behavior of a sequential circuit is determined from the inputs, the outputs, and the states of its flip-flops. Both the outputs and the next state are a function of the inputs and the present state. The analysis of sequential circuits consists of obtaining a table or a diagram for the time sequence of inputs, outputs, and internal states. It is also possible to write Boolean expressions that describe the behavior of sequential circuits. However, these expressions must include the necessary time sequence either directly or indirectly.

A logic diagram is recognized as the circuit of a sequential circuit if it includes flip-flops. The flip-flops may be of any type and the logic diagram may or may not include combinational gates. In this section, we first introduce a specific example of a clocked sequential circuit and then present various methods for describing the behavior of sequential circuits. The specific example will be used throughout the discussion to illustrate the various methods.

An Example of a Sequential Circuit

An example of a clocked sequential circuit is shown in Fig. 6-15. It has one input variable x, one output variable y, and two clocked RS flip-flops labeled A and B. The cross-connections from outputs of flip-flops to inputs of gates are not shown by line drawings so as to facilitate the tracing of the circuit. Instead, the connections are recognized from the letter symbol marked in each input. For example, the input marked x' in gate 1 designates an input from the complement of x. The second input marked A designates a connection to the normal output of flip-flop A.

We shall assume negative edge triggering in both flip-flops and in the source that produces the external input x. Therefore, the signals for a given present state are available during the time from the termination of a clock pulse to the termination of the next clock pulse, at which time the circuit goes to the next state.

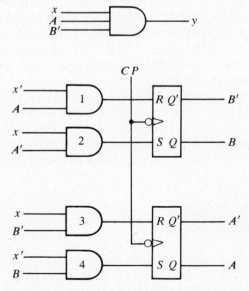

Figure 6-15 Example of a clocked sequential circuit

State Table

The time sequence of inputs, outputs, and flip-flop states may be enumerated in a *state table*.* The state table for the circuit of Fig. 6-15 is shown in Table 6-1. It consists of three sections labeled *present state*, *next state*, and *output*. The *present state* designates the states of flip-flops before the occurrence of a clock pulse. The *next state* shows the states of flip-flops after the application of a clock pulse, and the *output* section lists the values of the output variables during the present state. Both the next state and output sections have two columns, one for $x = 0$ and the other for $x = 1$.

TABLE 6-1 State table for circuit of Fig. 6-15

Present State	Next state		Output	
	$x = 0$	$x = 1$	$x = 0$	$x = 1$
AB	AB	AB	y	y
00	00	01	0	0
01	11	01	0	0
10	10	00	0	1
11	10	11	0	0

The derivation of the state table starts from an assumed initial state. The initial state of most practical sequential circuits is defined to be the state with 0's in all flip-flops. Some sequential circuits have a different initial state and some have none at all. In either case, the analysis can always start from any arbitrary state. In this example, we start deriving the state table from the initial state 00.

When the present state is 00, $A = 0$ and $B = 0$. From the logic diagram, we see that with both flip-flops cleared and $x = 0$, none of the AND gates produce a logic-1 signal. Therefore, the next state remains unchanged. With $AB = 00$ and $x = 1$, gate 2 produces a logic-1 signal at the S input of flip-flop B and gate 3 produces a logic-1 signal at the R input of flip-flop A. When a clock pulse triggers the flip-flops, A is cleared and B is set, making the next state 01. This information is listed in the first row of the state table.

In a similar manner, we can derive the next state starting from the other three possible present states. In general, the next state is a function of the inputs, the present state, and the type of flip-flop used. With RS flip-flops, for example, we must remember that a 1 in input S sets the flip-flop and a 1 in input R clears the flip-flop, regardless of its previous state. A 0 in both the S and R inputs leaves the

---

*Switching circuit theory books call this table a *transition table*. They reserve the name *state table* for a table with internal states represented by arbitrary symbols.

flip-flop unchanged, whereas a 1 in both the S and R inputs shows a bad design and an indeterminate state table.

The entries for the output section are easier to derive. In this example, output y is equal to 1 only when $x = 1$, $A = 1$, and $B = 0$. Therefore, the output columns are marked with 0's, except when the present state is 10 and input $x = 1$, for which y is marked with a 1.

The state table of any sequential circuit is obtained by the same procedure used in the example. In general, a sequential circuit with m flip-flops and n input variables will have 2^m rows, one for each state. The next state and output sections each will have 2^n columns, one for each input combination.

The external outputs of a sequential circuit may come from logic gates or from memory elements. The output section in the state table is necessary only if there are outputs from logic gates. Any external output taken directly from a flip-flop is already listed in the present state column of the state table. Therefore, the output section of the state table can be excluded if there are no external outputs from logic gates.

State Diagram

The information available in a state table may be represented graphically in a *state diagram*. In this diagram, a state is represented by a circle, and the transition between states is indicated by directed lines connecting the circles. The state diagram of the sequential circuit of Fig. 6-15 is shown in Fig. 6-16. The binary number inside each circle identifies the state the circle represents. The directed lines are labeled with two binary numbers separated by a /. The input value that causes the state transition is labeled first; the number after the symbol / gives the value of the output during the present state. For example, the directed line from state 00 to 01 is labeled 1/0, meaning that the sequential circuit is in a present state 00 while $x = 1$ and $y = 0$, and that on the termination of the next clock pulse, the

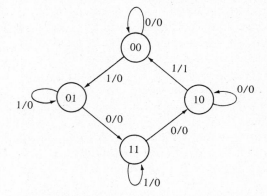

Figure 6-16 State diagram for the circuit of Fig. 6-15

circuit goes to next state 01. A directed line connecting a circle with itself indicates that no change of state occurs. The state diagram provides the same information as the state table and is obtained directly from Table 6-1.

There is no difference between a state table and a state diagram except in the manner of representation. The state table is easier to derive from a given logic diagram and the state diagram follows directly from a state table. The state diagram gives a pictorial view of state transitions and is in a form suitable for human interpretation of the circuit operation. The state diagram is often used as the initial design specification of a sequential circuit.

State Equations

A *state equation* (also known as an *application equation*) is an algebraic expression that specifies the conditions for a flip-flop state transition. The left side of the equation denotes the next state of a flip-flop and the right side, a Boolean function that specifies the present state conditions that make the next state equal to 1. A state equation is similar in form to a flip-flop characteristic equation, except that it specifies the next state conditions in terms of external input variables and other flip-flop values. The state equation is derived directly from a state table. For example, the state equation for flip-flop A is derived from inspection of Table 6-1. From the next state columns, we note that flip-flop A goes to the 1 state four times: when $x = 0$ and $AB = 01$ or 10 or 11, or when $x = 1$ and $AB = 11$. This can be expressed algebraically in a state equation as follows:

$$A(t + 1) = (A'B + AB' + AB)x' + ABx$$

The right-hand side of the state equation is a Boolean function for a *present state*. When this function is equal to 1, the occurrence of a clock pulse causes flip-flop A to have a next state of 1. When the function is equal to 0, the clock pulse causes A to have a next state of 0. The left side of the equation identifies the flip-flop by its letter symbol, followed by the time function designation $(t + 1)$, to emphasize that this value is to be reached by the flip-flop one pulse sequence later.

The state equation is a Boolean function with time included. It is applicable only in clock sequential circuits, since $A(t + 1)$ is defined to change value with the occurrence of a clock pulse at discrete instants of time.

The state equation for flip-flop A is simplified by means of a map as shown in Fig. 6-17(a). With some algebraic manipulation, the function can be expressed in the following form:

$$A(t + 1) = Bx' + (B'x)'A$$

If we let $Bx' = S$ and $B'x = R$, we obtain the relationship:

$$A(t + 1) = S + R'A$$

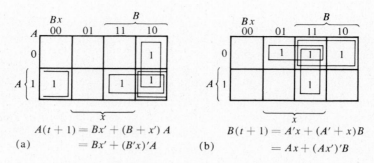

$$A(t+1) = Bx' + (B+x')A$$
$$= Bx' + (B'x)'A$$

(a)

$$B(t+1) = A'x + (A'+x)B$$
$$= Ax + (Ax')'B$$

(b)

Figure 6-17 State equations for flip-flops A and B

which is the characteristic equation of an RS flip-flop [Fig. 6-4(d)]. This relationship between the state equation and the flip-flop characteristic equation can be justified from inspection of the logic diagram of Fig. 6-15. In it we see that the S input of flip-flop A is equal to the Boolean function Bx' and the R input is equal to $B'x$. Substituting these functions into the flip-flop characteristic equation results in its state equation for this sequential circuit.

The state equation for a flip-flop in a sequential circuit may be derived from a state table or from a logic diagram. The derivation from the state table consists of obtaining the Boolean function specifying the conditions that make the next state of the flip-flop a 1. The derivation from a logic diagram consists of obtaining the functions of the flip-flop inputs and substituting them into the flip-flop characteristic equation.

The derivation of the state equation for flip-flop B from the state table is shown in the map of Fig. 6-17(b). The 1's marked in the map are the present state and input combinations that cause the flip-flop to go to a next state of 1. These conditions are obtained directly from Table 6-1. The simplified form obtained in the map is manipulated algebraically, and the state equation obtained is:

$$B(t + 1) = A'x + (Ax')'B$$

The state equation can be derived directly from the logic diagram. From Fig. 6-15, we see that the signal for input S of flip-flop B is generated by the function $A'x$ and the signal for input R by the function Ax'. Substituting $S = A'x$ and $R = Ax'$ into an RS flip-flop characteristic equation given by:

$$B(t + 1) = S + R'B$$

we obtain the state equation derived above.

The state equations of all flip-flops, together with the output functions, fully specify a sequential circuit. They represent, algebraically, the same information a state table represents in tabular form and a state diagram represents in graphical form.

222

Flip-flop Input Functions

The logic diagram of a sequential circuit consists of memory elements and gates. The type of flip-flops and their characteristic table specify the logical properties of the memory elements. The interconnections among the gates form a combinational circuit and may be specified algebraically with Boolean functions. Thus, knowledge of the type of flip-flops and a list of the Boolean functions of the combinational circuit provide all the information needed to draw the logic diagram of a sequential circuit. The part of the combinational circuit that generates external outputs is described algebraically by the *circuit output functions*. The part of the circuit that generates the inputs to flip-flops are described algebraically by a set of Boolean functions called *flip-flop input functions* or sometimes *input equations*.

We shall adopt the convention of using two letters to designate a flip-flop input variable: the first to designate the name of the input and the second the name of the flip-flop. As an example, consider the following flip-flop input functions:

$$JA = BC'x + B'Cx'$$
$$KA = B + y$$

JA and *KA* designate two Boolean variables. The first letter in each denotes the *J* and *K* input, respectively, of a *JK* flip-flop. The second letter *A* is the symbol name of the flip-flop. The right side of each equation is a Boolean function for the corresponding flip-flop input variable. The implementation of the two input functions is shown in the logic diagram of Fig. 6-18. The *JK* flip-flop has an output symbol *A* and two inputs labeled *J* and *K*. The combinational circuit drawn in the diagram is the implementation of the algebraic expression given by the input functions. The outputs of the combinational circuit are denoted by *JA* and *KA* in the input functions and go to the *J* and *K* inputs, respectively, of flip-flop *A*.

From this example, we see that a flip-flop input function is an algebraic expression for a combinational circuit. The two-letter designation is a variable

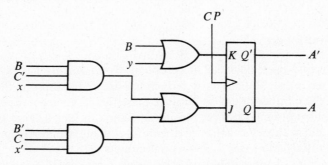

Figure 6-18 Implementation of the flip-flop input functions
$JA = BC'x + B'Cx'$ and $KA = B + y$

name for an *output* of the combinational circuit. This output is always connected to the *input* (designated by the first letter) of a flip-flop (designated by the second letter).

The sequential circuit of Fig. 6-15 has one input x, one output y, and two RS flip-flops denoted by A and B. The logic diagram can be expressed algebraically with four flip-flop input functions and one circuit output function as follows:

$$SA = Bx' \qquad RA = B'x$$
$$SB = A'x \qquad RB = Ax'$$
$$y = AB'x$$

This set of Boolean functions fully specifies the logic diagram. Variables SA and RA specify an RS flip-flop labeled A; variables SB and RB specify a second RS flip-flop labeled B. Variable y denotes the output. The Boolean expressions for the variables specify the combinational circuit part of the sequential circuit.

The flip-flop input functions constitute a convenient algebraic form for specifying a logic diagram of a sequential circuit. They imply the type of flip-flop from the first letter of the input variable and they fully specify the combinational circuit that drives the flip-flop. Time is not included explicitly in these equations but is implied from the clock pulse operation. It is sometimes convenient to specify a sequential circuit algebraically with circuit output functions and flip-flop input functions instead of drawing the logic diagram.

6-5 STATE REDUCTION AND ASSIGNMENT*

The analysis of sequential circuits starts from a circuit diagram and culminates in a state table or diagram. The design of a sequential circuit starts from a set of specifications and culminates in a logic diagram. Design procedures are presented starting from Section 6-7. This section discusses certain properties of sequential circuits that may be used to reduce the number of gates and flip-flops during the design.

State Reduction

Any design process must consider the problem of minimizing the cost of the final circuit. The two most obvious cost reductions are reductions in the number of flip-flops and the number of gates. Because these two items seem the most obvious, they have been extensively studied and investigated. In fact, a large portion of the subject of switching theory is concerned with finding algorithms for minimizing the number of flip-flops and gates in sequential circuits.

The reduction of the number of flip-flops in a sequential circuit is referred to as the *state reduction* problem. State reduction algorithms are concerned with

---

*This section may be omitted without loss of continuity.

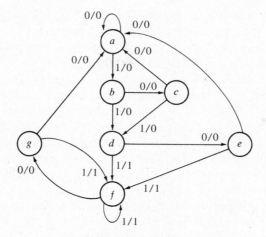

Figure 6-19 State diagram

procedures for reducing the number of states in a state table while keeping the external input-output requirements unchanged. Since m flip-flops produce 2^m states, a reduction in the number of states may (or may not) result in a reduction in the number of flip-flops. An unpredictable effect in reducing the number of flip-flops is that sometimes the equivalent circuit (with less flip-flops) may require more combinational gates.

We shall illustrate the need for state reduction with an example. We start with a sequential circuit whose specification is given in the state diagram of Fig. 6-19. In this example, only the input-output sequences are important; the internal states are used merely to provide the required sequences. For this reason, the states marked inside the circles are denoted by letter symbols instead of by their binary values. This is in contrast to a binary counter, where the binary value sequence of the states themselves are taken as the outputs.

There are an infinite number of input sequences that may be applied to the circuit; each results in a unique output sequence. As an example, consider the input sequence 01010110100 starting from the initial state a. Each input of 0 or 1 produces an output of 0 or 1 and causes the circuit to go to the next state. From the state diagram, we obtain the output and state sequence for the given input sequence as follows: With the circuit in initial state a, an input of 0 produces an output of 0 and the circuit remains in state a. With present state a and input of 1, the output is 0 and the next state is b. With present state b and input of 0, the output is 0 and next state is c. Continuing this process, we find the complete sequence to be as follows:

state	a	a	b	c	d	e	f	f	g	f	g	a
input	0	1	0	1	0	1	1	0	1	0	0	
output	0	0	0	0	0	1	1	0	1	0	0	

225

In each column, we have the present state, input value, and output value. The next state is written on top of the next column. It is important to realize that in this circuit the states themselves are of secondary importance because we are interested only in output sequences caused by input sequences.

Now let us assume that we have found a sequential circuit whose state diagram has less than seven states and we wish to compare it with the circuit whose state diagram is given by Fig. 6-19. If identical input sequences are applied to the two circuits and identical outputs occur for all input sequences, then the two circuits are said to be equivalent (as far as the input-output is concerned) and one may be replaced by the other. The problem of state reduction is to find ways of reducing the number of states in a sequential circuit without altering the input-output relationships.

We shall now proceed to reduce the number of states for this example. First, we need the state table; it is more convenient to apply procedures for state reduction here than in state diagrams. The state table of the circuit is listed in Table 6-2 and is obtained directly from the state diagram of Fig. 6-19.

TABLE 6-2   State table

Present state	Next state		Output	
	$x = 0$	$x = 1$	$x = 0$	$x = 1$
a	a	b	0	0
b	c	d	0	0
c	a	d	0	0
d	e	f	0	1
e	a	f	0	1
f	g	f	0	1
g	a	f	0	1

An algorithm for the state reduction of a completely specified state table is given here without proof: "Two states are said to be equivalent if, for each member of the set of inputs, they give exactly the same output and send the circuit either to the same state or to an equivalent state. When two states are equivalent, one of them can be removed without altering the input-output relationships."

We shall apply this algorithm to Table 6-2. Going through the state table, we look for two present states that go to the same next state and have the same output for both input combinations. States g and e are two such states; they both go to states a and f and have outputs of 0 and 1 for $x = 0$ and $x = 1$, respectively. Therefore, states g and e are equivalent; one can be removed. The procedure of removing a state and replacing it by its equivalent is demonstrated in Table 6-3. The row with present state g is crossed out and state g is replaced by state e each time it occurs in the next state columns.

TABLE 6-3   Reducing the state table

Present state	Next state		Output	
	$x = 0$	$x = 1$	$x = 0$	$x = 1$
a	a	b	0	0
b	c	d	0	0
c	a	d	0	0
d	e	$\not{f}\,d$	0	1
e	a	$\not{f}\,d$	0	1
$\not{f}$	$\not{g}\,e$	f	0	1
$\not{g}$	a	f	0	1

Present state f now has next states e and f and outputs 0 and 1 for $x = 0$ and $x = 1$, respectively. The same next states and outputs appear in the row with present state d. Therefore, states f and d are equivalent; state f can be removed and replaced by d. The final reduced table is shown in Table 6-4. The state diagram for the reduced table consists of only five states and is shown in Fig. 6-20. This state diagram satisfies the original input-output specifications and will produce the required output sequence for any given input sequence. The following list derived from the state diagram of Fig. 6-20 is for the input sequence used previously. We note that the same output sequence results although the state sequence is different:

state	a	a	b	c	d	e	d	d	e	d	e	a
input	0	1	0	1	0	1	1	0	1	0	0	
output	0	0	0	0	0	1	1	0	1	0	0	

In fact, this sequence is exactly the same as that obtained for Fig. 6-19, if we replace e by g and d by f.

TABLE 6-4   Reduced state table

Present state	Next state		Output	
	$x = 0$	$x = 1$	$x = 0$	$x = 1$
a	a	b	0	0
b	c	d	0	0
c	a	d	0	0
d	e	d	0	1
e	a	d	0	1

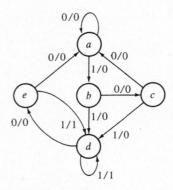

Figure 6-20 Reduced state diagram

It is worth noting that the reduction in the number of states of a sequential circuit is possible if one is interested only in external input-output relationships. When external outputs are taken directly from flip-flops, the outputs must be independent of the number of states before state reduction algorithms are applied.

The sequential circuit of this example was reduced from seven to five states. In either case, the representation of the states with physical components requires that we use three flip-flops, because m flip-flops can represent up to 2^m distinct states. With three flip-flops, we can formulate up to eight binary states denoted by binary numbers 000 through 111, with each bit designating the state of one flip-flop. If the state table of Table 6-2 is used, we must assign binary values to seven states; the remaining state is unused. If the state table of Table 6-4 is used, only five states need binary assignment, and we are left with three unused states. Unused states are treated as don't-care conditions during the design of the circuit. Since don't-care conditions usually help in obtaining a simpler Boolean function, it is more likely that the circuit with five states will require fewer combinational gates than the one with seven states. In any case, the reduction from seven to five states does not reduce the number of flip-flops. In general, reducing the number of states in a state table is likely to result in a circuit with less equipment. However, the fact that a state table has been reduced to fewer states does not guarantee a saving in the number of flip-flops or the number of gates.

State Assignment

The cost of the combinational circuit part of a sequential circuit can be reduced by using the known simplification methods for combinational circuits. However, there is another factor, known as the *state assignment* problem, that comes into play in minimizing the combinational gates. State assignment procedures are concerned with methods for assigning binary values to states in such a way as to reduce the cost of the combinational circuit that drives the flip-flops. This is particularly helpful when a sequential circuit is viewed from its external input-output terminals. Such a circuit may follow a sequence of internal states, but the binary values of the

TABLE 6-5 Three possible binary state assignments

State	Assignment 1	Assignment 2	Assignment 3
a	001	000	000
b	010	010	100
c	011	011	010
d	100	101	101
e	101	111	011

TABLE 6-6 Reduced state table with binary assignment 1

Present state	Next state		Output	
	$x = 0$	$x = 1$	$x = 0$	$x = 1$
001	001	010	0	0
010	011	100	0	0
011	001	100	0	0
100	101	100	0	1
101	001	100	0	1

individual states may be of no consequence as long as the circuit produces the required sequence of outputs for any given sequence of inputs. This does not apply to circuits whose external outputs are taken directly from flip-flops with binary sequences fully specified.

The binary state assignment alternatives available can be demonstrated in conjunction with the sequential circuit specified in Table 6-4. Remember that, in this example, the binary values of the states are immaterial as long as their sequence maintains the proper input-output relationships. For this reason, any binary number assignment is satisfactory as long as each state is assigned a unique number. Three examples of possible binary assignments are shown in Table 6-5 for the five states of the reduced table. Assignment 1 is a straight binary assignment for the sequence of states from a through e. The other two assignments are chosen arbitrarily. In fact, there are 140 different distinct assignments for this circuit (11).

Table 6-6 is the reduced state table with binary assignment 1 substituted for the letter symbols of the five states.* It is obvious that a different binary assignment will result in a state table with different binary values for the states, while the input-output relationships remain the same. The binary form of the state table is used to derive the combinational circuit part of the sequential circuit. The complexity of the combinational circuit obtained depends on the binary state assignment chosen. The design of the sequential circuit presented in this section is completed in Example 6-1 of Section 6-7.

*A state table with binary assignment is sometimes called a *transition table*.

Various procedures have been suggested that lead to a particular binary assignment from the many available. The most common criterion is that the chosen assignment should result in a simple combinational circuit for the flip-flop inputs. However, to date, there are no state assignment procedures that guarantee a minimal-cost combinational circuit. State assignment is one of the challenging problems of switching theory. The interested reader will find a rich and growing literature on this topic. Techniques for dealing with the state assignment problem are beyond the scope of this book.

6-6 FLIP-FLOP EXCITATION TABLES

The characteristic tables for the various flip-flops were presented in Section 6-2. A characteristic table defines the logical property of the flip-flop and completely characterizes its operation. Integrated-circuit flip-flops are sometimes defined by a characteristic table tabulated somewhat differently. This second form of the characteristic tables for RS, JK, D, and T flip-flops is shown in Table 6-7. They represent the same information as the characteristic tables of Figs. 6-4(c) through 6-7(c).

Table 6-7 defines the state of each flip-flop as a function of its inputs and previous state. $Q(t)$ refers to the present state and $Q(t + 1)$ to the next state after the occurrence of a clock pulse. The characteristic table for the RS flip-flop shows that the next state is equal to the present state when inputs S and R are both 0. When the R input is equal to 1, the next clock pulse clears the flip-flop. When the S input is equal to 1, the next clock pulse sets the flip-flop. The question mark for the next state when S and R are both equal to 1 simultaneously designates an indeterminate next state.

TABLE 6-7   Flip-flop characteristic tables

S	R	$Q(t + 1)$
0	0	$Q(t)$
0	1	0
1	0	1
1	1	?

(a) RS

J	K	$Q(t + 1)$
0	0	$Q(t)$
0	1	0
1	0	1
1	1	$Q'(t)$

(b) JK

D	$Q(t + 1)$
0	0
1	1

(c) D

T	$Q(t + 1)$
0	$Q(t)$
1	$Q'(t)$

(d) T

The table for the *JK* flip-flop is the same as that for the *RS* when *J* and *K* are replaced by *S* and *R*, respectively, except for the indeterminate case. When both *J* and *K* are equal to 1, the next state is equal to the complement of the present state, i.e., $Q(t + 1) = Q'(t)$. The next state of the *D* flip-flop is completely dependent on the input *D* and independent of the present state. The next state of the *T* flip-flop is the same as the present state if $T = 0$ and complemented if $T = 1$.

The characteristic table is useful for analysis and for defining the operation of the flip-flop. It specifies the next state when the inputs and present state are known. During the design process we usually know the transition from present state to next state and wish to find the flip-flop input conditions that will cause the required transition. For this reason, we need a table that lists the required inputs for a given change of state. Such a list is called an *excitation table*.

Table 6-8 presents the excitation tables for the four flip-flops. Each table consists of two columns, $Q(t)$ and $Q(t + 1)$, and a column for each input to show how the required transition is achieved. There are four possible transitions from present state to next state. The required input conditions for each of the four transitions are derived from the information available in the characteristic table. The symbol *X* in the tables represents a don't-care condition, i.e., it does not matter whether the input is 1 or 0.

RS Flip-flop

The excitation table for the *RS* flip-flop is shown in Table 6-8(a). The first row shows the flip-flop in the 0-state at time *t*. It is desired to leave it in the 0-state after the occurrence of the pulse. From the characteristic table, we find that if *S*

TABLE 6-8   Flip-flop excitation tables

$Q(t)$	$Q(t + 1)$	S	R
0	0	0	X
0	1	1	0
1	0	0	1
1	1	X	0

(a) *RS*

$Q(t)$	$Q(t + 1)$	J	K
0	0	0	X
0	1	1	X
1	0	X	1
1	1	X	0

(b) *JK*

$Q(t)$	$Q(t + 1)$	D
0	0	0
0	1	1
1	0	0
1	1	1

(c) *D*

$Q(t)$	$Q(t + 1)$	T
0	0	0
0	1	1
1	0	1
1	1	0

(d) *T*

and R are both 0, the flip-flop will not change state. Therefore, both S and R inputs should be 0. However, it really doesn't matter if R is made a 1 when the pulse occurs, since it results in leaving the flip-flop in the 0-state. Thus, R can be 1 or 0 and the flip-flop will remain in the 0-state at $t + 1$. Therefore, the entry under R is marked by the don't-care condition X.

If the flip-flop is in the 0-state and it is desired to have it go to the 1-state, then from the characteristic table, we find that the only way to make $Q(t + 1)$ equal to 1 is to make $S = 1$ and $R = 0$. If the flip-flop is to have a transition from the 1-state to the 0-state, we must have $S = 0$ and $R = 1$.

The last condition that may occur is for the flip-flop to be in the 1-state and remain in the 1-state. Certainly R must be 0; we do not want to clear the flip-flop. However, S may be either a 0 or a 1. If it is 0, the flip-flop does not change and remains in the 1-state; if it is 1, it sets the flip-flop to the 1-state as desired. Therefore, S is listed as a don't-care condition.

JK Flip-Flop

The excitation table for the JK flip-flop is shown in Table 6-8(b). When both present state and next state are 0, the J input must remain at 0 and the K input can be either 0 or 1. Similarly, when both present state and next state are 1, the K input must remain at 0 while the J input can be 0 or 1. If the flip-flop is to have a transition from the 0-state to the 1-state, J must be equal to 1 since the J input sets the flip-flop. However, input K may be either 0 or a 1. If $K = 0$, the $J = 1$ condition sets the flip-flop as required; if $K = 1$ and $J = 1$, the flip-flop is complemented and goes from the 0-state to the 1-state as required. Therefore the K input is marked with a don't-care condition for the 0-to-1 transition. For a transition from the 1-state to the 0-state, we must have $K = 1$, since the K input clears the flip-flop. However, the J input may be either 0 or 1, since $J = 0$ has no effect, and $J = 1$ together with $K = 1$ complements the flip-flop with a resultant transition from the 1-state to the 0-state.

The excitation table for the JK flip-flop illustrates the advantage of using this type when designing sequential circuits. The fact that it has so many don't-care conditions indicates that the combinational circuits for the input functions are likely to be simpler because don't-care terms usually simplify a function.

D Flip-Flop

The excitation table for the D flip-flop is shown in Table 6-8(c). From the characteristic table, Table 6-7(c), we note that the next state is always equal to the D input and independent of the present state. Therefore, D must be 0 if $Q(t + 1)$ has to be 0, and 1 if $Q(t + 1)$ has to be 1, regardless of the value of $Q(t)$.

T Flip-Flop

The excitation table for the T flip-flop is shown in Table 6-8(d). From the characteristic table, Table 6-7(d), we find that when input $T = 1$, the state of the flip-flop is complemented; when $T = 0$, the state of the flip-flop remains unchanged. Therefore, when the state of the flip-flop must remain the same, the requirement is that $T = 0$. When the state of the flip-flop has to be complemented, T must equal 1.

Other Flip-Flops

The design procedure to be described in this chapter can be used with any flip-flop. It is necessary that the flip-flop characteristic table, from which it is possible to develop a new excitation table, be known. The excitation table is then used to determine the flip-flop input functions, as explained in the next section.

6-7 DESIGN PROCEDURE

The design of a clocked sequential circuit starts from a set of specifications and culminates in a logic diagram or a list of Boolean functions from which the logic diagram can be obtained. In contrast to a combinational circuit, which is fully specified by a truth table, a sequential circuit requires a state table for its specification. The first step in the design of sequential circuits is to obtain a state table or an equivalent representation, such as a state diagram or state equations.

A synchronous sequential circuit is made up of flip-flops and combinational gates. The design of the circuit consists of choosing the flip-flops and then finding a combinational gate structure which, together with the flip-flops, produces a circuit that fulfills the stated specifications. The number of flip-flops is determined from the number of states needed in the circuit. The combinational circuit is derived from the state table by methods presented in this chapter. In fact, once the type and number of flip-flops are determined, the design process involves a transformation from the sequential circuit problem into a combinational circuit problem. In this way the techniques of combinational circuit design can be applied.

This section presents a procedure for the design of sequential circuits. Although intended to serve as a guide for the beginner, this procedure can be shortened with experience. The procedure is first summarized by a list of consecutive recommended steps as follows:

1. The word description of the circuit behavior is stated. This may be accompanied by a state diagram, a timing diagram, or other pertinent information.

2. From the given information about the circuit, obtain the state table.

3. The number of states may be reduced by state reduction methods if the sequential circuit can be characterized by input-output relationships independent of the number of states.

4. Assign binary values to each state if the state table obtained in step 2 or 3 contains letter symbols.

5. Determine the number of flip-flops needed and assign a letter symbol to each.

6. Choose the type of flip-flop to be used.

7. From the state table, derive the circuit excitation and output tables.

8. Using the map or any other simplification method, derive the circuit output functions and the flip-flop input functions.

9. Draw the logic diagram.

The word specification of the circuit behavior usually assumes that the reader is familiar with digital logic terminology. It is necessary that the designer use intuition and experience to arrive at the correct interpretation of the circuit specifications, because word descriptions may be incomplete and inexact. However, once such a specification has been set down and the state table obtained, it is possible to make use of the formal procedure to design the circuit.

The reduction of the number of states and the assignment of binary values to the states were discussed in Section 6-5. The examples that follow assume that the number of states and the binary assignment for the states are known. As a consequence, steps 3 and 4 of the design will not be considered in subsequent discussions.

It has already been mentioned that the number of flip-flops is determined from the number of states. A circuit may have unused binary states if the total number of states is less than 2^m. The unused states are taken as don't-care conditions during the design of the combinational circuit part of the circuit.

The type of flip-flop to be used may be included in the design specifications or may depend on what is available to the designer. Many digital systems are constructed entirely with JK flip-flops because they are the most versatile available. When many types of flip-flops are available, it is advisable to use the RS or D flip-flop for applications requiring transfer of data (such as shift registers), the T type for applications involving complementation (such as binary counters), and the JK type for general applications.

The external output information is specified in the output section of the state table. From it we can derive the circuit output functions. The excitation table for the circuit is similar to that of the individual flip-flops, except that the input conditions are dictated by the information available in the present state and next state columns of the state table. The method of obtaining the excitation table and the simplified flip-flop input functions is best illustrated by an example.

We wish to design the clocked sequential circuit whose state diagram is given in Fig. 6-21. The type of flip-flop to be used is JK.

The state diagram consists of four states with binary values already assigned. Since the directed lines are marked with a single binary digit without a $/$, we conclude that there is one input variable and no output variables. (The state of the flip-flops may be considered the outputs of the circuit.) The two flip-flops needed to represent the four states are designated A and B. The input variable is designated x.

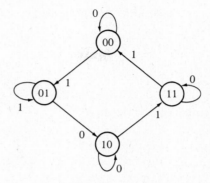

Figure 6-21 State diagram

The state table for this circuit, derived from the state diagram, is shown in Table 6-9. Note that there is no output section for this circuit. We shall now show the procedure for obtaining the excitation table and the combinational gate structure.

The derivation of the excitation table is facilitated if we arrange the state table in a different form. This form is shown in Table 6-10, where the present state and input variables are arranged in the form of a truth table. The next state value for each present state and input conditions is copied from Table 6-9. The excitation table of a circuit is a list of flip-flop input conditions that will cause the required state transitions and is a function of the type of flip-flop used. Since this example specified JK flip-flops, we need columns for the J and K inputs of flip-flops A (denoted by JA and KA) and B (denoted by JB and KB).

The excitation table for the JK flip-flop was derived in Table 6-8(b). This table is now used to derive the excitation table of the circuit. For example, in the first row of Table 6-10 we have a transition for flip-flop A from 0 in the present state to 0 in the next state. In Table 6-8(b) we find that a transition of states from 0 to 0 requires that input $J = 0$ and input $K = X$. So 0 and X are copied in the first row under JA and KA, respectively. Since the first row also shows a transition for flip-flop B from 0 in the present state to 0 in the next state, 0 and X are copied

TABLE 6-9 State table

Present state		Next state			
		$x = 0$		$x = 1$	
A	B	A	B	A	B
0	0	0	0	0	1
0	1	1	0	0	1
1	0	1	0	1	1
1	1	1	1	0	0

TABLE 6-10   Excitation table

Inputs of combinational circuit			Next state		Outputs of combinational circuit			
Present state		Input			Flip-flop inputs			
A	B	x	A	B	JA	KA	JB	KB
0	0	0	0	0	0	X	0	X
0	0	1	0	1	0	X	1	X
0	1	0	1	0	1	X	X	1
0	1	1	0	1	0	X	X	0
1	0	0	1	0	X	0	0	X
1	0	1	1	1	X	0	1	X
1	1	0	1	1	X	0	X	0
1	1	1	0	0	X	1	X	1

in the first row under JB and KB. The second row of Table 6-10 shows a transition for flip-flop B from 0 in the present state to 1 in the next state. From Table 6-8(b) we find that a transition from 0 to 1 requires that input $J = 1$ and input $K = X$. So 1 and X are copied in the second row under JB and KB, respectively. This process is continued for each row of the table and for each flip-flop, with the input conditions as specified in Table 6-8(b) being copied into the proper row of the particular flip-flop being considered.

Let us now pause and consider the information available in an excitation table such as Table 6-10. We know that a sequential circuit consists of a number of flip-flops and a combinational circuit. Figure 6-22 shows the two JK flip-flops needed for the circuit and a box to represent the combinational circuit. From the block diagram, it is clear that the outputs of the combinational circuit go to flip-flop inputs and external outputs (if specified). The inputs to the combinational circuit are the external inputs and the present state values of the flip-flops. Moreover, the Boolean functions that specify a combinational circuit are derived from a truth table that shows the input-output relations of the circuit. The truth table that describes the combinational circuit is available in the excitation table. The combinational circuit *inputs* are specified under the present state and input columns, and the combinational circuit *outputs* are specified under the flip-flop input columns. Thus, an excitation table transforms a state diagram to the truth table needed for the design of the combinational circuit part of the sequential circuit.

The simplified Boolean functions for the combinational circuit can now be derived. The inputs are the variables A, B, and x; the outputs are the variables JA, KA, JB, and KB. The information from the truth table is transferred into the maps

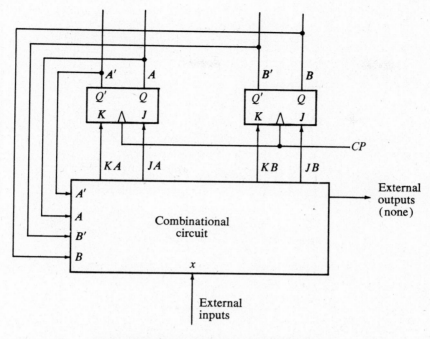

Figure 6-22 Block diagram of sequential circuit

of Fig. 6-23, where the four simplified flip-flop input functions are derived:

$$JA = Bx' \qquad KA = Bx$$
$$JB = x \qquad KB = A \odot x$$

The logic diagram is drawn in Fig. 6-24 and consists of two flip-flops, two AND gates, one equivalence gate, and one inverter.

  With some experience, it is possible to reduce the amount of work involved in the design of the combinational circuit. For example, it is possible to obtain the information for the maps of Fig. 6-23 directly from Table 6-9, without having to derive Table 6-10. This is done by systematically going through each present state and input combination in Table 6-9 and comparing it with the binary values of the corresponding next state. The required input conditions as specified by the flip-flop excitation in Table 6-8 is then determined. Instead of inserting the 0, 1, or X thus obtained into the excitation table, it can be written down directly into the appropriate square of the appropriate map.

  The excitation table of a sequential circuit with m flip-flops, k inputs per flip-flop, and n external inputs consists of $m + n$ columns for the present state and input variables and up to 2^{m+n} rows listed in some convenient binary count. The next state section has m columns, one for each flip-flop. The flip-flop input values are listed in mk columns, one for each input of each flip-flop. If the circuit contains j outputs, the table must include j columns. The truth table of the

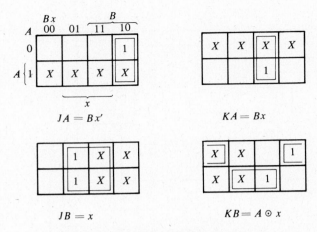

$$JA = Bx'$$

$$KA = Bx$$

$$JB = x$$

$$KB = A \odot x$$

Figure 6-23 Maps for combinational circuit

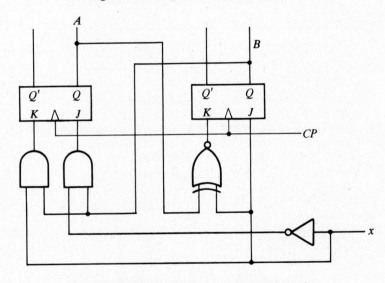

Figure 6-24 Logic diagram of sequential circuit

combinational circuit is taken from the excitation table by considering the $m + n$ present state and input columns as *inputs* and the $mk + j$ flip-flop input values and external outputs as *outputs*.

Design with Unused States

A circuit with m flip-flops would have 2^m states. There are occasions when a sequential circuit may use less than this maximum number of states. States that are not used in specifying the sequential circuit are not listed in the state table. When simplifying the input functions to flip-flops, the unused states can be treated as don't-care conditions.

TABLE 6-11 Excitation table for Example 6-1

Present state			Input	Next state			Flip-flop inputs						Output
A	B	C	x	A	B	C	SA	RA	SB	RB	SC	RC	y
0	0	1	0	0	0	1	0	X	0	X	X	0	0
0	0	1	1	0	1	0	0	X	1	0	0	1	0
0	1	0	0	0	1	1	0	X	X	0	1	0	0
0	1	0	1	1	0	0	1	0	0	1	0	X	0
0	1	1	0	0	0	1	0	X	0	1	X	0	0
0	1	1	1	1	0	0	1	0	0	1	0	1	0
1	0	0	0	1	0	1	X	0	0	X	1	0	0
1	0	0	1	1	0	0	X	0	0	X	0	X	1
1	0	1	0	0	0	1	0	1	0	X	X	0	0
1	0	1	1	1	0	0	X	0	0	X	0	1	1

EXAMPLE 6-1: Complete the design of the sequential circuit presented in Section 6-5. Use the reduced state table with assignment 1 as given in Table 6-6. The circuit is to employ *RS* flip-flops.

The state table of Table 6-6 is redrawn in Table 6-11 in the form convenient for obtaining the excitation table. The flip-flop input conditions are derived from the present state and next state columns of the state table. Since *RS* flip-flops are used, we need to refer to Table 6-8(a) for the excitation conditions of this type of flip-flop. The three flip-flops are given variable names *A*, *B*, and *C*. The input variable is *x* and the output variable is *y*. The excitation table of the circuit provides all the information needed for the design.

There are three unused states in this circuit: binary states 000, 110, and 111. When an input of 0 or 1 is included with these unused states, we obtain six don't-care minterms: 0, 1, 12, 13, 14, and 15. These six binary combinations are not listed in the table under present state and input and are treated as don't-care terms.

The combinational circuit part of the sequential circuit is simplified in the maps of Fig. 6-25. There are seven maps in the diagram. Six maps are for simplifying the input functions for the three *RS* flip-flops. The seventh map is for simplifying the output *y*. Each map has six *X*'s in the squares of the don't-care minterms 0, 1, 2, 13, 14, and 15. The other don't-care terms in the maps come from the *X*'s in the flip-flop input columns of the table. The simplified functions are listed under each map. The logic diagram obtained from these Boolean functions is drawn in Fig. 6-26.

One factor neglected up to this point in the design is the initial state of a sequential circuit. When power is first turned on in a digital system, one does not

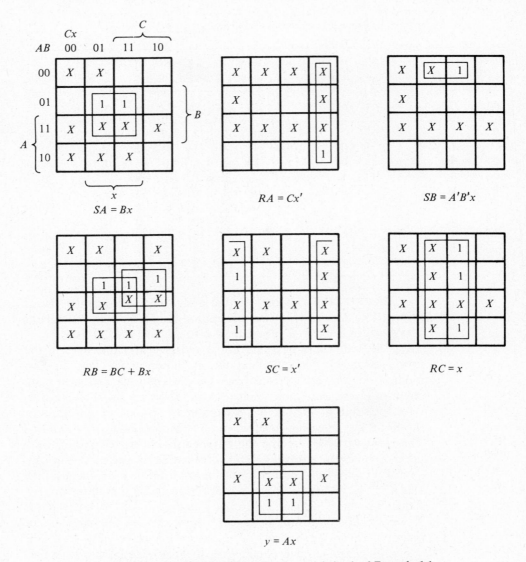

Figure 6-25 Maps for simplifying the sequential circuit of Example 6-1

know in what state the flip-flops will settle. It is customary to provide a *master-re-set* input whose purpose is to initialize the states of all flip-flops in the system. Typically, the master reset is a signal applied to all flip-flops asynchronously before the clocked operations start. In most cases flip-flops are cleared to 0 by the master-reset signal, but some may be set to 1. For example, the circuit of Fig. 6-26 may initially be reset to a state $ABC = 001$, since state 000 is not a valid state for this circuit.

But what if a circuit is not reset to an initial valid state? Or worse, what if, because of a noise signal or any other unforeseen reason, the circuit finds itself in

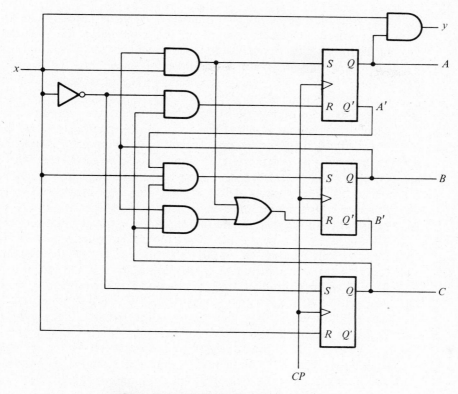

Figure 6-26 Logic diagram for Example 6-1

one of its invalid states? In that case it is necessary to ensure that the circuit eventually goes into one of the valid states so it can resume normal operation. Otherwise, if the sequential circuit circulates among invalid states, there will be no way to bring it back to its intended sequence of state transitions. Although one can assume that this undesirable condition is not supposed to occur, a careful designer must ensure that this situation never occurs.

It was stated previously that unused states in a sequential circuit can be treated as don't-care conditions. Once the circuit is designed, the m flip-flops in the system can be in any one of 2^m possible states. If some of these states were taken as don't-care conditions, the circuit must be investigated to determine the effect of these unused states. The next state from invalid states can be determined from the analysis of the circuit. In any case, it is always wise to analyze a circuit obtained from a design to ensure that no mistakes were made during the design process.

> **EXAMPLE 6-2:** Analyze the sequential circuit obtained in Example 6-1 and determine the effect of the unused states.
>
> The unused states are 000, 110, and 111. The analysis of the circuit is done by the method outlined in Section 6-4. The maps of

Fig. 6-25 may also help in the analysis. What is needed here is to start with the circuit diagram of Fig. 6-26 and derive the state table or diagram. If the derived state table is identical to Table 6-6 (or the state-table part of Table 6-11), then we know that the design is correct. In addition, we must determine the next states from the unused states 000, 110, and 111.

The maps of Fig. 6-25 can help in finding the next state from each of the unused states. Take, for instance, the unused state 000. If the circuit, for some reason, happens to be in the present state 000, an input $x = 0$ will transfer the circuit to some next state and an input $x = 1$ will transfer it to another (or the same) next state. We first investigate minterm $ABCx = 0000$. From the maps, we see that this minterm is not included in any function except for SC, i.e., the set input of flip-flop C. Therefore, flip-flops A and B will not change but flip-flop C will be set to 1. Since the present state is $ABC = 000$, the next state will be $ABC = 001$. The maps also show that minterm $ABCx = 0001$ is included in the functions for SB and RC. Therefore, B will be set and C will be cleared. Starting with $ABC = 000$ and setting B, we obtain the next state $ABC = 010$ (C is already cleared). Investigation of the map for output y shows that y will be 0 for these two minterms.

The result of the analysis procedure is shown in the state diagram of Fig. 6-27. The circuit operates as intended, as long as it stays within the states 001, 010, 011, 100, and 101. If it ever finds itself in one of the invalid states 000, 110, or 111, it goes to one of the valid states within one or two clock pulses. Thus the circuit is self-starting and self-correcting, since it eventually goes to a valid state from which it continues to operate as required.

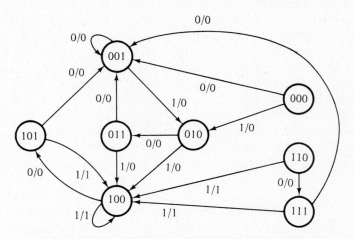

Figure 6-27 State diagram for the circuit of Fig. 6-26

An undesirable situation would have occurred if the next state of 110 for $x = 1$ happened to be 111 and the next state of 111 for $x = 0$ or 1 happened to be 110. Then, if the circuit starts from 110 or 111, it will circulate and stay between these two states forever. Unused states that cause such undesirable behavior should be avoided; if they are found to exist, the circuit should be redesigned. This can be done most easily by specifying a valid next state for any unused state that is found to circulate among invalid states.

6-8 DESIGN OF COUNTERS

A sequential circuit that goes through a prescribed sequence of states upon the application of input pulses is called a *counter*. The input pulses, called *count pulses*, may be clock pulses, or they may originate from an external source and may occur at prescribed intervals of time or at random. In a counter, the sequence of states may follow a binary count or any other sequence of states. Counters are found in almost all equipment containing digital logic. They are used for counting the number of occurrences of an event and are useful for generating timing sequences to control operations in a digital system.

Of the various sequences a counter may follow, the straight binary sequence is the simplest and most straightforward. A counter that follows the binary sequence is called a *binary counter*. An *n*-bit binary counter consists of *n* flip-flops and can count in binary from 0 to $2^n - 1$. As an example, the state diagram of a 3-bit counter is shown in Fig. 6-28. As seen from the binary states indicated inside the circles, the flip-flop outputs repeat the binary count sequence with a return to 000 after 111. The directed lines between circles are not marked with input-output values as in other state diagrams. Remember that state transitions in clocked sequential circuits occur during a clock pulse; the flip-flops remain in their present states if no pulse occurs. For this reason, the clock pulse variable *CP* does not

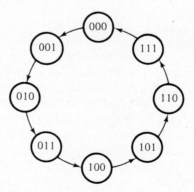

Figure 6-28 State diagram of a 3-bit binary counter

appear explicitly as an input variable in a state diagram or state table. From this point of view, the state diagram of a counter does not have to show input-output values along the directed lines. The only input to the circuit is the count pulse, and the outputs are directly specified by the present states of the flip-flops. The next state of a counter depends entirely on its present state, and the state transition occurs every time the pulse occurs. Because of this property, a counter is completely specified by a list of the *count sequence*, i.e., the sequence of binary states that it undergoes.

The count sequence of a 3-bit binary counter is given in Table 6-12. The next number in the sequence represents the next state reached by the circuit upon the application of a count pulse. The count sequence repeats after it reaches the last value, so that state 000 is the next state after 111. The count sequence gives all the information needed to design the circuit. It is not necessary to list the next states in a separate column because they can be read from the next number in the sequence. The design of counters follows the same procedure as that outlined in Section 6-7, except that the excitation table can be obtained directly from the count sequence.

TABLE 6-12   Excitation table for a 3-bit binary counter

Count sequence			Flip-flop inputs		
A_2	A_1	A_0	TA_2	TA_1	TA_0
0	0	0	0	0	1
0	0	1	0	1	1
0	1	0	0	0	1
0	1	1	1	1	1
1	0	0	0	0	1
1	0	1	0	1	1
1	1	0	0	0	1
1	1	1	1	1	1

Table 6-12 is the excitation table for the 3-bit binary counter. The three flip-flops are given variable designations A_2, A_1, and A_0. Binary counters are most efficiently constructed with T flip-flops (or JK flip-flop with J and K tied together). The flip-flop excitation for the T inputs is derived from the excitation table of the T flip-flop and from inspection of the state transition from a given count (present state) to the next below it (next state). As an illustration, consider the flip-flop input entries for row 001. The present state here is 001 and the next state is 010, which is the next count in the sequence. Comparing these two counts, we note that A_2 goes from 0 to 0; so TA_2 is marked with a 0 because flip-flop A_2 must remain unchanged when a clock pulse occurs. A_1 goes from 0 to 1; so TA_1 is marked with a 1 because this flip-flop must be complemented in the next clock pulse. Similarly, A_0 goes from 1 to 0, indicating that it must be complemented; so TA_0 is marked

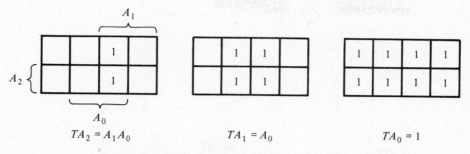

$$TA_2 = A_1 A_0 \qquad\qquad TA_1 = A_0 \qquad\qquad TA_0 = 1$$

Figure 6-29 Maps for a 3-bit binary counter

with a 1. The last row with present state 111 is compared with the first count 000 which is its next state. Going from all 1's to all 0's requires that all three flip-flops be complemented.

The flip-flop input functions from the excitation tables are simplified in the maps of Fig. 6-29. The Boolean functions listed under each map specify the combinational-circuit part of the counter. Including these functions with the three flip-flops, we obtain the logic diagram of the counter as shown in Fig. 6-30.

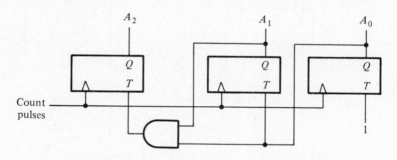

Figure 6-30 Logic diagram of a 3-bit binary counter

A counter with n flip-flops may have a binary sequence of less than 2^n numbers. A BCD counter counts the binary sequence from 0000 to 1001 and returns to 0000 to repeat the sequence. Other counters may follow an arbitrary sequence which may not be the straight binary sequence. In any case, the design procedure is the same. The count sequence is listed and the excitation table is obtained by comparing a present count with the next count listed below it. A tabulated count sequence always assumes a repeated count, so that the next state of the last entry is the first count listed.

EXAMPLE 6-3: Design a counter that has a repeated sequence of six states as listed in Table 6-13.

In this sequence, flip-flops B and C repeat the binary count 00, 01, 10, while flip-flop A alternates between 0 and 1 every three

TABLE 6-13   Excitation table for Example 6-3

Count sequence			Flip-flop inputs					
A	B	C	JA	KA	JB	KB	JC	KC
0	0	0	0	X	0	X	1	X
0	0	1	0	X	1	X	X	1
0	1	0	1	X	X	1	0	X
1	0	0	X	0	0	X	1	X
1	0	1	X	0	1	X	X	1
1	1	0	X	1	X	1	0	X

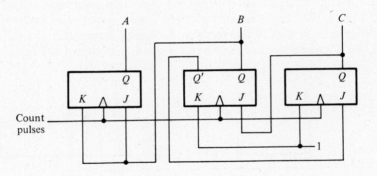

(a) Logic diagram of counter.

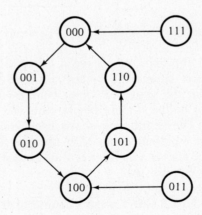

(b) State diagram of counter.

Figure 6-31   Solution to Example 6-3

counts. The count sequence for A, B, C is not straight binary and two states, 011 and 111, are not used. The choice of JK flip-flops results in the excitation table of Table 6-13. Inputs KB and KC have only 1's and X's in their columns, so these inputs are always 1. The other flip-flop input functions can be simplified using minterms 3 and 7 as don't-care conditions. The simplified functions are:

$$JA = B \qquad KA = B$$
$$JB = C \qquad KB = 1$$
$$JC = B' \qquad KC = 1$$

The logic diagram of the counter is shown in Fig. 6-31(a). Since there are two unused states, we analyze the circuit to determine their effect. The state diagram so obtained is drawn in Fig. 6-31(b). If the circuit ever goes to an invalid state, the next count pulse transfers it to one of the valid states, and it continues to count correctly. Thus the counter is self-starting. A self-starting counter is one that can start from any state but eventually reaches the normal count sequence.

6-9   DESIGN WITH STATE EQUATIONS

A sequential circuit can be designed by means of state equations rather than an excitation table. As shown in Section 6-4, a state equation is an algebraic expression that gives the conditions for the next state as a function of the present state and input variables. The state equations of a sequential circuit express in algebraic form the same information which is expressed in tabular form in a state table.

The state equation method is convenient when the circuit is already specified in this form or when the state equations are easily derived from the state table. This is the preferred method when D flip-flops are used. The method may sometimes be convenient to use with JK flip-flops. The application of this procedure to circuits with RS or T flip-flops is possible but involves a considerable amount of algebraic manipulation. Here we will show the application of this method to sequential circuits employing D or JK flip-flops. The starting point in each case is the flip-flop characteristic equation derived in Section 6-2.

Sequential Circuits with *D* Flip-flops

The characteristic equation of the D flip-flop is derived in Fig. 6-5(d):

$$Q(t + 1) = D$$

This equation states that the next state of the flip-flop is equal to the present value of its D input and is independent of the value of the present state. This means that the entries for the next state in the state table are exactly the same as the D inputs. Therefore, it is not necessary to derive the flip-flop input conditions for the excitation table because this information is already available in the next state columns.

Take, for example, the excitation table of Table 6-10. The next state column for A has four 1's, and so does the column for the next state of B. To design this circuit with D flip-flops, we write the state equations and equate them to the corresponding D inputs:

$$A(t + 1) = DA(A, B, x) = \Sigma(2, 4, 5, 6)$$
$$B(t + 1) = DB(A, B, x) = \Sigma(1, 3, 5, 6)$$

where DA and DB are the flip-flop input functions for D flip-flops A and B, respectively, and each function is expressed as the sum of four minterms. The simplified functions can be obtained by means of two three-variable maps. The simplified flip-flop input functions are:

$$DA = AB' + Bx'$$
$$DB = A'x + B'x + ABx'$$

If there are unused states in the sequential circuit, they must be considered, together with the inputs, as don't-care combinations. The don't-care minterms thus obtained can be used to simplify the state equations of the D flip-flop input functions.

EXAMPLE 6-4: Design a sequential circuit with four flip-flops, A, B, C, and D. The next states of B, C, and D are equal to the present states of A, B, and C, respectively. The next state of A is equal to the exclusive-OR of the present states of C and D.

From the statement of the problem, it is convenient to first write the state equations for the circuit:

$$A(t + 1) = C \oplus D$$
$$B(t + 1) = A$$
$$C(t + 1) = B$$
$$D(t + 1) = C$$

This circuit specifies a *feedback shift register*. In a feedback shift register, each flip-flop transfers or shifts its content to the next flip-flop when a clock pulse occurs, but the next state of the first flip-flop (A in this case) is some function of the present state of other flip-flops. Since the state equations are very simple, the most convenient flip-flop to use is the D type.

The flip-flop input functions for this circuit are taken directly from the state equations, with the next state variable replaced by the flip-flop input variable:

$$DA = C \oplus D$$
$$DB = A$$
$$DC = B$$
$$DD = C$$

The circuit can be constructed with four D flip-flops and one exclusive-OR gate.

State Equations with *JK* Flip-flops*

The characteristic equation for the JK flip-flop is derived in Fig. 6-6(d):

$$Q(t + 1) = (J)Q' + (K')Q$$

Input variables J and K are enclosed in parentheses so as not to confuse the AND terms of the characteristic equation with the two-letter convention which has been used to represent the flip-flop input variables.

The sequential circuit can be derived directly from the state equations without having to draw the excitation table. This is done by means of a matching process between the state equation for each flip-flop and the general characteristic equation of the JK flip-flop. The matching process consists of manipulating each state equation until it is in the form of the characteristic equation. Once this is done, the functions for inputs J and K can be extracted and simplified. This must be done for each state equation listed, and its flip-flop variable name A, B, C, etc., must replace the letter Q in the characteristic equation.

A given state equation for $Q(t + 1)$ may be already expressed as a function of Q and Q'. More often, either Q or Q' or both would be absent in the Boolean expression. It is then necessary to mainpulate the expression algebraically until both Q and Q' are included in the expression. The following example demonstrates all the possibilities that may be encountered.

EXAMPLE 6-5: Design a sequential circuit with JK flip-flops to satisfy the following state equations:

$$A(t + 1) = A'B'CD + A'B'C + ACD + AC'D'$$
$$B(t + 1) = A'C + CD' + A'BC'$$
$$C(t + 1) = B$$
$$D(t + 1) = D'$$

*This part may be omitted without loss of continuity.

The input functions for flip-flop A are derived by this method by arranging the state equation and matching it with the characteristic equation as follows:

$$A(t + 1) = (B'CD + B'C)A' + (CD + C'D')A$$
$$= (J)A' + (K')A$$

From the equality of the two equations, we deduce the input functions for flip-flop A to be:

$$J = B'CD + B'C = B'C$$
$$K = (CD + C'D')' = CD' + C'D$$

The state equation for flip-flop B can be arranged as follows:

$$B(t + 1) = (A'C + CD') + (A'C')B$$

However, this form is not suitable for matching with the characteristic equation because the variable B' is missing. If the first quantity in parentheses is ANDed with $(B' + B)$, the equation remains the same but with the variable B' included. Thus:

$$B(t + 1) = (A'C + CD')(B' + B) + (A'C')B$$
$$= (A'C + CD')B' + (A'C + CD' + A'C')B$$
$$= (J)B' + (K')B$$

From the equality of the two equations, we deduce the input functions for flip-flop B:

$$J = A'C + CD'$$
$$K = (A'C + CD' + A'C')' = AC' + AD$$

The state equation for flip-flop C can be manipulated as follows:

$$C(t + 1) = B = B(C' + C) = BC' + BC$$
$$= (J)C' + (K')C$$

The input functions for flip-flop C are:

$$J = B$$
$$K = B'$$

Finally, the state equation for flip-flop D may be manipulated for the purpose of matching as follows:

$$D(t + 1) = D' = 1.D' + 0.D$$
$$= (J)D' + (K')D$$

which gives the input function:

$$J = K = 1$$

The derived input functions can be accumulated and listed together. The two-letter convention to designate the flip-flop input variable, not used in the above derivation, is used below:

$$JA = B'C \qquad KA = CD' + C'D$$
$$JB = A'C + CD' \qquad KB = AC' + AD$$
$$JC = B \qquad KC = B'$$
$$JD = 1 \qquad KD = 1$$

The design procedure introduced here is an alternative method for determining the flip-flop input functions of a sequential circuit when JK flip-flops are employed. To use this procedure when a state diagram or state table is initially specified, it is necessary that the state equations be derived by the procedure outlined in Section 6-4. The state-equation method for finding flip-flop input functions can be extended to cover unused states which are considered as don't-care conditions. The don't-care minterms are written in the form of a state equation and manipulated until they are in the form of the characteristic equation for the particular flip-flop considered. The J and K functions in the don't-care state equation are then taken as don't-care minterms when simplifying the input functions for a particular flip-flop.

REFERENCES

1. Marcus, M. P., *Switching Circuits for Engineers*, 3rd ed. Englewood Cliffs, N.J.: Prentice-Hall, 1975.

2. McCluskey, E. J., *Introduction to the Theory of Switching Circuits*. New York: McGraw-Hill Book Co., 1965.

3. Miller, R. E., *Switching Theory*, two volumes. New York: John Wiley and Sons, 1965.

4. Krieger, M., *Basic Switching Circuit Theory*. New York: The Macmillan Co., 1967.

5. Hill, F. J., and G. R. Peterson, *Introduction to Switching Theory and Logical Design*. New York: John Wiley and Sons, 1974.

6. Givone, D. D., *Introduction to Switching Circuit Theory*. New York: McGraw-Hill Book Co., 1970.

7. Kohavi, Z., *Switching and Finite Automata Theory*. New York: McGraw-Hill Book Co., 1970.

8. Phister M., *The Logical Design of Digital Computers*. New York: John Wiley and Sons, 1958.

9. Paull, M. C., and S. H. Unger, "Minimizing the Number of States in Incompletely Specified Sequential Switching Functions." *IRE Trans. on Electronic Computers*, Vol. EC-8, No. 3 (September 1959), 356–66.

10. Hartmanis, J., "On the State Assignment Problem for Sequential Machines I." *IRE Trans. on Electronic Computers*, Vol. EC-10, No. 2 (June 1961), 157–65.

11. McCluskey, E. J., and S. H. Unger, "A Note on the Number of Internal Assignments for Sequential Circuits." *IRE Trans. on Electronic Computer*, Vol. EC-8, No. 4 (December 1959), 439–40.

PROBLEMS

6-1.   Show the logic diagram of a clocked *RS* flip-flop with four NAND gates.

6-2.   Show the logic diagram of a clocked *D* flip-flop with AND and NOR gates.

6-3.   Show that the clocked *D* flip-flop of Fig. 6-5(a) can be reduced by one gate.

6-4.   Consider a *JK'* flip-flop, i.e., a *JK* flip-flop with an inverter between external input *K'* and internal input *K*.
(a) Obtain the flip-flop characteristic table.
(b) Obtain the characteristic equation.
(c) Show that tying the two external inputs together forms a *D* flip-flop.

6-5.   A set-dominate flip-flop has a set and a reset input. It differs from a conventional *RS* flip-flop in that an attempt to simultaneously set and reset results in setting the flip-flop.
(a) Obtain the characteristic table and characteristic equation for the set-dominate flip-flop.
(b) Obtain a logic diagram for an asynchronous set-dominate flip-flop.

6-6.   Obtain the logic diagram of a master-slave *JK* flip-flop with AND and NOR gates. Include a provision for setting and clearing the flip-flop asynchronously (without a clock).

6-7.   This problem investigates the operation of the master-slave *JK* flip-flop through the binary transition in the internal gates of Fig. 6-11. Evaluate the binary values (0 or 1) in the outputs of the nine gates when the inputs to the circuit go through the following sequence:
(a) $CP = 0$, $Y = 0$, $Q = 0$, and $J = K = 1$.
(b) After CP goes to 1 (Y should go to 1; Q remains at 0).
(c) After CP goes to 0 and immediately after that J goes to 0 (Q should go to 1; Y is unaffected).
(d) After CP goes to 1 again (Y should go to 0).
(e) After CP goes back to 0 and immediately after that K goes to 0 (Q should go to 0).
(f) All succeeding pulses have no effect as long as J and K remain at 0.

6-8.   Draw the logic diagram (showing all gates) of a master-slave *D* flip-flop. Use NAND gates.

6-9.   Connect an asynchronous clear terminal to the inputs of gates 2 and 6 of the flip-flop in Fig. 6-12.

(a) Show that when the clear input is 0, the flip-flop is cleared, and remains cleared, regardless of the values of CP and D inputs.

(b) Show that when the clear input is 1, it has no effect on the normal clocked operations.

6-10.   The full-adder of Fig. P6-10 receives two external inputs x and y; the third input z comes from the output of a D flip-flop. The carry output is transferred to the flip-flop every clock pulse. The external S output gives the sum of x, y, and z. Obtain the state table and state diagram of the sequential circuit.

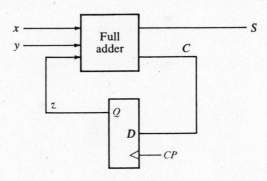

Figure P6-10

6-11.   Derive the state table and state diagram of the sequential circuit of Fig. P6-11. What is the function of the circuit?

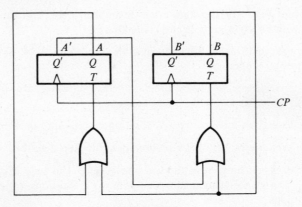

Figure P6-11

6-12.   A sequential circuit has four flip-flops A, B, C, D and an input x. It is described by the following state equations:

$$A(t + 1) = (CD' + C'D)x + (CD + C'D')x'$$
$$B(t + 1) = A$$
$$C(t + 1) = B$$
$$D(t + 1) = C$$

(a) Obtain the sequence of states when $x = 1$, starting from state $ABCD = 0001$.

(b) Obtain the sequence of states when $x = 0$, starting from state $ABCD = 0000$.

6-13. A sequential circuit has two flip-flops (A and B), two inputs (x and y), and an output (z). The flip-flop input functions and the circuit output function are as follows:

$$JA = xB + y'B' \qquad KA = xy'B'$$
$$JB = xA' \qquad KB = xy' + A$$
$$z = xyA + x'y'B$$

Obtain the logic diagram, state table, state diagram, and state equations.

6-14. Reduce the number of states in the following state table and tabulate the reduced state table.

Present state	Next state		Output	
	$x = 0$	$x = 1$	$x = 0$	$x = 1$
a	f	b	0	0
b	d	c	0	0
c	f	e	0	0
d	g	a	1	0
e	d	c	0	0
f	f	b	1	1
g	g	h	0	1
h	g	a	1	0

6-15. Starting from state a of the state table in problem 6-14, find the output sequence generated with an input sequence 01110010011.

6-16. Repeat problem 6-15 using the reduced table of problem 6-14. Show that the same output sequence is obtained.

6-17. Substitute binary assignment 2 of Table 6-5 to the states in Table 6-4 and obtain the binary state table. Repeat with binary assignment 3.

6-18. Obtain the excitation table of the JK' flip-flop described in problem 6-4.

6-19. Obtain the excitation table of the set-dominate flip-flop described in problem 6-5.

6-20. A sequential circuit has one input and one output. The state diagram is shown in Fig. P6-20. Design the sequential circuit with (a) T flip-flops, (b) RS flip-flops, and (c) JK flip-flops.

6-21. Design the circuit of a 4-bit register that converts the binary number stored in the register to its 2's complement value when input $x = 1$. The flip-flops of the register are of the RST type. This flip-flop has three inputs: two inputs have RS capabilities and one has a T capability. The RS inputs are used to transfer the 4-bit number when an input $y = 1$. Use the T input for the conversion.

6-22. Repeat Example 6-1 with binary assignment 3 of Table 6-5. Use JK flip-flops.

6-23. Design a BCD counter with JK flip-flops.

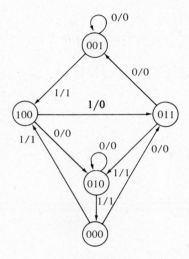

Figure P6-20

6-24. Design a counter that counts the decimal digits according to the 2, 4, 2, 1 code (Table 1-2). Use T flip-flops.

6-25. Design the binary counters having the following repeated binary sequence. Use JK flip-flops.
(a) 0, 1, 2
(b) 0, 1, 2, 3, 4
(c) 0, 1, 2, 3, 4, 5, 6

6-26. Design a counter with the following binary sequence: 0, 1, 3, 2, 6, 4, 5, 7 and repeat. Use RS flip-flops.

6-27. Design a counter with the following binary sequence: 0, 1, 3, 7, 6, 4 and repeat. Use T flip-flops.

6-28. Design a counter with the following binary sequence: 0, 4, 2, 1, 6 and repeat. Use JK flip-flops.

6-29. Repeat Example 6-5 using D flip-flops.

6-30. Verify the circuit obtained in Example 6-5 by using the excitation table method.

6-31. Design the sequential circuit described by the following state equations. Use JK flip-flops.

$$A(t + 1) = xAB + yA'C + xy$$
$$B(t + 1) = xAC + y'BC'$$
$$C(t + 1) = x'B + yAB'$$

6-32. (a) Derive the state equations for the sequential circuit specified by Table 6-6, Section 6-5. List the don't-care terms. (b) Derive the flip-flop input functions from the state equations (and don't-care terms) using the method outlined in Example 6-5. Use JK flip-flops.

Registers, Counters, and the Memory Unit

7

7-1   INTRODUCTION

A clocked sequential circuit consists of a group of flip-flops and combinational gates connected to form a feedback path. The flip-flops are essential because, in their absence, the circuit reduces to a purely combinational circuit (provided there is no feedback path). A circuit with only flip-flops is considered a sequential circuit even in the absence of combinational gates.

An MSI circuit that contains storage cells within it is, by definition, a sequential circuit. MSI circuits that include flip-flops or other storage cells are usually classified by the function they perform rather than by the name "sequential circuit." These MSI circuits are classified in one of three categories: registers, counters, or random-access memory. This chapter presents various registers and counters available in IC form and explains their operation. The organization of the random-access memory is also presented.

A *register* is a group of binary storage cells suitable for holding binary information. A group of flip-flops constitutes a register, since each flip-flop is a binary cell capable of storing one bit of information. An n-bit register has a group of n flip-flops and is capable of storing any binary information containing n bits. In addition to the flip-flops, a register may have combinational gates that perform certain data-processing tasks. In its broadest definition, a register consists of a group of flip-flops and gates that effect their transition. The flip-flops hold binary information and the gates control when and how new information is transferred into the register.

Counters were introduced in Section 6-8. A counter is essentially a register that goes through a predetermined sequence of states upon the application of input pulses. The gates in a counter are connected in such a way as to produce a prescribed sequence of binary states in the register. Although counters are a special type of register, it is common to differentiate them by giving them a special name.

A memory unit is a collection of storage cells together with associated circuits needed to transfer information in and out of storage. A random-access memory

(RAM) differs from a read-only memory (ROM) in that a RAM can transfer the stored information out (read) and is also capable of receiving new information in for storage (write). A more appropriate name for such a memory would be *read-write memory*.

Registers, counters, and memories are extensively used in the design of digital systems in general and digital computers in particular. Registers can also be used to facilitate the design of sequential circuits. Counters are useful for generating timing variables to sequence and control the operations in a digital system. Memories are essential for storage of programs and data in a digital computer. Knowledge of the operation of these components is indispensable for the understanding of the organization and design of digital systems.

7-2   REGISTERS

Various types of registers are available in MSI circuits. The simplest possible register is one that consists of only flip-flops without any external gates. Figure 7-1 shows such a register constructed with four D-type flip-flops and a common clock pulse input. The clock pulse input, CP, enables all flip-flops so that the information presently available at the four inputs can be transferred into the 4-bit register. The four outputs can be sampled to obtain the information presently stored in the register.

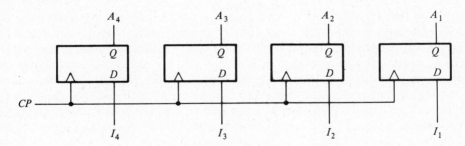

Figure 7-1   4-bit register

The way that the flip-flops in a register are triggered is of primary importance. If the flip-flops are constructed with gated D-type latches as in Fig. 6-5, then information present at a data (D) input is transferred to the Q output when the enable (CP) is 1, and the Q output follows the input data as long as the CP signal remains 1. When CP goes to 0, the information that was present at the data input just before the transition is retained at the Q output. In other words, the flip-flops are sensitive to the pulse duration, and the register is enabled for as long as $CP = 1$. A register that responds to the pulse duration is commonly called a *gated latch*, and the CP input is frequently labeled with the variable G (instead of CP). Latches are suitable for use as temporary storage of binary information that is to be transferred to an external destination. They should not be used in the design of sequential circuits that have feedback connections.

As explained in Section 6-3, a flip-flop can be used in the design of clocked sequential circuits provided it is sensitive to the pulse transition rather than the pulse duration. This means that the flip-flops in the register must be of the edge-triggered or master-slave type. Normally, it is not possible to distinguish from a logic diagram whether a flip-flop is a gated latch, edge-triggered, or master-slave, because the graphic symbols for all three are the same. The distinction must be made from the name given to the unit. A group of flip-flops sensitive to pulse duration is usually called a *latch*, whereas a group of flip-flops sensitive to pulse transition is called a *register*.* A register can always replace a latch, but the converse should be done with caution to make sure that outputs from a latch never go to other flip-flop inputs that are triggered with the same common clock pulse. In subsequent discussions, we will always assume that any group of flip-flops drawn constitutes a *register* and that all flip-flops are of the edge-triggered or master-slave type. If the register is sensitive to the pulse duration, it will be referred to as a *latch*.

Register with Parallel Load

The transfer of new information into a register is referred to as *loading* the register. If all the bits of the register are loaded simultaneously with a single clock pulse, we say that the loading is done in parallel. A pulse applied to the *CP* input of the register of Fig. 7-1 will load all four inputs in parallel. In this configuration, the clock pulse must be inhibited from the *CP* terminal if the content of the register must be left unchanged. In other words, the *CP* input acts as an enable signal which controls the loading of new information into the register. When *CP* goes to 1, the input information is loaded into the register. If *CP* remains at 0, the content of the register is not changed. Note that the change of state in the outputs occurs at the positive edge of the pulse. If a flip-flop changes state at the negative edge, there will be a small circle under the triangle symbol in the *CP* input of the flip-flop.

Most digital systems have a master-clock generator that supplies a continuous train of clock pulses. All clock pulses are applied to all flip-flops and registers in the system. The master-clock generator acts like a pump that supplies a constant beat to all parts of the system. A separate control signal then decides what specific clock pulses will have an effect on a particular register. In such a system, the clock pulses must be ANDed with the control signal, and the output of the AND gate is then applied to the *CP* terminal of the register shown in Fig. 7-1. When the control signal is 0, the output of the AND gate is 0, and the stored information in the register remains unchanged. Only when the control signal is a 1 does the clock pulse pass through the AND gate and into the *CP* terminal for new information to be loaded into the register. Such a control variable is called a *load* control input.

---

*For example, IC type 7475 is a 4-bit latch, whereas type 74175 is a 4-bit register.

Inserting an AND gate in the path of clock pulses means that logic is performed with clock pulses. The insertion of logic gates produces propagation delays between the master-clock generator and the clock inputs of flip-flops. To fully synchronize the system, we must ensure that all clock pulses arrive at the same time to all inputs of all flip-flops so that they can all change simultaneously. Performing logic with clock pulses inserts variable delays and may throw the system out of synchronism. For this reason, it is advisable (but not necessary, as long as the delays are taken into consideration) to apply clock pulses directly to all flip-flops and control the operation of the register with other inputs, such as the R and S inputs of an RS flip-flop.

A 4-bit register with a load control input using RS flip-flops is shown in Fig. 7-2. The CP input of the register receives continuous synchronized pulses which are applied to all flip-flops. The inverter in the CP path causes all flip-flops to be triggered by the negative edge of the incoming pulses. The purpose of the inverter

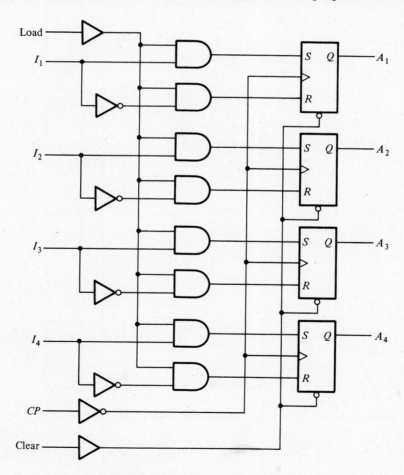

Figure 7-2 4-bit register with parallel load

is to reduce the loading of the master-clock generator. This is because the *CP* input is connected to only one gate (the inverter) instead of the four-gate inputs that would have been required if the connections were made directly into the flip-flop clock inputs (marked with small triangles).

The *clear* input goes to a special terminal in each flip-flop through a noninverting buffer gate. When this terminal goes to 0, the flip-flop is cleared asynchronously. The clear input is useful for clearing the register to all 0's prior to its clocked operation. The clear input must be maintained at 1 during normal clocked operations (see Fig. 6-14).

The *load* input goes through a buffer gate (to reduce loading) and through a series of AND gates to the R and S inputs of each flip-flop. Although clock pulses

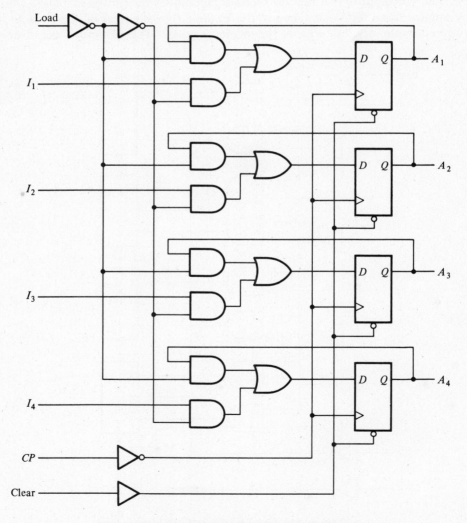

Figure 7-3 Register with parallel load using D flip-flops

are continuously present, it is the load input that controls the operation of the register. The two AND gates and the inverter associated with each input I determine the values of R and S. If the load input is 0, both R and S are 0, and no change of state occurs with any clock pulse. Thus, the load input is a control variable which can prevent any information change in the register as long as its input is 0. When the load control goes to 1, inputs I_1 through I_4 specify what binary information is loaded into the register on the next clock pulse. For each I that is equal to 1, the corresponding flip-flop inputs are $S = 1$, $R = 0$. For each I that is equal to 0, the corresponding flip-flop inputs are $S = 0$, $R = 1$. Thus, the input value is transferred into the register provided the load input is 1, the clear input is 1, and a clock pulse goes from 1 to 0. This type of transfer is called a *parallel-load* transfer because all bits of the register are loaded simultaneously. If the buffer gate associated with the load input is changed to an inverter gate, then the register is loaded when the load input is 0 and inhibited when the load input is 1.

A register with parallel load can be constructed with D flip-flops as shown in Fig. 7-3. The clock and clear inputs are the same as before. When the load input is 1, the I inputs are transferred into the register on the next clock pulse. When the load input is 0, the circuit inputs are inhibited and the D flip-flops are reloaded with their present value, thus maintaining the content of the register. The feedback connection in each flip-flop is necessary when D type is used because a D flip-flop does not have a "no-change" input condition. With each clock pulse, the D input determines the next state of the output. To leave the output unchanged, it is necessary to make the D input equal to the present Q output in each flip-flop.

Sequential Logic Implementation

We saw in Chapter 6 that a clocked sequential circuit consists of a group of flip-flops and combinational gates. Since registers are readily available as MSI circuits, it becomes convenient at times to employ a register as part of the sequential circuit. A block diagram of a sequential circuit that uses a register is shown in Fig. 7-4. The present state of the register and the external inputs determine the next state of the register and the values of external outputs. Part of

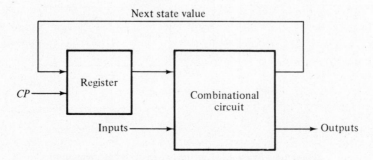

Figure 7-4 Block diagram of a sequential circuit

the combinational circuit determines the next state and the other part generates the outputs. The next state value from the combinational circuit is loaded into the register with a clock pulse. If the register has a load input, it must be set to 1; otherwise, if the register has no load input (as in Fig. 7-1), the next state value will be transferred automatically every clock pulse.

The combinational circuit part of a sequential circuit can be implemented by any of the methods discussed in Chapter 5. It can be constructed with SSI gates, with ROM, or with a programmable logic array (PLA). By using a register, it is possible to reduce the design of a sequential circuit to that of a combinational circuit connected to a register.

EXAMPLE 7-1: Design the sequential circuit whose state table is listed in Fig. 7-5(a).

The state table specifies two flip-flops A_1 and A_2, one input x, and one output y. The next state and output information is obtained directly from the table:

$$A_1(t + 1) = \Sigma(4, 6)$$
$$A_2(t + 1) = \Sigma(1, 2, 5, 6)$$
$$y(A_1, A_2, x) = \Sigma(3, 7)$$

The minterm values are for variables A_1, A_2, and x, which are the present state and input variables. The functions for the next state and output can be simplified by means of maps to give:

$$A_1(t + 1) = A_1 x'$$
$$A_2(t + 1) = A_2 \oplus x$$
$$y = A_2 x$$

The logic diagram is shown in Fig. 7-5(b).

Present state A_1	A_2	Input x	Next state A_1	A_2	Output y
0	0	0	0	0	0
0	0	1	0	1	0
0	1	0	0	1	0
0	1	1	0	0	1
1	0	0	1	0	0
1	0	1	0	1	0
1	1	0	1	1	0
1	1	1	0	0	1

(a) State Table

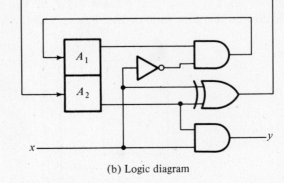

(b) Logic diagram

Figure 7-5 Example of sequential-circuit implementation

ROM truth table

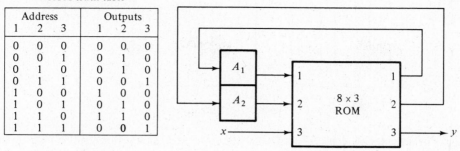

Address			Outputs		
1	2	3	1	2	3
0	0	0	0	0	0
0	0	1	0	1	0
0	1	0	0	1	0
0	1	1	0	0	1
1	0	0	1	0	0
1	0	1	0	1	0
1	1	0	1	1	0
1	1	1	0	0	1

Figure 7-6 Sequential circuit using a register and a ROM

EXAMPLE 7-2: Repeat Example 7-1, but now use a ROM and a register.

The ROM can be used to implement the combinational circuit and the register will provide the flip-flops. The number of inputs to the ROM is equal to the number of flip-flops plus the number of external inputs. The number of outputs of the ROM is equal to the number of flip-flops plus the number of external outputs. In this case we have three inputs and three outputs for the ROM; so its size must be 8×3. The implementation is shown in Fig. 7-6. The ROM truth table is identical to the state table with "present state" and "inputs" specifying the address of ROM and "next state" and "outputs" specifying the ROM outputs. The next state values must be connected from the ROM outputs to the register inputs.

7-3 SHIFT REGISTERS

A register capable of shifting its binary information either to the right or to the left is called a *shift register*. The logical configuration of a shift register consists of a chain of flip-flops connected in cascade, with the output of one flip-flop connected to the input of the next flip-flop. All flip-flops receive a common clock pulse which causes the shift from one stage to the next.

The simplest possible shift register is one that uses only flip-flops, as shown in Fig. 7-7. The Q output of a given flip-flop is connected to the D input of the flip-flop at its right. Each clock pulse shifts the contents of the register one bit position to the right. The *serial input* determines what goes into the leftmost flip-flop during the shift. The *serial output* is taken from the output of the rightmost flip-flop prior to the application of a pulse. Although this register shifts its contents to the right, if we turn the page upside down, we find that the register shifts its contents to the left. Thus a unidirectional shift register can function either as a shift-right or as a shift-left register.

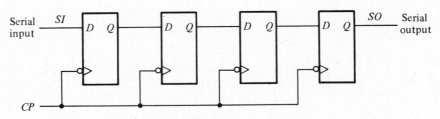

Figure 7-7 Shift register

The register in Fig. 7-7 shifts its contents with every clock pulse during the negative edge of the pulse transition. (This is indicated by the small circle associated with the clock input in all flip-flops.) If we want to control the shift so that it occurs only with certain pulses but not with others, we must control the CP input of the register. It will be shown later that the shift operations can be controlled through the D inputs of the flip-flops rather than through the CP input. If, however, the shift register in Fig. 7-7 is used, the shift can easily be controlled by means of an external AND gate as shown below.

Serial Transfer

A digital system is said to operate in a serial mode when information is transferred and manipulated one bit at a time. The content of one register is transferred to another by shifting the bits from one register to the other. The information is transferred one bit at a time by shifting the bits out of the source register into the destination register.

The serial transfer of information from register A to register B is done with shift registers, as shown in the block diagram of Fig. 7-8(a). The serial output (SO) of register A goes to the serial input (SI) of register B. To prevent the loss of information stored in the source register, the A register is made to circulate its information by connecting the serial output to its serial input terminal. The initial content of register B is shifted out through its serial output and is lost unless it is transferred to a third shift register. The shift-control input determines when and by how many times the registers are shifted. This is done by the AND gate that allows clock pulses to pass into the CP terminals only when the shift-control is 1.

Suppose the shift registers have four bits each. The control unit that supervises the transfer must be designed in such a way that it enables the shift registers, through the shift-control signal, for a fixed time duration equal to four clock pulses. This is shown in the timing diagram of Fig. 7-8(b). The shift-control signal is synchronized with the clock and changes value just after the negative edge of a clock pulse. The next four clock pulses find the shift-control signal in the 1 state, so the output of the AND gate connected to the CP terminals produces the four pulses T_1, T_2, T_3, and T_4. The fourth pulse changes the shift control to 0 and the shift registers are disabled.

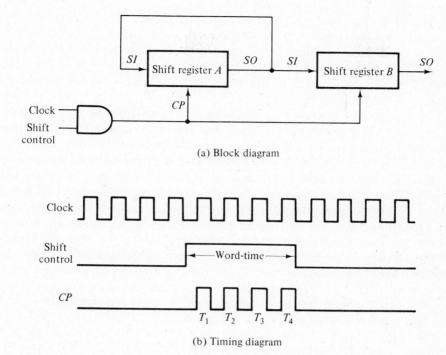

(a) Block diagram

(b) Timing diagram

Figure 7-8 Serial transfer from register A to register B

Assume that the binary content of A before the shift is 1011 and that of B, 0010. The serial transfer from A to B will occur in four steps as shown in Table 7-1. After the first pulse T_1, the rightmost bit of A is shifted into the leftmost bit of B and, at the same time, this bit is circulated into the leftmost position of A. The other bits of A and B are shifted once to the right. The previous serial output from B is lost and its value changes from 0 to 1. The next three pulses perform identical operations, shifting the bits of A into B, one at a time. After the fourth shift, the shift control goes to 0 and both registers A and B have the value 1011. Thus, the content of A is transferred into B while the content of A remains unchanged.

TABLE 7-1 Serial transfer example

Timing pulse	Shift register A				Shift register B				Serial output of B
Initial value	1	0	1	1	0	0	1	0	0
After T_1	1	1	0	1	1	0	0	1	1
After T_2	1	1	1	0	1	1	0	0	0
After T_3	0	1	1	1	0	1	1	0	0
After T_4	1	0	1	1	1	0	1	1	1

The difference between serial and parallel modes of operation should be apparent from this example. In the parallel mode, information is available from all bits of a register and all bits can be transferred simultaneously during one clock pulse. In the serial mode, the registers have a single serial input and a single serial output. The information is transferred one bit at a time while the registers are shifted in the same direction.

Computers may operate in a serial mode, a parallel mode, or in a combination of both. Serial operations are slower because of the time it takes to transfer information in and out of shift registers. Serial computers, however, require less hardware to perform operations because one common circuit can be used over and over again to manipulate the bits coming out of shift registers in a sequential manner. The time interval between clock pulses is called the *bit time*, and the time required to shift the entire contents of a shift register is called the *word time*. These timing sequences are generated by the control section of the system. In a parallel computer, control signals are enabled during one clock pulse interval. Transfers into registers are in parallel, and they occur upon application of a single clock pulse. In a serial computer, control signals must be maintained for a period equal to one word time. The pulse applied every bit time transfers the result of the operation, one at a time, into a shift register. Most computers operate in a parallel mode because this is a faster mode of operation.

Bidirectional Shift Register with Parallel Load

Shift registers can be used for converting serial data to parallel data, and vice versa. If we have access to all the flip-flop outputs of a shift register, then information entered serially by shifting can be taken out in parallel from the outputs of the flip-flops. If a parallel load capability is added to a shift register, then data entered in parallel can be taken out in serial fashion by shifting the data stored in the register.

Some shift registers provide the necessary input and output terminals for parallel transfer. They may also have both shift-right and shift-left capabilities. The most general shift register has all the capabilities listed below. Others may have only some of these functions, with at least one shift operation.

1. A *clear* control to clear the register to 0.

2. A *CP* input for clock pulses to synchronize all operations.

3. A *shift-right* control to enable the shift-right operation and the *serial input* and *output* lines associated with the shift-right.

4. A *shift-left* control to enable the shift-left operation and the *serial input* and *output* lines associated with the shift-left.

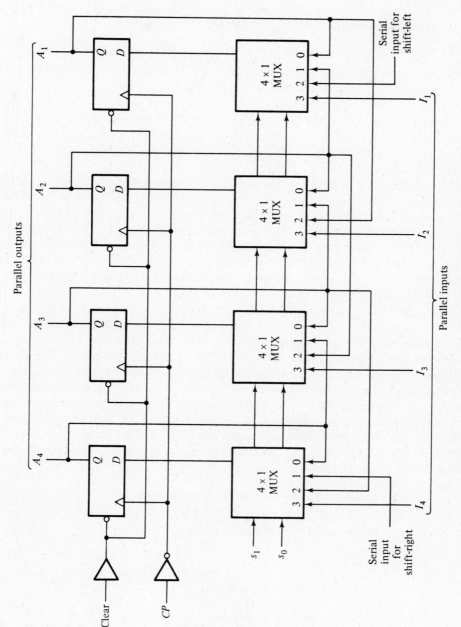

Figure 7-9 4-bit bidirectional shift register with parallel load

5. A *parallel-load* control to enable a parallel transfer and the *n* input lines associated with the parallel transfer.

6. *n* parallel output lines.

7. A control state that leaves the information in the register unchanged even though clock pulses are continuously applied.

A register capable of shifting both right and left is called a *bidirectional shift register*. One that can shift in only one direction is called a *unidirectional shift register*. If the register has both shift and parallel-load capabilities, it is called a *shift register with parallel load*.

The diagram of a shift register that has all the capabilities listed above is shown in Fig. 7-9.* It consists of four D flip-flops, although RS flip-flops could be used provided an inverter is inserted between the S and R terminals. The four multiplexers (MUX) are part of the register and are drawn here in block diagram form. (See Fig. 5-16 for the logic diagram of the multiplexer.) The four multiplexers have two common selection variables, s_1 and s_0. Input 0 in each MUX is selected when $s_1 s_0 = 00$, input 1 is selected when $s_1 s_0 = 01$, and similarly for the other two inputs to the multiplexers.

The s_1 and s_0 inputs control the mode of operation of the register as specified in the function entries of Table 7-2. When $s_1 s_0 = 00$, the present value of the register is applied to the D inputs of the flip-flops. This condition forms a path from the output of each flip-flop into the input of the same flip-flop. The next clock pulse transfers into each flip-flop the binary value it held previously, and no change of state occurs. When $s_1 s_0 = 01$, terminals 1 of the multiplexer inputs have a path to the D inputs of the flip-flops. This causes a shift-right operation, with the serial input transferred into flip-flop A_4. When $s_1 s_0 = 10$, a shift-left operation results, with the other serial input going into flip-flop A_1. Finally, when $s_1 s_0 = 11$, the binary information on the parallel input lines is transferred into the register simultaneously during the next clock pulse.

TABLE 7-2   Function table for the register of Fig. 7-9

Mode control		Register operation
s_1	s_2	
0	0	No change
0	1	Shift right
1	0	Shift left
1	1	Parallel load

*This is similar to IC type 74194.

A bidirectional shift register with parallel load is a general-purpose register capable of performing three operations: shift left, shift right, and parallel load. Not all shift registers available in MSI circuits have all these capabilities. The particular application dictates the choice of one MSI shift register over another.

Serial Addition

Operations in digital computers are mostly done in parallel because this is a faster mode of operation. Serial operations are slower but require less equipment. To demonstrate the serial mode of operation, we present here the design of a serial adder. The parallel counterpart was discussed in Section 5-2.

The two binary numbers to be added serially are stored in two shift registers. Bits are added one pair at a time, sequentially, through a single full-adder (FA) circuit, as shown in Fig. 7-10. The carry out of the full-adder is transferred to a D flip-flop. The output of this flip-flop is then used as an input carry for the next pair of significant bits. The two shift registers are shifted to the right for one word-time period. The sum bits from the S output of the full-adder could be transferred into a third shift register. By shifting the sum into A while the bits of A are shifted out, it is possible to use one register for storing both the augend and the sum bits. The serial input (SI) of register B is able to receive a new binary number while the addend bits are shifted out during the addition.

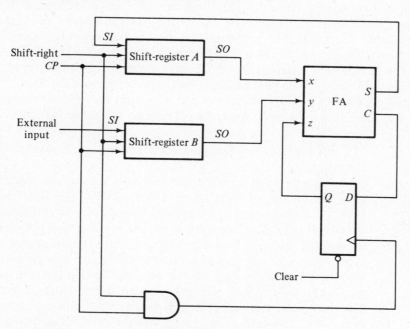

Figure 7-10 Serial adder

The operation of the serial adder is as follows. Initially, the A register holds the augend, the B register holds the addend, and the carry flip-flop is cleared to 0. The serial outputs (SO) of A and B provide a pair of significant bits for the full-adder at x and y. Output Q of the flip-flop gives the input carry at z. The shift-right control enables both registers and the carry flip-flop; so at the next clock pulse, both registers are shifted once to the right, the sum bit from S enters the leftmost flip-flop of A, and the output carry is transferred into flip-flop Q. The shift-right control enables the registers for a number of clock pulses equal to the number of bits in the registers. For each succeeding clock pulse, a new sum bit is transferred to A, a new carry is transferred to Q, and both registers are shifted once to the right. This process continues until the shift-right control is disabled. Thus, the addition is accomplished by passing each pair of bits together with the previous carry through a single full-adder circuit and transferring the sum, one bit at a time, into register A.

If a new number has to be added to the contents of register A, this number must be first transferred serially into register B. Repeating the process once more will add the second number to the previous number in A.

Comparing the serial adder with the parallel adder described in Section 5-2, we note the following differences. The parallel adder must use registers with parallel-load capability, whereas the serial adder uses shift registers. The number of full-adder circuits in the parallel adder is equal to the number of bits in the binary numbers, whereas the serial adder requires only one full-adder circuit and a carry flip-flop. Excluding the registers, the parallel adder is a purely combinational circuit, whereas the serial adder is a sequential circuit. The sequential circuit in the serial adder consists of a full-adder circuit and a flip-flop that stores the output carry. This is typical in serial operations because the result of a bit-time operation may depend not only on the present inputs but also on previous inputs.

To show that bit-time operations in serial computers may require a sequential circuit, we will redesign the serial adder by considering it a sequential circuit.

> **EXAMPLE 7-3:** Design a serial adder using a sequential-logic procedure.
>
> First, we must stipulate that two shift registers are available to store the binary numbers to be added serially. The serial outputs from the registers are designated by variables x and y. The sequential circuit to be designed will not include the shift registers; they will be inserted later to show the complete unit. The sequential circuit proper has two inputs, x and y, that provide a pair of significant bits, an output S that generates the sum bit, and flip-flop Q for storing the carry. The present state of Q provides the present value of the carry. The clock pulse that shifts the registers enables flip-flop Q to load the next carry. This carry is then used with the next pair of bits in x and y. The state table that specifies the sequential circuit is given in Table 7-3.

TABLE 7-3 Excitation table for a serial adder

Present state	Inputs		Next state	Output	Flip-flop inputs	
Q	x	y	Q	S	JQ	KQ
0	0	0	0	0	0	X
0	0	1	0	1	0	X
0	1	0	0	1	0	X
0	1	1	1	0	1	X
1	0	0	0	1	X	1
1	0	1	1	0	X	0
1	1	0	1	0	X	0
1	1	1	1	1	X	0

The present state of Q is the present value of the carry. The present carry in Q is added together with inputs x and y to produce the sum bit in output S. The next state of Q is equivalent to the output carry. Note that the state table entries are identical to the entries in a full-adder truth table, except that the input carry is now the present state of Q and the output carry is now the next state of Q.

If we use a D flip-flop for Q, we obtain the same circuit as in Fig. 7-10 because the input requirements of the D input are the same as the next state values. If we use a JK flip-flop for Q, we obtain the input excitation requirements listed in Table 7-3. The three Boolean functions of interest are the flip-flop input functions for JQ and KQ and output S. These functions are specified in the excitation table

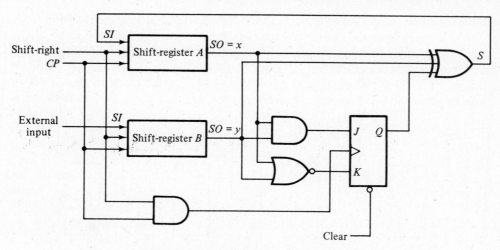

Figure 7-11 Second form of a serial adder

and can be simplified by means of maps:

$$JQ = xy$$
$$KQ = x'y' = (x + y)'$$
$$S = x \oplus y \oplus Q$$

As shown in Fig. 7-11, the circuit consists of three gates and a *JK* flip-flop. The two shift registers are also included in the diagram to show the complete serial adder. Note that output *S* is a function not only of *x* and *y* but also of the present state of *Q*. The next state of *Q* is a function of the present values of *x* and *y* that come out of the serial outputs of the shift registers.

7-4 RIPPLE COUNTERS

MSI counters come in two categories: ripple counters and synchronous counters. In a ripple counter, the flip-flop output transition serves as a source for triggering other flip-flops. In other words, the *CP* inputs of all flip-flops (except the first) are triggered not by the incoming pulses but rather by the transition that occurs in other flip-flops. In a synchronous counter, the input pulses are applied to all *CP* inputs of all flip-flops. The change of state of a particular flip-flop is dependent on the present state of other flip-flops. Synchronous MSI counters are discussed in the next section. Here we present some common MSI ripple counters and explain their operation.

Binary Ripple Counter

A binary ripple counter consists of a series connection of complementing flip-flops (*T* or *JK* type), with the output of each flip-flop connected to the *CP* input of the next higher-order flip-flop. The flip-flop holding the least significant bit receives the incoming count pulses. The diagram of a 4-bit binary ripple counter is shown in Fig. 7-12. All *J* and *K* inputs are equal to 1. The small circle in the *CP* input indicates that the flip-flop complements during a negative-going transition or when

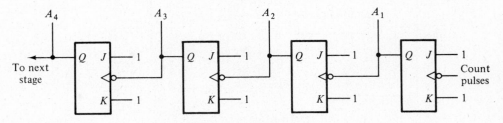

Figure 7-12   4-bit binary ripple counter

TABLE 7-4   Count sequence for a binary ripple counter

Count sequence				Conditions for complementing flip-flops
A_4	A_3	A_2	A_1	
0	0	0	0	Complement A_1
0	0	0	1	Complement A_1 A_1 will go from 1 to 0 and complement A_2
0	0	1	0	Complement A_1
0	0	1	1	Complement A_1 A_1 will go from 1 to 0 and complement A_2; A_2 will go from 1 to 0 and complement A_3
0	1	0	0	Complement A_1
0	1	0	1	Complement A_1 A_1 will go from 1 to 0 and complement A_2
0	1	1	0	Complement A_1
0	1	1	1	Complement A_1 A_1 will go from 1 to 0 and complement A_2; A_2 will go from 1 to 0 and complement A_3; A_3 will go from 1 to 0 and complement A_4
1	0	0	0	and so on . . .

the output to which it is connected goes from 1 to 0. To understand the operation of the binary counter, refer to its count sequence given in Table 7-4. It is obvious that the lowest-order bit A_1 must be complemented with each count pulse. Every time A_1 goes from 1 to 0, it complements A_2. Every time A_2 goes from 1 to 0, it complements A_3, and so on. For example, take the transition from count 0111 to 1000. The arrows in the table emphasize the transitions in this case. A_1 is complemented with the count pulse. Since A_1 goes from 1 to 0, it triggers A_2 and complements it. As a result, A_2 goes from 1 to 0, which in turn complements A_3. A_3 now goes from 1 to 0, which complements A_4. The output transition of A_4, if connected to a next stage, will not trigger the next flip-flop since it goes from 0 to 1. The flip-flops change one at a time in rapid succession, and the signal propagates through the counter in a *ripple* fashion. Ripple counters are sometimes called *asynchronous counters*.

A binary counter with a reverse count is called a binary *down-counter*. In a down-counter, the binary count is decremented by 1 with every input count pulse. The count of a 4-bit down-counter starts from binary 15 and continues to binary counts 14, 13, 12, . . . , 0 and then back to 15. The circuit of Fig. 7-12 will function as a binary down-counter if the outputs are taken from the complement terminals Q' of all flip-flops. If only the normal outputs of flip-flops are available, the circuit must be modified slightly as described below.

A list of the count sequence of a count-down binary counter shows that the lowest-order bit must be complemented with every count pulse. Any other bit in the sequence is complemented if its previous lower-order bit goes from 0 to 1. Therefore, the diagram of a binary down-counter looks the same as in Fig. 7-12, provided all flip-flops trigger on the positive edge of the pulse. (The small circles in

273

the CP inputs must be absent.) If negative-edge-triggered flip-flops are used, then the CP input of each flip-flop must be connected to the Q' output of the previous flip-flop. Then when Q goes from 0 to 1, Q' will go from 1 to 0 and complement the next flip-flop as required.

BCD Ripple Counter

A decimal counter follows a sequence of ten states and returns to 0 after the count of 9. Such a counter must have at least four flip-flops to represent each decimal digit, since a decimal digit is represented by a binary code with at least four bits. The sequence of states in a decimal counter is dictated by the binary code used to represent a decimal digit. If BCD is used, the sequence of states is as shown in the state diagram of Fig. 7-13. This is similar to a binary counter, except that the state after 1001 (code for decimal digit 9) is 0000 (code for decimal digit 0).

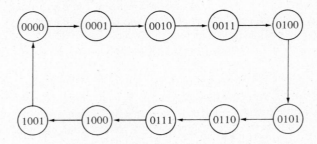

Figure 7-13   State diagram of a decimal BCD counter

The design of a decimal ripple counter or of any ripple counter not following the binary sequence is not a straightforward procedure. The formal tools of logic design can serve only as a guide. A satisfactory end product requires the ingenuity and imagination of the designer.

The logic diagram of a BCD ripple counter is shown in Fig. 7-14.* The four outputs are designated by the letter symbol Q with a numeric subscript equal to the binary weight of the corresponding bit in the BCD code. The flip-flops trigger on the negative edge, i.e., when the CP signal goes from 1 to 0. Note that the output of Q_1 is applied to the CP inputs of both Q_2 and Q_8 and the output of Q_2 is applied to the CP input of Q_4. The J and K inputs are connected either to a permanent 1 signal or to outputs of flip-flops, as shown in the diagram.

A ripple counter is an asynchronous sequential circuit and cannot be described by Boolean equations developed for describing clocked sequential circuits. Signals that affect the flip-flop transition depend on the order in which they change from 1 to 0. The operation of the counter can be explained by a list of conditions for flip-flop transitions. These conditions are derived from the logic diagram and from knowledge of how a JK flip-flop operates. Remember that when the CP

*This circuit is similar to IC type 7490.

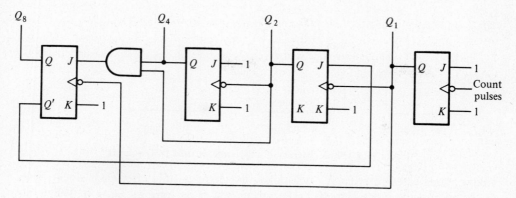

Figure 7-14 Logic diagram of a BCD ripple counter

input goes from 1 to 0, the flip-flop is set if $J = 1$, is cleared if $K = 1$, is complemented if $J = K = 1$, and is left unchanged if $J = K = 0$. The following are the conditions for each flip-flop state transition:

1. Q_1 is complemented on the negative edge of every count pulse.

2. Q_2 is complemented if $Q_8 = 0$ and Q_1 goes from 1 to 0. Q_2 is cleared if $Q_8 = 1$ and Q_1 goes from 1 to 0.

3. Q_4 is complemented when Q_2 goes from 1 to 0.

4. Q_8 is complemented when $Q_4 Q_2 = 11$ and Q_1 goes from 1 to 0. Q_8 is cleared if either Q_4 or Q_2 is 0 and Q_1 goes from 1 to 0.

To verify that these conditions result in the sequence required by a BCD ripple counter, it is necessary to verify that the flip-flop transitions indeed follow a sequence of states as specified by the state diagram of Fig. 7-13. Another way to verify the operation of the counter is to derive the timing diagram for each flip-flop from the conditions listed above. This diagram is shown in Fig. 7-15 with the

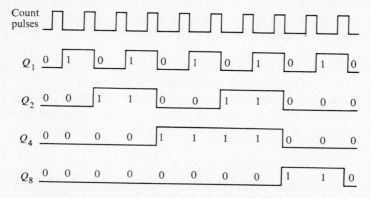

Figure 7-15 Timing diagram for the decimal counter of Fig. 7-14

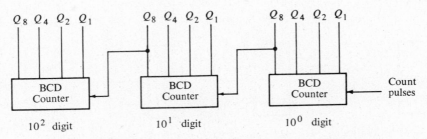

Figure 7-16 Block diagram of a 3-decade decimal BCD counter

binary states listed after each clock pulse. Q_1 changes state after each clock pulse. Q_2 complements every time Q_1 goes from 1 to 0 as long as $Q_8 = 0$. When Q_8 becomes 1, Q_2 remains cleared at 0. Q_4 complements every time Q_2 goes from 1 to 0. Q_8 remains cleared as long as Q_2 or Q_4 is 0. When both Q_2 and Q_4 become 1's, Q_8 complements when Q_1 goes from 1 to 0. Q_8 is cleared on the next transition of Q_1.

The BCD counter of Fig. 7-14 is a *decade* counter, since it counts from 0 to 9. To count in decimal from 0 to 99, we need a two-decade counter. To count from 0 to 999, we need a three-decade counter. Multiple-decade counters can be constructed by connecting BCD counters in cascade, one for each decade. A three-decade counter is shown in Fig. 7-16. The inputs to the second and third decades come from Q_8 of the previous decade. When Q_8 in one decade goes from 1 to 0, it triggers the count for the next higher-order decade while its own decade goes from 9 to 0. For instance, the count after 399 will be 400.

7-5 SYNCHRONOUS COUNTERS

Synchronous counters are distinguished from ripple counters in that clock pulses are applied to the *CP* inputs of *all* flip-flops. The common pulse triggers all the flip-flops simultaneously, rather than one at a time in succession as in a ripple counter. The decision whether a flip-flop is to be complemented or not is determined from the values of the *J* and *K* inputs at the time of the pulse. If $J = K = 0$, the flip-flop remains unchanged. If $J = K = 1$, the flip-flop complements.

A design procedure for any type of synchronous counter was presented in Section 6-8. The design of a 3-bit binary counter was carried out in detail and is illustrated in Fig. 6-30. In this section, we present some typical MSI synchronous counters and explain their operation. It must be realized that there is no need to design a counter if it is already available commerically in IC form.

Binary Counter

The design of synchronous binary counters is so simple that there is no need to go through a rigorous sequential-logic design process. In a synchronous binary counter, the flip-flop in the lowest-order position is complemented with every pulse.

This means that its J and K inputs must be maintained at logic-1. A flip-flop in any other position is complemented with a pulse provided all the bits in the lower-order positions are equal to 1, because the lower-order bits (when all 1's) will change to 0's on the next count pulse. The binary count dictates that the next higher-order bit be complemented. For example, if the present state of a 4-bit counter is $A_4A_3A_2A_1 = 0011$, the next count will be 0100. A_1 is always complemented. A_2 is complemented because the present state of $A_1 = 1$. A_3 is complemented because the present state of $A_2A_1 = 11$. But A_4 is not complemented because the present state of $A_3A_2A_1 = 011$, which does not give an all-1's condition.

Synchronous binary counters have a regular pattern and can easily be constructed with complementing flip-flops and gates. The regular pattern can be clearly seen from the 4-bit counter depicted in Fig. 7-17. The CP terminals of all flip-flops are connected to a common clock-pulse source. The first stage A_1 has its J and K equal to 1 if the counter is enabled. The other J and K inputs are equal to 1 if all previous low-order bits are equal to 1 and the count is enabled. The chain of AND gates generates the required logic for the J and K inputs in each stage. The counter can be extended to any number of stages, with each stage having an additional flip-flop and an AND gate that gives an output of 1 if all previous flip-flop outputs are 1's.

Note that the flip-flops trigger on the negative edge of the pulse. This is not essential here as it was with the ripple counter. The counter could also be triggered on the positive edge of the pulse.

Binary Up-Down Counter

In a synchronous count-down binary counter, the flip-flop in the lowest-order position is complemented with every pulse. A flip-flop in any other position is complemented with a pulse provided all the lower-order bits are equal to 0. For example, if the present state of a 4-bit count-down binary counter is $A_4A_3A_2A_1 = 1100$, the next count will be 1011. A_1 is always complemented. A_2 is complemented because the present state of $A_1 = 0$. A_3 is complemented because the present state of $A_2A_1 = 00$. But A_4 is not complemented because the present state of $A_3A_2A_1 = 100$, which is not an all-0's condition.

A count-down binary counter can be constructed as shown in Fig. 7-17, except that the inputs to the AND gates must come from the complement outputs Q' and not from the normal outputs Q of the previous flip-flops. The two operations can be combined in one circuit. A binary counter capable of counting either up or down is shown in Fig. 7-18. The T flip-flops employed in this circuit may be considered as JK flip-flops with the J and K terminals tied together. When the *up* input control is 1, the circuit counts up, since the T inputs are determined from the previous values of the normal outputs in Q. When the *down* input control is 1, the circuit counts down, since the complement outputs Q' determine the states of the T inputs. When both the *up* and *down* signals are 0's, the register does not change state but remains in the same count.

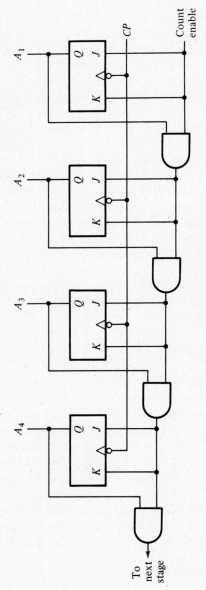

Figure 7-17 4-bit synchronous binary counter

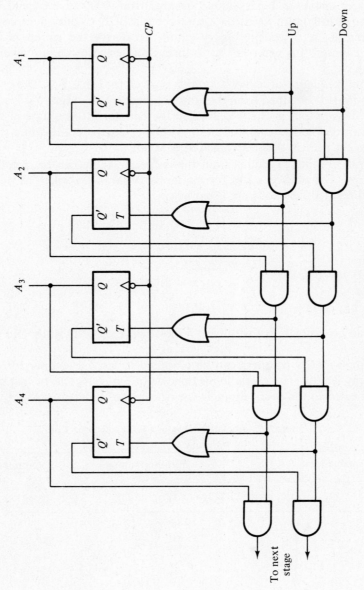

Figure 7-18 4-bit up-down binary counter

BCD Counter

A BCD counter counts in binary-coded decimal from 0000 to 1001 and back to 0000. Because of the return to 0 after a count of 9, a BCD counter does not have a regular pattern as in a straight binary count. To derive the circuit of a BCD synchronous counter, it is necessary to go through a design procedure as discussed in Section 6-8.

The count sequence of a BCD counter is given in Table 7-5. The excitation for the T flip-flops is obtained from the count sequence. An output y is also shown in the table. This output is equal to 1 when the counter present state is 1001. In this way, y can enable the count of the next-higher-order decade while the same pulse switches the present decade from 1001 to 0000.

The flip-flop input functions from the excitation table can be simplified by means of maps. The unused states for minterms 10 to 15 are taken as don't-care terms. The simplified functions are listed below:

$$TQ_1 = 1$$
$$TQ_2 = Q_8'Q_1$$
$$TQ_4 = Q_2Q_1$$
$$TQ_8 = Q_8Q_1 + Q_4Q_2Q_1$$
$$y = Q_8Q_1$$

The circuit can be easily drawn with four T flip-flops, five AND gates, and one OR gate.

Synchronous BCD counters can be cascaded to form a counter for decimal numbers of any length. The cascading is done as in Fig. 7-16, except that output y must be connected to the count input of the next-higher-order decade.

TABLE 7-5 Excitation table for a BCD counter

Count sequence				Flip-flop inputs				Output carry
Q_8	Q_4	Q_2	Q_1	TQ_8	TQ_4	TQ_2	TQ_1	y
0	0	0	0	0	0	0	1	0
0	0	0	1	0	0	1	1	0
0	0	1	0	0	0	0	1	0
0	0	1	1	0	1	1	1	0
0	1	0	0	0	0	0	1	0
0	1	0	1	0	0	1	1	0
0	1	1	0	0	0	0	1	0
0	1	1	1	1	1	1	1	0
1	0	0	0	0	0	0	1	0
1	0	0	1	1	0	0	1	1

Binary Counter with Parallel Load

Counters employed in digital systems quite often require a parallel-load capability for transferring an initial binary number prior to the count operation. Figure 7-19 shows the logic diagram of a register that has a parallel-load capability and can also operate as a counter.* The input load control, when equal to 1, disables the count sequence and causes a transfer of data from inputs I_1 through I_4 into flip-flops A_1 through A_4, respectively. If the load input is 0 and the count input control is 1, the circuit operates as a counter. The clock pulses then cause the state of the flip-flops to change according to the binary count sequence. If both control inputs are 0, clock pulses do not change the state of the register.

The carry-out terminal becomes a 1 if all flip-flops are equal to 1 while the count input is enabled. This is the condition for complementing the flip-flop holding the next-higher-order bit. This output is useful for expanding the counter to more than four bits. The speed of the counter is increased if this carry is generated directly from the outputs of all four flip-flops instead of going through a chain of AND gates. Similarly, each flip-flop is associated with an AND gate that receives all previous flip-flop outputs directly to determine when the flip-flop should be complemented.

The operation of the counter is summarized in Table 7-6. The four control inputs: clear, CP, load, and count determine the next output state. The clear input is asynchronous and, when equal to 0, causes the counter to be cleared to all 0's, regardless of the presence of clock pulses or other inputs. This is indicated in the table by the X entries, which symbolize don't-care conditions for the other inputs, so their value can be either 0 or 1. The clear input must go to the 1 state for the clocked operations listed in the next three entries in the table. With the load and count inputs both at 0, the outputs do not change, whether a pulse is applied in the CP terminal or not. A load input of 1 causes a transfer from inputs I_1-I_4 into the register during the positive edge of an input pulse. The input information is loaded into the register regardless of the value of the count input, because the count input is inhibited when the load input is 1. If the load input is maintained at 0, the count input controls the operation of the counter. The outputs change to the next binary count on the positive-edge transition of every clock pulse, but no change of state occurs if the count input is 0.

The 4-bit counter shown in Fig. 7-19 can be enclosed in one IC package. Two ICs are necessary for the construction of an 8-bit counter; four ICs for a 16-bit counter; and so on. The carry output of one IC must be connected to the count input of the IC holding the four next-higher-order bits of the counter.

Counters with parallel-load capability having a specified number of bits are very useful in the design of digital systems. Later we will refer to them as registers with load and increment capabilities. The *increment* function is an operation that adds 1 to the present content of a register. By enabling the count control during one clock pulse period, the content of the register can be incremented by 1.

*This is similar but not identical to IC type 74161.

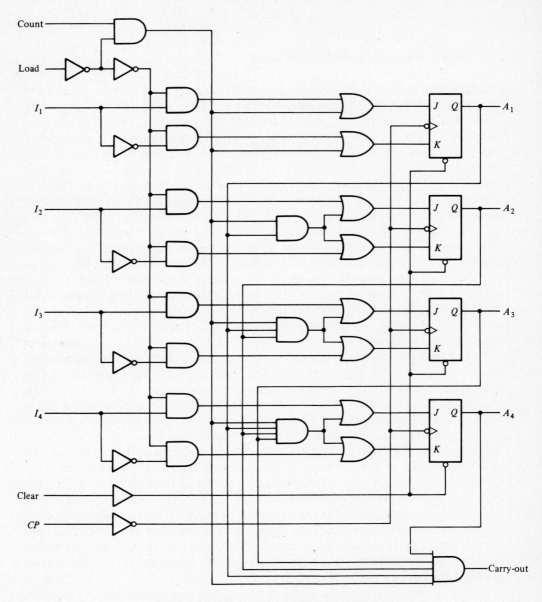

Figure 7-19 4-bit binary counter with parallel load

TABLE 7-6 Function table for the counter of Fig. 7-19

Clear	CP	Load	Count	Function
0	X	X	X	Clear to 0
1	X	0	0	No change
1	↑	1	X	Load inputs
1	↑	0	1	Count next binary state

A counter with parallel load can be used to generate any desired number of count sequences. A modulo-N (abbreviated mod N) counter is a counter that goes through a repeated sequence of N counts. For example, a 4-bit binary counter is a mod-16 counter. A BCD counter is a mod-10 counter. In some applications, one may not be concerned with the particular N states that a mod-N counter uses. If this is the case, then a counter with parallel load can be used to construct any mod-N counter, with N being any value desired. This is shown in the following example.

EXAMPLE 7-4: Construct a mod-6 counter using the MSI circuit specified in Fig. 7-19.

Figure 7-20 shows four ways in which a counter with parallel load can be used to generate a sequence of six counts. In each case the count control is set to 1 to enable the count through the pulses in the *CP* input. We also use the facts that the load control inhibits the count and that the clear operation is independent of other control inputs.

The AND gate in Fig. 7-20(a) detects the occurrence of state 0101 in the output. When the counter is in this state, the load input is enabled and an all-0's input is loaded into the register. Thus, the counter goes through binary states 0, 1, 2, 3, 4, and 5 and then returns to 0. This produces a sequence of six counts.

The clear input of the register is asynchronous, i.e., it does not depend on the clock. In Fig. 7-20(b), the NAND gate detects the count of 0110, but as soon as this count occurs, the register is cleared. The count 0110 has no chance of staying on for any appreciable time because the register goes immediately to 0. A momentary spike occurs in output A_2 as the count goes from 0101 to 0110 and immediately to 0000. This momentary spike may be undesirable and for this reason this configuration is not recommended. If the counter has a synchronous clear input, it would be possible to clear the counter with the clock after an occurrence of the 0101 count.

Instead of using the first six counts, we may want to choose the last six counts from 10 to 15. In this case it is possible to take advantage of the output carry to load a number in the register. In Fig. 7-20(c), the counter starts with count 1010 and continues to 1111. The output carry generated during the last state enables the load control, which then loads the input which is set at 1010.

It is also possible to choose any intermediate count of six states. The mod-6 counter of Fig. 7-20(d) goes through the count sequence 3, 4, 5, 6, 7, and 8. When the last count 1000 is reached, output A_4 goes to 1 and the load control is enabled. This loads into the register the value of 0011, and the binary count continues from this state.

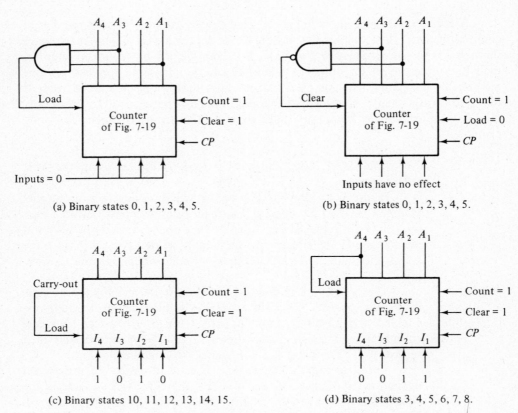

(a) Binary states 0, 1, 2, 3, 4, 5.

(b) Binary states 0, 1, 2, 3, 4, 5.

(c) Binary states 10, 11, 12, 13, 14, 15.

(d) Binary states 3, 4, 5, 6, 7, 8.

Figure 7-20 Four ways to achieve a mod-6 counter using a counter with parallel load

7-6 TIMING SEQUENCES

The sequence of operations in a digital system are specified by a control unit. The control unit that supervises the operations in a digital system would normally consist of timing signals that determine the time sequence in which the operations are executed. The timing sequences in the control unit can be easily generated by means of counters or shift registers. This section demonstrates the use of these MSI functions in the generation of timing signals for a control unit.

Word-time Generation

First, we demonstrate a circuit that generates the required timing signal for serial mode of operation. Serial transfer of information was discussed in Section 7-3, with an example depicted in Fig. 7-8. The control unit in a serial computer must generate a *word-time* signal that stays on for a number of pulses equal to the number of bits in the shift registers. The word-time signal can be generated by means of a counter that counts the required number of pulses.

Assume that the word-time signal to be generated must stay on for a period of eight clock pulses. Figure 7-21(a) shows a counter circuit that accomplishes this task. Initially, the 3-bit counter is cleared to 0. A start signal will set flip-flop Q. The output of this flip-flop supplies the word-time control and also enables the counter. After the count of eight pulses, the flip-flop is reset and Q goes to 0. The timing diagram of Fig. 7-21(b) demonstrates the operation of the circuit. The start signal is synchronized with the clock and stays on for one clock pulse period. After Q is set to 1, the counter starts counting the clock pulses. When the counter reaches the count of 7 (binary 111), it sends a stop signal to the reset input of the flip-flop. The stop signal becomes a 1 after the negative-edge transition of pulse 7. The next clock pulse switches the counter to the 000 state and also clears Q. Now the counter is disabled and the word-time signal stays at 0. Note that the word-time control stays on for a period of eight pulses. Note also that the stop signal in this circuit can be used to start another word-count control in another circuit just as the start signal is used in this circuit.

Timing Signals

In a parallel mode of operation, a single clock pulse can specify the time at which an operation should be executed. The control unit in a digital system that operates in the parallel mode must generate timing signals that stay on for only one clock

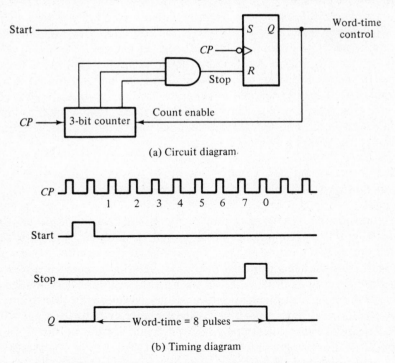

(a) Circuit diagram

(b) Timing diagram

Figure 7-21   Generation of a word-time control for serial operations

pulse period, but these timing signals must be distinguished from each other.

Timing signals that control the sequence of operations in a digital system can be generated with a shift register or a counter with a decoder. A *ring counter* is a circular shift register with only one flip-flop being set at any particular time; all others are cleared. The single bit is shifted from one flip-flop to the other to produce the sequence of timing signals. Figure 7-22(a) shows a 4-bit shift register connected as a ring counter. The initial value of the register is 1000, which produces the variable T_0. The single bit is shifted right with every clock pulse and circulates back from T_3 to T_0. Each flip-flop is in the 1 state once every four clock pulses and produces one of the four timing signals shown in Fig. 7-22(c). Each output becomes a 1 after the negative-edge transition of a clock pulse and remains 1 during the next clock pulse.

The timing signals can be generated also by continuously enabling a 2-bit counter that goes through four distinct states. The decoder shown in Fig. 7-22(b) decodes the four states of the counter and generates the required sequence of timing signals.

The timing signals, when enabled by the clock pulses, will provide multiple-phase clock pulses. For example, if T_0 is ANDed with CP, the output of the AND gate will generate clock pulses at one-fourth the frequency of the master-clock pulses. Multiple-phase clock pulses can be used for controlling different registers with different time scales.

To generate 2^n timing signals, we need either a shift register with 2^n flip-flops or an n-bit counter together with an n-to-2^n line decoder. For example, 16 timing signals can be generated with a 16-bit shift register connected as a ring counter or with a 4-bit counter and a 4-to-16 line decoder. In the first case, we need 16 flip-flops. In the second case, we need four flip-flops and 16 4-input AND gates for the decoder. It is also possible to generate the timing signals with a combination of a shift register and a decoder. In this way, the number of flip-flops is less than in a ring counter, and the decoder requires only 2-input gates. This combination is sometimes called a *Johnson counter*.

Johnson Counter

A k-bit ring counter circulates a single bit among the flip-flops to provide k distinguishable states. The number of states can be doubled if the shift register is connected as a *switch-tail* ring counter. A switch-tail ring counter is a circular shift register with the complement output of the last flip-flop connected to the input of the first flip-flop. Figure 7-23(a) shows such a shift register. The circular connection is made from the complement output of the rightmost flip-flop to the input of the leftmost flip-flop. The register shifts its contents once to the right with every clock pulse, and at the same time, the complement value of the E flip-flop is transferred into the A flip-flop. Starting from a cleared state, the switch-tail ring counter goes through a sequence of eight states as listed in Fig. 7-23(b). In general,

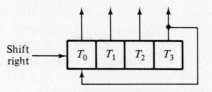

(a) Ring-counter (initial value = 1000)

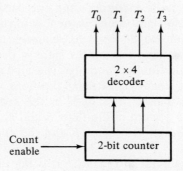

(b) Counter and decoder

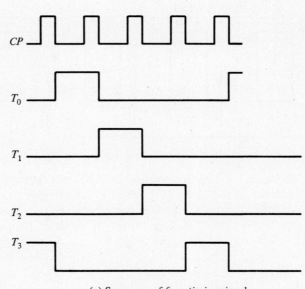

(c) Sequence of four timing signals

Figure 7-22 Generation of timing signals

a k-bit switch-tail ring counter will go through a sequence of $2k$ states. Starting from all 0's, each shift operation inserts 1's from the left until the register is filled with all 1's. In the following sequences, 0's are inserted from the left until the register is again filled with all 0's.

A Johnson counter is a k-bit switch-tail ring counter with $2k$ decoding gates to provide outputs for $2k$ timing signals. The decoding gates are not shown in Fig. 7-23 but are specified in the last column of the table. The eight AND gates listed in the table, when connected to the circuit, will complete the construction of the Johnson counter. Since each gate is enabled during one particular state sequence, the outputs of the gates generate eight timing sequences in succession.

The decoding of a k-bit switch-tail ring counter to obtain $2k$ timing sequences follows a regular pattern. The all-0's state is decoded by taking the complement of the two extreme flip-flop outputs. The all-1's state is decoded by taking the normal outputs of the two extreme flip-flops. All other states are decoded from an adjacent 1, 0 or 0, 1 pattern in the sequence. For example, sequence 7 has an adjacent 0, 1 pattern in flip-flops B and C. The decoded output is then obtained by taking the complement of B and the normal output of C, or $B'C$.

One disadvantage of the circuit in Fig. 7-23(a) is that, if it finds itself in an unused state, it will persist in moving from one invalid state to another and never

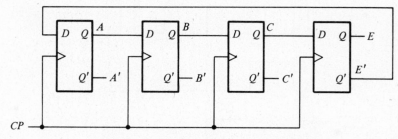

(a) 4-stage switch-tail ring counter

Sequence number	Flip-flop outputs				AND gate required for output
	A	B	C	E	
1	0	0	0	0	$A'E'$
2	1	0	0	0	AB'
3	1	1	0	0	BC'
4	1	1	1	0	CE'
5	1	1	1	1	AE
6	0	1	1	1	$A'B$
7	0	0	1	1	$B'C$
8	0	0	0	1	$C'E$

(b) Count sequence and required decoding.

Figure 7-23 Construction of a Johnson counter

find its way to a valid state. This difficulty can be corrected by modifying the circuit to avoid this undesirable condition. One correcting procedure is to disconnect the output from flip-flop B that goes to the D input of flip-flop C, and instead enable the input of flip-flop C by the function:*

$$DC = (A + C)B$$

where DC is the flip-flop input function for the D input of flip-flop C.

Johnson counters can be constructed for any number of timing sequences. The number of flip-flops needed is one-half the number of timing signals. The number of decoding gates is equal to the number of timing signals and only 2-input gates are employed.

7-7 THE MEMORY UNIT

The registers in a digital computer may be classified as either operational or storage type. An *operational* register is capable of storing binary information in its flip-flops and, in addition, has combinational gates capable of data-processing tasks. A *storage* register is used solely for temporary storage of binary information. This information cannot be altered when transferred in and out of the register. A *memory unit* is a collection of storage registers together with the associated circuits needed to transfer information in and out of the registers. The storage registers in a memory unit are called *memory registers*.

The bulk of the registers in a digital computer are memory registers, to which information is transferred for storage and from which information is available when needed for processing. Comparatively few operational registers are found in the processor unit. When data processing takes place, the information from selected registers in the memory unit is first transferred to the operational registers in the processor unit. Intermediate and final results obtained in the operational registers are transferred back to selected memory registers. Similarly, binary information received from input devices is first stored in memory registers; information transferred to output devices is taken from registers in the memory unit.

The component that forms the binary cells of registers in a memory unit must have certain basic properties, the most important of which are: (1) It must have a reliable two-state property for binary representation. (2) It must be small in size. (3) The cost per bit of storage should be as low as possible. (4) The time of access to a memory register should be reasonably fast. Examples of memory unit components are magnetic cores, semiconductor ICs, and magnetic surfaces on tapes, drums, or disks.

A memory unit stores binary information in groups called *words*, each word being stored in a memory register. A word in memory is an entity of n bits that moves in and out of storage as a unit. A memory word may represent an operand,

---

*This is the way it is done in IC type 4022.

an instruction, a group of alphanumeric characters, or any binary-coded information. The communication between a memory unit and its environment is achieved
through two control signals and two external registers. The control signals specify
the direction of transfer required, that is, whether a word is to be stored in a
memory register or whether a word previously stored is to be transferred out of a
memory register. One external register specifies the particular memory register
chosen out of the thousands available; the other specifies the particular bit
configuration of the word in question. The control signals and the registers are
shown in the block diagram of Fig. 7-24.

The memory *address register* specifies the memory word selected. Each word
in memory is assigned a number identification starting from 0 up to the maximum
number of words available. To communicate with a specific memory word, its
location number, or *address*, is transferred to the address register. The internal
circuits of the memory unit accept this address from the register and open the paths
needed to select the word called. An address register with n bits can specify up to
2^n memory words. Computer memory units can range from 1024 words, requiring
an address register of 10 bits, to $1,048,576 = 2^{20}$ words, requiring a 20-bit address
register.

The two control signals applied to the memory unit are called *read* and *write*.
A write signal specifies a transfer-in function; a read signal specifies a transfer-out
function. Each is referenced from the memory unit. Upon accepting one of the
control signals, the internal control circuits inside the memory unit provide the

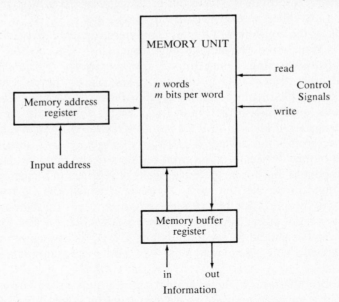

Figure 7-24 Block diagram of a memory unit showing
communication with environment

desired function. Certain types of storage units, because of their component characteristics, destroy the information stored in a cell when the bit in that cell is read out. Such a unit is said to be a destructive read-out memory, as opposed to a nondestructive memory where the information remains in the cell after it is read out. In either case, the old information is always destroyed when new information is written. The sequence of internal control in a destructive read-out memory must provide control signals that will cause the word to be restored into its binary cells if the application calls for a nondestructive function.

The information transfer to and from registers in memory and the external environment is communicated through one common register called the memory *buffer register* (other names are *information register* and *storage register*). When the memory unit receives a *write* control signal, the internal control interprets the contents of the buffer register to be the bit configuration of the word to be stored in a memory register. With a *read* control signal, the internal control sends the word from a memory register into the buffer register. In each case the contents of the address register specify the particular memory register referenced for writing or reading.

Let us summarize the information transfer characteristics of a memory unit by an example. Consider a memory unit of 1024 words with eight bits per word. To specify 1024 words, we need an address of ten bits, since $2^{10} = 1024$. Therefore, the address register must contain ten flip-flops. The buffer register must have eight flip-flops to store the contents of words transferred into and out of memory. The memory unit has 1024 registers with assigned address numbers from 0 to 1023.

Figure 7-25 shows the initial contents of three registers: memory address register (MAR), memory buffer register (MBR), and the memory register addressed

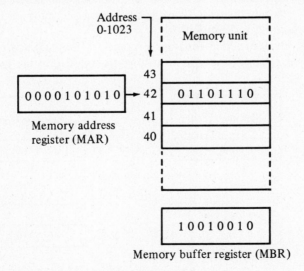

Figure 7-25 Initial values of registers

by MAR. Since the equivalent binary number in MAR is decimal 42, the memory register addressed by MAR is the one with address number 42.

The sequence of operations needed to communicate with the memory unit for the purpose of transferring a word out to the MBR is:

1. Transfer the address bits of the selected word into MAR.

2. Activate the *read* control input.

The result of the read operation is depicted in Fig. 7-26(a). The binary information presently stored in memory register 42 is transferred into MBR.

The sequence of operations needed to store a new word into memory is:

1. Transfer the address bits of the selected word into MAR.

2. Transfer the data bits of the word into MBR.

3. Activate the *write* control input.

The result of the write operation is depicted in Fig. 7-26(b). The data bits from MBR are stored in memory register 42.

In the above example, we assumed a memory unit with nondestructive read-out property. Such memories can be constructed with semiconductor ICs. They retain the information in the memory register when the register is sampled during the reading process so that no loss of information occurs. Another component commonly used in memory units is the magnetic core. A magnetic core characteristically has destructive read-out, i.e., it loses the stored binary information during the reading process. Examples of semiconductor and magnetic-core memories are presented in Section 7-8.

Because of its destructive read-out property, a magnetic-core memory must provide additional control functions to restore the word into the memory register.

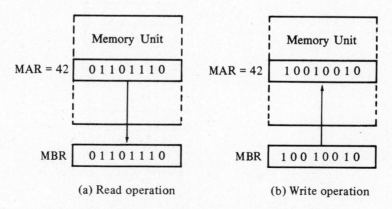

(a) Read operation   (b) Write operation

Figure 7-26 Information transfer during read and write operations

A read control signal applied to a magnetic-core memory transfers the content of the addressed word into an external register and, at the same time, the memory register is automatically cleared. The sequence of internal control in a magnetic-core memory then provides appropriate signals to cause the restoration of the word into the memory register. The information transfer in a magnetic-core memory during a read operation is depicted in Fig. 7-27. A destructive read operation transfers the selected word into MBR but leaves the memory register with all 0's. Normal memory operation requires that the content of the selected word remain in memory after a read operation. Therefore, it is necessary to go through a *restore* operation that writes the value in MBR into the selected memory register. During the restore operation, the contents of MAR and MBR must remain unchanged.

A write control input applied to a magnetic-core memory causes a transfer of information as depicted in Fig. 7-28. To transfer new information into a selected register, the old information must first be erased by clearing all the bits of the word to 0. After this is done, the content of MBR can be transferred to the selected word. MAR must not change during the operation to ensure that the same selected word that is cleared is the one that receives the new information.

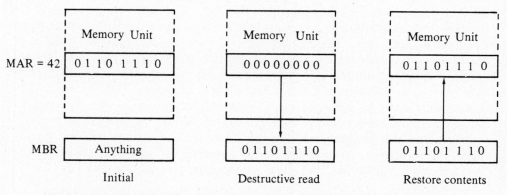

Figure 7-27   Information transfer in a magnetic-core memory during a read operation

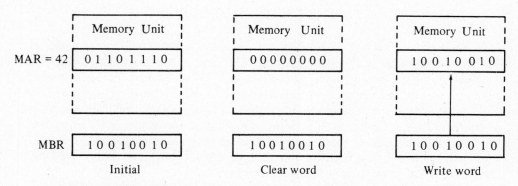

Figure 7-28   Information transfer in a magnetic-core memory during a write operation

A magnetic-core memory requires two half-cycles either for reading or writing. The time it takes for the memory to go through both half-cycles is called the *memory-cycle* time.

The mode of access of a memory system is determined by the type of components used. In a *random-access* memory, the registers may be thought of as being separated in space, with each register occupying one particular spatial location as in a magnetic-core memory. In a *sequential-access* memory, the information stored in some medium is not immediately accessible but is available only at certain intervals of time. A magnetic-tape unit is of this type. Each memory location passes the read and write heads in turn, but information is read out only when the requested word has been reached. The *access time* of a memory is the time required to select a word and either read or write it. In a random-access memory, the access time is always the same regardless of the word's particular location in space. In a sequential memory, the access time depends on the position of the word at the time of request. If the word is just emerging from storage at the time it is requested, the access time is just the time necessary to read or write it. But, if the word happens to be in the last position, the access time also includes the time required for all the other words to move past the terminals. Thus, the access time in a sequential memory is variable.

Memory units whose components lose stored information with time or when the power is turned off are said to be *volatile*. A semiconductor memory unit is of this category since its binary cells need external power to maintain the needed signals. In contrast, a nonvolatile memory unit, such as magnetic core or magnetic disk, retains its stored information after removal of power. This is because the stored information in magnetic components is manifested by the direction of magnetization, which is retained when power is turned off. A nonvolatile property is desirable in digital computers because many useful programs are left permanently in the memory unit. When power is turned off and then on again, the previously stored programs and other information are not lost but continue to reside in memory.

7-8 EXAMPLES OF RANDOM-ACCESS MEMORIES

The internal construction of two different types of random-access memories are presented diagramatically in this section. The first is constructed with flip-flops and gates and the second with magnetic cores. To be able to include the entire memory unit in one diagram, a limited storage capacity must be used. For this reason, the memory units presented here have a small capacity of 12 bits arranged in four words of three bits each. Commercial random-access memories may have a capacity of thousands of words and each word may range somewhere between 8 and 64 bits. The logical construction of large-capacity memory units would be a direct extension of the configuration shown here.

Integrated-circuit Memory

The internal construction of a random-access memory of m words with n bits per word consists of $m \times n$ binary storage cells and the associated logic for selecting individual words. The binary storage cell is the basic building block of a memory unit. The equivalent logic of a binary cell that stores one bit of information is shown in Fig. 7-29. Although the cell is shown to include gates and a flip-flop, internally it is constructed with two transistors having multiple inputs. A binary storage cell must be very small in order to be able to pack as many cells as possible in the small area available in the integrated-circuit chip. The binary cell has three inputs and one output. The select input enables the cell for reading or writing. The read/write input determines the cell operation when it is selected. A 1 in the read/write input forms a path from the flip-flop to the output terminal. The information in the input terminal is transferred into the flip-flop when the read/write control is 0. Note that the flip-flop operates without clock pulses and that its purpose is to store the information bit in the binary cell.

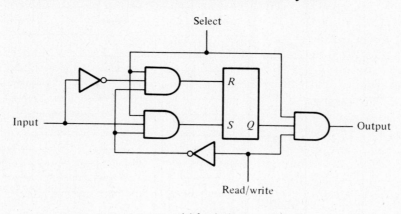

(a) Logic diagram

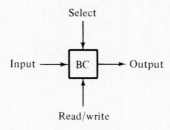

(b) Block diagram

Figure 7-29 Memory cell

Integrated-circuit memories sometimes have a single line for the read and write control. One binary state in the single line specifies a read operation and the other state specifies a write operation. In addition, one or more enable lines are included to provide means for selecting the IC and for expanding several packages into a memory unit with a larger number of words. The logical construction of a IC RAM is shown in Fig. 7-30. It consists of 4 words of 3 bits each, for a total of 12 binary cells. The small boxes labeled BC represent a binary cell, and the three inputs and one output in each BC are as specified in the diagram of Fig. 7-29.

The two address input lines go through an internal 2-to-4 line decoder. The decoder is enabled with the memory-enable input. When the memory enable is 0,

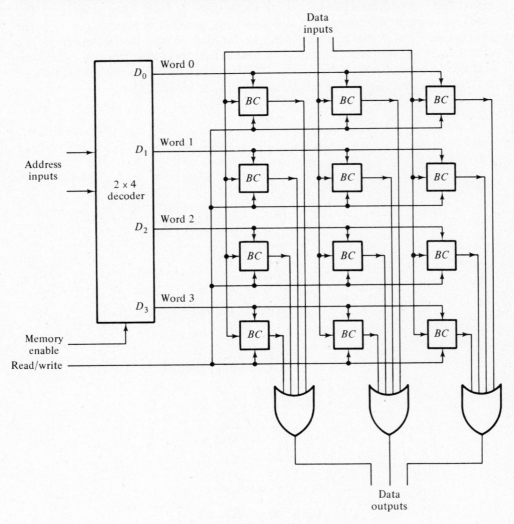

Figure 7-30   Integrated-circuit memory

all the outputs of the decoder are 0 and none of the memory words are selected. With the memory enable at 1, one of the four words is selected, depending on the value of the two address lines. Now, with the read/write control at 1, the bits of the selected word go through the three OR gates to the output terminals. The nonselected binary cells produce 0's in the inputs of the OR gates and have no effect on the outputs. With the read/write control at 0, the information available on the input lines is transferred into the binary cells of the selected word. The nonselected binary cells in the other words are disabled by their selection inputs and their previous values remain unchanged. With the memory-enable control at 0, the contents of all cells in the memory remain unchanged, regardless of the value of the read/write control.

IC RAMs are constructed internally with cells having a wired-OR capability. This eliminates the need for the OR gates in the diagram. The external output lines can also form wired logic to facilitate the connection of two or more IC packages to form a memory unit with a larger number of words.

Magnetic-core Memory

A magnetic-core memory uses magnetic cores to store binary information. A magnetic core is a doughnut-shaped toroid made of magnetic material. In contrast to a semiconductor flip-flop that needs only one physical quantity such as voltage for its operation, a magnetic core employs three physical quantities: current, magnetic flux, and voltage. The signal that excites the core is a *current* pulse in a wire passing through the core. The binary information stored is represented by the direction of *magnetic flux* within the core. The output binary information is extracted from a wire linking the core in the form of a *voltage* pulse.

The physical property that makes a magnetic core suitable for binary storage is its hysteresis loop, shown in Fig. 7-31(c). This is a plot of current vs magnetic flux, and it has the shape of a square loop. With zero current, a flux which is either positive (counterclockwise direction) or negative (clockwise direction) remains in the magnetized core. One direction, say counterclockwise magnetization, is used to represent a 1 and the other to represent a 0.

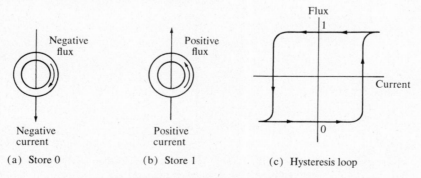

(a) Store 0   (b) Store 1   (c) Hysteresis loop

Figure 7-31 Storing a bit into a magnetic core

A pulse of current applied to the winding through the core can shift the direction of magnetization. As shown in Fig. 7-31(a), current in the downward direction produces flux in the clockwise direction, causing the core to go to the 0 state. Figure 7-31(b) shows the current and flux directions for storing a 1. The path that the flux takes when the current pulse is applied is indicated by arrows in the hysteresis loop.

Reading out the binary information stored in the core is complicated by the fact that flux cannot be detected when it is not changing. However, if flux is changing with respect to time, it induces a voltage in a wire that links the core. Thus, read-out could be accomplished by applying a current in the negative direction as shown in Fig. 7-32. If the core is in the 1 state, the current reverses the direction of magnetization, and the resulting change of flux produces a voltage pulse in the sense wire. If the core is already in the 0 state, the negative current leaves the core magnetized in the same direction, causing a very slight disturbance of magnetic flux which results in a very small output voltage in the sense wire. Note that this is a destructive read-out, since the read current always returns the core to the 0 state. The previously stored value is lost.

Figure 7-33 shows the organization of a magnetic-core memory containing four words with three bits each. Comparing it with the IC memory unit of Fig. 7-30, we note that the binary cell now is a magnetic core and the wires linking it. The excitation of the core is accomplished by means of a current pulse generated in a driver (DR). The output information goes through a sense amplifier (SA) whose outputs set corresponding flip-flops in the buffer register. Three wires link each core. The word wire is excited by a word driver and goes through the three cores of a word. A bit wire is excited by a bit driver and goes through four cores in the same bit position. The sense wire links the same cores as the bit wire and is applied to a sense amplifier that shapes the voltage pulse when a 1 is read and rejects the small disturbance when a 0 is read.

During a read operation, a word-driver current pulse is applied to the cores of the word selected by the decoder. The read current is in the negative direction (Fig. 7-32) and causes all cores of the selected word to go to the 0 state, regardless of their previous state. Cores which previously contained a 1 switch their flux and

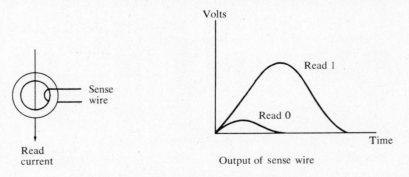

Figure 7-32 Reading a bit from a magnetic core

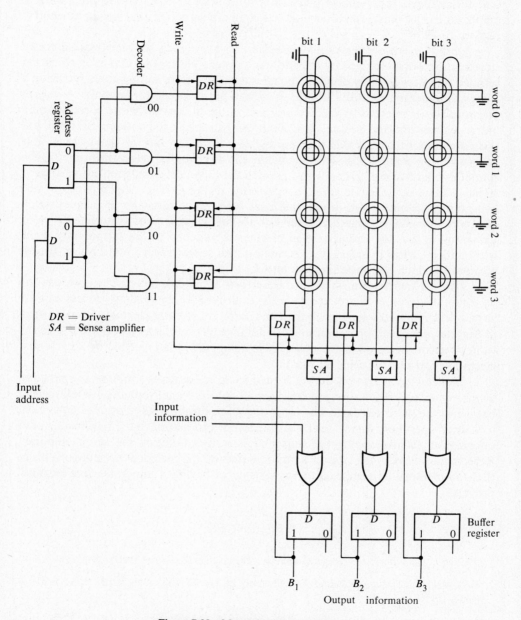

Figure 7-33 Magnetic-core memory unit

299

induce a voltage into their sense wire. The flux of cores which already contained a 0 is not changed. The voltage pulse on a sense wire of cores with a previous 1 is amplified in the sense amplifier and sets the corresponding flip-flop in the buffer register.

During a write operation, the buffer register holds the information to be stored in the word specified by the address register. We assume that all cores in the selected word are initially cleared, i.e., all are in the 0 state so that cores requiring a 1 need to undergo a change of state. A current pulse is generated simultaneously in the word driver selected by the decoder and in the bit driver, whose corresponding buffer register flip-flop contains a 1. Both currents are in the positive direction, but their magnitude is only half that needed to switch the flux to the 1 state. This half-current by itself is too small to change the direction of magnetization. But the sum of two half-currents is enough to switch the direction of magnetization to the 1 state. A core switches to the 1 state only if there is a coincidence of two half-currents from a word driver and a bit driver. The direction of magnetization of a core does not change if it receives only half-current from one of the drivers. The result is that the magnetization of cores is switched to the 1 state only if the word and bit wires intersect, that is, only in the selected word and only in the bit position in which the buffer register is a 1.

The read and write operations described above are incomplete, because the information stored in the selected word is destroyed by the reading process and the write operation works properly only if the cores are initially cleared. As mentioned in Section 7-7, a read operation must be followed by another cycle that restores the values previously stored in the cores. A write operation is preceded by a cycle that clears the cores of the selected word.

The restore operation during a read cycle is equivalent to a write operation which, in effect, writes the previously read information from the buffer register back into the word selected. The clear operation during a write cycle is equivalent to a read operation which destroys the stored information but prevents the read information from reaching the buffer register by inhibiting the sense amplifier. Restore and clear cycles are normally initiated by the memory internal control, so that the memory unit appears to the outside as having a nondestructive read-out property.

REFERENCES

1. *The TTL Data Book for Design Engineers*. Dallas, Texas: Texas Instruments, Inc., 1976.

2. Blakeslee, T. R., *Digital Design with Standard MSI and LSI*. New York: John Wiley & Sons, 1975.

3. Barna A., and D. I. Porat, *Integrated Circuits in Digital Electronics*. New York: John Wiley & Sons, 1973.

4. Taub, H., and D. Schilling, *Digital Integrated Electronics*. New York: McGraw-Hill Book Co., 1977.

5. Grinich, V. H., and H. G. Jackson, *Introduction to Integrated Electronics*. New York: McGraw-Hill Book Co., 1975.

6. Kostopoulos, G. K., *Digital Engineering*. New York: McGraw-Hill Book Co., 1975.

7. Scott, N. R., *Electronic Computer Technology*. New York: McGraw-Hill Book Co., 1970, chap. 10.

8. Kline, R. M., *Digital Computer Design*. Englewood Cliffs, N.J.: Prentice-Hall, Inc., 1977, chap. 9.

PROBLEMS

7-1.   The register of Fig. 7-1 transfers the input information into the flip-flops when the *CP* input goes through a positive-edge transition. Modify the circuit so that the input information is transferred into the register when a clock pulse goes through a negative-edge transition, provided a load input control is equal to binary 1.

7-2.   The register of Fig. 7-3 loads the inputs during a negative transition of a clock pulse. What internal changes are necessary for the inputs to be loaded during the positive edge of a pulse?

7-3.   Verify the circuit of Fig. 7-5 using maps to simplify the next-state equations.

7-4.   Design the sequential circuit whose state table is given below using a 2-bit register and combinational gates.

Present state		Input	Next state	
A	*B*	*x*	*A*	*B*
0	0	0	0	0
0	0	1	0	1
0	1	0	1	0
0	1	1	0	1
1	0	0	1	0
1	0	1	1	1
1	1	0	1	0
1	1	1	0	1

7-5.   Design a sequential circuit whose state diagram is given in Fig. 6-27 using a 3-bit register and a 16 × 4 ROM.

7-6.   The content of a 4-bit shift register is initially 1101. The register is shifted six times to the right, with the serial input being 101101. What is the content of the register after each shift?

7-7.   What is the difference between serial and parallel transfer? What type of register is used in each case?

7-8. The 4-bit bidirectional shift register of Fig. 7-9 is enclosed within one IC package.
(a) Draw a block diagram of the IC showing all inputs and outputs.
(b) Draw a block diagram using three ICs to produce a 12-bit bidirectional shift register.

7-9. The serial adder of Fig. 7-10 uses two 4-bit shift registers. Register A holds the binary number 0101 and register B holds 0111. The carry flip-flop Q is initially cleared. List the binary values in register A and flip-flop Q after each shift.

7-10. What changes are needed in the circuit of Fig. 7-11 to convert it to a circuit that subtracts the content of B from the content of A?

7-11. Design a serial counter; in other words, determine the circuit that must be included externally with a shift register in order to obtain a counter that operates in a serial fashion.

7-12. Draw the diagram of a 4-bit binary ripple counter using flip-flops that trigger on the positive edge.

7-13. A flip-flop has a 20-ns delay from the time its CP input goes from 1 to 0 to the time the output is complemented. What is the maximum delay in a 10-bit binary ripple counter that uses these flip-flops? What is the maximum frequency the counter can operate at reliably?

7-14. How many flip-flops must be complemented in a 10-bit binary ripple counter to reach the next count after 0111111111?

7-15. Draw the diagram of a 4-bit binary ripple down-counter using flip-flops that trigger on the (a) positive-edge transition and (b) negative-edge transition.

7-16. Draw a timing diagram similar to that in Fig. 7-15 for the binary ripple counter of Fig. 7-12.

7-17. Determine the next state for each of the six unused states in the BCD ripple counter of Fig. 7-14. Is the counter self-starting?

7-18. The ripple counter shown in Fig. P7-18 uses flip-flops that trigger on the negative-edge transition of the CP input. Determine the count sequence of the counter. Is the counter self-starting?

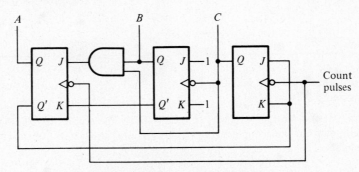

Figure P7-18 Ripple counter

7-19.   What happens to the counter of Fig. 7-18 if both the up and down inputs are equal to 1 at the same time? Modify the circuit so that it will count up if this condition occurs.

7-20.   Verify the flip-flop input functions of the synchronous BCD counter specified in Table 7-5. Draw the logic diagram of the BCD counter and include a count-enable control input.

7-21.   Design a synchronous BCD counter with *JK* flip-flops.

7-22.   Show the external connections of four IC binary counters with parallel load (Fig. 7-19) to produce a 16-bit binary counter. Use a block diagram for each IC.

7-23.   Construct a BCD counter using the MSI circuit of Fig. 7-19.

7-24.   Construct a mod-12 counter using the MSI circuit specified in Fig. 7-19. Give four alternatives.

7-25.   Using two MSI circuits as specified in Fig. 7-19, construct a binary counter that counts from 0 to binary 64.

7-26.   Using the *stop* variable from Fig. 7-21 as a start signal, construct a second word-time control that stays on for a period of 16 clock pulses.

7-27.   Show that an n-bit binary counter connected to an n-to-2^n line decoder is equivalent to a ring counter with 2^n flip-flops. Draw the block diagrams of both circuits for $n = 3$. How many timing signals are generated?

7-28.   Include an enable input to the decoder of Fig. 7-22(b) and connect it to the clock pulses. Draw the timing signals that are now generated at the outputs of the decoder.

7-29.   Complete the design of the Johnson counter of Fig. 7-23, showing the outputs of the eight timing signals.

7-30.   (a) List the eight unused states in the switch-tail ring counter of Fig. 7-23. Determine the next state for each unused state and show that, if the circuit finds itself in an invalid state, it does not return to a valid state. (b) Modify the circuit as recommended in the text and show that (1) the circuit produces the same sequence of states as listed in Fig. 7-23(b), and (2) the circuit reaches a valid state from any one of the unused states.

7-31.   Construct a Johnson counter with ten timing signals.

7-32.   (a) The memory unit of Fig. 7-24 has a capacity of 8192 words of 32 bits per word. How many flip-flops are needed for the memory address register and memory buffer register? (b) How many words will the memory unit contain if the address register has 15 bits?

7-33.   When the number of words to be selected in a memory is too large, it is convenient to use a binary storage cell with two select inputs: one X (horizontal) and one Y (vertical) select input. Both X and Y must be enabled to select the cell.
        (a) Draw a binary cell similar to that in Fig. 7-29 with X and Y select inputs.
        (b) Show how two 4×16 decoders can be used to select a word in a 256-word memory.

7-34.   (a) Draw a block diagram of the 4 × 3 memory of Fig. 7-30, showing all inputs and outputs. (b) Construct an 8 × 3 memory using two such units. Use a block diagram construction.

7-35.   It is required to construct a memory with 256 words, 16 bits per word, organized as in Fig. 7-33. Cores are available in a matrix of 16 rows and 16 columns.

   (a) How many matrices are needed?

   (b) How many flip-flops are in the address and buffer registers?

   (c) How many cores receive current during a read cycle?

   (d) How many cores receive at least half-current during a write cycle?

Register-Transfer Logic

8

8-1 INTRODUCTION

A digital system is a sequential logic system constructed with flip-flops and gates. It was shown in previous chapters that a sequential circuit can be specified by means of a state table. To specify a large digital system with a state table would be very difficult, if not impossible, because the number of states would be prohibitively large. To overcome this difficulty, digital systems are invariably designed using a modular approach. The system is partitioned into modular subsystems, each of which performs some functional task. The modules are constructed from such digital functions as registers, counters, decoders, multiplexers, arithmetic elements, and control logic. The various modules are interconnected with common data and control paths to form a digital computer system. A typical digital system module would be the processor unit of a digital computer.

The interconnection of digital functions to form a digital system module cannot be described by means of combinational or sequential logic techniques. These techniques were developed to describe a digital system at the gate and flip-flop level and are not suitable for describing the system at the digital function level. To describe a digital system in terms of functions such as adders, decoders, and registers, it is necessary to employ a higher-level mathematical notation. The register-transfer logic method fulfills this requirement. In this method, the registers are selected to be the primitive components in the digital system, rather than the gates and flip-flops as in sequential logic. In this way it is possible to describe, in a concise and precise manner, the information flow and processing tasks among the data stored in the registers. The register-transfer logic method uses a set of expressions and statements which resemble the statements used in programming languages. This notation provides the necessary tools for specifying a prescribed set of interconnections between various digital functions. An important characteristic of the register-transfer logic method of presentation is that it is closely related to the way people would prefer to specify the operations of a digital system.

The basic components of this method are those that describe a digital system from the operational level. The operation of a digital system is best described by specifying:

1. The set of registers in the system and their functions.

2. The binary-coded information stored in the registers.

3. The operations performed on the information stored in the registers.

4. The control functions that initiate the sequence of operations.

These four components form the basis of the register-transfer logic method for describing digital systems.

A *register*, as defined in the register-transfer logic notation, not only implies a register as defined in Chapter 7, but also encompasses all other types of registers, such as shift registers, counters, and memory units. A counter is considered to be a register whose function is to increment by 1 the information stored within it. A memory unit is considered to be a collection of storage registers where information can be stored. A flip-flop standing alone is taken to be a 1-bit register. In fact, the flip-flops and associated gates of any sequential circuit are called a register by this method of designation.

The *binary information* stored in registers may be binary numbers, binary-coded decimal numbers, alphanumeric characters, control information, or any other binary-coded information. The operations that are performed on the data stored in registers depend on the type of data encountered. Numbers are manipulated with arithmetic operations, whereas control information is usually manipulated with logic operations such as setting and clearing specified bits in the register.

The operations performed on the data stored in registers are called *microoperations*. A microoperation is an elementary operation that can be performed in parallel during one clock pulse period. The result of the operation may replace the previous binary information of a register or may be transferred to another register. Examples of microoperations are shift, count, add, clear, and load. The digital functions introduced in Chapter 7 are registers that implement microoperations. A counter with parallel load is capable of performing the microoperations increment and load. A bidirectional shift register is capable of performing the shift-right and shift-left microoperations. The combinational MSI functions introduced in Chapter 5 can be used in some applications to perform microoperations. A binary parallel adder is useful for implementing the *add* microoperation on the contents of two registers that hold binary numbers. A microoperation requires only one clock pulse for execution if the operation is done in parallel. In serial computers, a microoperation requires a number of pulses equal to the word time in the system. This is equal to the number of bits in the shift registers that transfer the information serially while a microoperation is being executed.

The *control functions* that initiate the sequence of operations consist of timing signals that sequence the operations one at a time. Certain conditions which depend on results of previous operations may also determine the state of control functions. A control function is a binary variable that, when in one binary state, initiates an operation and, when in the other binary state, inhibits the operation.

The purpose of this chapter is to introduce the components of the register-transfer logic method in some detail. The chapter introduces a symbolic notation for representing registers, for specifying operations on the contents of registers, and for specifying control functions. This symbolic notation is sometimes called a *register-transfer language* or *computer hardware description language*. The register-transfer language adopted here is believed to be as simple as possible. It should be realized, however, that no standard symbology exists for a register-transfer language, and different sources adopt different conventions.

A statement in a register-transfer language consists of a control function and a list of microoperations. The control function (which may be omitted sometimes) specifies the control condition and timing sequence for executing the listed microoperations. The microoperations specify the elementary operations to be performed on the information stored in registers. The types of microoperations most often encountered in digital systems can be classified into four categories:

1. *Interregister-transfer* microoperations do not change the information content when the binary information moves from one register to another.

2. *Arithmetic* microoperations perform arithmetic on numbers stored in registers.

3. *Logic* microoperations perform operations such as AND and OR on individual pairs of bits stored in registers.

4. *Shift* microoperations specify operations for shift registers.

Sections 8-2 through 8-4 define a basic set of microoperations. Special symbols are assigned to the microoperations in the set, and each symbol is shown to be associated with corresponding digital hardware that implements the stated microoperation. It is important to realize that the register-transfer logic notation is directly related to, and cannot be separated from, the registers and the digital functions that it defines.

The microoperations performed on the information stored in registers depend on the type of data that reside in the registers. The binary information commonly found in registers of digital computers can be classified into three categories:

1. Numerical data such as binary numbers or binary-coded decimal numbers used in arithmetic computations.

2. Nonnumerical data such as alphanumeric characters or other binary-coded symbols used for special applications.

3. Instruction codes, addresses, and other control information used to specify the data-processing requirements in the system.

Sections 8-5 through 8-9 discuss the representation of numerical data and their relationship to the arithmetic microoperations. Section 8-10 explains the use of logic microoperations for processing nonnumerical data. The representation of instruction codes and their manipulation with microoperations are presented in Sections 8-11 and 8-12.

8-2 INTERREGISTER TRANSFER

The registers in a digital system are designated by capital letters (sometimes followed by numerals) to denote the function of the register. For example, the register that holds an address for the memory unit is usually called the memory address register and is designated MAR. Other designations for registers are A, B, $R1$, $R2$, and IR. The cells or flip-flops of an n-bit register are numbered in sequence from 1 to n (or from 0 to $n-1$) starting either from the left or from the right. Figure 8-1 shows four ways to represent a register in block diagram form. The most common way to represent a register is by a rectangular box with the name of the register inside, as shown in Fig. 8-1(a). The individual cells can be distinguished as in (b), with each cell assigned a letter with a subscript number. The numbering of cells from right to left can be marked on top of the box as in the 12-bit register MBR in (c). A 16-bit register is partitioned into two parts in (d). Bits 1 through 8 are assigned the symbol letter L (for low) and bits 9 through 16 are assigned the symbol letter H (for high). The name of the 16-bit register is PC. The symbol $PC(H)$ refers to the eight high-ordered cells and $PC(L)$ refers to the eight low-ordered cells of the register.

Registers can be specified in a register-transfer language with a declaration statement. For example, the registers of Fig. 8-1 can be defined with declaration

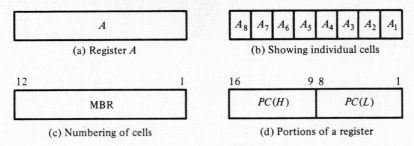

(a) Register A (b) Showing individual cells

(c) Numbering of cells   (d) Portions of a register

Figure 8-1 Block diagram of registers

statements such as:

> DECLARE REGISTER $A(8)$, $MBR(12)$, $PC(16)$
> DECLARE SUBREGISTER $PC(L) = PC(1\text{--}8)$, $PC(H) = PC(9\text{--}16)$

However, in this book we will not use declaration statements to define registers; instead, the registers will be shown in block diagram form as in Fig. 8-1. Registers shown in a block diagram can be easily converted into declaration statements for simulation purposes.

Information transfer from one register to another is designated in symbolic form by means of the *replacement operator*. The statement:

$$A \leftarrow B$$

denotes the transfer of the *contents* of register B into register A. It designates a replacement of the contents of A by the contents of B. By definition, the contents of the source register B do not change after the transfer.

A statement that specifies a register transfer implies that circuits are available from the outputs of the source register to the cell inputs of the destination register. Normally, we do not want this transfer to occur with every clock pulse, but only under a predetermined condition. The condition that determines when the transfer is to occur is called a *control function*. A control function is a Boolean function that can be equal to 1 or 0. The control function is included with the statement as follows:

$$x'T_1:\quad A \leftarrow B$$

The control function is terminated with a colon. It symbolizes the requirement that the transfer operation be executed by the hardware only when the Boolean function $x'T_1 = 1$, i.e., when variable $x = 0$ and timing variable $T_1 = 1$.

Every statement written in a register-transfer language implies a hardware construction for implementing the transfer. Figure 8-2 shows the implementation of the statement written above. The outputs of register B are connected to the inputs of register A, and the number of lines in this connection is equal to the

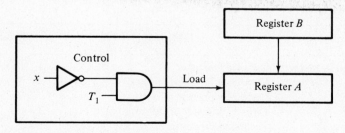

Figure 8-2   Hardware implementation of the statement $x'T_1$: $A \leftarrow B$

number of bits in the registers. Register A must have a load control input so that it can be enabled when the control function is 1. Although not shown, it is assumed that register A has an additional input that accepts continuous synchronized clock pulses. The control function is generated by means of an inverter and an AND gate. It is also assumed that the control unit that generates the timing variable T_1 is synchronized with the same clock pulses that are applied to register A. The control function stays on during one clock pulse period (when the timing variable is equal to 1), and the transfer occurs during the next transition of a clock pulse.

The basic symbols of the register-transfer logic are listed in Table 8-1. Registers are denoted by capital letters, and numerals may follow the letters. Subscripts are used to distinguish individual cells of the register. Parentheses are used to define a portion of a register. The arrow denotes a transfer of information and the direction of transfer. A colon terminates a control function, and the comma is used to separate two or more operations that are executed at the same time. The statement:

$$T_3: \quad A \leftarrow B, \quad\quad B \leftarrow A$$

denotes an exchange operation that swaps the contents of two registers during one common clock pulse. This simultaneous operation is possible in registers with master-slave or edge-triggered flip-flops.

The square brackets are used in conjunction with memory transfer. The letter M designates a memory word, and the register enclosed inside the square brackets provides the address for the memory. This is explained in more detail below.

There are occasions when a destination register receives information from two sources, but evidently not at the same time. Consider the two statements:

$$T_1: \quad C \leftarrow A$$

$$T_5: \quad C \leftarrow B$$

The first line states that the contents of register A are to be transferred to register C when timing variable T_1 occurs. The second statement uses the same destination register as the first, but with a different source register and a different timing

TABLE 8-1   Basic symbols for register-transfer logic

Symbol	Description	Examples
Letters (and numerals)	Denotes a register	A, MBR, $R2$
Subscript	Denotes a bit of a register	A_2, B_6
Parentheses ( )	Denotes a portion of a register	$PC(H)$, $MBR(OP)$
Arrow $\leftarrow$	Denotes transfer of information	$A \leftarrow B$
Colon :	Terminates a control function	$x'T_0:$
Comma ,	Separates two microoperations	$A \leftarrow B$, $B \leftarrow A$
Square brackets [ ]	Specifies an address for memory transfer	$MBR \leftarrow M[MAR]$

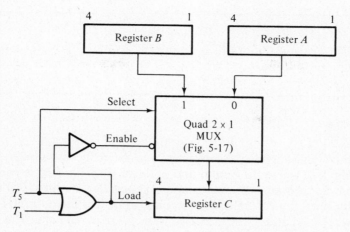

Figure 8-3 Use of a multiplexer to transfer information from two sources into a single destination

variable. The connection of two source registers to the same destination register cannot be done directly, but requires a multiplexer circuit to select between two possible paths. The block diagram of the circuit that implements the two statements is shown in Fig. 8-3. For registers with four bits each, we need a quadruple 2-to-1 line multiplexer, similar to the one previously given in Fig. 5-17, in order to select either register A or register B. When $T_5 = 1$, register B is selected, but when $T_1 = 1$, register A is selected (because T_5 must be 0 when T_1 is 1). The multiplexer and the load input of register C are enabled every time T_1 or T_5 occurs. This causes a transfer of information from the selected source register into the destination register.

Bus Transfer

Quite often a digital system has many registers, and paths must be provided to transfer information from one register to another register. Consider, for example, the requirement for transfer among three registers as shown in Fig. 8-4. There are six data paths, and each register requires a multiplexer to select between two sources. If each register consists of n flip-flops, there is a need for $6n$ lines and three multiplexers. As the number of registers increases, the number of interconnection lines and multiplexers increases. If we restrict the transfer to one at a time,

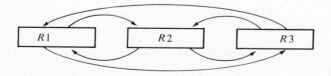

Figure 8-4 Transfer among three registers

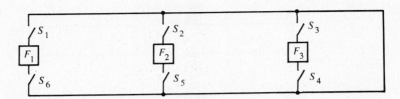

Figure 8-5 Transfer through one common line

the number of paths among the registers can be reduced considerably. This is shown in Fig. 8-5, where the output and input of each flip-flop is connected to a common line through an electronic circuit that acts like a switch. All the switches are normally open until a transfer is required. For a transfer from F_1 to F_3, for example, switches S_1 and S_4 are closed to form the required path. This scheme can be extended to registers with n flip-flops, and it requires n common lines.

A group of wires through which binary information is transferred one at a time among registers is called a *bus*. For parallel transfer, the number of lines in the bus is equal to the number of bits in the registers. The idea of a bus transfer is analogous to a central transportation system used to bring commuters from one point to another. Instead of each commuter using private transportation to go from one location to another, a bus system is used, and the commuters wait in line until transportation is available.

A common-bus system can be constructed with multiplexers, and a destination register for the bus transfer can be selected by means of a decoder. The multiplexers select one source register for the bus, and the decoder selects one destination register to transfer the information from the bus. The construction of a bus system for four registers is depicted in Fig. 8-6. The four bits in the same significant position in the registers go through a 4-to-1 line multiplexer to form one line of the bus. Only two multiplexers are shown in the diagram: one for the low-order significant bits and one for the high-order significant bits. For registers of n bits, n multiplexers are needed to produce an n-line bus. The n lines in the bus are connected to the n inputs of all registers. The transfer of information from the bus into one destination register is accomplished by activating the load control of that register. The particular load control activated is selected by the outputs of the decoder when enabled. If the decoder is not enabled, no information will be transferred, even though the multiplexers place the contents of a source register onto the bus.

To illustrate with a particular example, consider the statement:

$$C \leftarrow A$$

The control function that enables this transfer must select register A for the bus and register C for the destination. The multiplexers and decoder select inputs must

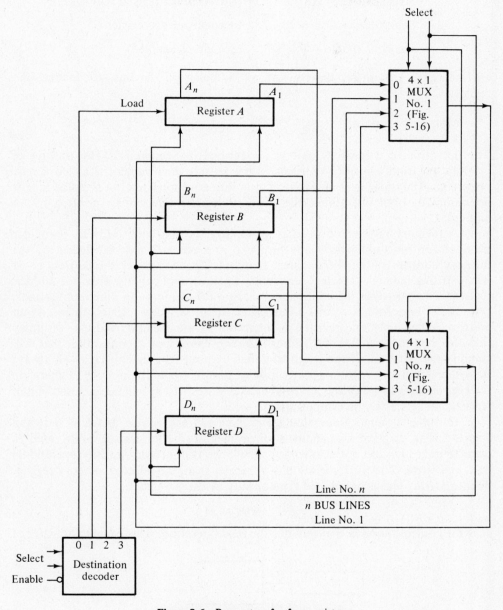

Figure 8-6 Bus system for four registers

be:

$$\text{Select source} = 00 \qquad \text{(MUXs select register } A)$$

$$\text{Select destination} = 10 \qquad \text{(decoder selects register } C)$$

$$\text{Decoder enable} = 0 \qquad \text{(decoder is enabled)}$$

On the next clock pulse, the contents of A, being on the bus, are loaded into register C.

Memory Transfer

The operation of a memory unit was described in Section 7-7. The transfer of information from a memory register to the outside environment is called a *read* operation. The transfer of new information into a memory register is called a *write* operation. In both operations, the memory register selected is specified by an address.

A memory register or word is symbolized by the letter M. The particular memory register among the many available in a memory unit is selected by the memory address during the transfer. It is necessary to specify the address of M when writing memory-transfer statements. In some applications, only one address register is connected to the address terminals of the memory. In other applications, the address lines form a common-bus system to allow many registers to specify an address. When only one register is connected to the memory address, we know that this register specifies the address and we can adopt a convention that will simplify the notation. If the letter M stands by itself in a statement, it will always designate a memory register selected by the address presently in MAR. Otherwise, the register that specifies the address (or the address itself) will be enclosed within square brackets after the symbol M.

Consider a memory unit that has a single address register, MAR, as shown in Fig. 8-7. The diagram also shows a single memory buffer register MBR used to transfer data into and out of memory. There are two memory-transfer operations: read and write. The read operation is a transfer from the selected memory register M into MBR. This is designated symbolically by the statement:

$$R: \quad MBR \leftarrow M$$

R is the control function that initiates the read operation. This causes a transfer of

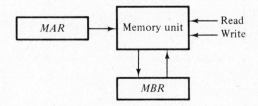

Figure 8-7   Memory unit that communicates with two external registers

information into MBR from the selected memory register M specified by the address in MAR. The write operation is a transfer from MBR to the selected memory register M. This is designated by the statement:

$$W: \quad M \leftarrow MBR$$

W is the control function that initiates the write operation. This causes a transfer of information from MBR into the memory register M selected by the address presently in MAR.

The access time of a memory unit must be synchronized with the master clock pulses in the system that triggers the processor registers. In fast memories, the access time may be shorter than or equal to a clock pulse period. In slow memories, it may be necessary to wait for a number of clock pulses for the transfer to be completed. In magnetic-core memories, the processor registers must wait for the memory cycle time to be completed. For a read operation, the cycle time includes the restoration of the word after reading. For a write operation, the cycle time includes the clearing of the memory word prior to writing.

In some systems, the memory unit receives addresses and data from many registers connected to common buses. Consider the case depicted in Fig. 8-8. The address to the memory unit comes from an address bus. Four registers are connected to this bus and any one may supply an address. The output of the memory can go to any one of four registers which are selected by a decoder. The data input to the memory comes from the data bus, which selects one of four registers. A memory word is specified in such a system by the symbol M followed by a register enclosed in square brackets. The contents of the register within the square brackets specify the address for M. The transfer of information from register $B2$ to a memory word selected by the address in register $A1$ is symbolized by the statement:

$$W: \quad M[A1] \leftarrow B2$$

This is a write operation, with register $A1$ specifying the address. The square brackets after the letter M give the address register used for selecting the memory register M. The statement does not specify the buses explicitly. Nevertheless, it implies the required selection inputs for the two multiplexers that form the address and data buses.

The read operation in a memory with buses can be specified in a similar manner. The statement:

$$R: \quad B0 \leftarrow M[A3]$$

symbolizes a read operation from a memory register whose address is given by $A3$. The binary information coming out of memory is transferred to register $B0$. Again, this statement implies the required selection inputs for the address multiplexer and the selection variables for the destination decoder.

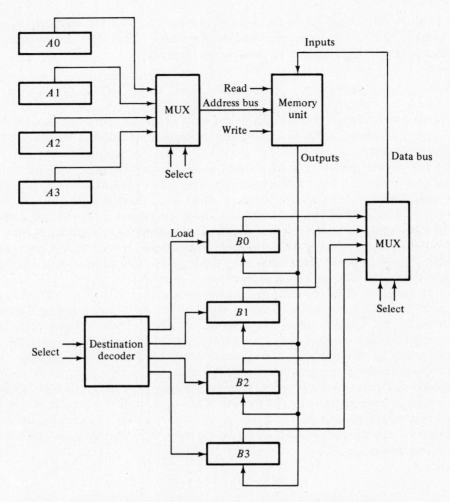

Figure 8-8 Memory unit that communicates with multiple registers

8-3 ARITHMETIC, LOGIC, AND SHIFT MICROOPERATIONS

The interregister-transfer microoperations do not change the information content when the binary information moves from the source register to the destination register. All other microoperations change the information content during the transfer. Among all possible operations that can exist in a digital system, there is a basic set from which all other operations can be obtained. In this section, we define a set of basic microoperations, their symbolic notation, and the digital hardware that implements them. Other microoperations with appropriate symbols can be defined if necessary to suit a particular application.

Arithmetic Microoperations

The basic arithmetic microoperations are add, subtract, complement, and shift. Arithmetic shifts are explained in Section 8-7 in conjunction with the type of binary data representation. All other arithmetic operations can be obtained from a variation or a sequence of these basic microoperations.

The arithmetic microoperation defined by the statement:

$$F \leftarrow A + B$$

specifies an *add* operation. It states that the contents of register A are to be added to the contents of register B, and the sum transferred to register F. To implement this statement, we require three registers, A, B, and F, and the digital function that performs the addition operation, such as a parallel adder. The other basic arithmetic operations are listed in Table 8-2. Arithmetic subtraction implies the availability of a binary parallel subtractor composed of full-subtractor circuits connected in cascade. Subtraction is most often implemented through complementation and addition as specified by the statement:

$$F \leftarrow A + \bar{B} + 1$$

$\bar{B}$ is the symbol for the 1's complement of B. Adding 1 to the 1's complement gives the 2's complement of B. Adding A to the 2's complement of B produces A minus B.

The increment and decrement microoperations are symbolized by a *plus-one* or *minus-one* operation executed on the contents of a register. These microoperations are implemented with an up-counter or down-counter, respectively.

There must be a direct relationship between the statements written in a register-transfer language and the registers and digital functions which are required for their implementation. To illustrate this relationship, consider the two statements:

$$T_2: \quad A \leftarrow A + B$$
$$T_5: \quad A \leftarrow A + 1$$

TABLE 8-2 Arithmetic microoperations

Symbolic designation	Description
$F \leftarrow A + B$	Contents of A plus B transferred to F
$F \leftarrow A - B$	Contents of A minus B transferred to F
$B \leftarrow \bar{B}$	Complement register B (1's complement)
$B \leftarrow \bar{B} + 1$	Form the 2's complement of the contents of register B
$F \leftarrow A + \bar{B} + 1$	A plus the 2's complement of B transferred to F
$A \leftarrow A + 1$	Increment the contents of A by 1 (count up)
$A \leftarrow A - 1$	Decrement the contents of A by 1 (count down)

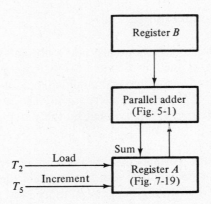

Figure 8-9 Implementation for the add and increment microoperations

Timing variable T_2 initiates an operation to add the contents of register B to the present contents of A. Timing variable T_5 increments register A. The incrementing can be easily done with a counter, and the sum of two binary numbers can be generated with a parallel adder. The transfer of the sum from the parallel adder into register A can be activated with a load input in the register. This dictates that the register be a counter with parallel-load capability. The implementation of the above two statements is shown in block diagram form in Fig. 8-9. A parallel adder receives input information from registers A and B. The sum bits from the parallel adder are applied to the inputs of A, and timing variable T_2 loads the sum into register A. Timing variable T_5 increments the register by enabling the increment input (or count input, as in Fig. 7-19).

Note that the arithmetic operations multiply and divide are not listed in Table 8-2. The multiplication operation can be represented by the symbol $*$, and the division by a $/$. These two operations are valid arithmetic operations but are not included in the basic set of microoperations. The only place where these operations can be considered as microoperations is in a digital system where they are implemented by means of combinational circuits. In such a case, the signals that perform these operations propagate through gates, and the result of the operation can be transferred into a destination register by a clock pulse as soon as the output signals progagate through the combinational circuit. In most computers, the multiplication operation is implemented with a sequence of add and shift microoperations. Division is implemented with a sequence of subtract and shift microoperations. To specify the hardware implementation in such a case requires a list of statements that use the basic microoperations of *add*, *subtract*, and *shift*.

Logic Microoperations

Logic microoperations specify binary operations for a string of bits stored in registers. These operations consider each bit in the registers separately and treat it as a binary variable. As an illustration, the exclusive-OR microoperation is symbolized by the statement:

$$F \leftarrow A \oplus B$$

It specifies a logic operation that considers each pair of bits in the registers as binary variables. If the content of register A is 1010 and that of register B 1100, the information transferred to register F is 0110:

1010	content of A
1100	content of B
0110	content of $F \leftarrow A \oplus B$

There are 16 different possible logic operations that can be performed with two binary variables. These logic operations are listed in Table 2-6. All 16 logic operations can be expressed in terms of the AND, OR, and complement operations. Special symbols will be adopted for these three microoperations to distinguish them from the corresponding symbols used to express Boolean functions. The symbol $\lor$ will be used to denote an OR microoperation and the symbol $\land$ to denote an AND microoperation. The complement microoperation is the same as the 1's complement and uses a bar on top of the letter (or letters) that denotes the register. By using these symbols, it will be possible to differentiate between a logic microoperation and a control (or Boolean) function. The symbols for the four logic microoperations are summarized in Table 8-3. The last two symbols are for the shift microoperations discussed below.

TABLE 8-3   Logic and shift microoperations

Symbolic designation	Description
$A \leftarrow \bar{A}$	Complement all bits of register A
$F \leftarrow A \lor B$	Logic OR microoperation
$F \leftarrow A \land B$	Logic AND microoperation
$F \leftarrow A \oplus B$	Logic exclusive-OR microoperation
$A \leftarrow \text{shl } A$	Shift-left register A
$A \leftarrow \text{shr } A$	Shift-right register A

A more important reason for adopting a special symbol for the OR microoperation is to differentiate the symbol $+$, when used as an arithmetic plus, from a logic OR operation. Although the $+$ symbol has two meanings, it will be possible to distinguish between them by noting where the symbol occurs. When this symbol occurs in a microoperation, it denotes an arithmetic plus. When it occurs in a control (or Boolean) function, it denotes a logic OR operation. For example, in the statement:

$$T_1 + T_2: \quad A \leftarrow A + B, \quad C \leftarrow D \lor F$$

the + between T_1 and T_2 is an OR operation between two timing variables of a control function. The + between A and B specifies an add microoperation. The OR microoperation is designated by the symbol $\lor$ between registers D and F.

The logic microoperations can be easily implemented with a group of gates. The complement of a register of n bits is obtained from n inverter gates. The AND microoperation is obtained from a group of AND gates, each of which receives a pair of bits from the two source registers. The outputs of the AND gates are applied to the inputs of the destination register. The OR microoperation requires a group of OR gates arranged in a similar fashion.

Shift Microoperations

Shift microoperations transfer binary information between registers in serial computers. They are also used in parallel computers for arithmetic, logic, and control operations. Registers can be shifted to the left or to the right. There are no conventional symbols for the shift operations. In this book, we adopt the symbols *shl* and *shr* for the shift-left and shift-right operations, respectively. For example:

$$A \leftarrow \text{shl } A, \qquad B \leftarrow \text{shr } B$$

are two microoperations that specify a 1-bit shift to the left of register A and a 1-bit shift to the right of register B. The register symbol must be the same on both sides of the arrow as in the increment operation.

While the bits of a register are shifted, the extreme flip-flops receive information from the serial input. The extreme flip-flop is in the leftmost position of the register during a shift-right operation and in the rightmost position during a shift-left operation. The information transferred into the extreme flip-flops is not specified by the *shl* and *shr* symbols. Therefore, a shift microoperation statement must be accompanied with another microoperation that specifies the value of the serial input for the bit transfer into the extreme flip-flop. For example:

$$A \leftarrow \text{shl } A, \qquad A_1 \leftarrow A_n$$

is a circular shift that transfers the leftmost bit from A_n into the rightmost flip-flop A_1. Similarly:

$$B \leftarrow \text{shr } B, \qquad A_n \leftarrow E$$

is a shift-right operation with the leftmost flip-flop A_n receiving the value of the 1-bit register E.

8-4 CONDITIONAL CONTROL STATEMENTS

It is sometimes convenient to specify a control condition by a conditional statement rather than a Boolean control function. A *conditional control* statement is symbolized by an *if-then-else* statement in the following manner:

$$P: \quad \textit{If } (\text{condition}) \textit{ then } [\text{microoperation(s)}] \textit{ else } [\text{microoperation(s)}]$$

The statement is interpreted to mean that if the control condition stated within the parentheses after the word *if* is true, then the microoperation (or microoperations) enclosed within the parentheses after the word *then* is executed. If the condition is not true, the microoperation listed after the word *else* is executed. In any case, the control function P must occur for anything to be done. If the *else* part of the statement is missing, then nothing is executed if the condition is not true.

The conditional control statement is more of a convenience than a necessity. It enables the writing of clearer statements that are easier for people to interpret. It can always be rewritten in a conventional statement without an if-then-else form. As an example, consider the conditional control statement:

$$T_2: \quad \text{If } (C = 0) \text{ then } (F \leftarrow 1) \text{ else } (F \leftarrow 0)$$

F is assumed to be a 1-bit register (flip-flop) that can be set or cleared. If register C is a 1-bit register, the statement is equivalent to the following two statements:

$$C'T_2: \quad F \leftarrow 1$$
$$CT_2: \quad F \leftarrow 0$$

Note that the same timing variable can occur in two separate control functions. The variable C can be either 0 or 1; therefore, only one of the microoperations will be executed during T_2, depending on the value of C.

If register C has more than one bit, the condition $C = 0$ means that all bits of C must be 0. Assume that register C has four bits C_1, C_2, C_3, and C_4. The condition for $C = 0$ can be expressed with a Boolean function:

$$x = C_1' C_2' C_3' C_4' = (C_1 + C_2 + C_3 + C_4)'$$

Variable x can be generated with a NOR gate. Using the definition of x as above, the conditional control statement is now equivalent to the two statements:

$$xT_2: \quad F \leftarrow 1$$
$$x'T_2: \quad F \leftarrow 0$$

Variable $x = 1$ if $C = 0$ but is equal to 0 if $C \neq 0$.

When writing conditional control statements, one must realize that the condition stated after the word *if* is part of the control function and not part of a microoperation statement. The condition must be clearly stated and must be implementable with a combinational circuit.

8-5 FIXED-POINT BINARY DATA

The binary information found in registers represents either data or control information. Data are operands and other discrete elements of information operated on to achieve required results. Control information is a bit or group of bits that specify the operations to be done. A unit of control information stored in digital computer registers is called an *instruction* and is a binary code that specifies the operations to be performed on the stored data. Instruction codes and their representation in registers are presented in Section 8-11. Some commonly used types of data and their representation in registers are presented in this and the following sections.

Sign and Radix-Point Representation

A register with n flip-flops can store a binary number of n bits; each flip-flop represents one binary digit. This represents the magnitude of the number but does not give information about its sign or the position of the binary point. The sign is needed for arithmetic operations, as it shows whether the number is positive or negative. The position of the binary point is needed to represent integers, fractions, or mixed integer-fraction numbers.

The sign of a number is a discrete quantity of information having two values: plus and minus. These two values can be represented by a code of one bit. The convention is to represent a plus with a 0 and a minus with a 1. To represent a sign binary number in a register, we need $n = k + 1$ flip-flops, k flip-flops for the magnitude and one for storing the sign of the number.

The representation of the binary point is complicated by the fact that it is characterized by a *position* between two flip-flops in the register. There are two possible ways of specifying the position of the binary point in a register: by giving it a *fixed-point* position or by employing a *floating-point* representation. The fixed-point method assumes that the binary point is always fixed in one position. The two positions most widely used are (1) a binary point in the extreme left of the register to make the stored number a fraction, and (2) a binary point in the extreme right of the register to make the stored number an integer. In both cases, the binary point is not physically visible but is assumed from the fact that the number stored in the register is treated as a fraction or as an integer. The floating-point representation uses a second register to store a number that designates the position of the binary point in the first register. Floating-point representation is explained in Section 8-9.

Signed Binary Numbers

When a fixed-point binary number is positive, the sign is represented by 0 and the magnitude by a positive binary number. When the number is negative, the sign is represented by 1 and the rest of the number may be represented in any one of three different ways. These are:

1. Sign-magnitude.

2. Sign-1's complement.

3. Sign-2's complement.

In the sign-magnitude representation, the magnitude is represented by a positive binary number. In the other two representations, the number is in either 1's or 2's complement. If the number is positive, the three representations are the same.

As an example, the binary number 9 is written below in the three representations. It is assumed that a 7-bit register is available to store the sign and the magnitude of the number.

	+9	−9
Sign-magnitude	0 001001	1 001001
Sign-1's complement	0 001001	1 110110
Sign-2's complement	0 001001	1 110111

A positive number in any representation has a 0 in the leftmost bit for a plus, followed by a positive binary number. A negative number always has a 1 in the leftmost bit for a minus, but the magnitude bits are represented differently. In the sign-magnitude representation, these bits are the positive number; in the 1's-complement representation, these bits are the complement of the binary number; and in the 2's-complement representation, the number is in its 2's-complement form.

The sign-magnitude representation of −9 is obtained from +9 (0 001001) by complementing *only* the sign bit. The sign-1's-complement representation of −9 is obtained by complementing *all* the bits of 0 001001 (+9), including the sign bit. The sign-2's-complement representation is obtained by taking the 2's complement of the positive number, *including* its sign bit.

Arithmetic Addition

The reason for using the sign-complement representation for negative numbers will become apparent after we consider the steps involved in forming the sum of two signed numbers. The sign-magnitude representation is the one used in everyday calculations. For example, +23 and −35 are represented with a sign, followed by the magnitude of the number. To add these two numbers, it is necessary to subtract the smaller magnitude from the larger magnitude and to use the sign of the larger number for the sign of the result, i.e., $(+23) + (-35) = -(35-23) = -12$. The process of adding two signed numbers when negative numbers are represented in sign-magnitude form requires that we compare their signs. If the two signs are the same, we add the two magnitudes. If the signs are not the same, we compare the relative magnitudes of the numbers and then subtract the smaller from the larger. It is necessary also to determine the sign of the result. This is a process that, when implemented with digital hardware, requires a sequence of control decisions as well as circuits that can compare, add, and subtract numbers.

Now compare the above procedure with the procedure that forms the sum of two signed binary numbers when negative numbers are in 1's- or 2's-complement representation. These procedures are very simple and can be stated as follows:

Addition with sign-2's-complement representation. The addition of two signed binary numbers with negative numbers represented by their 2's complement is obtained from the addition of the two numbers including their sign bits. A carry in the most significant (sign) bit is discarded.

Addition with sign-1's-complement representation. The addition of two signed binary numbers with negative numbers represented by their 1's complement is obtained from the addition of the two numbers, including their sign bits. If there is a carry out of the most significant (sign) bit, the result is incremented by 1 and its carry is discarded.

Numerical examples for addition with negative numbers represented by their 2's complement are shown below. Note that negative numbers must be initially in 2's-complement representation and that the sum obtained after addition is always in the required representation.

$$
\begin{array}{rl} \quad\quad +\;\;6 & 0\;\,000110 \\ +\;\;9 & 0\;\,001001 \\ \hline +\;15 & 0\;\,001111 \end{array}
\qquad\qquad
\begin{array}{rl} -\;\;6 & 1\;\,111010 \\ +\;\;9 & 0\;\,001001 \\ \hline +\;\;3 & 0\;\,000011 \end{array}
$$

$$
\begin{array}{rl} \quad\quad +\;\;6 & 0\;\,000110 \\ -\;\;9 & 1\;\,110111 \\ \hline -\;\;3 & 1\;\,111101 \end{array}
\qquad\qquad
\begin{array}{rl} -\;\;9 & 1\;\,110111 \\ -\;\;9 & 1\;\,110111 \\ \hline -\;18 & 1\;\,101110 \end{array}
$$

The two numbers in the four examples are added, including their sign bits. Any carry out of the sign bit is discarded, and negative results are automatically in their 2's-complement form.

The four examples are repeated below with negative numbers represented by their 1's complement. The carry out of the sign bit is returned and added to the least significant bit (end-around carry).

$$
\begin{array}{ll}
+\ 6 & 0\ 000110 \\
& \qquad\qquad + \\
+\ 9 & 0\ 001001 \\ \hline
+\ 15 & 0\ 001111
\end{array}
\qquad
\begin{array}{ll}
-\ 6 & 1\ 111001 \\
& \qquad\qquad + \\
+\ 9 & 0\ 001001 \\ \hline
& 10\ 000010 \\
& \qquad\qquad + \\
& \qquad\qquad 1 \\ \hline
+\ 3 & 0\ 000011
\end{array}
$$

$$
\begin{array}{ll}
+\ 6 & 0\ 000110 \\
& \qquad\qquad + \\
-\ 9 & 1\ 110110 \\ \hline
-\ 3 & 1\ 111100
\end{array}
\qquad
\begin{array}{ll}
-\ 9 & 1\ 110110 \\
& \qquad\qquad + \\
-\ 9 & 1\ 110110 \\ \hline
& 11\ 101100 \\
& \qquad\qquad + \\
& \qquad\qquad 1 \\ \hline
-\ 18 & 1\ 101101
\end{array}
$$

The advantage of the sign-2's-complement representation over the sign-1's-complement form (and the sign-magnitude form) is that it contains only one type of zero. The other two representations have both a positive zero and a negative zero. For example, adding $+9$ to -9 in the 1's-complement representation, one obtains:

$$
\begin{array}{ll}
+\ 9 & 0\ 001001 \\
-\ 9 & 1\ 110110 \\ \hline
-\ 0 & 1\ 111111
\end{array}
$$

and the result is a negative zero, i.e., the complement of 0 000000 (positive zero).

A zero with an associated sign bit will appear in a register in one of the following forms, depending on the representation used for negative numbers:

	+0	−0
In sign-magnitude	0 0000000	1 0000000
In sign-1's complement	0 0000000	1 1111111
In sign-2's complement	0 0000000	none

Both the sign-magnitude and the 1's-complement representations have associated with them the possiblity of a negative zero. The sign-2's-complement representation has only a positive zero. This occurs because the 2's complement of 0 000000 (positive zero) is 0 000000 and may be obtained from the 1's complement plus 1 (i.e., 1 111111 + 1) provided the end carry is discarded.

The range of binary integer numbers that can be accommodated in a register of $n = k + 1$ bits is $\pm(2^k - 1)$, where k bits are reserved for the number and one bit for the sign. A register with 8 bits can store binary numbers in the range of $\pm(2^7 - 1) = \pm 127$. However, since the sign-2's-complement representation has only one zero, it should accommodate one more number than the other two representations. Consider the representation of the largest and smallest numbers:

	sign-1's complement	sign-2's complement
+126 = 0 1111110	− 126 = 1 0000001	1 0000010
+127 = 0 1111111	− 127 = 1 0000000	1 0000001
+128 (impossible)	− 128 (impossible)	1 0000000

In the sign-2's-complement representation, it is possible to represent − 128 with eight bits. In general, the sign-2's-complement representation can accommodate numbers in the range $+(2^k - 1)$ to -2^k, where $k = n - 1$ and n is the number of bits in the register.

Arithmetic Subtraction

Subtraction of two signed binary numbers when negative numbers are in the 2's-complement form is very simple and can be stated as follows: *Take the 2's complement of the subtrahend (including the sign bit) and add it to the minuend (including sign bit)*. This procedure uses the fact that a subtraction operation can be changed to an addition operation if the sign of the subtrahend is changed. This is demonstrated by the following relationships (*B* is the subtrahend):

$$(\pm A) - (- B) = (\pm A) + (+ B)$$
$$(\pm A) - (+ B) = (\pm A) + (- B)$$

But changing a positive number to a negative number is easily done by taking its 2's complement (including the sign bit). The reverse is also true because the complement of the complement restores the number to its original value.

The subtraction with 1's-complement numbers is similar except for the end-around carry. Subtraction with sign-magnitude requires that only the sign bit of the subtrahend be complemented. Addition and subtraction of binary numbers in sign-magnitude representation is demonstrated in Section 10-3.

Because of the simple procedure for adding and subtracting binary numbers when negative numbers are in sign-2's-complement form, most computers adopt this representation over the more familiar sign-magnitude form. The reason 2's complement is usually chosen over the 1's complement is to avoid the end-around carry and the occurrence of a negative zero.

8-6 OVERFLOW

When two numbers of n digits each are added and the sum occupies $n + 1$ digits, we say that an *overflow* occurs. This is true for binary numbers or decimal numbers whether signed or unsigned. When one performs the addition with paper and pencil, an overflow is not a problem, since we are not limited by the width of the page to write down the sum. An overflow is a problem in a digital computer because the lengths of all registers, including memory registers, are of finite length. A result of $n + 1$ bits cannot be accommodated in a register of standard length n. For this reason, many computers check for the occurrence of an overflow, and when it occurs, they set an overflow flip-flop for the user to check.

An overflow cannot occur after an addition if one number is positive and the other is negative, since adding a positive number to a negative number produces a result (positive or negative) which is smaller than the larger of the two original numbers. An overflow may occur if the two numbers are added and both are positive or both are negative. When two numbers in sign-magnitude representation are added, an overflow can be easily detected from the carry out of the number bits. When two numbers in sign-2's-complement representation are added, the sign bit is treated as part of the number and the end carry does not necessarily indicate an overflow.

The algorithm for adding two numbers in sign-2's-complement representation, as previously stated, gives an incorrect result when an overflow occurs. This arises because an overflow of the number bits always changes the sign of the result and gives an erroneous n-bit answer. To see how this happens, consider the following example. Two signed binary numbers, 35 and 40, are stored in two 7-bit registers. The maximum capacity of the register is $(2^6 - 1) = 63$ and the minimum capacity is $-2^6 = -64$. Since the sum of the numbers is 75, it exceeds the capacity of the register. This is true if the numbers are both positive or both negative. The operations in binary are shown below together with the last two carries of the addition:

carries:	0 1		carries:	1 0
$+35$	0 100011		-35	1 011101
$+40$	0 101000		-40	1 011000
$+75$	1 001011		-75	0 110101

In either case, we see that the 7-bit result that should have been positive is negative, and vice versa. Obviously, the binary answer is incorrect and the algorithm for adding binary numbers represented in 2's complement as stated previously fails to give correct results when an overflow occurs. Note that if the carry out of the sign-bit position is taken as the sign for the result, then the 8-bit answer so obtained will be correct.

An overflow condition can be detected by observing the carry *into* the sign-bit position and the carry *out* of the sign-bit position. If these two carries are not equal, an overflow condition is produced. This is indicated in the example above where the two carries are explicitly shown. The reader can try a few examples of numbers that do not produce an overflow to see that these two carries will always come out to be either both 0's or both 1's. If the two carries are applied to an exclusive-OR gate, an overflow would be detected when the output of the gate is 1.

The addition of two signed binary numbers when negative numbers are represented in sign-2's-complement form is implemented with digital functions as shown in Fig. 8-10. Register A holds the augend, with the sign bit in position A_n. Register B holds the addend, with the sign bit in B_n. The two numbers are added by means of an n-bit parallel adder. The full-adder (FA) circuit in stage n (the sign bits) is shown explicitly. The carry going into this full-adder is C_n. The carry out of the full-adder is C_{n+1}. The exclusive-OR of these two carries is applied to an overflow flip-flop V. If, after the addition, $V = 0$, then the sum loaded into A is correct. If $V = 1$, there is an overflow and the n-bit sum is incorrect. The circuit shown in Fig. 8-10 can be specified by the following statement:

$$T: \quad A \leftarrow A + B, \quad V \leftarrow C_n \oplus C_{n+1}$$

The variables in the statement are defined in Fig. 8-10. Note that variables C_n and C_{n+1} do not represent registers; they represent output carries from a parallel adder.

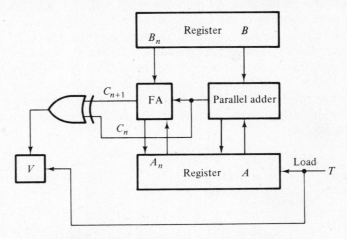

Figure 8-10   Addition of sign-2's-complement numbers

8-7 ARITHMETIC SHIFTS

An arithmetic shift is a microoperation that shifts a *signed* binary number to the left or right. An arithmetic shift-left multiplies a signed binary number by 2. An arithmetic shift-right divides the number by 2. Arithmetic shifts must leave the sign unchanged because the sign of the number remains the same when it is multiplied or divided by 2.

The leftmost bit in a register holds the sign bit, and the remaining bits hold the number. Figure 8-11 shows a register of n bits. Bit A_n in the leftmost position holds the sign bit and is designated by $A(S)$. The number bits are stored in the portion of the register designated by $A(N)$. A_1 refers to the least significant bit, A_{n-1} refers to the most significant position in the number bits, and A refers to the entire register.

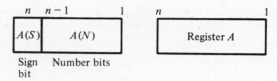

Figure 8-11   Defining register A for arithmetic shifts

Binary fixed-point numbers can be represented in three different ways. The manner of shifting the number stored in a register is different for each representation.

Consider first the arithmetic shift-right that divides a number by 2. This can be symbolized by one of the following statements:

$A(N) \leftarrow$ shr $A(N)$, $A_{n-1} \leftarrow 0$ for sign-magnitude

$A \leftarrow$ shr A, $A(S) \leftarrow A(S)$ for sign-1's or sign-2's complement

In the sign-magnitude representation, the arithmetic shift-right requires a shift of the number bits with 0 inserted into the most significant position. The sign bit is not affected. In the sign-1's- or 2's-complement representation, the entire register is shifted while the sign bit remains unaltered. This is because a positive number must insert a 0 in the most significant position but a negative number must insert a 1. The following numerical examples demonstrate the procedure.

Positive number	+12:	0 01100	+6:	0 00110
Sign-magnitude	−12:	1 01100	−6:	1 00110
Sign-1's complement	−12:	1 10011	−6:	1 11001
Sign-2's complement	−12:	1 10100	−6:	1 11010

In each case the arithmetic shift-right of 12 produces a 6 without altering the sign.

For positive numbers, the result is the same in all three representations. A number in sign-magnitude, whether positive or negative, when shifted, receives a 0 in the most significant position. In the two sign-complement representations, the most significant position receives the sign bit. The latter case is sometimes called *shifting with sign extension*.

Consider now the arithmetic shift-left that multiplies a number by 2. This can be symbolized by one of the following statements:

$$A(N) \leftarrow \text{shl } A(N), \quad A_1 \leftarrow 0 \qquad \text{for sign-magnitude}$$

$$A \leftarrow \text{shl } A, \quad A_1 \leftarrow A(S) \qquad \text{for sign-1's complement}$$

$$A \leftarrow \text{shl } A, \quad A_1 \leftarrow 0 \qquad \text{for sign-2's complement}$$

In the sign-magnitude representation, the number bits are shifted left with 0 inserted in the least significant position. In the sign-1's complement, the entire register is shifted and the sign bit is inserted into the least significant position. The sign-2's complement is similar, except that 0 is shifted into the least significant position. Consider the number 12 shifted to the left to produce 24:

Positive number	0 01100	0 11000
Sign-magnitude	1 01100	1 11000
Sign-1's complement	1 10011	1 00111
Sign-2's complement	1 10100	1 01000

A number shifted to the left may cause an overflow to occur. An overflow will occur after the shift if the following condition exists *before* the shift:

$$A_{n-1} = 1 \qquad \text{for sign-magnitude}$$

$$A_n \oplus A_{n-1} = 1 \qquad \text{for sign-1's or sign-2's complement}$$

In the sign-magnitude case, a 1 in the most significant position will be shifted out and lost. In the sign-complement case, overflow will occur if the sign bit $A_n = A(S)$ is not the same as the most significant bit. Consider the following numerical example with sign-1's-complement numbers:

Initial value	9:	0 1001	Initial value	−9:	1 0110
shift-left	−2:	1 0010	shift-left	+2:	0 1101

The shift-left should produce 18, but since the original sign is lost, we obtain an incorrect result with a sign reversal. If the sign bit after the shift is not the same as the sign bit before the shift, an overflow occurs. The correct result would be a number of $n + 1$ bits, with the $(n + 1)$th bit position containing the original sign of the number which is lost after the shift.

8-8 DECIMAL DATA

The representation of decimal numbers in registers is a function of the binary code used to represent a decimal digit. A four-bit decimal code, for example, requires four flip-flops for each decimal digit. The representation of $+4385$ in BCD requires at least 17 flip-flops: one flip-flop for the sign and four for each digit. This number is represented in a register with 25 flip-flops as follows:

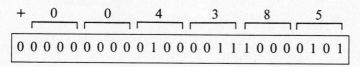

By representing numbers in decimal, we waste a considerable amount of storage space since the number of flip-flops needed to store a decimal number in a binary code is greater than the number of flip-flops needed for its equivalent binary representation. Also, the circuits required to perform decimal arithmetic are much more complex. However, there are some advantages in the use of decimal representation, mostly because computer input and output data are generated by people that always use the decimal system. A computer that uses binary representation for arithmetic operations requires data conversion from decimal to binary prior to performing calculations. Binary results must be converted back to decimal for output. This procedure is time consuming; it is worth using provided the amount of arithmetic operations is large, as is the case with scientific applications. Some applications, such as business data processing, require small amounts of arithmetic calculations. For this reason, some computers perform arithmetic calculations directly on decimal data (in binary code) and thus eliminate the need for conversion to binary and back to decimal. Large-scale computer systems usually have hardware for performing arithmetic calculations both in binary and in decimal representation. The user can specify by programmed instructions whether the computer is to perform calculations on binary or decimal data. A decimal adder was introduced in Section 5-3.

There are three ways to represent negative fixed-point decimal numbers. They are similar to the three representations of a negative binary number except for the radix change:

1. Sign-magnitude.

2. Sign-9's complement.

3. Sign-10's complement.

For all three representations, a positive decimal number is represented by 0 (for plus) followed by the magnitude of the number. It is in regard to negative numbers that the representations differ. The sign of a negative number is represented by 1, and the magnitude of the number is positive in sign-magnitude representation. In the other two representations, the magnitude is represented by the 9's or 10's complement.

The sign of a decimal number is sometimes taken as a 4-bit quantity to conform with the 4-bit representation of digits. It is customary to represent a plus with four 0's and a minus with the BCD equivalent of 9, i.e., 1001. In this way all procedures developed for sign-2's-complement numbers apply also to the sign-10's-complement numbers. The addition is done by adding all digits, including the sign digit, and discarding the end carry. For example, $+375 + (-240)$ is done with sign-10's-complement representation as follows:

$$
\begin{array}{r}
0\ 375 \\
+\quad\ \ \\
9\ 760 \\
\hline
0\ 135
\end{array}
$$

The 9 in the second number represents a minus, and 760 is the 10's complement of 240. An overflow is detected in this representation from the exclusive-OR of the carries into and out of the sign digits position.

Decimal arithmetic operations may employ the same symbols as binary operations provided the base of the numbers is understood to be 10 instead of 2. The statement:

$$ A \leftarrow A + \bar{B} + 1 $$

can be used to express the addition of the decimal number stored in register A to the 10's complement of the decimal number in register B. $\bar{B}$ in this case denotes the 9's complement of the decimal number. The arithmetic shifts are also applicable to decimal numbers, except that a shift-left corresponds to a multiplication by 10 and a shift-right to a division by 10. The sign-9's complement is similar to the sign-1's complement, and the sign-magnitude representation in both radix representations have similar arithmetic procedures.

If the adoption of similar symbols for binary and decimal operations were not acceptable, it would be necessary to formulate different symbols for the operations with decimal data. Sometimes the register-transfer operations are used to simulate the system by means of a computer program. In that case the two types of data can be specified by declaration statements as is done in programming languages.

8-9 FLOATING-POINT DATA

Floating-point representation of numbers needs two registers. The first represents a signed fixed-point number and the second, the position of the radix point. For example, the representation of the decimal number $+6132.789$ is as follows:

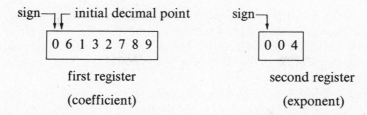

sign — initial decimal point   sign

first register   second register

(coefficient)   (exponent)

The first register has a 0 in the most significant flip-flop position to denote a plus. The magnitude of the number is stored in a binary code in 28 flip-flops, with each decimal digit occupying 4 flip-flops. The number in the first register is considered a fraction, so the decimal point in the first register is fixed at the left of the most significant digit. The second register contains the decimal number $+4$ (in binary code) to indicate that the *actual* position of the decimal point is four decimal positions to the right. This representation is equivalent to the number expressed by a fraction times 10 to an exponent, i.e., $+6132.789$ is represented as $+.6132789 \times 10^{+4}$. Because of this analogy, the contents of the first register are called the *coefficient* (and sometimes *mantissa* or *fractional part*) and the contents of the second register are called the *exponent* (or *characteristic*).

The position of the actual decimal point may be outside the range of digits of the coefficient register. For example, assuming sign-magnitude representation, the following contents:

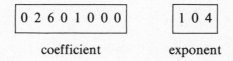

coefficient   exponent

represent the number $+.2601000 \times 10^{-4} = +.000026010000$, which produces four more 0's on the left. On the other hand, the following contents:

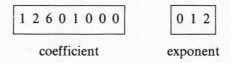

coefficient   exponent

represent the number $-.2601000 \times 10^{12} = -260100000000$, which produces five more 0's on the right.

In these examples, we have assumed that the coefficient is a fixed-point fraction. Some computers assume it to be an integer, so the initial decimal point in the coefficient register is to the right of the least significant digit.

Another arrangement used for the exponent is to remove its sign bit altogether and consider the exponent as being "biased." For example, numbers between 10^{+49} and 10^{-50} can be represented with an exponent of two digits (without sign bit) and a bias of 50. The exponent register always contains the number $E + 50$, where E is the actual exponent. The subtraction of 50 from the contents of the register gives the desired exponent. This way, positive exponents are represented in the register in the range of numbers from 50 to 99. The subtraction of 50 gives the positive values from 00 to 49. Negative exponents are represented in the register in the range of 00 to 49. The subtraction of 50 gives the negative values in the range of -50 to -1.

A floating-point binary number is similarly represented with two registers, one to store the coefficient and the other, the exponent. For example, the number $+1001.110$ can be represented as follows:

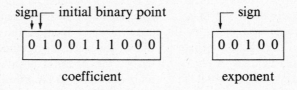

The coefficient register has ten flip-flops: one for sign and nine for magnitude. Assuming that the coefficient is a fixed-point fraction, the actual binary point is four positions to the right, so the exponent has the binary value $+4$. The number is represented in binary as $.100111000 \times 10^{100}$ (remember that 10^{100} in binary is equivalent to decimal 2^4).

Floating-point is always interpreted to represent a number in the following form:

$$c \cdot r^e$$

where c represents the contents of the coefficient register and e, the contents of the exponent register. The radix (base) r and the radix-point position in the coefficient are always assumed. Consider, for example, a computer that assumes integer representation for the coefficient and base 8 for the exponent. The octal number $+17.32 = +1732 \times 8^{-2}$ will look like this:

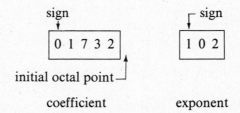

When the octal representation is converted to binary, the binary value of the registers becomes:

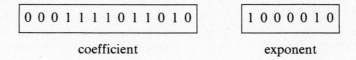

A floating-point number is said to be *normalized* if the most significant position of the coefficient contains a nonzero digit. In this way, the coefficient has no leading zeros and contains the maximum possible number of significant digits. Consider, for example, a coefficient register that can accomodate five decimal digits and a sign. The number $+.00357 \times 10^3 = 3.57$ is not normalized because it has two leading zeros and the unnormalized coefficient is accurate to three significant digits. The number can be normalized by shifting the coefficient two positions to the left and decreasing the exponent by 2 to obtain: $+.35700 \times 10^1 = 3.5700$, which is accurate to five significant digits.

Arithmetic operations with floating-point number representation are more complicated than arithmetic operations with fixed-point numbers and their execution takes longer and requires more complex hardware. However, floating-point representation is more convenient because of the scaling problems involved with fixed-point operations. Many computers have a built-in capability to perform floating-point arithmetic operations. Those that do not have this hardware are usually programmed to operate in this mode.

Adding or subtracting two numbers in floating-point representation requires first an alignment of the radix point, since the exponent part must be made equal before the coefficients are added or subtracted. This alignment is done by shifting one coefficient while its exponent is adjusted until it is equal to the other exponent. Floating-point multiplication or division requires no alignment of the radix point. The product can be formed by multiplying the two coefficients and adding the two exponents. Division is accomplished from the division with the coefficients and the subtraction of the divisior exponent from the exponent of the dividend.

8-10 NONNUMERIC DATA

The types of data considered thus far represent numbers that a computer uses as operands for arithmetic operations. However, a computer is not a machine that only stores numbers and does high-speed arithmetic. Very often, a computer manipulates symbols rather than numbers. Most programs written by computer users are in the form of characters, i.e., a set of symbols comprised of letters, digits, and various special characters. A computer is capable of accepting characters (in a binary code), storing them in memory, and performing operations on and transferring characters to an output device. A computer can function as a character-string-manipulating machine. By a *character string* is meant a finite sequence of characters written one after another.

Characters are represented in computer registers by a binary code. In Table 1-5, we listed three different character codes in common use. Each member of the code represents one character and consists of either six, seven, or eight bits, depending on the code. The number of characters that can be stored in one register depends on the length of the register and the number of bits used in the code. For example, a computer with a word length of 36 bits that uses a character code of 6 bits can store six characters per word. Character strings are stored in memory in consecutive locations. The first character in the string can be specified from the address of the first word. The last character of the string may be found from the address of the last word, or by specifying a character count, or by a special mark designating end of character string. The manipulation of characters is done in the registers of the processor unit, with each character representing a unit of information.

Various other symbols can be stored in computer registers in binary-coded form. A binary code can be adopted to represent musical notes for the production of music by computer. Special binary codes are needed to represent speech patterns for an automatic speech-recognition system. The display of characters through a dot matrix in a CRT (cathode-ray tube) screen requires a binary-coded representation for each symbol that is displayed. Status information to supervise the operation of a controlled process or a power-distribution system uses predetermined binary-coded information. The chess board and pieces to run a chess game by computer require some form of binary-coded information representation.

The operations mostly done on nonnumerical data are transfers, logic, shifts, and control decisions. The transfer operations can prepare the binary-coded information in some required order in memory and transfer the information to and from external units. Logic and shift operations provide a capability to perform data manipulation tasks that help in the decision-making process.

Logic microoperations are very useful for manipulating individual bits stored in a register or a group of bits that comprise a given binary-coded symbol. Logic operations can change bit values, delete a group of bits, or insert new bit values into a register. The following examples show how the bits of one register are manipulated by logic and shift microoperations as a function of logic operands that are prestored in memory.

The OR microoperation can be used to set a bit or a selected group of bits in a register. The Boolean relations $x + 1 = 1$ and $x + 0 = x$ dictate that the binary variable x, when ORed with a 1, produces a 1 regardless of the binary value of x; but, when ORed with a 0, it does not change the value of x. By ORing a given bit A_i in a register with a 1, it is possible to set bit A_i to 1 regardless of its previous value. Consider the following specific example:

$$
\begin{array}{ll}
0101\ 0101 & A \\
\underline{1111\ 0000} & B \\
1111\ 0101 & A \leftarrow A \vee B
\end{array}
$$

The logic operand in B has 1's in the four high-order bit positions. By ORing this value with the present value of A, it is possible to set the four high-order bits of A to 1's but leave the four low-order bits unchanged. Thus, the OR microoperation can be used to selectively set bits of a register.

The AND microoperation can be used to clear a bit or a selected group of bits in a register. The Boolean relationships $x \cdot 0 = 0$ and $x \cdot 1 = x$ dictate that binary variable x, when ANDed with a 0, produces a 0 regardless of the binary value of x; but, when ANDed with a 1, it does not change the value of x. A given bit A_i in register A can be cleared to 0 if it is ANDed with a 0. Consider a logic operand $B = 0000\ 1111$. When this operand is ANDed with the contents of a register, it will clear the four high-order bits of the register but leave the four low-order bits unchanged:

$$
\begin{array}{ll}
0101\ 0101 & A \\
\underline{0000\ 1111} & B \\
0000\ 0101 & A \leftarrow A \wedge B
\end{array}
$$

The AND microoperation can be used to selectively clear bits of a register. The AND operation is sometimes called a *mask* operation because it masks or removes all 1's from a selected portion of a register.

The AND operation followed by an OR operation can be used to change a bit or a group of bits from a given value to a new desired value. This is done by first masking the bits in question and then ORing the new value. For example, suppose an A register contains eight bits, 0110 0101. To replace the four high-order bits by the value 1100, we first mask the four unwanted bits:

$$
\begin{array}{ll}
0110\ 0101 & A \\
\underline{0000\ 1111} & B1 \\
0000\ 0101 & A \leftarrow A \wedge B1
\end{array}
$$

and then insert the new value:

$$
\begin{array}{ll}
0000\ 0101 & A \\
\underline{1100\ 0000} & B2 \\
1100\ 0101 & A \leftarrow A \vee B1
\end{array}
$$

The mask operation is an AND microoperation and the insert operation is an OR microoperation.

The XOR (exclusive-OR) microoperation can be used to complement a bit or a selected group of bits in a register. The Boolean relationships $x \oplus 1 = x'$ and $x \oplus 0 = x$ dictate that the binary variable x be complemented when XORed with a 1 and remain unchanged otherwise. By XORing a given bit in a register with a 1, it is possible to complement the selected bit. Consider the numerical example:

$$
\begin{array}{ll}
1101\ 0101 & A \\
\underline{1111\ 0000} & B \\
0010\ 0101 & A \leftarrow A \oplus B
\end{array}
$$

The four high-order bits of A are complemented after the exclusive-OR operation with operand B. The XOR microoperation can be used to selectively complement bits of a register. If the operand B has all 1's, the XOR operation will complement all the bits of A. If the contents of A are XORed with their own value, the register will be cleared, since $x \oplus x = 0$:

$$
\begin{array}{ll}
0101\ 0101 & A \\
\underline{0101\ 0101} & A \\
0000\ 0000 & A \leftarrow A \oplus A
\end{array}
$$

The value of individual bits in a register can be determined by first masking all bits, except the one in question, and then checking if the register is equal to 0. Suppose we want to determine if bit 4 in register A is 0 or 1:

$$
\begin{array}{ll}
101x010 & A \\
\underline{0001000} & B \\
000x000 & A \leftarrow B \wedge A
\end{array}
$$

The bit marked x can be 0 or 1. When all other bits are masked with the operand in B, register A will contain all 0's if bit 4 was a 0. If bit 4 was originally a 1, this bit will remain a 1. By checking if the contents of A are 0 or not, we determine whether bit 4 was 0 or 1.

If each bit in a register must be checked for 0 or 1, it is more convenient to shift the register to the left and transfer the high-order bit into a special 1-bit register which is usually called the carry flip-flop. After every shift, the carry can be checked for 0 or 1 and a decision made depending on the outcome.

Shift operations are useful for packing and unpacking binary-coded information. Packing of binary-coded information such as characters is an operation that groups two or more characters in one word. Unpacking is a reverse operation that separates two or more characters stored in one word into individual characters. Consider the packing of BCD digits that are first entered as ASCII characters. The ASCII character code for digits 5 and 9 are obtained from Table 1-5. Each contains seven bits and a 0 is inserted in the high-order position as shown below. The character 5 is transferred to register A, and 9 to register B. The four high-order bits are of no use for BCD representation, so they are masked out. The packing of the two BCD digits into register A consists of shifting register A four times to the left (with 0's inserted in the low-order bit positions) and then ORing the contents of the registers:

	A	B
ASCII 5 =	0011 0101	0011 1001 = ASCII 9
AND with 0000 1111	0000 0101	0000 1001
Shift A left four times	0101 0000	
$A \leftarrow A \vee B$	0101 1001 = BCD 59	

A shift operation with 0 inserted in the extreme bit is considered a logical shift microoperation.

The binary information available in a register during logical operations is called a *logical word*. A logical word is interpreted to be a bit string as opposed to character strings or numerical data. Each bit in a logical word functions in exactly the same way as every other bit; in other words, the unit of information of a logical word is a bit.

8-11   INSTRUCTION CODES

The internal organization of a digital system is defined by the registers it employs and the sequence of microoperations it performs on data stored in the registers. In a *special-purpose* digital system, the sequence of microoperations is fixed and the system performs the same specific task over and over again. A digital computer is a *general-purpose* digital system capable of executing various operations and, in addition, can be instructed as to what specific sequence of operations it must perform. The user of a computer can control the process by means of a *program*, i.e., a set of instructions that specify the operations, operands, and the sequence in which processing has to occur. The data-processing task may be altered simply by specifying a new program with different instructions or by specifying the same instructions with different data. Instruction codes, together with data, are stored in memory. The control reads each instruction from memory and places it in a control register. The control then interprets the instruction and proceeds to execute it by issuing a sequence of control functions. Every general-purpose computer has its own unique instruction repertoire. The ability to store and execute instructions, the stored-program concept, is the most important property of a general-purpose computer.

An *instruction code* is a group of bits that tell the computer to perform a specific operation. It is usually divided into parts, each having its own particular interpretation. The most basic part of an instruction code is its operation part. The *operation code* of an instruction is a group of bits that define an operation such as add, subtract, multiply, shift, and complement. The set of machine operations formulated for a computer depends on the processing it is intended to carry out. The total number of operations thus obtained determines the set of machine operations. The number of bits required for the operation part of the instruction code is a function of the total number of operations used. It must consist of at least n bits for a given 2^n (or less) distinct operations. The designer assigns a bit combination (a code) to each operation. The control unit of the computer is designed to accept this bit configuration at the proper time in a sequence and to supply the proper command signals to the required destinations in order to execute the specified operation. As a specific example, consider a computer using 32 distinct operations, one of them being an ADD operation. The operation code may consist of five bits, with a bit configuration 10010 assigned to the ADD operation.

When the operation code 10010 is detected by the control unit, a command signal is applied to an adder circuit to add two numbers.

The operation part of an instruction code specifies the operation to be performed. This operation must be executed on some data, usually stored in computer registers. An instruction code, therefore, must specify not only the operation but also the registers where the operands are to be found as well as the register where the result is to be stored. These registers may be specified in an instruction code in two ways. A register is said to be specified *explicitly* if the instruction code contains special bits for its identification. For example, an instruction may contain not only an operation part but also a memory address. We say that the memory address specifies explicitly a memory register. On the other hand, a register is said to be specified *implicitly* if it is included as part of the definition of the operation, i.e., if the register is implied by the operation part of the code.

Instruction-Code Formats

The format of an instruction is usually depicted in a rectangular box symbolizing the bits of the instruction as they appear in memory words or in a control register. The bits of the instruction are sometimes divided into groups that subdivide the instruction into parts. Each group is assigned a symbolic name, such as *operation-code* part or *address* part. The various parts specify different functions for the instruction, and when shown together they constitute the instruction-code format.

Consider, for example, the three instruction-code formats specified in Fig. 8-12. The instruction format in (a) consists of an operation code which implies a register in the processor unit. It can be used to specify operations such as "clear a processor register," or "complement a register," or "transfer the contents of one register to a second register." The instruction format in (b) has an operation code followed by an operand. This is called an *immediate* operand instruction because the operand follows immediately after the operation-code part of the instruction. It

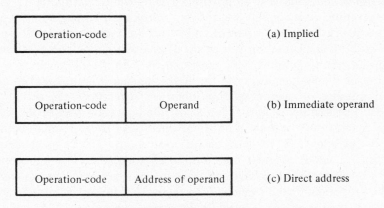

Figure 8-12 Three possible instruction formats

can be used to specify operations such as "add the operand to the present contents of a register" or "transfer the operand to a processor register," or it can specify any other operation to be done between the contents of a register and the given operand. The instruction format specified in Fig. 8-12(c) is similar to the one in (b) except that the operand must be extracted from memory at the location specified by the address part of the instruction. In other words, the operation specified by the operation code is done between a processor register and an operand which can be stored in memory anywhere. The address of this operand in memory is included in the instruction.

Let us assume that we have a memory unit with 8 bits per word and that an operation code contains 8 bits. The placement of the three instruction codes in memory is depicted in Fig. 8-13. At address 25, we have an implied instruction that specifies an operation: "transfer the contents of processor register R into processor register A." This operation can be symbolized by the statement:

$$A \leftarrow R$$

In memory addresses 35 and 36, we have an immediate operand instruction that occupies two words. The first word at address 35 is the operation code for the instruction, "transfer the operand to register A," symbolized as:

$$A \leftarrow \text{operand}$$

The operand itself is stored immediately after the operation code at address 36.

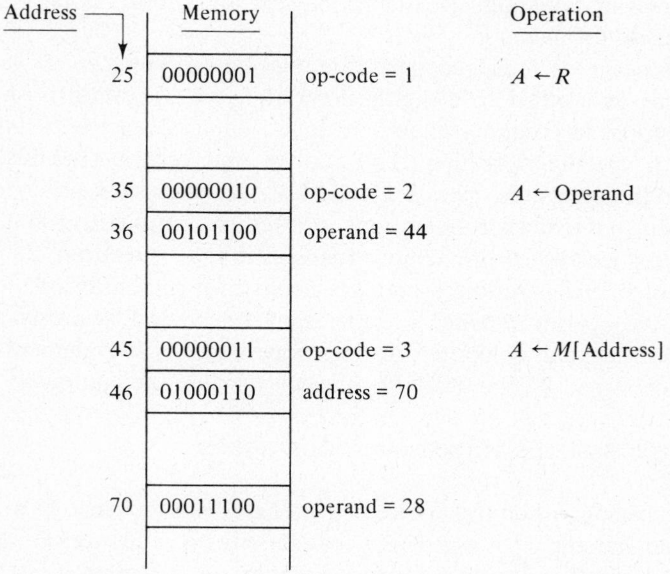

Address	Memory		Operation
25	00000001	op-code = 1	$A \leftarrow R$
35	00000010	op-code = 2	$A \leftarrow \text{Operand}$
36	00101100	operand = 44	
45	00000011	op-code = 3	$A \leftarrow M[\text{Address}]$
46	01000110	address = 70	
70	00011100	operand = 28	

Figure 8-13 Memory representation of instructions

In addresses 45 and 46, there is a direct address instruction that specifies the operation:

$$A \leftarrow M[\text{address}]$$

This symbolizes a memory-transfer operation of an operand which is specified by the address part of the instruction. The second word of the instruction at address 46 contains the *address*, and its value is binary 70. Therefore, the operand to be transferred to register A is the one stored in address 70, and its value is shown to be binary 28. Note that the instruction is stored in memory at some address. This instruction has an address part which gives the address of the operand. To avoid the confusion of saying the word "address" so many times, it is customary to refer to a memory address as a "location." Thus the direct address instruction is stored in locations 45 and 46. The address of the operand is in location 46, and the operand is available from location 70.

It must be realized that the placing of instructions in memory as shown in Fig. 8-13 is only one of many possible alternatives. Only very small computers have 8-bit words. Large computers may have from 16 to 64 bits per word. In most computers, the entire instruction can be placed in one word, and in some, even two or more instructions can be placed in a single memory word.

The instruction formats shown in Fig. 8-12 are three of many possible formats that can be formulated for digital computers. They are presented here just as an example and should not be considered the only possibilities. Subsequent chapters, especially Chapters 11 and 12, present and discuss other instructions and instruction-code formats.

At this point we must recognize the relationship between an *operation* and a *microoperation* as applied to a digital computer. An operation is specified by an instruction stored in computer memory. It is a binary code that tells the computer to perform a specific operation. The control unit receives the instruction from memory and interprets the operation-code bits. It then issues a sequence of control functions that perform microoperations in internal computer registers.

For every instruction in memory that specifies an operation, the control issues a sequence of microoperations which are needed for the hardware implementation of the specified operation code. An operation is specified by a user in the form of an instruction to the computer. A microoperation is an elementary operation which is constrained by the available hardware inside the computer.

Macrooperations versus Microoperations

There are occasions when it is convenient to express a sequence of microoperations with a single statement. A statement that requires a sequence of microoperations for its implementation is called a *macrooperation*. A statement in the register-transfer method of notation that defines an instruction is a *macrooperation* statement, although macrooperation statements can be used on other occasions as well. The register-transfer method can be used to define the operation specified by a computer instruction because all instructions specify some register-transfer operation which must be executed by computer hardware.

One cannot tell from looking at an isolated register-transfer statement whether it represents a macro- or microoperation, since both types of statements denote some register-transfer statement. The only way to distinguish between them is to recognize from the context and the internal hardware of the system in question whether the statement is executed with one control function or not. If the statement can be executed with a single control function, it represents a microoperation. If the hardware execution of the statement requires two or more control functions, the statement is taken to be a macrooperation. Only if one knows the hardware constraints of the system can this question be answered.

Consider, for example, the instruction in Fig. 8-13 symbolized by the statement:

$$A \leftarrow \text{operand}$$

This statement is a macrooperation because it specifies a computer instruction. To execute the instruction, the control unit must issue control functions for the following sequence of microoperations:

1. Read the operation code from address 35.

2. Transfer the operation code to a control register.

3. The control decodes the operation code and recognizes it as an immediate operand instruction, so it reads the operand from address 36.

4. The operand read from memory is transferred into register A.

The microoperation in step 4 executes the instruction, but steps 1 through 3 are needed prior to it for the control to interpret the instruction itself.

The statement that symbolizes the instruction:

$$A \leftarrow R$$

is also a macrooperation because the control has to first read the operation code at address 25 to decode and recognize it. The interregister transfer itself is executed with a second control function.

The register-transfer method is suitable for describing the operations among the registers in a digital system. It can be used at different levels of presentation provided one interprets the statements properly. Specifically, it can be used for the following tasks.

1. To define computer instructions concisely by macrooperation statements.

2. To express any desired operation by means of a macrooperation statement without being concerned with specific hardware implementation.

3. To define the internal organization of digital systems by means of control functions and microoperations.

4. To design a digital system by specifying the hardware components and their interconnections.

The set of instructions for a given computer can be explained in words, but when defined with macrooperation statements, the definition can be stated precisely and with a minimum of ambiguity. The use of other macrooperation statements may facilitate the initial specifications of a system and can be used to simulate the system when it is desired to check its intended operation. The internal organization of a digital system is best described by a set of control functions and microoperations. The list of register-transfer statements that describe the organization of the system can be used to derive the digital functions from which the system can be designed.

The next section shows by example how the register-transfer method is used in each of the four tasks listed above. This is done by defining and designing a very simple computer.

8-12 DESIGN OF A SIMPLE COMPUTER

The block diagram of a simple computer is shown in Fig. 8-14. The system consists of a memory unit, seven registers, and two decoders. The memory unit has 256 words of 8 bits each, which is very small for a real computer, but sufficient for demonstrating the basic operations found in most computers. Instructions and data are stored in the memory unit, but all information processing is done in the registers. The registers are listed in Table 8-4, together with a brief description of their function and the number of bits they contain.

The memory address register, MAR, holds the address for the memory. The memory buffer register, MBR, holds the contents of the memory word read from or written into memory. Registers A and R are general-purpose processor registers.

The program counter PC, the instruction register IR, and the timing counter T are part of the control unit. The IR receives the operation code of instructions. The decoder associated with this register supplies one output for each operation code encountered. Thus $q_1 = 1$ if the operation code is binary 1, $q_2 = 1$ if the operation code is binary 2, and so on. The T counter is also decoded to supply eight timing variables, t_0 through t_7 (see Section 7-6). This counter is incremented with every clock pulse, but it can be cleared at any time to start a new sequence from t_0.

The PC goes through a step-by-step counting sequence and causes the computer to read successive instructions previously stored in memory. The PC always holds the address of the next instruction in memory. To read an instruc-

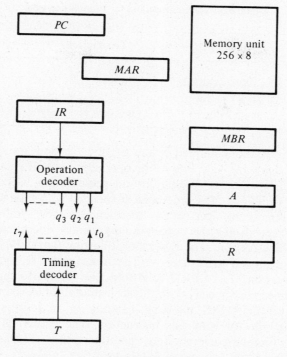

Figure 8-14 Block diagram of a simple computer

tion, the contents of *PC* are transferred into *MAR* and a memory-read cycle is initiated. The *PC* is then incremented by 1 so it holds the next address in the sequence of instructions. An operation code read from memory into *MBR* is then transferred into *IR*. If the memory-address part of an instruction is read into *MBR*, this address is transferred into *MAR* to read the operand. Thus, *MAR* can receive addresses either from *PC* or from *MBR*.

TABLE 8-4 List of registers for the simple computer

Symbol	Number of bits	Name of register	Function
MAR	8	Memory address register	Holds address for memory
MBR	8	Memory buffer register	Holds contents of memory word
A	8	*A* register	Processor register
R	8	*R* register	Processor register
PC	8	Program counter	Holds address of instruction
IR	8	Instruction register	Holds current operation code
T	3	Timing counter	Sequence generator

TABLE 8-5 Three instructions for a simple computer

Operation code	Mnemonic		Description	Function
00000001	MOV	R	Move R to A	$A \leftarrow R$
00000010	LDI	OPRD	Load OPRD into A	$A \leftarrow OPRD$
00000011	LDA	ADRS	Load operand specified by ADRS into A	$A \leftarrow M[ADRS]$

The three instructions defined in the previous section are specified again in Table 8-5. Since there are eight bits in the operation code, it is possible to specify up to 256 different operations. To simplify the presentation, we consider here only the three listed instructions. The mnemonic associated with each instruction can be used by programmers to specify the instructions with symbolic names. The mnemonic MOV stands for the corresponding binary operation code and symbolizes a "move" instruction. The R symbol following the MOV indicates that the contents of R are moved to register A. The mnemonic LDI symbolizes a "load immediate" instruction. The OPRD following LDI stands for an actual operand that the programmer must specify with this instruction. LDA is an abbreviation for "load into A," and the ADRS following it stands for an address number that the programmer must specify with this instruction. The actual OPRD and ADRS values, together with their corresponding operation codes, will be stored in memory as in Fig. 8-13.

Table 8-5 gives a word description for each instruction. This word description is not precise. The statements listed under the function column give a concise and precise definition of each instruction.

A computer with only three instructions is not very useful. We must assume that this computer has many more instructions, even though only three of them are considered here. A program written for the computer is stored in memory. This program consists of many instructions, but once in a while the instruction used will be one of the three listed. We now consider the internal operations needed to execute the instructions that are stored in memory.

Instruction Fetch Cycle

Program counter PC must be initialized to contain the first address of the program stored in memory. When a "start" switch is activated, the computer sequence follows a basic pattern. An operation code whose address is in PC is read from memory into MBR. The PC is incremented by 1 to prepare it for the next address in sequence. The operation code is transferred from MBR to IR, where it is decoded by the control. This sequence is called the instruction *fetch* cycle, since it fetches the operation code from memory and places it in a control register. The timing variables, t_0, t_1, and t_2, out of the timing decoder are used as control functions to sequence the microoperations for reading an operation code (op-code) and placing it into IR:

t_0: $MAR \leftarrow PC$ transfer op-code address

t_1: $MBR \leftarrow M, PC \leftarrow PC + 1$ read op-code, increment PC

t_2: $IR \leftarrow MBR$ transfer op-code to IR

It is assumed that the timing counter, T, starts from a value 000 which produces a t_0 timing variable out of the decoder. The T register is incremented with every clock pulse and automatically produces the next timing variable in sequence. The first three timing variables execute the microoperation sequence which may be symbolized with the macrooperation statement:

$$IR \leftarrow M[PC], \quad PC \leftarrow PC + 1$$

This states that the memory word specified by the address in PC is transferred into IR and then the PC is incremented. The hardware constraint in the simple computer is that only MAR and MBR can communicate with the memory. Since PC and IR cannot communicate directly with the memory, the above macrooperation must be executed with a sequence of three microoperations. Another hardware constraint is that the PC cannot be incremented while its value is being used to supply the address for a memory read. Only after the read operation is completed can the PC be incremented. By transferring the contents of PC into MAR, the PC can be incremented while the memory reads the word addressed by MAR.

The fetch cycle is common to all instructions. The microoperations and control functions that follow the fetch cycle are determined in the control section from the decoded operation code. This is available from outputs q_i, $i = 1, 2, 3, \ldots$ in the operation decoder.

Execution of Instructions

During timing variable t_3, the operation code is in IR and one output of the operation decoder is equal to 1. The control uses the q_i variables to determine the next microoperations in sequence. The MOV R instruction has an operation code that makes $q_1 = 1$. The execution of this instruction requires the microoperation:

$$q_1 t_3: \quad A \leftarrow R, T \leftarrow 0$$

Thus, when $q_1 = 1$ at time t_3, the contents of R are transferred into register A and the timing register T is cleared. By clearing T, control goes back to produce timing variable t_0 and thus starts the fetch cycle again to read the operation code of the next instruction in sequence. Remember that PC was incremented during time t_1, so now it holds the address of the next instruction in sequence.

The LDI OPRD instruction has an operation code that makes $q_2 = 1$. The microoperations that execute this instruction are:

$q_2 t_3$: $MAR \leftarrow PC$ transfer operand address

$q_2 t_4$: $MBR \leftarrow M, PC \leftarrow PC + 1$ read operand, increment PC

$q_2 t_5$: $A \leftarrow MBR, T \leftarrow 0$ transfer operand, go to fetch cycle.

The three timing variables that follow the fetch cycle while $q_2 = 1$ read the operand from memory and transfer it into register A. Since the operand is in a memory location following the operation code, it is read from memory from the address specified in PC. The operand read into MBR is then transferred to A. Note that PC is incremented once again to prepare it for the address of the next operation code before going back to the fetch cycle.

The LDA ADRS instruction has an operation code that makes $q_3 = 1$. The microoperations needed to execute this instruction are listed below:

$q_3 t_3$: $MAR \leftarrow PC$ transfer next instruction address

$q_3 t_4$: $MBR \leftarrow M, PC \leftarrow PC + 1$ read ADRS, increment PC

$q_3 t_5$: $MAR \leftarrow MBR$ transfer operand address

$q_3 t_6$: $MBR \leftarrow M$ read operand

$q_3 t_7$: $A \leftarrow MBR, T \leftarrow 0$ transfer operand to A, go to fetch cycle

The address of the operand, symbolized by ADRS, is placed in memory right after the operation code. Since PC was incremented at t_1 during the fetch cycle, it now holds the address where ADRS is stored. The value of ADRS is read from memory at time t_4. PC is incremented at this time to prepare it for the fetch cycle of the next instruction. At time t_5, the value of ADRS is transferred from MBR to MAR. Since ADRS specifies the address of the operand, a memory read during time t_6 causes the operand to be placed in MBR. The operand from MBR is transferred to register A and control goes back to the fetch cycle.

The control functions and microoperations for the simple computer are summarized in Table 8-6. The first three timing variables constitute the fetch cycle which reads the operation code into IR. The microoperations that are executed during time t_3 depend on the operation-code value in IR. There are three control functions that are a function of t_3, but either q_1 or q_2 or q_3 can be equal to 1 at this time. The particular microoperation executed at time t_3 is the one whose corresponding control function has a q variable that is equal to 1. The same can be said for the other timing variables.

A practical computer has many instructions, and each instruction requires a fetch cycle for reading its operation code. The microoperations needed for the execution of the particular instructions are specified by the timing variables and by

TABLE 8-6 Register-transfer statements for a simple computer

FETCH	t_0:	$MAR \leftarrow PC$
	t_1:	$MBR \leftarrow M, PC \leftarrow PC + 1$
	t_2:	$IR \leftarrow MBR$
MOV	$q_1 t_3$:	$A \leftarrow R, T \leftarrow 0$
LDI	$q_2 t_3$:	$MAR \leftarrow PC$
	$q_2 t_4$:	$MBR \leftarrow M, PC \leftarrow PC + 1$
	$q_2 t_5$:	$A \leftarrow MBR, T \leftarrow 0$
LDA	$q_3 t_3$:	$MAR \leftarrow PC$
	$q_3 t_4$:	$MBR \leftarrow M, PC \leftarrow PC + 1$
	$q_3 t_5$:	$MAR \leftarrow MBR$
	$q_3 t_6$:	$MBR \leftarrow M$
	$q_3 t_7$:	$A \leftarrow MBR, T \leftarrow 0$

the particular q_i, $i = 0, 1, 2, 3, \ldots , 255$, which happens to be in the 1-state at that time. The list of control functions and microoperations for a practical computer would be much longer than the one shown in Table 8-6. Obviously, the simple computer is not a practical device, but by using only three instructions, the basic functions of a digital computer can be clearly demonstrated. The extension of this principle to a computer with more instructions and more processor registers should be apparent from this example. In Chapter 11, we use the principles presented here to design a more realistic computer.

Design of Computer

It was shown previously that the register-transfer logic is suitable for defining the operations specified by computer instructions. We have just shown that the register-transfer logic is a convenient method for specifying the sequence of internal control functions in a digital computer, together with the microoperations they execute. It will be shown now that the list of control functions and microoperations for a digital system is a convenient starting point for the design of the system. The list of microoperations specifies the types of registers and associated digital functions that must be incorporated in the system. The list of control functions specifies the logic gates required for the control unit. To demonstrate this procedure, we will go through the design of the simple computer from the list of register-transfer statements given in Table 8-6.

The first step in the design is to scan the register-transfer statements listed in Table 8-6 and retrieve all those statements that perform the same microoperation on the same register. For example, the microoperation $MAR \leftarrow PC$ is listed in the first line with control function t_0, in the fifth line with control function $q_2 t_3$, and in the eighth line with control function $q_3 t_3$. The three lines are combined into one statement:

$$t_0 + q_2 t_3 + q_3 t_3: \quad MAR \leftarrow PC$$

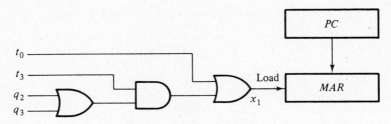

Figure 8-15 Implementation of x_1: $MAR \leftarrow PC$

Remember that a control function is a Boolean function. The $+$ between the control functions denotes a Boolean OR operation, and the absence of an operator between q_2 and t_3 denotes a Boolean AND operation. The above statement combines all the control conditions for the transfer from PC into MAR. The hardware implementation of the above statement is depicted in Fig. 8-15. The control function can be manipulated as a Boolean function to give:

$$x_1 = t_0 + q_2t_3 + q_3t_3 = t_0 + (q_2 + q_3)t_3$$

The binary variable x_1 is applied to the load input of MAR and the outputs from PC are applied to the inputs of MAR. When $x_1 = 1$, the next clock pulse transfers the contents of PC into MAR. The binary variables that cause x_1 to be a 1 come from the operation and timing decoders in the control unit.

There are eight different microoperations listed in Table 8-6. For each distinct microoperation, we accumulate the associated control functions and OR them together. The result is as shown in Table 8-7. The combined control functions obtained for each microoperation are equated to a binary variable x_i, $i = 1, 2, \ldots, 8$. The eight x variables can be easily generated with AND and OR gates, and will not be done here.

The design of the simple computer can be now obtained from the register-transfer information given in Table 8-7. The block diagram design is shown in Fig. 8-16. Here we again have the seven registers, the memory unit, and two decoders. In addition, there is a box labeled "combinational circuit." The combinational-circuit block generates the eight control functions, x_1 through x_8, according to the

TABLE 8-7 Hardware specification for a simple computer

$x_1 = t_0 + q_2t_3 + q_3t_3$:	$MAR \leftarrow PC$
$x_2 = q_3t_5$:	$MAR \leftarrow MBR$
$x_3 = t_1 + q_2t_4 + q_3t_4$:	$PC \leftarrow PC + 1$
$x_4 = x_3 + q_3t_6$:	$MBR \leftarrow M$
$x_5 = q_2t_5 + q_3t_7$:	$A \leftarrow MBR$
$x_6 = q_1t_3$:	$A \leftarrow R$
$x_7 = x_5 + x_6$:	$T \leftarrow 0$
$x_8 = t_2$:	$IR \leftarrow MBR$

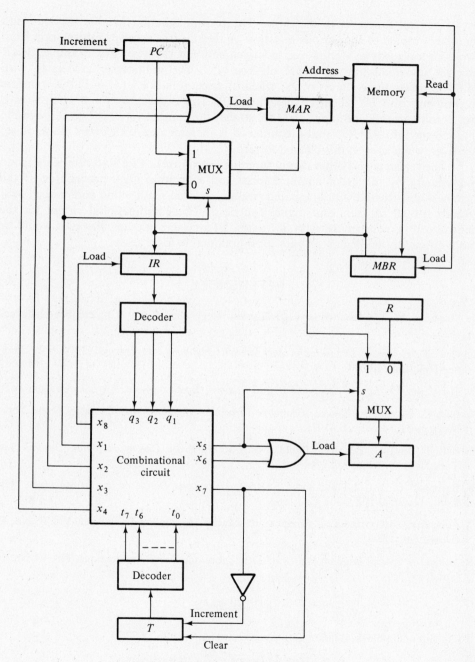

Figure 8-16 Design of a simple computer

list of control functions in the table. The control functions enable the load and increment inputs of the various registers. A register that receives information from two sources needs a multiplexer to select between the two. For example, MAR receives information from MBR or from PC. The multiplexer associated with MAR transfers the contents of PC when its select line is a 1 ($x_1 = 1$) but transfers the contents of MBR when the select line is 0. This is because $x_1 = 0$ when $x_2 = 1$, but x_2 initiates the load input of MAR so that the contents of MBR go through the multiplexer into MAR. Timing counter T is incremented with every clock pulse; however, when $x_7 = 1$, it is cleared to zero.

The registers and other digital functions specified in Fig. 8-16 can be designed individually by means of combinational and sequential logic procedures. If the system is constructed with integrated circuits, one can readily find commercial MSI circuits for all registers and digital functions. The combinational circuit for the control can be constructed with SSI gates. In a large computer, this part would be more efficiently implemented with a programmable logic array.

REFERENCES

1. Mano, M. M., *Computer System Architecture*. Englewood Cliffs, N.J.: Prentice-Hall, Inc., 1976.

2. Chu, Y., *Computer Organization and Microprogramming*. Englewood Cliffs, N.J.: Prentice-Hall, Inc., 1972.

3. Dietmeyer, D., *Logical Design of Digital Systems*. Boston, Mass.: Allyn and Bacon, 1971.

4. Bell, C. G., and A. Newell, *Computer Structures*: *Readings and Examples*. New York: McGraw-Hill Book Co., 1971.

5. Hill, F., and G. Peterson, *Digital Systems*: *Hardware Organization and Design*. New York: John Wiley & Sons, 1973.

6. Bartee, T. C., I. L. Lebow, and I. S. Reed, *Theory and Design of Digital Machines*. New York: McGraw-Hill Book Co., 1962.

7. *Computer*, Special Issue on Computer Hardware Description Languages, Vol. 7, No. 12 (December, 1974).

8. *Computer*, Special Issue on Hardware Description Language Applications, Vol. 10, No. 16 (June, 1977).

PROBLEMS

8-1.   Show the block diagram that executes the statement:

$$xT_3: \quad A \leftarrow B, \quad B \leftarrow A$$

8-2.   A constant value can be transferred to a register by applying to each input a binary signal equivalent to logic-1 or logic-0. Show the implementation of the transfer:

$$T: \quad A \leftarrow 11010110$$

8-3.   An 8-bit register A has one input x. The register operation is described symbolically as:

$$P: \quad A_8 \leftarrow x, \quad A_i \leftarrow A_{i+1} \quad\quad i = 1, 2, 3, \ldots, 7$$

What is the function of the register? The cells are numbered from right to left.

8-4.   Show the hardware implementation for each of the following statements. The registers are 4-bits in length:

T_0: $A \leftarrow R0$
T_1: $A \leftarrow R1$
T_2: $A \leftarrow R2$
T_3: $A \leftarrow R3$

8-5.   Let s_1, s_0 be the selection variables for the multiplexer of Fig. 8-6, and let $d_1 \, d_0$ be the selection variables for the destination decoder. Variable e is used to enable the decoder.

(a) State the transfers that occur when the selection variables $s_1 s_0 d_1 d_0 e$ are equal to: (1) 00010; (2) 01000; (3) 11100; (4) 01101.
(b) Give the values of the selection variables for the following transfers: (1) $A \leftarrow B$; (2) $B \leftarrow C$; (3) $D \leftarrow A$.

8-6.   A memory unit has two control inputs labeled *enable* and *read/write* (as explained in conjunction with Fig. 7-30). The memory data inputs and outputs are connected to an *MBR* register as in Fig. 8-7. The *MBR* can receive information either from an external register *EXR* or from the memory unit after a read operation. The *MBR* provides the data for the memory-write operation. Draw a block diagram using multiplexers and gates that shows the connection of *MBR* to memory. The system must have a capability of implementing the following three transfers:

W: $M \leftarrow MBR$ write into memory
R: $MBR \leftarrow M$ read from memory
E: $MBR \leftarrow EXR$ load *MBR* from *EXR*

8-7.   The following memory transfers are specified for the system of Fig. 8-8.
(a) $M[A2] \leftarrow B3$
(b) $B2 \leftarrow M[A3]$
Specify the memory operation and determine the binary selection variables for the two multiplexers and the destination decoder.

8-8.   Using the quadruple 2-to-1 line multiplexers of Fig. 5-17 and four inverters, draw a block diagram for implementing the statements:

T_1: $R2 \leftarrow R1$
T_2: $R2 \leftarrow \overline{R2}$
T_3: $R2 \leftarrow 0$

8-9.   Consider a 4-bit register A with bit A_4 being in the most significant position. What is the operation specified by the following statement:

$$A_4' C: \quad A \leftarrow A + 1$$
$$A_4: \quad\quad A \leftarrow 0$$

Show the implementation of the system using a counter with parallel load.

8-10. Show the hardware required to implement the following logic microoperations:

(a) T_1: $F \leftarrow A \wedge B$
(b) T_2: $G \leftarrow C \vee D$
(c) T_3: $E \leftarrow \bar{E}$

8-11. What is the difference between these two statements?

$$A + B: \quad F \leftarrow C \vee D$$

and

$$C + D: \quad F \leftarrow A + B$$

8-12. Specify the serial transfer depicted in Fig. 7-8 in symbolic form. Let S be the shift control function. Assume that S is enabled for a period of four pulses.

8-13. Show the hardware that implements the following statement. Include the logic gates for the control function.

$$xy'T_0 + T_1 + x'yT_2: \quad A \leftarrow A + B$$

8-14. A digital system has three registers: AR, BR, and PR. Three flip-flops provide the control functions for the system: S is a flip-flop which is enabled by an external signal to start the system's operation; F and R are used for sequencing the micro-operations. A fourth flip-flop, D, is set by the digital system when the operation is completed. The function of the system is described by the following register-transfer operations:

$$S: \quad PR \leftarrow 0, \quad S \leftarrow 0, \quad D \leftarrow 0, \quad F \leftarrow 1$$

$$F: \quad F \leftarrow 0, \quad \text{if } (AR = 0) \text{ then } (D \leftarrow 1) \text{ else } (R \leftarrow 1)$$

$$R: \quad PR \leftarrow PR + BR, \quad AR \leftarrow AR - 1, \quad R \leftarrow 0, \quad F \leftarrow 1$$

What is the function that the system performs?

8-15. Perform the arithmetic operations $(+42) + (-13)$ and $(-42) - (-13)$ in binary using:

(a) Sign-1's-complement representation.
(b) Sign-2's-complement representation.

8-16. The binary numbers listed below have a sign bit in the leftmost position and, if negative, are in 2's-complement form. Perform the arithmetic operations indicated using the algorithms for addition and subtraction stated in the text. Check your results by doing the arithmetic with equivalent decimal numbers.

(a) $001110 + 110010$
(b) $010101 + 000011$
(c) $111001 + 001010$
(d) $101011 + 111000$
(e) $010101 - 000111$
(f) $001010 - 111001$
(g) $111001 - 001010$
(h) $101011 - 100110$

8-17. What is the range of numbers that can be accommodated in a 16-bit register when the binary numbers are represented in:

(a) Sign-magnitude.
(b) Sign-2's complement.
Give the answers in equivalent decimal representation.

8-18. Perform the arithmetic operations listed below with binary numbers in sign-2's-complement representation and by applying the algorithm stated in the text. Use eight bits to accommodate each number together with its sign.

(1) $(+65) + (+78)$ (4) $(+65) + (-78)$
(2) $(-65) + (-78)$ (5) $(-65) + (+78)$
(3) $(+35) + (+40)$ (6) $(-35) + (-40)$

Inspect the 8-bit answer in each case and:
(a) Determine if there is an overflow.
(b) List the carries into and out of the sign-bit position.
(c) Determine the sign of the result (the eighth bit).
(d) State the relationship between (a) and (b).
(e) State the relationship between (a) and (c).

8-19. (a) Show the contents of an 8-bit register that stores the numbers $+36$ and -36 in binary and in three different representations, i.e., sign-magnitude, sign-1's complement, and sign-2's complement. (b) Show the contents of the register after the numbers are shifted arithmetically one position to the right (in all three representations). (c) Repeat (b) for arithmetic shift-left.

8-20. Two numbers in sign-2's-complement representation are added as shown in Fig. 8-10, and the sum is transferred to register A. Show that the arithmetic right-shift symbolized by:

$$A \leftarrow \text{shr } A, \qquad A_n \leftarrow A_n \oplus V$$

will always produce the correct sum divided by 2 whether or not there was an overflow in the original sum.

8-21. Represent $+149$ and -178 in BCD using sign-10's-complement representation. Use one bit for the sign. Add the two BCD numbers, including the sign bit, and interpret the answer obtained.

8-22. The algorithms for adding and subtracting decimal numbers in sign-10's-complement representation is similar to the algorithms for binary numbers in sign-2's-complement representation.

(a) State the algorithms for decimal addition and subtraction in sign-10's-complement representation. A positive sign is represented by a 0 and a negative sign is represented by a 9 in the most significant position.
(b) Apply the algorithms for the decimal computations $(-638) + (785)$ and $(-638) - (185)$.

8-23. A 36-bit floating-point binary number has 8 bits plus sign for the exponent. The coefficient is assumed to be a normalized fraction. The numbers in the coefficient and exponent are in sign-magnitude form. What are the largest and smallest positive quantities that can be accommodated, excluding zero?

8-24. A 30-bit register holds a decimal floating-point number represented in BCD. The coefficient occupies 21 bits of the register and is assumed to be a normalized integer. The numbers in the coefficient and exponent are assumed to be in sign-magnitude representation. What are the largest and smallest positive quantities that can be accommodated, excluding zero?

8-25. Represent the number $(+31.5)_{10}$ with a normalized integer coefficient of 13 bits and an exponent of 7 bits as:

(a) A binary number (assumed base of 2).

(b) A binary-coded octal number (assumed base of 8).

(c) A binary-coded hexadecimal number (assumed base of 16).

8-26. Register A holds the binary information 11011001. Determine the B operand and the logic microoperation to be performed between A and B to change the value in A to:

(a) 01101101

(b) 11111101

8-27. Determine the logic operation that will selectively clear bits in register A in those positions where there are 1's in the bits of register B.

8-28. A digital computer has a memory unit with 24 bits per word. The instruction set consists of 190 different operations. Each instruction is stored in one word of memory and consists of an operation-code part and an address part.

(a) How many bits are needed for the operation code?

(b) How many bits are left for the address part of the instruction?

(c) How many words can be accommodated in the memory unit?

(d) What is the largest signed fixed-point binary number that can be stored in one word of memory?

8-29. Specify an instruction format for a computer that performs the following operation:

$$A \leftarrow M[\text{address}] + R$$

where R can be any one of eight possible registers in the processor.

8-30. Assume that the memory unit of Fig. 8-14 has 65,536 words of 8 bits each.

(a) What should be the number of bits in the first five registers listed in Table 8-4?

(b) How many words of memory are required to store the instruction:

LDA   ADRS

as specified in Table 8-5?

(c) List the sequence of microoperations needed to execute the instruction. Register R can be used to temporarily hold part of an address.

8-31. An immediate instruction for the simple computer defined in Fig. 8-14 has an operation code 00000100. The instruction is specified as follows:

LRI   OPRD   (Load OPRD into R) $R \leftarrow OPRD$

List the sequence of microoperations for executing this instruction.

8-32. Repeat the design of the simple computer presented in Section 8-12. Replace the instructions in Table 8-5 by the following instructions:

Operation code	Mnemonic		Description	Function
00000001	ADD	R	Add R to A	$A \leftarrow A + R$
00000010	ADI	OPRD	Add operand to A	$A \leftarrow A + \text{OPRD}$
00000011	ADA	ADRS	Add direct to A	$A \leftarrow A + M[\text{ADRS}]$

8-33. Draw a block diagram showing the hardware implementation of the system specified in problem 8-14. Include a *start* input to set flip-flop S and a *done* output from flip-flop D.

Processor Logic Design

9-1 INTRODUCTION

A processor unit is that part of a digital system or a digital computer that implements the operations in the system. It is comprised of a number of registers and the digital functions that implement arithmetic, logic, shift, and transfer microoperations. The processor unit, when combined with a control unit that supervises the sequence of microoperations, is called a *central processor unit* or CPU. This chapter is concerned with the organization and design of the processor unit. The next chapter deals with the logic design of the control unit. In Chapter 11, we demonstrate the organization and design of a computer CPU.

The number of registers in a processor unit may vary from just one processor register to as many as 64 registers or more. Some older computers came with only one processor register. In some cases a special-purpose digital system may employ a single processor register. However, since registers and other digital functions are inexpensive when constructed with integrated circuits, all recent computers employ a large number of processor registers and route the information among them through common buses.

An operation may be implemented in a processor unit either with a single microoperation or with a sequence of microoperations. For example, the multiplication of two binary numbers stored in two registers may be implemented with a combinational circuit that performs the operation by means of gates. As soon as the signals propagate through the gates, the product is available and can be transferred to a destination register with a single clock pulse. Alternatively, the multiplication operation may be performed with a sequence of add and shift microoperations. The method chosen for the implementation dictates the amount and type of hardware in the processor unit.

All computers, except the very large and fast ones, implement the involved operations by means of a sequence of microoperations. In this way, the processor unit need only have circuits that implement simple, basic microoperations such as add and shift. Other operations, such as multiplication, division, and floating-point arithmetic, are generated in conjunction with the control unit. The processor unit by itself is designed to implement basic microoperations of the type discussed in Chapter 8. The control unit is designed to sequence the microoperations to achieve other operations which are not included in the basic set.

The digital function that implements the microoperations on the information stored in processor registers is commonly called an *arithmetic logic unit* or ALU. To perform a microoperation, the control routes the source information from registers into the inputs of the ALU. The ALU receives the information from the registers and performs a given operation as specified by the control. The result of the operation is then transferred to a destination register. By definition, the ALU is a combinational circuit; thus the entire register-transfer operation can be performed during one clock pulse interval. All register-transfer operations, including interregister transfers, in a typical processor unit are performed in one common ALU; otherwise, it would be necessary to duplicate the digital functions for each register. The shift microoperations are often performed in a separate unit. The shift unit is usually shown separately, but sometimes this unit is implied to be part of the overall arithmetic and logic unit.

A computer CPU must manipulate not only data but also instruction codes and addresses coming from memory. The register that holds and manipulates the operation code of instructions is considered to be part of the control unit. The registers that hold addresses are sometimes included as part of the processor unit, and the address information is manipulated by the common ALU. In some computers, the registers that hold addresses are connected to a separate bus and the address information is manipulated with separate digital functions.

This chapter presents a few alternatives for the organization and design of a processor unit. The design of a particular arithmetic logic unit is undertaken to show the design process involved in formulating and implementing a common digital function capable of performing a large number of microoperations. Other digital functions considered and designed in this chapter are a shifter unit and a general-purpose processor register, commonly called an *accumulator*.

9-2 PROCESSOR ORGANIZATION

The processor part of a computer CPU is sometimes referred to as the *data path* of the CPU because the processor forms the paths for the data transfers between the registers in the unit. The various paths are said to be controlled by means of *gates* that open the required path and close all others. A processor unit can be designed to fulfill the requirements of a set of data paths for a specific application. The design of a special-purpose processor was demonstrated in Section 8-9. Figure

8-16 showed the various data paths for a particular, very limited processor. The gating of the data paths is achieved through the decoders and combinational circuit which comprise the control section of the unit.

In a well-organized processor unit, the data paths are formed by means of buses and other common lines. The control gates that formulate the given path are essentially multiplexers and decoders whose selection lines specify the required path. The processing of information is done by one common digital function whose data path can be specified with a set of common selection variables. A processor unit that has a well-structured organization can be used in a wide variety of applications. If constructed within an integrated circuit, it becomes available to many users, each of which may have a different application.

In this section, we investigate a few alternatives for organizing a general-purpose processor unit. All organizations employ a common ALU and shifter. The differences in organizations are mostly manifested in the organization of the registers and their common path to the ALU.

Bus Organization

When a large number of registers are included in a processor unit, it is most efficient to connect them through common buses or arrange them as a small memory having very fast access time. The registers communicate with each other not only for direct data transfers, but also while performing various microoperations. A bus organization for four processor registers is shown in Fig. 9-1. Each register is connected to two multiplexers (MUX) to form input buses A and B. The selection lines of each multiplexer select one register for the particular bus. The A and B buses are applied to a common arithmetic logic unit. The function selected in the ALU determines the particular operation that is to be performed. The shift microoperations are implemented in the shifter. The result of the microoperation goes through the output bus S into the inputs of all registers. The destination register that receives the information from the output bus is selected by a decoder. When enabled, this decoder activates one of the register load inputs to provide a transfer path between the data on the S bus and the inputs of the selected destination register.

The output bus S provides the terminals for transferring data to an external destination. One input of multiplexer A or B can receive data from the outside environment when it is necessary to transfer external data into the processor unit.

The operation of the multiplexers, the buses, and the destination decoder is explained in Section 8-2 in conjunction with Fig. 8-6. The ALU and shifter are discussed later in this chapter.

A processor unit may have more than four registers. The construction of a bus-organized processor with more registers requires larger multiplexers and decoder; otherwise, it is similar to the organization depicted in Fig. 9-1.

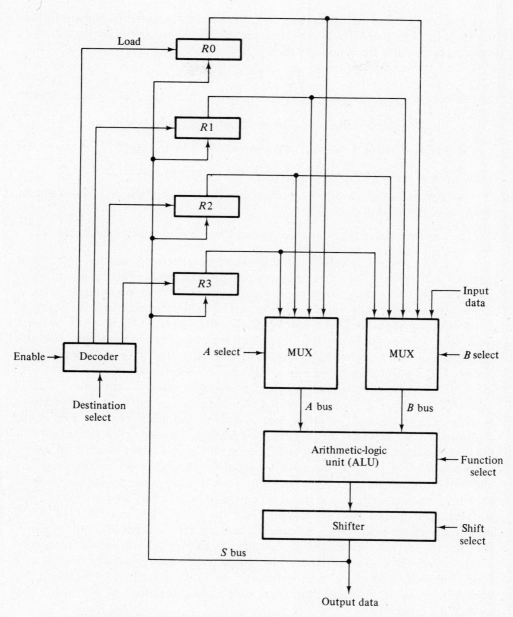

Figure 9-1 Processor registers and ALU connected through common buses

The control unit that supervises the processor bus system directs the information flow through the ALU by selecting the various components in the unit. For example, to perform the microoperation:

$$R1 \leftarrow R2 + R3$$

the control must provide binary selection variables to the following selector inputs:

1. MUX A selector: to place the contents of $R2$ onto bus A.

2. MUX B selector: to place the contents of $R3$ onto bus B.

3. ALU function selector: to provide the arithmetic operation $A + B$.

4. Shift selector: for direct transfer from the output of the ALU onto output bus S (no shift).

5. Decoder destination selector: to transfer the contents of bus S into $R1$.

The five control selection variables must be generated simultaneously and must be available during one common clock pulse interval. The binary information from the two source registers propagates through the combinational gates in the multiplexers, the ALU, and the shifter, to the output bus, and into the inputs of the destination register, all during one clock pulse interval. Then, when the next clock pulse arrives, the binary information on the output bus is transferred into $R1$. To achieve a fast response time, the ALU is constructed with carry look-ahead circuits and the shifter is implemented with combinational gates.

When enclosed in an IC package, a processor unit is sometimes called a *register and arithmetic logic unit* or RALU. It is also called by some vendors a *bit-slice microprocessor*. The prefix *micro* refers to the small physical size of the integrated circuit in which the processor is enclosed. *Bit-slice* refers to the fact that the processor can be expanded to a processor unit with a larger number of bits by using a number of ICs. For example, a 4-bit-slice microprocessor contains registers and ALU for manipulating 4-bit data. Two such ICs can be combined to construct an 8-bit processor unit. For a 16-bit processor, it is necessary to use four ICs and connect them in cascade. The output carry from one ALU is connected to the input carry of the next higher-order ALU, and the serial output and input lines of the shifters are also connected in cascade. A *bit-slice microprocessor* should be distinguished from another type of IC called a *microprocessor*. The former is a processor unit, whereas a microprocessor refers to an entire computer CPU enclosed in one IC package. Microprocessors and associated equipment are discussed in Chapter 12.

Scratchpad Memory

The registers in a processor unit can be enclosed within a small memory unit. When included in a processor unit, a small memory is sometimes called a *scratchpad* memory. The use of a small memory is a cheaper alternative to connecting processor registers through a bus system. The difference between the two systems is the manner in which information is selected for transfer into the ALU. In a bus system, the information transfer is selected by the multiplexers that form the buses. On the other hand, a single register in a group of registers organized as a small memory must be selected by means of an address to the memory unit. A memory register can function just as any other processor register as long as its only function is to hold binary information to be processed in the ALU.

A scratchpad memory should be distinguished from the main memory of the computer. Contrary to the main memory which stores instructions and data, a small memory in a processor unit is merely an alternative to connecting a number of processor registers through a common transfer path. The information stored in the scratchpad memory would normally come from the main memory by means of instructions in the program.

Consider, for example, a processor unit that employs eight registers of 16 bits each. The registers can be enclosed within a small memory of eight words of 16 bits each, or an 8×16 RAM. The eight memory words can be designated $R0$ through $R7$, corresponding to addresses 0 through 7, and constitute the registers for the processor.

A processor unit that uses a scratchpad memory is shown in Fig. 9-2. A source register is selected from memory and loaded into register A. A second source register is selected from memory and loaded into register B. The selection is done by specifying the corresponding word address and activating the memory-read input. The information in A and B is manipulated in the ALU and shifter. The result of the operation is transferred to a memory register by specifying its word address and activating the memory-write input control. The multiplexer in the input of the memory can select input data from an external source.

Assume that the memory has eight words, so that an address must be specified with three bits. To perform the operation:

$$R1 \leftarrow R2 + R3$$

the control must provide binary selection variables to perform the following sequence of three microoperations:

T_1: $A \leftarrow M[010]$ read $R2$ into register A

T_2: $B \leftarrow M[011]$ read $R3$ into register B

T_3: $M[001] \leftarrow A + B$ perform operation in ALU
                      and transfer result to $R1$

Control function T_1 must supply an address of 010 to the memory and activate the *read* and *load A* inputs. Control function T_2 must supply an address 011 to the memory and activate the *read* and *load B* inputs. Control function T_3 must supply the function code to the ALU and shifter to perform an-*add* operation (with no

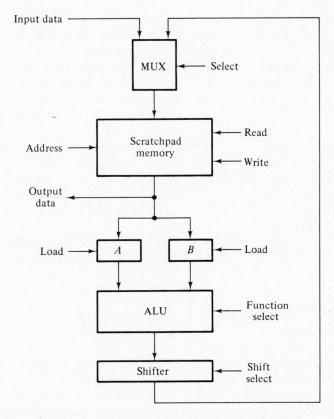

Figure 9-2 Processor unit employing a scratchpad memory

shift), apply an address 001 to the memory, select the output of the shifter for the MUX, and activate the memory *write* input. The symbol $M[xxx]$ designates a memory word (or register) specified by the address given in the binary number *xxx*.

The reason for a sequence of three microoperations, instead of just one as in a bus-organized processor, is due to the limitation of the memory unit. Since the memory unit has only one set of address terminals but two source registers are to be accessed, two accesses to memory are needed to read the source information. The third microoperation is needed to address the destination register. If the destination register is the same as the second source register, the control could activate the read input to extract the second-source information, followed by a write signal to activate the destination transfer, without having to change the address value.

Some processors employ a 2-port memory in order to overcome the delay caused when reading two source registers. A 2-port memory has two separate address lines to select two words of memory simultaneously. In this way, the two source registers can be read at the same time. If the destination register is the same

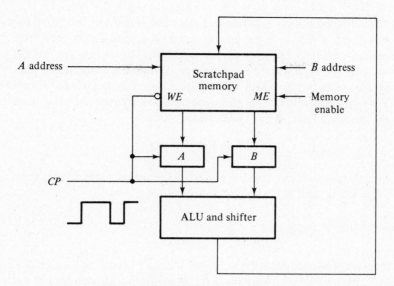

Figure 9-3 Processor unit with a 2-port memory

as one of the source registers, then the entire microoperation can be done within one clock pulse period.

The organization of a processor unit with a 2-port scratchpad memory is shown in Fig. 9-3.* The memory has two sets of addresses, one for port A and the other for port B. Data from any word in memory are read into the A register by specifying an A address. Likewise, data from any word in memory are read into the B register by specifying a B address. The same address can be applied to the A address and the B address, in which case the identical word will appear in both A and B registers. When enabled by the memory enable (ME) input, new data can be written into the word specified by the B address. Thus the A and B addresses specify two source registers simultaneously, and the B address always specifies the destination register. Figure 9-3 does not show a path for external input and output data, but they can be included as in previous organizations.

The A and B registers are, in effect, latches that accept new information as long as the clock pulse, CP, is in the 1-state. When CP goes to 0, the latches are disabled, and they hold the information that was stored when CP was a 1. This eliminates any possible race conditions that could occur while new information is being written into memory. The clock input controls the memory read and write operations through the write enable (WE) input. It also controls the transfers into the A and B latches. The waveform of one clock pulse interval is shown in the diagram.

When the clock input is 1, the A and B latches are open and accept the information coming from memory. The WE input is also in the 1-state. This

*This organization is similar to the 4-bit-slice microprocessor, type 2901.

disables the write operation and enables the read operation in the memory. Thus, when $CP = 1$, the words selected by the A and B addresses are read from memory and placed in registers A and B, respectively. The operation in the ALU is performed with the data stored in A and B. When the clock input goes to 0, the latches are closed and they retain the last data entered. If the ME input is enabled while $WE = 0$, the result of the microoperation is written into the memory word defined by the B address. Thus, a microoperation:

$$R1 \leftarrow R1 + R2$$

can be done within one clock pulse period. Memory register $R1$ must be specified with the B address, and $R2$ with the A address.

Accumulator Register

Some processor units separate one register from all others and call it an *accumulator* register, abbreviated AC or A register. The name of this register is derived from the arithmetic addition process encountered in digital computers. The process of adding many numbers is carried out by initially storing these numbers in other processor registers or in the memory unit of the computer and clearing the accumulator to 0. The numbers are then added to the accumulator one at a time, in consecutive order. The first number is added to 0, and the sum transferred to the accumulator. The second number is added to the contents of the accumulator, and the newly formed sum replaces its previous value. This process is continued until all numbers are added and the total sum is formed. Thus, the register "accumulates" the sum in a step-by-step manner by performing sequential additions between a new number and the previously accumulated sum.

The accumulator register in a processor unit is a multipurpose register capable of performing not only the add microoperation, but many other microoperations as well. In fact, the gates associated with an accumulator register provide all the digital functions found in an ALU.

Figure 9-4 shows the block diagram of a processor unit that employs an accumulator register. The A register is distinguished from all other processor registers. In some cases the entire processor unit is just the accumulator register and its associated ALU. The register itself can function as a shift register to provide the shift microoperations. Input B supplies one external source information. This information may come from other processor registers or directly from the main memory of the computer. The A register supplies the other source information to the ALU at input A. The result of an operation is transferred back to the A register and replaces its previous content. The output from the A register may go to an external destination or into the input terminals of other processor registers or memory unit.

To form the sum of two numbers stored in processor registers, it is necessary

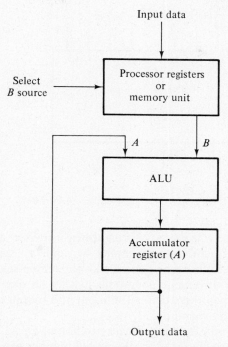

Input data

Select
B source

Processor registers
or
memory unit

A   B

ALU

Accumulator
register (A)

Output data

Figure 9-4 Processor with an accumulator register

to add them in the A register using the following sequence of microoperations:

$$T_1: \quad A \leftarrow 0 \qquad\qquad \text{clear } A$$

$$T_2: \quad A \leftarrow A + R1 \qquad \text{transfer } R1 \text{ to } A$$

$$T_3: \quad A \leftarrow A + R2 \qquad \text{add } R2 \text{ to } A$$

Register A is first cleared. The first number in $R1$ is transferred into the A register by adding it to the present zero content of A. The second number in $R2$ is then added to the present value of A. The sum formed in A may be used for other computations or may be transferred to a required destination.

9-3 ARITHMETIC LOGIC UNIT

An arithmetic logic unit (ALU) is a multioperation, combinational-logic digital function. It can perform a set of basic arithmetic operations and a set of logic operations. The ALU has a number of selection lines to select a particular operation in the unit. The selection lines are decoded within the ALU so that k selection variables can specify up to 2^k distinct operations.

Figure 9-5 shows the block diagram of a 4-bit ALU. The four data inputs from A are combined with the four inputs from B to generate an operation at the F

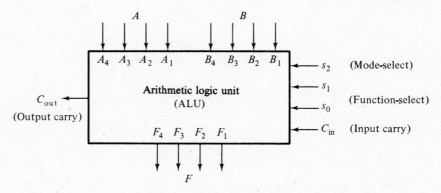

Figure 9-5 Block diagram of a 4-bit ALU

outputs. The mode-select input s_2 distinguishes between arithmetic and logic operations. The two function-select inputs s_1 and s_0 specify the particular arithmetic or logic operation to be generated. With three selection variables, it is possible to specify four arithmetic operations (with s_2 in one state) and four logic operations (with s_2 in the other state). The input and output carries have meaning only during an arithmetic operation.

The input carry in the least significant position of an ALU is quite often used as a fourth selection variable that can double the number of arithmetic operations. In this way, it is possible to generate four more operations, for a total of eight arithmetic operations.

The design of a typical ALU will be carried out in three stages. First, the design of the arithmetic section will be undertaken. Second, the design of the logic section will be considered. Finally, the arithmetic section will be modified so that it can perform both arithmetic and logic operations.

9-4 DESIGN OF ARITHMETIC CIRCUIT

The basic component of the arithmetic section of an ALU is a parallel adder. A parallel adder is constructed with a number of full-adder circuits connected in cascade (see Section 5-2). By controlling the data inputs to the parallel adder, it is possible to obtain different types of arithmetic operations. Figure 9-6 demonstrates the arithmetic operations obtained when one set of inputs to a parallel adder is controlled externally. The number of bits in the parallel adder may be of any value. The input carry C_{in} goes to the full-adder circuit in the least significant bit position. The output carry C_{out} comes from the full-adder circuit in the most significant bit position.

The arithmetic addition is achieved when one set of inputs receives a binary number A, the other set of inputs receives a binary number B, and the input carry is maintained at 0. This is shown in Fig. 9-6(a). By making $C_{in} = 1$ as in Fig.

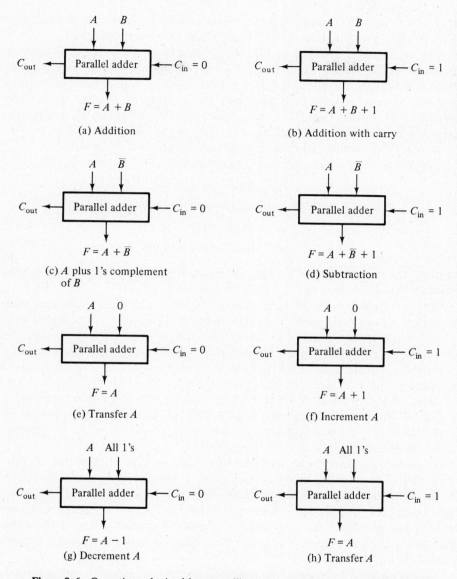

Figure 9-6 Operations obtained by controlling one set of inputs to a parallel adder

9-6(b), it is possible to add 1 to the sum in F. Now consider the effect of complementing all the bits of input B. With $C_{in} = 0$, the output produces $F = A + \overline{B}$, which is the sum of A plus the 1's complement of B. Adding 1 to this sum by making $C_{in} = 1$, we obtain $F = A + \overline{B} + 1$, which produces the sum of A plus the 2's complement of B. This operation is similar to a subtraction operation if the output carry is discarded. If we force all 0's into the B terminals, we obtain

369

$F = A + 0 = A$, which transfers input A into output F. Adding 1 through C_{in} as in Fig. 9-6(f), we obtain $F = A + 1$, which is the increment operation.

The condition illustrated in Fig. 9-6(g) inserts all 1's into the B terminals. This produces the decrement operation $F = A - 1$. To show that this condition is indeed a decrement operation, consider a parallel adder with n full-adder circuits. When the output carry is 1, it represents the number 2^n because 2^n in binary consists of a 1 followed by n 0's. Subtracting 1 from 2^n, we obtain $2^n - 1$, which in binary is a number of n 1's. Adding $2^n - 1$ to A, we obtain $F = A + 2^n - 1 = 2^n + A - 1$. If the output carry 2^n is removed, we obtain $F = A - 1$.

To demonstrate with a numerical example, let $n = 8$ and $A = 9$. Then:

$$
\begin{aligned}
A &= \quad\;\; 0000 \;\; 1001 = (9)_{10} \\
2^n &= 1 \;\; 0000 \;\; 0000 = (256)_{10} \\
2^n - 1 &= \quad\;\; 1111 \;\; 1111 = (255)_{10} \\
A + 2^n - 1 &= 1 \;\; 0000 \;\; 1000 = (256 + 8)_{10}
\end{aligned}
$$

Removing the output carry $2^n = 256$, we obtain $8 = 9 - 1$. Thus, we have decremented A by 1 by adding to it a binary number with all 1's.

The circuit that controls input B to provide the functions illustrated in Fig. 9-6 is called a *true/complement, one/zero* element. This circuit is illustrated in Fig. 9-7. The two selection lines s_1 and s_0 control the input of each B terminal. The diagram shows one typical input designated by B_i and an output designated by Y_i. In a typical application, there are n such circuits for $i = 1, 2, \ldots, n$. As shown in the table of Fig. 9-7, when both s_1 and s_0 are equal to 0, the output $Y_i = 0$, regardless of the value of B_i. When $s_1 s_0 = 01$, the top AND gate generates the value of B_i while the bottom gate output is 0; so $Y_i = B_i$. With $s_1 s_0 = 10$, the bottom AND gate generates the complement of B_i to give $Y_i = B_i'$. When $s_1 s_0 = 11$, both gates are active and $Y_i = B_i + B_i' = 1$.

A 4-bit arithmetic circuit that performs eight arithmetic operations is shown in Fig. 9-8. The four full-adder (FA) circuits constitute the parallel adder. The carry into the first stage is the input carry. The carry out of the fourth stage is the output carry. All other carries are connected internally from one stage to the next. The selection variables are s_1, s_0, and C_{in}. Variables s_1 and s_0 control all of the B inputs to the full-adder circuits as in Fig. 9-7. The A inputs go directly to the other inputs of the full adders.

The arithmetic operations implemented in the arithmetic circuit are listed in Table 9-1. The values of the Y inputs to the full-adder circuits are a function of

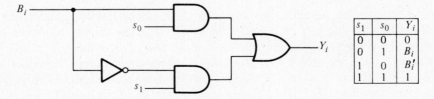

s_1	s_0	Y_i
0	0	0
0	1	B_i
1	0	B_i'
1	1	1

Figure 9-7 True/complement, one/zero circuit

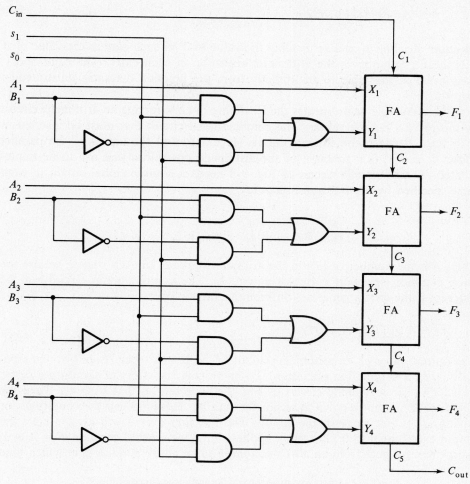

Figure 9-8 Logic diagram of arithmetic circuit

TABLE 9-1 Function table for the arithmetic circuit of Fig. 9-8

Function select			Y equals	Output equals	Function
s_1	s_0	C_{in}			
0	0	0	0	$F = A$	Transfer A
0	0	1	0	$F = A + 1$	Increment A
0	1	0	B	$F = A + B$	Add B to A
0	1	1	B	$F = A + B + 1$	Add B to A plus 1
1	0	0	$\overline{B}$	$F = A + \overline{B}$	Add 1's complement of B to A
1	0	1	$\overline{B}$	$F = A + \overline{B} + 1$	Add 2's complement of B to A
1	1	0	All 1's	$F = A - 1$	Decrement A
1	1	1	All 1's	$F = A$	Transfer A

selection variables s_1 and s_0. Adding the value of Y in each case to the value of A plus the C_{in} value gives the arithmetic operation in each entry. The eight operations listed in the table follow directly from the function diagrams illustrated in Fig. 9-6.

This example demonstrates the feasibility of constructing an arithmetic circuit by means of a parallel adder. The combinational circuit that must be inserted in each stage between the external inputs A_i and B_i and the inputs of the parallel adder X_i and Y_i is a function of the arithmetic operations that are to be implemented. The arithmetic circuit of Fig. 9-8 needs a combinational circuit in each stage specified by the Boolean functions:

$$X_i = A_i$$
$$Y_i = B_i s_0 + B_i' s_1 \qquad i = 1, 2, \ldots, n$$

where n is the number of bits in the arithmetic circuit. In each stage i, we use the same common selection variables s_1 and s_0. The combinational circuit will be different if the circuit generates different arithmetic operations.

Effect of Output Carry

The output carry of an arithmetic circuit or ALU has special significance, especially after a subtraction operation. To investigate the effect of the output carry, we expand the arithmetic circuit of Fig. 9-8 to n bits so that $C_{out} = 1$ when the output of the circuit is equal to or greater than 2^n. Table 9-2 lists the conditions for having an output carry in the circuit. The function $F = A$ will always have the output carry equal to 0. The same applies to the increment operation $F = A + 1$, except when it goes from an all-1's condition to an all-0's condition, at which time

TABLE 9-2   Effect of output carry in the arithmetic circuit of Fig. 9-8

Function select			Arithmetic function	$C_{out} = 1$ if	Comments
s_1	s_0	C_{in}			
0	0	0	$F = A$		C_{out} is always 0
0	0	1	$F = A + 1$	$A = 2^n - 1$	$C_{out} = 1$ and $F = 0$ if $A = 2^n - 1$
0	1	0	$F = A + B$	$(A + B) \geqslant 2^n$	Overflow occurs if $C_{out} = 1$
0	1	1	$F = A + B + 1$	$(A + B) \geqslant (2^n - 1)$	Overflow occurs if $C_{out} = 1$
1	0	0	$F = A - B - 1$	$A > B$	If $C_{out} = 0$, then $A \leqslant B$ and $F = $ 1's complement of $(B - A)$
1	0	1	$F = A - B$	$A \geqslant B$	If $C_{out} = 0$, then $A < B$ and $F = $ 2's complement of $(B - A)$
1	1	0	$F = A - 1$	$A \neq 0$	$C_{out} = 1$, except when $A = 0$
1	1	1	$F = A$		C_{out} is always 1

it produces an output carry of 1. An output carry of 1 after an addition operation denotes an overflow condition. It indicates that the sum is greater than or equal to 2^n and that the sum consists of $n + 1$ bits.

The operation $F = A + \bar{B}$ adds the 1's complement of B to A. Remember from Section 1-5 that the complement of B can be expressed arithmetically as $2^n - 1 - B$. The arithmetic result in the output will be:

$$F = A + 2^n - 1 - B = 2^n + A - B - 1$$

If $A > B$, then $(A - B) > 0$ and $F > (2^n - 1)$, so that $C_{out} = 1$. Removing the output carry 2^n from this result gives:

$$F = A - B - 1$$

which is a subtraction with borrow. Note that if $A \leqslant B$, then $(A - B) \leqslant 0$ and $F \leqslant (2^n - 1)$, so that $C_{out} = 0$. For this condition it is more convenient to express the arithmetic result as:

$$F = (2^n - 1) - (B - A)$$

which is the 1's complement of $B - A$.

The condition for output carry when $F = A + \bar{B} + 1$ can be derived in a similar manner. $\bar{B} + 1$ is the symbol for the 2's complement of B. Arithmetically, this is an operation that produces a number equal to $2^n - B$. The result of the operation can be expressed as:

$$F = A + 2^n - B = 2^n + A - B$$

If $A \geqslant B$, then $(A - B) \geqslant 0$ and $F \geqslant 2^n$, so that $C_{out} = 1$. Removing the output carry 2^n, we obtain:

$$F = A - B$$

which is a subtraction operation. If, however, $A < B$, then $(A - B) < 0$ and $F < 2^n$, so that $C_{out} = 0$. The arithmetic result for this condition can be expressed as:

$$F = 2^n - (B - A)$$

which is the 2's complement of $B - A$. Thus, the output of the arithmetic subtraction is correct as long as $A \geqslant B$. The output should be $B - A$ if $B > A$, but the circuit generates the 2's complement of this number.

The decrement operation is obtained from $F = A + (2^n - 1) = 2^n + A - 1$. The output carry is always 1 except when $A = 0$. Subtracting 1 from 0 gives -1, and -1 in 2's complement is $2^n - 1$, which is a number with all 1's. The last entry in Table 9-2 generates $F = (2^n - 1) + A + 1 = 2^n + A$. This operation transfers A into F and gives an output carry of 1.

Design of Other Arithmetic Circuits

The design of any arithmetic circuit that generates a set of basic operations can be undertaken by following the procedure outlined in the previous example. Assuming that all operations in the set can be generated through a parallel adder, we start by obtaining a function diagram as in Fig. 9-6. From the function diagram, we obtain a function table that relates the inputs of the full-adder circuit to the external inputs. From the function table, we obtain the combinational gates that must be added to each full-adder stage. This procedure is demonstrated in the following example.

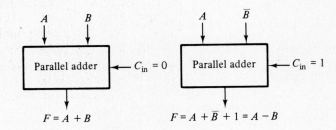

(a) Function specification

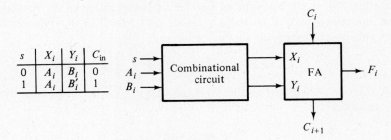

(b) Specifying combinational circuit

s	A_i	B_i	X_i	Y_i
0	0	0	0	0
0	0	1	0	1
0	1	0	1	0
0	1	1	1	1
1	0	0	0	1
1	0	1	0	0
1	1	0	1	1
1	1	1	1	0

$$X_i = A_i$$

$$Y_i = B_i \oplus s$$

$$C_{in} = s$$

(c) Truth table and simplified equations

Figure 9-9 Derivation of an adder/subtractor circuit

EXAMPLE 9-1: Design an adder/subtractor circuit with one selection variable s and two inputs A and B. When $s = 0$ the circuit performs $A + B$. When $s = 1$ the circuit performs $A - B$ by taking the 2's complement of B.

The derivation of the arithmetic circuit is illustrated in Fig. 9-9. The function diagram is shown in Fig. 9-9(a). For the addition part, we need $C_{in} = 0$. For the subtraction part, we need the complement of B and $C_{in} = 1$. The function table is listed in Fig. 9-9(b). When $s = 0$, X_i and Y_i of each full adder must be equal to the external inputs A_i and B_i, respectively. When $s = 1$, we must have $X_i = A_i$ and $Y_i = B_i'$. The input carry must be equal to the value of s. The diagram in (b) shows the position of the combinational circuit in one typical stage of the arithmetic circuit. The truth table in (c) is obtained by listing the eight values of the binary input variables. Output X_i is made to be equal to input A_i in all eight entries. Output Y_i is equal to B_i for the four entries when $s = 0$. It is equal to the

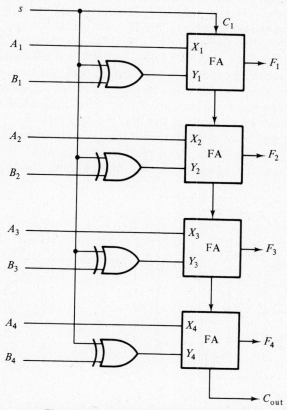

Figure 9-10   4-bit adder/subtractor circuit

complement of B_i for the last four entries where $s = 1$. The simplified output functions for the combinational circuit are:

$$X_i = A_i$$
$$Y_i = B_i \oplus s$$

The diagram of the 4-bit adder/subtractor circuit is shown in Fig. 9-10. Each input B_i requires an exclusive-OR gate. The selection variable s goes to one input of each gate and also to the input carry of the parallel adder. The 4-bit adder/subtractor can be constructed with two ICs. One IC is the 4-bit parallel adder and the other is a quadruple exclusive-OR gates.

9-5 DESIGN OF LOGIC CIRCUIT

The logic microoperations manipulate the bits of the operands separately and treat each bit as a binary variable. Table 2-6 listed 16 logic operations that can be performed with two binary variables. The 16 logic operations can be generated in one circuit and selected by means of four selection lines. Since all logic operations can be obtained by means of AND, OR, and NOT (complement) operations, it may be more convenient to employ a logic circuit with just these operations. For three operations, we need two selection variables. But two selection lines can select among four logic operations, so we choose also the exclusive-OR (XOR) function for the logic circuit to be designed in this and the next section.

The simplest and most straightforward way to design a logic circuit is shown in Fig. 9-11. The diagram shows one typical stage designated by subscript i. The circuit must be repeated n times for an n-bit logic circuit. The four gates generate

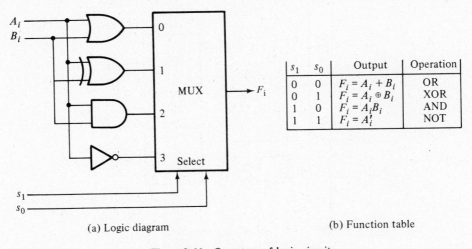

s_1	s_0	Output	Operation
0	0	$F_i = A_i + B_i$	OR
0	1	$F_i = A_i \oplus B_i$	XOR
1	0	$F_i = A_i B_i$	AND
1	1	$F_i = A_i'$	NOT

(a) Logic diagram   (b) Function table

Figure 9-11 One stage of logic circuit

the four logic operations OR, XOR, AND, and NOT. The two selection variables in the multiplexer select one of the gates for the output. The function table lists the output logic generated as a function of the two selection variables.

The logic circuit can be combined with the arithmetic circuit to produce one arithmetic logic unit. Selection variables s_1 and s_0 can be made common to both sections provided we use a third selection variable, s_2, to differentiate between the two. This configuration is illustrated in Fig. 9-12. The outputs of the logic and arithmetic circuits in each stage go through a multiplexer with selection variable s_2. When $s_2 = 0$, the arithmetic output is selected, but when $s_2 = 1$, the logic output is selected. Although the two circuits can be combined in this manner, this is not the best way to design an ALU.

A more efficient ALU can be obtained if we investigate the possibility of generating logic operations in an already available arithmetic circuit. This can be done by inhibiting all input carries into the full-adder circuits of the parallel adder. Consider the Boolean function that generates the output sum in a full-adder circuit:

$$F_i = X_i \oplus Y_i \oplus C_i$$

The input carry C_i in each stage can be made to be equal to 0 when a selection variable s_2 is equal to 1. The result would be:

$$F_i = X_i \oplus Y_i$$

This expression is valid because of the property of the exclusive-OR operation $x \oplus 0 = x$. Thus, with the input carry to *each* stage equal to 0, the full-adder circuits generate the exclusive-OR operation.

Now consider the arithmetic circuit of Fig. 9-8. The value of Y_i can be selected by means of the two selection variables to be equal to either 0, B_i, B_i', or 1.

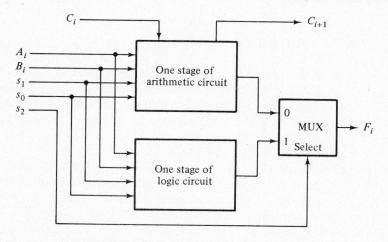

Figure 9-12 Combining logic and arithmetic circuits

TABLE 9-3 Logic operations in one stage of arithmetic circuit

s_2	s_1	s_0	X_i	Y_i	C_i	$F_i = X_i \oplus Y_i$	Operation	Required operation
1	0	0	A_i	0	0	$F_i = A_i$	Transfer A	OR
1	0	1	A_i	B_i	0	$F_i = A_i \oplus B_i$	XOR	XOR
1	1	0	A_i	B_i'	0	$F_i = A_i \odot B_i$	Equivalence	AND
1	1	1	A_i	1	0	$F_i = A_i'$	NOT	NOT

The value of X_i is always equal to input A_i. Table 9-3 shows the four logic operations obtained when a third selection variable $s_2 = 1$. This selection variable forces C_i to be equal to 0 while s_1 and s_0 choose a particular value for Y_i. The four logic operations obtained by this configuration are transfer, exclusive-OR, equivalence, and complement. The third entry is the equivalence operation because:

$$A_i \oplus B_i' = A_i B_i + A_i' B_i' = A_i \odot B_i$$

The last entry in the table is the NOT or complement operation because:

$$A_i \oplus 1 = A_i'$$

The table has one more column which lists the four logic operations we want to include in the ALU. Two of these operations, XOR and NOT, are already available. The question that must be answered is whether it is possible to modify the arithmetic circuit further so that it will generate the logic functions OR and AND instead of the transfer and equivalence functions. This problem is investigated in the next section.

9-6 DESIGN OF ARITHMETIC LOGIC UNIT

In this section, we design an ALU with eight arithmetic operations and four logic operations. Three selection variables s_2, s_1, and s_0 select eight different operations, and the input carry C_{in} is used to select four additional arithmetic operations. With $s_2 = 0$, selection variables s_1 and s_0 together with C_{in} will select the eight arithmetic operations listed in Table 9-1. With $s_2 = 1$, variables s_1 and s_0 will select the four logic operations OR, XOR, AND, and NOT.

The design of an ALU is a combinational-logic problem. Because the unit has a regular pattern, it can be broken into identical stages connected in cascade through the carries. We can design one stage of the ALU and then duplicate it for the number of stages required. There are six inputs to each stage: A_i, B_i, C_i, s_2, s_1, and s_0. There are two outputs in each stage: output F_i and the carry out C_{i+1}. One can formulate a truth table with 64 entries and simplify the two output functions.

Here we choose to employ an alternate procedure that uses the availability of a parallel adder.

The steps involved in the design of an ALU are as follows:

1. Design the arithmetic section independent of the logic section.

2. Determine the logic operations obtained from the arithmetic circuit in step 1, assuming that the input carries to all stages are 0.

3. Modify the arithmetic circuit to obtain the required logic operations.

The third step in the design is not a straightforward procedure and requires a certain amount of ingenuity on the part of the designer. There is no guarantee that a solution can be found or that the solution uses the minimum number of gates. The example presented here demonstrates the type of logical thinking sometimes required in the design of digital systems.

It must be realized that various ALUs are available in IC packages. In a practical situation, all that one must do is search for a suitable ALU or processor unit among the ICs that are available commercially. Yet, the internal logic of the IC selected must have been designed by a person familiar with logic design techniques.

The solution to the first design step is shown in Fig. 9-8. The solution to the second design step is presented in Table 9-3. The solution of the third step is carried out below.

From Table 9-3, we see that when $s_2 = 1$, the input carry C_i in each stage must be 0. With $s_1 s_0 = 00$, each stage as it stands generates the function $F_i = A_i$. To change the output to an OR operation, we must change the input to each full-adder circuit from A_i to $A_i + B_i$. This can be accomplished by ORing B_i and A_i when $s_2 s_1 s_0 = 100$.

The other selection variables that give an undesirable output occur when $s_2 s_1 s_0 = 110$. The unit as it stands generates an output $F_i = A_i \odot B_i$, but we want to generate the AND operation $F_i = A_i B_i$. Let us investigate the possibility of ORing each input A_i with some Boolean function K_i. The function so obtained is then used for X_i when $s_2 s_1 s_0 = 110$:

$$F_i = X_i \oplus Y_i = (A_i + K_i) \oplus B_i' = A_i B_i + K_i B_i + A_i' K_i' B_i'$$

Careful inspection of the result reveals that if the variable $K_i = B_i'$, we obtain an output:

$$F_i = A_i B_i + B_i' B_i + A_i B_i B_i' = A_i B_i$$

Two terms are equal to 0 because $B_i B_i' = 0$. The result obtained is the AND operation as required. The conclusion is that, if A_i is ORed with B_i' when $s_2 s_1 s_0 = 110$, the output will generate the AND operation.

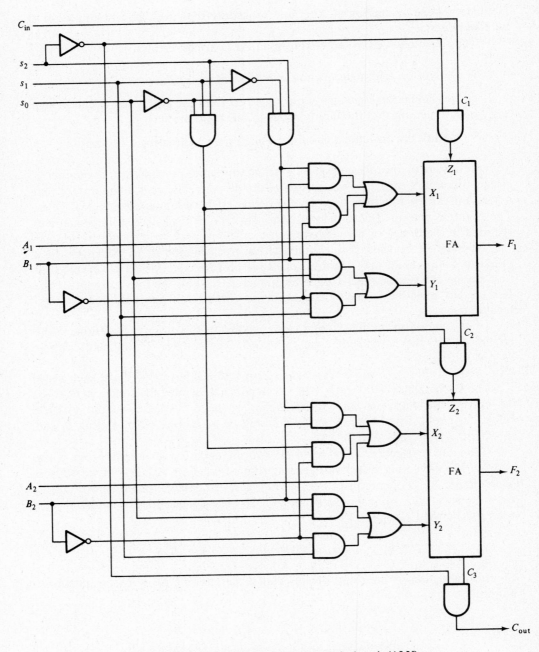

Figure 9-13 Logic diagram of arithmetic logic unit (ALU)

The final ALU is shown in Fig. 9-13. Only the first two stages are drawn, but the diagram can be easily extended to more stages. The inputs to each full-adder circuit are specified by the Boolean functions:

$$X_i = A_i + s_2 s_1' s_0' B_i + s_2 s_1 s_0' B_i'$$
$$Y_i = s_0 B_i + s_1 B_i'$$
$$Z_i = s_2' C_i$$

When $s_2 = 0$, the three functions reduce to:

$$X_i = A_i$$
$$Y_i = s_0 B_i + s_1 B_i'$$
$$Z_i = C_i$$

which are the functions for the arithmetic circuit of Fig. 9-8. The logic operations are generated when $s_2 = 1$. For $s_2 s_1 s_0 = 101$ or 111, the functions reduce to:

$$X_i = A_i$$
$$Y_i = s_0 B_i + s_1 B_i'$$
$$C_i = 0$$

Output F_i is then equal to $X_i \oplus Y_i$ and produces the exclusive-OR and complement operations as specified in Table 9-3. When $s_2 s_1 s_0 = 100$, each A_i is ORed with B_i to provide the OR operation as discussed above. When $s_2 s_1 s_0 = 110$, each A_i is ORed with B_i' to provide the AND operation as explained previously.

The 12 operations generated in the ALU are summarized in Table 9-4. The particular function is selected through s_2, s_1, s_0, and C_{in}. The arithmetic operations

TABLE 9-4   Function table for the ALU of Fig. 9-13

	Selection				
s_2	s_1	s_0	C_{in}	Output	Function
0	0	0	0	$F = A$	Transfer A
0	0	0	1	$F = A + 1$	Increment A
0	0	1	0	$F = A + B$	Addition
0	0	1	1	$F = A + B + 1$	Add with carry
0	1	0	0	$F = A - B - 1$	Subtract with borrow
0	1	0	1	$F = A - B$	Subtraction
0	1	1	0	$F = A - 1$	Decrement A
0	1	1	1	$F = A$	Transfer A
1	0	0	X	$F = A \vee B$	OR
1	0	1	X	$F = A \oplus B$	XOR
1	1	0	X	$F = A \wedge B$	AND
1	1	1	X	$F = \overline{A}$	Complement A

are identical to the ones listed for the arithmetic circuit. The value of C_{in} for the four logic functions has no effect on the operation of the unit and those entries are marked with don't-care X's.

9-7   STATUS REGISTER

The relative magnitudes of two numbers may be determined by subtracting one number from the other and then checking certain bit conditions in the resultant difference. If the two numbers are unsigned, the bit conditions of interest are the output carry and a possible zero result. If the two numbers include a sign bit in the highest-order position, the bit conditions of interest are the sign of the result, a zero indication, and an overflow condition. It is sometimes convenient to supplement the ALU with a status register where these status-bit conditions are stored for further analysis. Status-bit conditions are sometimes called *condition-code* bits or *flag* bits.

Figure 9-14 shows the block diagram of an 8-bit ALU with a 4-bit status register. The four status bits are symbolized by C, S, Z, and V. The bits are set or cleared as a result of an operation performed in the ALU.

1. Bit C is set if the output carry of the ALU is 1. It is cleared if the output carry is 0.

2. Bit S is set if the highest-order bit of the result in the output of the ALU (the sign bit) is 1. It is cleared if the highest-order bit is 0.

3. Bit Z is set if the output of the ALU contains all 0's, and cleared otherwise. $Z = 1$ if the result is zero, and $Z = 0$ if the result is nonzero.

4. Bit V is set if the exclusive-OR of carries C_8 and C_9 is 1, and cleared otherwise. This is the condition for overflow when the numbers are in sign-2's-complement representation (see Section 8-5). For the 8-bit ALU, V is set if the result is greater than 127 or less than -128.

The status bits can be checked after an ALU operation to determine certain relationships that exist between the values of A and B. If bit V is set after the addition of two signed numbers, it indicates an overflow condition. If Z is set after an exclusive-OR operation, it indicates that $A = B$. This is so because $x \oplus x = 0$, and the exclusive-OR of two equal operands gives an all-0's result which sets the Z bit. A single bit in A can be checked to determine if it is 0 or 1 by masking all bits except the bit in question and then checking the Z status bit. For example, let $A = 101x1100$, where x is the bit to be checked. The AND operation of A with $B = 00010000$ produces a result $000x0000$. If $x = 0$, the Z status bit is set, but if $x = 1$, the Z bit is cleared since the result is not zero.

The *compare* operation is a subtraction of B from A, except that the result of the operation is not transferred into a destination register, but the status bits are affected. The status register then provides the information about the relative

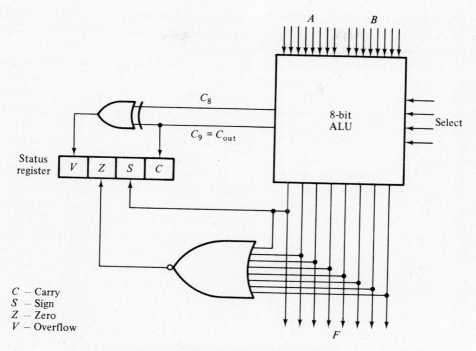

Figure 9-14 Setting bits in a status register

magnitudes of A and B. The status bits to consider depend on whether we take the two numbers to be unsigned or signed and in 2's-complement representation.

Consider the operation $A - B$ done with two *unsigned* binary numbers. The relative magnitudes of A and B can be determined from the values transferred to the C and Z status bits. If $Z = 1$, then we know that $A = B$, since $A - B = 0$. If $Z = 0$, then we know that $A \neq B$. From Table 9-2, we have that $C = 1$ if $A \geqslant B$ and $C = 0$ if $A < B$. These conditions are listed in Table 9-5. The table lists two other conditions. For A to be greater than but not equal to B ($A > B$), we must have $C = 1$ and $Z = 0$. Since C is set when the result is 0, we must check Z to

TABLE 9-5 Status bits after the subtraction of unsigned numbers ($A - B$)

Relation	Condition of status bits	Boolean function
$A > B$	$C = 1$ and $Z = 0$	CZ'
$A \geqslant B$	$C = 1$	C
$A < B$	$C = 0$	C'
$A \leqslant B$	$C = 0$ or $Z = 1$	$C' + Z$
$A = B$	$Z = 1$	Z
$A \neq B$	$Z = 0$	Z'

ensure that the result is not 0. For A to be less than or equal to B ($A \leqslant B$), the C bit must be 0 (for $A < B$) or the Z bit must be 1 (for $A = B$). Table 9-5 also lists the Boolean functions that must be satisfied for each of the six relationships.

Some computers consider the C bit to be a borrow bit after a subtraction operation $A - B$. An end borrow does not occur if $A \geqslant B$, but an extra bit must be borrowed when $A < B$. The condition for a borrow is the complement of the output carry obtained when the subtraction is done by taking the 2's complement of B. For this reason, a processor that considers the C bit to be a borrow after a subtraction will complement the C bit after a subtraction or compare operation and denote this bit as a borrow.

Now consider the operation $A - B$ done with two *signed* binary numbers when negative numbers are in 2's-complement form. The relative magnitudes of A and B can be determined from the values transferred to the Z, S, and V status bits. If $Z = 1$, then we know that $A = B$; when $Z = 0$, we have that $A \neq B$. If $S = 0$, the sign of the result is positive, so A must be greater than B. This is true if there was no overflow and $V = 0$. If the result overflows, we obtain an erroneous result. It was shown in Section 8-5 that an overflow condition changes the sign of the result. Therefore, if $S = 1$ and $V = 1$, it indicates that the result should have been positive and therefore A must be greater than B.

Table 9-6 lists the six possible relationships that can exist between A and B and the corresponding values of Z, S, and V in each case. For $A - B$ to be greater than but not equal to zero ($A > B$), the result must be positive and nonzero. Since a zero result gives a positive sign, we must ensure that the Z bit is 0 to exclude the possibility of $A = B$. For $A \geqslant B$, it is sufficient to check for a positive sign when no overflow occurs or a negative sign when an overflow occurs. For $A < B$, the result must be negative. If the result is negative or zero, we have that $A \leqslant B$. The Boolean functions listed in the table express the status-bit conditions in algebraic form.

TABLE 9-6   Status bits after the subtraction of sign-2's complement numbers ($A - B$)

Relation	Condition of status bits	Boolean function
$A > B$	$Z = 0$ and ($S = 0, V = 0$ or $S = 1, V = 1$)	$Z'(S \odot V)$
$A \geqslant B$	$S = 0, V = 0$ or $S = 1, V = 1$	$S \odot V$
$A < B$	$S = 1, V = 0$ or $S = 0, V = 1$	$S \oplus V$
$A \leqslant B$	$S = 1, V = 0$ or $S = 0, V = 1$ or $Z = 1$	$(S \oplus V) + Z$
$A = B$	$Z = 1$	Z
$A \neq B$	$Z = 0$	Z'

9-8   DESIGN OF SHIFTER

The shift unit attached to a processor transfers the output of the ALU onto the output bus. The shifter may transfer the information directly without a shift, or it may shift the information to the right or left. Provision is sometimes made for no transfer from the ALU to the output bus. The shifter provides the shift microoperations commonly not available in an ALU.

An obvious circuit for a shifter is a bidirectional shift-register with parallel load. The information from the ALU can be transferred to the register in parallel and then shifted to the right or left. In this configuration, a clock pulse is needed for the transfer to the shift register, and another pulse is needed for the shift. These two pulses are in addition to the pulse required to transfer the information from the shift register to a destination register.

The transfer from a source register to a destination register can be done with one clock pulse if the shifter is implemented with a combinational circuit. In a combinational-logic shifter, the signals from the ALU to the output bus propagate through gates without the need for a clock pulse. Hence, the only clock pulse needed in the processor system is for loading the data from the output bus into the destination register.

A combinational-logic shifter can be constructed with multiplexers as shown in Fig. 9-15. The two selection variables, H_1 and H_0, applied to all four multiplexers select the type of operation in the shifter. With $H_1 H_0 = 00$, no shift is executed and the signals from F go directly to the S lines. The next two selection variables cause a shift-right operation and a shift-left operation. When $H_1 H_0 = 11$, the multiplexers select the inputs attached to 0 and as a consequence the S outputs are also equal to 0, blocking the transfer of information from the ALU to the output bus. Table 9-7 summarizes the operation of the shifter.

The diagram of Fig. 9-15 shows only four stages of the shifter. The shifter, of course, must consist of n stages in a system with n parallel lines. Inputs I_R and I_L

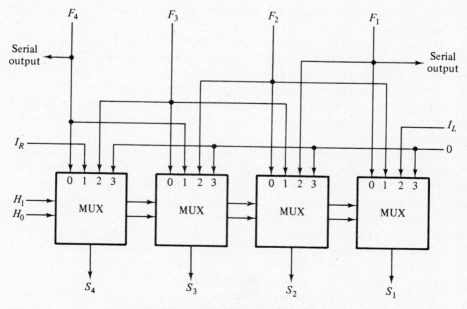

Figure 9-15   4-bit combinational-logic shifter

TABLE 9-7   Function table for shifter

H_1	H_0	Operation	Function
0	0	$S \leftarrow F$	Transfer F to S (no shift)
0	1	$S \leftarrow \text{shr } F$	Shift-right F into S
1	0	$S \leftarrow \text{shl } F$	Shift-left F into S
1	1	$S \leftarrow 0$	Transfer 0's into S

serve as serial inputs for the last and first stages during a shift-right or shift-left, respectively. Another selection variable may be employed to specify what goes into I_R or I_L during the shift. For example, a third selection variable, H_2, when in one state can select a 0 for the serial input during the shift. When H_2 is in the other state, the information can be circulated around together with the value of the carry status bit. In this way, a carry produced during an addition operation can be shifted to the right and into the most significant bit position of a register.

9-9   PROCESSOR UNIT

The selection variables in a processor unit control the microoperations executed within the processor during any given clock pulse. The selection variables control the buses, the ALU, the shifter, and the destination register. We will now demonstrate by means of an example how the control variables select the microoperations in a processor unit. The example defines a processor unit together with all selection variables. Then we will discuss the choice of control variables for some typical microoperations.

A block diagram of a processor unit is shown in Fig. 9-16(a). It consists of seven registers $R1$ through $R7$ and a status register. The outputs of the seven registers go through two multiplexers to select the inputs to the ALU. Input data from an external source are also selected by the same multiplexers. The output of the ALU goes through a shifter and then to a set of external output terminals. The output from the shifter can be transferred to any one of the registers or to an external destination.

There are 16 selection variables in the unit, and their function is specified by a *control word* in Fig. 9-16(b). The 16-bit control word, when applied to the selection variables in the processor, specifies a given microoperation. The control word is partitioned into six fields, with each field designated by a letter name. All fields, except C_{in}, have a code of three bits. The three bits of A select a source register for the input to left side of the ALU. The B field is the same, but it selects the source information for the right input of the ALU. The D field selects a destination register. The F field, together with the bit in C_{in}, selects a function for the ALU. The H field selects the type of shift in the shifter unit.

The functions of all selection variables are specified in Table 9-8. The 3-bit binary code listed in the table specifies the code for each of the five fields A, B, D,

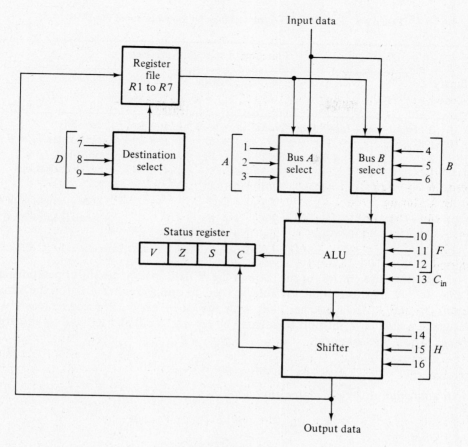

Input data

Output data

(a) Block diagram

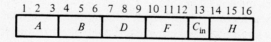

1 2 3	4 5 6	7 8 9	10 11 12	13	14 15 16
A	B	D	F	C_{in}	H

(b) Control word

Figure 9-16 Processor unit with control variables

F, and H. The register selected by A, B, and D is the one whose decimal number is equivalent to the binary number in the code. When the A or B field is 000, the corresponding multiplexer selects the input data. When $D = 000$, no destination register is selected. The three bits in the F field, together with the input carry C_{in}, provide the 12 operations of the ALU as specified in Table 9-4. Note that there are two possibilities for $F = A$. In one case the carry bit C is cleared, and in the other case it is set to 1 (see Table 9-2).

Binary code	A	B	D	F with $C_{in} = 0$	F with $C_{in} = 1$	H
				Function of selection variables		
0 0 0	Input data	Input data	None	$A, C \leftarrow 0$	$A + 1$	No shift
0 0 1	$R1$	$R1$	$R1$	$A + B$	$A + B + 1$	Shift-right, $I_R = 0$
0 1 0	$R2$	$R2$	$R2$	$A - B - 1$	$A - B$	Shift-left, $I_L = 0$
0 1 1	$R3$	$R3$	$R3$	$A - 1$	$A, C \leftarrow 1$	0's to output bus
1 0 0	$R4$	$R4$	$R4$	$A \lor B$	—	—
1 0 1	$R5$	$R5$	$R5$	$A \oplus B$	—	Circulate-right with C
1 1 0	$R6$	$R6$	$R6$	$A \land B$	—	Circulate-left with C
1 1 1	$R7$	$R7$	$R7$	$\overline{A}$	—	—

The first four entries for the code in the H field specify the shift operations of Table 9-7. A third selection variable is used to specify either a 0 for the serial inputs I_R and I_L or a circular shift with the carry bit C. For convenience, we designate a circular right-shift with carry by crc and a circular left-shift with carry by clc. Thus, the statement:

$$R \leftarrow crc \ R$$

is an abbreviation for the statement:

$$R \leftarrow shr \ R, \qquad R_n \leftarrow C, \qquad C \leftarrow R_1$$

R is shifted to the right, its least significant bit R_1 goes to C, and the value of C goes into the most significant bit position R_n.

A control word of 16 bits is needed to specify a microoperation for the processor unit. The most efficient way to generate control words with so many bits is to store them in a memory unit which functions as a *control memory* where all control words are stored. The sequence of control words is then read from the control memory, one word at a time, to initiate the desired sequence of microoperations. This type of control organization is called *microprogramming* and is discussed in more detail in Chapter 10.

The control word for a given microoperation can be derived directly from the selection variables defined in Table 9-8. The subtract microoperation:

$$R1 \leftarrow R1 - R2$$

specifies $R1$ for the left input of the ALU, $R2$ for the right input of the ALU, $A - B$ for the ALU operation, no shift for the shifter, and $R1$ for the destination register. From Table 9-8, we derive the control word for this operation to be

0010100010101000:

$$
\begin{array}{cccccc}
A & B & D & F & C_{\text{in}} & H \\
001 & 010 & 001 & 010 & 1 & 000
\end{array}
$$

The control words for this microoperation and a few others are listed in Table 9-9.

The *compare* operation is similar to the subtract microoperation, except that the difference is not transferred to a destination register; only the status bits are affected. The destination field D for this case must be 000. The transfer of $R4$ into $R5$ requires an ALU operation $F = A$. The source A is 100 and the destination D is 101. The B selection code could be anything because the ALU does not use it. This field is marked with 000 in the table for convenience, but any other 3-bit code could be used.

To transfer the input data into $R6$, we must have $A = 000$ to select the external input and $D = 110$ to select the destination register. Again the value of B does not matter and the ALU function is $F = A$. To output data from $R7$, we make $A = 111$ and $D = 000$ (or 111). The ALU operation $F = A$ places the information from $R7$ into the output bus.

It is sometimes necessary to clear or set the carry bit before a circular-shift operation. This can be done with an ALU select code 0000 or 0111. With the first select code the C bit is cleared, and with the second code the C bit is set. The transfer $R1 \leftarrow R1$, $C \leftarrow 0$ does not change the contents of the register, but it clears C and V. The A and S status bits are affected in the usual manner. If $R1 = 0$, then Z is set to 1; otherwise, it is cleared. The S bit is set to the value of the sign bit in $R1$.

The clock pulse that triggers the destination register also transfers the status bits from the ALU into the status register. The status bits are affected after the arithmetic operations. The C and V status bits are left unchanged during a logic operation, since these bits have no meaning for the logic operations. In some

TABLE 9-9   Examples of microoperations for processor

Microoperation	Control word						Function
	A	B	D	F	C_{in}	H	
$R1 \leftarrow R1 - R2$	001	010	001	010	1	000	Subtract $R2$ from $R1$
$R3 - R4$	011	100	000	010	1	000	Compare $R3$ and $R4$
$R5 \leftarrow R4$	100	000	101	000	0	000	Transfer $R4$ to $R5$
$R6 \leftarrow$ Input	000	000	110	000	0	000	Input data to $R6$
Output $\leftarrow R7$	111	000	000	000	0	000	Output data from $R7$
$R1 \leftarrow R1, C \leftarrow 0$	001	000	001	000	0	000	Clear carry bit C
$R3 \leftarrow$ shl $R3$	011	011	011	100	0	010	Shift-left $R3$ with $I_L = 0$
$R1 \leftarrow$ crc $R1$	001	001	001	100	0	101	Circulate-right $R1$ with carry
$R2 \leftarrow 0$	000	000	010	000	0	011	Clear $R2$

processors, it is customary not to change the value of carry bit C after an increment or decrement operation as well.

If we want to place the contents of a register into the shifter without changing the carry bit, we can use the OR logic operation with the same register selected for both ALU inputs A and B. The operation:

$$R \leftarrow R \vee R$$

does not change the value of register R. However, it does place the contents of R into the inputs of the shifter, and it *does not change* the values of status bits C and V.

The examples in Table 9-9 discussed thus far use the shift-select code 000 for the H field to indicate a no-shift operation. To shift the contents of a register, the value of the register must be placed into the shifter without any change through the ALU. The shift-left microoperation statement:

$$R3 \leftarrow \text{shl } R3$$

specifies the code for the shift select but not the code for the ALU. The contents of $R3$ can be placed into the shifter by specifying an OR operation between $R3$ and itself. The shifted information returns to $R3$ if $R3$ is specified as the destination register. This requires that select fields A, B, and D have the code 011 for $R3$, that the ALU function code be 1000 for the OR operation, and that the shift-select H be 010 for the shift-left.

The circular shift-right with carry of register $R1$ is symbolized by the statement:

$$R1 \leftarrow \text{crc } R1$$

This statement specifies the code for the shifter, but not the code for the ALU. To place the contents of $R3$ into the output terminals of the ALU without affecting the C bit, we use the OR operation as before. In this way, the C bit is not affected by the ALU operation but may be changed because of the circular shift.

The last example in Table 9-9 shows the control word for clearing a register to 0. To clear register $R2$, the output bus is made to contain al 0's, with $H = 011$. The destination field D is made equal to the code for register $R2$.

It is obvious from these examples that many more microoperations can be generated in the processor unit. A processor unit with a complete set of microoperations is a general-purpose device that can be adapted for many applications. The register-transfer method is a convenient tool for specifying the operations in symbolic form in a digital system that employs a general-purpose processor unit. The system is first defined with a sequence of microoperation statements in the register-transfer method of notation or in any other suitable equivalent notation. A control function here is represented not by a Boolean function, but rather by a string of binary variables called a control word. The control word for each microoperation is derived from the function table of the processor.

The sequence of control words for the system is stored in a control memory. The output of the control memory is applied to the selection variables of the processor. By reading consecutive control words from memory, it is possible to sequence the microoperations in the processor. Thus, the entire design can be done by means of the register-transfer method which, in this particular case, is referred to as the *microprogramming method.* This method of controlling the processor unit is demonstrated in Section 10-5.

9-10 DESIGN OF ACCUMULATOR

Some processor units distinguish one register from all others and call it an accumulator register. The organization of a processor unit with an accumulator register is shown in Fig. 9-4. The ALU associated with the register may be constructed as a combinational circuit of the type discussed in Section 9-5. In this configuration, the accumulator register is essentially a bidirectional shift register with parallel load which is connected to an ALU. Because of the feedback connection from the output of the register to one of the inputs in the ALU, the accumulator register and its associated logic, when taken as one unit, constitute a sequential circuit. Because of this property, an accumulator register can be designed by sequential-circuit techniques instead of using a combinational-circuit ALU.

The block diagram of an accumulator that forms a sequential circuit is shown in Fig. 9-17. The A register and the associated combinational circuit constitute a sequential circuit. The combinational circuit replaces the ALU but cannot be separated from the register, since it is only the combinational-circuit part of a sequential circuit. The A register is referred to as the accumulator register and is sometimes denoted by the symbol AC. Here, accumulator refers to both the A register and its associated combinational circuit. The external inputs to the accumulator are the data inputs from B and the control variables that determine the

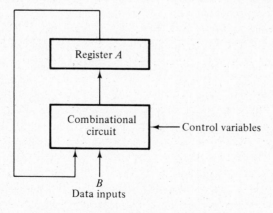

Figure 9-17 Block diagram of accumulator

microoperations for the register. The next state of register A is a function of its present state and of the external inputs.

In Chapter 7, we considered various registers that perform specific functions such as parallel load, shift operations, and counting. The accumulator is similar to these registers but is more general, since it can perform not only the above functions, but also other data-processing operations. An accumulator is a multi-function register that, by itself, can be made to perform all of the microoperations in a processor unit. The microoperations included in an accumulator depend on the operations that must be included in the particular processor. To demonstrate the logic design of a multipurpose operational register such as an accumulator, we will design the circuit with nine microoperations. The procedure outlined in this section can be used to extend the register to other microoperations.

The set of microoperations for the accumulator is given in Table 9-10. Control variables p_1 through p_9 are generated by control logic circuits and should be considered as control functions that initiate the corresponding register-transfer operations. Register A is a source register in all the listed microoperations. In essence, this represents the present state of the sequential circuit. The B register is used as a second source register for microoperations that need two operands. The B register is assumed to be connected to the accumulator and supplies the inputs to the sequential circuit. The destination register for all microoperations is always register A. The new information transferred to A constitutes the next state of the sequential circuit. The nine control variables are also considered as inputs to the sequential circuit. These variables are mutually exclusive and only one variable must be enabled when a clock pulse occurs. The last entry in Table 9-10 is a conditional control statement. It produces a binary 1 in an output variable Z when the content of register A is 0, i.e., when all flip-flops in the register are cleared.

TABLE 9-10 List of microoperations for an accumulator

Control variable	Microoperation	Name
p_1	$A \leftarrow A + B$	Add
p_2	$A \leftarrow 0$	Clear
p_3	$A \leftarrow \overline{A}$	Complement
p_4	$A \leftarrow A \wedge B$	AND
p_5	$A \leftarrow A \vee B$	OR
p_6	$A \leftarrow A \oplus B$	Exclusive-OR
p_7	$A \leftarrow \text{shr } A$	Shift-right
p_8	$A \leftarrow \text{shl } A$	Shift-left
p_9	$A \leftarrow A + 1$	Increment
	If $(A = 0)$ then $(Z = 1)$	Check for zero

Design Procedure

The accumulator consists of n stages and n flip-flops, $A_1, A_2, \ldots, A_n$, numbered consecutively starting from the rightmost position. It is convenient to partition the accumulator into n similar stages, with each stage consisting of one flip-flop denoted by A_i, one data input denoted by B_i, and the combinational logic associated with the flip-flop. In the design procedure that follows, we consider only one typical stage i with the understanding that an n-bit accumulator consists of n stages for $i = 1, 2, \ldots, n$. Each stage A_i is interconnected with the neighboring stage A_{i-1} on its right and stage A_{i+1} on its left. The first stage, A_1, and the last stage, A_n, have no neighbors on one side and require special attention. The register will be designed using JK-type flip-flops.

Each control variable p_j, $j = 1, 2, \ldots, 9$, initiates a particular microoperation. For the operation to be meaningful, we must ensure that only one control variable is enabled at any given time. Since the control variables are mutually exclusive, it is possible to separate the combinational circuit of a stage into smaller circuits, one for each microoperation. Thus, the accumulator is to be partitioned into n stages, and each stage is to be partitioned into those circuits that are needed for each microoperation. In this way, we can simplify the design process considerably. Once the various pieces are designed separately, it will be possible to combine them to obtain one typical stage of the accumulator and then to combine the stages into a complete accumulator.

Add B to A (p_1): The add microoperation is initiated when control variable p_1 is 1. This part of the accumulator can use a parallel adder composed of full-adder circuits as was done with the ALU. The full-adder in each stage i will accept as inputs the present state of A_i, the data input B_i, and a previous carry bit C_i. The sum bit generated in the full-adder must be transferred to flip-flop A_i, and the output carry C_{i+1} must be applied to the input carry of the next stage.

The internal construction of a full-adder circuit can be simplified if we consider that it operates as part of a sequential circuit. The state table of a full-adder, when considered as a sequential circuit, is shown in Fig. 9-18. The value of flip-flop A_i before a clock pulse specifies the present state in the sequential circuit. The value of A_i after the application of a clock pulse specifies the next state. The next state of A_i is a function of its present state and inputs B_i and C_i. The present state and inputs in the state table correspond to the inputs of a ful-adder. The next state and output C_{i+1} correspond to the outputs of a full-adder. But because it is a sequential circuit, A_i appears in both the present and next-state columns. The next state of A_i gives the sum bit that must be transferred to the flip-flop.

The excitation inputs for the JK flip-flop are listed in columns JA_i and KA_i. These values are obtained by the method outlined in Section 6-7. The flip-flop input functions and the Boolean function for the output are simplified in the maps

Present state	Inputs		Next state	Flip-flop inputs		Output
A_i	B_i	C_i	A_i	JA_i	KA_i	C_{i+1}
0	0	0	0	0	X	0
0	0	1	1	1	X	0
0	1	0	1	1	X	0
0	1	1	0	0	X	1
1	0	0	1	X	0	0
1	0	1	0	X	1	1
1	1	0	0	X	1	1
1	1	1	1	X	0	1

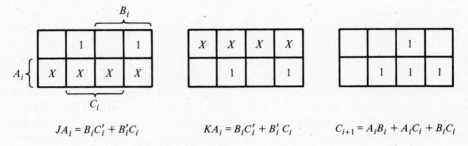

$$JA_i = B_iC_i' + B_i'C_i \qquad KA_i = B_iC_i' + B_i'C_i \qquad C_{i+1} = A_iB_i + A_iC_i + B_iC_i$$

Figure 9-18 Excitation table for add microoperation

of Fig. 9-18. The J input of flip-flop A_i, designated by JA_i, and the K input of flip-flop A_i, designated by KA_i, do not include the control variable p_1. These two equations should affect the flip-flop only when p_1 is enabled; therefore, they should be ANDed with control variable p_1. The part of the combinational circuit associated with the add microoperation can be expressed with three Boolean functions:

$$JA_i = B_iC_i'p_1 + B_i'C_ip_1$$
$$KA_i = B_iC_i'p_1 + B_i'C_ip_1$$
$$C_{i+1} = A_iB_i + A_iC_i + B_iC_i$$

The first two equations are identical, and they specify a condition for complementing A_i. The third equation generates the carry for the next stage.

Clear (p_2): Control variable p_2 clears all flip-flops in register A. To cause this transition in a JK flip-flop, we need only apply control variable p_2 to the K input of the flip-flop. The J input will be assumed to be 0 if nothing is applied to it. The input functions for the clear microoperation are:

$$JA_i = 0$$
$$KA_i = p_2$$

Complement (p_3): Control variable p_3 complements the state of register A. To cause this transition in a JK flip-flop, we need to apply p_3 to both the J and K inputs:

$$JA_i = p_3$$
$$KA_i = p_3$$

AND (p_4): The AND microoperation is initiated with control variable p_4. This operation forms the logic AND operation between A_i and B_i and transfers the result to A_i. The excitation table for this operation is given in Fig. 9-19(a). The next state of A_i is 1 only when both B_i and the present state of A_i are equal to 1. The flip-flop input functions which are simplified in the two maps dictate that the

Present state A_i	Input B_i	Next state A_i	Flip-flop inputs JA_i	KA_i
0	0	0	0	X
0	1	0	0	X
1	0	0	X	1
1	1	1	X	0

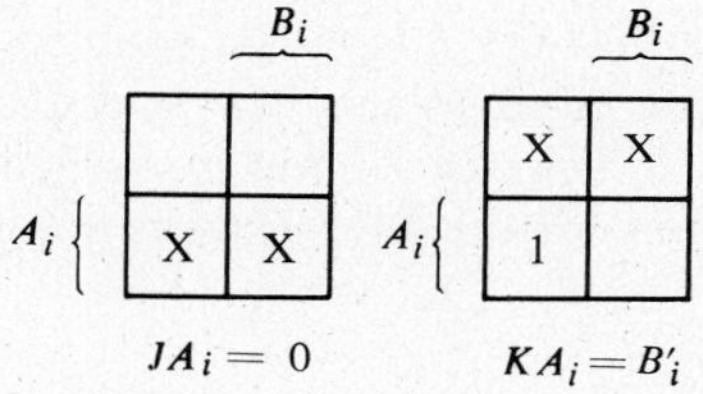

$$JA_i = 0 \qquad KA_i = B'_i$$

(a) AND

Present state A_i	Input B_i	Next state A_i	Flip-flop inputs JA_i	KA_i
0	0	0	0	X
0	1	1	1	X
1	0	1	X	0
1	1	1	X	0

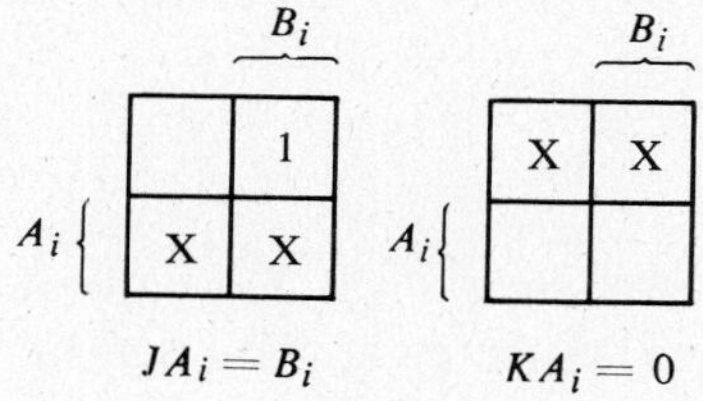

$$JA_i = B_i \qquad KA_i = 0$$

(b) OR

Present state A_i	Input B_i	Next state A_i	Flip-flop inputs JA_i	KA_i
0	0	0	0	X
0	1	1	1	X
1	0	1	X	0
1	1	0	X	1

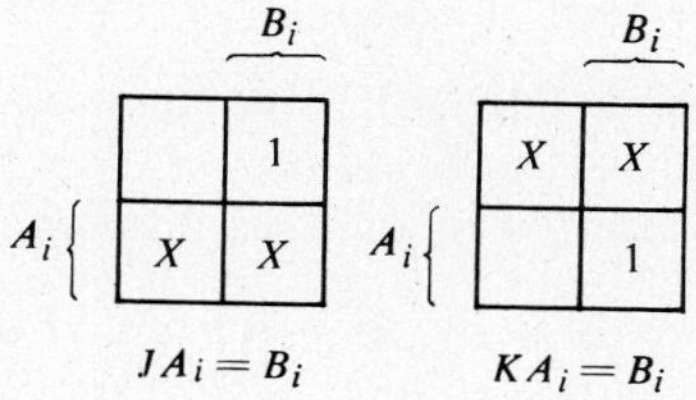

$$JA_i = B_i \qquad KA_i = B_i$$

(c) Exclusive-OR

Figure 9-19 Excitation tables for logic microoperations

K input of the flip-flop be enabled with the complement value of B_i. This result can be verified from the conditions listed in the state table. If $B_i = 1$, the present state and next state of A_i are the same, so the flip-flop does not have to undergo a change of state. If $B_i = 0$, the next state of A_i must go to 0, and this is accomplished by enabling the K input of the flip-flop. The input functions for the AND microoperation must include the control variable that initiates this microoperation:

$$JA_i = 0$$
$$KA_i = B_i'p_4$$

OR (p_5): Control variable p_5 initiates the logic OR operation between A_i and B_i, with the result transferred to A_i. Figure 9-19(b) shows the derivation of the flip-flop input functions for this operation. The simplified equations in the maps dictate that the J input be enabled when $B_i = 1$. This result can be verified from the state table. When $B_i = 0$, the present state and next state of A_i are the same. When $B_i = 1$, the J input is enabled and the next state of A_i becomes 1. The input functions for the OR microoperation are:

$$JA_i = B_ip_5$$
$$KA_i = 0$$

Exclusive-OR (p_6): This operation forms the logic exclusive-OR between A_i and B_i and transfers the result to A_i. The pertinent information for this operation is shown in Fig. 9-19(c). The flip-flop input functions are:

$$JA_i = B_ip_6$$
$$KA_i = B_ip_6$$

Shift-right (p_7): This operation shifts the contents of the A register one position to the right. This means that the value of flip-flop A_{i+1}, which is one position to the left of stage i, must be transferred into flip-flop A_i. This transfer is expressed by the input functions:

$$JA_i = A_{i+1}p_7$$
$$KA_i = A_{i+1}'p_7$$

Shift-left (p_8): This operation shifts the A register one position to the left. For this case, the value of A_{i-1}, which is one position to the right of stage i, must be transferred to A_i. This transfer is expressed by the input functions:

$$JA_i = A_{i-1}p_8$$
$$KA_i = A_{i-1}'p_8$$

Increment (p_9): This operation increments the contents of the A register by one; in other words, the register behaves like a synchronous binary counter with p_9 enabling the count. A 3-bit synchronous counter is shown in Fig. 9-20. It is similar

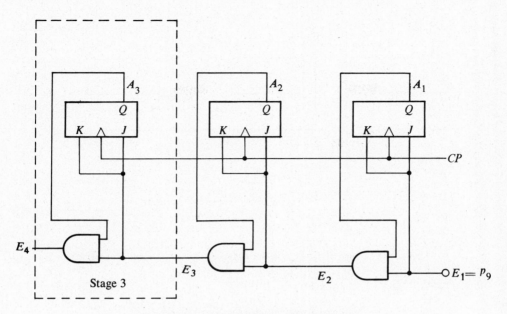

Figure 9-20 3-bit synchronous binary counter

to the counter in Fig. 7-17 of Section 7-5, where the operation of synchronous binary counters are discussed in detail. From the diagram, we see that each stage is complemented when an input carry $E_i = 1$. Each stage also generates an output carry, E_{i+1}, for the next stage on its left. The first stage is an exception, since it is complemented with the count-enable p_9. The Boolean functions for a typical stage can be expressed as follows:

$$JA_i = E_i$$
$$KA_i = E_i$$
$$E_{i+1} = E_iA_i \qquad i = 1, 2, \ldots, n$$
$$E_1 = p_9$$

The input carry, E_i, into the stage is used to complement flip-flop A_i. Each stage generates a carry for the next stage by ANDing the input carry with A_i. The input carry into the first stage is E_1 and must be equal to control variable p_9 which enables the count.

Check for Zero (Z): Variable Z is an output from the accumulator used to indicate a zero content in the A register. This output is equal to binary 1 when all the flip-flops are cleared. When a flip-flop is cleared, its complement output, Q', is equal to 1. Figure 9-21 shows the first three stages of the accumulator that checks for a zero content. Each stage generates a variable z_{i+1} by ANDing the complement output of A_i to an input variable z_i. In this way, a chain of AND gates through all stages will indicate if all flip-flops are cleared. The Boolean functions

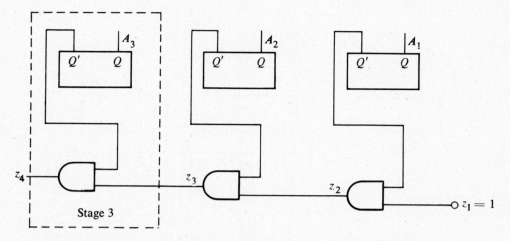

Figure 9-21 Chain of AND gates for checking the zero content of a register

for a typical stage can be expressed as follows:

$$z_{i+1} = z_i A'_i \qquad i = 1, 2, \ldots, n$$
$$z_1 = 1$$
$$z_{n+1} = Z$$

Variable Z becomes 1 if the output signal from the last stage, z_{n+1}, is 1.

One Stage of Accumulator

A typical accumulator stage consists of all the circuits that were derived for the individual microoperations. Control variables p_1 through p_9 are mutually exclusive; therefore, the corresponding logic circuits can be combined with an OR operation. Combining all the input functions for the J and the K inputs of flip-flop A_i produces a composite set of input Boolean functions for a typical stage:

$$JA_i = B_i C'_i p_1 + B'_i C_i p_1 + p_3 + B_i p_5 + B_i p_6 + A_{i+1} p_7 + A_{i-1} p_8 + E_i$$
$$KA_i = B_i C'_i p_1 + B'_i C_i p_1 + p_2 + p_3 + B'_i p_4 + B_i p_6 + A'_{i+1} p_7$$
$$+ A'_{i-1} p_8 + E_i$$

Each stage in the accumulator must also generate the carries for the next stage:

$$C_{i+1} = A_i B_i + A_i C_i + B_i C_i$$
$$E_{i+1} = E_i A_i$$
$$z_{i+1} = z_i A'_i$$

The logic diagram of one typical stage of the accumulator is shown in Fig. 9-22. It is a direct implementation of the Boolean functions listed above. The

398

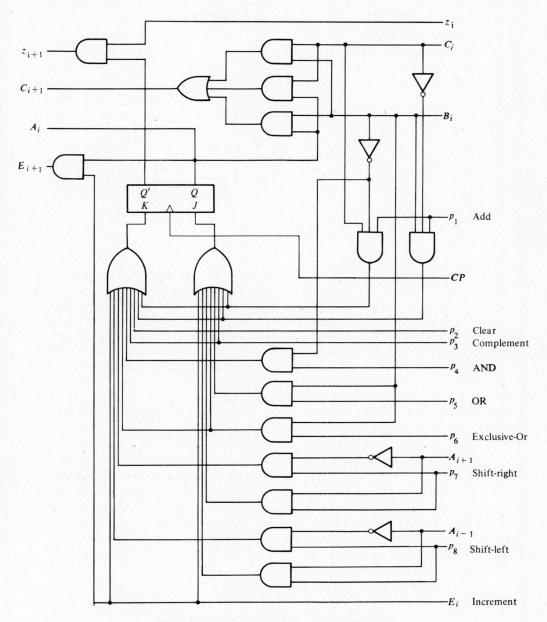

Figure 9-22 One typical stage of the accumulator

diagram is a composite circuit that includes the individual circuits associated with each microoperation. The various circuits are combined with two OR gates in the J and K inputs of flip-flop A_i.

Each accumulator stage has eight control inputs, p_1 through p_8, that initiate one of eight possible microoperations. Control variable p_9 is applied only to the first stage to enable the increment operation through input E_i. There are six other inputs in the circuit. B_i is the data bit from the B terminals that provide the inputs to the accumulator. C_i is the input carry from the previous stage on the right. A_{i-1} comes from the output of the flip-flop one position to the right, and A_{i+1} comes from the flip-flop one position to the left. E_i is the carry input for the increment operation, and z_i is used to form the chain for zero detection. The circuit has four outputs: A_i is the output of the flip-flop, C_{i+1} is a carry for the next stage, E_{i+1} is the increment carry for the next stage, and z_{i+1} is for the next stage on the left to form the chain for zero detection.

Complete Accumulator

An accumulator with n bits requires n stages connected in cascade, with each stage having the circuit shown in Fig. 9-22. All control variables, except p_9, must be applied to each stage. The other inputs and outputs in each stage must be connected in cascade to form a complete accumulator.

The interconnection among stages to form a complete accumulator is illustrated in the 4-bit accumulator shown in Fig. 9-23. Each block in the diagram represents the circuit of Fig. 9-22. The number on top of each block represents the bit position in the accumulator. All blocks receive eight control variables, p_1 through p_8, and the clock pulses from CP. The other six inputs and four outputs in each block are identical to those of a typical stage, except that subscript i is now replaced by the particular number in each block.

The circuit has four B inputs. The zero-detect chain is obtained by connecting the z variables in cascade, with the first block receiving a binary constant 1. The last stage in this chain produces the zero-detect variable Z. The carries for the arithmetic addition are connected in cascade as in full-adder circuits. The serial input for the shift-left operation goes to input A_0, which corresponds to input A_{i-1} in the first stage. The serial input for the shift-right operation goes to input A_5, which corresponds to A_{i+1} in the fourth and last stage. The increment operation is enabled with control variable p_9 in the first stage. The other blocks receive the increment carry from the previous stage.

The total number of terminals in the 4-bit accumulator is 25, including terminals for the A outputs. Incorporating two more terminals for power supply, the circuit can be enclosed within one IC package having 27 or 28 pins. The number of terminals for the control variables can be reduced from nine to four if a decoder is inserted in the IC. In such a case, the IC pin count can be reduced to 22 and the accumulator can be extended to 16 microoperations without adding external pins.

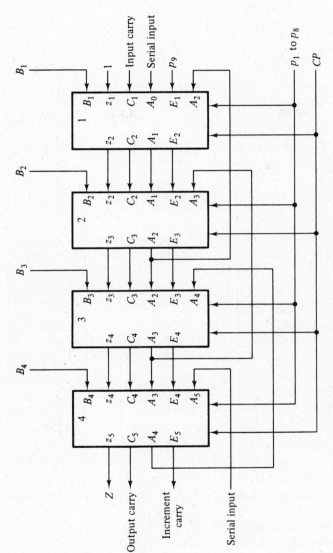

Figure 9-23 4-bit accumulator constructed with four stages

REFERENCES

1. Mano, M. M., *Computer System Architecture*. Englewood Cliffs, N.J.: Prentice-Hall, Inc., 1976.

2. *The TTL Data Book for Design Engineers*. Dallas, Texas: Texas Instruments, Inc., 1976.

3. *The Am2900 Bipolar Microprocessor Family Data Book*. Sunnyvale, Calif.: Advanced Micro Devices, Inc., 1976.

4. Sobel, H. S., *Introduction to Digital Computer Design*. Reading, Mass.: Addison-Wesley Publishing Co., 1970.

5. Kline, R. M., *Digital Computer Design*. Englewood Cliffs, N.J.: Prentice-Hall, Inc., 1977.

6. Chirlian, P. M., *Analysis and Design of Digital Circuits and Computer Systems*. Champaign, Ill.: Matrix Publishing, Inc., 1976.

PROBLEMS

9-1. Modify the processor unit of Fig. 9-1 so that the selected destination register is always the same register that is selected for the A bus. How does this effect the number of multiplexers and the number of selection lines used?

9-2. A bus-organized processor as in Fig. 9-1 consists of 15 registers. How many selection lines are there in each multiplexer and in the destination decoder?

9-3. Assume that each register in Fig. 9-1 is 8 bits long. Draw a detailed block diagram for the box labeled MUX that selects the register for the A bus. Show that the selection can be done with eight 4-to-1 line multiplexers.

9-4. A processor unit employs a scratchpad memory as in Fig. 9-2. The processor consists of 64 registers of eight bits each.

(a) What is the size of the scratchpad memory?

(b) How many lines are needed for the address?

(c) How many lines are there for the input data?

(d) What is the size of the MUX that selects between the input data and the output of the shifter?

9-5. Show a detailed block diagram for the processor unit of Fig. 9-4 when the B inputs come from:

(a) Eight processor registers forming a bus system.

(b) A memory unit with address and buffer registers.

9-6. The 4-bit ALU of Fig. 9-5 is enclosed within one IC package. Show the connections among three such ICs to form a 12-bit ALU. Designate the input and output carries in the 12-bit ALU.

9-7. TTL IC type 7487 is a 4-bit true/complement, zero/one element. One stage of this IC is shown in Fig. P9-7.

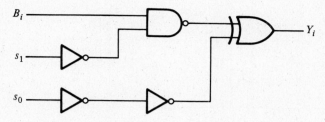

Figure P9-7 True/complement, one/zero circuit

(a) Derive the Boolean function for output Y_i as a function of inputs B_i, s_1, and s_0.

(b) Draw the truth table for the circuit.

(c) Draw a function table (similar to the one shown in Fig. 9-7) and verify the circuit operation.

9-8. Modify the arithmetic circuit of Fig. 9-8 by including a third selection variable, s_2. When $s_2 = 1$, the modified circuit is identical to the original circuit. When $s_2 = 0$, all the A inputs to the full-adders are inhibited and 0's are inserted instead.

(a) Draw the logic diagram of one stage of the modified circuit.

(b) Go over an analysis similar to that in Fig. 9-6 to determine the eight operations obtained when $s_2 = 0$.

(c) List the new output functions in tabular form.

9-9. Determine the arithmetic operations obtained in the eight blocks of Fig. 9-6 if, in each case, input A is changed to $\overline{A}$ (complement of A).

9-10. Design an arithmetic circuit with one selection variable s and two data inputs A and B. When $s = 0$, the circuit performs the addition operation $F = A + B$. When $s = 1$, the circuit performs the increment operation $F = A + 1$.

9-11. The straight binary subtraction $F = A - B$ produces a correct difference if $A \geqslant B$. What would be the result if $A < B$? Determine the relationship between the result obtained in F and a borrow in the most significant position.

9-12. Design an arithmetic circuit with two selection variables, s_1 and s_0, that generates the following arithmetic operations. Draw the logic diagram of one typical stage.

s_1	s_0	$C_{in} = 0$	$C_{in} = 1$
0	0	$F = A + B$	$F = A + B + 1$
0	1	$F = A$	$F = A + 1$
1	0	$F = \overline{B}$	$F = \overline{B} + 1$
1	1	$F = A + \overline{B}$	$F = A + \overline{B} + 1$

9-13. Design an arithmetic circuit with two selection variables, s_1 and s_0, that generates the following arithmetic operations. Draw the logic diagram of one typical stage.

s_1	s_0	$C_{in} = 0$	$C_{in} = 1$
0	0	$F = A$	$F = A + 1$
0	1	$F = A - B - 1$	$F = A - B$
1	0	$F = B - A - 1$	$F = B - A$
1	1	$F = A + B$	$F = A + B + 1$

9-14. The following relationships of the exclusive-OR operation were used in deriving the logic operations of Table 9-3.

(a) $x \oplus 0 = x$

(b) $x \oplus 1 = x'$

(c) $x \oplus y' = x \odot y$

Prove that these relationships are valid.

9-15. Derive a minimal combinational circuit that generates all 16 logic functions listed in Table 2-5. Use four selection variables. *Hint*: Try a 4×1 multiplexer in reverse, i.e., use the normal inputs of the multiplexer as the selection lines for the logic unit.

9-16. Modify the arithmetic circuit of Fig. 9-8 into an ALU with mode-select variable s_2. When $s_2 = 0$, the ALU is identical to the arithmetic circuit. When $s_2 = 1$, the ALU generates the logic functions according to the following table:

s_2	s_1	s_0	Output	Function
1	0	0	$F = A \wedge B$	AND
1	0	1	$F = A \oplus B$	XOR
1	1	0	$F = A \vee B$	OR
1	1	1	$F = \bar{A}$	NOT

9-17. An arithmetic logic unit is similar to the one shown in Fig. 9-13 except that the inputs to each full-adder circuit are according to the following Boolean functions:

$$X_i = A_i B_i + (s_2 s_1' s_0')' A_i + s_2 s_1 s_0' B_i$$
$$Y_i = s_0 B_i + s_1 B_i' (s_2 s_1 s_0')'$$
$$Z_1 = s_2' C_i$$

Determine the 12 functions of the ALU.

9-18. The operation performed in an ALU is $F = A + \bar{B}$ (A plus 1's complement of B).

(a) Determine the output value of F when $A = B$. Let this condition set a·status bit E.

(b) Determine the condition for $C_{out} = 1$. Let this condition set a status bit C.

(c) Derive a table for the six relationships listed in Table 9-5 in terms of the status bit conditions E and C defined above.

9-19. A processor unit has a status register of ten bits, one for each of the conditions listed in Tables 9-5 and 9-6. (The equal and unequal conditions are common to both

404

tables.) Draw a logic diagram showing the gates from the outputs of the ALU to the ten bits of the status register.

9-20. Two signed numbers are added in an ALU, and their sum transferred to register R. The status bits S (sign) and V (overflow) are affected during the transfer. Prove that the sum can now be divided by 2 according to the statement:

$$R \leftarrow \text{shr } R, \qquad R_n \leftarrow S \oplus V$$

where R_n is the sign bit (leftmost position) of register R.

9-21. Add another multiplexer to the shifter of Fig. 9-15 with two separate selection lines G_1 and G_0. This multiplexer is used to specify the serial input I_R during a shift-right operation in the following manner:

G_1	G_0	Function
0	0	Insert 0 into I_R
0	1	Perform a circular shift
1	0	Perform a circular shift with carry
1	1	Insert the value of $S \oplus V$ for arithmetic shift (see problem 9-20)

Show the connection of the multiplexer between the status register and the shifter.

9-22. The shift-select H defined for the processor of Fig. 9-16 has three variables, H_2, H_1, and H_0. The last two selection variables are used for the shifter specified in Table 9-7. Design the circuit associated with selection variable H_2.

9-23. Specify the control word that must be applied to the processor of Fig. 9-16 to implement the following microoperations:

(a) $R2 \leftarrow R1 + 1$ (e) $R1 \leftarrow \text{shr } R1$

(b) $R3 \leftarrow R4 + R5$ (f) $R2 \leftarrow \text{clc } R2$

(c) $R6 \leftarrow \overline{R6}$ (g) $R3 \leftarrow R4 \oplus R5$

(d) $R7 \leftarrow R7 - 1$ (h) $R6 \leftarrow R7$

9-24. It is necessary to compute the average value of four unsigned binary numbers stored in registers $R1$, $R2$, $R3$, and $R4$ of the processor defined in Fig. 9-16. The average value is to be stored in register $R5$. The other two registers in the processor can be used for intermediate results. Care must be taken not to cause an overflow.

(a) List the sequence of microoperations in symbolic form.

(b) List the corresponding binary control words.

9-25. The following sequence of microoperations is performed in the accumulator defined in Section 9-10:

$$p_3: \quad A \leftarrow \overline{A}$$

$$p_9: \quad A \leftarrow A + 1$$

$$p_1: \quad A \leftarrow A + B$$

$$p_3: \quad A \leftarrow \overline{A}$$

$$p_9: \quad A \leftarrow A + 1$$

(a) Determine the content of A after each microoperation if initially $A = 1101$ and the B input is 0110.

(b) Repeat with initial $A = 0110$ and $B = 1101$.

(c) Repeat with initial $A = 0110$ and $B = 0110$.

(d) Prove that the above sequence of microoperations performs $(A - B)$ if $A \geqslant B$, or the 2's complement of $(B - A)$ if $A < B$.

9-26. Using JK flip-flops, design one typical stage of an A register that performs the subtract microoperation:

$$p_{10}: \quad A \leftarrow A - B$$

Use full-subtracter circuits (Section 4-4) with input and output borrows K_i and K_{i+1}.

9-27. Using JK flip-flops, design one typical stage of a register that performs the following logic microoperations:

$$p_{11}: \quad A \leftarrow \overline{A \vee B} \qquad \text{NOR}$$

$$p_{12}: \quad A \leftarrow \overline{A \wedge B} \qquad \text{NAND}$$

$$p_{13}: \quad A \leftarrow A \odot B \qquad \text{Equivalence}$$

9-28. Derive the Boolean functions for a typical stage of a decrement microoperation:

$$p_{14}: \quad A \leftarrow A - 1$$

9-29. Using T-type flip-flops, design a 4-bit register that performs the 2's-complement microoperation:

$$P: \quad A \leftarrow \overline{A} + 1$$

From the result obtained, show that a typical stage can be expressed by the following Boolean functions:

$$TA_i = PE_i \qquad i = 1, 2, 3, \ldots, n$$

$$E_{i+1} = A_i + E_i$$

$$E_1 = 0$$

9-30. A 4-bit accumulator performs 15 microoperations with control variables p_1 through p_{15}. The circuit is enclosed in one IC package with only four terminals available for selecting a microoperation. Design the circuit (within the IC) that must be inserted between the four terminals and the 15 control variables. Include a no-operation condition.

Control Logic Design

10-1 INTRODUCTION

The process of logic design is a complex undertaking. Many installations develop various computer-automated design techniques to facilitate the design process. However, the specifications for the system and the development of algorithmic procedures for achieving the required data-processing tasks cannot be automated and require the mental reasoning of a human designer.

The most challenging and creative part of the design is the establishment of design objectives and the formulation of algorithms and procedures for achieving the stated objectives. This task requires a considerable amount of experience and ingenuity on the part of the designer. An *algorithm* is a procedure for obtaining a solution to a problem. A *design algorithm* is a procedure for implementing the problem with a given piece of equipment. The development of a design algorithm cannot start until the designer is certain of two things. First, the problem at hand must be thoroughly understood. Second, an initial configuration of equipment must be assumed for implementing the procedure. Starting from the problem statement and equipment availability, a solution is then found and an algorithm formed. The algorithm is stated by a finite number of well-defined procedural steps.

The binary information found in a digital system is stored in processor or memory registers, and it can be either data or control information. Data are discrete elements of information that are manipulated by microoperations. Control information provides command signals for specifying the sequence of microoperations. The logic design of a digital system is a process for deriving the digital circuits that perform data processing and the digital circuits that provide control signals.

The timing for all registers in a synchronous digital system is controlled by a master-clock generator. The clock pulses are applied to all flip-flops and registers in the system, including the flip-flops and registers in the control unit. The continuous clock pulses do not change the state of a register unless the register is enabled by a control signal. The binary variables that control the selection variables and enable inputs of registers are generated in the control unit. The outputs of the control unit select and enable the data-processor part of the system and also determine the next state of the control unit itself.

The relationship between the control and the data processor in a digital system is shown in Fig. 10-1. The data processor part may be a general-purpose processor unit, or it may consist of individual registers and associated digital functions. The control initiates all microoperations in the data processor. The control logic that generates the signals for sequencing the microoperations is a sequential circuit whose internal states dictate the control functions for the system. At any given time, the state of the sequential control initiates a prescribed set of microoperations. Depending on status conditions or other inputs, the sequential control goes to the next state to initiate other microoperations. Thus, the digital circuit that acts as the control logic provides a time sequence of signals for initiating the microoperations in the data-processor part of the system.

The design of a digital system that requires a control sequence starts with the assumption of the availability of timing variables. We designate each timing variable in the sequence by a state and then form a state diagram or an equivalent representation for the transition between states. Concurrent with the development of the control sequence, we develop a list of microoperations to be initiated for each control state. If the system is too complicated for a state diagram, it may be convenient to specify the system entirely in the register-transfer method by means of control functions and microoperation statements.

The control sequence and register-transfer relationships may be derived directly from the word specification of the problem. However, it is sometimes convenient to use an intermediate representation to describe the needed sequence of operations for the system. Two representations which are helpful in the design of systems that need a control are timing diagrams and flowcharts.

A *timing diagram* clarifies the timing sequence and other relationships among the various control signals in the system. In a clocked sequential circuit, the clock

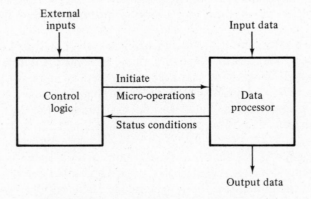

Figure 10-1   Control and data-processor interaction

pulses synchronize all operations, including signal transitions in control variables. In an asynchronous system, a signal transition in one control variable may cause a change of another control variable. A timing diagram is very useful in asynchronous control because it provides a pictorial representation of required changes and transitions of all control variables.

A *flowchart* is a convenient way to specify the sequence of procedural steps and decision paths for an algorithm. A flowchart for a design algorithm would normally use the variable names of registers defined in the initial equipment configuration. It translates an algorithm from its word statement to an information-flow diagram that enumerates the sequence of register-transfer operations together with the conditions necessary for their execution.

A flowchart is a diagram that consists of blocks connected by directed lines. Within the blocks, we specify the procedural steps for implementing the algorithm. The directed lines between blocks designate the path to be taken from one procedural step to the next. Two major types of blocks are used: A rectangular block designates a *function* block within which the microoperations are listed. A diamond-shaped block is a *decision* block within which is listed a given status condition. A decision block has two or more alternate paths, and the path that is taken depends on the value of the status condition specified within the block.

A flowchart is very similar to a state diagram. Each function block in the flowchart is equivalent to a state in the state diagram. The decision block in the flowchart is equivalent to the binary information written along the directed lines that connect two states in a state diagram. As a consequence, it is sometimes convenient to express an algorithm by means of a flowchart from which the control state diagram may be readily derived.

In this chapter, we first present four possible configurations for a control unit. The various configurations are presented in block diagram form to emphasize the differences in organization. We then demonstrate the various procedures available for control logic design by going through specific examples.

The design of control logic cannot be separated from the algorithmic development necessary for solving a design problem. Moreover, the control logic is directly related to the data-processor part of the system that it controls. As a consequence, the examples presented in this chapter start with the development of an algorithm for implementing the given problem. The data-processing part of the system is then derived from the stated algorithm. Only after this is done can we proceed to show the design of the control that sequences the data processor according to the steps specified by the algorithm.

10-2 CONTROL ORGANIZATION

Once a control sequence has been established, the sequential system that implements the control operations must be designed. Since the control is a sequential circuit, it can be designed by a sequential logic procedure as outlined in Chapter 6.

However, in most cases this method is impractical because of the large number of states that the control circuit may have. Design methods that use state and excitation tables can be used in theory, but in practice they are cumbersome and difficult to manage. Moreover, the control circuit obtained by this method usually requires an excessive number of flip-flops and gates, which implies the use of SSI circuits. This type of implementation is inefficient with respect to the number of IC packages used and the number of wires that must be interconnected. One major goal of control logic design should be the development of a circuit that implements the desired control sequence in a logical and straightforward manner. The attempt to minimize the number of circuits would tend to produce an irregular network which would make it difficult for anyone but the designer to recognize the sequence of events that the control undergoes. As a consequence, it may be difficult to service and maintain the equipment when it is in operation.

Because of the reasons cited above, experienced logic designers use specialized methods for control logic design which may be considered an extension of the classical sequential-logic method combined with the register-transfer method. In this section, we consider four methods of control organization:

1. One flip-flop per state method.

2. Sequence register and decoder method.

3. PLA control.

4. Microprogram control.

The first two methods result in a circuit that must use SSI and MSI circuits for the implementation. The various circuits are interconnected by wires to form the control network. A control unit implemented with SSI and MSI devices is said to be a hard-wired control. If any alterations or modifications are needed, the circuits must be rewired to fulfill the new requirements. This is in contrast to the PLA or microprogram control which uses an LSI device such as a programmable logic array or a read-only memory. Any alterations or modifications in a microprogram control can be easily achieved without wiring changes by removing the ROM from its socket and inserting another ROM programmed to fulfill the new specifications.

We shall now explain each method in general terms. The subsequent sections of this chapter deal with specific examples that demonstrate the detailed design of control units by each of the four methods.

One Flip-Flop per State Method

This method uses one flip-flop per state in the control sequential circuit. Only one flip-flop is set at any particular time; all others are cleared. A single bit is made to propagate from one flip-flop to the other under the control of decision logic. In such an array, each flip-flop represents a state and is activated only when the control bit is transferred to it.

It is obvious that this method does not use a minimum number of flip-flops for the sequential circuit. In fact, it uses a maximum number of flip-flops. For example, a sequential circuit with 12 states requires a minimum of four flip-flops because $2^3 < 12 < 2^4$. Yet by this method, the control circuit uses 12 flip-flops, one for each state.

The advantage of the one flip-flop per state method is the simplicity with which it can be designed. This type of controller can be designed by inspection from the state diagram that describes the control sequence. At first glance, it may seem that this method would increase system cost since more flip-flops are used. But the method offers other advantages which may not be apparent at first. For example, it offers a savings in design effort, an increase in operational simplicity, and a potential decrease in the combinational circuits required to implement the complete sequential circuit.

Figure 10-2 shows the configuration of a four-state sequential control logic that uses four D-type flip-flops: one flip-flop per state T_i, $i = 0, 1, 2, 3$. At any

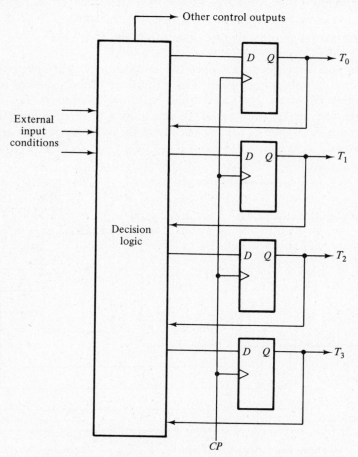

Figure 10-2 Control logic with one flip-flop per state

given time interval between two clock pulses, only one flip-flop is equal to 1; all others are equal to 0. The transition from the present state to the next is a function of the present T_i that is a 1 and certain input conditions. The next state is manifested when the previous flip-flop is cleared and a new one is set. Each of the flip-flop outputs is connected to the data-processing section of the digital system to initiate certain microoperations. The other control outputs shown in the diagram are a function of the T's and external inputs. These outputs may also initiate microoperations.

If the control circuit does not need external inputs for its sequencing, the circuit reduces to a straight shift register with a single bit shifted from one position to the next. If the control sequence must be repeated over and over again, the control reduces to a ring counter. A *ring counter* is a shift register with the output of the last flip-flop connected to the input of the first flip-flop. In a ring counter, the single bit continuously shifts from one position to the next in a circular manner. For this reason, the one flip-flop per state method is sometimes called a *ring-counter controller*.

Sequence Register and Decoder Method

This method uses a register to sequence the control states. The register is decoded to provide one output for each state. For *n* flip-flops in the sequence register, the circuit will have 2^n states and the decoder will have 2^n outputs. For example, a 4-bit register can be in any one of 16 states. A 4×16 decoder will have 16 outputs, one for each state of the register. Both the sequence register and decoder are MSI devices.

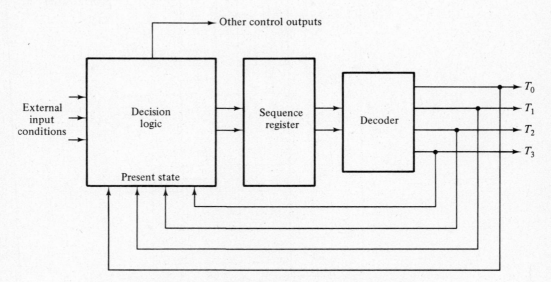

Figure 10-3   Control logic with sequence register and decoder

Figure 10-3 shows the configuration of a four-state sequential control logic. The sequence register has two flip-flops and the decoder establishes separate outputs for each state in the register. The transition to the next state in the sequence register is a function of the present state and the external input conditions. Since the outputs of the decoder are available anyway, it is convenient to use them as present-state variables rather than use the direct flip-flop outputs. Other outputs which are a function of the present state and external inputs may initiate microoperations in addition to the decoder outputs.

If the control circuit of Fig. 10-3 does not need external inputs, the sequence register reduces to a counter that continuously sequences through the four states. For this reason, this method is sometimes called a *counter-decoder* method. The counter-decoder method and the ring-counter method were explained in Chapter 7 in conjunction with Fig. 7-22.

PLA Control

The programmable logic array was introduced in Section 5-8. It was shown there that the PLA is an LSI device that can implement any complex combinational circuit. The PLA control is essentially similar to the sequence register and decoder method except that all combinational circuits are implemented with a PLA, including the decoder and the decision logic. By using a PLA for the combinational circuit, it is possible to reduce the number of ICs and the number of interconnection wires.

Figure 10-4 shows the configuration of a PLA controller. An external sequence register establishes the present state of the control circuit. The PLA outputs determine which microoperations should be initiated, depending on external input conditions and the present state of the sequence register. At the same time, other PLA outputs determine the next state of the sequence register.

The sequence register is external to the PLA if the unit implements only combinational circuits. However, some PLAs are available which include not only

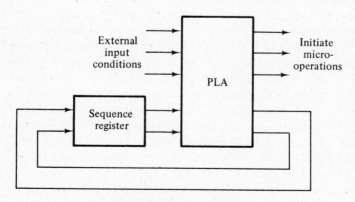

Figure 10-4 PLA control logic

gates, but also flip-flops within the unit. This type of PLA can implement a sequential circuit by specifying the links that must be connected to the flip-flops in the same manner that the gate links are specified.

Microprogram Control

The purpose of the control unit is to initiate a series of sequential steps of microoperations. During any given time, certain operations are to be initiated while all others remain idle. Thus, the control variables at any given time can be represented by a string of 1's and 0's called a *control word*. As such, control words can be programmed to initiate the various components in the system in an organized manner. A control unit whose control variables are stored in a memory is called a *microprogrammed control unit*. Each control word of memory is called a *microinstruction*, and a sequence of microinstructions is called a *microprogram*. Since alteration of the microprogram is seldom needed, the control memory can be a ROM. The use of a microprogram involves placing all control variables in words of the ROM for use by the control unit through successive read operations. The content of the word in the ROM at a given address specifies the microoperations for the system.

A more advanced development known as *dynamic* microprogramming permits a microprogram to be loaded initially from the computer console or from an auxiliary memory such as a magnetic disk. Control units that use dynamic microprogramming employ a *writable control memory* (WCM). This type of memory can be used for writing (to change the microprogram) but is used mostly for reading. A ROM, PLA, or WCM, when used in a control unit, is referred to as a *control memory*.

Figure 10-5 illustrates the general configuration of the microprogram control unit. The control memory is assumed to be a ROM, within which all control information is permanently stored. The control memory address register specifies the control word read from control memory. It must be realized that a ROM operates as a combinational circuit, with the address value as the input and the corresponding word as the output. The content of the specified word remains on the output wires as long as the address value remains in the address register. No read signal is needed as in a random-access memory. The word out of the ROM should be transferred to a buffer register if the address register changes while the ROM word is still in use. If the change in address and ROM word can occur simultaneously, no buffer register is needed.

The word read from control memory represents a microinstruction. The microinstruction specifies one or more microoperations for the components of the system. Once these operations are executed, the control unit must determine its next address. The location of the next microinstruction may be the next one in sequence, or it may be located somewhere else in the control memory. For this reason, it is necessary to use some bits of the microinstruction to control the generation of the address for the next microinstruction. The next address may also

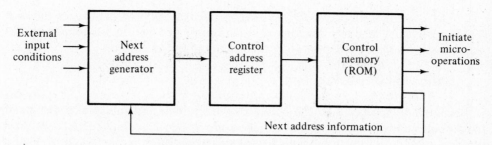

Figure 10-5 Microprogram control logic

be a function of external input conditions. While the microoperations are being executed, the next address is computed in the next-address generator circuit and then transferred (with the next clock pulse) into the control address register to read the next microinstruction. The detailed construction of the next address generator depends on the particular application.

The remainder of this chapter deals with specific examples of control logic design. The first example in Section 10-3 demonstrates the one flip-flop per state method, and Section 10-4 presents the same example with a microprogram control. Section 10-6 uses a second example to demonstrate the sequence register and decoder method, and Section 10-7 implements the second example with a PLA. Sections 10-5 and 10-8 consider the microprogram control method in more detail.

10-3 HARD-WIRED CONTROL—EXAMPLE 1

This example demonstrates the development of a design algorithm. We start from the statement of the problem and proceed through the design to obtain the control logic for the system. The design is carried out in five consecutive steps.

1. The problem is stated.

2. An initial equipment configuration is assumed.

3. An algorithm is formulated.

4. The data-processor part is specified.

5. The control logic is designed.

An initial equipment configuration is necessary in order to formulate the design algorithm in terms of the register-transfer method. The algorithm is formulated by means of a flowchart that specifies the sequence of microoperations for the system. Once we have a list of microoperations, we can choose the digital functions necessary for their implementation. In essence, this supplies the data-processor part of the system. The control is then designed to sequence the required microoperations in the data processor.

415

The control logic derived in this section is a hard-wired control of the one flip-flop per state method. The digital system presented here is used again in the next section to demonstrate an example of microprogram control.

Statement of the Problem

In Section 8-5, an algorithm was stated for the addition and subtraction of binary fixed-point numbers when negative numbers are in sign-2's-complement form. The problem here is to implement with hardware the addition and subtraction of two fixed-point binary numbers represented in sign-magnitude form. Complement arithmetic may be used, provided the final result is in sign-magnitude form.

The addition of two numbers stored in registers of finite length may result in a sum that exceeds the storage capacity of the register by one bit. The extra bit is said to cause an overflow. The circuit must provide a flip-flop for storing a possible overflow bit.

Equipment Configuration

The two signed binary numbers to be added or subtracted contain n bits. The magnitudes of the numbers contain $k = n - 1$ bits and are stored in registers A and B. The sign bits are stored in flip-flops A_s and B_s. Figure 10-6 shows the registers and associated equipment. The ALU performs the arithmetic operations and the 1-bit register E serves as the overflow flip-flop. The output carry from the ALU is transferred to E.

It is assumed that the two numbers and their signs have been transferred to their respective registers and that the result of the operation is to be available in registers A and A_s. Two input signals in the control specify the add (q_a) and subtract (q_s) operations. Output variable x indicates the end of the operation. The control logic communicates with the outside environment through the input and output variables. Control recognizes input signal q_a or q_s and provides the required

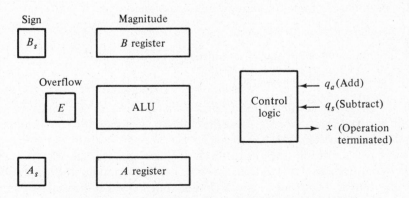

Figure 10-6 Register configuration for the adder-subtractor

operation. Upon completion of the operation, control informs the external environment with output x that the sum or difference is in registers A and A_s and that the overflow bit is in E.

Derivation of the Algorithm

The representation of numbers by sign-magnitude is familiar because it is used for paper and pencil arithmetic calculations. The procedure for adding or subtracting two signed binary numbers with paper and pencil is simple and straightforward. A review of this procedure will be helpful for deriving the design algorithm.

We designate the *magnitude* of the two numbers by A and B. When the numbers are added or subtracted algebraically, we find that there are eight different conditions to consider, depending on the sign of the numbers and the operation performed. The eight conditions may be expressed in a compact form as follows:

$$(\pm A) \pm (\pm B)$$

If the arithmetic operation specified is subtraction, we change the sign of B and add. This is evident from the relations:

$$(\pm A) - (+B) = (\pm A) + (-B)$$
$$(\pm A) - (-B) = (\pm A) + (+B)$$

This reduces the number of possible conditions to four, namely:

$$(\pm A) + (\pm B)$$

When the signs of A and B are the same, we add the two magnitudes and the sign of the result is the same as the common sign. When the signs of A and B are not the same, we subtract the smaller number from the larger and the sign of the result is the sign of the larger number. This is evident from the following relationships:

	if $A \geqslant B$	if $A < B$
$(+A) + (+B) = +(A + B)$		
$(+A) + (-B) =$	$+(A - B) =$	$-(B - A)$
$(-A) + (+B) =$	$-(A - B) =$	$+(B - A)$
$(-A) + (-B) = -(A + B)$		

The flowchart of Fig. 10-7 shows how we can implement sign-magnitude addition and subtraction with the equipment of Fig. 10-6. An operation is initiated by either input q_s or input q_a. Input q_s initiates a subtraction operation, so the sign

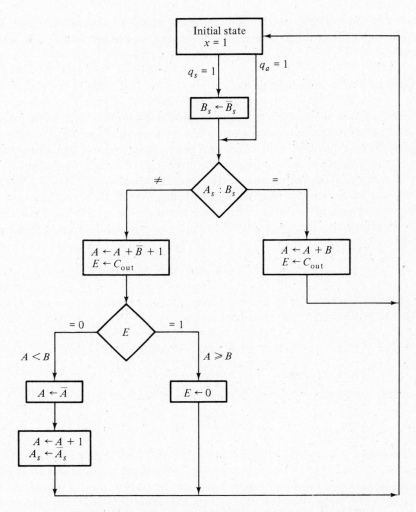

Figure 10-7 Flowchart for sign-magnitude addition and subtraction

of B is complemented. Input q_a initiates an add operation, and the sign of B is left unchanged. The next step is to compare the two signs. The decision block marked with $A_s : B_s$ symbolizes this decision. If the signs are equal, we take the path marked by the symbol $=$; otherwise, we take the path marked by the symbol $\neq$. For equal signs, the content of A is added to the content of B and the sum is transferred to A. The value of the end carry in this case is an overflow; so the E flip-flop is made equal to the output carry C_{out}. The circuit then goes to its initial state and output x becomes 1. The sign of the result in this case is the same as the original sign of A_s; so the sign bit is left unchanged.

The two magnitudes are subtracted if the signs are not the same. The subtraction of the magnitudes is done by adding A to the 2's complement of B. No overflow can occur if the numbers are subtracted; so E is cleared to 0. A 1 in E

indicates that $A \geqslant B$ and the number in A is the correct result. The sign of the result again is equal to the original value of A_s. A 0 in E indicates that $A < B$. For this case, it is necessary to form the 2's complement of the value in A and complement the sign in A_s. The 2's complement of A can be done with one microoperation, $A \leftarrow \bar{A} + 1$. However, we want to use the ALU of Chapter 9 and this ALU does not have the 2's complement operation. For this reason, the 2's complement is obtained from the complement and increment operations which are available in the ALU.

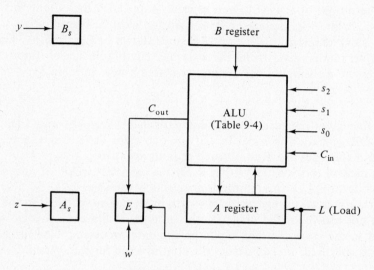

(a) Data processor registers and ALU

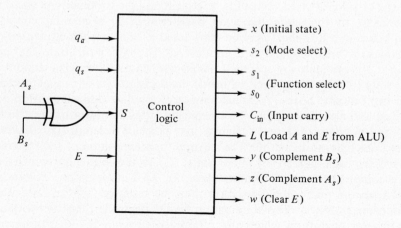

(b) Control block diagram

Figure 10-8   System block diagram

Data Processor Specification

The flowchart algorithm lists all the microoperations for the data-processor part of the system. The operations between A and B can be done with the ALU. The operations with A_s, B_s, and E must be initiated with separate control variables. Figure 10-8(a) shows the data-processor with the required control variables. As mentioned before, the ALU is from Chapter 9 and its function is specified in Table 9-4. This ALU has four selection variables, as shown in the diagram. The variable L loads the output of the ALU into register A and also the output carry into E. Variables y, z, and w complement B_s and A_s and clear E, respectively.

The block diagram of the control logic is shown in Fig. 10-8(b). The control receives five inputs: two from the external environment and three from the data-processor. To simplify the design, we define a new variable S:

$$S = A_s \oplus B_s$$

This variable gives the result of the comparison between the two sign bits. The exclusive-OR operation is equal to 1 if the two signs are not the same, and it is equal to 0 if the signs are both positive or both negative.

The control provides an output x for the external circuit. It also selects the operations in the ALU through the four selection variables s_2, s_1, s_0, and C_{in}. The other four outputs go to registers in the data-processor as specified in the diagram. Although not shown in the diagram, the outputs of the control logic should be connected to the corresponding inputs in the data-processor. Now that the data-processor is specified, we can design the control logic for the system.

Control State Diagram

The design of a hard-wired control is a sequential-logic problem. As such, it may be convenient to formulate the state diagram of the sequential control. The function boxes in a flowchart may be considered as states of the sequential circuit, and the decision boxes as next-state conditions. The microoperations that must be executed at a given state are specified within the function box. The conditions for the next state transition are specified inside the decision box or in the directed lines between two function boxes. Although one can formulate this relationship between a flowchart and a state diagram, the conversion from one form to the other is not unique. Consequently, different designers may produce different state diagrams for the same flowchart, and each may be a correct representation of the system.

We start by assigning an initial state, T_0, to the sequential controller. We then determine the transition to other states T_1, T_2, T_3, and so on. For each state, we determine the microoperations that must be initiated by the control circuit. This procedure produces the state diagram for the controller, together with a list of register-transfer operations which are to be initiated while the control circuit is in each and every state.

The control state diagram and the corresponding register-transfer operations are derived in Fig. 10-9. The information for this design is taken directly from the

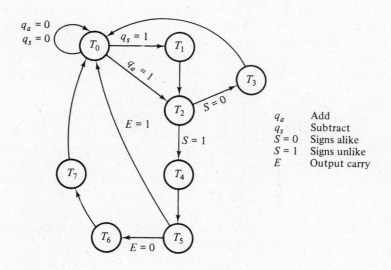

(a) State diagram

	Control outputs							
x	s_2	s_1	s_0	C_{in}	L	y	z	w

T_0: Initial state $x = 1$ 1 0 0 0 0 0 0 0 0

T_1: $B_s \leftarrow \bar{B}_s$ 0 0 0 0 0 0 1 0 0

T_2: nothing   0 0 0 0 0 0 0 0 0

T_3: $A \leftarrow A + B$, $E \leftarrow C_{out}$ 0 0 0 1 0 1 0 0 0

T_4: $A \leftarrow A + \bar{B} + 1$, $E \leftarrow C_{out}$ 0 0 1 0 1 1 0 0 0

T_5: $E \leftarrow 0$ 0 0 0 0 0 0 0 0 1

T_6: $A \leftarrow \bar{A}$ 0 1 1 1 0 1 0 0 0

T_7: $A \leftarrow A + 1$, $A_s \leftarrow \bar{A}_s$ 0 0 0 0 1 1 0 1 0

(b) Sequence of register transfers

Figure 10-9   Control state diagram and sequence of microoperations

flowchart of Fig. 10-7 and the variables defined in the block diagram of Fig. 10-8. The initial control state is T_0. While the control is in this state, variable x is made equal to 1. This variable is 0 in all other states. As long as q_a and q_s are 0, the control stays in its initial state. If q_s becomes 1, the control performs a subtraction operation by going to state T_1. In this state, sign bit B_s is complemented. Control then goes to state T_2 to add the two numbers. If q_a becomes 1, control goes directly to state T_2.

The next state after T_2 depends on the relative values of the sign bits which are determined from input variable S. If the signs are alike, S is 0 and control goes to state T_3. In this state, the two magnitudes are added and the overflow bit set. Once this is done, control goes back to the initial state. If the signs are unlike, S is 1 and control goes from state T_2 to state T_4. In this state, the two magnitudes are subtracted by taking the 2's complement of B. The end carry is transferred to E during the subtraction, and control then goes to state T_5.

It must be realized that the end carry from the ALU is transferred to E with a clock pulse. This happens with the same clock pulse that causes the control to go from state T_4 to T_5. Although we show the microoperation:

$$E \leftarrow C_{out}$$

with timing variable T_4 this operation is not executed until a clock pulse occurs. Once this clock pulse executes the operation, control finds itself in state T_5. Therefore, the value of E for an end carry should not be checked until control reaches state T_5. The value of E is checked to determine the relative magnitudes of A and B. If $E = 1$, it indicates that $A \geqslant B$. For this case, E must be cleared and the operation is completed. If $E = 0$, it indicates that $A < B$. Control then goes to states T_6 and T_7 to complement A and A_s. Note that E is cleared while the control is in state T_5. This is done whether E is 1 or 0, since trying to clear a flip-flop that is already 0 leaves the flip-flop in the 0 state anyway. Note also that E is cleared with the clock pulse that causes control to go out of state T_5. It must be realized that clearing E and transferring control to state T_0 or T_6 is done with one common clock pulse without a conflict. The original value of E at time T_5 determines the next state even though this flip-flop is cleared while the clock pulse goes through an edge transition.

It should be apparent from this example that the interpretation of a flowchart may result in a different state diagram for the same control logic. This is acceptable as long as the hardware constraints are taken into consideration and the system functions according to the specifications. For example, instead of checking E at time T_5, we could have chosen to check C_{out} at time T_4. If C_{out} is 1, control goes to state T_5 to clear E. If it is 0, control can go directly to state T_6, bypassing state T_5 in this case.

Design of Hard-wired Control

The control outputs are a function of the control states and are listed in Fig. 10-9(b). These outputs are defined in the block diagram of Fig. 10-8(b). The values for the ALU selection variables are determined from Table 9-4. The L (load

A) variable must be made equal to 1 every time the output of the ALU is transferred to register *A*. Otherwise, *L* is 0 and the ALU outputs have no effect on the register. To design the control for this system, we need to design the state diagram of Fig. 10-9(a) and provide the control outputs as specified in Fig. 10-9(b).

The control can be designed using the classical sequential-logic procedure. This procedure requires a state table with eight states, four inputs, and nine outputs. The sequential circuit to be derived from such a state table will not be easy to obtain because of the large number of variables. The circuit obtained by using this method may have a minimum number of gates, but it will have an irregular pattern and will be difficult to analyze if a malfunction occurs. These difficulties are removed if the control is designed by the one flip-flop per state method.

A control organization that uses one flip-flop per state has the convenient characteristic that the circuit can be derived directly from the state diagram by inspection. No state or excitation tables are needed if *D* flip-flops are employed. Remember that the next state of a *D* flip-flop is a function of the *D* input and is independent of the present state. Since the method requires one flip-flop for each state, we choose eight *D* flip-flops and label their outputs $T_0, T_1, T_2, \ldots, T_7$. The condition for setting a given flip-flop is specified in the state diagram. For example, flip-flop T_2 is set with the next clock pulse if $T_1 = 1$ or if $T_0 = 1$ and $q_a = 1$. This condition can be defined with the Boolean function:

$$DT_2 = q_a T_0 + T_1$$

where DT_2 designates the *D* input of flip-flop T_2. In fact, the condition for setting a flip-flop to 1 is obtained from the condition specified in the directed lines going into a given flip-flop state ANDed with the previous flip-flop state. If there is more than one directed line going into a state, all conditions must be ORed. Using this procedure for the other flip-flops, we obtain the input functions given in Table 10-1.

Initially, flip-flop T_0 is set and all others are cleared. At any given time, only one *D* input is in the 1 state while all others are maintained at 0. The next clock pulse sets the flip-flop whose *D* input is 1 and clears all others. For example, if

TABLE 10-1 Boolean functions for control

Flip-flop input functions	Boolean functions for output control
$DT_0 = q'_a q'_s T_0 + T_3 + ET_5 + T_7$	$x = T_0$
$DT_1 = q_s T_0$	$s_2 = T_6$
$DT_2 = q_a T_0 + T_1$	$s_1 = T_4 + T_6$
$DT_3 = S' T_2$	$s_0 = T_3 + T_6$
$DT_4 = S T_2$	$C_{in} = T_4 + T_7$
$DT_5 = T_4$	$L = T_3 + T_4 + T_6 + T_7$
$DT_6 = E' T_5$	$y = T_1$
$DT_7 = T_6$	$z = T_7$
	$w = T_5$

presently $T_0 = 1$, then if $q_a = 0$ and $q_s = 0$, the D input of T_0 will be 1 and the next pulse will leave flip-flop T_0 in the 1 state. If during the interval between two pulses q_s becomes a 1, the D input of T_0 will change to 0; but the D input of T_1 will be 1, so the next pulse will set T_1 and clear T_0. The flip-flop input functions are mutually exclusive and only one flip-flop can be set at any given time; all others are cleared because their D inputs are 0's.

We now need to specify the control outputs as a function of flip-flop states. This is done with the Boolean functions given in Table 10-1. These Boolean functions are obtained by inspection from Fig. 10-9(b). For example, the L output must be 1 during state T_3, T_4, T_6, or T_7. These variables are available from outputs of flip-flops. What is needed here is a 4-input OR gate to generate output control L.

The circuit for the control logic is not drawn but can be easily obtained from the Boolean functions in Table 10-1. The circuit can be constructed with eight D flip-flops, seven AND gates, six OR gates, and four inverters. Note that five control outputs are taken directly from the flip-flop outputs.

10-4   MICROPROGRAM CONTROL

In a microprogram control, the control variables that initiate microoperations are stored in memory. The control memory is usually a ROM, since the control sequence is permanent and needs no alteration. The control variables stored in memory are read one at a time to initiate the sequence of microoperations for the system.

The words stored in a control memory are microinstructions, and each microinstruction specifies one or more microoperations for the components in the system. Once these microoperations are executed, the control unit must determine its next address. Therefore, a few bits of the microinstruction are used to control the generation of the address for the next microinstruction. Thus, a microinstruction contains bits for initiating microoperations and bits that determine the next address for the control memory itself.

In addition to the control memory, a microprogram control unit must include special circuits for selecting the next address as specified by the microinstruction. These circuits and the configuration of the microinstruction bits stored in memory vary from one unit to another. Instead of dwelling on all the possibilities encountered in different situations, we choose here to introduce the microprogram concept by means of a simple example.

The control logic to be designed is for the sign-magnitude adder-subtractor developed in the previous section. The hard-wired control designed in Section 10-3 will be replaced by a microprogram control to be designed subsequently. Realize, however, that the digital system considered here is too small for a microprogram controller and, in practice, a hard-wired control would be more efficient. The microprogram control organization is more efficient in large, complicated systems.

A state in control memory is represented by the address of a microinstruction. An address for control memory specifies a control word within a microinstruction, just as a state in a sequential circuit specifies a microoperation. The control we wish to design is specified in Fig. 10-9. Since there are eight states in the control, we choose a control memory with eight words having addresses 0 through 7. The address of the control memory corresponds to the subscript number under the T's in the state diagram.

Inspection of the state diagram reveals that the address sequencing in the microprogram control must have the following capabilities.

1. Provision for loading an external address as a result of the occurrence of external signals q_a and q_s.

2. Provision for sequencing consecutive addresses.

3. Provision for choosing between two addresses as a function of present values of the status variables S and E.

Each microinstruction must contain a number of bits to specify the way that the next address is to be selected.

Hardware Configuration

The organization of the microprogram control unit is shown in Fig. 10-10. The control memory is an 8-word by 14-bit ROM. The first nine bits of a microinstruction word contain the control variables that initiate the microoperations. The last five bits provide information for selecting the next address. The control address register (CAR) holds the address for the control memory. This register receives an input value when its load control is enabled; otherwise, it is incremented by 1. CAR is essentially a counter with parallel-load capability.

Bits 10, 11, and 12 of a microinstruction contain an address for CAR. Bits 13 and 14 select an input for a multiplexer. Bit 1 provides the initial state condition denoted by variable x and also enables an external address when q_s or q_a is equal to 1. We stipulate that when $x = 1$, the address field of the microinstruction must be 000. Then if $q_s = 1$, address 001 is available at the inputs of CAR, but if $q_a = 1$, address 010 is applied to CAR. If both q_s and q_a are 0's, the zero address from bits 10, 11, and 12 are applied to the inputs of CAR. In this way, the control memory stays at address zero until an external variable is enabled.

The multiplexer (MUX) has four inputs that are selected with bits 13 and 14 of the microinstruction. The functions of the multiplexer select bits are tabulated in Fig. 10-10. If bits 13 and 14 are 00, a multiplexer input that is equal to 0 is selected. The output of the multiplexer is 0, and the increment input to CAR is enabled. This configuration increments CAR to choose the next address in sequence. An input of 1 is selected by the multiplexer when bits 13 and 14 are equal to 01. The output of the multiplexer is 1 and the external input is loaded into CAR. Status variable S is selected when bits 13 and 14 are equal to 10. If $S = 1$, the output of the multiplexer is 1 and the address bits of the microinstruction are loaded into CAR (provided $x = 0$). If $S = 0$, the output of the multiplexer is 0 and CAR is incremented. With bits 13 and 14 equal to 11, status variable E is selected

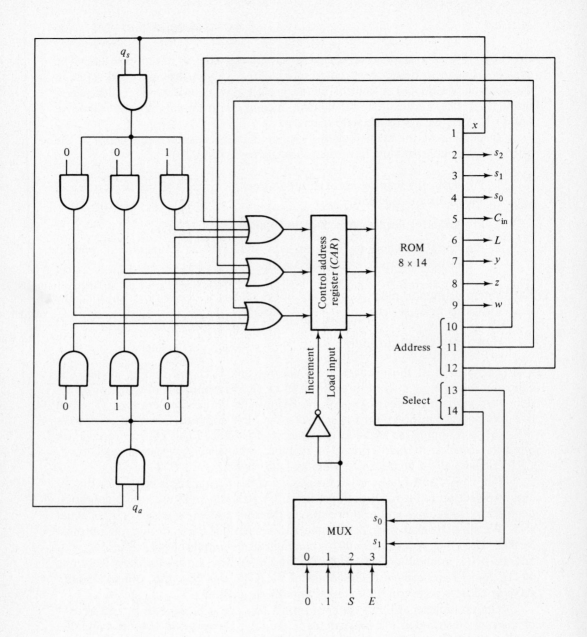

Figure 10-10 Microprogram control block diagram

and the address field is loaded into CAR if $E = 1$, but CAR is incremented if $E = 0$. Thus, the multiplexer allows the control to choose between two addresses, depending on the value of the status bit selected.

The Microprogram

Once the configuration of a microprogram control unit is established, the designer's task is to generate the microcode for the control memory. This code generation is called microprogramming and is a process that determines the bit configuration for each and all words in control memory. To appreciate this process, we will derive the microprogram for the adder-subtractor example. The control memory has eight words and each word contains 14 bits. To microprogram the control memory, we must determine the bit values of each of the eight words.

The register-transfer method can be adopted for developing a microprogram. The microoperation sequence can be specified with register-transfer statements. There is no need for listing control functions with Boolean variables since, in this case, the control variables are the control words stored in control memory. Instead of a control function, we specify an address with each register-transfer statement. The address associated with each symbolic statement corresponds to the address where the microinstruction is to be stored in memory. The sequencing from one address to the next can be indicated by means of conditional control statements. This type of statement can specify the address to which control goes, depending on status conditions. Thus, instead of thinking in terms of the 1's and 0's that must be inserted for each microinstruction, it is more convenient to think in terms of symbols in the register-transfer method. Once the symbolic microprogram is established, it is possible to translate the register-transfer statements to their equivalent binary form.

The microprogram in symbolic form is given in Table 10-2. The eight addresses of the ROM are listed in the first column. In the second column, the microinstruction that must be stored at each address is given in symbolic form.

TABLE 10-2　Symbolic microprogram for control memory

ROM address	Microinstruction	Comments
0	$x = 1$, if $(q_s = 1)$ then (go to 1), if $(q_a = 1)$ then (go to 2), if $(q_s \wedge q_a = 0)$ then (go to 0)	Load 0 or external address
1	$B_s \leftarrow \bar{B}_s$	$q_s = 1$, start subtraction
2	If $(S = 1)$ then (go to 4)	$q_a = 1$, start addition
3	$A \leftarrow A + B$, $E \leftarrow C_{out}$, go to 0	Add magnitudes and return
4	$A \leftarrow A + \bar{B} + 1$, $E \leftarrow C_{out}$,	Subtract magnitudes
5	If $(E = 1)$ then (go to 0), $E \leftarrow 0$	Operation terminated if $E = 1$
6	$A \leftarrow \bar{A}$	$E = 0$, complement A
7	$A \leftarrow A + 1$, $A_s \leftarrow \bar{A}_s$, go to 0	Done, return to address 0

The comments are used to clarify the register-transfer statements. Address 0 is equivalent to the initial state and produces an output $x = 1$. The next address depends on the values of external variables q_s and q_a. The three conditional control statements in this microinstruction use a *go to* statement after the word *then*. This is interpreted to mean that if the condition is satisfied, control goes to the address written after the words *go to*. Thus, if both q_s and q_a are 0, control stays in address 0 to repeat the microinstruction. If q_s or q_a is 1, control goes to address 1 or 2, respectively.

The conditional control statements in the other microinstructions use the status variables S and E. The *go to* statement without a condition attached specifies an unconditional branch to the indicated address. For example, go to 0 means that control goes to address 0 after the present microinstruction is executed. If there is no *go to* statement in the microinstruction, it implies that the next microinstruction is taken from the next address in sequence. Also, if the condition after an *if* statement is not satisfied, control goes to the next address in sequence.

The microinstructions associated with the eight addresses are derived directly from the control specifications of Fig. 10-9. The microoperations listed are identical to the ones listed in Fig. 10-9(b). The conditional control statement specifies the address sequence as given by the state diagram of Fig. 10-9(a). Note that each address number is the same as the subscript number under the T's in the state diagram. It should be obvious that the conditional control statements provide a different way to specify a state diagram. This shows that the register-transfer method can be used to specify a sequential circuit.

The microprogram in Table 10-2 could have been derived directly from the flowchart of Fig. 10-7. This flowchart was used to specify the algorithm for the system that we are attempting to design. Although the microprogram developed here seems to require many intermediate steps, it must be realized that this was done for explanatory purposes. Once the microprogram concept is understood, there is no reason we could not specify the algorithm directly as a symbolic microprogram without the need for a state diagram. Once the equipment configuration for the data processor and the microprogram control is established, the algorithm can be developed by means of a microprogram.

The symbolic designation is a convenient method for developing the microprogram in a way that people can read and understand. But this is not the way that the microprogram is stored in control memory. The symbolic microprogram must be translated to binary because this is the form that goes into memory. The translation is done by dividing the bits of each microinstruction into their functional parts called *fields*. Here we have three functional parts. Bits 1 through 9 specify the control word for initiating the microoperations. Bits 10 through 12 specify an address field, and bits 13 and 14 select a multiplexer input. For each microinstruction listed in symbolic form, we must choose the appropriate bits in the corresponding microinstruction fields.

The equivalent binary form of the microprogram is given in Table 10-3. The addresses for the ROM control memory are listed in binary. The content of each

TABLE 10-3 Binary microprogram for control memory

ROM address	x	s_2	s_1	s_0	C_{in}	L	y	z	w	Address			Select	
	1	2	3	4	5	6	7	8	9	10	11	12	13	14
0 0 0	1	0	0	0	0	0	0	0	0	0	0	0	0	1
0 0 1	0	0	0	0	0	0	1	0	0	0	1	0	0	1
0 1 0	0	0	0	0	0	0	0	0	0	1	0	0	1	0
0 1 1	0	0	0	1	0	1	0	0	0	0	0	0	0	1
1 0 0	0	0	1	0	1	1	0	0	0	1	0	1	0	1
1 0 1	0	0	0	0	0	0	0	0	1	0	0	0	1	1
1 1 0	0	1	1	1	0	1	0	0	0	1	1	1	0	1
1 1 1	0	0	0	0	1	1	0	1	0	0	0	0	0	1

word of ROM is also given in binary. This table constitutes the truth table needed for programming the ROM.

The first nine bits in each ROM word give the control word that initiates the specified microoperations. These bit values are taken directly from Fig. 10-9(b). The last five bits in each ROM word are derived from the conditional control statements in the symbolic program.

At address 000, we have 01 for the *select* field. This allows an external address to be loaded into CAR if q_s or q_a is equal to 1. Otherwise, address 000 is transferred to CAR. In address 001, the microinstruction select field is 01 and the address field is 010. From the table in Fig. 10-10, we find that the clock pulse that initiates the microoperation $B_s \leftarrow \bar{B}_s$ (because $y = 1$) also transfers the address field into CAR. The next microinstruction out of ROM will be the one stored in address 010. The select field at address 001 could have been chosen to be 00. This would have caused CAR to increment and go to address 010.

Inspection of the select field in bits 13 and 14 shows that when these two bits are equal to 01, the address field is the next address. When these two bits are 10, status variable S is selected, and when they are 11, status variable E is selected. In the last two cases, the next address is the one specified in the address field if the selected status bit is equal to 1. If the selected status bit is equal to 0, the next address is the one next in sequence because CAR is incremented.

10-5 CONTROL OF PROCESSOR UNIT

The hardware configuration of the microprogram control unit used in the preceding section is suitable for the particular example considered. In a practical situation, the hardware organization of a microprogram control unit must have a general-purpose configuration to suit a wide variety of situations. A general-purpose microprogram control unit must have a control memory large enough to store many microinstructions. Provisions must be made to include all possible control variables in the system—not only for controlling an ALU. The multiplexer and select bits must include all other possible status bits that one may want to check in the system. A provision must be available to accept an external address to initiate many operations rather than just two operations such as add and subtract.

The main advantage of the microprogram control is the fact that, once the hardware configuration is established, there should be no need for further hardware or wiring changes. If we want to establish a different control sequence for the system, all we need to do is specify a different set of microinstructions for the control memory. The hardware configuration should not change for different operations; the only change should be in the microprogram residing in control memory.

To show the general property of the microprogram organization, we will expand the hardware configuration to include the control of an entire processor unit. A general-purpose processor unit was introduced in Section 9-9. Referring to Fig. 9-16, we note that the processor unit has seven registers, an ALU, a shifter, and a status register. A microoperation is selected with a control word of 16 bits. The bits for a given control word can be formulated from the binary code listed in Table 9-8.

A microprogram organization for controlling the processor unit is shown in Fig. 10-11. It has a control memory of 64 words, with 26 bits per word. To select 64 words, we need an address of 6 bits. To select 8 status bits, we need 3 selection lines for the multiplexer. One bit of the microinstruction selects between an external address and the address field of the microinstruction. Adding the 16 bits for selecting the microoperation in the processor requires a total of 26 bits for each microinstruction.

The processor unit is included in the diagram to show its connection to the microprogram control unit. The first 16 bits of the microinstruction select the microoperation for the processor. The other 10 bits select the next address for the control address register. The status bits from the processor are applied to the inputs of a multiplexer. Both the normal and complement values are used, except for the overflow bit V. Input 0 of MUX 2 is connected to a binary constant which is always 1. The load input to CAR is enabled when this input is selected by bits 18, 19, and 20 in the microinstruction. This causes a transfer of information from the output of MUX 1 into CAR. The input into CAR is a function of bit 17 in the microinstruction. If bit 17 is 1, CAR receives the address field of the microinstruction. If bit 17 is 0, an external address is loaded into CAR. The external address is for the purpose of initiating a new sequence of microinstructions which can be specified by the external environment. The status bit (or its complement) selected by bits 18, 19, and 20 of the microinstruction may be equal to 1 or 0. The input address is loaded into CAR if the selected bit is 1, but CAR is incremented if the selected bit is 0.

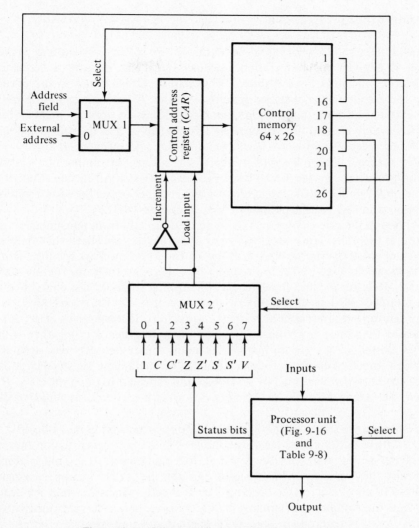

Figure 10-11 Microprogram control for processor unit

To construct correct microprograms, it is necessary to specify exactly how the status bits are affected by each microoperation in the processor. The S (sign) and Z (zero) bits are affected by all operations. The C (carry) and V (overflow) bits *do not change* after the following ALU operations:

1. The four logic operations OR, AND, XOR, and complement.

2. The increment and decrement operations.

For all other operations, the output carry from the ALU goes into the C bit of the status register. The C bit is also affected after a circular shift with carry operation.

Microprogram Example

We now demonstrate by means of an example how a microprogram is written to implement a given macrooperation. A macrooperation initiates a sequence of microinstructions in control memory. This sequence constitutes a microprogram *routine* for executing the specified macrooperation. A macrooperation is initiated by an external address that supplies the first address in control memory for the microinstruction routine. The routine is terminated with a microinstruction that loads a new external address to start executing the next macrooperation.

The macrooperation we wish to implement counts the number of 1's presently stored in processor register $R1$ and sets processor register $R2$ to that number. For example, if $R1 = 00110101$, the microprogram routine counts the four 1's stored in the register and sets register $R2$ to the binary number 100.

Although the microprogram can be derived directly from the statement of the problem, it may be convenient to first construct a flowchart that shows the sequence of microoperations and decision paths. The flowchart for the microprogram is shown in Fig. 10-12. We assume that the microprogram routine starts at address 8. Register $R2$ and the C (carry) bit are first set to 0. The content of $R1$ is then examined. If it is 0, it signifies that there are no 1's stored in it; so the microprogram routine terminates with $R2$ equal to 0. If the content of $R1$ is not 0, it indicates that there are some 1's stored in it. Register $R1$, together with the carry, is shifted in a circular manner as many times as necessary until a 1 is transferred into C. For every 1 detected in C, we increment register $R2$ and then go back to check if $R1$ is equal to 0. This loop is repeated until all the 1's in $R1$ are counted. Note that the value of C is always 0 when it is circulated with the content of $R1$.

The microprogram routine in symbolic form is presented in Table 10-4. The routine starts at address 8 by clearing register $R2$. The microinstruction in address 9 clears the C bit and sets the Z bit if $R1$ contains all 0's. This is done by transferring the content of $R1$ into itself through the ALU. The microinstruction in address 10 checks the value of the Z bit. If it is 1, it indicates that $R1$ contains all 0's, and the routine is terminated by accepting a new external address to start executing another macrooperation. If Z is not equal to 1, control continues with address 11. The circular right-shift with carry (crc) places the least significant bit of $R1$ into C. Next we check the value of C. If it is 0, control goes back to address 11 to circulate again until C becomes a 1. When $C = 1$, control goes to address 13 to increment $R2$ and then returns to address 9 to check the content of $R1$ for an all 0's state.

The binary microprogram is given in Table 10-5. The 16 bits for the conrtol word that selects the processor microoperations are derived from Table 9-8. In fact, most of the control words listed were explained in Section 9-9 in conjunction with Table 9-9. The multiplexer select bits select the inputs to the two multiplexers. Bit 17 is 0 in address 10 for selecting an external address. In all other cases, it is 1 to

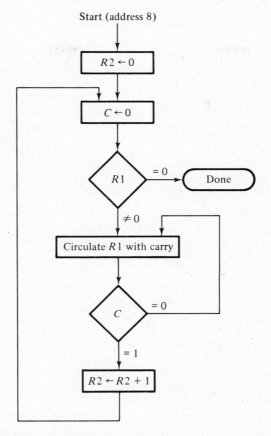

Start (address 8)

$R2 \leftarrow 0$

$C \leftarrow 0$

$R1$ — $= 0$ → Done

$\neq 0$

Circulate $R1$ with carry

C — $= 0$

$= 1$

$R2 \leftarrow R2 + 1$

Figure 10-12 Flowchart for counting the number of 1's in register $R1$

select the address field of the microinstruction. When bits 18, 19, and 20 are 000, the next address is determined directly from the address field. When these bits are 011, they select the Z bit for MUX 2. If $Z = 1$, an external address is transferred to CAR. If $Z = 0$, CAR is incremented and the next address is the next one in sequence. The microinstruction at address 12 selects the complement of the carry bit or C'. If $C = 0$, then $C' = 1$ and the address field (binary 1011) is transferred into CAR. If $C = 1$, then $C' = 0$ and CAR is incremented to give 13 for the next address.

The reader familiar with machine- or assembly-language programming for a computer will realize that writing microprograms is very similar to writing machine-language programs for a computer. Thus, the microprogram concept is a systematic procedure for designing the control unit of a digital system. Once the

TABLE 10-4 Symbolic microprogram to count the number of 1's in $R1$

ROM address	Microinstruction	Comments
8	$R2 \leftarrow 0$	Clear $R2$ counter
9	$R1 \leftarrow R1, C \leftarrow 0$	Clear C, set status bits
10	If $(Z = 1)$ then (go to external address)	Done if $R1 = 0$
11	$R1 \leftarrow$ crc $R1$	Circulate $R1$ right with carry
12	If $(C = 0)$ then (go to 11)	Circulate again if $C = 0$
13	$R2 \leftarrow R2 + 1$, go to 9	Carry $= 1$, increment $R2$

TABLE 10-5 Binary microprogram to count the number of 1's in $R1$

ROM address	ROM content														
	Microoperation select					MUX select				Address field					
	A	B	D	F	H	17			20	21					26
	1				16										
001000	000	000	010	0000	011	1	0	0	0	0	0	1	0	0	1
001001	001	000	001	0000	000	1	0	0	0	0	0	1	0	1	0
001010	001	001	000	1000	000	0	0	1	1	0	0	0	0	0	0
001011	001	001	001	1000	101	1	0	0	0	0	0	1	1	0	0
001100	001	001	000	1000	000	1	0	1	0	0	0	1	0	1	1
001101	010	000	010	0001	000	1	0	0	0	0	0	1	0	0	1

microinstruction format is established, the design is done by writing a microprogram, which is similar to writing a program for a computer. For this reason, the microprogram method is sometimes referred to as *firmware* to distinguish it from the hardware method (which we called a hard-wired control) and the software concept which constitutes a programming method.

10-6 HARD-WIRED CONTROL—EXAMPLE 2

The example presented in this section demonstrates the development of a second arithmetic algorithm and a different method for designing the control logic. As in the previous example, we first develop the design algorithm together with the hardware configuration for the processor part of the system. After this is done, we formulate the control logic specification for the system.

The control organization chosen for this example is the sequence register and decoder method. In the next section, we design the control logic by means of a

PLA. This example demonstrates the direct relationship that exists between the sequence register and decoder method and its corresponding PLA control implementation.

Statement of the Problem

We wish to design an arithmetic circuit that multiplies two fixed-point binary numbers in sign-magnitude representation. The product obtained from the multiplication of two binary numbers whose magnitudes consist of k bits each can be up to $2k$ bits long. The sign of each number occupies one additional bit.

Multiplication of two fixed-point binary numbers in sign-magnitude representation is done with paper and pencil by successive additions and shifting. This process is best illustrated with a numerical example. Let us multiply the two binary numbers 10111 and 10011:

$$
\begin{array}{rll}
23 & 10111 & \text{multiplicand} \\
\times & & \\
19 & 10011 & \text{multiplier} \\
\hline
 & 10111 & \\
 & 10111 & \\
 & 00000 & + \\
 & 00000 & \\
 & 10111 & \\
\hline
437 & 110110101 & \text{product}
\end{array}
$$

The process consists of looking at successive bits of the multiplier, least significant bit first. If the multiplier bit is a 1, the multiplicand is copied down; otherwise, zeros are copied down. The numbers copied down in successive lines are shifted one position to the left from the previous number. Finally, the numbers are added; their sum forms the product.

The sign of the product is determined from the signs of the multiplicand and multiplier. If they are alike, the sign of the product is plus. If they are unlike, the sign of the product is minus.

When the above process is implemented in a digital machine, it is convenient to change the process slightly. First, instead of providing digital circuits to store and add simultaneously as many binary numbers as there are 1's in the multiplier, it is convenient to provide circuits for the summation of only two binary numbers and successively accumulate the partial products in a register. Second, instead of shifting the multiplicand to the left, the partial product is shifted to the right, which results in leaving the partial product and the multiplicand in the required relative positions. Third, when the corresponding bit of the multiplier is a 0, there is no need to add all zeros to the partial product since it will not alter its value. The previous numerical example is repeated here to clarify the proposed multiplication process:

multiplicand:	10111
multiplier:	10011
1st multiplier bit = 1, copy multiplicand	10111
shift right to obtain 1st partial product	010111
2nd multiplier bit = 1, copy multiplicand	10111
add multiplicand to previous partial product	1000101
shift right to obtain 2nd partial product	1000101
3rd multiplier bit = 0, shift right to obtain 3rd partial product	01000101
4th multiplier bit = 0, shift right to obtain 4th partial product	001000101
5th multiplier bit = 1, copy multiplicand	10111
add multiplicand to previous partial product	110110101
shift right to obtain 5th partial product = final product	0110110101

Equipment Configuration

The register configuration for the binary multiplier is shown in Fig. 10-13. The multiplicand is stored in register B, the multiplier is stored in register Q, and the partial product is formed in register A. The sign of the multiplicand is in B_s, the sign of the multiplier is in Q_s, and the sign of the product is formed in A_s. The E flip-flop stores the output carry after the addition of B to A. The two numbers to be multiplied consist of n bits. One of these bits holds the sign and the other $k = n - 1$ bits hold the magnitude of the number. The P counter is initially set to hold a binary number equal to the number of bits in the multiplier magnitude. This counter is decremented after the formation of each new partial product.

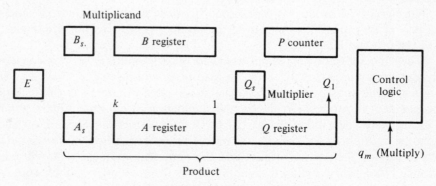

Figure 10-13   Registers for binary multiplier

When the contents of the counter reaches zero, the product is formed in registers A and Q and the process stops.

The control logic stays in an initial state until variable q_m becomes 1. The control then performs the multiplication. The sum of A and B forms a partial product which is transferred to A. If there is a carry out of the addition, it is transferred to E. Both the partial product in A and the multiplier in Q are shifted to the right. After the right-shift of A and Q, one bit of the partial product is transferred into Q while the multiplier bits in Q are shifted one position to the right. In this manner, the rightmost bit in register Q, designated by Q_1, always holds the bit of the multiplier which must be inspected next.

Derivation of Algorithm

The flowchart for the binary multiplier is shown in Fig. 10-14. Initially, the multiplicand is in B and the multiplier in Q. Their corresponding signs are in B_s and Q_s. The multiplication process is initiated when $q_m = 1$. The two signs are compared by means of an exclusive-OR gate. If the two signs are alike, the exclusive-OR operation produces a 0 which is transferred to A_s to give a plus for the product. If the signs are unlike, a 1 is transferred to A_s to give a negative sign for the product. Registers A and E are cleared and the sequence counter P is set to a binary number k, which is equal to the number of bits in the multiplier.

Next we enter a loop that keeps forming the partial products. The multiplier bit in Q_1 is checked, and if it is equal to 1, the multiplicand in B is added to the present partial product in A. Any carry from the addition is transferred to E. The partial product in A is left unchanged if $Q_1 = 0$. The P counter is decremented by 1 regardless of the value of Q_1. Registers A, Q, and E are then shifted once to the right to obtain a new partial product. This shift operation is symbolized in the flowchart in compact form with the statement:

$$AQ \leftarrow \text{shr } EAQ, E \leftarrow 0$$

EAQ is a composite register made up of registers E, A, and Q. If we use the individual register symbols, the shift operation can be described by the following microoperations:

$$A \leftarrow \text{shr } A, Q \leftarrow \text{shr } Q, A_k \leftarrow E, Q_k \leftarrow A_1, E \leftarrow 0$$

Both registers A and Q are shifted right. The leftmost position of A, designated by A_k, receives the carry from E. The leftmost bit of Q, or Q_k, receives the bit from the rightmost position of A in A_1; and E is cleared. In essence, this is a long shift of the composite register EAQ with 0 inserted into the leftmost position, which is in E.

The value in the P counter is checked after the formation of each partial product. If P is not 0, the process is repeated and a new partial product is formed. The process stops after the kth partial product when $P = 0$. Note that the partial

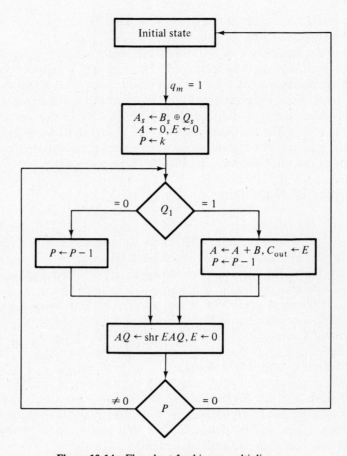

Figure 10-14 Flowchart for binary multiplier

product formed in A is shifted into Q one bit at a time and eventually replaces the multiplier. The final product is available in A and Q, with A holding the most significant bits and Q holding the least significant bits. The sign of the product is in A_s.

Control Specifications

The design algorithm given in the flowchart can be specified more precisely by a state diagram and a list of register-transfer operations. It was mentioned previously that the conversion from a flowchart to a state diagram is not unique. The flowchart may be considered a preliminary formulation of the algorithm. The control state diagram, together with a list of microoperations, is more precise since it takes into consideration the hardware constraints of the system.

The control sequence of operations is defined in Fig. 10-15. The control has four states, and the register-transfer operations for each state are listed below the

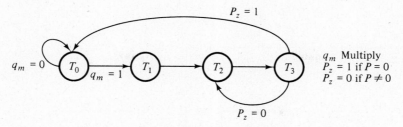

(a) State diagram

$$
\begin{aligned}
&T_0: &&\text{Initial state} \\
&T_1: &&A_s \leftarrow B_s \oplus Q_s, A \leftarrow 0, E \leftarrow 0, P \leftarrow k \\
&Q_1 T_2: &&A \leftarrow A + B, E \leftarrow C_{\text{out}} \\
&T_2: &&P \leftarrow P - 1 \\
&T_3: &&AQ \leftarrow \text{shr } EAQ, E \leftarrow 0
\end{aligned}
$$

(b) Sequence of register transfers

Figure 10-15 Control state diagram and sequence of micro-operations for multiplier

state diagram. Control stays in an initial state T_0 until q_m becomes 1. It then goes to state T_1 to initialize registers A, E, and P and to form the sign of the product. Control then goes to state T_2. In this state, register P is decremented and the contents of B are added to A if $Q_1 = 1$; otherwise, A is left unchanged. The two control functions at time T_2 are:

$$
\begin{aligned}
Q_1 T_2: &\quad A \leftarrow A + B, E \leftarrow C_{\text{out}} \\
T_2: &\quad P \leftarrow P - 1
\end{aligned}
$$

The second statement is always executed when $T_2 = 1$. The first statement is executed at time T_2 only if $Q_1 = 1$. Thus, a status variable (here Q_1) can be included with a timing variable to form a control function. Note that it is convenient to decrement P at state T_2 so that its new value can be checked at state T_3.

Control goes to T_3 after T_2. At state T_3, the composite register EAQ is shifted to the right and the contents of P are checked for zeros. The binary variable P_z is 1 if the P register contains all 0's; otherwise, P_z is 0. If $P_z = 1$, the operation is terminated and control goes to the initial state. If $P_z = 0$, control goes to state T_2 to form a new partial product. Note that P refers to the contents of the register, whereas P_z is a binary variable.

Data-Processor Specification

The data-processor part of the system can be derived from the microoperations list of Fig. 10-15(b). A block diagram of the data processor is shown in Fig. 10-16. A parallel adder is inserted between registers A and B to form the sum, which is

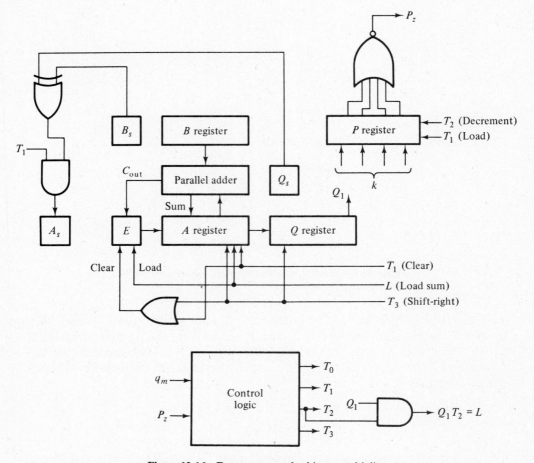

Figure 10-16 Data processor for binary multiplier

transferred to A. The sign of the product is formed by an exclusive-OR gate, and binary variable P_z is generated with a NOR gate. The outputs of the control logic initiate the microoperations for the data processor. Variable T_1 loads the sign of the product into A_s and the number k into P, and it clears registers A and E. Variable T_2 decrements register P, and if $Q_1 = 1$, it generates variable L which loads the sum from the parallel adder into A and E. Variable T_3 shifts A and Q to the right and clears E. Variable T_0 has no effect on the data processor since it only indicates that the system is in an initial state.

The inputs to the control logic are the external signal, q_m, and the two status conditions, P_z and Q_1. The outputs are T_1, T_2, L, and T_3. Although not shown in the diagram, these outputs should be connected to the corresponding inputs in the data processor. The AND gate that generates variable L is shown separately, although it is part of the control logic.

Design of Hard-wired Control

The control logic for the binary multiplier is specified in the state diagram of Fig. 10-15. The state diagram has four states and two inputs. To implement it by the sequence register and decoder method, two flip-flops and a 2×4 decoder are needed. Although this is a simple example, the procedure outlined below applies to more complicated situations as well.

We start with the excitation table of the sequential circuit given in Fig. 10-17(a). The state table part is obtained directly from the state diagram. The flip-flop input conditions are for two JK flip-flops labeled G_1 and G_2. Note that the excitation table has don't-care entries in most of the inputs. Note also that a present state is listed more than once if it has two or more next-state conditions. The variables T_0 through T_3 are listed along with the binary states for identification. The flip-flop input excitations are obtained directly from the excitation table of the JK flip-flop as shown in Table 6-8(b).

The sequential circuit can be designed from the excitation table by means of the classical procedure. This example has a small number of states and inputs; in most other control logic applications, the number of states and inputs is much larger. The application of the classical method requires an excessive amount of work to obtain the simplified input functions for the flip-flops. The design can be simplified if we take into consideration the fact that the decoder outputs are available for use in the design. Instead of using the flip-flop outputs as the present-state conditions, we might as well use the outputs of the decoder to supply this information. If the outputs of the decoder are designated by variables T_0, T_1, T_2, and T_3, these variables can be used to supply the present-state conditions for the circuit.

Instead of using maps for simplifying the flip-flop input functions, one can simply decide to obtain these functions directly from the excitation table. Although this may not result in a minimal circuit, the possible waste of a few gates may be worth the time saved. For example, from the excitation table we note that the J input of G_2 (designated by JG_2 in the table) must receive a binary 1 only when the present output of the decoder is T_1. The K input of G_2 must receive a 1 when the decoder output is T_3, provided $P_z = 1$. These observations can be written in algebraic form as:

$$JG_2 = T_1$$
$$KG_2 = T_3 P_z$$

In all other cases, both the J and K inputs of G_2 will receive a 0 and the state of the flip-flop will not change. This is acceptable because all other entries under JG_2 and KG_2 have either 0's or don't-care X's.

In a similar fashion, it is possible to derive the flip-flop input functions for G_1, by inspection, from the excitation table. The input functions so obtained are:

$$JG_1 = T_0 q_m + T_2$$
$$KG_1 = 1$$

	Present State		Inputs		Next state		Flip-flop inputs			
	G_2	G_1	q_m	P_z	G_2	G_1	JG_2	KG_2	JG_1	KG_1
T_0	0	0	0	X	0	0	0	X	0	X
T_0	0	0	1	X	0	1	0	X	1	X
T_1	0	1	X	X	1	0	1	X	X	1
T_2	1	0	X	X	1	1	X	0	1	X
T_3	1	1	X	0	1	0	X	0	X	1
T_3	1	1	X	1	0	0	X	1	X	1

(a) Excitation table

$$JG_2 = T_1 \qquad\qquad KG_2 = T_3P_z$$
$$JG_1 = T_0q_m + T_2 \quad KG_1 = 1$$

(b) Flip-flop input functions

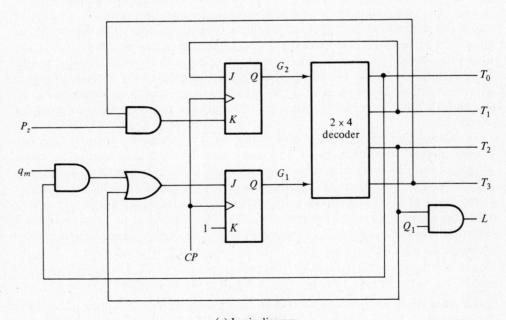

(c) Logic diagram

Figure 10-17 Design of control for binary multiplier

The reason for KG_1 being always 1 is that all entries in the table for this input variable are either 1's or X's.

When deriving input functions by inspection from the excitation table, we cannot be sure that the functions have been simplified in the best way possible. For this reason, one should always analyze the circuit to ensure that the derived equations do indeed produce the required state transitions as specified in the state table.

The logic diagram of the control logic is drawn in Fig. 10-17(c). It consists of two flip-flops, G_1 and G_2, and a decoder. The outputs of the decoder are used to obtain the next state of the circuit according to the Boolean functions listed in Fig. 10-17(b). The outputs of the controller should be connected to the data-processor part of the system as shown in Fig. 10-16.

10-7 PLA CONTROL

We have seen from the two examples presented in this chapter that the design of a control circuit is essentially a sequential-logic design problem. In Section 7-2 we showed that a sequential circuit can be constructed by means of a register connected to a combinational circuit. In Section 5-8 we investigated the programmable logic array and showed that it can be used to implement any combinational circuit. By replacing the combinational circuit with a PLA, it is then possible to design a control circuit with a register connected to a PLA. The register operates as a sequence register that determines the state of the control. The PLA is programmed to provide the control outputs and the next state for the sequence register.

The design of a control unit with a PLA is very similar to the design using the sequence register and decoder methods. In fact, the sequence register in both methods is the same. The difference in the methods is in the way the combinational-logic part of the control is implemented. The PLA essentially replaces the decoder and all other decision logic circuits required in the hard-wired implementation.

The internal organization of the PLA was presented in Section 5-8. It was also shown there how to obtain the PLA program table. The reader is advised to review this section to make sure that the meaning of a PLA program table is understood. The internal paths inside the PLA are "programmed" according to the specifications given in the program table.

The design of a PLA control requires that we obtain the state table for the circuit. The PLA method should be used if the state table contains many don't-care entries; otherwise, it may be advantageous to use a ROM instead of a PLA. The state table gives essentially all the information required for obtaining the PLA program table (or the ROM truth table).

TABLE 10-6 State table for control circuit

Present state		Inputs			Next state		Outputs				
G_2	G_1	q_m	P_z	Q_1	G_2	G_1	T_0	T_1	T_2	L	T_3
0	0	0	X	X	0	0	1	0	0	0	0
0	0	1	X	X	0	1	1	0	0	0	0
0	1	X	X	X	1	0	0	1	0	0	0
1	0	X	X	0	1	1	0	0	1	0	0
1	0	X	X	1	1	1	0	0	1	1	0
1	1	X	0	X	1	0	0	0	0	0	1
1	1	X	1	X	0	0	0	0	0	0	1

To demonstrate the procedure with an example, consider the control circuit for the binary multiplier presented in the previous section. The control specifications for the binary multiplier are given in Fig. 10-15. From this information, we obtain the state table of Table 10-6. The present state is determined from flip-flops G_1 and G_2. The input variables for the control circuit are q_m, P_z, and Q_1. The next state of G_1 and G_2 may be a function of one of the inputs or it may be independent of any inputs. If an input variable does not influence the next state, we mark it with a don't-care X. If the next state is a function of a particular input, the present state is repeated in the table but the next states are assigned different binary values. The table also lists all control outputs as a function of the present state and input conditions. Note that input Q_1 does not affect the next state but only determines the value of output L when output T_2 is equal to 1.

The block diagram of the PLA control is shown in Fig. 10-18(a). The PLA is connected to a sequence register with two flip-flops G_1 and G_2. The inputs to the PLA are the values of the present state of the sequence register and the three external inputs. The outputs of the PLA provide the next state for the sequence register and the control output variables. At any given time, the present state of the sequence register, together with input conditions, determines the output values and the next state for the sequence register. The next clock pulse initiates the microoperations specified by the outputs and transfers the next state into the sequence register. This provides a new control state and possible different input values. Thus, the PLA acts as the combinational-logic part of a sequential circuit to provide the control outputs and the next state values for the sequence register.

A PLA is specified by the number of inputs, the number of product terms, and the number of outputs. For this case, we have five inputs and seven outputs. The number of product terms is a function of the circuit we wish to implement.

The PLA program table can be obtained directly from the state table without the need for simplification procedures. The PLA program table in Fig. 10-18(b) specifies seven product terms, one for each row in the state table. The input and

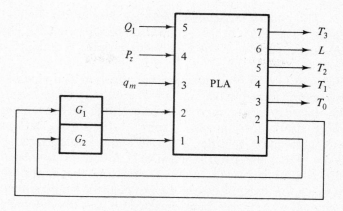

(a) Block diagram

Product term	Inputs					Outputs							Comments
	1	2	3	4	5	1	2	3	4	5	6	7	
1	0	0	0	–	–	–	–	1	–	–	–	–	$T_0 = 1$, $q_m = 0$
2	0	0	1	–	–	–	1	1	–	–	–	–	$T_0 = 1$, $q_m = 1$
3	0	1	–	–	–	1	–	–	1	–	–	–	$T_1 = 1$
4	1	0	–	–	0	1	1	–	–	1	–	–	$T_2 = 1$, $Q_1 = 0$
5	1	0	–	–	1	1	1	–	–	1	1	–	$T_2 = 1$, $L = 1$, $Q_1 = 1$
6	1	1	–	0	–	1	–	–	–	–	–	1	$T_3 = 1$, $P_z = 0$
7	1	1	–	1	–	–	–	–	–	–	–	1	$T_3 = 1$, $P_z = 1$

(b) PLA program table

Figure 10-18 PLA control for binary multiplier

output terminals are marked with numbers, and the variables applied to these numbered terminals are indicated in the block diagram. The comments are not part of the table but are included for clarification.

According to the rules established in Section 5-8, a no connection for a PLA path is indicated by a dash (–) in the table. The X's in the state table designate don't-care conditions and imply no connection for the PLA. The 0's in the output columns also indicate no connections to the OR gates within the PLA. The translation from the state table to a PLA program table is very simple: The X's in the input columns and the 0's in the output columns are changed to dashes, and all other entries remain the same. Note that the inputs to the PLA are the same as the present state and inputs in the state table. The outputs of the PLA are the same as the next state and outputs in the state table.

The procedure for designing control logic with a PLA should be evident from this example. From the specifications of the system, we first obtain a state table for

445

the controller. The number of states determines the number of flip-flops for the sequence register. The PLA is then connected to the sequence register and to the input and output variables. The PLA program table is obtained directly from the state table.

The PLA unit in a PLA control may be visualized as a control memory that stores control information for the system. The outputs of the sequence register, together with external inputs, may be considered to be an address for such a control memory. The outputs provide a control word for the data processor, and the next-state information specifies a partial value for the next address in the control memory. From this point of view, a PLA control may be classified as a microprogram control unit with the PLA replacing the ROM for the control memory. However, the organization of the two methods is different, although there is a certain amount of similarity between the PLA and the microprogram control methods.

The control examples introduced in this chapter demonstrate four methods of control logic design. These should not be considered the only possible methods. A resourceful designer may be able to formulate a control configuration to suit a particular application. This configuration may consist of a combination of methods or may constitute a control organization other than the ones presented here.

The design of the control logic for a digital computer follows the same procedure as outlined in this chapter. The role of the microprogram control in the organization of a general-purpose computer is presented in the next section. Chapter 11 presents the detailed design of a digital computer and shows how to implement its control unit by means of a hard-wired method, a PLA method, and a microprogram method.

10-8 MICROPROGRAM SEQUENCER

A microprogram control unit should be viewed as consisting of two parts: the control memory that stores the microinstructions and the associated circuits that control the generation of the next address. The address-generation part is sometimes called a microprogram *sequencer*, since it sequences the microinstructions in control memory. A microprogram sequencer can be constructed with MSI circuits to suit a particular application. However, just as general-purpose processor units are available in IC packages, so are general-purpose sequencers suited for the construction of microprogram control units. To guarantee a wide range of acceptability, an IC sequencer must provide an internal organization that can be adapted to a wide range of applications.*

A microprogram sequencer attached to a control memory inspects certain bits of the microinstruction, from which it determines the next address for control

---

*Some commercial microprogram sequencers are IC type 8X02 (Signetics), 9408 (Fairchild), and 2910 (Advanced Micro Devices).

memory. A typical sequencer provides the following address-sequencing capabilities:

1. Increments the present address for control memory.

2. Branches to an address as specified by the address field of the microinstruction.

3. Branches to a given address if a specified status bit is equal to 1.

4. Transfers control to a new address as specified by an external source.

5. Has a facility for subroutine calls and returns.

In most cases the microinstructions are read from control memory in succession. This type of sequencing can be easily accomplished by incrementing the address register of the control memory. In some microinstruction formats, each microinstruction contains an address field even for sequential addresses. This eliminates the need to increment the control memory address register, because the address field available in each microinstruction specifies the address of the next microinstruction. In any case, provision must be available for branching to an address out of normal sequence.

Once in a while, control must be transferred to a nonsequential microinstruction; thus, the sequencer must provide the capability for branching to any one of two addresses, depending on whether a status bit is 0 or 1. The simplest way to accomplish this is to branch to the address specified by the address field of the microinstruction if the status bit specified is equal to 1, but go to the next address in sequence if the status bit is equal to 0. This configuration requires the capability of incrementing the address register.

The sequencer transfers a new address for control memory to start executing a new macrooperation. The external address transfers control to the first microinstruction in a microprogram routine that executes the specified macrooperation.

Subroutines are programs used by other routines to accomplish a particular task. Subroutines can be called from any point within the main body of the microprogram. Frequently, many microprograms contain identical sections of code. Microinstructions can be saved by employing subroutines which use common sections of microcode. Microprograms that use subroutines must have a provision for storing the return address during a subroutine call and restoring the address during a subroutine return. This may be accomplished by placing the return address into a special register and then branching to the beginning of the subroutine. This special register can then become the address source for setting the address register for the return to the main routine. The best way to organize a register file that stores addresses for subroutine calls and returns is to use a last-in, first-out (LIFO) stack. The stack organization and its use in subroutine calls and returns are explained in more detail in Section 12-5.

The block diagram of a microprogram sequencer is shown in Fig. 10-19. It consists of a multiplexer that selects an address from four sources and routes it into a control address register. The output from CAR provides the address for the control memory. The contents of CAR are incremented and applied to the multiplexer and to the stack register file. The register selected in the stack is determined by the stack pointer. Inputs I_0, I_1, and I_2 specify the operation for the sequencer, and input T is a test point for a status bit. The address register can be cleared to zero to initialize the system and the clock pulses synchronize the loading into the registers.

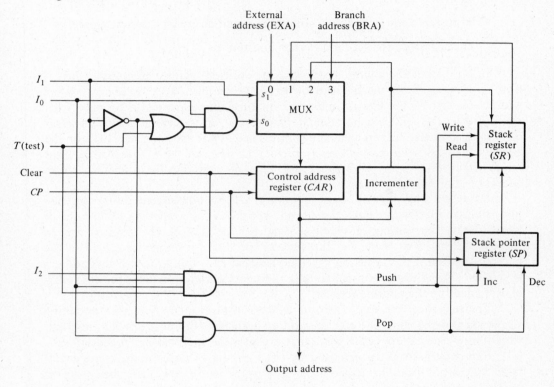

Function table

I_2	I_1	I_0	T	s_1	s_0	Operation	Comments
X	0	0	X	0	0	$CAR \leftarrow EXA$	Transfer external address
X	0	1	X	0	1	$CAR \leftarrow SR$	Transfer from register stack
X	1	0	X	1	0	$CAR \leftarrow CAR + 1$	Increment address
0	1	1	0	1	0	$CAR \leftarrow CAR + 1$	Increment address
0	1	1	1	1	1	$CAR \leftarrow BRA$	Transfer branch address
1	1	1	0	1	0	$CAR \leftarrow CAR + 1$	Increment address
1	1	1	1	1	1	$CAR \leftarrow BRA, SR \leftarrow CAR + 1$	Branch to subroutine

Figure 10-19 Typical microprogram sequencer organization

The function table listed in the diagram specifies the operation of the sequencer. Inputs I_1 and I_0 determine the selection variables for the multiplexer. An external address (EXA) is transferred into CAR when $I_1 I_0 = 00$. The transfer from the stack register (SR) occurs when $I_1 I_0 = 01$, and CAR is incremented when $I_1 I_0 = 10$. The T and I_2 inputs have no effect during these three operations and they are marked with don't-care X entries. When $I_1 I_0 = 11$, the sequencer executes a conditional branch operation dependent on the value of the test bit in T. If I_2 is also equal to 1, the operation is a conditional call to subroutine. In either case, CAR is incremented if the test bit T is 0. The branch address (BRA) is transferred to CAR if $T = 1$. Thus, with $I_1 I_0 = 11$, the sequencer branches to the BRA if the status bit in T is equal to 1, but increments CAR if the status bit is 0. The branch address normally comes from the address field of the microinstruction.

The conditional subroutine call ($I_2 = 1$) is similar to the conditional branch ($I_2 = 0$), except that the former uses the stack and the latter does not. The address stored in the stack during a subroutine call is taken from the incrementer. This is the address next in sequence, and it is called the *return address*. The return address is transferred back into CAR with a subroutine return operation ($I_1 I_0 = 01$).

The operation of the stack register and stack pointer will be better understood after reading Section 12-5. A register (or memory) stack is similar to a memory unit, except that the address for the stack is determined from the value in the stack-pointer register. The access to the stack is in a last-in, first-out sequence and is controlled by incrementing or decrementing the stack pointer. Initially, the stack pointer is cleared and is said to *point* at address 0 in the stack. The *write* or the transfer of information into the stack is called *push*. It consists of writing the input information into the stack at the address specified by the stack pointer and then incrementing the stack-pointer register. In this way, information is transferred into the stack, and the stack pointer points at the next empty location in the stack. The *read* or the transfer of information out of the stack is called *pop*. It consists of first decrementing the stack-pointer register and then reading out the contents of the register (or word) specified by the new value in the stack pointer.

A call to subroutine is executed when $I_2 I_1 I_0 = 111$ and $T = 1$. This causes a *push-stack* operation and a branch to the address specified by BRA. This is implemented by first storing the incremented value from CAR into the stack. When clock pulse CP goes through a positive-edge transition, the BRA address is transferred to CAR and the write input to the stack is inhibited. The stack-pointer register is incremented later when CP goes through its negative-edge transition. This is illustrated in Fig. 10-20(a).

The return from subroutine is executed when $I_1 I_0 = 01$. This causes a *pop-stack* operation and a branch to the address stored on top of the stack. This is implemented by first decrementing the stack-pointer register on the negative-edge transition of CP. The value in the stack, given by the address presently available in the stack pointer, is then read and transferred to CAR on the positive-edge transition of CP. This is illustrated in Fig. 10-20(b). Note that CAR is triggered

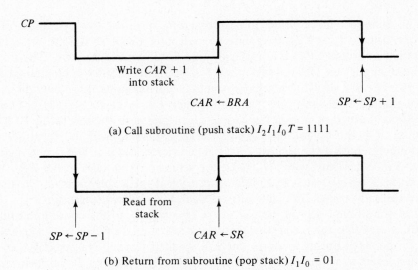

(a) Call subroutine (push stack) $I_2 I_1 I_0 T = 1111$

(b) Return from subroutine (pop stack) $I_1 I_0 = 01$

Figure 10-20 Stack operations in microprogram sequencer

during the positive edge and SP during the negative edge of a clock pulse. The stack pointer is incremented after the transfer into CAR and decremented prior to the transfer into CAR.

Microprogrammed CPU Organization

A digital computer consists of a central processor unit (CPU), a memory unit, and input-output devices. The CPU can be classified into two distinct but interactive functional sections. One section is the processing section and the other is the control section. A processor unit is a useful device for constructing the processor section of a CPU. The microprogram sequencer is a convenient element for constructing a microprogram control for a CPU. We now develop a computer CPU to show the usefulness of the microprogram sequencer defined in Fig. 10-19.

A block diagram of a microprogrammed computer is shown in Fig. 10-21. It consists of a memory unit, two processor units, a microprogram sequencer, a control memory, and few other digital functions. This configuration may be compared with the simple computer that was designed in Section 8-9 and whose block diagram is given in Fig. 8-16.

The memory unit stores the instructions and data supplied by the user through an input device. The data processor manipulates the data, and the address processor manipulates the address information received from memory. The two processors can be combined into one unit, but sometimes it is convenient to separate them in order to provide a distinct bus for the memory address. An instruction extracted from memory during the fetch cycle goes into the instruction register. The instruction-code bits in the instruction register specify a macrooperation for control memory. A code transformation is sometimes needed to convert

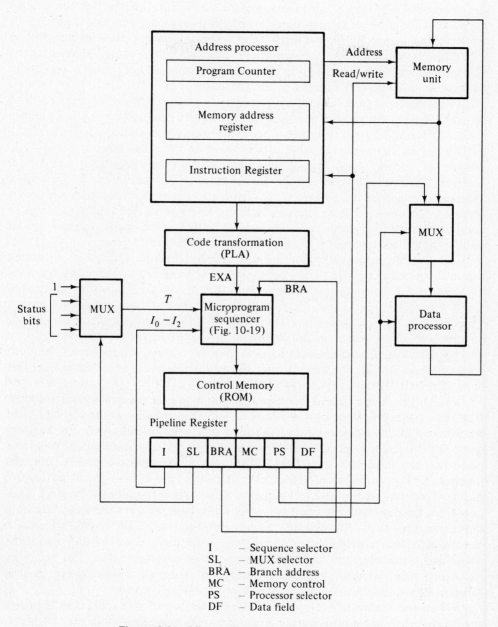

Figure 10-21 Microprogrammed computer organization

451

the operation-code bits of an instruction into a starting address for the control memory. This code transformation constitutes a mapping function and can be implemented with a ROM or a PLA. The mapping concept provides a flexibility for adding instructions or macrooperations for control memory as the need arises. The address generated in the code transformation mapping function is applied to the external address (*EXA*) input of the sequencer.

The microprogram control unit consists of the sequencer of Fig. 10-19, a control memory for storing the microinstructions, a multiplexer, and a pipeline register. The multiplexer selects one of many status bits and applies it to the *T* (test) input of the sequencer, One of the inputs to the multiplexer is always 1 to provide an unconditional branch operation. The pipeline register is not always necessary, because the outputs from control memory can go directly to the control inputs of the various units in the CPU. However, a pipeline register speeds up the control operation. It allows the next address to be generated and the output of control memory to change while the current control word in the pipeline register initiates the microoperations given by the present microinstruction.

A possible microinstruction format for the control memory is illustrated within the pipeline register. The I field consists of three bits and supplies the input information for the sequencer. The *SL* field selects a status bit for the multiplexer. The *BRA* field is the address field of the microinstruction and supplies a branch address (*BRA*) to the sequencer. These three fields of a microinstruction provide information to the sequencer to determine the next address for control memory. The sequencer generates the next address and the control memory reads the next microinstruction while the present microoperations are being executed in the other units of the CPU.

The other three fields in the microinstruction are for controlling the microoperations in the processor and memory units. The memory control (*MC*) field controls the address processor and the read and write operations in the memory unit. The processor select (*PS*) field controls the operations in the data processor unit. The last field is a data field (*DF*) used to introduce constants into the processor. The procedure of introducing data into the system from the control memory is a frequently used technique in many microprogrammed systems. Outputs from the data field may be used to set up control registers and introduce data in processor registers. For example, a constant in the data field may be added to a processor register to increment its contents by a specified value. Another use of the data field is in setting a sequence counter to a constant value. The sequence counter is then used to count the number of times a microprogram loop is traversed, as is usually required in a multiply or divide routine.

Once the hardware configuration of a microprogrammed CPU is established, the designer can use it to construct any one of many possible computer configurations. First, the instruction set for the computer is formulated and then a microprogram is written for control memory. One can change the microprogram in control memory if a different computer with a different set of instructions is desired. No hardware changes are required if the computer's specifications change;

the change is only in the control memory ROM. This involves removing the present ROM from its socket and replacing it with another unit with a different microprogram.

The construction of a CPU from LSI components as shown in Fig. 10-21 provides the freedom to define the instruction set for a computer system. It must be realized, however, that integrated circuits are available that contain a complete CPU within a single package. This type of CPU is called a *microprocessor*. If a microprocessor is used instead of a custom-made CPU, one must be satisfied with the fixed instruction set of the microprocessor chosen. In other words, a microprocessor is a ready-made CPU with a fixed set of computer instructions. A custom-made microprogrammed CPU is a flexible unit that allows the formulation of instructions suited to a particular application. Microprocessors are discussed in Chapter 12.

REFERENCES

1. Mano, M. M., *Computer System Architecture*. Englewood Cliffs, N. J.: Prentice-Hall, Inc., 1976

2. Rhyne, V. T., *Fundamentals of Digital Systems Design*. Englewood Cliffs, N. J.: Prentice-Hall, Inc., 1973

3. Chu, Y., *Computer Organization and Microprogramming*. Englewood Cliffs, N. J.: Prentice-Hall, Inc., 1972

4. Mick, J. R., and J. Brick, *Microprogramming Handbook*. Sunnyvale, Calif.: Advance Micro Devices, Inc., 1977

5. *Bipolar Microcomputer Components Data Book*. Dallas, Texas: Texas Instruments, Inc., 1977.

6. Agrawala, A.K., and T. G. Rauscher, *Foundations of Microprogramming*. New York: Academic Press, 1976.

7. *Signetics Field Programmable Logic Array: An Application Manual*. Sunnyvale, Calif.: Signetics Corp., 1977

8. Clare, C. R., *Designing Logic Systems Using State Machines*. New York: McGraw-Hill Book Co., 1973

9. Alexandridis, N. A., "Bit-sliced Microprocessor Architecture", *Computer*, Vol. 11, no. 6, (June 1978), pp 56-80.

PROBLEMS

10-1.   (a) Show that the ring-counter control of Fig. 7-22(a) is a special case of the one flip-flop per state control depicted in Fig. 10-2. Indicate how the latter can be reduced to the former. (b) Show that the counter and decoder control of Fig. 7-22(b) is a special case of the sequence register and decoder control depicted in Fig. 10-3. Indicate how the latter can be reduced to the former.

10-2.   What is the difference between hard-wired control and microprogram control? What are the advantages and disadvantages in each method?

10-3.   The adder-subtractor system designed in Section 10-3 employs an ALU. Redraw the system block diagram of Fig. 10-8 without using an ALU. Instead, use the adder-subtractor circuit of Fig. 9-10 and a register with complement, increment, and load capabilities. Revise the control outputs of Fig. 10-9(b).

10-4.   Go over the flowchart of Fig. 10-7 to find out if a negative zero may result at the end of the computation. A negative zero occurs if $A = 0$ and $A_s = 1$.

10-5.   Design a digital system that adds and subtracts two binary fixed-point numbers represented in sign-2's-complement form. Include an overflow indication.

10-6.   Revise the control state diagram of Fig. 10-9 if the value of C_{out} is checked at time T_4, instead of checking the value of E at time T_5.

10-7.   The number of states for the control of Fig. 10-9 can be reduced if the S variable is used together with q_a and q_s to determine the next state after the initial state. Also, register A can be complemented during the same state that E is cleared if E' is included in the control function for the complement operation. Show that the adder-subtractor system can be implemented with six control states.

10-8.   Derive the input functions for flip-flops B_s, A_s, and E of Fig. 10-8(a). Use JK flip-flops.

10-9.   Design the control specified by the state diagram of Fig. 10-15(a) by the one flip-flop per state method. Draw the logic diagram using gates and four D flip-flops.

10-10. Obtain a second listing for the binary microprogram of Table 10-3 by using 00 for ROM bits 13 and 14 every time that CAR is incremented unconditionally.

10-11. Redesign the input circuit of Fig. 10-10 by replacing the AND gates associated with q_a and q_s with a dual 2-to-1 line multiplexer with enable input.

10-12. The microprogram control unit of Fig. 10-10, together with the associated data processor of Fig. 10-8(a), is to be used for adding and subtracting two binary numbers in sign-2's-complement representation. The sign bits reside in the leftmost bit position of registers A and B. Since the signs are included with A and B, there is no need for A_s and B_s and variable S. Instead, let S now be a flip-flop that stores the carry C_n that goes into the sign-bit position, just as E stores the carry $C_{n+1} = C_{out}$ coming out of the sign-bit position. Let variables y and z be two control signals that set and clear an overflow flip-flop V. If an overflow occurs, V is set with control variable y. If no overflow occurs, V is cleared with control variable z.

(a) Write the microprogram in symbolic form.
(b) List the ROM truth table in binary.

10-13. Give a microinstruction in binary form for the control memory of Fig. 10-11 that will keep the system in a no-operation loop as long as the external address is the same as the address where the microinstruction is located in memory. The values that go into the status register are not important.

10-14. Write a microprogram in symbolic form for the system of Fig. 10-11 that checks the sign of the number stored in register $R1$. The number is in sign-2's complement representation. If the number is positive, it is divided by 2. If negative, it is multiplied by 2. If an overflow occurs, $R1$ is cleared to zero.

10-15. Write a microprogram that compares two unsigned binary numbers stored in $R1$ and $R2$. The register containing the smaller number is then cleared. If the two numbers are equal, both registers are cleared. Use the microprogram system of Fig. 10-11.

10-16. The processor of Fig. 9-16 is used for multiplying two unsigned binary numbers. The multiplicand is in $R1$, the multiplier is in $R3$, and the product is formed in $R2$ and $R3$. Register $R4$ holds a binary number equal to the number of bits in the multiplier. Derive the algorithm in flowchart form.

10-17. List the contents of registers E, A, Q, and P (Fig. 10-16) after each clock pulse during the process of multiplication of the two magnitudes 10111 (multiplicand) and 10011 (multiplier).

10-18. The control state diagram of Fig. 10-15(a) does not use variable Q_1 as a condition for state transition. Instead, Q_1 is used as part of a control function in the list of register transfers. Redesign the control so that Q_1 appears as a condition in the state diagram and removed from the list of control functions. Show that for this case the state diagram must have at least five states.

10-19. Determine the time it takes to process the multiplication operation in the digital system described in Fig. 10-15. Assume that the Q register has k bits and the interval between two clock pulses is t seconds.

10-20. Design the control logic of Fig. 10-16 using two T flip-flops and a decoder.

10-21. Change the P register of Fig. 10-16 to an up-counter with parallel load. Input T_2 will now increment the P register. What is the initial value that must be loaded into P at time T_1?

10-22. Prove that the multiplication of two n-digit numbers in any base r gives a product of no more than $2n$ digits in length. Show that this statement implies that no overflow can occur in the multiplier designed in Section 10-6.

10-23. Design the control specified in Fig. 10-9 by the sequence register and decoder method. Use three JK flip-flops G_3, G_2, and G_1.

10-24. Design the control specified in Fig. 10-9 using a sequence register and a PLA. List the PLA program table.

10-25. The register configuration and flowchart of a digital system that multiplies two unsigned binary numbers by the repeated addition method is shown in Fig. P10-25.
   (a) Convince yourself that the system multiplies the contents of A and B and places the product in register P.

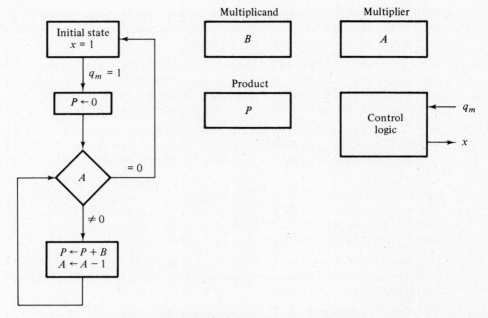

Figure P10-25 Multiplication by successive additions

(b) Let $A = 0100$ and $B = 0011$. Going through the steps in the flowchart, show that the system returns to the initial state, with register P having the product 1100.

(c) Draw a state diagram for the control and list the register transfers to be executed in each control state.

(d) Draw the block diagram of the data-processor part.

(e) Design the control by the one flip-flop per state method.

10-26. The following register-transfer operations specify a four-state control of the sequence register and decoder type. G is a 2-bit sequence register and T_0, T_1, T_2, and T_3 are the outputs of the decoder.

$$
\begin{aligned}
xT_0: & \quad G \leftarrow G + 1 \\
yT_0: & \quad G \leftarrow 10 \\
zT_0: & \quad G \leftarrow 11 \\
T_1 + T_2 + T_3: & \quad G \leftarrow G + 1
\end{aligned}
$$

(a) Draw the state diagram of the control.

(b) Design the sequence register with JK flip-flops.

10-27. A control unit has two inputs x and y and eight states. The control state diagram is shown in Fig. P10-27.

(a) Design the control using eight D flip-flops.

(b) Design the control using a register, a decoder, and a PLA.

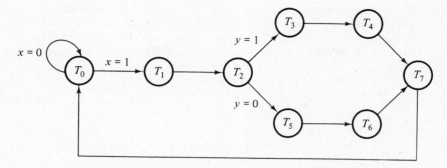

Figure P10-27 Control state diagram for problem 10-27

10-28. The state diagram of a control unit is shown in Fig. P10-28. It has four states and two inputs x and y. Design the control by the sequence register and decoder method with two JK flip-flops G_2 and G_1.

(a) Use the decoder outputs as conditions for the present states.

(b) Use the flip-flop outputs as conditions for the present states. Compare the two results and comment on the advantages and disadvantages in each case.

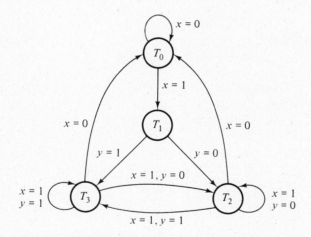

Figure P10-28 Control state diagram for problem 10-28

10-29. The pipeline register in Fig. 10-21 has one additional output labeled P for controlling the polarity of the T input in the sequencer. When $P = 0$, the value of the status bit selected by SL is applied to the T input. When $P = 1$, the complement of the selected status bit is applied to T.

(a) What does the polarity control P accomplish?

(b) Design the circuit that must be placed between the multiplexer selected by SL and the test input T.

10-30. The microprogrammed computer of Fig. 10-21 has a control address register (CAR) inside the sequencer and a pipeline register (PLR) in the output of control memory. The speed of operation can be improved if only one register is used. Compare the speed of operation by comparing the propagation delays encountered when the system uses:

(a) A CAR without a PLR.

(b) A PLR without a CAR.

Computer Design

11

11-1 INTRODUCTION

This chapter presents a small general-purpose digital computer starting from its functional specifications and culminating in its design. Although the computer is small, it is far from useless. Its scope is quite limited when compared with commercial electronic data-processing systems, yet it encompasses enough functional capabilities to demonstrate the design process. It is suitable for construction in the laboratory with ICs, and the finished product can be a useful system capable of processing digital data.*

The computer consists of a central processor unit, a memory unit, and a teletypewriter input-output unit. The logic design of the central processor unit will be derived here. The other two units are assumed to be available as finished products with known external characteristics.

The hardware design of a digital computer may be divided into three interrelated phases: system design, logic design, and circuit design. System design is concerned with the specifications and general properties of the system. This task includes the establishment of design objective and design philosophy, the formulation of computer instructions, and the investigation of its economic feasibility. The specifications of the computer structure are translated by the logic designer to provide the hardware implementation of the system. The circuit design specifies the components for the various logic circuits, memory circuits, electromechanical equipment, and power supplies. The computer hardware design is greatly influenced by the software system, which is normally developed concurrently and which constitutes an integral part of the total computer system.

The design of a digital computer is a complicated task. One cannot expect to cover all aspects of the design in one chapter. Here we are concerned with the system and logic design of a small digital computer whose specifications are formulated somewhat arbitrarily in order to establish a minimum configuration for

---

*The instructions for the computer are a subset of the instructions in the PDP-8 computer.

a very small, yet practical machine. The procedure outlined in this chapter can be useful in the logic design of more complicated systems.

The design process is divided into six phases:

1. The decomposition of the digital computer into registers which specify the general configuration of the system.

2. The specification of computer instructions.

3. The formulation of a timing and control network.

4. The listing of the register-transfer operations needed to execute all computer instructions.

5. The design of the processor section.

6. The design of the control section.

The design process is carried out by means of tabular listings that summarize the specifications and register-transfer operations in compact form. The processor section is defined by means of a block diagram consisting of registers and multiplexers. It is assumed that the reader has sufficient information to replace the blocks in the diagram with MSI circuits. The control section is designed by each of the three methods outlined in Chapter 10.

11-2 SYSTEM CONFIGURATION

The configuration of the computer is shown in Fig. 11-1. Each block represents a register, except for the memory unit, the master-clock generator, and the control logic. This configuration is assumed to satisfy the final system structure. In a practical situation, the designer starts with a tentative system configuration and constantly modifies it during the design process. The name of each register is written inside the block, together with a symbolic designation in parentheses.

The master-clock generator is a common clock-pulse source, usually an oscillator, which generates a periodic train of pulses. These pulses are fanned out by means of amplifiers and distributed over the entire system. Each pulse must reach every flip-flop and register at the same time. Phasing delays may be needed intermittently so that the difference in transmission delays is uniform throughout. The frequency of the pulses is a function of the speed with which the system operates. We shall assume a frequency of 1 megahertz, which gives one pulse every microsecond. This pulse frequency is chosen for the sake of having a round number and to avoid problems of circuit propagation delays.

The memory unit has a capacity of 4096 words of 16 bits each. This capacity is large enough for meaningful processing. A smaller size may be used if the computer is to be constructed in the laboratory under economic restrictions. Twelve bits of an instruction are needed to specify the address of an operand,

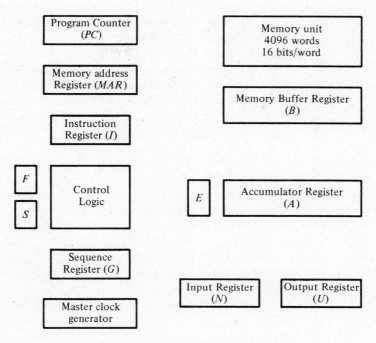

Figure 11-1 Block diagram of digital computer

TABLE 11-1 List of registers for computer

Symbolic designation	Name	Number of bits	Function
A	Accumulator register	16	Processor register
B	Memory buffer register	16	Holds contents of memory word
PC	Program counter	12	Holds address of next instruction
MAR	Memory address register	12	Holds address of memory word
I	Instruction register	4	Holds current operation-code
E	Extension flip-flop	1	Accumulator extension
F	Fetch flip-flop	1	Controls fetch and execute cycles
S	Start-stop flip-flop	1	Starts and stops computer
G	Sequence register	2	Provides timing signals
N	Input register	9	Holds information from input device
U	Output register	9	Holds information for output device

which leaves four bits for the operation part of the instruction. The access time of the memory is assumed to be less than 1 microsecond so that a word can be read or written during the interval between two clock pulses.

The part of the digital computer to be designed is decomposed into register subunits. The following paragraphs explain why each register is needed and what function it performs. A list of the registers and a brief description of their functions is presented in Table 11-1. Registers that hold memory words are 16 bits long. Those that hold an address are 12 bits long. Other registers have different numbers of bits, depending on their function.

Memory Address and Memory Buffer Registers

The memory address register, MAR, is used to address specific memory locations. MAR is loaded from PC when an instruction is to be read from memory, and from the 12 least significant bits of the B register when an operand is to be read from memory. Memory buffer register B holds the word read from or written into memory. The operation part of an instruction word placed in B is transferred into the I register, and the address part is left in the B register for transfer to MAR. An operand word placed in the B register is accessible for operation with the A register. A word to be stored in memory must be loaded into the B register before a write operation is initiated.

Program Counter

Program counter PC holds the address of the next instruction to be read from memory. This register goes through a step-by-step counting sequence and causes the computer to read successive instructions previously stored in memory. When the program calls for a transfer to another location or for skipping the next instruction in sequence, the PC is modified accordingly, causing the program to continue from a memory location out of the counting sequence. To read an instruction, the contents of PC are transferred to MAR and a read operation is initiated. The program counter is always incremented by 1 while a memory write operation reads the present instruction. Therefore, the address of the next instruction, one higher than the one presently being executed in the processor, is always available in PC.

Accumulator Register

Accumulator register A is a processor register that operates on data previously stored in memory. This register is used to execute most instructions and for accepting data from the input device or transferring data to the output device. The A register, together with the B register, makes up the bulk of the processor unit for the computer. Although most data processing systems include more registers for the processor unit, we have chosen to include only one accumulator here in order not to complicate the design. With a single accumulator as the arithmetic element, it is possible to implement only the add operation. Other arithmetic operations such as subtraction, multiplication, and division must be implemented with a sequence of instructions that form a subroutine.

Instruction Register

Instruction register I holds the operation-code bits of the current instruction. This register has only four bits since the operation-code of instructions is four bits long. The operation-code bits are transferred to the I register from the B register, while the address part of the instruction is left in B. The operation-code part must be taken out of the B register because an operand read from memory into the B register will destroy the previously held instruction. The operation part of the instruction is needed by the control to determine what is to be done to the operand just read.

Sequence Register

Sequence register G is a counter that produces the timing signals for the computer. The G register is decoded to supply four timing variables for the control unit. The timing variables, together with other control variables, produce the control functions that initiate all the microoperations for the computer.

E, *F*, and *S* Flip-flops

Each of these flip-flops is considered a one-bit register. The E flip-flop is an extension of the A register. It is used during shifting operations, receives the end carry during addition, and otherwise is a useful flip-flop that can simplify the data processing capabilities of the computer. The F flip-flop distinguishes between the fetch and execute cycles. When F is 0, the word read from memory is treated as an instruction. When F is 1, the word is treated as an operand. S is a start-stop flip-flop that can be cleared by program control and manipulated manually. When S is 1, the computer runs according to a sequence determined by the program stored in memory. When S is 0, the computer stops its operation.

Input and Output Registers

The input-output (I/0) device is not shown in the block diagram of Fig. 11-1. It is assumed to be a teletypewriter unit with a keyboard and a printer. The teletypewriter sends and receives serial information. Each quantity of information has 8 bits of an alphanumeric code. The serial information from the keyboard is shifted into the input register. The serial information for the printer is stored in the output register. These two registers communicate with the teletypewriter serially and with the accumulator register in parallel.

Input register N consists of nine bits. Bits 1 through 8 hold alphanumeric input information; bit 9 is a control bit called an input *flag*. The flag bit is set when a new character is available from the input device and cleared when the character is accepted by the computer. The flag bit is needed to synchronize the slow rate by which the input device operates compared to the high-speed circuits in the computer. The process of information transfer is as follows. Initially, the flag bit in N_9 is cleared. When a key is struck on the keyboard, an 8-bit code is shifted into the input register $(N_1 - N_8)$. As soon as the shift operation is completed, the flag bit in N_9 is set to 1. The computer checks the flag bit; if it is 1, the character code from the N register is transferred in parallel into the A register and the flag bit is cleared. Once the flag is cleared, a new character can be shifted into the N register by striking another key.

Output register U works in a similar fashion, but the direction of information flow is reversed. Initially, the output flag in U_9 is set to 1. The computer checks the flag bit; if it is 1, a character code from the A register is transferred in parallel to the output register $(U_1 - U_8)$ and the flag bit U_9 is cleared to 0. The output device accepts the coded information and prints the corresponding character; when the operation is completed, it sets the flag bit to 1. The computer does not load a new character into the output register when the flag is 0, because this condition indicates that the output device is in the process of printing the previous character.

11-3 COMPUTER INSTRUCTIONS

The number of instructions available in a computer and their efficiency in solving the problem at hand are a good indication of how well the system designer foresaw the intended application of the machine. Medium- to large-scale computing systems may have hundreds of instructions, while most small computers limit the list to less than 100. The instructions must be chosen carefully to supply sufficient capabilities to the system for solving a wide range of data processing problems. The minimum requirements of such a list should include a capability for storing and loading words from memory, a sufficient set of arithmetic and logic operations, some address-modification capabilities, unconditional branching and branching under test conditions, register manipulation capabilities, and I/O instructions. The instruction list chosen for our computer is believed to be close to the absolute minimum required for a restricted but practical data processor.

The formulation of a set of instructions for the computer goes hand in hand with the formulation of the formats for data and instruction words. A memory word consists of 16 bits. A word may represent either a unit of data or an instruction. The formats of data words are shown in Fig. 11-2. Data for arithmetic operations are represented by a 15-bit binary number, with the sign in the 16th bit position. Negative numbers are assumed to be in their 2's-complement equivalent. Logical operations are performed on individual bits of the word, with bit 16 treated as any other bit. When the computer communicates with the I/O device, the

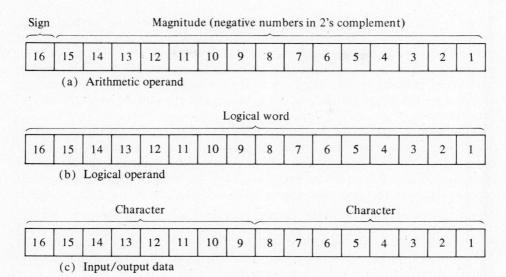

Sign   Magnitude (negative numbers in 2's complement)

16	15	14	13	12	11	10	9	8	7	6	5	4	3	2	1

(a) Arithmetic operand

Logical word

16	15	14	13	12	11	10	9	8	7	6	5	4	3	2	1

(b) Logical operand

Character   Character

16	15	14	13	12	11	10	9	8	7	6	5	4	3	2	1

(c) Input/output data

Figure 11-2   Data formats

information transferred is considered to be 8-bit alphanumeric characters. Two such characters can be accommodated in one computer word.

The formats of instruction words are shown in Fig. 11-3. The operation part of the instruction contains four bits; the meaning of the remaining 12 bits depends on the operation-code encountered. A *memory-reference* instruction uses the remaining 12 bits to specify an address. A *register-reference* instruction implies an

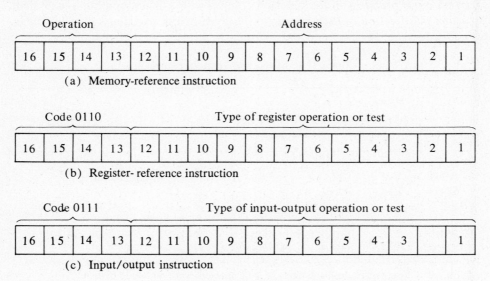

Operation   Address

16	15	14	13	12	11	10	9	8	7	6	5	4	3	2	1

(a) Memory-reference instruction

Code 0110   Type of register operation or test

16	15	14	13	12	11	10	9	8	7	6	5	4	3	2	1

(b) Register- reference instruction

Code 0111   Type of input-output operation or test

16	15	14	13	12	11	10	9	8	7	6	5	4	3		1

(c) Input/output instruction

Figure 11-3   Instruction formats

operation on, or a test of, the A or E register. An operand from memory is not needed; therefore, the 12 least significant bits are used to specify the operation or test to be executed. A register-reference instruction is recognized by the code 0110 in the operation part. Similarly, an *input-output* instruction does not need a reference to memory and is recognized by the operation code 0111. The remaining 12 bits are used to specify the particular device and the type of operation or test performed.

Only four bits of the instruction are available for the operation code. It would seem, then, that the computer is restricted to a maximum of 16 distinct operations. However, since register-reference and input-output instructions use the remaining 12 bits as part of the operation-code, the total number of instructions can exceed 16. In fact, the total number of instructions chosen for the computer is 22.

Of the 16 distinct operations that can be formulated with four bits, only eight have been utilized by the computer because the leftmost bit of all instructions (bit 16) is always a 0. This leaves open the possibility of adding new instructions and extending the computer capabilities if desired.

The six memory-reference instructions for the computer are listed in Table 11-2. The symbolic designation is a three-letter word and represents an abbreviation intended for use by programmers and users when writing symbolic programs for the computer. The hexadecimal code listed is an equivalent hexadecimal number of the binary code adopted for the operation-code. A memory-reference instruction uses one hexadecimal digit (4 bits) for the operation-code; the remaining three hexadecimal digits (12 bits) of the instruction represent an address designated by the letter m. Each instruction has a brief word description and is specified more precisely in the function column with a macrooperation statement. A further clarification of each instruction is given below, together with an explanation of its use.

TABLE 11-2   Memory-reference instructions

Symbol	Hexa-decimal code	Description	Function
AND	0 m*	AND to A	$A \leftarrow A \wedge M$*
ADD	1 m	Add to A	$A \leftarrow A + M, E \leftarrow$ Carry
STO	2 m	Store in A	$M \leftarrow A$
ISZ	3 m	Increment and skip if zero	$M \leftarrow M + 1$, if $(M + 1 = 0)$ then $(PC \leftarrow PC + 1)$
BSB	4 m	Branch to subroutine	$M \leftarrow PC + 5000, PC \leftarrow m + 1$
BUN	5 m	Branch unconditionally	$PC \leftarrow m$

*m is the address part of the instruction. M is the memory word addressed by m.

AND to *A*

This is a logic operation that performs the AND operation on corresponding pairs of bits in *A*, with the memory word *M* specified by the address part of the instruction. The result of the operation is left in register *A*, replacing its previous contents. Any computer must have a basic set of logic operations for manipulating nonnumerical data. The most common logic operations found in computer instructions are AND, OR, exclusive-OR, and complement. Here we use only the AND and complement. The latter is included as a register-reference instruction. These two logic operations constitute a minimal set from which all other logic operations can be derived, because together the AND and the complement perform a NAND operation. In Section 4-7 we saw that this is a universal operation from which any other logic operation can be obtained.

ADD to *A*

This instruction adds the contents of the memory word *M*, specified by the address part of the instruction, to the present contents of register *A*. The addition is done assuming that negative numbers are in their 2's-complement form. This requires that the sign bit be added in the same way as all other bits are added. The end-carry out of the sign-bit position is transferred to the *E* flip-flop. This instruction, together with the register-reference instructions, is sufficient for writing programs to implement all other arithmetic operations. Subtraction is achieved by complementing and incrementing the subtrahend. Multiplication is achieved by adding and shifting. The increment and shift are register-reference instructions.

The ADD instruction must be used for loading a word from memory into the *A* register. This is done by first clearing the *A* register with the register-reference instruction CLA (defined in Table 11-3). The required word is then loaded from memory by adding it to the cleared *A* register.

STORE in *A*

This instruction stores the contents of the *A* register into the memory word specified by the instruction address. The first three memory-reference instructions are used to manipulate data between memory words and the *A* register. The next three instructions are control instructions that cause a change in normal program sequence.

Increment and Skip if Zero (ISZ)

The increment-and-skip instruction is useful for address modification and for counting the number of times a program loop is executed. A negative number previously stored in memory at address *m* is read by the ISZ instruction. This number is incremented by 1 and stored back into memory. If, after it is incremented, the number reaches 0, the next instruction is skipped. Thus, at the end of a program loop, one inserts an ISZ instruction followed by a branch unconditionally (BUN) instruction to the beginning of the program loop. If the stored number does not reach 0, the program returns to execute the loop again. If it reaches 0, the next instruction (BUN) is skipped and the program continues to execute instructions after the program loop.

Branch Unconditionally (BUN)

This instruction transfers control unconditionally to the instruction at the location specified by the address part m. Remember that the program counter holds the address of the next instruction to be read and executed. Normally, the PC is incremented to give the address of the next instruction in sequence. The programmer has the prerogative of specifying any other instruction out of sequence by using the BUN instruction. This instruction tells the computer to take the address part m and transfer it into PC. The address of the next instruction to be executed is now in PC and is the one which was previously the address part of the BUN instruction.

The BUN instruction is listed with the memory-reference instructions because it needs an address part m. However, it does not need a reference to memory to access a memory word (designated by the symbol M), as is required by the other memory-reference instructions.

Branch to Subroutine (BSB)

This instruction is useful for branching to a subroutine portion of a program. When executed, the instruction stores the address of the next instruction in sequence which is presently held in PC (called the *return address*) into the memory word specified by the address part of the instruction. It also stores the operation code of BUN (hexadecimal 5) in the same memory location. The contents of the address part m plus 1 are transferred into PC to start executing the subroutine program at this location. After the subroutine is executed, control is transferred back to the calling program by means of a BUN instruction placed at the end of the subroutine.

The process of branching to a subroutine and the return to the calling program is demonstrated in Fig. 11-4 by means of a specific numerical example. The calling program is now in location 32. The subroutine program starts at location 65. The BSB instruction causes a transfer to the subroutine, and the last instruction in the subroutine causes a branch back to location 33 in the calling program. The numerical example in Fig. 11-4 shows a BSB instruction in location 32 with an address part m equal to binary 64. While this instruction is being executed, PC holds the address of the next instruction in sequence, which is 33.

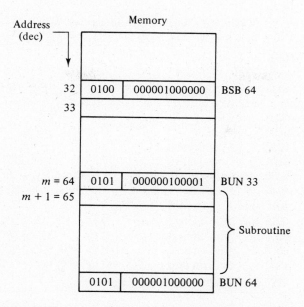

Figure 11-4 Demonstration of branch-to-subroutine instruction

The BSB instruction performs the macrooperation (see Table 11-2):

$$M \leftarrow PC + 5000, \quad PC \leftarrow m + 1$$

The contents of *PC* plus hexadecimal 5000 (code for BUN) are transferred into location 64. This transfer produces an instruction BUN 33. The address part of the instruction is incremented and placed in *PC*. *PC* now holds the binary equivalent of 65, so the computer starts executing the subroutine at this location. The last instruction in the subroutine is BUN 64. When this instruction is executed, control is transferred to the instruction in location 64. But in address 64, there is now an instruction that branches back to address 33. The address stored in location 64 by the BSB instruction will always have the proper return address no matter where the BSB instruction is located. In this way, the subroutine return is always to a location one higher than the location of the BSB instruction. Note that the address number of the BUN instruction placed at the end of the subroutine must always be equal to the address number where the return address is temporarily stored, which is 64 in this case.

Register-reference Instructions

The 12 register-reference instructions for the computer are listed in Table 11-3. Each register-reference instruction has.an operation code 0110 (hexadecimal 6) and contains a single 1 in one of the remaining 12 bits of the instruction. These

TABLE 11-3 Register-reference instructions

Symbol	Hexa-decimal code	Description	Function
CLA	6800	Clear A	$A \leftarrow 0$
CLE	6400	Clear E	$E \leftarrow 0$
CMA	6200	Complement A	$A \leftarrow \bar{A}$
CME	6100	Complement E	$E \leftarrow \bar{E}$
SHR	6080	Shift-right A and E	$A \leftarrow \text{shr } A, A_{16} \leftarrow E, E \leftarrow A_1$
SHL	6040	Shift-left A and E	$A \leftarrow \text{shl } A, A_1 \leftarrow E, E \leftarrow A_{16}$
INC	6020	Increment A	$A \leftarrow A + 1$
SPA	6010	Skip on positive A	If $(A_{16} = 0)$ then $(PC \leftarrow PC + 1)$
SNA	6008	Skip on negative A	If $(A_{16} = 1)$ then $(PC \leftarrow PC + 1)$
SZA	6004	Skip on zero A	If $(A = 0)$ then $(PC \leftarrow PC + 1)$
SZE	6002	Skip on zero E	If $(E = 0)$ then $(PC \leftarrow PC + 1)$
HLT	6001	Halt computer	$S \leftarrow 0$

instructions are specified with four hexadecimal digits which represent all 16 bits of an instruction word. The first seven instructions perform an operation on the A or E register and are self-explanatory. The next four are skip instructions used for program control, conditioned on certain status bits. To skip the next instruction, the PC is incremented by 1 once again. The first increment occurs when the present instruction is read. In this way, the next instruction read from memory is two locations up from the location of the present (skip) instruction.

The status bits for the skip instructions are the sign bit in A, which is in flip-flop A_{16}, and a zero condition for A or E. If the designated status condition is present, the next instruction in sequence is skipped; otherwise, the computer continues from the next instruction in sequence because PC is not incremented.

The halt instruction is usually placed at the end of a program if one wishes to stop the computer. Its execution clears the start-stop flip-flop, which prevents further operations.

Input-Output Instructions

The computer has four input-output instructions and they are listed in Table 11-4. These instructions have an operation code 0111 (hexadecimal 7), and each contains a 1 in only one of the remaining 12 bits of the instruction word. The input-output instructions are specified with four hexadecimal digits starting with 7.

The INP instruction transfers the input character from N to A and also clears the input flag in N_9. The OUT instruction transfers an 8-bit character code from A into the output register and also clears the output flag in U_9. The two skip instructions check the corresponding status flags and cause a skip of the next

TABLE 11-4 Input-output instructions

Symbol	Hexadecimal code	Description	Function
SKI	7800	Skip on input flag	If $(N_9 = 1)$ then $(PC \leftarrow PC + 1)$
INP	7400	Input to A	$A_{1-8} \leftarrow N_{1-8}, N_9 \leftarrow 0$
SKO	7200	Skip on output flag	If $(U_9 = 1)$ then $(PC \leftarrow PC + 1)$
OUT	7100	Output from A	$U_{1-8} \leftarrow A_{1-8}, U_9 \leftarrow 0$

instruction if the flag bit is 1. The instruction that is skipped is normally a BUN instruction. The BUN instruction is not skipped if the flag bit is 0; this causes a branch back to the skip instruction to check the flag again. If the flag bit is 1, the BUN instruction is skipped and an input or output operation is executed. Thus, the computer stays in a two-instruction loop (skip on flag and branch back to previous instruction) until the flag bit is set by the external device. The next instruction in sequence must be an input or output instruction.

11-4 TIMING AND CONTROL

All operations in the computer are synchronized by the master-clock generator whose clock pulses are applied to all flip-flops in the system. In addition, a certain number of timing variables are available in the control unit to sequence the operation in the proper order. These timing variables are designated t_0, t_1, t_2, and t_3 and are shown in Fig. 11-5. The clock pulses occur once every microsecond (μs). Each timing variable is 1 μs long and occurs once every 4 μs. We assume that the triggering of flip-flops occurs during the negative edge of the clock pulses. By applying one of the timing variables to the enable input of a given register, we can control the specific clock pulse that triggers the register. The timing variables repeat continuously in such a way that t_0 always appears after t_3. Four timing variables are sufficient for the execution of any instruction in the computer we are considering here. In other situations, it may be necessary to employ a different number of timing variables.

We assume that the memory access time is less than 1 μs. A memory read or write operation can be initiated with one of the timing variables when it goes high. The memory operation will be completed by the time the next clock pulse arrives.

The digital computer operates in discrete steps controlled by the timing signals. An instruction is read from memory and executed in registers by a sequence of microoperations. When the control receives an instruction, it generates the appropriate control functions for the required microoperations. A block diagram of the control logic is shown in Fig. 11-6. An instruction read from memory is placed in the memory buffer register B. The instruction has an operation code of 4 bits, designated by the symbol OP. If it is a memory-reference instruction, it has

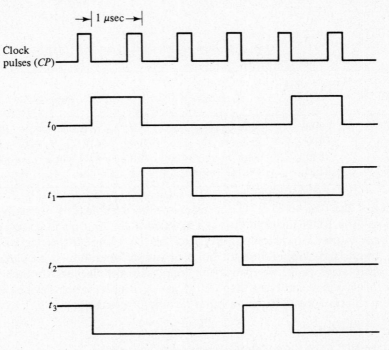

Figure 11-5 Computer timing signals

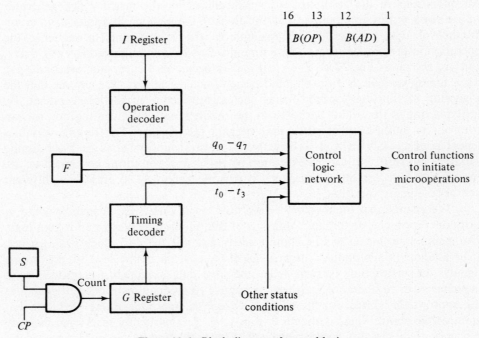

Figure 11-6 Block diagram of control logic

an address part designated by the symbol AD. The operation code is always transferred to the instruction register I. The operation code in I is decoded into eight outputs q_0–q_7, the subscript number being equal to the hexadecimal code for the operation. The G register is a 2-bit counter that continuously counts the clock pulses as long as start-stop flip-flop S is set. The outputs of the G register are decoded into the four timing variables t_0–t_3. The F flip-flop distinguishes between the fetch and execute cycles. Other status conditions are sometimes needed to determine the sequence of control. The outputs of the control logic network initiate all microoperations for the computer. The block diagram of the control logic is helpful in visualizing the control unit of the computer when the register-transfer operations are derived during the logic design process.

The control logic network is a combinational circuit consisting of a random connection of gates. Its implementation constitutes a hard-wired control. We shall see in Section 11-7 that the control part of the computer can also be implemented with programmable logic arrays. The PLA configuration will replace the control logic network as well as the operation and timing decoders. It will also be shown in Section 11-7 that the control can be partially implemented with a microprogram unit. The microprogram control configuration will replace the control logic network, the two decoders, and the I and G registers.

11-5   EXECUTION OF INSTRUCTIONS

Up to this point, we have considered the system design of the computer. We have specified the register configuration, the set of computer instructions, a timing sequence, and the configuration of the control unit. In this section, we start with the logic design phase of the computer. The first step is to specify the microoperations, together with the control functions, needed to execute each machine instruction.

The register-transfer operations describe in concise form the process of information transfer within the registers of the computer. Each statement in the description consists of a control function, followed by a colon, followed by one or more microoperations in symbolic notation. The control function is a Boolean function whose variables are the timing signals t_0–t_3, the decoded operation q_0–q_7, and certain status-bit conditions. The microoperations are specified in accordance with the symbolic notation defined in the register-transfer method.

Once a "start" switch is activated, the computer sequence follows a basic pattern. An instruction whose address is in PC is read from memory. Its operation part is transferred to register I, and PC is incremented by 1 to prepare it for the address of the next instruction. If the instruction is a memory-reference type, it may be necessary to access the memory again to read an operand. Thus, words read from memory into the B register can be either instructions or data. The F flip-flop is used to distinguish between the two. When $F = 0$, the word read from memory is interpreted to be an instruction and the computer is said to be in an instruction *fetch* cycle. When $F = 1$, the word read from memory is taken as an operand and the computer is said to be in a data *execute* cycle.

Fetch Cycle

An instruction is read from memory during the fetch cycle. The register-transfer relations that specify this process are:

$$F't_0: \quad MAR \leftarrow PC$$
$$F't_1: \quad B \leftarrow M, PC \leftarrow PC + 1$$
$$F't_2: \quad I \leftarrow B(OP)$$

When $F = 0$, timing signals t_0, t_1, and t_2 initiate a sequence of operations that transfer the contents of PC into MAR, initiate a memory read, increment PC, and transfer the operation code of the instruction to the I register. All microoperations are executed when the control function is logic 1 and when a clock pulse occurs. The microoperations in registers and the transfer of the memory word into B are executed during the negative edge of a clock pulse. This occurs just prior to the time that the specified timing variable goes to 0.

The operation code in the I register is decoded at time t_3. The next step depends on the value of q_i, $i = 0, 1, \ldots, 7$, that produces a 1 in the output of the decoder. If the decoded output is a memory-reference instruction, an operand may be needed. If not, the instruction can be executed during time t_3.

The BUN instruction and the register-reference and input-output instructions do not need a second access to memory. When an operation code 0, 1, 2, 3, or 4 is encountered, the computer has to go to an execute cycle to access the memory again. This condition is detected from the operation decoder which causes a transfer to the execute cycle by setting F to 1:

$$F'(q_0 + q_1 + q_2 + q_3 + q_4)t_3: \quad F \leftarrow 1$$

The register-transfer operations common to all instructions during the fetch cycle are listed in Table 11-5.

TABLE 11-5   Register-transfer operations during fetch cycle

$F't_0$:	$MAR \leftarrow PC$	Transfer instruction address
$F't_1$:	$B \leftarrow M, PC \leftarrow PC + 1$	Read instruction, increment PC
$F't_2$:	$I \leftarrow B(OP)$	Transfer operation code
$F'(q_0 + q_1 + q_2 + q_3 + q_4)t_3$:	$F \leftarrow 1$	Go to execute cycle
$q_5 t_3$:	$PC \leftarrow B(AD)$	Branch unconditionally (BUN)
$q_6 t_3$:	See Table 11-8	Register-reference instruction
$q_7 t_3$:	See Table 11-9	Input-output instruction

The BUN instruction has an operation code 5, and its corresponding output from the operation decoder is q_5. This instruction does not need an operand from memory, even though it is listed as a memory-reference instruction. It merely specifies that the next instruction be taken from a location given by the address part m. The address part of the instruction is in $B(AD)$ at time t_3 of the fetch cycle. The instruction can be executed during the fetch cycle at this time:

$$q_5 t_3: \quad PC \leftarrow B(AD)$$

There is no need to include F in the control function because the only time that q_5 can be 1 is during the fetch cycle. The microoperation that executes the instruction specifies a transfer of bits 1 through 12 of register B into the PC. The next timing variable after t_3 is always t_0. Since F remains 0 for this instruction, the computer returns to the beginning of the fetch cycle to read the instruction given by PC.

The register-reference instructions are recognized from the decoder output q_6, and the input-output instructions from q_7. Since these instructions require only one more microoperation for their execution, they can be terminated at time t_3 during the fetch cycle. This fact is indicated in Table 11-5. The specific microoperations are listed in later tables.

Execute Cycle

Flip-flop F is equal to 1 during the execute cycle. The four timing variables that occur during this cycle perform the microoperations for executing one of the memory-reference instructions. The instruction to be executed is specified by variable q_i, $i = 0, 1, 2, 3, 4$, available from the operation decoder. At the end of the fetch cycle, the address part of the instruction is in bits 1 through 12 of register B, symbolized by $B(AD)$. This address is transferred to MAR at the beginning of the execute cycle to serve as the memory address for the subsequent memory word:

$$F t_0: \quad MAR \leftarrow B(AD)$$

The instructions that need an operand from memory are the AND (q_0), ADD (q_1), and ISZ (q_3). The other two instructions, STO (q_2) and BSB (q_4), store a value into memory and are excluded during the next memory read operation:

$$F(q_0 + q_1 + q_3)t_1: \quad B \leftarrow M$$

The particular decoded instruction is executed with timing variables t_2 and t_3. At time t_3, the F flip-flop is cleared for the computer to return to the fetch cycle:

$$F t_3: \quad F \leftarrow 0$$

The next timing variable after t_3 is t_0. But now F is equal to 0, so the next control function is $F' t_0$. This is the first control function in the fetch cycle. Thus, after executing the current instruction, control always returns to the fetch cycle to read the next instruction whose address is in PC. The common operations performed during the execute cycle are listed in Table 11-6.

The five memory-reference instructions and their corresponding register-transfer operations are listed in Table 11-7. These instructions are executed when $F = 1$ and with timing variables t_2 and t_3. The decoded operation q_i determines the particular instruction that is executed.

TABLE 11-6   Common operations for execute cycle

Ft_0:	$MAR \leftarrow B(AD)$	Transfer address part
$F(q_0 + q_1 + q_3)t_1$:	$B \leftarrow M$	Read operand
$F(t_2 + t_3)$:	See Table 11-7	Execute memory-reference instruction
Ft_3:	$F \leftarrow 0$	Return to fetch cycle

TABLE 11-7   Execution of memory-reference instructions

AND	Fq_0t_3:	$A \leftarrow A \wedge B$	AND microoperation
ADD	Fq_1t_3:	$A \leftarrow A + B, E \leftarrow$ carry	Add microoperation
STO	Fq_2t_2:	$B \leftarrow A$	Transfer A to B
	Fq_2t_3:	$M \leftarrow B$	Store in memory
ISZ	Fq_3t_2:	$B \leftarrow B + 1$	Increment memory word
	Fq_3t_3:	$M \leftarrow B$	Store back in memory
	$Fq_3B_zt_3$:	$PC \leftarrow PC + 1$	Skip if $B_z = 1$ $(B = 0)$
BSB	Fq_4t_2:	$B(AD) \leftarrow PC, B(OP) \leftarrow 0101,$	Transfer return address,
		$PC \leftarrow MAR$	transfer address to PC
	Fq_4t_3:	$M \leftarrow B, PC \leftarrow PC + 1$	Store return address, increment
			address in PC

The AND and ADD instructions are executed with timing variable t_3, although they could use timing variable t_2 instead. The operand from memory has been transferred to B with timing variable t_1. The corresponding operation can be performed now between the B and A registers.

The STO instruction specifies a transfer of the contents of A into the memory word whose address was transferred to MAR with timing variable t_0. The contents of A are first transferred into B, and a write operation transfers the contents of B into the memory word specified by MAR:

$$Fq_2t_2: \quad B \leftarrow A$$

$$Fq_2t_3: \quad M \leftarrow B$$

The ISZ instruction is executed with the following microoperations:

$$Fq_3t_2: \quad B \leftarrow B + 1$$

$$Fq_3t_3: \quad M \leftarrow B$$

$$Fq_3B_zt_3: \quad PC \leftarrow PC + 1 \qquad B_z = 1 \text{ if } B = 0$$

The word from location M was placed in B during time t_1 (see Table 11-6). The B register is incremented at time t_2 and the new value is stored back in memory. All this time MAR does not change, so it always specifies the address of M. Remember that a memory word cannot be incremented while residing in memory. It must be transferred to a processor register where the counting can be implemented. While the incremented number is being stored in memory, its value in B is checked; if it is 0, PC is incremented to cause a skip of one instruction. Variable B_z used in the last statement above is a zero-detect variable and is equal to binary 1 if register B contains an all-0's number.

The BSB instruction is the most complicated instruction available in the computer. A possible way to execute this instruction is as follows:

$$Fq_4t_2: \quad B(AD) \leftarrow PC, B(OP) \leftarrow 0101, PC \leftarrow MAR$$

$$Fq_4t_3: \quad M \leftarrow B, PC \leftarrow PC + 1$$

The return address available in PC is transferred to the address part of register B and the code 0101 (BUN) is transferred to the operation-code part of the same register. Remember that the address register MAR contains the address part of the instruction designated by m. The transfer from MAR to PC results in transferring m into PC. All this is done during timing variable t_2. The return address is stored in memory at time t_3. PC is also incremented at this time, so the instruction to be read during the next fetch cycle will be from location $m + 1$.

Register-reference Instructions

The register microoperations that execute the register-reference instructions are listed in Table 11-8. These instructions are recognized from operation decoder output q_6 and are executed during time t_3 of the fetch cycle. For convenience, we define a new variable $r = q_6t_3$ and use it in all register-reference control functions. The rest of the control function is determined from one of the bits in the B register, where the rest of the instruction resides at this time. For example, the instruction CLA has the hexadecimal code 6800, which corresponds to a binary code 0110 1000 0000 0000. The operation code is decoded from the I register and is equal to q_6. Bit 12 in the B register is 1; so the control function that executes this instruction is $q_6t_3B_{12} = rB_{12}$.

TABLE 11-8 Execution of register-reference instructions

		$r = q_6 t_3$	
CLA	rB_{12}:	$A \leftarrow 0$	Clear A
CLE	rB_{11}:	$E \leftarrow 0$	Clear E
CMA	rB_{10}:	$A \leftarrow \bar{A}$	Complement A
CME	rB_9:	$E \leftarrow \bar{E}$	Complement E
SHR	rB_8:	$A \leftarrow$ shr $A, A_{16} \leftarrow E, E \leftarrow A_1$	Shift-right A and E
SHL	rB_7:	$A \leftarrow$ shl $A, A_1 \leftarrow E, E \leftarrow A_{16}$	Shift-left A and E
INC	rB_6:	$A \leftarrow A + 1$	Increment A
SPA	$rB_5 A'_{16}$:	$PC \leftarrow PC + 1$	Increment PC if A is positive
SNA	$rB_4 A_{16}$:	$PC \leftarrow PC + 1$	Increment PC if A is negative
SZA	$rB_3 A_z$:	$PC \leftarrow PC + 1$	Increment PC if A is zero
SZE	$rB_2 E'$:	$PC \leftarrow PC + 1$	Increment PC if E is zero
HLT	rB_1:	$S \leftarrow 0$	Clear start-stop flip-flop

The first seven register-reference instructions perform the clear, complement, shift, and increment operations on the A or E register. The next four instructions are skip instructions executed only if the stated condition is satisfied. The skipping of the instruction is achieved by incrementing PC again, in addition to the incrementing at time t_1 (see Table 11-5). The status-bit condition for skipping becomes part of the control function. Thus the accumulator is positive if $A_{16} = 0$ and negative if $A_{16} = 1$. The symbol A_z is a binary variable equal to 1 when the A register contains all 0's. E' is equal to 1 when the E flip-flop contains 0.

The halt instruction clears the start-stop flip-flop S and stops the timing sequence. The sequence register G stops counting while its value is 0. This causes the computer to idle, with t_0 always being at the output of the timing decoder. Since F is also 0, the control function $F't_0$ is the only one produced while the computer is halted. This control function transfers the contents of PC to MAR continuously (see Table 11-5). We could tolerate this continuous transfer when the computer halts. If this is undesirable, we can remove the clock pulses from MAR as well to prevent this transfer from occurring when $S = 0$. The computer can resume when the "start" switch is activated, which sets flip-flop S. This causes the clock pulses to reach the sequence register G and start producing the other timing variables.

Input-Output Instructions

The register-transfer microoperations that execute the four input-output instructions are listed in Table 11-9. These instructions are recognized from operation-decoder output q_7 and are executed during time t_3. We define a new variable $p = q_7 t_3$ and use it in all input-output control functions. The control functions for these

TABLE 11-9 Execution of input-output instructions

	$p = q_7 t_3$		
SKI	$pB_{12}N_9$:	$PC \leftarrow PC + 1$	Increment PC if input flag $N_9 = 1$
INP	pB_{11}:	$A_{1-8} \leftarrow N_{1-8},\ N_9 \leftarrow 0$	Input to A, clear flag
SKO	$pB_{10}U_9$:	$PC \leftarrow PC + 1$	Increment PC if output flag $U_9 = 1$
OUT	pB_9:	$U_{1-8} \leftarrow A_{1-8},\ U_9 \leftarrow 0$	Output from A, clear flag

instructions contain a single bit from the B register which is part of the instruction-code definition. The two skip instructions depend on the status condition of flag bits N_9 and U_9.

11-6 DESIGN OF COMPUTER REGISTERS

The design of a synchronous digital system follows a prescribed procedure. From a knowledge of the system requirements, one formulates a control network and obtains a list of register-transfer operations for the system. Once this list is derived, the rest of the design is straightforward. Some installations utilize computer design automation techniques for translating the register-transfer statements to a circuit diagram composed of integrated circuits.

Section 11-5 specified the register-transfer statements for the computer in five separate tables. The entries in the tables consist of control functions and microoperations. The list of control functions provides the Boolean functions for the gates in the control logic network. The list of microoperations gives an indication of the types of registers that must be chosen for the computer. Although these tables are sufficient to complete the logic design of the system, it may be convenient to rearrange the information in the tables in a more convenient way during the actual implementation process.

Register Operations

To determine the type of control input that must be provided in each register, we must obtain the list of microoperations that affect each register separately. This can be done by scanning the tables in Section 11-5 and retrieving all those statements that change the contents of a particular register. This also applies to the read and write operations in the memory unit. For example, a memory-read operation is symbolized with the microoperation:

$$B \leftarrow M$$

The statement also indicates that the contents of register B will change in value. This statement is found twice in the list of microoperations. In Table 11-5, we find it with control function $F't_1$, and in Table 11-6, with control function $F(q_0 + q_1 + q_3)t_1$. Since both control functions produce the same operation, they can be combined with an OR into one statement:

$$R = F't_1 + F(q_0 + q_1 + q_3)t_1: \quad B \leftarrow M$$

The symbol R is used for convenience to designate the *read* operation with a single Boolean control variable. The equal sign after R designates its equality with the control function listed.

This procedure is repeated for the memory-write operation and for all the registers in the computer. The result is as shown in Table 11-10. Each control function listed in the table is assigned a control-variable name. The single-letter variable names are not necessary, but they help shorten the algebraic expressions of input control for the registers. In most cases, the control variable is assigned a lowercase letter identical to the capital letter reserved to symbolize the corresponding register. The control variables common to the same register are distinguished by different numerical subscripts.

Table 11-10 is derived directly from Tables 11-5 through 11-9. The register to which a microoperation belongs is recognized by the presence of its symbol on the left side of the arrow. To recognize the microoperations belonging to register A, we scan the operations listed in Tables 11-5 through 11-9 and retrieve all those that have an A as a destination register. The microoperations for the other registers are obtained in a similar manner. If the microoperation occurs more than once, the corresponding control functions are ORed to form a composite control function.

The operations for the E flip-flop must be separated from the operations for the A register, even though they were listed together in the previous tables. The circular shift-right operation, for example, is stated in Table 11-8 as:

$$rB_8: \quad A \leftarrow \text{shr } A, A_{16} \leftarrow E, E \leftarrow A_1$$

Note that r is a variable equal to q_6t_3, and rB_8 is assigned a control variable a_5. In Table 11-10 under the A register, we have:

$$a_5 = rB_8: \quad A \leftarrow \text{shr } A, A_{16} \leftarrow E$$

which is the part of the shift operation that changes the contents of A. Under the E flip-flop, we have:

$$a_5 = rB_8: \quad E \leftarrow A_1$$

which shows the part of the shift operation that changes the E flip-flop. Thus, the shift-right control variable a_5 shifts the contents of A to the right and inserts the value of E into the leftmost bit of A. It also transfers the rightmost bit of A into E.

The sequence register G does not have any listed microoperations in the previous tables. This register is shown in Fig. 11-6 to be a counter whose clock pulses are enabled by the start-stop flip-flop S. This is included in Table 11-10 with the statement:

$$S: \quad G \leftarrow G + 1$$

TABLE 11-10 Microoperations for registers

Memory Control

$R = F't_1 + F(q_0 + q_1 + q_3)t_1$: $B \leftarrow M$ Memory read

$W = F(q_2 + q_3 + q_4)t_3$: $M \leftarrow B$ Memory write

A Register

$a_1 = Fq_0t_3$: $A \leftarrow A \wedge B$ AND

$a_2 = Fq_1t_3$: $A \leftarrow A + B$ Add

$a_3 = rB_{12}$: $A \leftarrow 0$ Clear

$a_4 = rB_{10}$: $A \leftarrow \overline{A}$ Complement

$a_5 = rB_8$: $A \leftarrow \text{shr } A, A_{16} \leftarrow E$ Shift-right

$a_6 = rB_7$: $A \leftarrow \text{shl } A, A_1 \leftarrow E$ Shift-left

$a_7 = rB_6$: $A \leftarrow A + 1$ Increment

$a_8 = pB_{11}$: $A_{1-8} \leftarrow N_{1-8}$ Transfer

B Register

$b_1 = Fq_2t_2$: $B \leftarrow A$ Transfer

$b_2 = Fq_3t_2$: $B \leftarrow B + 1$ Increment

$b_3 = Fq_4t_2$: $B(AD) \leftarrow PC, B(OP) \leftarrow 0101$ Transfer

PC Register

$c_1 = F't_1$

    $+ (q_3B_z + q_4)Ft_3$

    $+ (B_5A'_{16} + B_4A_{16}$

    $+ B_3A_z + B_2E')r$

    $+ (B_{12}N_9 + B_{10}U_9)p$: $PC \leftarrow PC + 1$ Increment

$c_2 = q_5t_3$: $PC \leftarrow B(AD)$ Transfer

$b_3 = Fq_4t_2$: $PC \leftarrow MAR$ Transfer

MAR Register

$d_1 = F't_0$: $MAR \leftarrow PC$ Transfer

$d_2 = Ft_0$: $MAR \leftarrow B(AD)$ Transfer

I Register

$i_1 = F't_2$: $I \leftarrow B(OP)$ Transfer

E Flip-Flop

$e_1 = rB_{11}$: $E \leftarrow 0$ Clear

$e_2 = rB_9$: $E \leftarrow \overline{E}$ Complement

$a_2 = Fq_1t_3$: $E \leftarrow \text{carry}$ Transfer

$a_5 = rB_8$: $E \leftarrow A_1$ Shift-right

$a_6 = rB_7$: $E \leftarrow A_{16}$ Shift-left

F Flip-Flop

$f_1 = F'(q_0 + q_1 + q_2$

    $+ q_3 + q_4)t_3$: $F \leftarrow 1$ Set

$f_2 = Ft_3$: $F \leftarrow 0$ Clear

S Flip-Flop

$s_1 = rB_1$: $S \leftarrow 0$ Clear

G Register

S: $G \leftarrow G + 1$ Count

U Register

$u_1 = pB_9$: $U_{1-8} \leftarrow A_{1-8}, U_9 \leftarrow 0$ Transfer

N Register

$a_8 = pB_{11}$: $N_9 \leftarrow 0$ Clear

Design of Computer

The list of microoperations given in Table 11-10 provides the information needed to design the registers of the computer. The operations to be performed on each register are clearly demonstrated by the listed statements. For example, program counter PC has three microoperations:

$$c_1: \quad PC \leftarrow PC + 1$$
$$c_2: \quad PC \leftarrow B(AD)$$
$$b_3: \quad PC \leftarrow MAR$$

This register must have increment and transfer capabilities. It can be implemented by means of a counter with parallel load of the type shown in Fig. 7-19. Since PC receives input information from two sources, it requires a multiplexer to select between the two inputs, as explained in conjunction with Fig. 8-3. The other registers are designed in a similar manner.

A block diagram showing the types of registers needed for the computer is given in Fig. 11-7. The memory unit is also included to show its connection to the processor. The control logic provides all the control variables for the registers. The design of the control logic is discussed in the next section. The control variables that are generated in the control unit are applied to the registers as indicated in the diagram. In addition to the registers, the processor uses four multiplexers to select from two or more sources. All the registers and multiplexers are MSI functions available in standard integrated circuits. The three flip-flops, E, F, and S, and their corresponding combinational logic must be designed with SSI gates and flip-flops.

All of the registers in the computer, except register A, require a load, increment, or both load and increment control inputs. One can choose to employ an MSI counter with parallel load for all registers. In this manner, it would be possible to have an inventory of just one standard type of IC component for the registers. A possible commercial component is IC type 74161. This MSI circuit contains a 4-bit counter with parallel load and an asynchronous clear input. The clear inputs of the registers can be connected to a master reset switch in the computer to clear all registers asynchronously prior to the clocked operations. The 12-bit registers, PC and MAR, will need three such ICs, and the 16-bit register, B, will require four ICs. The I and G registers can be implemented with one IC each. The 4-bit counter, IC, can be converted to a 2-bit counter for G by the method outlined in Section 7-5, in conjunction with Fig. 7-20.

The A register is the most complicated register because it performs all the processing tasks for the computer. This register is an accumulator register of the type designed in Section 9-10 and can use the configuration shown in Fig. 9-22. It can also be implemented with a bidirectional shift register with parallel load, as shown in Fig. 7-9, together with an ALU of the type discussed in Section 9-6. A better choice would be to use an accumulator MSI circuit such as type 74S281 IC.

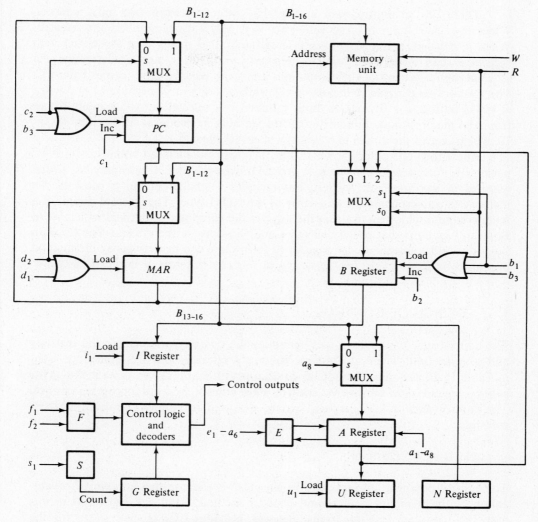

Figure 11-7 Detailed block diagram for computer

When implemented with an ALU or accumulator IC, the control unit must generate the corresponding control variables to select the required microoperations in the ALU. These will be different from the single control functions defined for the control unit in this design.

Input register N and output register U can be part of a standard teletypewriter interface. Integrated circuits that interface with a teletypewriter unit are available commercially and are usually called *universal asynchronous receiver-transmitters* (abbreviated UART). Such an IC includes an input register and an output register within the unit, together with the two flags required for synchronizing the transfer.

Three of the multiplexers in Fig. 11-7 select between two input sources. When the select input marked with an *s* is 1, MUX input number 1 is selected. When $s = 0$, MUX input number 0 is selected. The multiplexer associated with register *B* has three input sources. Selection variables s_1 and s_0 determine the selected input. When both selection lines are 0, the selected input comes from *PC*. The memory-read signal *R* makes $s_0 = 1$ while s_1 remains 0 (because $b_1 = 0$ when $R = 1$). With $s_1s_0 = 01$, MUX input number 1 is selected and this input comes from the memory unit. Similarly, control variable b_1 produces a selection $s_1s_0 = 10$, which causes the contents of register *A* to be selected.

The entire computer shown in Fig. 11-7 can be enclosed within a single IC package to form a *microcomputer*. A typical microcomputer IC normally has added features in the processor section, but includes a smaller memory. Most of the memory in a microcomputer is usually of the ROM type. The internal design of a microcomputer chip requires that the logic of the computer be defined with a set of Boolean functions that specify all gates and flip-flops in the system. The Boolean functions that implement each register in the system can be derived by the method presented in Section 9-10 for the design of registers in terms of Boolean functions.

11-7   DESIGN OF CONTROL

The control unit of the computer generates the control variables for the registers and memory unit. There are 24 distinct control variables and all of them are listed in Table 11-10 as control functions. In Chapter 10, we presented three methods for control logic design: hard-wired control, PLA control, and microprogram control. The control unit of the computer can be designed using any one of these three methods.

Hard-wired Control

The control organization presented in Fig. 11-6 is essentially a hard-wired organization of the sequence register and decoder method. Sequence register *G* in this case is a counter, and the timing decoder provides four control states for the system. A second decoder is used for the operation code stored in the *I* register. The control-logic-network block generates all the control functions for the computer.

The implementation of the control logic network in Fig. 11-6 completes the design of the hard-wired control. This implementation consists of combinational gates that generate the 24 control functions listed in Table 11-10. The Boolean functions listed as control functions specify the Boolean equations from which the combinational circuit can be derived. This circuit will not be drawn here but can be easily obtained from the 24 Boolean functions that define the control variables R, W, a_1 through a_8, b_1, b_2, b_3, c_1, c_2, d_1, d_2, i_1, e_1, e_2, f_1, f_2, s_1, and u_1.

PLA Control

The PLA control is similar to the sequence register and decoder method, except that all combinational circuits are implemented within the PLA. The two decoders are included inside the PLA implementation, since they are combinational circuits. The total number of control outputs is 24. The total number of PLA inputs is also 24. A 24-input, 24-output PLA may not be available in one commercial IC package. For this reason, the control unit should be partitioned in such a way so it can be implemented with a minimum number of PLA ICs.

One way to partition the control is according to the function tables presented in Section 11-5. The register-transfer statements in this section are listed in Tables 11-5 through 11-9. The PLA control partitioned according to these tables is shown in Fig. 11-8. This implementation replaces the hard-wired control of Fig. 11-6.

Figure 11-8 shows three PLAs and two registers for the control unit. The two decoders are not needed here, since they are implemented inside the PLA. Note that there are no connections from the outputs of any PLA to the inputs of sequence register G. A feedback connection is not necessary because the G register is a counter and the next state is predetermined from the continuous count sequence. PLA 1 implements the control variables listed in Table 11-5 (fetch cycle) and Table 11-6 (common operations for execute cycle). These control variables depend on the timing variables from G, the operation code from I, and the cycle control in F. PLA 2 implements the control functions listed in Table 11-7 (execution of memory-reference instructions). These control functions have the same input variables as PLA 1, with the addition of binary variable B_z. Remember that B_z is a binary variable equal to 1 when the B register contains all 0's.

The third PLA generates the register-reference and input-output control functions listed in Tables 11-8 and 11-9. These control functions have two common variables:

$$r = q_6 t_3 \qquad \text{for the register-reference operations}$$

$$p = q_7 t_3 \qquad \text{for the input-output operations}$$

These two common variables are generated in PLA 1 and applied as inputs to PLA 3. The other inputs to the third PLA come from register B (bits 1–12) and other status-bit conditions.

Control variable c_1 increments the program counter. This control variable is generated in all three PLAs. The three outputs must be combined with an external OR gate to provide a single output. This output is applied to the increment input of PC.

The derivation of the program tables for the three PLAs completes the control design. The PLA 1 program table can be obtained from the control functions listed in Tables 11-5 and 11-6. These functions are repeated again in

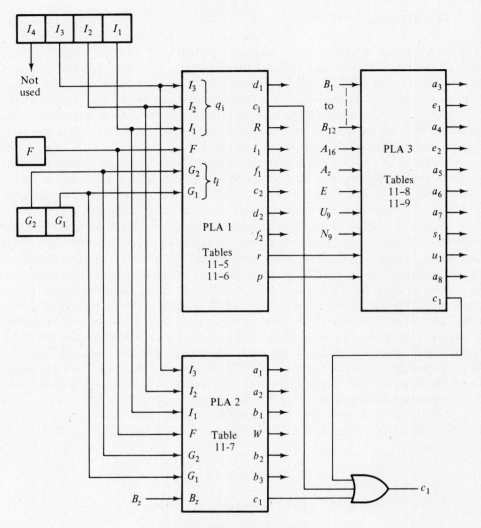

Figure 11-8 PLA control for computer

Table 11-11 for convenience. Some of the functions have been simplified for entry in the program table. For example, the read control variable R was originally listed as:

$$R = F't_1 + F(q_0 + q_1 + q_3)t_3$$

The decoded output variables q_0, q_1, and q_3 are a function of the variables in the I register and can be simplified as follows:

$$q_0 + q_1 + q_3 = I_3'I_2'I_1' + I_3'I_2'I_1 + I_3'I_2I_1 = I_3'I_1 + I_3'I_2'$$

TABLE 11-11 Control functions for PLA 1

$d_1 = F't_0$:	$MAR \leftarrow PC$
$c_1 = F't_1$:	$PC \leftarrow PC + 1$
$R = F't_1 + F(I_3'I_1 + I_3'I_2')t_1$:	$B \leftarrow M$
$i_1 = F't_2$:	$I \leftarrow B(OP)$
$f_1 = F'(I_3' + I_2'I_1')t_3$:	$F \leftarrow 1$
$c_2 = q_5t_3$:	$PC \leftarrow B(AD)$
$d_2 = Ft_0$:	$MAR \leftarrow B(AD)$
$f_2 = Ft_3$:	$F \leftarrow 0$
$r = q_6t_3$:	Register reference
$p = q_7t_3$:	Input-output

Since the PLA accepts the I variables rather than the q variables, it is more convenient to use the two-term function rather than the three-term function. Control variable f_1 is simplified in a similar manner. The other Boolean variables need a translation from the t designation to a state in the sequence register G and from the q designation to the corresponding operation code in the I register.

The program table for PLA 1 is given in Table 11-12. The PLA has 6 inputs, 12 product terms, and 10 outputs. The entries for G_2 and G_1 are 00, 01, 10, and 11 and correspond to timing variables t_0, t_1, t_2, and t_3, respectively. The entry for I_3, I_2, and I_1 is a binary number equal to the value of subscript i in q_i, unless the function is simplified. Note that register I has four bits, but I_4 is not used since it is always 0. The procedure for obtaining a PLA program table from a set of Boolean functions is explained in Section 5-8.

TABLE 11-12 Program table for PLA 1

Product term	Inputs						Outputs										
	I_3	I_2	I_1	F	G_2	G_1	d_1	c_1	R	i_1	f_1	c_2	d_2	f_2	r	p	
1	–	–	–	0	0	0	1	–	–	–	–	–	–	–	–	–	$F't_0$
2	–	–	–	0	0	1	–	1	1	–	–	–	–	–	–	–	$F't_1$
3	0	–	1	1	0	1	–	–	1	–	–	–	–	–	–	–	$FI_3'I_1t_1$
4	0	0	–	1	0	1	–	–	1	–	–	–	–	–	–	–	$FI_3'I_2't_1$
5	–	–	–	0	1	0	–	–	–	1	–	–	–	–	–	–	$F't_2$
6	0	–	–	0	1	1	–	–	–	–	1	–	–	–	–	–	$F'I_3't_3$
7	–	0	0	0	1	1	–	–	–	–	1	–	–	–	–	–	$F'I_2'I_1't_3$
8	1	0	1	–	1	1	–	–	–	–	–	1	–	–	–	–	q_5t_3
9	–	–	–	1	0	0	–	–	–	–	–	–	1	–	–	–	Ft_0
10	–	–	–	1	1	1	–	–	–	–	–	–	–	1	–	–	Ft_3
11	1	1	0	–	1	1	–	–	–	–	–	–	–	–	1	–	q_6t_3
12	1	1	1	–	1	1	–	–	–	–	–	–	–	–	–	1	q_7t_3

The program table for PLA 2 can be derived in a similar manner, although it is not listed here. The third PLA requires 12 AND terms and a 6-input OR gate (to generate control variable c_1). This part of the control may be implemented more economically with SSI gates or with a field-programmable gate array (FPGA). The FPGA is similar to the FPLA in concept, except that it contains only programmable AND gates. A typical FPGA has 9 AND (or NAND) gates sharing 16 common inputs.* Two such FPGA integrated circuits are required to replace PLA 3 in Fig. 11-8. The external OR gate can be combined with the other lines that generate variable c_1.

Microprogram Control

The organization of the control unit for the computer is more suitable for a PLA control than for a microprogram control, mostly because of the way the register-reference instructions were originally formulated. The microprogram control configuration to be developed here implements the control functions for the fetch cycle and the memory-reference instructions. The register-reference and input-output operations can be implemented more efficiently with a hard-wired or PLA control.

The microprogram control does not need the I, G, and F registers. The operation code is in $B(OP)$ at the end of the fetch cycle, and this code can be used to specify a macrooperation address for control memory without the need for an I register. The timing variables generated in the sequence register G can be replaced by a sequence of clock pulses that read consecutive microinstructions from control memory. The transfer from the fetch cycle to the execute cycle can be done in control memory by a branch microinstruction that transfers control to the next cycle without the use of the F flip-flop. The microprogram control configuration to be developed here replaces the entire hard-wired control of Fig. 11-6 (except the B register).

Going over Tables 11-5, 11-6, and 11-7, we note that all microinstructions can be sequenced by incrementing the control memory address, except for going to execute a particular memory-reference instruction or for returning to the fetch cycle. A particular memory-reference instruction routine can be accessed with an external macrooperation address. If we start the fetch cycle from address 0, it would be possible to branch to the fetch cycle by clearing the control memory address register CAR. Therefore, the address-sequencing part of the microprogram control needs only three operations:

1. Increment CAR to read the next microinstruction in sequence.

2. Clear CAR to start the fetch cycle.

3. Provide a bit transformation from $B(OP)$ to an external address for CAR.

*IC type 82S103 from Signetics.

A possible microprogram control for the computer is shown in Fig. 11-9. The control memory ROM has 32 words of 7 bits each. The first four bits are encoded to provide 16 bit combinations, one for each control function. Although the computer has 24 control functions, 16 are sufficient to generate those control functions associated with the fetch cycle and the execution of the memory-reference instructions. Instead of using 16 bits of ROM to specify 16 outputs, we chose to employ only 4 bits and decode them through a 4-to-16 line decoder to provide up to 16 distinguishable output variables. This scheme saves ROM bits but requires an external decoder. It also limits the capability of the microinstructions because only one control function can be specified in any given microinstruction.

The address-sequencing part of the microprogram unit does not require a multiplexer to select status-bit conditions. There is only one status bit to be considered and we will show later how this can be included with an external circuit. There is no need for an address field in the microinstruction because no branching capabilities are provided except to return to the beginning of the fetch cycle or to transfer an external address. The last three bits of a microinstruction determine the next address. Bit 7 increments the control address register. Bit 6 clears CAR, which causes a return to the fetch cycle. Bit 5 loads an external address into CAR. The input address must contain 5 bits because the ROM has $32 = 2^5$ words. Three of these bits come from the B-register part that holds the operation-code. The last two bits are always equal to 11. This is a code transformation from the operation-code bits of the instruction to an external address for control memory. This transformation causes the AND instruction whose operation code is 000 to be changed into an address for CAR equal to 00011. The ADD instruction transforms from 001 to 00111; and so on, up to an input-output instruction whose operation

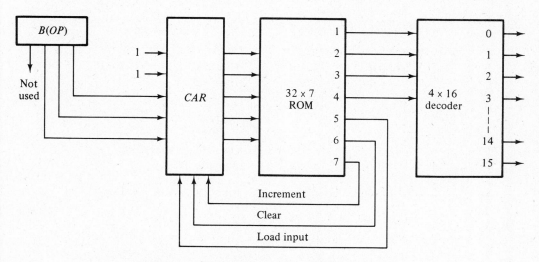

Figure 11-9 Microprogram control unit for computer

code is 111 and whose address transformation is 11111. The most significant bit in $B(OP)$ is not used because it is always 0.

The microprogram control unit shown in Fig. 11-9 is very simple and requires only three MSI circuits. Because of its simplicity, it is not very flexible and, as shown subsequently, requires additional circuits for a complete control-unit implementation.

The microoperations for the fetch cycle and the execution of memory-reference instructions are listed in Tables 11-5, 11-6, and 11-7. The microoperations for the I and F registers are not needed, since these registers are not used. The remaining microoperations and their encoded control functions are listed in Table 11-13. The first four bits of a ROM word in control memory provide 16 combinations, and each combination specifies a microoperation. The all-0's and all-1's combinations do not initiate a microoperation. The other 14 combinations are decoded to provide control variables for the listed microoperations. Decoder output 14 initiates the memory-write operation, $M \leftarrow B$, and also specifies a conditional control for incrementing PC dependent on variable B_z. The reason for repeating these two microoperations in one microinstruction will be clarified later. Note that the memory-write microoperation is also initiated with decoder output 11, and the control variable that increments PC is also available from decoder output 2.

The microprogram for control memory is given in Table 11-14. This is also the truth table for programming the ROM. There are 32 words of ROM, and the

TABLE 11-13   Encoding of ROM bits for microoperations

ROM bits 1 2 3 4	Decoder output	Control function	Microoperation
0 0 0 0	0	—	None
0 0 0 1	1	d_1	$MAR \leftarrow PC$
0 0 1 0	2	c_1	$PC \leftarrow PC + 1$
0 0 1 1	3	R	$B \leftarrow M$
0 1 0 0	4	c_2	$PC \leftarrow B(AD)$
0 1 0 1	5	d_2	$MAR \leftarrow B(AD)$
0 1 1 0	6	r	Register-reference operation
0 1 1 1	7	p	Input-output operation
1 0 0 0	8	a_1	$A \leftarrow A \wedge B$
1 0 0 1	9	a_2	$A \leftarrow A + B, E \leftarrow$ carry
1 0 1 0	10	b_1	$B \leftarrow A$
1 0 1 1	11	W	$M \leftarrow B$
1 1 0 0	12	b_2	$B \leftarrow B + 1$
1 1 0 1	13	b_3	$B(AD) \leftarrow PC, B(OP) \leftarrow 0101, PC \leftarrow MAR$
1 1 1 0	14	W, c_1	$M \leftarrow B$, if $(B_z = 1)$ then $(PC \leftarrow PC + 1)$
1 1 1 1	15	—	None

TABLE 11-14 ROM truth table for microprogram control

Instruction	ROM address	ROM outputs 1	2	3	4	5	6	7	Symbolic designation Microoperations	Next address
FETCH	00000	0	0	0	1	0	0	1	$MAR \leftarrow PC$	$CAR \leftarrow CAR + 1$
	00001	0	0	1	1	0	0	1	$B \leftarrow M$	$CAR \leftarrow CAR + 1$
	00010	0	0	1	0	1	0	0	$PC \leftarrow PC + 1$	$CAR \leftarrow 2^2 B(OP) + 3$
AND	00011	0	1	0	1	0	0	1	$MAR \leftarrow B(AD)$	$CAR \leftarrow CAR + 1$
	00100	0	0	1	1	0	0	1	$B \leftarrow M$	$CAR \leftarrow CAR + 1$
	00101	1	0	0	0	0	1	0	$A \leftarrow A \wedge B$	$CAR \leftarrow 0$
	00110	0	0	0	0	0	1	0	None	$CAR \leftarrow 0$
ADD	00111	0	1	0	1	0	0	1	$MAR \leftarrow B(AD)$	$CAR \leftarrow CAR + 1$
	01000	0	0	1	1	0	0	1	$B \leftarrow M$	$CAR \leftarrow CAR + 1$
	01001	1	0	0	1	0	1	0	$A \leftarrow A + B, E \leftarrow$ carry	$CAR \leftarrow 0$
	01010	0	0	0	0	0	1	0	None	$CAR \leftarrow 0$
STO	01011	0	1	0	1	0	0	1	$MAR \leftarrow B(AD)$	$CAR \leftarrow CAR + 1$
	01100	1	0	1	0	0	0	1	$B \leftarrow A$	$CAR \leftarrow CAR + 1$
	01101	1	0	1	1	0	1	0	$M \leftarrow B$	$CAR \leftarrow 0$
	01110	0	0	0	0	0	1	0	None	$CAR \leftarrow 0$
ISZ	01111	0	1	0	1	0	0	1	$MAR \leftarrow B(AD)$	$CAR \leftarrow CAR + 1$
	10000	0	0	1	1	0	0	1	$B \leftarrow M$	$CAR \leftarrow CAR + 1$
	10001	1	1	0	0	0	0	1	$B \leftarrow B + 1$	$CAR \leftarrow CAR + 1$
	10010	1	1	1	0	0	1	0	$M \leftarrow B$, if $(B_z = 1)$ then $(PC \leftarrow PC + 1)$	$CAR \leftarrow 0$
BSB	10011	0	1	0	1	0	0	1	$MAR \leftarrow B(AD)$	$CAR \leftarrow CAR + 1$
	10100	1	1	0	1	0	0	1	$B(AD) \leftarrow PC, PC \leftarrow MAR$	$CAR \leftarrow CAR + 1$
	10101	1	0	1	1	0	0	1	$M \leftarrow B$	$CAR \leftarrow CAR + 1$
	10110	0	0	1	0	0	1	0	$PC \leftarrow PC + 1$	$CAR \leftarrow 0$
BUN	10111	0	1	0	0	0	1	0	$PC \leftarrow B(AD)$	$CAR \leftarrow 0$
	11000	0	0	0	0	0	1	0	None	$CAR \leftarrow 0$
	11001	0	0	0	0	0	1	0	None	$CAR \leftarrow 0$
	11010	0	0	0	0	0	1	0	None	$CAR \leftarrow 0$
REGISTER	11011	0	1	1	0	0	1	0	Register operation	$CAR \leftarrow 0$
	11100	0	0	0	0	0	1	0	None	$CAR \leftarrow 0$
	11101	0	0	0	0	0	1	0	None	$CAR \leftarrow 0$
	11110	0	0	0	0	0	1	0	None	$CAR \leftarrow 0$
I/O	11111	0	1	1	1	0	1	0	Input-output operation	$CAR \leftarrow 0$

address and content of each word are specified in the table. The table is subdivided into nine routines showing the microinstructions that belong to the fetch cycle and the microinstructions for executing each of the computer instructions. The symbolic designation column gives the microprogram in symbolic form and the address sequencing for *CAR*.

The fetch cycle starts from address 0. The three consecutive microoperations in the fetch routine transfer the contents of *PC* to *MAR*, read the instruction into the *B* register, and increment *PC*. At address 2 (0010), bit 5 of the microinstruction is equal to 1. The same clock pulse that increments *PC* also performs the microoperation:

$$CAR \leftarrow 2^2 B(OP) + 3$$

$B(OP)$ contains the three bits of the operation code. These bits are shifted twice to the left (multiplied by 2^2) and binary 3 (11) is added to form an address for *CAR*. The address received in *CAR* transfers control to one of the routines listed in the table, and control continues to execute the specified instruction. The implementation of this code transformation is depicted in Fig. 11-9.

This configuration assigns four words of ROM for each instruction, except for the I/O instruction. For example, the ISZ instruction has operation code 011. The beginning of the routine that executes this instruction is at address $4 \times 3 + 3 = 15$, which is binary 01111. The four ROM words for this routine are at addresses 15, 16, 17, and 18. We cannot use the word at address 19 because this address contains the first microinstruction for the BSB routine. Since there are no branching capabilities in this microprogram unit, we cannot branch to an unused ROM word; therefore, each routine must be completed with no more than four microinstructions.

The AND routine can be implemented with three microinstructions. The address of the instruction is transferred into *MAR*, the operand is read from memory into *B*, and the AND microoperation is performed between the *A* and *B* registers. The last microinstruction at address 5 (00101) has bit 6 equal to 1. This causes *CAR* to be cleared, and control returns to address 0 to start the fetch cycle again. The first two microinstructions of the AND routine have bit 7 equal to 1, which causes *CAR* to be incremented. The last word in this routine at address 6 is not used. This word cannot be left empty because we must specify something for the ROM truth table. The best way to fill in this word is to specify no microoperation in bits 1 through 4 and to clear *CAR* with bit 6. In this way, if a malfunction occurs and control memory finds itself in address 6, no operation will be executed and control will return to the fetch cycle.

The ADD and STO routines need three microinstructions. The BSB instruction uses all four words available for the routine. The BUN instruction needs only one microinstruction. A register-reference instruction initiates a control variable *r*, which must be used in conjunction with a bit in the *B* register to initiate one of the specified operations. The same applies to an input-output (I/O) instruction.

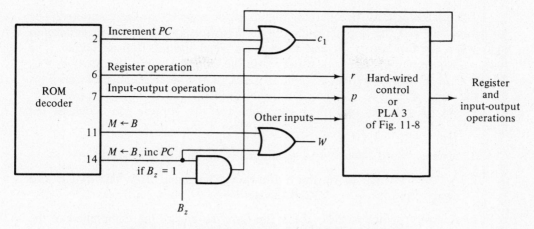

Figure 11-10 Additional circuits for microprogram control

The ISZ routine needs four microoperations and a conditional operation dependent on the value of B_z. This imposes a problem, because there are only four ROM words available for this routine and the microprogram configuration has no facility for checking status-bit conditions. This problem can be solved by including two microoperations in one microinstruction and checking the status bit with an external AND gate. To compensate for this unorthodox configuration, we insert an external circuit as shown in Fig. 11-10. The ROM decoder has two outputs for a memory-write operation $M \leftarrow B$: one in output 11 and the other in output 14. These two outputs are ORed externally to provide one common output. Output 14 of the decoder is enabled during the fourth microinstruction of the ISZ routine. This output is ANDed externally with status bit B_z to provide the increment-PC control function. Decoder output 2 also specifies an increment-PC. Some of the operations in the register-reference and input-output instructions specify this operation as well. The three outputs must be ORed together to form a single output for incrementing PC. Variables r and p from the ROM decoder are used in conjunction with other status-bit conditions to generate the remaining control variables for the computer. These control variables can be generated with an external hard-wired configuration or with a PLA as indicated in the diagram.

11-8 COMPUTER CONSOLE

Any computer has a control panel or console with switches and lamps to allow manual and visual communication between an operator and the computer. This communication is needed for starting the operation of the computer (bootstrapping) and for maintenance purposes. For the sake of completeness, we shall enumerate a set of useful console functions for the computer, although the circuits required to implement these functions will not be shown.

Lamps indicate to the operator the status of registers in the computer. The normal output of a flip-flop connected to an indicator lamp will cause the lamp to light when the flip-flop is set and to turn off when the flip-flop is cleared. The registers whose outputs are to be observed in the computer console are: A, B, PC, MAR, I, E, F and S. When a count is made of the total number of flip-flops involved, we find that 63 indicator lamps are needed.

A set of switches and their functions for the console may include the following:

1. Sixteen "word" switches to set manually the bits of one word.

2. A "start" switch to set the S flip-flop. The signal from this switch also clears flip-flop F, N_9, U_9 and register G.

3. A "stop" switch to clear the S flip-flop. To ensure the completion of the current instruction, the signal from the switch is ANDed with the Boolean function $(F + q_5 + q_6 + q_7)t_3$ before it is applied to clear S.

4. A "load address" switch to transfer an address to the PC register. When this switch is activated, the contents of 12 "word" switches are transferred to PC.

5. A "deposit" switch to manually store words into memory. When this switch is activated, the content of PC is transferred to MAR and a memory cycle is initiated. After 1 μs, the contents of the 16 "word" switches are transferred into the B register and PC is incremented by 1.

6. A "display" switch to examine the content of a word in memory. When this switch is activated, the content of PC is transferred to MAR, a memory cycle is initiated, and PC is incremented by 1. The contents of the memory word specified by the address in PC are in register B and can be seen in the corresponding indicator lamps.

To ensure that the computer is not running when the power is turned on, the S flip-flop must have a special circuit that forces it to always turn to the clear position right after the application of power to the machine.

REFERENCES

1. Mano, M. M., *Computer System Architecture*. Englewood Cliffs, N.J.: Prentice-Hall, Inc., 1976.

2. *Small Computer Handbook*. Maynard, Mass.: Digital Equipment Corp., 1973.

3. Booth, T. H., *Digital Networks and Computer Systems*. New York: John Wiley & Sons, Inc., 1971.

4. Hill, F. J., and G. R. Peterson, *Digital Systems: Hardware Organization and Design.* New York: John Wiley & Sons, Inc., 1973.

5. Bell, C. G., J. Grason, and A. Newell, *Designing Computers and Digital Systems.* Maynard, Mass.: Digital Press, 1972.

6. Kline, R. M., *Digital Computer Design.* Englewood Cliffs, N.J.: Prentice-Hall, Inc., 1977.

7. Soucek, B., *Minicomputers in Data Processing and Simulation.* New York: John Wiley & Sons, Inc., 1972.

PROBLEMS

11-1.   Go over the instruction set of the computer designed in this chapter (Tables 11-2, 11-3, and 11-4) and list all those instructions that are useful for:

(a) transfers between memory and accumulator;

(b) transfers between input-output and accumulator;

(c) arithmetic manipulations;

(d) logic operations;

(e) shift operations;

(f) control decisions based on status conditions;

(g) subroutine branch and return.

11-2.   List the sequence of instructions for the computer that will set flip-flop E.

11-3.   (a) List the sequence of instructions for the computer to perform an arithmetic right-shift of a number stored in the accumulator. The number is in sign-2's-complement representation. (b) Repeat for an arithmetic left-shift. Indicate how an overflow can be detected.

11-4.   Show that the list of instructions obtained in problem 11-1(d) constitutes a sufficient set for implementing all 16 logic operations listed in Table 2-6.

11-5.   (a) Write a sequence of three instructions to be stored in memory locations 1, 2, and 3. They should check if a character is available in the input device and, if so, transfer it to the accumulator. (b) Write a sequence of three instructions to be stored in memory locations 5, 6, and 7. They should check if the output device is empty and, if so, transfer a character from the accumulator.

11-6.   The computer described in this chapter does not have an overflow indication after two signed numbers are added. Assume that the two numbers added with the ADD instruction are in sign-2's-complement representation. Derive an algorithm in flowchart form for a computer program that will add the two numbers and detect an overflow.

11-7.   The following program is a list of instructions in hexadecimal code. The computer executes the instructions starting from hexadecimal location 100.

(a) Write the program in symbolic form. Note that the last two values are operands.

(b) Determine the contents of register A when the computer halts, and explain what the program accomplishes.

Location	Instruction
100	6800
101	1106
102	6200
103	6020
104	1107
105	6001
106	0063
107	0074

11-8. An instruction in address $(021)_{16}$ in the computer has the operation-code of the AND instruction and an address part $(083)_{16}$. The memory word at address $(083)_{16}$ contains the number $(B8F2)_{16}$. Register A contains $(A937)_{16}$. Tabulate the contents of registers PC, MAR, B, A, and I, after the instruction is executed. Repeat the problem five more times, each time starting with the operation-code of another memory-reference instruction.

11-9. Register A contains $(A937)_{16}$ and the value of E is 1. Tabulate the contents of registers E, A, B, and PC after the execution of the CLA instruction. Repeat the problem 11 more times, each time starting from another one of the register-reference instructions. The initial value of PC is $(021)_{16}$.

11-10. The memory access time for the computer was assumed to be less than 1 μs, so a memory read or write operation can be terminated during a clock pulse interval. Now assume that the memory has an access time of 2 μs. How many microseconds would it take to execute the ISZ instruction, including the time to fetch the instruction from memory?

11-11. The ADD instruction assumes that the numbers are either unsigned or in sign-2's-complement form, since all 16 bits of the numbers are added. It is required to change the hardware execution of this instruction (hexadecimal code 1) so that it will add numbers in sign-1's complement representation

(a) Modify the register-transfer statements for the ADD instruction in Table 11-7.

(b) Can the modified instruction be used to add two unsigned binary numbers?

(c) What is the circuit that is now needed to detect the zero content of register A for the SZA instruction?

11-12. The computer designed in this chapter does not use the hexadecimal operation codes 8 to F, even though the instruction has four bits for the operation part. We now add the following instructions to the computer. List the register-transfer statements that must be added to Tables 11-5, 11-6, and 11-7 for the execution of these new instructions.

Symbol	Hexadecimal code	Description	Function
ORA	8 m	OR to A	$A \leftarrow A \vee M$
XRA	9 m	Exclusive-OR to A	$A \leftarrow A \oplus M$
SWP	A m	Swap A with memory	$A \leftarrow M, M \leftarrow A$
SUB	B m	Subtract A from memory	$A \leftarrow M - A$
BSA	C m	Branch and save address in A	$A \leftarrow PC, PC \leftarrow m$
BPA	D m	Branch on positive A	If $(A \geqslant 0)$ then $(PC \leftarrow m)$
BNA	E m	Branch on negative A	If $(A < 0)$ then $(PC \leftarrow m)$
BZA	F m	Branch on zero A	If $(A = 0)$ then $(PC \leftarrow m)$

11-13. The computer designed in this chapter uses an F flip-flop to distinguish between the fetch and execute cycles. This flip-flop is not needed if the sequence register G is a 3-bit counter and its decoder supplies eight timing signals, t_0 through t_7. The G register can be cleared as soon as the execution of the instruction is completed. (This is the way the control was designed in the simple computer of Section 8-12.)
  (a) Revise Tables 11-5, 11-6, and 11-7 to conform with this new control scheme.
  (b) Determine the time of execution of each instruction, including the time to fetch the instruction.

11-14. List the register-transfer statements for the execution of the instructions listed below. Assume that the computer does not have an F flip-flop, but that the sequence register G has 16 timing variables, t_0 through t_{15}. The G register must be cleared when the execution of the instruction is completed. The fetch cycle for the computer now is:

$$t_0: \quad PC \leftarrow MAR$$

$$t_1: \quad B \leftarrow M, PC \leftarrow PC + 1$$

$$t_2: \quad I \leftarrow B(OP)$$

Each of the following instructions starts the execute cycle from timing variable t_3. The last statement must include the microoperation $G \leftarrow 0$.

Symbol	Hexadecimal code	Description	Function
SBA	8 m	Subtract from A	$A \leftarrow A - M$
ADM	9 m	Add to memory	$M \leftarrow A + M$ (A does not change)
BEA	A m	Branch if A equal	If $(A = M)$ then $(PC \leftarrow m)$ (A does not change)

11-15. Compare the register-transfer statements for the A register listed in Table 11-10 with the accumulator designed in Section 9-10. Design one typical stage of the A register for the computer using the procedure outlined in Section 9-10. Include the circuit for the zero-detection variable A_z.

11-16. Draw the logic gates that generate control functions a_1 through a_8 for register A (Table 11-10).

11-17. Starting from the register-transfer statement given in Table 11-10 for the E flip-flop, derive the input Boolean functions for E. Use a JK flip-flop.

11-18. One way to simplify a circuit when using the register-transfer method is to use common paths while developing the list of statements. To illustrate with a particular example, consider the multiplexer for the input to PC in Fig. 11-7. This multiplexer will not be needed if we can replace the statement:

$$b_3: \quad PC \leftarrow MAR$$

by the statement:

$$b_3: \quad PC \leftarrow B(AD)$$

in the BSB instruction of Table 11-7. Explain why this can be done and how it results in the removal of the multiplexer from the block diagram of the computer.

11-19. A 4-bit counter with parallel load is enclosed in one IC package. How many ICs are needed to construct the following computer registers: PC, MAR, I, and G?

11-20. Design the G register of the computer using a 4-bit counter with parallel load of the type shown in Fig. 7-19.

11-21. List the program table for PLA 2 of Fig. 11-8.

11-22. Change the AND instruction of the computer to an OR instruction and modify the microprogram of Table 11-14 accordingly. Assign the OR microoperation to decoder output 15 in Table 11-13.

11-23. Change the BSB instruction of the computer to the BSA instruction defined in problem 11-12. Modify the microprogram of Table 11-14 to conform with this change. The encoding of ROM bits in Table 11-13 may also need a change.

11-24. Design a microprogram control unit for a computer that implements the fetch cycle and the execution of the memory-reference instructions listed in Table 11-2 and problem 11-12. Include two outputs for register-reference and input-output operations.

Microcomputer System Design

12-1 INTRODUCTION

A digital system is defined by the registers it contains and the operations performed on the binary information stored in the registers. Once a digital system is specified, the role of the designer is to develop the hardware that implements the required sequence of operations. The number of distinct microoperations in a given system is finite. The complexity of the design is in sequencing the operations to achieve the intended data processing task. This involves the formulation of control functions or the development of a microprogram. A third alternative is to use a microcomputer to implement the digital system. With a microcomputer, the sequence of operations can be formulated with a set of instructions that constitutes a program.

A digital system can be constructed by means of MSI circuits such as registers, decoders, ALU, memory, and multiplexers. Such a custom-made system has the advantage that it can be tailored to the needs of the particular application. However, a digital system constructed with MSI circuits would require a large number of IC packages. Moreover, any modifications that may be required after the system has been constructed must be accomplished by means of wiring changes among the components.

Some digital systems are suitable for LSI design with components such as processor unit, microprogram sequencer, and memory unit. These systems can be microprogrammed to fit the required specifications. The microprogram method operates at the register-transfer level and must specify each microoperation in the system. The microprogram LSI organization uses fewer ICs than the MSI implementation.

The number of IC packages can be further reduced if the digital system is suitable for construction with microcomputer LSI components. These components can be classified by function as follows:

1. A *microprocessor*, which is a central processor unit (CPU) enclosed in one LSI package.

499

2. *Random-access memory* (RAM) and *read-only memory* (ROM) chips that can be combined to form any memory size needed for an application.

3. *Programmable interface* units whose function is to interface between the CPU or memory and a wide variety of input and output devices.

The user can interconnect these LSI components to form a microcomputer system that fits the design requirements and thus reduce drastically the number of IC packages.

A microprocessor combined with memory and interface modules is called a *microcomputer*. The word *micro* is used to indicate the small physical size of the components involved. The second part of the word in micro*processor* and micro*computer* is what really sets them apart. *Processor* is used to indicate that section of the system which performs the basic functions to execute instructions and to process data as specified by a program. This part is usually called the CPU. The term *microcomputer* is used to indicate a small-size computer system consisting of the three basic units: CPU, memory, and input-output interface. The microprocessor is usually enclosed in one IC package called a *microprocessor chip*. A microcomputer in most cases refers to an interconnection of LSI components. On the other hand, some microprocessor chips include within the package not only the CPU, but also a portion of the memory as well. Such an LSI component is sometimes called a *one-chip microcomputer*.

A microcomputer can be used as a low-cost, general-purpose computer to provide processing capabilities similar to those of any other computer system. Although this is an important application, it is not the one we want to emphasize. In many applications, the microcomputer is used as a special-purpose digital system to provide the register-transfer operations for the system. This has the advantage that a few LSI packages replace the large number of MSI circuits that would be otherwise needed to generate these operations. Another advantage is that the register-transfer operations for the system can now be specified with a program. The program for a special-purpose application is unalterable, and for this reason it can be stored in a read-only memory. Once a fixed program resides in ROM, there is no behavioral difference between a microcomputer-controlled digital system and a custom hardware design.

The most important feature of the microcomputer is that a special-purpose digital system having a dedicated application can be designed by writing a program for a general-purpose digital computer. The execution of the fixed, unalterable program causes the microcomputer to behave in a prescribed manner, just as a corresponding MSI-based digital system would behave. This method of digital design was not economically feasible to implement before the development of small, inexpensive microcomputer components.

The program stored in the ROM part of a microcomputer system is a computer program that needs no alterations. Since RAM is a volatile memory, turning power off and on again destroys the binary information stored in it. The ROM is a nonvolatile memory and the program stored in it is available every time power is turned on. A special-purpose digital system constructed with a microcomputer starts operating as soon as power is supplied since its program resides in ROM. For this reason, the ROM part of a microcomputer system is also called the *program* memory.

At this point we should distinguish between a microprogram and a microcomputer. Although both use the prefix *micro*, the former is derived from the concept of microoperations, whereas the latter refers to the small size of the components. Both use a ROM to store a program that specifies the operations in the system. A microprogram stored in control memory implements the control unit in the CPU. The instructions stored in a microcomputer may be considered as macrooperations for the CPU rather than microinstructions for processor registers. Furthermore, the word microprogram refers to the way the control unit is implemented. A microcomputer is a small-size computer whose CPU may or may not have a microprogram control unit.

The low-cost, small-size microcomputer has changed the direction of digital logic design. Instead of realizing a set of register-transfer operations by control functions or a microprogram, logic functions are realized by specifying a set of instructions which are stored in ROM and executed in the microprocessor CPU. This method of design may be classified as a *programmable logic* method since the sequential operations are specified with a program stored in memory.

The microprocessor is a central component in a microcomputer system. The amount and type of memory in the system, as well as the nature of the I/O interface units that are used, are a function of the particular application. The fixed program that resides in the ROM of a particular microcomputer system is also dependent on the specific application.

The design of a microcomputer system may be divided into two parts: hardware design and software design. The hardware design considers the interconnection of the physical components to provide a complete digital system. The software design is concerned with the development of the programs for a particular application. Writing programs for a microcomputer is essentially the same as writing programs for any other computer. The only difference is that a microcomputer programmer must be familiar with the hardware configuration and must take into consideration the problems associated with the particular application. Writing programs for an established general-purpose computer usually involves computational procedures which require very little, if any, knowledge of the hardware construction of the computer itself.

This chapter covers the hardware aspects of microcomputers without considering software problems. Writing a program for a microcomputer is similar to writing a microprogram for control memory, except that one must use the set of instructions for the commercial microprocessor selected. The study of software design is a subject that by itself could fill an entire volume.

In this chapter, we first define the various components of a microcomputer system and the way they communicate with each other. The organization of a typical microprocessor is then presented, and its internal and external operations are explained. Some important features common to all microprocessors are discussed. We then show the organization of the memory section and explain the various types of interface units commonly used in the design of microcomputer systems.

12-2   MICROCOMPUTER ORGANIZATION

A typical microcomputer system consists of a microprocessor plus memory and I/O interface. The various components that form the system are linked through buses that transfer instructions, data, addresses, and control information among the IC components. Figure 12-1 shows the block diagram of a microcomputer system. Typically, the microcomputer has a single microprocessor. If many processors are included, then we have a multiprocessor system—which is a valid possibility. A number of RAM and ROM chips are combined to form a given memory size. The interface units communicate with various external devices through the I/O bus. At any given time, the microprocessor selects one of the units through its address bus. Data are transferred to and from the selected unit and the microprocessor via the data bus. Control information is usually transferred through individual lines, each specifying a particular control function.

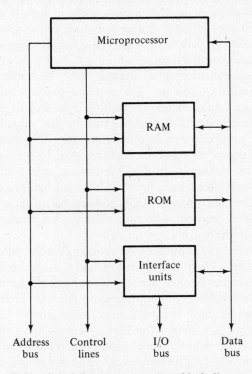

Figure 12-1   Microcomputer system block diagram

The purpose of the microprocessor is to provide a CPU which interprets instruction codes received from memory and to perform arithmetic, logic, and control operations on data stored in internal registers, memory words, or interface units. The microprocessor contains a number of registers, an arithmetic logic unit, and timing and control logic. Externally, it provides a bus system for transferring instructions, data, and control information to and from the modules connected to it. The internal operations of a typical microprocessor and the functions of the control lines are described in Section 12-3.

The random-access memory is a read-write memory type and consists of a number of IC packages connected together. The RAM is used to store data, variable parameters, and intermediate results that need updating and are subject to change. The ROM consists of a number of IC packages and is used for storing programs and tables of constants that are not subject to change once the production of the microcomputer system is completed. The method of connecting memory chips to the microprocessor is described in Section 12-6.

The interface units provide the necessary paths for transferring information between the microprocessor and external input and output devices connected to the I/O bus. The microprocessor receives status and data information from external devices through the interface. It responds by sending control and data information for the external devices through the interface. This communication is specified by programmed instructions that direct data through the buses in the microcomputer system. The various interface modules available in microcomputers and their operation are presented in Section 12-7.

The communication between the LSI components in a microcomputer takes place via the address and data buses. The address bus is unidirectional from the microprocessor to the other units. The binary information that the microprocessor places on the address bus specifies a particular memory word in RAM or ROM. The address bus is also used to select one of many interface units connected to the system or to a particular register within an interface unit. A memory word and an interface register may be distinguished by assigning a different address to each. Alternatively, a control signal may be used to specify whether the address on the bus is for a memory word or for an interface register. The number of lines available in the address bus determines the maximum memory size that can be accommodated in the system. For n lines, the address bus can specify up to 2^n words of memory. The typical length of a microprocessor address bus is 16, providing a maximum memory capacity of $2^{16} = 65,536$ words. The amount of memory employed in a microcomputer system depends on the particular application and quite often is less than the maximum available in the address bus.

The data bus transfers data to and from the microprocessor and the memory or interface which is selected by the address bus. The data bus is bidirectional, which means that the binary information can flow in either direction. A bidirectional data bus is used to save pins in the IC package. If a unit did not use a bidirectional data bus, it would be necessary to provide separate input and output terminals in the IC package. The number of lines in the microprocessor data bus ranges from 4 to 16, with 8 lines being the most common.

A set of separate data and address buses is the most common transfer path found in microprocessors. The advantage of this scheme is that a microprocessor can select a word in memory and transfer the data word at the same time. Some microprocessors use one common bus which is time-multiplexed for transfer of addresses or data. For example, a common 16-line bus can be used to transfer a 16-bit address, followed by a 16-bit data word to be written in memory. The advantage of this scheme is that fewer terminal pins are needed and yet data can be 16 bits wide. The disadvantages are the time lost in the sequential use of the common bus and the need for an external latch to hold the address for memory. Some microprocessors share only part of the system bus between data and address. A 16-line bus can use 8 bidirectional lines for data transfer and all 16 lines for transferring an address. This requires sharing of the data bus, since the address is split between the 8 data-bus lines and the remaining available 8 lines.

Instead of using a microprocessor chip as shown in Fig. 12-1, some applications replace this block with a microcomputer chip. Typically, a microcomputer chip contains a CPU together with 64 words of RAM and about 1024 words of ROM, all within one IC package. It also provides some features of an interface. If the digital system to be designed does not require more memory or additional interface capabilities, then the entire microcomputer system can be constructed with the single-chip microcomputer component. Thus a one-chip microcomputer can be used as a low-cost, small-size component for a stand-alone application. Most microcomputer chips can be expanded with external ROM, RAM, and interface capability to provide a more powerful control application. In subsequent discussions, the memory and interface will be separated from the CPU, but it must be realized that some of the memory and interface may be included within the IC package that contains the CPU.

To facilitate the development of special-purpose digital systems by means of a microcomputer, many sources offer a complete microcomputer unit on a single printed-circuit (PC) board. The microprocessor and a number of RAM, ROM, and interface ICs together with any other MSI and SSI chips needed to build a microcomputer unit, are all mounted on a single PC board. The IC terminals are connected through printed wires along the board to form a complete microcomputer unit. The user is given access to the interface for the I/O devices through the pins of the board connector. The connector also provides enough pins to accommodate all buses and allow for memory and interface expansion external to the board. Memory and interface expansion is also available in ready-made PC boards.

Bus Buffer

The bus system in a microprocessor is commonly implemented by means of bus buffers constructed with three-state gates. A three-state (or tri-state) gate is a digital circuit that exhibits three output states. Two of the states are signals equivalent to binary 1 and 0 as in conventional gates. The third state is called a *high-impedance state.* The high-impedance state behaves as if the output is disabled or "floating," which means that it cannot affect or be affected by an external signal at the terminal. The electronic circuit of a three-state gate is explained in Section 13-5 in conjunction with Fig. 13-16.

The graphic symbol of a three-state buffer gate is shown in Fig. 12-2. It has a normal input and a control input that determines the output state. When the control input is equal to binary 1, the gate behaves as any conventional buffer, with the output equal to the normal input. When the control input is 0, the output is disabled and the gate goes to the high-impedance state, regardless of the value in the normal input. The high-impedance state of a three-state gate provides a feature not available in other gates. Because of this feature, a large number of three-state gate outputs can be connected with wires to form a common bus line without endangering loading effects. However, no more than one gate may be in the active state at any given time. The connected gates must be controlled so that only one three-state gate has access to the bus line while all other gates are in a high-impedance state.

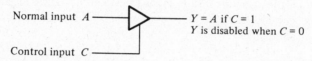

Normal input A — $Y = A$ if $C = 1$
Y is disabled when $C = 0$

Control input C

Figure 12-2   Graphic symbol for a three-state buffer gate

A bidirectional bus can be constructed with bus buffers to control the direction of information flow. One line of a bidirectional bus is shown in Fig. 12-3. The bus control has two selection lines, s_i for input transfer and s_o for output transfer. These selection lines control two three-state buffers. When $s_i = 1$ and $s_o = 0$, the bottom buffer is enabled and the top buffer is disabled by going to a high-impedance state. This forms a path for input data coming from the bus to pass through the bottom buffer and into the system. When $s_o = 1$ and $s_i = 0$, the top buffer is enabled and the bottom buffer goes to a high-impedance state. This

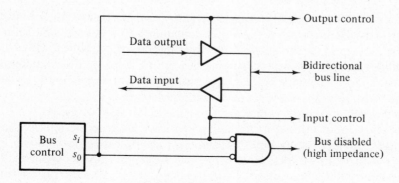

Figure 12-3   Bidirectional bus buffer

forms a path for output data coming from the system to pass through the upper gate and out to the bus line. The bus line can be disabled by making s_i and s_o both 0. This puts both buffers into a high-impedance state, which prevents any input or output transfer of information through the bus line. This condition must exist when an external source is using the common bus line to communicate with some other component. The two selection lines can be used to inform the external modules connected to the bus of the state in which the bidirectional bus is at any given time.

In most cases, the drive capability of a microprocessor bus is limited, i.e., it can drive only a small number of external loads. When the bus is connected to a large number of external units, the drive capability of the microprocessor must be enhanced with external bus buffers, which are also available in IC form. Furthermore, any component that has separate input and output terminals must be connected to the microcomputer bus system through external bus buffers in order to isolate the component when it is not communicating with the bus. Thus, a microcomputer system quite often needs external bus buffers between the microprocessor and the other LSI components and between certain LSI components and the common-bus system.

12-3 MICROPROCESSOR ORGANIZATION

To guarantee a wide range of acceptability, a microprocessor must provide an internal organization suited for a wide range of applications. The organizations of commercial microprocessors differ from each other, but they all have the common property of a central processor unit. As such, they are capable of interpreting instruction codes received from memory and of performing data processing tasks specified by a program. They also respond to external control commands and generate control signals for external modules to use.

Typical Set of Control Signals

Proper operation of a microprocessor requires that certain control and timing signals be provided to accomplish specific functions and that other control lines be monitored to determine the state of the microprocessor. A typical set of control lines available in most microprocessors is shown in Fig. 12-4. For completion, the diagram also shows the data bus, address bus, and power supply input to the unit. The power requirement for a particular microprocessor is specified by the voltage level and current consumption that must be supplied to operate the IC.

The *clock* input is used by the microprocessor to generate multiphase clock pulses that provide timing and control for internal functions. Some microprocessors require an external clock generator to supply the clock pulses. In this case, the output clock is available from the clock generator rather than from the microprocessor itself. Some units generate the clock within the chip but require an

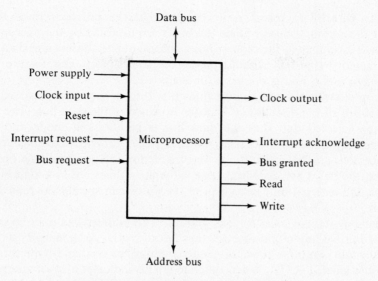

Figure 12-4 Control signals in a microprocessor

external crystal or circuit to control the frequency of the clock. The clock pulses are used by external modules to synchronize their operations with the operations of the microprocessor.

The *reset* input is used to reset and start the microprocessor after power is turned on or any time the user wants to start the process from the beginning. The effect of a reset signal is to initialize the microprocessor by forcing a given address into the program counter. The program then starts executing with the first instruction at this address. The simplest way to initiate a reset is to clear the program counter and start the program from address zero. Some microprocessors respond to the reset signal by transferring the contents of a specified memory location into the program counter. The designer must then store the beginning address of the program at the adopted memory location.

The *interrupt* request into the microprocessor typically comes from an interface module to inform the microprocessor that it is ready to transfer information. When the microprocessor acknowledges the interrupt request, it suspends the execution of the current program and branches to a program that services the interface module. At the completion of the service routine, the microprocessor returns to the previous program. The interrupt facility is included to provide a change in program sequence as a result of external conditions. The interrupt concept and the method of responding to an interrupt request are discussed in Section 12-5.

The *bus-request* control input is a request to the microprocessor to temporarily suspend its operation and drive all buses into their high-impedance state. When the request is acknowledged, the microprocessor responds by enabling the *bus-granted* control output line. Thus, when an external device wishes to transfer information directly to memory, it requests that the microprocessor relinquish control of the common buses. Once the buses are disabled by the microprocessor, the device that originated the request takes control of the address and data buses to conduct memory transfers without processor intervention. This feature is called *direct memory access* and is discussed in Section 12-8.

The *read* and *write* are control lines that inform the component selected by the address bus of the direction of transfer expected in the data bus. The read line informs the selected unit that the data bus is in an input mode and that the microprocessor will accept data from the data bus. The write line indicates that the microprocessor is in an output mode and that valid data are available on the data bus. When the buses are disabled, these two control lines are in a high-impedance state; thus, the external unit in control of the buses can specify the read and write operations.

Other possibilities exist for bus control. The address bus may be controlled with an additional line to indicate whether the address is for a memory word or for an interface unit. Another possibility is to combine the read and write control lines into one line labeled R/W. When this line is 1, it indicates a read, and when 0, it indicates a write. A second control line is then needed to indicate when a valid address is on the address bus, so that the external components respond to the R/W line only when requested with a valid address.

The control signals enumerated in Fig. 12-4 constitute a minimum set of control functions for a microprocessor. Most microprocessors have additional control features for special functions. Different units may use different mnemonic names for identical control functions, and not necessarily the names used here.

CPU Example

To appreciate the tasks performed by a microprocessor, it will be instructive to investigate the internal organization of a typical unit. Figure 12-5 shows the block diagram of a central processor unit enclosed within a microprocessor chip.* Externally, it provides a bidirectional data bus, an address bus, and a number of control lines. Here we show only the control lines associated with the bus transfer. The data bus is designated by the symbol DBUS and consists of eight lines. The information contained in the eight lines is called a *byte*, which is the name used to denote an *8-bit word*. The address bus, designated by the symbol ABUS, consists of 16 lines to specify $2^{16} = 64$K (K = 1024) possible addresses. Thus the microprocessor is capable of communicating with a memory unit of 64K bytes.

Internally, the microprocessor has six processor registers labeled *B* through *G*, an accumulator register designated by the letter *A*, and a temporary register, *T*. These registers are 8-bits wide and can accommodate a byte. The ALU operates on the data stored in *A* and *T*, and the result of the operation is transferred to *A* or,

---

*This is similar to the 8080/85 microprocessor except that the *F* and *G* registers are called *H* and *L* in the 8080/85.

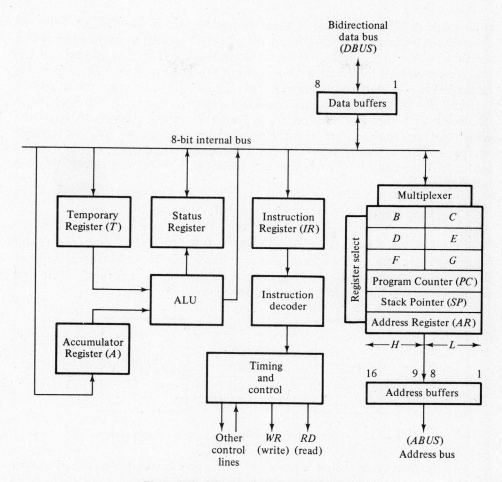

Figure 12-5 Block diagram of microprocessor

through an internal bus, to any one of the other six processor registers. The status register holds the status bits of an operation, such as end carry from the ALU, the sign-bit value, and a zero-result indication.* The operation code of an instruction is transferred to the instruction register (*IR*), where it is decoded to determine the sequence of microoperations needed to execute the instruction. The timing and control supervise all internal operations in the CPU and the external control lines in the microprocessor.

The address buffers receive information from three sources: the program counter (*PC*), the stack pointer (*SP*), and the address register (*AR*). *PC* maintains the memory address of the current program instruction and is incremented after every instruction fetch. *AR* is used for temporary storage of addresses that are read

---

*The status register was discussed in Sec. 9-7.

from memory. The functions of these two registers will be clarified when we describe the sequence of operations in the CPU. *SP* is used in conjunction with a memory stack and its function is explained in Section 12-5. The address bus can also receive address information from a pair of processor registers. Three pairs can be formed to provide a 16-bit address. They are labeled with the combined register symbols *BC*, *DE*, and *FG*. Each processor register contains 8 bits and, when combined with the one adjacent to it, forms a register pair of 16 bits. It is sometimes convenient to partition the three 16-bit registers *PC*, *SP*, and *AR* into two parts. The symbol *H* designates the 8 high-order bits, and the symbol *L*, the 8 low-order bits. Thus *PC(L)* refers to bits 1 through 8 of *PC* and *PC(H)* refers to bits 9 through 16.

Memory Cycle

The memory unit consists of both RAM and ROM. It is connected to the microprocessor through the address and data buses and the read and write control. This is shown schematically in Fig. 12-6. A memory cycle is defined as the time required to access the memory to read or write a byte.

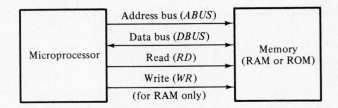

Figure 12-6 Communication between microprocessor and memory

In the *read* cycle, the microprocessor places an address in *ABUS* and enables control line *RD*. The memory responds by reading the byte and placing it in *DBUS*. The microprocessor then accepts the byte and transfers it to an internal register. To express the read cycle symbolically, assume that the address is to come from *AR* and the data byte is to be transferred to register *A*:

$$ABUS \leftarrow AR, RD \leftarrow 1 \qquad \text{address in bus for reading}$$

$$DBUS \leftarrow M[ABUS] \qquad \text{memory reads byte}$$

$$A \leftarrow DBUS, RD \leftarrow 0 \qquad \text{byte transferred to } A$$

First, the microprocessor places the memory address into *ABUS* and informs the memory that a valid address is available for reading. The memory responds to *RD* by reading the byte at the address given by *ABUS* and placing it in *DBUS*. The microprocessor then transfers the byte from *DBUS* to *A*. At the same time, control signal *RD* is disabled, indicating the end of the memory transfer.

The three operations listed above can be combined into one statement:

$$A \leftarrow M[AR]$$

This is a read operation that transfers the memory byte addressed by *AR* into the *A* register.

In the *write* cycle, the microprocessor places an address in *ABUS* and a data byte in *DBUS*. At the same time, the control line *WR* is enabled. The memory responds to *WR* by writing the byte from *DBUS* into a memory location specified by the address in *ABUS*. This process can be expressed symbolically:

$$ABUS \leftarrow AR, DBUS \leftarrow A, WR \leftarrow 1$$

$$M[ABUS] \leftarrow DBUS, WR \leftarrow 0$$

This states that the contents of register *A* are transferred to a memory byte at the address given by *AR*. Again, it is possible to write this operation with one composite statement:

$$M[AR] \leftarrow A$$

Memory transfers to and from the microprocessor must conform with certain timing relationships that must exist between the control signals and the information on the buses. These timing relationships are specified in timing waveforms that are included with the product specifications of the units involved. The time interval of a memory cycle is a function of the internal clock frequency of the microprocessor and the access time of the memory. Once the microprocessor sends an address, it expects a response within a given interval of time. A memory that is capable of responding within the processor time interval can be directly controlled by the microprocessor memory cycle.

If the microprocessor communicates with a slow memory, it may take longer to access the memory than the allowable timing interval. To be able to use slow memories, a microprocessor must be able to delay the transfer until the memory access is completed. One way is to extend the microprocessor clock period by reducing the clock frequency to fit the access time of the memory. Some microprocessors provide a special control input called *ready* to allow the memory to set its own memory cycle time. If, after sending an address out, the microprocessor does not receive a *ready* input from memory, it enters a *wait* state for as long as the ready line is in the 0-state. When the memory access is completed, the ready line goes to the 1-state to indicate that the memory is ready for the specified transfer.

Microprocessor Sequencing

The timing and control in the microprocessor determine the sequence of transfers through the internal and external buses, the ALU, and the processor registers. During the fetch cycle, the control reads an operation code from memory and deposits it into its instruction register. The instruction is decoded and translated into specific processing activities. Further references to memory depend on the operation code decoded. Let us assume that all operation codes consist of eight bits and are stored in one byte of memory. Operands are also one byte long because the data bus is eight bits wide. An address is specified with two bytes or 16 bits. Now consider three add instructions with different format lengths.

1. *Add* B *to* A. This is an instruction to add the contents of register *B* to the present contents of the accumulator. All the information necessary to specify the instruction is contained within the one-byte operation code.

2. *Add immediate operand to* A. This is an instruction that adds an operand to the present contents of the accumulator. The operand byte is placed in memory following the operation-code byte. This instruction occupies two bytes of memory.

3. *Add operand specified by an address to* A. This is an instruction that adds a byte stored anywhere in memory to the present contents of the accumulator. The address of the operand is placed in memory following the operation-code byte. This instruction occupies three bytes of memory since the address itself occupies two bytes.

The format and function of the three instructions are summarized in Table 12-1. Each instruction has at least one byte for the operation code. The control unit is designed to recognize the number of bytes in a particular instruction from the decoded operation code of the first byte.

The memory representation of the three instructions is depicted in Fig. 12-7. The first instruction is assumed to be in location 81, with an operation code of 8 bits assigned arbitrarily. The other two instructions occupy two and three bytes, respectively. The address of the third instruction is 260 and is determined from the 16-bit binary number in locations 85 and 86:

$$(00000001 \ 00000100)_2 = (260)_{10}$$

The operand for this instruction is shown to reside in memory location 260. In a

TABLE 12-1 Three typical instructions for microprocessor

Instruction	Byte 1	Byte 2	Byte 3	Function
Add *B* to *A*	Operation code	—	—	$A \leftarrow A + B$
Add immediate operand to *A*	Operation code	Operand	—	$A \leftarrow A + \text{byte 2}$
Add operand specified by an address to *A*	Operation code	High-order half of address	Low-order half of address	$A \leftarrow A + M[address]$

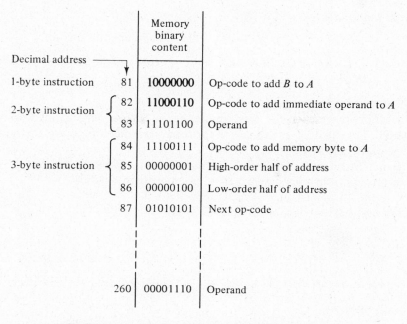

	Memory binary content	
1-byte instruction 81	**10000000**	Op-code to add *B* to *A*
2-byte instruction { 82	**11000110**	Op-code to add immediate operand to *A*
83	11101100	Operand
3-byte instruction { 84	11100111	Op-code to add memory byte to *A*
85	00000001	High-order half of address
86	00000100	Low-order half of address
87	01010101	Next op-code
260	00001110	Operand

Figure 12-7 Memory representation of three instructions

typical application, the three instructions will normally reside in ROM, while the operand in location 260 will be in RAM. This operand must reside in RAM because it must be assumed that its value is subject to change during the computation. Otherwise, if the operand value does not change, there is no need to associate it with an address.

Referring to Fig. 12-5 for the names of registers and buses, we can now list the sequence of operations required to process each instruction. We assume that the program counter initially contains 81.

Add B *to* A:

$$IR \leftarrow M[PC], PC \leftarrow PC + 1 \qquad \text{read operation code}$$
$$T \leftarrow B \qquad\qquad\qquad\qquad \text{transfer } B \text{ to } T$$
$$A \leftarrow A + T \qquad\qquad\qquad \text{add } T \text{ to } A$$

The first line represents the fetch cycle for reading the operation code into the instruction register. The decoded operation specifies a processor register; so the contents of *B* are transferred to *T* and the add operation is performed in the ALU. Note that *PC* has been incremented and now contains the number 82.

The one-byte instruction is executed with one memory cycle because all operands reside in processor registers. If an operand resides in memory, it is necessary to access the memory to read the operand.

Add immediate operand to A:

$$IR \leftarrow M[PC], PC \leftarrow PC + 1 \qquad \text{read operation code}$$

$$T \leftarrow M[PC], PC \leftarrow PC + 1 \qquad \text{read operand}$$

$$A \leftarrow A + T \qquad\qquad\qquad \text{add operand to } A$$

The first line represents the fetch cycle again. *PC* is incremented to contain address 83. The operand at this address is read from memory and placed in *T*, and the addition is performed in the ALU.

If the instruction contains the address of the operand, the microprocessor must go through four memory cycles to execute the instruction.

Add operand specified by an address to A:

$$IR \leftarrow M[PC], PC \leftarrow PC + 1 \qquad \text{read operation code}$$

$$AR(H) \leftarrow M[PC], PC \leftarrow PC + 1 \qquad \text{read first byte of address}$$

$$AR(L) \leftarrow M[PC], PC \leftarrow PC + 1 \qquad \text{read second byte of address}$$

$$T \leftarrow M[AR] \qquad\qquad\qquad \text{read operand}$$

$$A \leftarrow A + T \qquad\qquad\qquad\quad \text{add operand to } A$$

The address part of the instruction is temporarily stored in the address register (*AR*). The 16-bit address formed in *AR* is then used to read the operand.

A large number of memory cycles is undesirable in microprocessors because they consume a considerable amount of processing time. This is one of the limiting factors on the speed of 8-bit microprocessors with 16-bit addresses. The number of accesses to memory can be reduced if a 16-bit data bus is used. 16-bit microprocessors require fewer references to memory compared to 8-bit microprocessors. Although we have chosen to describe the operation of an 8-bit microprocessor, the operation with a 16-bit data bus would be similar, taking into consideration the differences in word lengths used for processor registers and memory words.

12-4 INSTRUCTIONS AND ADDRESSING MODES

The logical structure of microprocessors is described in reference manuals provided by the manufacturer. A reference manual for a particular microprocessor describes the internal organization of the CPU, the function of all input and output terminals, and the processor registers available from the user's point of view. The manual describes all the instructions available in the computer and explains their functions. It also shows how status bits are affected by each instruction. The internal code for each instruction is listed in binary, octal, or hexadecimal. In most cases, either the octal or hexadecimal equivalent code is adopted because these codes need fewer digits than the binary representation. When a program is written for the computer, each instruction is assigned a symbolic name to identify it.

Symbolic names and codes assigned to instructions used in one microprocessor are different from the names and codes used in a different microprocessor, even for similar instructions. For this reason, the user must study and remember the set of instructions and their symbolic names every time a different microprocessor is employed. Although the instruction sets of different microprocessors differ from one another, there are certain instructions that perform basic operations and are included in all microprocessors.

Basic Set of Microprocessor Instructions

Microprocessor instructions may be classified into three distinct types.

1. *Transfer* instructions that move data among registers, memory words, and interface registers without changing the binary information content.

2. *Operation* instructions that perform operations on data stored in registers or memory words.

3. *Control* instructions used to test status conditions in registers and, depending on results, cause a change in program sequence.

The instruction set of a particular microprocessor specifies the register-transfer operations and control decisions that are available in the microcomputer system. A specific program for a microcomputer is equivalent to specifying the sequence of operations for the particular digital system that the microcomputer implements.

Transfer-type instructions in microprocessors are indicated by various names. A *move* instruction causes a transfer of data from source to destination. Either the source or the destination may be a processor register or a memory location. The *load* and *store* instructions are similar to the move instruction, except that they usually refer to transfers from and to memory and accumulator. The *exchange* instruction swaps information between two registers or between a register and a memory word. The *push* and *pop* instructions transfer data among processor registers and a memory stack. The *input* and *output* instructions transfer data among processor registers and interface registers.

Operation-type instructions perform arithmetic, logic, and shift operations among processor registers or memory words. They also set, clear, or complement status or flag bits. Typical operation instructions are add, subtract, AND, OR, complement, and set carry. Most of the operation-type instructions also change the status bits in the status register of the processor.

Control-type instructions provide decision-making capabilities and change the path taken by the program when executed in the computer. Instructions are stored in consecutive memory locations and are executed one after the other in sequence. The programmer inserts a control instruction every time that control must be transferred to an instruction out of normal sequence. Control instructions may be conditional or unconditional. A conditional control instruction causes a branch out of normal program sequence only when a specified status condition is detected. An unconditional control instruction causes a branch unconditionally. The branch out of normal program sequence is accomplished by changing the program counter so it contains the address of the instruction that is to be executed next.

There are three types of control instructions and each type may be conditional or unconditional:

1. Jump or branch instructions.

2. Call to and return from subroutine instructions.

3. Skip instructions.

The words *jump* and *branch* are used interchangeably to mean the same thing, but sometimes they are used to denote different addressing modes. These instructions are associated with an address that specifies where the jump or branch is to be made. The call-to-subroutine and return-from-subroutine instructions are explained in the next section in conjunction with the memory stack. A skip instruction skips the next instruction in sequence. By placing an unconditional branch instruction after the skip instruction, it is possible to branch to one of two possible locations, depending on the value of a specified status-bit condition.

Instructions for Microprocessor

The number of distinct instructions in a particular microprocessor may range from 50 to 250. These instructions must be studied and memorized by the user who writes programs for the microcomputer. A partial list of instructions formulated for the microprocessor of Fig. 12-5 is presented in Table 12-2. The instructions are divided into three sections to give examples of transfer-, operation-, and control-type instructions.

The hexadecimal code listed in the table is a 2-digit number equivalent to the 8-bit operation code assigned to the instruction. (The equivalent 4-bit representation for the 16 hexadecimal digits was given in Table 1-1.) The symbolic name for each instruction is a 2- to 4-letter designation followed by one or two symbols for a register, an operand, or a memory address. The description column explains the instruction in words, and the function column defines the instruction precisely with a register-transfer statement. Note that computer instructions specify macrooperations for the computer and can be symbolized with appropriate statements in the register-transfer method. However, for various practical reasons, computer instructions are written with specialized symbols as in the second column of the table. These special symbols are assigned by the computer manufacturer and tend to be different in different computers.

TABLE 12-2 Partial list of instructions for microprocessor

Hexa-decimal code	Instruction symbol		Description	Function*
78	MOV	A, B	Move B to A	$A \leftarrow B$
3E	MVI	A, D8	Move immediate operand to A	$A \leftarrow D8$
7E	MOV	A, FG	Move to A with register indirect	$A \leftarrow M[FG]$
77	MOV	FG, A	Move A with register indirect	$M[FG] \leftarrow A$
3A	LDA	AD16	Load A direct	$A \leftarrow M[AD16]$
32	STA	AD16	Store A direct	$M[AD16] \leftarrow A$
01	LXI	FG, D16	Load register pair immediate	$FG \leftarrow D16$
80	ADD	B	Add B to A	$A \leftarrow A + B$
C6	ADI	D8	Add immediate operand to A	$A \leftarrow A + D8$
86	ADD	FG	Add to A with register indirect	$A \leftarrow A + M[FG]$
90	SUB	B	Subtract B from A	$A \leftarrow A - B$
A0	ANA	B	AND B to A	$A \leftarrow A \wedge B$
B0	ORA	B	OR B to A	$A \leftarrow A \vee B$
04	INR	B	Increment B	$B \leftarrow B + 1$
05	DCR	B	Decrement B	$B \leftarrow B - 1$
03	INX	BC	Increment register pair BC	$BC \leftarrow BC + 1$
0B	DCX	BC	Decrement register pair BC	$BC \leftarrow BC - 1$
2F	CMA		Complement A	$A \leftarrow \bar{A}$
07	RLC		Rotate A left with carry	$A \leftarrow \text{clc } A$
0F	RRC		Rotate A right with carry	$A \leftarrow \text{crc } A$
37	STC		Set carry bit to 1	$C \leftarrow 1$
C3	JMP	AD16	Jump unconditionally	$PC \leftarrow AD16$
DA	JC	AD16	Jump on carry	If $(C = 1)$ then $(PC \leftarrow AD16)$
C2	JNZ	AD16	Jump on nonzero	If $(Z = 0)$ then $(PC \leftarrow AD16)$
CD	CALL	AD16	Call subroutine	$Stack \leftarrow PC$, $PC \leftarrow AD16$
C9	RET		Return from subroutine	$PC \leftarrow stack$
76	HLT		Halt processor	

*A = accumulator register; B = B register; FG = register pair F and G; BC = register pair B and C; $D8$ = 8-bit data operand (1 byte); $D16$ = 16-bit data operand (2 bytes); $AD16$ = 16-bit address (2 bytes).

The first four instructions in Table 12-2 are move instructions that transfer information from a given source to a given destination. The next three are load and store instructions that accomplish a similar function. A representative number of operation-type instructions are listed in the second part of the table. The last section lists a few control instructions.

The move with register-indirect instruction:

$$\text{MOV} \quad \text{A, FG}$$

symbolizes the register-transfer operation $A \leftarrow M[FG]$. It transfers the memory byte whose address is in register pair FG into register A. This is called a register-indirect instruction because register pair FG specifies the address of the operand rather than the operand itself.

The load-immediate instruction:

$$\text{LXI} \quad \text{FG, D16}$$

symbolizes the register-transfer operation $FG \leftarrow D16$, where $D16$ is a 2-byte number that may represent an address. This instruction can be used to transfer an address into register pair FG. When used in this manner, register pair FG constitutes a *data counter* or a *pointer* that points to an address in memory where an operand is stored. FG can be incremented with the increment-register-pair instruction:

$$\text{INX} \quad \text{FG}$$

which symbolizes the register-transfer operation $FG \leftarrow FG + 1$. In this way, the data counter or pointer can be incremented to point at consecutive addresses in memory where the programmer stores a table of consecutive data bytes.

The operation instructions provide the common arithmetic, logic, and shift operations. Note that more instructions of the same type can be formulated if we specify one of the other five processor registers C, D, E, F, or G instead of specifying register B. Similarly, an instruction that specifies a register pair can be duplicated by using any one of the three possible register pairs BE, DE, or FG.

The last six instructions in the table are control instructions. The jump and call instructions need a 16-bit address symbolized by $AD16$. The return and halt instructions are one-byte instructions. Those that include the symbol $AD16$ or $D16$ are three-byte instructions and those that use a $D8$ symbol are two-byte instructions. All others are one-byte instructions whether they do or do not specify a register.

The best way to appreciate the instruction set of a computer is to write programs that perform meaningful data-processing tasks. The programs written for a microcomputer system require the same logical reasoning involved in writing microprograms for a digital system as exemplified in Chapter 10.

Addressing Modes

The operation code of the instruction specifies the operation that will be executed after it is read from memory and placed in the control unit of the CPU. The control unit must also know where to find the operand or operands upon which the operation is to be performed. Operands may be located in processor registers, in memory words, or in interface registers. The way the operands are determined during program execution is determined from the *addressing mode* of the instruction. In large computers, the addressing mode of an instruction is specified with a binary code just as the operation code is specified. In 8-bit microprocessors, the first byte of an instruction is a combined binary code that specifies both the operation and the mode of the instruction. This byte, when placed in the instruction register during the fetch cycle, is interpreted by the control to determine not only the operation that must be executed but also the way to go about locating the operands.

An example of three addressing modes for the same operation can be found in Table 12-1. The table defines three types of addressing modes for the add-to-*A* instruction. By specifying a different mode, the operation can refer to a register, to an immediate operand, or to an operand specified by a memory address. A computer can use a variety of addressing modes for the same operation to provide different ways for locating operands. To the inexperienced user, the variety of addressing modes in some computers may seem excessively complicated. However, the availability of different addressing schemes gives the experienced programmer flexibility for writing programs that are more efficient with respect to the number of instructions and execution time.

We have already discussed several addressing modes in previous examples and they are summarized here for reference.

Implied Mode: In this mode the operand is specified implicitly in the definition of the instruction. Instructions of this type are 1-byte instructions. For example, the instruction "complement accumulator" is an implied-mode instruction because the operand in the accumulator register is implied in the definition of the instruction.

Register Mode: In this mode the operands are in registers which reside within the CPU. Register-mode instructions are 1-byte instructions and can be executed within the CPU without the need to reference memory for operands.

Register-indirect Mode: In this mode the instruction specifies a register or a pair of registers in the processor whose contents give the address of the operand in memory. This mode uses 1-byte instructions even though the operand is in memory. Before using a register-indirect-mode instruction, the programmer must ensure that the address of the operand is placed in the processor register with a previous transfer-type instruction. A reference to the register is then equivalent to specifying a memory address.

Immediate Mode: In this mode the operand is specified in the instruction itself. In an 8-bit microprocessor, the operand is placed in memory immediately after the operation-code byte. An immediate-mode instruction having an 8-bit operand is a 2-byte instruction. One with a 16-bit operand is a 3-byte instruction.

Direct-addressing Mode: In this mode the operand resides in memory and its address is given directly in the address part of the instruction. In 8-bit microprocessors with 16-bit addresses, a direct instruction consists of 3 bytes. In computers with wider memory words, the address part is combined with the operation and mode code bits to combine the entire instruction in one memory word. Most direct-mode instructions assume that the other operands reside in processor registers. If more than one operand resides in memory, the instruction must include additional addresses to specify their locations.

Some 8-bit microprocessors with 16-bit addresses have special direct-addressing modes that require only one byte to specify an address. Such microprocessors divide the 2^{16} bytes of memory into blocks called *pages*. Each page is usually assigned 256 bytes of consecutive memory space. A page in memory is then specified by the 8 high-order bits of an address. The 8 low-order bits give the byte within the page. Thus, a 64K memory can be divided into 256 pages of 256 bytes each. The first page is called page 0 and the last is page 255. By means of the paging scheme, it is possible to develop some variations in the direct mode of addressing.

Zero-page Addressing: This is similar to the direct-addressing mode except that the address part of the instruction contains only 1 byte. This is a 2-byte instruction, with the second byte specifying the 8 low-order bits of a memory address. The 8 high-order bits of the address are assumed to be all 0's. This restricts the range of addresses to the lowest 256 bytes of memory (0–255) which is defined to be page 0.

Present-page Addressing: This mode assumes that the operand resides in memory within the same memory page as the instruction that uses it. Since the program counter always holds the address of the next instruction, its 8 high-order bits also contain the present page number. This mode of addressing uses 2-byte instructions, with an 8-bit address part. The address of the operand is obtained from the page number catenated with the address part of the instruction. The 16-bit address of the operand is computed from:

$$PC(H) + AD8$$

where $PC(H)$ denotes the eight high-order bits of PC, and $AD8$ is the 8-bit address of the instruction. The result is a 16-bit address, with $PC(H)$ giving the first 8 bits and $AD8$ the other 8 bits.

Relative Addressing: This is similar to the present-page addressing mode except that it is not sensitive to page boundaries. A relative-mode instruction is a 2-byte instruction, with the second byte specifying a signed number in the range between -128 and $+127$. This is accomplished by representing the number in sign-2's-complement form. The 16-bit address of the operand is computed by adding the 16-bit content presently available in the program counter to the 8-bit signed address in the instruction. If the latter is denoted by $AD8$, the address computation can be symbolized as:

$$PC + AD8$$

This requires that the operand (or the location where a branch relative instruction transfers control) be within 127 and -128 bytes away from the address of the next instruction. Page boundaries are of no consequence in the relative mode because the entire 16 bits of the program counter are used in the calculation.

The address part of an instruction is used by the control unit in the CPU to obtain the operand from memory. Sometimes this address is the address of the operand, but sometimes it is just an address from which the address of the operand is calculated. Computers use various other addressing modes to calculate the address of an operand. To differentiate among the various addresses involved in the computation, we must distinguish between the address given in the instruction and the actual address used by the control when it executes the instruction. The address of the operand or the address where control branches in response to a jump, branch, or call instruction is called the *effective address*. In a direct-mode instruction, the effective address is equal to the address part of the instruction. In the relative mode, the effective address is computed from the value in PC plus the address part of the instruction.

The computation of the effective address for the last four addressing modes discussed above are listed in Table 12-3. The table also lists five other addressing modes commonly found in microprocessors (and in larger computers as well). The symbol $AD16$ denotes a 2-byte address, and $AD8$ denotes a 1-byte address. PC is the program counter and XR is an index register. XR is a CPU register used in many computers for storing an address. The address stored in XR can be referenced with an indexed-mode instruction. An address is placed initially into XR by means of a transfer-type instruction. The computation of the effective address in each mode is specified in the table with a register computational expression. The computed effective address is then used to access memory to read an operand or becomes the branch address in a control-type instruction. The other addressing modes listed in the table are explained below.

TABLE 12-3 Computation of effective address for various addressing modes

Address mode	Effective address	Comments
Direct	$AD\,16$	16-bit address part of instruction
Zero page	$AD\,8$	8-bit address part of instruction
Present page	$PC(H) + AD\,8$	8 highest-order bits of PC catenated with $AD\,8$
Relative	$PC + AD\,8$	Contents of PC plus signed $AD\,8$
Indexed	$XR + AD\,16$	Contents of XR plus $AD\,16$
Base register	$XR + AD\,8$	Contents of XR plus $AD\,8$
Indirect	$M[AD\,16]$	Address stored in location given by $AD\,16$
Indexed-indirect	$M[XR + AD\,8]$	Address stored in location $(XR + AD\,8)$
Indirect-indexed	$M[AD\,8] + XR$	Address stored in location $AD\,8$ plus contents of XR

Indexed Addressing: Instructions in this mode contain 3 bytes, with the last two giving a 16-bit address. The address part of the instruction is added to the value presently stored in the index register to obtain the effective address. The index register is often incremented or decremented to facilitate the execution of program loops and to access tables of data stored in memory.

Base-register Addressing: This is similar to the indexed-addressing mode, except that the address part of the instruction consists of a number of bits that is less than the number of bits required for a full address. The effective address is calculated by adding the contents of the index register to the partial address in the instruction. The register used in this mode is sometimes called a *base register* instead of an index register. The base register holds a base address, and the truncated address in the instruction specifies a displacement with respect to the base address.

Indirect Addressing: In this mode the address part of the instruction specifies the address where the effective address is stored. Control reads the address part of the instruction and uses it to address memory again to read the effective address. Memory must be accessed again to read the operand if the instruction is of the operation type. In a control-type instruction, the effective address is the branch address which is transferred to PC.

Indexed-indirect Addressing: This is an indirect-addressing mode, except that the address part of the instruction is added to the contents of the index register to determine the address where the effective address is stored in memory.

Indirect-indexed Addressing: In this mode the value stored in the memory location specified by the address part of the instruction is added to the contents of the index register to obtain the effective address.

Specific microprocessors employ several addressing modes, but very seldom would one unit have all the addressing modes enumerated here. To be able to write programs for a microcomputer, it is necessary to know the type of instructions available and also to be thoroughly familiar with the addressing modes used in the microprocessor.

12-5   STACK, SUBROUTINES, AND INTERRUPT

A very useful feature included in many computers is a memory stack, also called a last-in first-out (LIFO) list. A stack is a storage device that stores information in such a manner that the item stored last is the first item retrieved. The operation of a stack is sometimes compared to a stack of trays. The last tray placed in the stack is the first to be taken off.

A stack is useful for a variety of applications and its organization possesses special features that facilitate many data processing tasks. For example, a stack is used in some electronic calculators and computers to facilitate the evaluation of arithmetic expressions. Its use in microprocessors is mostly for handling of subroutines and interrupts. In this section, we explain the operation of a stack and restrict the discussion to those applications found in microprocessors.

Memory Stack

A *memory stack* is essentially a portion of a memory unit accessed by an address that is always incremented or decremented after the memory access. The register that holds the address for a stack is called a *stack pointer* (*SP*) because its value always points to the top item in the stack. The two operations of a stack are the insertion and deletion of items. The operation of insertion is called *push* and it can be thought of as the result of pushing a new item onto the top of the stack. The operation of deletion is called *pop* and it can be thought of as the result of removing one item so that the stack pops out. However, nothing is physically pushed or popped in a memory stack. Those operations are simulated by incrementing or decrementing the stack pointer register.

It must be realized that a stack can be placed within the microprocessor without the need to refer to memory. In such a case, the stack is constructed with registers and is called a *register stack*. The size of a register stack is limited by the number of registers it contains. A memory stack can grow and may occupy the entire memory space if necessary. We will explain the organization of the stack assuming that it resides in memory. The same organization also applies to a register stack, except that the push and pop operations are executed within the microprocessor without reference to memory.

Figure 12-8 shows a portion of a memory unit organized as a stack. The stack pointer register *SP* holds a binary number whose value is equal to the address

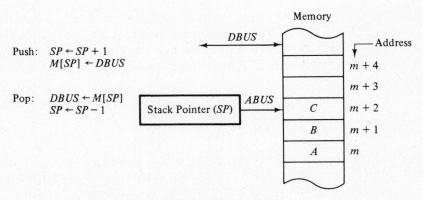

Push: $SP \leftarrow SP + 1$
       $M[SP] \leftarrow DBUS$

Pop: $DBUS \leftarrow M[SP]$
       $SP \leftarrow SP - 1$

Figure 12-8 Memory stack operations

of the item which is currently on top of the stack. Three items are presently stored in the stack: A, B, and C in consecutive addresses m, $m + 1$, and $m + 2$, respectively. Item C at address $m + 2$ is on top of the stack, so SP now contains $m + 2$. To remove the top item, the stack is popped by reading the item at address $m + 2$ and decrementing SP. Item B is now on top of the stack since SP contains address $m + 1$. To insert a new item, the stack is pushed by incrementing SP and writing a new item on top of the stack. Note that item C has been read out but not physically removed. This does not matter as far as the stack operation is concerned, because when the stack is pushed, a new item is written on top of the stack regardless of what was there before.

The position of the stack pointer in a microprocessor can be found in the block diagram of Fig. 12-5. The SP can specify an address for memory through the address bus, $ABUS$. The data transferred to and from the memory stack and the microprocessor go through the data bus, $DBUS$. To write meaningful register-transfer statements for the stack operations, we assume that the data are transferred to and from register A.

The *push A* operation is defined by the statements:

$$SP \leftarrow SP + 1$$
$$M[SP] \leftarrow A$$

SP is incremented to point at the next empty location in the stack. The contents of register A are placed in $DBUS$, the contents of SP are placed in $ABUS$, and a WR (write) operation is initiated. This inserts the contents of A into the top of the stack, and SP points at that location.

The *pop A* operation is defined by the statements:

$$A \leftarrow M[SP]$$
$$SP \leftarrow SP - 1$$

The contents of SP are placed in $ABUS$, and a RD (read) operation is initiated.

The memory reads the word at the given address and places it in *DBUS*. The microprocessor accepts the word from *DBUS* and transfers it to register *A*. *SP* is then decremented to point at the byte one address down, which is now on top of the stack.

The two operations for either push or pop stack are (1) an access to memory through *SP*, and (2) updating *SP*. Which of the two operations is done first and whether *SP* is updated by incrementing or decrementing depend on the organization of the stack. In Fig. 12-8 the stack grows by *increasing* the memory address. The stack may be made to grow by *decreasing* the memory address as shown in Fig. 12-9. In such a case *SP* is decremented for the push operation and incremented for a pop operation. A stack may be organized so that *SP* points at the next *empty* location on top of the stack. In this case, the sequence of operations of updating *SP* and memory access must be interchanged. This last configuration was demonstrated in Fig. 10-20 for the register stack defined in Fig. 10-19.

The stack pointer is loaded with an initial value by means of a transfer-type instruction. This initial value must be the bottom address of an assigned stack in memory. Henceforth, *SP* is automatically incremented or decremented with every push or pop operation. The advantage of a memory stack is that the processor can refer to it without having to specify an address, since the address is always available and automatically updated in the stack pointer. Thus, a processor can reference a memory stack without specifying an address. For this reason, instructions involving stack operations are referred to as *zero address* or *implied* instructions.

Subroutines

A subroutine is a self-contained sequence of instructions that performs a given task. During normal execution of a program, a subroutine may be called to perform its function many times at various points in the main program. Each time a subroutine is called, a branch is executed to the beginning of the subroutine to start executing its set of instructions. After the subroutine has been executed, a branch is made back to the main program. Because branching to a subroutine and returning to the main program is a common operation, all processors provide special instructions to facilitate subroutine entry and return.

The instruction that transfers control to a subroutine is known by different names. The most common names used are *call subroutine, jump to subroutine,* and *branch to subroutine*. A *call-subroutine* instruction consists of an operation code together with the address that specifies the beginning of the subroutine. The instruction is executed by the performance of two tasks: (1) Control is transferred to the beginning of the subroutine. (2) The address of the next instruction in the calling program is stored in a temporary location so that the subroutine knows where to return. The last instruction of every subroutine, commonly called *return from subroutine*, transfers control to the instruction in the calling program whose address was originally stored in the temporary location.

Microprocessors use the stack for storing the return address when handling subroutines. This is accomplished by pushing the return address into the stack every time a subroutine is called. The return-from-subroutine instruction is accomplished by popping the stack to read the return address and transferring control to the program at this address.

Figure 12-9 demonstrates by example the process of subroutine call and return in an 8-bit microprocessor. Three separate portions of memory are shown: the main program, a subroutine program, and a memory stack. The computer is now executing the main program, with *PC* pointing at the instruction in location 3500. The subroutine program starts at location 2673, and the top of the stack is specified by *SP* at address 7803. This is shown in Fig. 12-9(a) with all addresses having hexadecimal values. The call-subroutine instruction has associated with it a two-byte address and each byte occupies one memory location. The last instruction of the subroutine in location 2686 has the operation code of the return-from-subroutine instruction. The top of the stack now contains a byte (designated by hexadecimal 46), but this is not important for the present discussion.

The execution of the call-subroutine instruction in the main program is carried out as follows: (1) The address associated with the instruction (2673) is transferred to *PC*. (2) The return address to the main program (3503) is pushed into the stack. The result of these two operations is shown in Fig. 12-9(b). *PC* now points at location 2673, which is the address of the first instruction in the subroutine. Return address 3503 is pushed into the stack and occupies two bytes of memory. The computer now continues by executing the instructions in the subroutine program, since *PC* points at the first instruction of the subroutine.

When the last instruction of the subroutine is reached at address 2686, the computer executes a return-from-subroutine instruction by popping the two top bytes in the stack and placing them into *PC*. The situation now is as depicted in Fig. 12-9(c). *PC* now holds address 3503 to continue the execution of the main program, and *SP* returns to its initial position.

The microprocessor shown in Fig. 12-5 executes the call-to-subroutine instruction by going through five memory cycles and six internal operations:

$IR \leftarrow M[PC], PC \leftarrow PC + 1$	read operation code
$AR(H) \leftarrow M[PC], PC \leftarrow PC + 1$	read first byte of address
$AR(L) \leftarrow M[PC], PC \leftarrow PC + 1$	read second byte of address
$SP \leftarrow SP - 1, M[SP] \leftarrow PC(H)$	push first byte of return address
$SP \leftarrow SP - 1, M[SP] \leftarrow PC(L)$	push second byte of return address
$PC \leftarrow AR$	branch to subroutine address

The return-from-subroutine instruction is executed with three memory cycles and

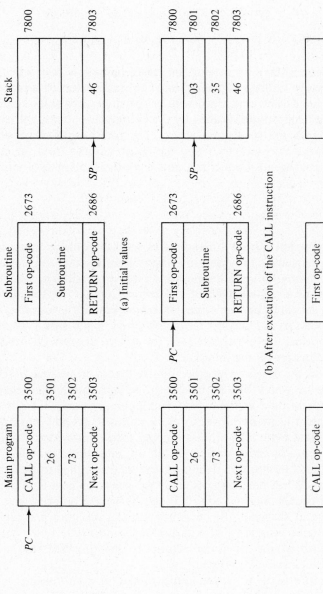

Figure 12-9 Numerical example for the call-subroutine and return-from-subroutine instructions

527

the updating of *PC* and *SP*:

$$IR \leftarrow M[PC], PC \leftarrow PC + 1 \qquad \text{read operation code}$$

$$PC(L) \leftarrow M[SP], SP \leftarrow SP + 1 \qquad \text{pop second byte of address}$$

$$PC(H) \leftarrow M[SP], SP \leftarrow SP + 1 \qquad \text{pop first byte of address}$$

The advantage of using a stack for storing the return address is that, when a subroutine is called, the return address is pushed into the stack automatically and the programmer does not have to be concerned with or remember where the return address is stored. If another subroutine is called by the current subroutine, the new return address is pushed into the stack, and so on. The return-from-subroutine instruction automatically pops the stack to obtain the return address from the last program that called it. Thus, the subroutine that exits is always the last subroutine that was called.

Interrupt

The concept of program interrupt is used to handle a variety of problems that arise out of normal program sequence. Program interrupt refers to the transfer of control from a currently running program to another service program as a result of an externally generated control signal. One of the control inputs in the micro-processor of Fig. 12-4 is labeled *interrupt*. Each interface module is capable of interrupting the microprocessors normal operation by providing a signal at this control input. The interrupt may be either a request for service or an acknowledg-ment of service performed earlier by the interface.

Consider, for example, the case of a microcomputer that is processing a large volume of data, portions of which are to be output to a printer. The micro-processor can output a byte of data within a few clock pulse intervals, but it may take the printer the equivalent of many processor clock pulses to actually print the character specified by the data byte. The processor could then remain idle, waiting until the printer can accept the next data byte. If an interrupt capability is available, the microprocessor can output a data byte and then continue to perform other data processing tasks. When the printer is ready to accept the next data byte, it can request an interrupt via the *interrupt* control input. When the microprocessor acknowledges the interrupt, it suspends the currently running program and auto-matically branches to a service program that will output the next data byte. After the byte is sent to the printer, the processor returns to the program that was interrupted while the character is being printed.

The interrupt procedure is, in principle, quite similar to a subroutine call, except that the branch is initiated by an external signal rather than by an instruction in the program. As in a subroutine call, an interrupt stores the return address in the stack. A subroutine-call instruction provides the branch address for the subroutine. With an interrupt procedure, the branch address to the service routine must be provided by the hardware. The way a microprocessor chooses the branch address in response to an interrupt request varies from one unit to another. In principle, there are two methods for accomplishing this. One is called *vectored* and the other *nonvectored* interrupt. In a nonvectored interrupt, the branch address either is a fixed location in memory or is stored in a fixed location in memory. The interrupt cycle stores the return address from PC into the stack and then sets PC to the predetermined branch address. In a vectored interrupt, the interrupting source itself supplies the branch information to the microprocessor. This information, transferred through the data bus, is called an *interrupt vector*. The interrupt cycle first stores the return address from PC into the stack. If the interrupt vector is an address, the microprocessor accepts it from the data bus and transfers it to PC. The interrupt vector in some microprocessors is assumed to be a subroutine-call instruction. The microprocessor accepts the instruction from the data bus, places it into its instruction register, and proceeds to execute it.

The return from the service routine back to the original interrupted program is similar to a subroutine return. The stack is popped and the return address previously stored there is transferred to PC.

A microprocessor may have single or multiple interrupt input lines. If there are more interrupt sources than there are interrupt inputs in the microprocessor, two or more sources are ORed together to form a common line for the microprocessor. An interrupt signal into a microprocessor may originate at any time during program execution. To ensure that no information is lost, the microprocessor acknowledges the interrupt only after the execution of the current instruction is completed and if the state of the processor warrants it. Figure 12-10

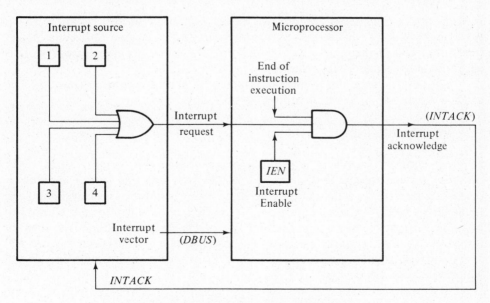

Figure 12-10 Vectored interrupt configuration

shows a possible vectored interrupt configuration. The diagram shows four sources ORed to a single interrupt-request input. The microprocessor has within it an interrupt enable (*IEN*) flip-flop that can be set or cleared with program instructions. When *IEN* is cleared, the interrupt request is neglected. If *IEN* is set and the microprocessor is at the end of instruction execution, the microprocessor acknowledges the interrupt by enabling *INTACK*. The interrupt source responds to *INTACK* by placing an interrupt vector into *DBUS*. The program controlled *IEN* flip-flop allows the programmer to decide whether to use the interrupt facility or not. If an instruction to clear *IEN* has been inserted in the program, it means that the programmer does not want the program to be interrupted. (*IEN* is also cleared with a reset signal.) An instruction to set *IEN* indicates that the interrupt facility will be used while the program is running. Some microprocessors use an interrupt mask bit in the status register instead of a separate *IEN* flip-flop.

Assume that the interrupt vector supplied to the data bus is an 8-bit address. The microprocessor responds to an interrupt request by performing the following operations:

$$SP \leftarrow SP + 1, M[SP] \leftarrow PC(H) \qquad \text{push first byte of return address}$$

$$SP \leftarrow SP + 1, M[SP] \leftarrow PC(L) \qquad \text{push second byte of return address}$$

$$INTACK \leftarrow 1 \qquad \text{enable interrupt acknowledge}$$

$$PC(H) \leftarrow 0, PC(L) \leftarrow DBUS \qquad \text{transfer vector address to } PC$$

$$IEN \leftarrow 0 \qquad \text{disable further interrupts}$$

In this manner, the interrupt source can specify any vector address from 0 to 255 to serve as the branch address to a service routine. *IEN* is cleared to disable further interrupts. The programmer can set *IEN* in the service program whenever it is appropriate to enable further interrupts.

The return from the interrupt is similar to a return from subroutine. The stack is popped and the return address is transferred to *PC*.

Priority Interrupt

In the preceding discussion, a method for generating the vector address of an interrupt service routine was described. If there is only one source capable of requesting service, the source of the interrupt is known and the service program can immediately begin the service routine. More often, several devices are allowed to originate interrupt requests, and the first task of the interrupt routine is to identify the source of the interrupt. There is also the possibility that several sources will simultaneously request service. In this case, the service program must also decide which source to service first.

The most common method of handling multiple interrupts is to begin the service routine by *polling* the interfaces to identify the one that generated the request. The service routine tests each source in sequence to find out if its interrupt signal is on. Once an interrupt is identified, all other interrupts are neglected until the service routine for the particular source is completed.

A *priority interrupt* is an interrupt system that establishes a priority over the various sources to determine which condition is to be serviced first when two or more requests arrive simultaneously. Establishing the priority of simultaneous interrupts can be done by software or hardware. In the software method, there is only one vector address for all interrupts. The service program begins at the vector address and polls the interrupt sources in sequence. The order in which the sources are tested determines the priority of each interrupt request. The highest-priority source is tested first and if its interrupt signal is on, control branches to a service routine for this source. Otherwise, the next lower-priority source is tested, and so on. Thus, the initial service routine for all interrupts consists of a program that tests the interrupt sources in sequence and branches to one of many possible service routines. The particular service routine reached belongs to the highest-priority source among all sources than can interrupt the processor.

Software techniques can, in theory, handle any number of interrupt sources to any sophisticated level of priority. In practice, if there are many sources of interrupt requests, the time required to poll them to find the appropriate interrupt can exceed the time available to service the I/O device. In this situation, an external hardware priority interrupt unit can be used to speed up the operation.

A hardware priority interrupt unit functions as an overall manager in an interrupt system environment. It accepts interrupt requests from many sources, determines which of the incoming requests is of the highest priority, and issues an interrupt to the processor based on this determination. To speed up the operation, each interrupt source has its own vector address to access directly to its own service routine. Thus, no polling is required because all the decisions are established by the hardware priority interrupt unit.

The basic circuit that implements the hardware priority function is a *priority encoder*. The logic of the priority encoder is such that, if two or more input levels arrive at the same time, then the input having the highest priority will take precedence. The output of the priority encoder generates a partial address for the interrupt vector that supplies the branch address. The truth table of a four-input priority encoder is given in Table 12-4. The X's in the table designate don't-care conditions. Input I_0 has the highest priority; so regardless of the values of other inputs, when this input is 1 the output generates the partial address $xy = 00$. I_1 has the next priority level. The output is 01 if $I_1 = 1$ provided $I_0 = 0$, regardless of the values of the other two lower-priority inputs. The partial address for I_2 is generated only if higher-priority inputs are 0, and so on down the priority level. The priority levels dictate that a low-level input generates its own partial address only if all higher-level inputs are not asking for service. An interrupt request R is generated for the microprocessor only when one or more inputs are requesting an interrupt. If all inputs are 0, the R output becomes 0 and the partial address at this time is of no consequence because it will not be used by the microprocessor.

TABLE 12-4 Priority encoder truth table

Input				Outputs		
(Interrupt source)				(Partial address)		(Interrupt request)
I_0	I_1	I_2	I_3	x	y	R
1	X	X	X	0	0	1
0	1	X	X	0	1	1
0	0	1	X	1	0	1
0	0	0	1	1	1	1
0	0	0	0	X	X	0

Usually a microprocessor will have more than four interrupt sources. A priority encoder with eight inputs, for example, will generate a partial address of three bits.

The partial address out of the encoder is used to form the vector address for each interrupt source. For example, the vector address supplied to the data bus after an interrupt acknowledge can be of the form:

$$000xy000$$

where x and y are the output bits from the priority encoder. The particular xy bits transferred will belong to the highest-priority interrupt source. By this procedure, the priority encoder can specify one of four possible branch addresses. Each vector address specifies the beginning address of an 8-byte service routine in the lower 32 bytes of memory.

12-6 MEMORY ORGANIZATION

A microprocessor must communicate with memory, both RAM and ROM, to read and write binary information such as instructions, data, and addresses. The size of the memory attached to a microprocessor depends on the number of instructions and data bytes needed for the particular application. A microprocessor may have an address bus with 16 lines to accommodate up to 64K bytes of memory. In many applications, the amount of memory needed may be less than 64K bytes. RAM and ROM chips are available in a variety of sizes and the individual chips must be interconnected to form a required memory size.

RAM and ROM Chips

A RAM chip is better suited for communicating with a microprocessor if it has one or more control inputs for selecting and enabling the unit only upon request. Another convenient feature is a bidirectional data bus to avoid inserting external bus buffers between the RAM and the data bus. The block diagram of a RAM chip suited for microcomputer applications is shown in Fig. 12-11. The capacity of the memory is 128 words of 8 bits each. This requires a 7-bit address and an 8-bit bidirectional data bus. The read and write inputs specify the memory operation, and the two chip select (CS) control inputs are for enabling the chip only when it is selected by the microprocessor. The availability of more than one control input to select the chip facilitates the decoding of the address lines when multiple chips are used in the microcomputer. The read and write inputs are sometimes combined into one line labeled R/W. When the chip is selected, the two binary states in this line specify the two operations of read and write.

The function table listed in Fig. 12-11(b) specifies the operation of the RAM chip. The unit is in operation only when $CS1 = 1$ and $\overline{CS2} = 0$. The bar on top of the second select variable indicates that this input is enabled when it is 0. If the chip select inputs are not enabled, or if they are enabled but the read and write inputs are not enabled, the memory is inhibited and its data bus is in a high-impedance state. When $CS1 = 1$ and $\overline{CS2} = 0$, the memory can be placed in a write or read mode. When the WR input is enabled, the memory stores a byte from the data bus into a location specified by the address input lines. When the RD input is enabled, the contents of the selected byte are placed on the data bus. The RD and WR signals control the memory operation as well as the bus buffers associated with the bidirectional data bus.

A ROM chip is organized externally in a similar manner. However, since a ROM can only read, the data bus can only be in an output mode. The block

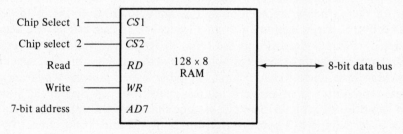

(a) Block diagram

$CS1$	$\overline{CS2}$	RD	WR	Memory function	State of data bus
0	0	X	X	Inhibit	High-impedance
0	1	X	X	Inhibit	High-impedance
1	0	0	0	Inhibit	High-impedance
1	0	0	1	Write	Input data to RAM
1	0	1	X	Read	Output data from RAM
1	1	X	X	Inhibit	High-impedance

(b) Function table

Figure 12-11 Typical RAM chip

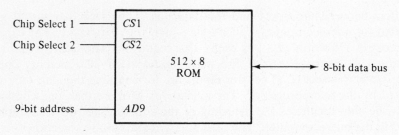

Figure 12-12 Typical ROM chip

diagram of a ROM chip is shown in Fig. 12-12. For the same-size chip, it is possible to have more bits of ROM than of RAM, because the internal binary cells in ROM occupy less space than in RAM. For this reason, the diagram specifies a 512-byte ROM, whereas the RAM has only 128 bytes.

The nine address lines in the ROM chip specify any one of the 512 bytes stored in it. The two chip select inputs must be $CS1 = 1$ and $\overline{CS2} = 0$ for the unit to operate. Otherwise, the data bus is in a high-impedance state. There is no need for a read or write control because the unit can only read. Thus, when the chip is enabled by the two select inputs, the byte selected by the address lines appears on the data bus.

Memory Address Map

The designer of a microcomputer system must calculate the amount of memory required for the particular application and assign it to either RAM or ROM. The interconnection between memory and microprocessor is then established according to the size of memory needed and the types of RAM and ROM chips available. The addressing of memory can be established by means of a table that specifies the memory address assigned to each chip. The table, called a *memory address map*, is a pictorial representation of assigned address space for each chip in the system.

To demonstrate with an example, assume that a microcomputer system needs 512 bytes of RAM and 512 bytes of ROM. The RAM and ROM chips to be used are specified in Figs. 12-11 and 12-12. The memory address map for this configuration is shown in Table 12-5. The component column specifies whether a RAM or a ROM chip is used. The hexadecimal address column assigns a range of hexadecimal equivalent addresses for each chip. The address bus lines are listed in the third column. Although there are 16 lines in the address bus, the table shows only 10 lines because the other 6 are not used in this example and are assumed to be zero. The small x's under the address bus lines designate those lines that must be connected to the address inputs in each chip. The RAM chips have 128 bytes and need 7 address lines. The ROM chip has 512 bytes and needs 9 address lines. The x's are always assigned to the low-order bus lines—lines 1 through 7 for the RAM and lines 1 through 9 for the ROM. It is now necessary to distinguish between four RAM chips by assigning to each a different address. For this particular example,

TABLE 12-5   Memory address map for microprocomputer

Component	Hexadecimal address	Address bus									
		10	9	8	7	6	5	4	3	2	1
RAM 1	0000–007F	0	0	0	x	x	x	x	x	x	x
RAM 2	0080–00FF	0	0	1	x	x	x	x	x	x	x
RAM 3	0100–017F	0	1	0	x	x	x	x	x	x	x
RAM 4	0180–01FF	0	1	1	x	x	x	x	x	x	x
ROM	0200–03FF	1	x	x	x	x	x	x	x	x	x

we choose bus lines 8 and 9 to represent four distinct binary combinations. Note that any other pair of unused bus lines can be chosen for this purpose. The table clearly shows that the 9 low-order bus lines constitute a memory space for RAM equal to $2^9 = 512$ bytes. The distinction between a RAM and ROM address is done with another bus line. For this purpose, we choose line 10. When line 10 is 0, the microprocessor selects a RAM, and when this line is 1, it selects the ROM.

The equivalent hexadecimal address for each chip is obtained from the information under the address bus assignment. The address bus lines are subdivided into groups of four bits each so that each group can be represented with a hexadecimal digit. The first hexadecimal digit represents lines 13–16 and is always 0. The next hexadecimal digit represents lines 9–12, but lines 11 and 12 are always 0. The range of hexadecimal addresses for each component is determined from the x's associated with it. These x's represent a binary number that can range from an all-0's to an all-1's value.

Memory Connection to Microprocessor

RAM and ROM chips are connected to a microprocessor through the data and address buses. The low-order lines in the address bus select the byte within the chips, and other lines in the address bus select a particular chip through its chip select inputs. The connection of memory chips to the microprocessor is shown in Fig 12-13. This configuration gives a memory capacity of 512 bytes of RAM and 512 bytes of ROM. It implements the memory map of Table 12-5. Each RAM receives the 7 low-order bits of the address bus to select one of 128 bytes possible. The particular RAM chip selected is determined from lines 8 and 9 in the address bus. This is done through a 2×4 decoder whose outputs go to the $CS1$ inputs in each RAM chip. Thus, when address lines 8 and 9 are equal to 00, the first RAM chip is selected. When 01, the second RAM chip is selected, and so on. The RD and WR outputs from the microprocessor are applied to the inputs of each RAM chip.

The selection between RAM and ROM is achieved through bus line 10. The RAMs are selected when the bit on this line is 0, and the ROM, when the bit is 1.

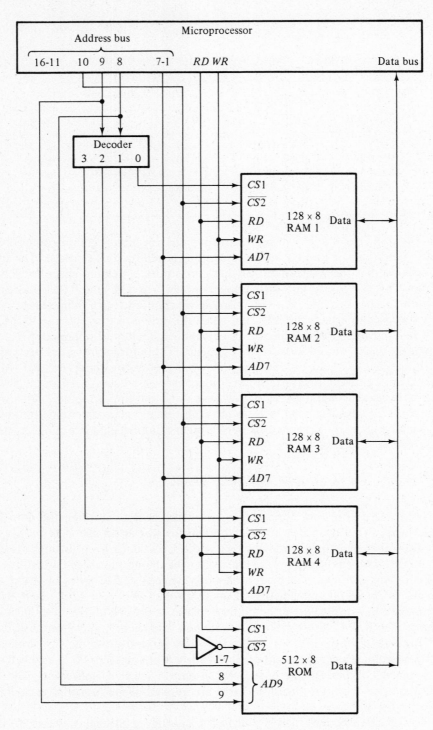

Figure 12-13 Memory connection to the microprocessor

The other chip select input in the ROM is connected to the RD control line for the ROM chip to be enabled only during a read operation. Bus lines 1–9 are applied to the input address of ROM without going through the decoder. This assigns addresses 0–511 to RAM and 512–1023 to ROM. The data bus of the ROM has only an output capability, whereas the data bus connected to the RAMs can transfer information in both directions.

The example just shown gives an indication of the interconnection complexity that can exist between memory chips and the microprocessor. The more chips connected, the more external decoders are required for selection among the chips. The designer must establish a memory map that assigns addresses to the various chips from which the required connections are determined. Since microprocessors also communicate with interface units, it is necessary to assign addresses to each interface as well. The communication between the microprocessor and interface is discussed in the next section.

12-7 INPUT-OUTPUT INTERFACE

An interface chip is an LSI component that provides the communication link between a microprocessor and an I/O device. When in the output mode, the interface receives binary information from the data bus at the microprocessor rate and mode of transfer and transmits it to an external device at the device rate and mode of transfer. The interface behaves in a similar manner in the input mode, except that the direction of transfer is in the opposite direction. An interface consists of a number of registers, selection logic, and control circuits that implement the required transfers. Interface logic is sometimes included within a RAM or ROM chip to provide an LSI component that includes both memory and interface capabilities within one IC package.

Most LSI interface components can be programmed to accommodate a variety of combinations of operating modes. The microprocessor, through program instructions, transfers a byte to a control register inside the interface unit. This control information puts the interface in one of the possible modes suitable for the particular device to which it is attached. By changing the control byte, it is possible to change the interface characteristics. For this reason, LSI interface units are often said to be *programmable*. The instructions that transfer control information into a programmable interface are included in the microcomputer program and they initialize the interface for a particular mode of operation.

Manufacturers of microprocessors supplement their product with a set of interface chips suitable for communication between the microprocessor and a variety of standard input and output devices. Interface components are usually designed to operate with a particular microprocessor system bus with no additional logic besides address decoding. There are a variety of interface components in commercial use and each can be classified to be in one of four categories:

1. A *parallel peripheral interface* transfers data in parallel between the microprocessor and a peripheral device.

2. A *serial communication interface* converts parallel data from the microprocessor into serial data for transmission and converts incoming serial data into parallel data for reception by the microprocessor.

3. A *special dedicated interface* is constructed to communicate with one particular input-output device, or can be programmed to operate with a particular device.

4. A *direct memory access* (DMA) interface is used for transferring data directly between an external device and memory. The bus buffers in the microprocessor are disabled and go into a high-impedance state during DMA transfer.

Commercial interface units may have different names from the ones listed here. Moreover, the internal and external characteristics vary considerably from one commercial unit to another. In this section, we discuss the common properties of interface components and explain in general terms the various modes of transfer that they provide. The direct memory access transfer is discussed in the next section.

Communication with Microprocessor

Large computers quite often use separate buses in the CPU to communicate with memory and I/O interface. An I/O bus in large computers consists of a data bus and an address bus similar to the buses that communicate with memory. The I/O data bus transfers information to and from the external devices, and the I/O address bus is used to select a particular I/O device through its interface. The number of address lines in an I/O bus is smaller than in a memory bus because there are fewer I/O units to select than words in the memory system.

A microprocessor has a limit to the number of terminals that can be accommodated in the IC package. There are just not enough pins in a microprocessor chip to provide separate buses for communicating separately with memory and I/O. Invariably, all microprocessors use a common bus system for selecting memory words and interface units. If an interface chip has a number of registers, each register is selected by its own address just as a memory word is selected. The microprocessor bus does not distinguish between an interface register and a memory word. It is the responsibility of the user, through program instructions, to specify the appropriate address that will select one or the other. There are two ways that addresses can be assigned for selecting both memory and interface registers. One method is called *memory-mapped* I/O and the other is called *isolated* I/O.

In the memory-mapped I/O method, the microprocessor treats an interface register as being part of the memory system. The assigned addresses for interface registers cannot be used for memory words, thus reducing the memory space available. In a memory-mapped I/O organization there are no input or output instructions because the microprocessor can manipulate I/O data residing in interface registers with the same instructions that are used to manipulate memory locations. Each interface is organized as a set of registers that respond to read and write commands in the normal address space of the microprocessor. Typically, a segment of the total address space is reserved for interface registers, but in general, they can be located at any address as long as there is not also a memory word that corresponds to that address.

The memory-mapped I/O organization is convenient for systems that do not need all the memory space available from the address bus lines. A microprocessor with a 16-bit address bus that requires a memory of less than 32K bytes can use the other 32K addresses available on the bus to access interface registers. A specific configuration for a memory-mapped I/O can be implemented by modifying slightly the address connections shown in Fig. 12-13. Address line 11 in the diagram is not used to access memory. We now let this line distinguish between memory and interface so that when the bit in this line is 1, the address bus selects a memory word, but when the bit is 0, it selects an interface register. To accomplish this new condition, each line going into $CS1$ in the RAMs and ROM in Fig. 12-13 must be ANDed with the bit from address line 11. The chip select inputs of all interface units must be conditioned on the complement value of line 11, in addition to their assigned address.

With the isolated I/O organization, the microprocessor itself specifies whether the address on the address bus is for a memory word or for an interface register. This is done by means of one or two additional control lines provided with the microprocessor. For example, a microprocessor may have an output control line labeled M/IO. When $M/IO = 1$, it is signifies that the address in the address bus is for a memory word. When $M/IO = 0$, the address is for an interface register. This control line must be connected to the chip select inputs of RAM, ROM, and interface chips in a similar fashion as bus line 11 was connected in the previous example for the memory-mapped I/O case.

In the isolated I/O organization, the microprocessor must provide distinct input and output instructions, and each of these instructions must be associated with an address. When the microprocessor fetches and decodes the operation code of an input or output instruction, it reads the address associated with the instruction and places it on the address bus. At the same time it makes control line M/IO equal to 0 to inform the external components that this address is for an interface and not for memory. Thus, during a fetch cycle or a memory-reference execute cycle, the microprocessor enables the read or write control and sets the M/IO line to 1. During the execution of an input or output instruction, the microprocessor enables the read or write control and sets the M/IO line to 0.

The isolated I/O method isolates memory and I/O addresses so that memory space is not affected by the interface address assignment. Because of this isolation, the full address space available by the address bus is unaffected by interface addressing as in the memory-mapped I/O method.

Parallel Peripheral Interface

A parallel peripheral interface is an LSI component that provides a path for transferring binary information in parallel between the microprocessor and a peripheral device. An interface chip normally contains two or more I/O ports that communicate with one or more external devices, and a single interface to communicate with the microprocessor bus system. The block diagram of a typical parallel peripheral interface is shown in Fig. 12-14. It consists of two ports. Each port has two registers, an 8-bit I/O bus, and a pair of lines labeled *handshake*. The information stored in the control register specifies the port's mode of operation. The port data register is used for transferring data to and from the data bus and the I/O bus.

The interface communicates with the microprocessor through the data bus and the chip select and read/write control. A circuit must be inserted externally (usually an AND gate) to detect the address assigned to the interface. This circuit enables the chip select input when the interface is selected through the address bus. Two register select inputs, $RS1$ and $RS2$ are usually connected to the lowest-order lines of the address bus. These two inputs select one of the four registers in the

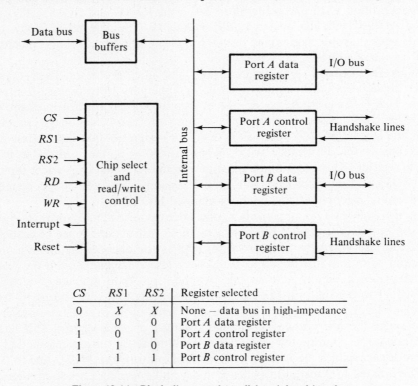

CS	$RS1$	$RS2$	Register selected
0	X	X	None — data bus in high-impedance
1	0	0	Port A data register
1	0	1	Port A control register
1	1	0	Port B data register
1	1	1	Port B control register

Figure 12-14 Block diagram of parallel peripheral interface

interface, as specified in the table accompanying the diagram. The contents of the selected register are transferred into the microprocessor through the data bus when the *RD* input is enabled. The microprocessor loads a byte into the selected register through the data bus when the *WR* input is enabled. The interrupt output is used for interrupting the microprocessor, and the reset input is for resetting the interface after power is turned on.

The microprocessor initializes each port by transferring a byte to its control register. By loading appropriate bits into a control register at system initialization, the program can define the mode of operation of the port. The characteristic of the port depends on the commercial unit used. In most cases, each port can be placed in an input or output mode. This is done by transferring bits in the control register that specify the direction of transfer in the bus buffers that drive the bidirectional I/O bus. In addition, the port can be made to function in a variety of operating modes. Three operating modes found in most interface chips are:

1. Direct transfer without handshake lines.

2. Transfer with handshaking.

3. Transfer with handshaking using interrupt.

An interface is placed in a direct-transfer mode of operation when the device attached to the I/O bus is always ready to transfer information. The handshake lines are not used in this mode, and some interface chips have a programming mode to convert these lines into data transfer lines. The direct transfer can operate in an input or output mode. In the input mode, a read operation transfers the contents of the I/O bus to the microprocessor data bus. In the output mode, a write operation transfers the contents of the data bus to the selected port data register. The received byte is then applied to the I/O bus. Direct input or output transfers are useful only if valid data can reside in the I/O bus for a long time compared with the microprocessor instruction execution time. If I/O data can be valid only for a short time, the interface must operate in the handshake mode.

Handshake lines are used to control the transfer between two devices operating asynchronously with each other, i.e., when they do not share a common clock. Handshaking is a commonly used procedure and is not restricted to interface chips alone. Two handshake lines, connected between a source device and a destination device, control the transfer by informing each other of the status of the transfer through a common bus. The source device informs the destination through one of the handshake lines when valid information is available on the bus. The destination device responds by enabling the second handshake line when the information on the bus has been accepted. Figure 12-14 shows two handshake lines in each port. One is an output line and the other is an input line. It is customary to refer to these lines with symbols, but the symbols adopted are always different in different commercial units. Because of the variety of symbols used to designate these lines, we prefer not to adopt one symbol over another, but refer to the two lines as the output or input handshake line. The input handshake line would normally set a bit in the control register inside the interface. We will call this bit a *flag*, realizing that the register that holds the flag bit (the control register in this case) can be read by the microprocessor to check the status of the transfer. The flag bit is automatically cleared by the interface after a read or write operation associated with the corresponding data register.

The detailed handshake sequence for a particular commercial interface chip is specified in timing diagrams accompanying the product specifications. Because of the variety of procedures encountered in practice, it would be better to explain the handshake method in general terms without a preference for one specific method. The transfer with handshaking depends on whether the port is in an output or input mode.

In the output handshake mode, the microprocessor writes a byte into the interface port data register. The interface then enables the output handshake line to inform the external device that a valid byte is available on the I/O bus. When the external device accepts the byte from the I/O bus, it enables the input handshake line. This sets a flag bit in the control register. The microprocessor reads the register containing the flag bit to determine if the transfer was completed. If so, the microprocessor can write a new byte into the data register of the interface port. Writing data into a given port automatically clears the flag bit associated with the output transfer. The process now can be repeated to output the next byte.

In the input handshake mode, the external device places a byte on the I/O bus and enables the interface input handshake line. The interface transfers the byte into its data register and also sets a flag bit in the control register. The microprocessor reads the register containing the flag bit to determine if an input transfer is requested. If the flag bit is set, the microprocessor reads the byte from the port data register and clears the flag bit. The interface then informs the device attached to the I/O bus, through the output handshake line, that a new byte can now be accepted. Once the output device has been informed that the interface is ready, it can initiate the transfer of the next byte by enabling the input handshake again.

In the handshake method just described, the microprocessor must periodically read the control register to check the status of the flag bit. If there are a number of ports attached to the microprocessor, it would be necessary to poll them in succession to determine the ones that require a transfer. This is a time-consuming operation that can be avoided if the interface is initialized to operate in the interrupt mode. The interrupt output shown in Fig. 12-14 is then used to request an interrupt from the microprocessor. Most commercial units provide a separate interrupt line for each port in the interface. Every time a flag is set in the port, the interrupt request belonging to the port is automatically enabled to inform the microprocessor that a transfer is to be initiated. The microprocessor responds to the interrupt signal from the port that requested the action and transfers the byte of data to or from the interface port data register.

Serial Communication Interface

An I/O device may transfer binary information either in parallel or serially. In parallel transmission, each information bit uses a separate line so that the n bits of an item can be transmitted simultaneously. For example, a parallel peripheral device can transmit a word of 16 bits all at once through two 8-bit buses of a parallel peripheral interface. In serial transmission, the bits of a word are transmitted in sequence, one bit at a time, and through a single line. Parallel transmission is faster but requires many lines. It is used for short distances and where speed is important. Serial transmission is slower but less expensive, since it requires only one line. Binary information transmitted from remote terminals through telephone wires or other communication media is of the serial type, because it would be expensive to subscribe to or lease a large number of lines. Examples of communication terminals are teletypewriters, CRT terminals, and remote computing devices.

The serial binary information transmitted to and from a terminal consists of binary-coded characters. The characters may represent alphanumeric information or control characters. The alphanumeric characters are referred to as *text* and include the letters of the alphabet, the decimal digits, and a number of graphic symbols such as period, plus, and comma. The control characters are used for the layout of printing or for specifying the format of the transmitted message. The number of bits assigned to each character code may be between five and eight, depending on the terminal.

The block diagram of a serial communication interface is shown in Fig. 12-15. It functions both as a transmitter and as a receiver and can be programmed to operate in a variety of transmission modes. The interface is initialized for a particular serial-transfer mode by means of a control byte which is loaded into its control register. The transmitter register accepts a data byte from the microprocessor through the data bus. This byte is transferred to a shift register for serial transmission. The receiver portion receives serial information into another shift register, and when a complete data byte is accumulated, it is transferred to the receiver register. The microprocessor can select the receiver register to read the byte through the data bus. The bits in the status register are used to set input and output flags and to detect certain errors that may occur during the transmission. The microprocessor can read the status register to check the status of the flag bits and to determine if any errors have occurred.

The chip select and read/write control lines communicate with the microprocessor. The chip select (CS) input is used to select the interface. The register select (RS) is associated with the RD and WR controls. Two registers accept information during a write operation and the other two supply information during a read operation. The register selected is then a function of the RD and WR status, as shown in the table accompanying the diagram.

The transmitter and receiver have a clock input to synchronize the bit rate at which the serial information is transferred. The transmit data line is connected to a

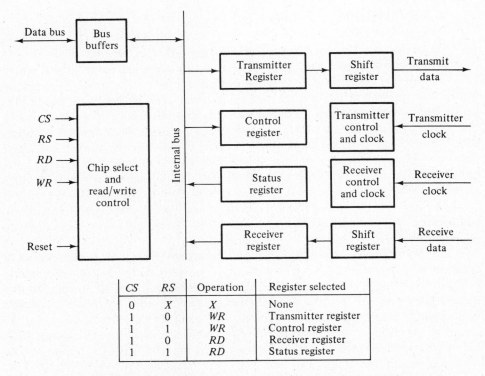

CS	RS	Operation	Register selected
0	X	X	None
1	0	WR	Transmitter register
1	1	WR	Control register
1	0	RD	Receiver register
1	1	RD	Status register

Figure 12-15 Block diagram of a typical serial communication interface

remote receiver and the receive data line comes from a remote transmitter. If the clock is also connected to the remote terminal, the transmission is said to be *synchronous*. If the clock is not shared with the remote terminal, the transmission is said to be *asynchronous*.

In the synchronous serial mode of transmission, the local and remote transmitter and receiver share a common clock. Bits are sent from the transmitter at equal intervals of time determined by the rate of the clock pulses. Since the receiver shares a common clock with the transmitter, it accepts the bits at the same clock rate. In asynchronous transmission, the two sides do not share a common clock. The interface transmitter and receiver clocks are supplied with a local clock rate that specifies the transfer rate of the remote communication terminal to which the interface is attached.

A common problem associated with serial transmission is concerned with framing the characters in a string of continuous bits. The transmitter and receiver can be programmed to recognize the number of bits in each character in the remote terminal. There remains the problem of detecting the first bit in each character so that a count can start to frame the next character. The way characters are framed in serial transmission depends on whether the mode of transfer is synchronous or asynchronous.

In synchronous serial transmission, one *communication control* character, called the *sync* character, is chosen to serve as a synchronizing agent between the transmitter and receiver. For example, when the 7-bit ASCII code is used with an odd-parity bit at the most significant position, the assigned sync character has the 8-bit code 00010110. When the transmitter starts sending 8-bit characters, it sends a few sync characters first and then sends the actual message. The initial continuous string of bits accepted by the receiver is checked for a sync character. In other words, with each clock pulse, the receiver checks the last eight bits received. If they do not match the bits of the sync character, the receiver accepts one more bit, rejects the previous high-order bit, and checks again the last 8 bits received for a sync character. This is repeated after each clock pulse and bit received until a sync character is recognized. Once a sync character is detected, the receiver has framed a character. From here on, the receiver counts every eight bits and acccepts them as a single character. Usually the receiver checks two consecutive sync characters to remove any doubt that the first sync character did not occur as a result of a noise signal on the line. Moreover, when the transmitter is idle and does not have any message characters to send, it sends a continuous string of sync characters. The receiver recognizes all sync characters as a condition for synchronizing the line and goes into a synchronous idle state. In this state, the two units maintain synchronism while no meaningful message is being communicated.

The standard procedure just described dictates that the transmitter in a synchronous communication interface be designed to send sync characters at the beginning of transmission and also when no characters are available from the microprocessor. The receiver in a synchronous communication interface must frame eight consecutive bits into characters and must be able to identify certain character codes such as the sync character. When the receiver recognizes sync characters, they are used to maintain synchronism with the transmitter; but sync characters are not sent to the microprocessor.

The standard procedure for framing characters during asynchronous transmission is to send at least two additional bits with each character. These additional bits are called the *stop* and *start* bits. For example, a teletype unit uses an 8-bit character code but sends 11 bits for each character transmitted. The first bit is the start bit. This is followed by the 8 bits of the character and then by two stop bits. The convention in this terminal is that it rests in the 1-state when no character is transmitted. The first bit is always 0 and represents the start bit to indicate the beginning of a character. The receiver can detect the start bit when the line goes from 1 to 0. A clock in the receiver knows the transfer rate and the number of character bits to expect. After the 8 bits of the character are received, the receiver checks for two stop bits which are always in the 1-state. The length of time the line stays in the 1 (stop)-state depends on the amount of time required for the terminal to resynchronize. A teletype requires two stop bits. Other terminals use just one stop bit, and some use a one-and-a-half bit time for the stop period. The line remains in the 1-state until another character is transmitted. Figure 12-16 shows the 11 bits of a typical character from a teletype. After the two stop bits have been

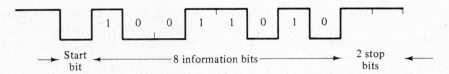

Figure 12-16 Asychronous serial transmission of a character

transmitted, the line may go to 0, indicating a start bit for a new character. The line will stay in the 1-state if no other character follows immediately.

The standard procedure just described dictates that the transmitter in an asynchronous communication interface inserts the start and stop bits prior to the serial transmission. The receiver must recognize the start and stop bits to frame the character. The receiver must also isolate the information bits for transfer to the microprocessor.

The standard framing procedures are incorporated with any serial communication interface. A serial communication interface may be asynchronous only, synchronous only, or both synchronous and asynchronous.

Dedicated Interface Components

In addition to the interface components that transfer information in parallel or serially, one can find in commercial use other interface chips that are dedicated to a particular interface application. A few of them are listed below.

Floppy disk controller

Keyboard and display interface

Priority interrupt controller

Interval timer

Universal peripheral interface

The floppy disk controller is an interface chip designed to control a small magnetic-disk storage device called *floppy disk*. The keyboard and display interface is suitable for scanning a matrix of keys to detect a closure and for driving a display of numeric or alphanumeric information. The priority interrupt controller facilitates the interrupt handling by establishing priorities and providing an interrupt vector for the microprocessor. An interval timer is a programmable counter that can be set to count for a given interval of time and to interrupt the microprocessor when the counter reaches a prescribed count.

A universal peripheral interface is an LSI component that acts as a slave I/O processor to the system CPU. It has its own processor, control logic, RAM, and ROM and in some ways resembles a microcomputer chip. Its funetion is to handle the operations of I/O devices rather than be involved in computational procedures.

The program stored in the ROM part of a universal peripheral interface is a dedicated, fixed program that handles the particular devices attached to it. The universal interface component is supervised by the program that is executed in the microprocessor. In essence, this is a two-processor configuration with the system CPU and the slave universal interface device operating in parallel.

12-8 DIRECT MEMORY ACCESS

The transfer of data between a mass storage device, such as magnetic disk or magnetic tape, and system memory is often limited by the speed of the microprocessor. Removing the processor during such a transfer and letting the peripheral device manage the transfer directly to memory would improve the speed of transfer and make the system more efficient. This transfer technique is called DMA (direct memory access). During DMA transfer, the processor is idle; so it no longer has control of the system bus. A DMA controller takes over the buses to manage the transfer directly between the peripheral device and memory.

The microprocessor may be made to idle in a variety of ways. The most common method is to disable the buses through a special control signal. Figure 12-17 shows two control signals useful for DMA transfer. The *bus request (BR)* input, when in the 1-state, is a request to the microprocessor to disable its buses. The microprocessor terminates the execution of its present instruction and then places its buses, including the *RD* (read) and *WR* (write) lines, into a high-impedance state. When this is done, the processor places the *bus granted (BG)* output in the 1-state. As long as $BG = 1$, the microprocessor is idle and its buses are disabled. The processor returns to its normal operation after the *BR* line returns to 0 by returning its *BG* line to 0 and enabling its buses. The bus request line is sometimes called a *hold* command, and the bus granted a *hold acknowledge*.

As soon as $BG = 1$, the DMA controller can take control of the bus system to communicate directly with the memory. The transfer can be made for an entire block of memory words, suspending the processor operation until the whole block is transferred. The transfer can be made one word at a time in between microprocessor instruction executions. Such a transfer is called *cycle stealing*. The

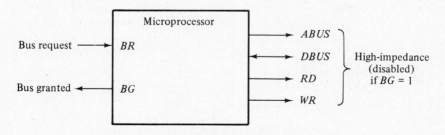

Figure 12-17 Control signals for DMA transfer

processor merely delays its operation for one memory cycle to allow the direct memory I/O transfer to *steal* one memory cycle.

The DMA controller needs the usual circuits of an interface to communicate with the microprocessor. In addition, it needs an address register, a byte count register, and a set of address lines. The address register and address lines are used for direct communication with the system RAM. The word count register specifies the number of words to be transferred. The data transfer is usually done directly between the peripheral device and memory under control of the DMA.

Figure 12-18 shows the block diagram of a typical DMA controller. The unit communicates with the microprocessor via the data bus and control lines. The registers in the DMA are selected by the microprocessor through its address lines by enabling *CS* (chip select) and *RS* (register select). The *RD* and *WR* lines in the DMA are bidirectional. With *BG* = 0, the microprocessor communicates with the DMA register through the data bus to read from or write into the DMA registers. When *BG* = 1, DMA can communicate directly with the memory by specifying an address in the address bus and activating its *RD* or *WR* control. The DMA communicates with an external peripheral device through the *request* and *acknowledge* lines.

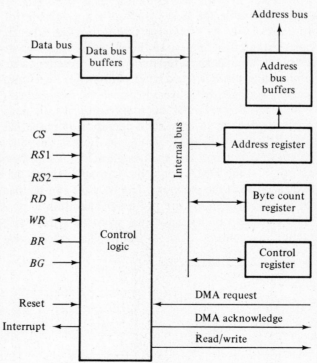

Figure 12-18 Block diagram of DMA controller

The DMA controller includes three registers: an address register, a byte count register, and a control register. The address register contains 16 bits that specify the desired location in memory. The address bits go through a bus buffer into the address bus. The address register is incremented after each DMA byte transfer. The byte count register holds the number of bytes to be transferred. This register is decremented after each byte transfer and internally tested for zero. The control register specifies the mode of transfer—whether it is into (write) or out of (read) memory. All registers in the DMA appear to the microprocessor as an I/O interface. Thus, the processor can read from or write into the DMA registers under program control via the data bus.

The DMA is first initialized by the microprocessor. After that, the DMA starts and continues to transfer data between memory and peripheral unit until an entire block is transferred. The initialization process is essentially a program consisting of I/O instructions that include the DMA address for selecting particular registers. The microprocessor initializes the DMA by sending the following information through the data bus:

1. The starting address of the memory block where data are available (for read) or where data are to be stored (for write).

2. The byte count, which is the number of bytes in the memory block.

3. Control bits to specify a read or write transfer.

4. A control bit to start the DMA.

The starting address is stored in the DMA address register. The byte count is stored in the DMA byte count register, and the control bits are stored in the DMA control register. Once the DMA is initialized, the microprocessor stops communicating with the DMA unless it receives an interrupt signal or if it wants to check how many bytes have been transferred.

The position of the DMA controller among other components in a microcomputer system is illustrated in Fig. 12-19. The microprocessor communicates with the DMA controller through the address and data buses as with any interface unit. The DMA has its own address which activates the *CS* and *RS* lines. The microprocessor initializes the DMA through the data bus. Once the DMA receives the start control bit, it can start the transfer between the peripheral device and system RAM.

When the peripheral device sends a DMA request, the DMA controller activates its *BR* line, informing the processor to relinquish the buses. The microprocessor responds with its *BG* line, informing the DMA that its buses are disabled. The DMA then puts the current value of its address register onto the address bus, initiates the *RD* or *WR* signal, and sends a DMA acknowledge to the peripheral device.

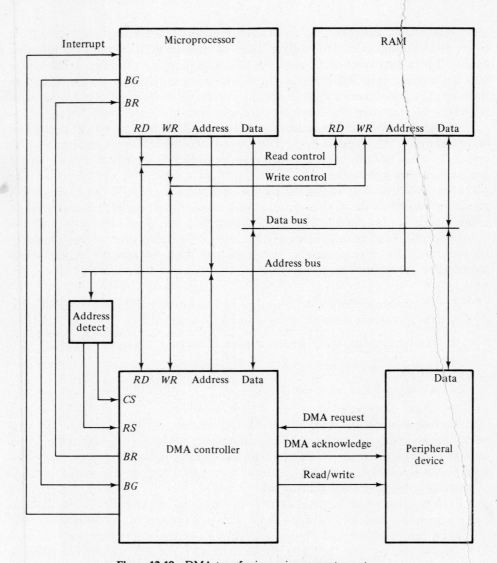

Figure 12-19 DMA transfer in a microcomputer system

The peripheral device then puts a byte on the data bus (for write) or receives a byte from the data bus (for read). Thus, the DMA controls the read or write operation and supplies the address for the memory. The peripheral unit can then communicate with RAM through the data bus for direct transfer between the two units while the microprocessor is momentarily disabled.

For each byte that is transferred, the DMA increments its address register and decrements its byte count register. If the byte count register does not reach zero, the DMA checks the request line coming from the peripheral. For a high-speed peripheral, this line will be activated as soon as the previous transfer is completed. A second transfer is then initiated, and the process continues until the entire block is transferred. If the peripheral speed is slower, the DMA request line may come somewhat later. In this case, the DMA removes its bus request line so the microprocessor can continue to execute its program. When the peripheral requests a transfer, the DMA requests the buses again.

If the byte count register reaches zero, the DMA stops any further transfer and removes its bus request. It also informs the microprocessor of the termination by means of an interrupt request. When the microprocessor responds to the DMA interrupt, it reads the contents of the byte count register. The zero value of this register indicates that all the bytes were successfully transferred. The microprocessor can read this register at any other time as well to check the number of bytes already transferred.

A DMA controller may have more than one channel. In this case, each channel has a DMA request/acknowedge pair of control signals and is connected to a separate peripheral device. Each channel also has its own address register and byte count register within the DMA. A priority among the channels may be established so that channels with high priority are serviced before channels with lower priority.

DMA transfer is very useful in many microcomputer system applications. It is used for fast transfer of information between floppy disks or magnetic-tape cassettes and system RAM. It is also useful for communication with interactive terminal systems having CRT screens or with television screens used for video games. Typically, an image of the screen display is kept in a memory which can be updated under processor control. The contents of the memory can be transferred to the screen periodically by means of DMA transfer.

A potential application for DMA is in a multiprocessor system forming a network of two or more processors. Communication between processors can be maintained with a shared memory that can be accessed by all processors. DMA is a convenient method for transferring information between the common memory and the various processors in the network.

REFERENCES

1. Peatman, J. B., *Microcomputer-Based Design.* New York: McGraw-Hill Book Co., 1977.

2. Klingman, E. K., *Microprocessor Systems Design.* Englewood Cliffs, N.J.: Prentice-Hall, Inc., 1977.

3. Hillburn, J. L., and P. N. Julich, *Microcomputers/Microprocessors: Hardware, Software, and Applications.* Englewood Cliffs, N.J.: Prentice-Hall, Inc., 1976.

4. Soucek, B., *Microprocessors and Microcomputers.* New York: John Wiley & Sons, 1976.

5. Osborn, A., *An Introduction to Microcomputers, Volume 1: Basic Concepts.* Berkeley, Calif.: Adam Osborn and Associates, 1976.

6. Osborn, A., *An Introduction to Microcomputers Volume 2: Some Real Products*. Berkeley, Calif.: Adam Osborn and Associates, 1977.

7. McGlynn, D. R., *Microprocessors Technology, Architecture and Applications*. New York: John Wiley & Sons, Inc., 1976.

8. *Intel 8080 Microcomputer Systems User's Manual*. Santa Clara, Calif.: Intel Corp., 1975.

9. Wakerly, J. F., "Microprocessor Input/Output Architecture." *Computer*, Vol. 10, No. 2 (February, 1977), pp 26–33.

10. Cosley, J., and S. Vasa, "Block Transfer with DMA Augments Microprocessor Efficiency." *Computer Design*, Vol. 16, No. 1 (January, 1977), pp 81–85.

PROBLEMS

12-1.   What is the difference between RAM and ROM? What function does each serve in a microcomputer system?

12-2.   Why is the data bus in most microprocessors bidirectional while the address bus is unidirectional?

12-3.   Microprocessors are typically categorized as being 4-bit, 8-bit, or 16-bit. What does the number of bits imply?

12-4.   A microprocessor data bus has 16 lines and its address bus contains 12 lines. What is the maximum memory capacity that can be connected to the microprocessor? How many bytes can be stored in memory?

12-5.   What is the difference between a microprocessor and a microcomputer? What is the difference between a single-chip microcomputer and a microprocessor chip?

12-6.   Consider an 8-bit LSI component (memory or interface) with separate input and output data terminals and no internal bus buffers. Using external three-state buffers, show how the input and output terminals of the component should be connected to a bidirectional data bus.

12-7.   A 16-bit microprocessor has a single 16-bit bus which is shared for transferring either a 16-bit address or a 16-bit data word. Explain why an external address latch or register would be required between the microprocessor and the address inputs of the memory. Formulate a possible set of control signals for communicating between the microprocessor and memory. List the sequence of transfers for a memory read and memory write.

12-8.   What will accumulator register A and the status bits C (carry), S (sign), Z (zero), and V (overflow) contain after each of the following instructions? The initial value of register A in each case is $(72)_{16}$. Assume that all status bits are affected after an arithmetic or logic operation.

(a) ADD immediate operand $(C6)_{16}$.

(b) ADD immediate operand $(1E)_{16}$.

(c) AND immediate operand $(8D)_{16}$.

(d) Exclusive-OR the accumulator to itself.

12-9. Specify the number of bytes in each instruction and list the sequence of register transfers that execute the following instructions from Table 12-2.

(a) STA AD16   Store A direct $M[AD16] \leftarrow A$

(b) ADD FG   Add with register indirect $A \leftarrow A + M[FG]$

(c) SUB B   Subtract B from A $A \leftarrow A - B$

(d) INR A   Increment A $A \leftarrow A + 1$

(e) JC AD16   Jump on carry   If $(C = 1)$ then $(PC \leftarrow AD16)$

12-10. Go over the list of instructions in Table 12-2 and indicate if the instruction occupies one, two, or three bytes.

12-11. The first instruction listed in Table 12-2 is a move instruction that transfers the contents of B to A. How many equivalent instructions are there for transferring the contents of register $R1$ to $R2$, where $R1$ or $R2$ is one of the registers A, B, C, D, E, F, or G? The source register can be the same as the destination register.

12-12. Table 12-1 lists three add-to A instructions with different addressing modes. Extend the table to include the following addressing modes:

(a) Zero-page addressing.

(b) Relative addressing.

(c) Index addressing.

List the sequence of operations required to process each instruction.

12-13. The operation code of an instruction is stored in memory location $(7128)_{16}$. The next byte in memory contains $(FB)_{16}$. Where should the operand be stored in memory if the instruction has the following addressing mode?

(a) Zero-page addressing.

(b) Present-page addressing.

(c) Relative addressing.

12-14. List the sequence of memory transfers required to process an indirect-addressing-mode instruction when the instruction is a control type (for example, jump unconditionally). How many memory cycles are needed?

12-15. Some microprocessors provide an internal (limited capacity) register stack within the microprocessor chip. Others provide a stack pointer register with access to memory for the stack. Discuss the advantages and disadvantages of each configuration.

12-16. If you are familiar with an electronic calculator that employs a stack for evaluating arithmetic expressions, explain how the stack mechanism operates when calculating the expression $3 \times 4 + 5 \times 6$.

12-17. A subroutine return address can be stored in an index register instead of a stack. Discuss the advantages and disadvantages of this configuration.

12-18. The top of the stack contains 5A and the next byte down the stack is 14 (all numbers are in hexadecimal). The stack pointer contains 3A56. A call subroutine to location 67AE instruction (three bytes) is located at memory address 013F. What are the contents of PC, SP, and the stack:

(a) Before the call instruction is executed?

(b) After the call instruction is executed?

(c) After the return from subroutine?

(d) After a second return from subroutine instruction following the one in (c)?

12-19. How would you sequence a program that needs two memory stacks maintained throughout the program with a microprocessor that has only one stack pointer?

12-20. What is the fundamental difference between a subroutine call and an interrupt request? Is it possible to employ a common memory stack for both?

12-21. A microprocessor responds to an interrupt request by pushing into the stack not only the return address,, but also the contents of processor registers that may be affected while servicing the interrupt.

   (a) List those registers from Fig. 12-5 whose contents should be pushed into the stack.

   (b) How many memory cycles would it now take to execute an interrupt request?

12-22. Obtain the circuit of the four-input priority encoder whose truth table is specified in Table 12-4.

12-23. Derive the truth table of an 8-input priority encoder.

12-24. Specify the four vector addresses (in hexadecimal) when x and y of Table 12-4 are bits 4 and 5 of the low-order byte. All other bits of the byte are 0. The high-order byte is always FF.

12-25. (a) How many 128×8 RAM chips are needed to provide a memory capacity of 2048 bytes?

   (b) How many lines of the address bus must be used to access 2048 bytes of memory? How many of these lines will be common to all chips?

   (c) How many lines must be decoded for chip select? Specify the size of the decoders.

12-26. A microprocessor uses RAM chips of 1024×1 capacity.

   (a) How many chips are needed and how should their address lines be connected to provide a memory capacity of 1024 bytes?

   (b) How many chips are needed to provide a memory capacity of 16K bytes?

   Explain in words how the chips are to be connected to the address bus.

12-27. A ROM chip of 1024×8 bits has four select inputs and operates from a 5-volt power supply. How many pins are needed for the IC package? Draw a block diagram and label all input and output terminals in the ROM.

12-28. Extend the memory system of Fig. 12-13 to 4096 bytes of RAM and 4096 bytes of ROM. List the memory-address map and indicate what size decoders are needed.

12-29. A microprocessor employs RAM chips of 256×8 and ROM chips of 1024×8. The microcomputer system needs 2K bytes of RAM, 4K bytes of ROM, and four interface units, each with four registers. A memory-mapped I/O configuration is used. The two highest-order bits of the address bus are assigned 00 for RAM, 01 for ROM, and 10 for interface registers.

   (a) How many RAM and ROM chips are needed?

(b) Draw a memory-address map for the system.

(c) Give the address range in hexadecimal for RAM, ROM, and interface.

12-30. An 8-bit microprocessor has a 16-bit address bus. The first 15 lines of the address are used to select a bank of 32K bytes of memory. The high-order bit of the address is used to select a register which receives the contents of the data bus. Explain how this configuration can be used to extend the memory capacity of the system to 8 banks of 32K bytes each, for a total of 256K bytes of memory.

12-31. The interface of Fig. 12-14 is connected to the address bus of a microprocessor. The data register of port A is selected with a hexadecimal address $XXXC$, where the X's can be any number.

(a) How should the address lines be connected to the chip select (CS) input?

(b) What are the hexadecimal addresses that select the other three registers in the interface?

12-32. What is the difference between direct transfer and a transfer with handshaking in a parallel peripheral interface?

12-33. What is the difference between synchronous and asynchronous serial transfer of information over long-distance communication lines?

12-34. Consider the possibility of connecting a number of microprocessors to one common set of data and address buses. How can an orderly transfer of information be established between the microprocessors and the common memory?

Digital Integrated Circuits

13

13-1 INTRODUCTION

The integrated circuit (IC) was introduced in Section 1-9, and the various IC digital logic families were discussed in Section 2-8. This chapter presents the basic electronic circuits in each IC digital logic family and analyzes their electrical operation. A basic knowledge of electronics is assumed.

The IC digital logic families to be considered here are:

RTL	Resistor-transistor logic
DTL	Diode-transistor logic
I^2L	Integrated-injection logic
TTL	Transistor-transistor logic
ECL	Emitter-coupled logic
MOS	Metal-oxide semiconductor
CMOS	Complementary metal-oxide semiconductor

The first two, RTL and DTL, have only historical significance since they are seldom used in new designs. RTL was the first commercial family to have been used extensively. It is included here because it represents a useful starting point for explaining the basic operation of digital gates. DTL circuits have been gradually replaced by TTL. In fact, TTL is a modification of the DTL gate. The operation of the TTL gate will be easier to understand after the DTL gate is discussed. The characteristics of TTL, ECL, and CMOS were presented in Section 2-8. These families have a large number of SSI circuits, as well as MSI and LSI circuits. I^2L and MOS are mostly used for constructing LSI functions.

The basic circuit in each IC digital logic family is either a NAND or a NOR gate. This basic circuit is the primary building block from which more complex functions are obtained. An *RS* latch is constructed from two NAND or two NOR gates connected back to back. A master-slave flip-flop is obtained from the interconnection of about ten basic gates. A register is obtained from the interconnection of flip-flops and basic gates. Each IC logic family has available a catalog of integrated-circuit packages that provide various digital logic functions. The differences in the logic functions available from each logic family are not so much in the function that they achieve as in the specific characteristics of the basic gate from which the function has been constructed.

NAND and NOR gates are usually defined by the Boolean functions they implement in terms of binary variables. When analyzing them as electronic circuits, it is more convenient to investigate their input-output relationships in terms of two voltage levels: a *high* level (H) and a *low* level (L) (see Fig. 2-10). Binary variables take the values 1 and 0. When positive logic is adopted, the high voltage level is assigned the binary value of 1, and the low voltage level a binary 0. From the truth table of a positive-logic NAND gate, we deduce its behavior in terms of high and low levels as stated in Fig. 13-1. The corresponding behavior of the NOR gate is also stated in the same figure. These statements must be remembered because they will be used during the analysis of all the gates in this chapter.

The various digital logic families are usually evaluated by comparing the characteristics of the basic gate in each family. The most important characteristics were discussed in Section 2-8. They are listed here again for reference.

1. *Fan-out* specifies the number of standard loads that the output of the gate can drive without impairment of its normal operation. A standard load is defined as the current flowing in the input of a gate in the same IC family.

Inputs		Output	NAND gate
x	*y*	*z*	(a) If *any* input is LOW, the output is HIGH.
L	L	H	(b) If *all* inputs are HIGH, the output is LOW.
L	H	H	
H	L	H	
H	H	L	

Inputs		Output	NOR gate
x	*y*	*z*	(a) If *any* input is HIGH, the output is LOW.
L	L	H	(b) If *all* inputs are LOW, the output is HIGH.
L	H	L	
H	L	L	
H	H	L	

Figure 13-1 Input-output conditions for positive-logic NAND and NOR gates

2. *Power dissipation* is the power consumed by the gate, which must be available from the power supply.

3. *Propagation delay* is the average transition delay time for the signal to propagate from input to output when the signals change in value.

4. *Noise margin* is the limit of a noise voltage which may be present without impairing the proper operation of the circuit.

The *bipolar* junction transistor (BJT) is the familiar *npn* or *pnp* junction transistor. In contrast, the field-effect transistor (FET) is said to be *unipolar*. The operation of a bipolar transistor depends on the flow of two types of carriers: electrons and holes. A unipolar transistor depends on the flow of only one type of majority carrier which may be eletrons (n-channel) or holes (p-channel). The first five logic families listed previously, RTL, DTL, TTL, ECL, and I²L, use bipolar transistors. The last two logic families, MOS and CMOS, employ a type of unipolar transistor called metal-oxide semiconductor field-effect transistor, abbreviated MOSFET, or MOS for short. We begin by describing the characteristics of the bipolar transistor and the basic gates used in the bipolar logic families. We then explain the operation of the MOS transistor in conjunction with its two logic families.

13-2 BIPOLAR TRANSISTOR CHARACTERISTICS

This section is devoted to a review of the bipolar transistor as applied to digital circuits. This information will be used for the analysis of the basic circuit in the five bipolar logic families. Bipolar transistors may be of the *npn* or *pnp* type. Moreover, they are constructed either with germanium or silicon semiconductor material. IC transistors, however, are made with silicon and are usually of the npn type.

The basic data needed for the analysis of digital circuits may be obtained from inspection of the typical characteristic curves of a common-emitter *npn* silicon transistor, shown in Fig. 13-2. The circuit in (a) is a simple inverter with two resistors and a transistor. The current marked I_C flows through resistor R_C and the collector of the transistor. Current I_B flows through resistor R_B and the base of the transistor. The emitter is connected to ground and its current $I_E = I_C + I_B$. The supply voltage is between V_{CC} and ground. The input is between V_i and ground, and the output is between V_o and ground.

We have assumed a positive direction for the currents as indicated. These are the directions in which the currents normally flow in an *npn* transistor. Collector and base currents I_C and I_B are positive when they flow into the transistor. Emitter current I_E is positive when it flows out of the transistor, as indicated by the arrow in the emitter terminal. The symbol V_{CE} stands for the voltage drop from collector

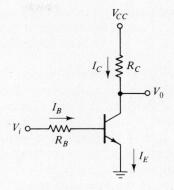

(a) Inverter circuit

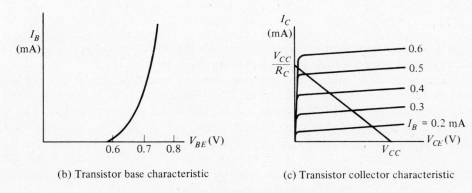

(b) Transistor base characteristic   (c) Transistor collector characteristic

Figure 13-2   Silicon *npn* transistor characteristics

to emitter and is always positive. Correspondingly, V_{BE} is the voltage drop across the base-to-emitter junction. This junction is forward biased when V_{BE} is positive. It is reverse biased when V_{BE} is negative.

The base-emitter graphical characteristic is shown in Fig. 13-2(b). This is a plot of V_{BE} versus I_B. If the base-emitter voltage is less than 0.6 V, the transistor is said to be *cutoff* and no base current flows. When the base-emitter junction is forward biased with a voltage greater than 0.6 V, the transistor conducts and I_B starts rising very fast while V_{BE} changes very little. The voltage V_{BE} across a conducting transistor seldom exceeds 0.8 V.

The graphical collector-emitter characteristics, together with the load line, are shown in Fig. 13-2(c). When V_{BE} is less than 0.6 V, the transistor is cutoff with $I_B = 0$ and a negligible current flows in the collector. The collector-to-emitter circuit then behaves like an open circuit. In the *active* region, collector voltage V_{CE} may be anywhere from about 0.8 V up to V_{CC}. Collector current I_C in this region can be calculated to be approximately equal to $I_B h_{FE}$, where h_{FE} is a transistor parameter called the *dc current gain*. The maximum collector current depends not on I_B, but rather on the external circuit connected to the collector. This is because V_{CE} is always positive and its lowest possible value is 0 V. For example, in the inverter shown, the maximum I_C is obtained by making $V_{CE} = 0$ to obtain $I_C = V_{CC}/R_C$.

It was stated that $I_C = h_{FE}I_B$ in the active region. The parameter h_{FE} varies widely over the operating range of the transistor, but still it is useful to employ an average value for the purpose of analysis. In a typical operating range, h_{FE} is about 50, but under certain conditions it could go down to as low as 20. It must be realized that the base current I_B may be increased to any desirable value, but the collector current I_C is limited by external circuit parameters. As a consequence, a situation can be reached where $h_{FE}I_B$ is greater than I_C. If this condition exists, then the transistor is said to be in the *saturation* region. Thus, the condition for saturation is determined from the relationship:

$$I_B \geqslant \frac{I_{CS}}{h_{FE}}$$

where I_{CS} is the maximum collector current flowing during saturation. V_{CE} is not exactly zero in the saturation region but is normally about 0.2V.

The basic data needed for analyzing bipolar transistor digital circuits are listed in Table 13-1. In the cutoff region, V_{BE} is less than 0.6 V, V_{CE} is considered as an open circuit, and both currents are negligible. In the active region, V_{BE} is about 0.7 V, V_{CE} may vary over a wide range, and I_C can be calculated as a function of I_B. In the saturation region, V_{BE} hardly changes but V_{CE} drops to 0.2 V. The base current must be large enough to satisfy the inequality listed. To simplify the analysis, we will assume that $V_{BE} = 0.7$ V if the transistor is conducting, whether in the active or saturation region.

TABLE 13-1 Typical npn silicon transistor parameters

Region	$V_{BE}(V)$*	V_{CE} (V)	Current relationship
Cutoff	<0.6	Open circuit	$I_B = I_C = 0$
Active	0.6–0.7	>0.8	$I_C = h_{FE}I_B$
Saturation	0.7–0.8	0.2	$I_B \geqslant I_{CS}/h_{FE}$

*V_{BE} will be assumed to be 0.7 V if the transistor is conducting, whether in the active or saturation region.

The analysis of digital circuits may be undertaken using a prescribed procedure: For each transistor in the circuit determine if its V_{BE} is less than 0.6 V. If so, then the transistor is cutoff and the collector-to-emitter circuit is considered an open circuit. If V_{BE} is greater than 0.6 V, the transistor may be in the active or saturation region. Calculate the base current, assuming that $V_{BE} = 0.7$ V. Then calculate the maximum possible value of collector current I_{CS}, assuming $V_{CE} = 0.2$

V. These calculations will be in terms of voltages applied and resistor values. Then, if the base current is large enough that $I_B \geqslant I_{CS}/h_{FE}$, we deduce that the transistor is in the saturation region with $V_{CE} = 0.2$ V. However, if the base current is smaller and the above relationship is not satisfied, the transistor is in the active region and we recalculate collector current I_C using the equation $I_C = h_{FE}I_B$.

To demonstrate with an example, consider the inverter circuit of Fig. 13-2(a) with the following parameters:

$$R_C = 1 \text{ k}\Omega \qquad V_{CC} = 5 \text{ V (voltage supply)}$$

$$R_B = 22 \text{ k}\Omega \qquad H = 5 \text{ V (high-level voltage)}$$

$$h_{FE} = 50 \qquad L = 0.2 \text{ V (low-level voltage)}$$

With input voltage $V_i = L = 0.2$ V, we have that $V_{BE} < 0.6$ V and the transistor is cutoff. The collector-emitter circuit behaves like an open circuit; so output voltage $V_o = 5$ V $= H$.

With input voltage $V_i = H = 5$ V, we deduce that $V_{BE} > 0.6$ V. Assuming that $V_{BE} = 0.7$, we calculate the base current:

$$I_B = \frac{V_i - V_{BE}}{R_B} = \frac{5 - 0.7}{22 \text{ } k\Omega} = 0.195 \text{ mA}$$

The maximum collector current, assuming $V_{CE} = 0.2$ V, is:

$$I_{CS} = \frac{V_{CC} - V_{CE}}{R_C} = \frac{5 - 0.2}{1 \text{ } k\Omega} = 4.8 \text{ mA}$$

We then check for saturation:

$$0.195 = I_B \geqslant \frac{I_{CS}}{h_{FE}} = \frac{4.8}{50} = 0.096 \text{ mA}$$

and find that the inequality is satisfied since $0.195 > 0.096$. We conclude that the transistor is saturated and output voltage $V_o = V_{CE} = 0.2$ V $= L$. Thus the circuit behaves as an inverter.

The procedure just described will be used extensively during the analysis of the circuits in the following sections. This will be done by means of a qualitative analysis, i.e., without writing down the specific numerical equations. The quantitative analysis and specific calculations will be left as execises in the Problems section at the end of the chapter.

There are occasions where not only transistors but also diodes are used in digital circuits. An IC diode is usually constructed from a transistor with its collector connected to the base, as shown in Fig. 13-3(a). The graphic symbol employed for a diode is shown in Fig. 13-3(b). The diode behaves essentially like the base-emitter junction of a transistor. Its graphical characteristic, shown in Fig.

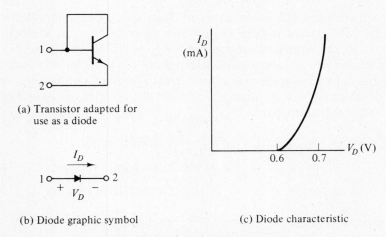

(a) Transistor adapted for
use as a diode

(b) Diode graphic symbol

(c) Diode characteristic

Figure 13-3   Silicon diode symbol and characteristic

13-3(c), is similar to the base-emitter characteristic of a transistor. We can then conclude that a diode is off and nonconducting when its forward voltage, V_D, is less than 0.6 V. When the diode conducts, current I_D flows in the direction shown in Fig. 13-3(b), and V_D stays at about 0.7 V. One must always provide an external resistor to limit the current in a conducting diode, since its voltage remains fairly constant at a fraction of a volt.

13-3   RTL AND DTL CIRCUITS

RTL Basic Gate

The basic circuit of the RTL digital logic family is the NOR gate shown in Fig. 13-4. Each input is associated with one resistor and one transistor. The collectors of the transistors are tied together at the output. The voltage levels for the circuit are 0.2 V for the low-level and from 1 to 3.6 V for the high-level.

The analysis of the RTL gate is very simple and follows the procedure outlined in the previous section. If any input of the RTL gate is high, the corresponding transistor is driven into saturation. This causes the output to be low, regardless of the states of the other transistors. If all inputs are low at 0.2 V, all transistors are cutoff because $V_{BE} < 0.6$ V. This causes the output of the circuit to be high, approaching the value of supply voltage V_{CC}. This confirms the conditions stated in Fig. 13-1 for the NOR gate. Note that the noise margin for low signal input is $0.6 - 0.2 = 0.4$ V.

The fan-out of the RTL gate is limited by the value of the output voltage when high. As the output is loaded with inputs of other gates, more current is consumed by the load. This current must flow through the 640-Ω resistor. A simple calculation (see Problem 13-1) will show that, if h_{FE} drops to 20, the output

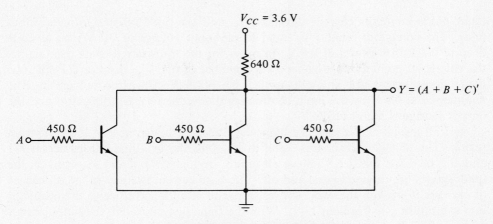

Figure 13-4 RTL basic NOR gate

voltage drops to about 1 V when the fan-out is 5. Any voltage below 1 V in the output may not drive the next transistor into saturation as required. The power dissipation of the RTL gate is about 12 mW and the propagation delay averages 25 ns.

DTL Basic Gates

The basic circuit in the DTL digital logic family is the NAND gate shown in Fig. 13-5. Each input is associated with one diode. The diodes and the 5-kΩ resistor form an AND gate. The transistor serves as a current amplifier while inverting the digital signal. The two voltage levels are 0.2 V for the low-level and between 4 and 5 V for the high-level.

 The analysis of the DTL gate should conform to the conditions listed in Fig. 13-1 for the NAND gate. If any input of the gate is low at 0.2 V, the corresponding

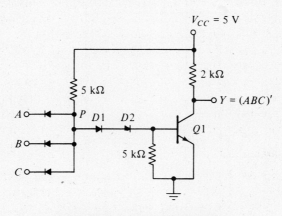

Figure 13-5 DTL basic NAND gate

input diode conducts current through V_{CC} and the 5-kΩ resistor into the input node. The voltage at point P is equal to the input voltage of 0.2 V plus a diode drop of 0.7 V, for a total of 0.9 V. In order for the transistor to start conducting, the voltage at point P must overcome a potential of one V_{BE} drop in $Q1$ plus two diode drops across $D1$ and $D2$, or $3 \times 0.6 = 1.8$ V. Since the voltage at P is maintained at 0.9 V by the input conducting diode, the transistor is cutoff and the output voltage is high at 5 V.

If all inputs of the gate are high, the transistor is driven into the saturation region. The voltage at P now is equal to V_{BE} plus the two diode drops across $D1$ and $D2$, or $0.7 \times 3 = 2.1$ V. Since all inputs are high at 5 V and $V_P = 2.1$ V, the input diodes are reverse biased and off. The base current is equal to the difference of currents flowing in the two 5-kΩ resistors and is sufficient to drive the transistor into saturation (see Problem 13-2). With the transistor saturated, the output drops to V_{CE} of 0.2 V, which is the low level for the gate.

The power dissipation of a DTL gate is about 12 mW and the propagation delay averages 30 ns. The noise margin is about 1 V and a fan-out as high as 8 is possible. The fan-out of the DTL gate is limited by the maximum current that can flow in the collector of the saturated transistor (see Problem 13-3).

The fan-out of a DTL gate may be increased by replacing one of the diodes in the base circuit with a transistor as shown in Fig. 13-6. Transistor $Q1$ is maintained in the active region when output transistor $Q2$ is saturated. As a consequence, the modified circuit can supply a larger amount of base current to the output transistor. The output transistor can now draw a larger amount of collector current before it goes out of saturation. Part of the collector current comes from the conducting diodes in the loading gates when $Q2$ is saturated. Thus, an increase in allowable collector saturated current allows more loads to be connected to the output, which increases the fan-out capability of the gate.

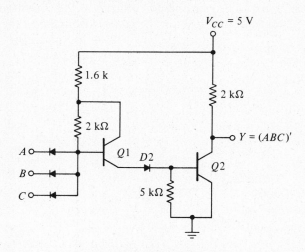

Figure 13-6 Modified DTL gate

High-Threshold Logic—HTL

There are occasions where digital circuits must operate in an environment which produces very high noise signals. For operation in such surroundings, there is available a type of DTL gate which possesses a high threshold to noise immunity. This type of gate is called a *high-threshold-logic* (HTL) gate.

The HTL gate is shown in Fig. 13-7. Comparing it with the modified DTL gate of Fig. 13-6, we note that the supply voltage has been raised to 15 V and a zener diode (Z) is used instead of a normal diode. The zener diode has the characteristic of maintaining a constant voltage of 6.9 V when reverse biased.

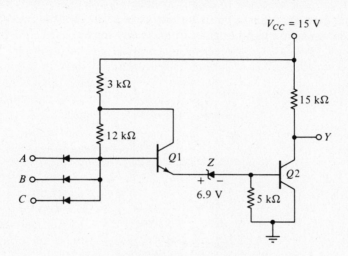

Figure 13-7   High-threshold-logic (HTL) gate

In order for output transistor $Q2$ to conduct, the emitter of $Q1$ must rise to a potential of one V_{BE} drop plus the fixed zener voltage of 6.9 V, for a total of about 7.5 V. The low level for the gate remains at 0.2 V, but the high level is about 15 V. With the input of 0.2 V, the base of $Q1$ is at 0.9 V and $Q2$ is off. The noise signal must be greater than 7.5 V to change the state of $Q2$. With all the inputs at 15 V, output transistor $Q2$ is saturated. The noise signal must be greater than 7.5 V (in the negative direction) to turn the transistor off. Thus, the noise margin of the HTL gate is about 7.5 V for both voltage levels.

13-4   INTEGRATED-INJECTION LOGIC (I²L)

Integrated-injection logic is the most recent digital logic family to be introduced commercially. Its main advantage is the high packing density of gates that can be achieved in a given area of semiconductor chip. This allows more circuits to be placed in the chip to form complex digital functions. As a consequence, this family is used mostly for LSI functions. It is not available in SSI packages containing individual gates.

The I^2L basic gate is similar in operation to the RTL gate, with few major differences: (1) The base resistor used in the RTL gate is removed altogether in the I^2L gate. (2) The collector resistor used in the RTL gate is replaced by a pnp transistor that acts as a load for the I^2L gate. (3) I^2L transistors use multiple collectors instead of the individual transistors employed in RTL.

The schematic diagram of the basic I^2L gate is shown in Fig. 13-8. It has an npn transistor, $Q1$, with multiple collectors for the outputs. The base circuit has a pnp transistor, $T1$, connected to supply voltage V_{BB}. Unlike other logic families, the I^2L basic gate operation cannot be analyzed when standing alone. One must show its interconnection to other gates to make any sense.

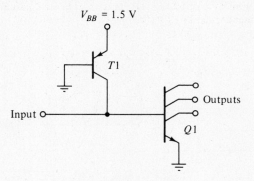

Figure 13-8 I^2L basic gate

Figure 13-9 shows the interaction of the basic gate formed by $Q1$ and $T1$ with other gates in its input and output. Here we see that one collector of $Q2$ supplies the input to the basic gate. Transistor $T1$ in the basic gate acts as a load that injects current to the collector of $Q2$. One of the collectors of $Q1$ acts as an output of the basic gate and is connected to the base of $Q3$. Transistor $T3$, connected to the base of $Q3$, acts as a load to inject current to the collector of $Q1$ in the basic gate. The basic gate here acts as an inverter and its equivalent circuit is shown in Fig. 13-9(b). Using multiple collectors and a pnp transistor instead of a load resistor turns out to be a more efficient method of construction, since they reduce the chip area required and allow the packing of more circuits. The pnp transistor, although shown to be connected to the base of a given gate, acts as a collector load for all the other gates that are connected to this base.

The basic I^2L gate, when connected to other gates, performs the NOR logic function. This is demonstrated in the circuit diagram shown in Fig. 13-10. The logic function that the circuit implements is drawn with graphic gate symbols in Fig. 13-10(a), which shows the interconnection of two NOR gates and an inverter. This is implemented with three I^2L gates, $Q1$, $Q2$, and $Q3$, as shown in Fig. 13-10(b). The output transistors are also shown for completeness. The collectors of

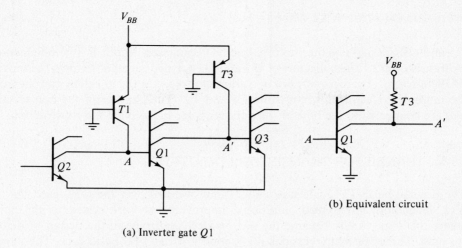

(b) Equivalent circuit

(a) Inverter gate $Q1$

Figure 13-9 Connection of other gates to the inputs and outputs of a basic I²L gate

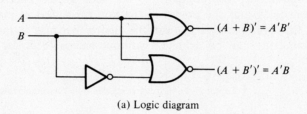

(a) Logic diagram

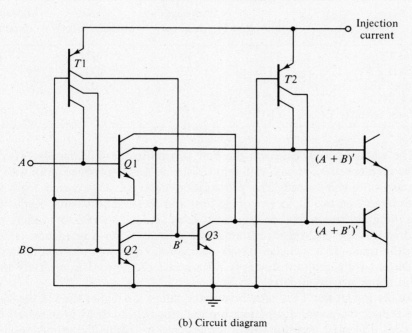

(b) Circuit diagram

Figure 13-10 Typical connections among I²L gates

$Q1$ and $Q2$ are tied together to form one NOR function. Input B is complemented by transistor $Q2$. The collectors of $Q3$ and $Q1$ are tied together to form the second NOR function. The base of each npn transistor receives the injection current from the multiple-collector pnp transistors $T1$ and $T2$. The emitters of the npn transistors are connected to the base of the pnp transistor to facilitate the construction.

13-5 TRANSISTOR-TRANSISTOR LOGIC (TTL)

The original basic TTL gate was a slight improvement over the DTL gate. As the TTL technology progressed, additional improvements were added to the point where this logic family became the most widely used type in the design of digital systems. There are many versions (or "series") of the TTL basic gate. The names and characteristics of five versions appear in Table 13-2, together with their propagation delay and power dissipation values. The speed-power product is an important parameter for comparing the basic gates. This is a product of the propagation delay and the power dissipation measured in picojoules (pJ). A low value for this parameter is a desirable figure, because it indicates that a given propagation delay can be achieved without excessive power dissipation, or vice versa.

TABLE 13-2 TTL versions and their characteristics

Name	Abbreviation	Propagation delay (ns)	Power dissipation (mW)	Speed-power product (pJ)
Standard TTL	TTL	10	10	100
Low-power TTL	LTTL	33	1	33
High-speed TTL	HTTL	6	22	132
Schottky TTL	STTL	3	19	57
Low-power Schottky TTL	LSTTL	9.5	2	19

The standard TTL gate was the first version in the TTL family. This basic gate was then constructed with different resistor values to produce gates with lower dissipation or higher speed. The propagation delay of a saturated logic family depends largely on two factors: storage time and RC time constants. Reducing the storage time decreases the propagation delay. Reducing resistor values in the circuit reduces the RC time constants and decreases the propagation delay. Of course, the trade-off is a higher power dissipation because lower resistances draw more current from the power supply. The speed of the gate is inversely proportional to the propagation delay.

In the low-power TTL gate the resistor values are higher than in the standard gate to reduce the power dissipation, but the propagation delay is increased. In the high-speed TTL gate, resistor values are lowered to reduce the propagation delay, but the power dissipation is increased. The Schottky TTL is a later improvement in the technology that removes the storage time of transistors by preventing them from going into saturation. This version increases the speed of operation without an excessive increase in power dissipation. The low-power Schottky TTL version sacrifices some speed for reduced power dissipation. It is about equal to standard TTL in propagation delay but has only one-fifth the power dissipation. It has the best speed-power product and, as a consequence, it became the most popular version in new designs.

All TTL versions are available in SSI packages and in more complex forms as MSI and LSI functions. The differences in the TTL versions are not in the digital functions that they perform, but rather in the values of resistors and type of transistor that their basic gate uses. In any case, TTL gates in all versions come in three different types of output configurations.

1. Open-collector output.

2. Totem-pole output.

3. Three-state (or tri-state) output.

These three types of outputs will be considered in conjunction with the circuit description of the basic TTL gate.

Open-collector Output Gate

The basic TTL gate shown in Fig. 13-11 is a modified circuit of the DTL gate. The multiple emitters in transistor $Q1$ are connected to the inputs. These emitters behave most of the time like the input diodes in the DTL gate since they form a *pn*

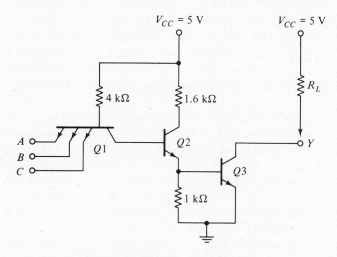

Figure 13-11   Open-collector TTL gate

junction with their common base. The base-collector junction of $Q1$ acts as another *pn* junction diode corresponding to $D1$ in the DTL gate (see Fig. 13-5). Transistor $Q2$ replaces the second diode, $D2$, in the DTL gate. The output of the TTL gate is taken from the open collector of $Q3$. A resistor connected to V_{CC} must be inserted external to the IC package for the output to "pull up" to the high voltage level when $Q3$ is off; otherwise, the output acts as an open circuit. The reason for not providing the resistor internally will be discussed later.

The two voltage levels of the TTL gate are 0.2 V for the low level and from 2.4 to 5 V for the high level. The basic circuit is a NAND gate. If any input is low, the corresponding base-emitter junction in $Q1$ is forward biased. The voltage at the base of $Q1$ is equal to the input voltage of 0.2 V plus a V_{BE} drop of 0.7 V or 0.9 V. In order for $Q3$ to start conducting, the path from $Q1$ to $Q3$ must overcome a potential of one diode drop in the base-collector *pn* junction of $Q1$ and two V_{BE} drops in $Q2$ and $Q3$, or $3 \times 0.6 = 1.8$ V. Since the base of $Q1$ is maintained at 0.9 V by the input signal, the output transistor cannot conduct and is cutoff. The output level will be high if an external resistor is connected between the output and V_{CC} (or an open circuit if a resistor is not used).

If all inputs are high, both $Q2$ and $Q3$ conduct and saturate. The base voltage of $Q1$ is equal to the voltage across its base-collector *pn* junction plus two V_{BE} drops in $Q2$ and $Q3$, or about $0.7 \times 3 = 2.1$ V. Since all inputs are high and greater than 2.4 V, the base-emitter junctions of $Q1$ are all reverse biased. When output transistor $Q3$ saturates (provided it has a current path), the output voltage goes low to 0.2 V. This confirms the conditions of a NAND operation.

In the above analysis, we said that the base-collector junction of $Q1$ acts like a *pn* diode junction. This is true in the steady-state condition. However, during the turn-off transition, $Q1$ does exhibit transistor action resulting in a reduction in propagation delay. When all inputs are high and then one of the inputs is brought to a low level, both $Q2$ and $Q3$ start turning off. At this time, the collector junction of $Q1$ is reverse biased and the emitter is forward biased; so transistor $Q1$ goes momentarily into the active region. The collector current of $Q1$ comes from the base of $Q2$ and quickly removes the excess charge stored in $Q2$ during its previous saturation state. This causes a reduction in the storage time of the circuit as compared to the DTL type of input. The result is a reduction of the turn-off time of the gate.

The open-collector TTL gate will operate without the external resistor when connected to inputs of other TTL gates, although this is not recommended because of the low noise immunity encountered. Without an external resistor, the output of the gate will be an open circuit when $Q3$ is off. An open circuit to an input of a TTL gate behaves as if it has a high-level input (but a small amount of noise can change this to a low level). When $Q3$ conducts, its collector will have a current path supplied by the input of the loading gate through V_{CC}, the 4-kΩ resistor, and the forward-biased base-emitter junction.

Open-collector gates are used in three major applications: driving a lamp or relay, performing wired logic, and for the construction of a common-bus system.

An open-collector output can drive a lamp placed in its output through a limiting resistor. When the output is low, the saturated transistor $Q3$ forms a path for the current that turns the lamp on. When the output transistor is off, the lamp turns off because there is no path for the current.

If the outputs of several open-collector TTL gates are tied together with a single external resistor, a wired-AND logic is performed. Remember that a positive-logic AND function gives a high level only if all variables are high; otherwise, the function is low. With outputs of open-collector gates connected together, the common output is high only when all output transistors are off (or high). If an output transistor conducts, it forces the output to the low state.

The wired logic performed with open-collector TTL gates is depicted in Fig. 13-12. The physical wiring in (a) shows how the outputs must be connected to a common resistor. The graphic symbol for such a connection is demonstrated in (b). The AND function formed by connecting together the two outputs is called a wired-AND function. The AND gate is drawn with the lines going through the center of the gate to distinguish it from a conventional gate. The wired-AND gate is not a physical gate but only a symbol to designate the function obtained from the indicated connection. The Boolean function obtained from the circuit of Fig. 13-12 is the AND operation between the outputs of the two NAND gates:

$$Y = (AB)' \cdot (CD)' = (AB + CD)'$$

The second expression is preferred since it shows an operation commonly referred to as an AND-OR-INVERT function (see Section 3-7).

Open-collector gates can be tied together to form a common bus. At any time, all gate outputs tied to the bus, except one, must be maintained in their high state. The selected gate may be either in the high or low state, depending on whether we want to transmit a 1 or 0 on the bus. Control circuits must be used to select the particular gate that drives the bus at any given time.

Figure 13-13 demonstrates the connection of four sources tied to a common bus line. Each of the four inputs drives an open-collector inverter, and the outputs of the inverters are tied together to form a single bus line. The figure shows that

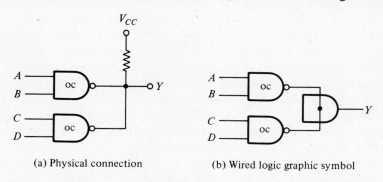

(a) Physical connection   (b) Wired logic graphic symbol

Figure 13-12   Wired-AND of two open-collector (oc) gates, $Y = (AB + CD)'$

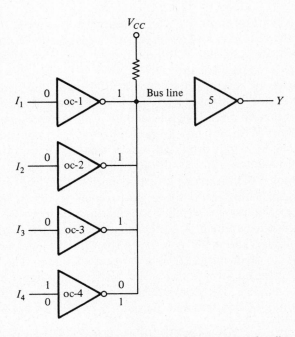

Figure 13-13 Open-collector gates forming a common bus line

three of the inputs are 0, which produces a 1 or high level on the bus. The fourth input, I_4, can now transmit information through the common bus line into inverter 5. Remember that an AND operation is performed in the wired logic. If $I_4 = 1$, the output of gate 4 is 0 and the wired-AND operation produces a 0. If $I_4 = 0$, the output of gate 4 is 1 and the wired-AND operation produces a 1. Thus, if all other outputs are maintained at 1, the selected gate can transmit its value through the bus. The value transmitted is the complement of I_4, but inverter 5 in the receiving end can easily invert this signal again to make $Y = I_4$.

Totem-pole Output

The output impedance of a gate is normally a resistive plus a capacitive load. The capacitive load consists of the capacitance of the output transistor, the capacitance of the fan-out gates, and any stray wiring capacitance. When the output changes from the low to the high state, the output transistor of the gate goes from saturation to cutoff and the total load capacitance, C, charges exponentially from the low to the high voltage level with a time constant equal to RC. For the open-collector gate, R is the external resistor marked R_L. For a typical operating value of $C = 15$ pF and $R_L = 4$ kΩ, the propagation delay of a TTL open-collector gate during the turn-off time is 35 ns. With an *active pull-up* circuit replacing the passive pull-up resistor R_L, the propagation delay is reduced to 10 ns. This

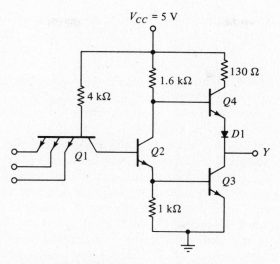

Figure 13-14 TTL gate with totem-pole output

configuration, shown in Fig. 13-14, is called a *totem-pole* output because transistor $Q4$ "sits" upon $Q3$.

The TTL gate with the totem-pole output is the same as the open-collector gate, except for the output transistor $Q4$ and the diode $D1$. When the output Y is in the low state, $Q2$ and $Q3$ are driven into saturation as in the open-collector gate. The voltage in the collector of $Q2$ is $V_{BE}(Q3) + V_{CE}(Q2)$ or $0.7 + 0.2 = 0.9$ V. The output $Y = V_{CE}(Q3) = 0.2$ V. Transistor $Q4$ is cutoff because its base must be one V_{BE} drop plus one diode drop, or $2 \times 0.6 = 1.2$ V, to start conducting. Since the collector of $Q2$ is connected to the base of $Q4$, the latter's voltage is only 0.9 V instead of the required 1.2 V, and so $Q4$ is cutoff. The reason for placing the diode in the circuit is to provide a diode drop in the output path and thus ensure that $Q4$ is cutoff when $Q3$ is saturated.

When the output changes to the high state because one of the inputs drops to the low state, transistors $Q2$ and $Q3$ go into cutoff. However, the output remains momentarily low because the voltages across the load capacitance cannot change instantaneously. As soon as $Q2$ turns off, $Q4$ conducts because its base is connected to V_{CC} through the 1.6-kΩ resistor. The current needed to charge the load capacitance causes $Q4$ to momentarily saturate, and the output voltage rises with a time constant RC. But R in this case is equal to 130 Ω, plus the saturation resistance of $Q4$, plus the resistance of the diode, for a total of approximately 150 Ω. This value of R is much smaller than the passive pull-up resistance used in the open-collector circuit. As a consequence, the transition from the low to high level is much faster.

As the capacitive load charges, the output voltage rises and the current in $Q4$ decreases, bringing the transistor into the active region. Thus, in contrast to the other transistors, $Q4$ is in the *active* region when in a steady-state condition. The final value of the output voltage is then 5 V, minus a V_{BE} drop in $Q4$, minus a diode drop in $D1$ to about 3.6 V. Transistor $Q3$ goes into cutoff very fast, but during the initial transition time both $Q3$ and $Q4$ are on and a peak current is drawn from the power supply. This current spike generates noise in the power supply distribution system. When the change of state is frequent, the transient current spikes increase the power supply current requirement and the average power dissipation of the circuit increases.

The wired-logic connection is not allowed with totem-pole output circuits. When two totem-poles are wired together with the output of one gate high and the output of the second gate low, the excessive amount of current drawn can produce enough heat to damage the transistors in the circuit (see Problem 13-7). Some TTL gates are constructed to withstand the amount of current that flows under this condition. In any case, the collector current in the low gate may be high enough to move the transistor into the active region and produce an output voltage in the wired connection greater than 0.8 V, which is not a valid binary signal for TTL gates.

Schottky TTL Gate

As mentioned before, a reduction in storage time results in a reduction of propagation delay. This is because the time needed for a transistor to come out of saturation delays the switching of the transistor from the on condition to the off condition. Saturation can be eliminated by placing a Schottky diode between the base and collector of each saturated transistor in the circuit. The Schottky diode is formed by the junction of a metal and semiconductor, in contrast to a conventional diode which is formed by the junction of p-type and n-type semiconductor material. The voltage across a conducting Schottky diode is only 0.4 V, as compared to 0.7 V in a conventional diode. The presence of a Schottky diode between the base and collector prevents the transistor from going into saturation. The resulting transistor is called a *Schottky transistor*. The use of Schottky transistors in a TTL decreases the propagation delay without a sacrifice of power dissipation.

The Schottky TTL gate is shown in Fig. 13-15. Note the special symbol used for the Schottky transistors and diodes. The diagram shows all transistors to be of the Schottky type except $Q4$. An exception is made of $Q4$ since it does not saturate but stays in the active region. Note also that resistor values have been reduced to further decrease the propagation delay.

In addition to using Schottky transistors and lower resistor values, the circuit of Fig. 13-15 includes other modifications not available in the standard gate of Fig. 13-14. Two new transistors, $Q5$ and $Q6$ have been added, and Schottky diodes are inserted between each input terminal and ground. There is no diode in the totem-pole circuit. However, the new combination of $Q5$ and $Q4$ still gives the two

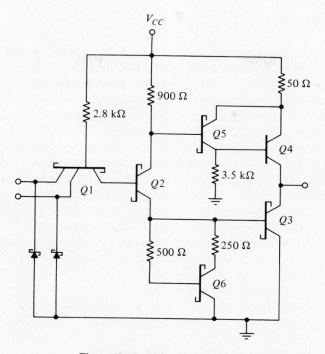

Figure 13-15 Schottky TTL gate

V_{BE} drops necessary to prevent $Q4$ from conducting when the output is low. This combination comprises a double emitter-follower called a *Darlington pair*. The Darlington pair provides a very high current gain and extremely low resistance. This is exactly what is needed during the low-to-high swing of the output, resulting in a decrease of propagation delay.

The diodes in each input shown in the circuit help clamp any ringing that may occur in the input lines. Under transient switching conditions, signal lines appear inductive; this, along with stray capacitance, cause signals to oscillate or "ring." When the output of a gate switches from the high to the low state, the ringing waveform at the input may have excursions below ground as great as 2–3 V, depending on line length. The diodes connected to ground help clamp this ringing since they conduct as soon as the negative voltage exceeds 0.4 V. When the negative excursion is limited, the positive swing is also reduced. The success of the clamp diodes in limiting line effects has been so successful that all versions of TTL gates use them.

The emitter resistor of $Q2$ in Fig. 13-14 has been replaced in Fig. 13-15 by a circuit consisting of transistor $Q6$ and two resistors. The effect of this circuit is to reduce the turn-off current spikes discussed previously. The analysis of this circuit, which helps to reduce the propagation time of the gate, is too involved to present in this brief discussion.

Three-state Gate

As mentioned earlier, the outputs of two TTL gates with totem-pole structures cannot be connected together as in open-collector outputs. There is, however, a special type of totem-pole gate that allows the wired connection of outputs for the purpose of forming a common-bus system. When a totem-pole output TTL gate has this property, it is called a *three-state* (or tri-state) gate.

A three-state gate exhibits three output states: (1) a low-level state when the lower transistor in the totem-pole is on and the upper transistor is off; (2) a high-level state when the upper transistor in the totem-pole is on and the lower transistor is off: and (3) a third state when both transistors in the totem-pole are off. The third state provides an open circuit or high-impedance state which allows a direct wire connection of many outputs to a common line. Three-state gates eliminate the need for open-collector gates in bus configurations.

Figure 13-16(a) shows the graphic symbol of a three-state buffer gate. When the control input C is high, the gate is enabled and behaves like a normal buffer with the output equal to the input binary value. When the control input is low, the output is an open circuit which gives a high impedance (the third state) regardless of the value of input A. Some three-state gates produce a high-impedance state when the control input is high. This is shown symbolically in Fig. 13-16(b). Here we have two small circles, one for the inverter output and the other to indicate that the gate is enabled when C is low.

The circuit diagram of the three-state inverter is shown in Fig. 13-16(c). Transistors $Q6$, $Q7$, and $Q8$ associated with the control input form a circuit similar to the open-collector gate. Transistors $Q1-Q5$, associated with the data input, form a totem-pole TTL circuit. The two circuits are connected together through diode $D1$. As in an open-collector circuit, transistor $Q8$ turns off when the control input at C is in the low-level state. This prevents diode $D1$ from conducting, and also, the emitter in $Q1$ connected to $Q8$ has no conduction path. Under this condition, transistor $Q8$ has no effect on the operation of the gate and the output in Y depends only on the data input at A.

When the control input is high, transistor $Q8$ turns on, and the current flowing from V_{CC} through diode $D1$ causes transistor $Q8$ to saturate. The voltage at the base of $Q5$ is now equal to the voltage across the saturated transistor, $Q8$, plus one diode drop, or 0.9 V. This voltage turns off $Q5$ and $Q4$ since it is less than two V_{BE} drops. At the same time, the low input to one of the emitters of $Q1$ forces transistor $Q3$ (and $Q2$) to turn off. Thus both $Q3$ and $Q4$ in the totem-pole are turned off and the output of the circuit behaves like an open circuit with a very high output impedance.

A three-state bus is created by wiring several three-state outputs together. At any given time, only one control input is enabled while all other outputs are in the high-impedance state. The single gate not in a high-impedance state can transmit binary information through the common bus. Extreme care must be taken that all except one of the outputs are in the third state; otherwise, we have the undesirable

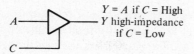

$Y = A$ if C = High
Y high-impedance
if C = Low

(a) Three-state buffer gate

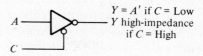

$Y = A'$ if C = Low
Y high-impedance
if C = High

(b) Three-state inverter gate

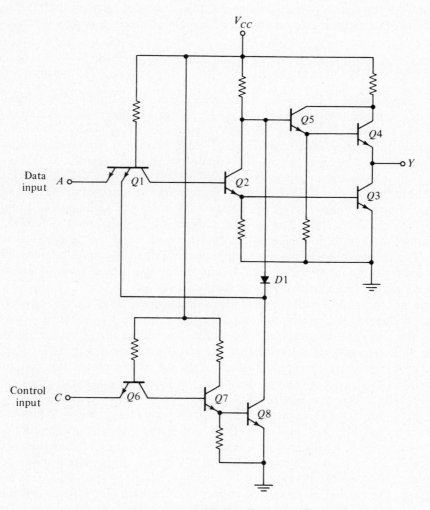

(c) Circuit diagram for the three-state inverter of (b)

Figure 13-16 Three-state TTL gate

condition of having two active totem-pole outputs connected together.

An important feature of most three-state gates is that the output enable delay is longer than the output disable delay. If a control circuit enables one gate and disables another at the same time, the disabled gate enters the high-impedance state before the other gate is enabled. This eliminates the situation of both gates being active at the same time.

There is a very small leakage current associated with the high-impedance condition in a three-state gate. Nevertheless, this current is so small that as many as 100 three-state outputs can be connected together to form a common bus line.

13-6   EMITTER-COUPLED LOGIC (ECL)

Emitter-coupled logic (ECL) is a nonsaturated digital logic family. Since transistors do not saturate, it is possible to achieve propagation delays of 2 ns and even below 1 ns. This logic family has the lowest propagation delay of any family and is used mostly in systems requiring very-high-speed operation. Its noise immunity and power dissipation, however, are the worst of all the logic families available.

A typical basic circuit of the ECL family is shown in Fig. 13-17. The outputs provide both the OR and NOR functions. Each input is connected to the base of a transistor. The two voltage levels are about -0.8 V for the high state and about -1.8 V for the low state. The circuit consists of a differential amplifier, a temperature- and voltage-compensated bias network, and an emitter-follower output. The emitter outputs require a pull-down resistor for current to flow. This is obtained from the input resistor, R_P, of another similar gate or from an external resistor connected to a negative voltage supply.

The internal temperature- and voltage-compensated bias circuit supplies a reference voltage to the differential amplifier. Bias voltage V_{BB} is set at -1.3 V, which is the midpoint of the signal logic swing. The diodes in the voltage divider, together with $Q6$, provide a circuit that maintains a constant V_{BB} value despite changes in temperature or supply voltage. Any one of the power supply inputs could be used as ground. However, the use of the V_{CC} node as ground and V_{EE} at -5.2 V results in best noise immunity.

If any input in the ECL gate is high, the corresponding transistor is turned on and $Q5$ is turned off. An input of -0.8 V causes the transistor to conduct and places -1.6 V on the emitters of all transistors (V_{BE} drop in ECL transistors is 0.8 V). Since $V_{BB} = -1.3$ V, the base voltage of $Q5$ is only 0.3 V more positive than its emitter. $Q5$ is cutoff because its V_{BE} voltage needs at least 0.6 V to start conducting. The current in resistor R_{C2} flows into the base of $Q8$ (provided there is a load resistor). This current is so small that only a negligible voltage drop occurs across R_{C2}. The OR output of the gate is one V_{BE} drop below ground, or -0.8 V, which is the high state. The current flowing through R_{C1} and the conducting transistor causes a drop of about 1 V below ground (see Problem 13-9). The NOR output is one V_{BE} drop below this level, or at -1.8 V, which is the low state.

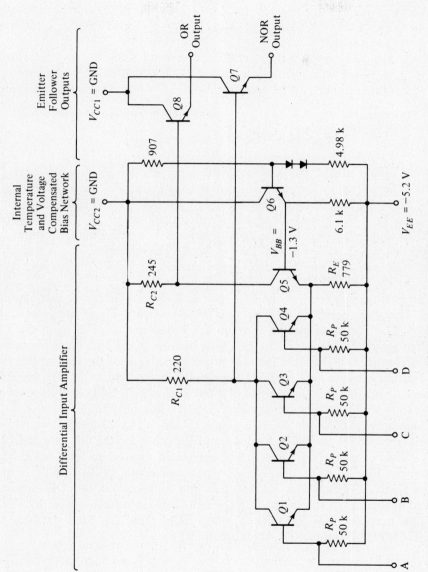

Figure 13-17 ECL basic gate

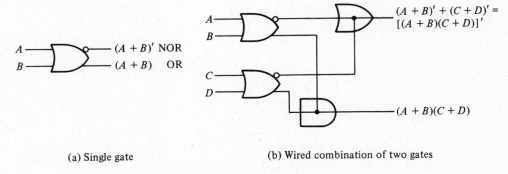

(a) Single gate

(b) Wired combination of two gates

Figure 13-18 Graphic symbols of ECL gates

If all inputs are at the low level, all input transistors turn off and $Q5$ conducts. The voltage in the common-emitter node is one V_{BE} drop below V_{BB} or -2.1 V. Since the base of each input is at a low level of -1.8 V, each base-emitter junction has only 0.3 V and all input transistors are cutoff. R_{C2} draws current through $Q5$ that results in a voltage drop of about 1 V, making the OR output one V_{BE} drop below this, at -1.8 V or the low level. The current in R_{C1} is negligible and the NOR output is one V_{BE} drop below ground, at -0.8 V or the high level. This verifies the OR and NOR operations of the circuit.

The propagation delay of the ECL gate is 2 ns, and the power dissipation is 25 mW. This gives a speed-power product of 50, which is about the same as for Schottky TTL. The noise margin is about 0.3 V and not as good as in the TTL gate. High fan-out is possible in the ECL gate because of the high input impedance of the differential amplifier and the low output impedance of the emitter-follower. Because of the extreme high speed of the signals, external wires act like transmission lines. Except for very short wires of a few centimeters, ECL outputs must use coaxial cables with a resistor termination to reduce line reflections.

The graphic symbol for the ECL gate is shown in Fig. 13-18(a). Two outputs are available: one for the NOR function and the other for the OR function. The outputs of two or more ECL gates can be connected together to form wired logic. As shown in Fig. 13-18(b), an *external* wired connection of two NOR outputs produces a wired-OR function. An *internal* wired connection of two OR outputs is employed in some ECL ICs to produce a wired-AND (sometimes called dot-AND) logic. This property may be utilized when ECL gates are used to form the OR-AND-INVERT and the OR-AND functions.

13-7 METAL-OXIDE SEMICONDUCTOR (MOS)

The field-effect transistor (FET) is a unipolar transistor, since its operation depends on the flow of only one type of carrier. There are two types of field-effect transistors: the junction field-effect transistor (JFET) and the metal-oxide semi-

580

conductor (MOS). The former is used in linear circuits and the latter in digital circuits. MOS transistors can be fabricated in less area than bipolar transistors.

The basic structure of the MOS transistor is shown in Fig. 13-19. The p-channel MOS consists of a lightly doped substrate of n-type silicon material. Two regions are heavily doped by diffusion with p-type impurities to form the *source* and *drain*. The region between the two p-type sections serves as the *channel*. The *gate* is a metal plate separated from the channel by an insulated dielectric of silicon dioxide. A negative voltage (with respect to the substrate) at the gate terminal causes an induced electric field in the channel which attracts p-type carriers from the substrate. As the magnitude of the negative voltage on the gate increases, the region below the gate accumulates more positive carriers, the conductivity increases, and current can flow from source to drain provided a voltage difference is maintained between these two terminals.

There are four basic types of MOS structures. The channel can be a p- or n-type, depending on whether the majority carriers are holes or electrons. The mode of operation can be enhancement or depletion, depending on the state of the channel region at zero gate voltage. If the channel is initially doped lightly with p-type impurity (diffused channel), a conducting channel exists at zero gate voltage and the device is said to operate in the *depletion* mode. In this mode, current flows unless the channel is depleted by an applied gate field. If the region beneath the gate is left initially uncharged, a channel must be induced by the gate field before current can flow. Thus, the channel current is enhanced by the gate voltage and such a device is said to operate in the *enhancement* mode.

The source is the terminal through which the majority carriers enter the bar. The drain is the terminal through which the majority carriers leave the bar. In a p-channel MOS, the source terminal is connected to the substrate and a negative voltage is applied to the drain terminal. When the gate voltage is above a threshold voltage V_T (about -2 V), no current flows in the channel and the drain-to-source path is like an open circuit. When the gate voltage is sufficiently negative below V_T, a channel is formed and p-type carriers flow from source to drain. P-type carriers are positive and correspond to a positive current flow from source to drain.

In the n-channel MOS, the source terminal is connected to the substrate and a positive voltage is applied to the drain terminal. When the gate voltage is below

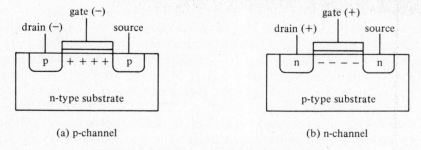

(a) p-channel   (b) n-channel

Figure 13-19 Basic structure of MOS transistor

the threshold voltage V_T (about 2 V) no current flows in the channel. When the gate voltage is sufficiently positive above V_T to form the channel, n-type carriers flow from source to drain. N-type carriers are negative, which corresponds to a positive current flow from drain to source. The threshold voltage may vary from 1 to 4 V depending on the particular process used.

The graphic symbols for the MOS transistors are shown in Fig. 13-20. The accepted symbol for the enhancement type is the one with the broken-line connection between source and drain. In this symbol, the substrate can be identified and is shown connected to the source. We will use an alternative symbol that omits the substrate; in this symbol, the arrow is placed in the source terminal to show the direction of *positive* current flow (from source to drain in the p-channel and from drain to source in the n-channel).

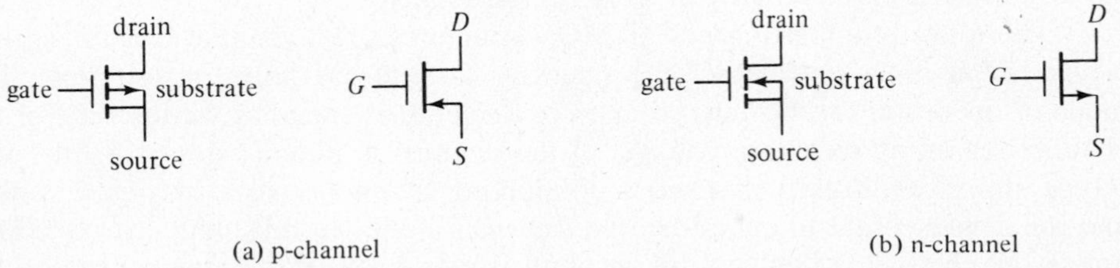

(a) p-channel   (b) n-channel

Figure 13-20   Symbols for MOS transistors

Because of the symmetrical construction of source and drain, the MOS transistor can be operated as a bilateral device. Although normally operated so that carriers flow from source to drain, there are circumstances when it is convenient to allow carrier flow from drain to source (see Problem 13-12).

One advantage of the MOS device is that it can be used not only as a transistor, but as a resistor as well. A resistor is obtained from the MOS by permanently biasing the gate terminal for conduction. The ratio of the source-drain voltage to the channel current then determines the value of the resistance. Different resistor values may be constructed during manufacturing by fixing the channel length and width of the MOS device.

Three logic circuits using MOS devices are shown in figure 13-21. For an n-channel MOS, supply voltage V_{DD} is positive (about 5 V) to allow positive current flow from drain to source. The two voltage levels are a function of the threshold voltage V_T. The low level is anywhere from zero to V_T, and the high level ranges from V_T to V_{DD}. The n-channel gates usually employ positive logic. The p-channel MOS circuits use a negative voltage for V_{DD} to allow positive current flow from source to drain. The two voltage levels are both negative above and below the negative threshold voltage V_T. P-channel gates usually employ negative logic.

The inverter circuit shown in Fig. 13-21(a) uses two MOS devices. $Q1$ acts as the load resistor and $Q2$ as the active device. The load resistor MOS has its gate connected to V_{DD}, thus maintaining it always in the conduction state. When the

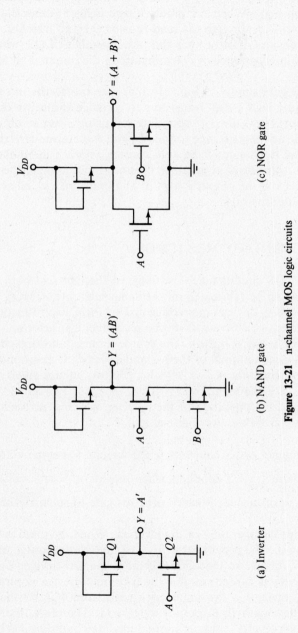

(a) Inverter

(b) NAND gate

(c) NOR gate

Figure 13-21 n-channel MOS logic circuits

input voltage is low (below V_T), $Q2$ turns off. Since $Q1$ is always on, the output voltage is at about V_{DD}. When the input voltage is high (above V_T), $Q2$ turns on. Current flows from V_{DD} through the load resistor $Q1$ and into $Q2$. The geometry of the two MOS devices must be such that the resistance of $Q2$, when conducting, is much less than the resistance of $Q1$ to maintain the output Y at a voltage below V_T.

The NAND gate shown in Fig. 13-21(b) uses transistors in series. Inputs A and B must both be high for all transistors to conduct and cause the output to go low. If either input is low, the corresponding transistor is turned off and the output is high. Again, the series resistance formed by the two active MOS devices must be much less than the resistance of the load resistor MOS. The NOR gate shown in Fig. 13-21(c) uses transistors in parallel. If either input is high, the corresponding transistor conducts and the output is low. If all inputs are low, all active transistors are off and the output is high.

13-8 COMPLEMENTARY MOS (CMOS)

Complementary MOS circuits take advantage of the fact that both n-channel and p-channel devices can be fabricated on the same substrate. CMOS circuits consist of both types of MOS devices interconnected to form logic functions. The basic circuit is the inverter, which consists of one p-channel transistor and one n-channel transistor as shown in Fig. 13-22(a). The source terminal of the p-channel device is at V_{DD}, and the source terminal of the n-channel device is at ground. The value of V_{DD} may be anywhere from $+3$ to $+18$ V. The two voltage levels are 0 V for the low level and V_{DD} for the high level.

To understand the operation of the inverter, we must review the behavior of the MOS transistor from the previous section:

1. The n-channel MOS conducts when its gate-to-source voltage is positive.

2. The p-channel MOS conducts when its gate-to-source voltage is negative.

3. Either type of device is turned off if its gate-to-source voltage is zero.

Now consider the operation of the inverter. When the input is low, both gates are at zero potential. The input is at $-V_{DD}$ relative to the source of the p-channel device and at 0 V relative to the source of the n-channel device. The result is that the p-channel device is turned on and the n-channel device is turned off. Under these conditions, there is a low-impedance path from V_{DD} to the output and a very-high-impedance path from output to ground. Therefore, the output voltage approaches the high level V_{DD} under normal loading conditions. When the input is high, both gates are at V_{DD} and the situation is reversed: The p-channel device is off and the n-channel device is on. The result is that the output approaches the low level of 0 V.

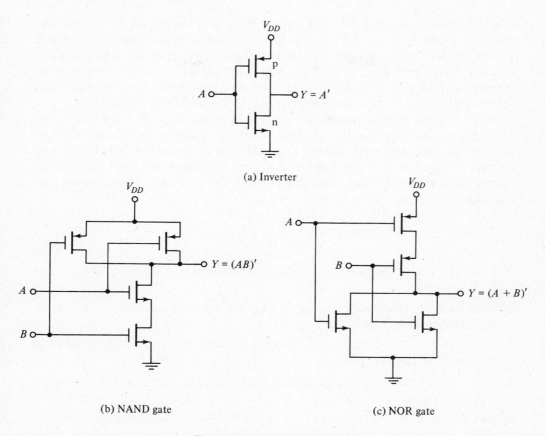

(a) Inverter

(b) NAND gate

(c) NOR gate

Figure 13-22 CMOS logic circuits

In either logic state, one MOS transistor is on while the other is off. Because one transistor is always turned off, the dc power dissipation of the CMOS circuit is extremely low, usually on the order of 10 nW. The major power drain occurs when the CMOS circuit changes state.

CMOS logic is usually specified for single-supply operation over the 5–15-V range, but some circuits may be operated at 3 V or 18 V. Operating CMOS at large values of supply voltage produces a greater power dissipation. The propagation delay time decreases and the noise margin improves with increased power supply voltage. The propagation delay of the inverter is about 25 ns. The noise margin is usually about 40% of the V_{DD} supply voltage value. The advantages of CMOS, i.e., low power dissipation, excellent noise immunity, high packing density, and a wide range of supply voltages, make it a strong contender for a popular standard as a digital circuit family.

Two other CMOS basic gates are shown in Fig. 13-22. A two-input NAND gate consists of two p-type units in parallel and two n-type units in series, as shown in Fig. 13-22(b). If all inputs are high, both p-channel transistors turn off and both n-channel transistors turn on. The output has a low impedance to ground and produces a low state. If any input is low, the associated n-channel transistor is turned off and the associated p-channel transistor is turned on. The output is coupled to V_{DD} and goes to the high state. Multiple-input NAND gates may be formed by placing equal numbers of p-type and n-type transistors in parallel and series, respectively, in an arrangement similar to that shown in Fig. 13-22(b).

A two-input NOR gate consists of two n-type units in parallel and two p-type units in series, as shown in Fig. 13-22(c). When all inputs are low, both p-channel units are on and both n-channel units are off. The output is coupled to V_{DD} and goes to the high state. If any input is high, the associated p-channel transistor is turned off and the associated n-channel transistor turns on. This connects the output to ground, causing a low-level output.

REFERENCES

1. Taub, H., and D. Schilling, *Digital Integrated Electronics*. New York: McGraw-Hill Book Co., 1977.

2. Grinich, V. H., and H. G. Jackson, *Introduction to Integrated Circuits*. New York: McGraw-Hill BookCo., 1975.

3. Morris, R. L., and J. R. Miller, Eds., *Designing with TTL Integrated Circuits*. New York: McGraw-Hill Book Co., 1971.

4. Garret, L. S., "Integrated-Circuit Digital Logic Families." *IEEE Spectrum* (October, November, December, 1970).

5. De Falco, J. A., "Comparison and Uses of TTL Circuits." *Computer Design* (February, 1972).

6. Blood, W. R. Jr., *MECL System Design Handbook*. Phoenix, Ariz.: Motorola Semiconductor Products Inc., 1972.

7. *Data Book Series SSD-203B: COS/MOS Digital Integrated Circuits*, Somerville, N.J.: RCA Solid State Division, 1974.

PROBLEMS

13-1.   (a) Determine the high-level output voltage of the RTL gate for a fan-out of 5. (b) Determine the minimum input voltage required to drive an RTL transistor to saturation when $h_{FE} = 20$. (c) From the results in (a) and (b), determine the noise margin of the RTL gate when the input is high and the fan-out is 5.

13-2.   Show that the output transistor of the DTL gate of Fig. 13-5 goes into saturation when all inputs are high. Assume that $h_{FE} = 20$.

13-3.   Connect the output Y of the DTL gate shown in Fig. 13-5 to N inputs of other similar gates. Assume that the output transistor is saturated and its base current is 0.44 mA. Let $h_{FE} = 20$.

(a) Calculate the current in the 2-kΩ resistor.

(b) Calculate the current coming from each input connected to the gate.

(c) Calculate the total collector current in the output transistor as a function of N.

(d) Find the value of N that will keep the transistor in saturation.

(e) What is the fan-out of the gate?

13-4.   Draw the interconnection of I^2L gates to form a 2×4 decoder.

13-5.   Let all inputs in the open-collector TTL gate of Fig. 13-11 be in the high state of 3 V.

(a) Determine the voltages in the base, collector, and emitter of all transistors.

(b) Determine the minimum h_{FE} of $Q2$ that ensures that this transistor saturates.

(c) Calculate the base current of $Q3$.

(d) Assume that the minimum h_{FE} of $Q3$ is 6.18. What is the maximum current that can be tolerated in the collector to ensure saturation of $Q3$?

(e) What is the minimum value of R_L that can be tolerated to ensure saturation of $Q3$?

13-6.   (a) Using the actual output transistors of two open-collector TTL gates, show (by means of a truth table) that when connected together to an external resistor and V_{CC}, the wired connection produces an AND function. (b) Prove that two open-collector TTL inverters when connected together produce the NOR function.

13-7.   It was stated in Section 13-5 that totem-pole outputs should not be tied together to form wired logic. To see why this is prohibitive, connect two such circuits together and let the output of one gate be in the high state and the output of the other gate be in the low state. Show that the load current (which is the sum of the base and collector currents of the saturated transistor $Q4$ in Fig. 13-14) is about 32 mA. Compare this value with the recommended load current in the high state of 0.4 mA.

13-8.   For the following conditions, list the transistors that are off and those that are conducting in the three-state TTL gate of Fig. 13-16(c). (For $Q1$ and $Q6$, it would be necessary to list the states in the base-emitter and base-collector junctions separately.)

(a) When C is low and A is low.

(b) When C is low and A is high.

(c) When C is high.

What is the state of the output in each case?

13-9.   Calculate the emitter current I_E across R_E in the ECL gate of Fig. 13-17 when:

(a) At least one input is high at -0.8 V.

(b) All inputs are low at -1.8 V.

Now assume that $I_C = I_E$. Calculate the voltage drop across the collector resistor in each case and show that it is about 1 V as required.

13-10.   Calculate the noise margin of the ECL gate.

13-11.   Using the NOR outputs of two ECL gates, show that when connected together to an external resistor and negative supply voltage, the wired connection produces an OR function.

13-12. The MOS transistor is bilateral, i. e., current may flow from source to drain or from drain to source. Using this property, derive a circuit that implements the Boolean function:

$$Y = (AB + CD + AED + CEB)'$$

using six MOS transistors.

13-13. (a) Show the circuit of a four-input NAND gate using CMOS transistors. (b) Repeat for a four-input NOR gate.

Appendix

ANSWERS TO SELECTED PROBLEMS

Chapter 1

1-1.   0, 1, 2, 10, 11, 12, 20, 21, 22, 100, 101, 102, 110, 111, 112, 120, 121, 122, 200, 201.

1-2.   (a) 1313, 102210
     (b) 223, 11314.52
     (c) 1304, 336313
     (d) 331, 13706

1-3. $(100021.1111 \ldots)_3$; $(3322.2)_4$; $(505.333 \ldots)_7$; $(372.4)_8$; $(FA.8)_{16}$.

1-4.   1100.0001; 10011100010000; 1010100001.00111; 11111001110.

1-5.   2.53125; 46.3125; 117.75; 109.875.

1-6.

decimal	binary	octal	hexadecimal
225.225	11100001.001110011	341.16314	E1.399
215.75	11010111.110	327.6	D7.C
403.9843	110010011.111111	623.77	193.FC
10949.8125	10101011000101.1101	25305.64	2AC5.D

1-7.   (a) 73.375
     (b) 151
     (c) 78.5
     (d) 580
     (e) 0.62037
     (f) 35
     (g) 8.333
     (h) 260

1-8. 1's complement: 0101010; 1000111; 1111110; 01111; 11111.
2's complement: 0101011; 1001000; 1111111; 10000; 00000.

1-9.   9's complement: 86420; 90099; 09909; 89999; 99999.
10's complement: 86421; 90100; 09910; 90000; 00000.

1-10. $(175)_{11}$.

1-14. (a) Six possible tables.
(b) Four possible tables.

1-15. (a) 1000 0110 0010 0000
(b) 1011 1001 0101 0011
(c) 1110 1100 0010 0000
(d) 1000011 0101100

1-17. 0000, 0001, 0010, 0011, 0100, 0101, 0110, 0111, 1011, 1100, 1101, 1110.

1-18. 00001, 01110, 01101, 01011, 01000, 10110, 10101, 10011, 10000, 11111.

1-20   000, 001, 010, 101, 110, 111, representing 0, 1, 2, 3, 4, 5, respectively.

1-21. Two bits for suit, four bits for number, J = 1011, Q = 1100, K = 1101.

1-23. (a) 0000 0000 0000 0001 0010 0111
(b) 0000 0000 0000 0010 1001 0101
(c) 1110 0111 1110 1000 1111 0101

1-24. (a) 597 in BCD
(b) 264 in excess-3
(c) Not valid for 2421 code of Table 1-2
(d) FG in alphanumeric

1-25. 00100000001 + 10000011010 = 10100011011.

1-26. L = (A + B) · C.

Chapter 2

2-1. Closure, associative, commutative, distributive; identity for + is 2; identity for · is 0; no inverses.

2-2. All postulates are satisfied except for postulate 5; there is no complement.

2-5. (a) x
(b) x
(c) y
(d) $z(x + y)$
(e) 0
(f) $y(x + w)$

2-6.   (a) $A'B' + B(A + C)$

    (b) $BC + AC'$

    (c) $A + CD$

    (d) $A + B'CD$

2-7.   (a) 1

    (b) $B'D' + A(D' + BC')$

    (c) 1

    (d) $(A' + B)(C + D)$

2-11.   (b) $F = (x' + y')' + (x + y)' + (y + z')'$ has only **OR** and **NOT** operators.

    (c) $F = [(xy)' \cdot (x'y')' \cdot (y'z)']'$ has only **AND** and **NOT** operators.

2-12.   (a) $T_1 = A'(B' + C')$

    (b) $T_2 = A + BC = T_1'$

2-13.   (a) $\Sigma(1, 3, 5, 7, 9, 11, 13, 15) = \Pi(0, 2, 4, 6, 8, 10, 12, 14)$

    (b) $\Sigma(1, 3, 5, 9, 12, 13, 14) = \Pi(0, 2, 4, 6, 7, 8, 10, 11, 15)$

    (c) $\Sigma(0, 1, 2, 8, 10, 12, 13, 14, 15) = \Pi(3, 4, 5, 6, 7, 9, 11)$

    (d) $\Sigma(0, 1, 3, 7) = \Pi(2, 4, 5, 6)$

    (e) $\Sigma(0, 1, 2, 3, 4, 5, 6, 7)$, no maxterms

    (f) $\Sigma(3, 5, 6, 7) = \Pi(0, 1, 2, 4)$

2-14.   (a) $\Pi(0, 2, 4, 5, 6)$

    (b) $\Pi(1, 3, 4, 5, 7, 8, 9, 10, 12, 15)$

    (c) $\Sigma(1, 2, 4, 5)$

    (d) $\Sigma(5, 7, 8, 9, 10, 11, 13, 14, 15)$

2-18. $F = x \oplus y = x'y + xy'$; (dual of F) $= (x' + y)(x + y') = xy + x'y' = F'$.

2-20. $F = xy + xz + yz$.

Chapter 3

3-1.   (a) y

    (b) $ABD + ABC + BCD$

    (c) $BCD + A'BD'$

    (d) $wx + w'x'y$

3-2.   (a) $xy + x'z'$

    (b) $C' + A'B$

    (c) $a' + bc$

    (d) $xy + xz + yz$

3-3.   (a) $D + B'C$

    (b) $BD + B'D' + A'B$ or $BD + B'D' + A'D'$

(c) $ln' + k'm'n$

(d) $B'D' + A'BD + ABC'$

(e) $xy' + x'z + wx'y$

3-4. (a) $A'B'D' + B'C'D' + AD'E$

(b) $DE + A'B'C + B'C'E'$

(c) $BDE' + B'CD' + B'D'E' + A'B'D' + CDE'$

3-5. (a) $F_1 = \Pi(0, 3, 5, 6); F_2 = \Pi(0, 1, 2, 4)$

(b) $F_1 = x'y'z + x'yz' + xy'z' + xyz; F_2 = xy + xz + yz$

(c) $F_1 = (x + y + z)(x + y' + z')(x' + y + z')(x' + y' + z);$
$F_2 = (x + y)(x + z)(y + z)$

3-6. (a) y

(b) $(B + C')(A + B)(A + C + D)$

(c) $(w + z')(x' + z')$

3-7. (a) $z' + xy = (x + z')(y + z')$

(b) $C'D + A'B'CD' + ABCD' = (A + B' + D)(A' + B + D)(C + D)$
$\qquad\qquad (C' + D')$

(c) $A'C' + AD' + B'D' = (A' + D')(C' + D')(A + B' + C')$

(d) $B'D' + A'CD' + A'BD = (A' + B')(B + D')(B' + C + D)$

(e) $w'z' + vw'x + v'wz = (v' + w')(w' + z)(w + x + z')(v + w + z')$

3-8. (a)

3-9. (a) $F_1 = A + D'E' + CD' = (A'D + A'C'E)'$

(b) $F_2 = A'B' + C'D' + B'C' = (BD + BC + AC)'$

3-11. (a) $F = BD + D'(AB'C' + A'B'C)$

3-12. (a) $(A' + B' + C')(A + B' + C + D')(A + B + C' + D')$

(b) $(C + D)(C' + D')(A + B)(A' + B')$

3-13. AND-AND → AND, AND-NAND → NAND, NOR-NAND → OR,
NOR-AND → NOR, OR-OR → OR, OR-NOR → NOR, NAND-NOR
→ AND, NAND-OR → NAND.

3-15. (a) $F = 1$

(b) $F = CD' + B'D' + ABC'D$

3-16. (a) $F = A'C + B'D'; A'(C + D')(B' + C)$

(b) $x'z' + w'z; (w' + z')(x' + z)$

(c) $AC + CE' + A'C'D; (A' + C)(C + D)(A + C' + D')$
or $AC + CD' + A'C'E; (A' + C)(C + E)(A + C' + E')$

(d) $A'B + B'E'; (A' + B')(B + E')$

3-17.   (a) $B'(A + C' + D')$

   (b) $A'D + ABC'$

   (c) $B'D + B'C + CD$

3-18. $F = x'y + xz$ (needs four NAND); $F = (x' + z)(x + y)$(needs four NOR).

3-19. $d = ABC'DE + AB'CDE' + ABCD'E$.

3-20. $B'D'(A' + C) + BD(A' + C')$; $[B' + D(A' + C')] [B + D'(A' + C)]$;
   $[D' + B(A' + C')] [D + B'(A' + C)]$.

3-21. $f \cdot g = x'yz' + w'y'z + wxy'z'$.

3-24.   (a) $F = A'CEF'G'$

   (b) $F = ABCDEFG + A'CEF'G' + BC'D'EF$

   (c) $F = A'B'C'DEF' + A'BC'D'E + CE'F + A'BD'EF$

Chapter 4

4-1.   **Inputs:** a, b, c, d.

   Outputs: $F = abc + abd + bcd + acd + a'b'c' + a'c'd' + a'b'd'$
   $+ b'c'd'$; $F = \Pi(3, 5, 6, 9, 10, 12)$(cannot be simplified further).

4-2.   **Inputs:** A_3, A_2, A_1.

   Outputs: B_6 to B_1; $B_1 = A_1$; $B_2 = 0$; $B_3 = A_1'A_2$; $B_4 = A_1(A_2A_3'$
   $+ A_2'A_3)$; $B_5 = A_3(A_1 + A_2')$; $B_6 = A_2A_3$.

4-3.   **Outputs:** w, x, y, z; $w = a_0a_1b_0b_1$; $x = a_1a_0'b_1 + a_1b_1b_0'$
   $y = a_1b_0b_1' + a_0a_1'b_1 + a_0b_0'b_1 + a_0'a_1b_0$; $z = a_0b_0$.

4-4.   **Outputs:** x, y, z; $x = a_1b_1 + a_1a_0b_0 + b_1b_0a_0$;
   $y = a_1'a_0'b_1 + a_1'b_1b_0' + a_1'a_0b_1'b_0 + a_1b_1'b_0' + a_1a_0'b_1' + a_1a_0b_1b_0$.
   $z = a_0b_0' + a_0'b_0$.

4-5.   **Inputs:** A, B, C, D.

   Outputs: w, x, y, z; $w = A'B'C'$; $x = BC' + B'C$; $y = C$; $z = D'$.

4-6.   **Inputs:** A, B, C, D.

   Outputs: $F_4F_3F_2F_1$; $F_1 = D$; $F_2 = CD' + C'D$; $F_3 = (C + D)$
   $B' + BC'D'$; $F_4 = (B + C + D)A' + AB'C'D'$.

4-7.   **Inputs:** $F_8F_4F_2F_1$.

   Outputs: $\underline{S_8S_4S_2S_1} \quad \underline{L_8L_4L_2L_1}$;
   $\qquad\qquad 10^1 \qquad\qquad 10^0$
   $L_2 = L_8 = S_8 = 0$; $L_1 = L_4 = F_1$; $S_1 = F_2$; $S_2 = F_4$;
   $S_4 = F_8$.

4-8.   **Inputs:** A, B, C, D.

   Output: $F = AB + AC$.

4-11.   Inputs: $A, B, C, D.$

Outputs: $w, x, y, z; w = AB + AC'D'; x = B'C + B'D + BC'D';$
$y = CD' + C'D; z = D.$

4-12.   Inputs: $A, B, C, D.$

Outputs: $w, x, y, z; w = A; x = A'C + BCD + A'B + A'D$
$y = AC'D' + A'C'D + ACD + A'CD'$ or $y = AC'D'$
$+ B'C'D + ACD + B'CD'; z = D.$

4-13.   Inputs: $w, x, y, z.$

Outputs: $E \;\underline{ABCD}\; ; E = wx + wy; A = wx'y';$
$10^1 \quad 10^0$
$B = w'x + xy; C = w'y + wxy'; D = z.$

4-14.   Inputs: A, B, C, D (Blank display for invalid input bit combinations)

Outputs: $a = A'C + A'BD + B'C'D' + AB'C'$
$b = A'B' + A'C'D' + A'CD + AB'C'$
$c = A'B + A'D + B'C'D' + AB'C'$
$d = A'CD' + A'B'C + B'C'D' + AB'C' + A'BC'D$
$e = A'CD' + B'C'D'$
$f = A'BC' + A'C'D' + A'BD' + AB'C'$
$g = A'CD' + A'B'C + A'BC' + AB'C'$

(Total of 21 NAND gates)

4-15.   Full-adder circuit.

4-16.   Full-adder circuit.

4-19.

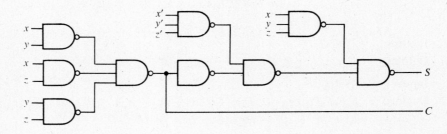

4-20. $F = ABC' + A'B + B' = A' + B' + C'$ (two NOR gates).

4-21.   (a) Full-adder, F_1 is the sum, F_2 is the carry

(b) $F = A'B'C' + A'BC + AB'C + ABC'$

4-28.   Input variables: A, B, C, D; output variables: $w, x, y, z.$
$w = A, x = A \oplus B, y = x \oplus C, z = y \oplus D.$

4-29. $C = x \oplus y \oplus z \oplus P$ (three exclusive-OR gates).

4-30.

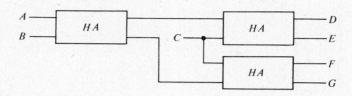

4-31. $F = (A \oplus B)(C \oplus D)$.

Chapter 5

5-1. Same as Fig. 5-2 except that $B = 1101$.

5-3. The exclusive-OR gate is used to form the 1's complement of B when $V = 1$.
The 2's complement is obtained by adding $1 = V$ to the input carry.

5-4. $C_5 = G_4 + P_4G_3 + P_4P_3G_2 + P_4P_3P_2G_1 + P_4P_3P_2P_1C_1.$

5-5. (b) $C_4 = (G_3'P_3' + G_3'G_2'P_2' + G_3'G_2'G_1'P_1' + G_3'G_2'G_1'C_1')'$

5-6. (c) $C_4 = (P_3' + G_3'P_2' + G_3'G_2'P_1' + G_3'G_2'G_1'C_1')'$

5-7. (a) 60 ns
(b) 120 ns

5-9. 312.

5-10. Inputs: x_8, x_4, x_2, x_1; outputs: y_8, y_4, y_2, y_1.
$y_1 = x_1', y_2 = x_2, y_4 = x_2 \oplus x_4, y_8 = (x_2 + x_4 + x_8)'$.

5-15. All ten AND gates require four inputs equivalent to the minterms m_0 through m_9.

5-17. $F_1(x, y, z) = \Sigma(0, 1, 6)$.
$F_2'(x, y, z) = \Sigma(4, 5)$ (use NOR gate).
$F_3(x, y, z) = \Sigma(0, 1, 6, 7) = F_1 + m_7$.

5-22. Inputs: $D_0D_1D_2D_3$; outputs: x, y, E. Priority given to input with highest subscript number.

$x = D_2 + D_3, \quad y = D_3 + D_1D_2', \quad E = D_0 + D_1 + D_2 + D_3.$

5-23. $F(C, A, B, D) = \Sigma(0, 1, 2, 4, 5, 9, 15), I_0$ through $I_7 = C', 1, C', 0, C', C', 0, C$.

5-29. (a) 1024×5
(b) 256×8
(c) 1024×2

Chapter 6

6-4.

Q	J	K'	$Q(t + 1) = JQ' + K'Q$
0	0	0	0
0	0	1	0
0	1	0	1
0	1	1	1
1	0	0	0
1	0	1	1
1	1	0	0
1	1	1	1

6-5.

Q	SD	R	$Q(t + 1) = S + R'Q$
0	0	0	0
0	0	1	0
0	1	0	1
0	1	1	1
1	0	0	1
1	0	1	0
1	1	0	1
1	1	1	1

6-7. Output of gate:

	1	2	3	4	5	6	7	8	9	
(a)	1	1	0	1	1	0	0	1	1	
(b)	0	1	1	0	1	1	0	1	0	
(c)	1	1	1	0	0	1	1	0	1	
(d)	1	0	0	1	1	1	1	0	0	
(e)	1	1	0	1	1	0	0	1	1	
(f)	1	1	0	1	1	1	0	1	0	$CP = 1$
	1	1	0	1	1	0	0	1	1	$CP = 0$

6-10.

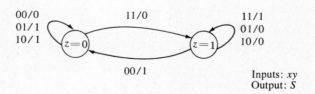

Inputs: xy
Output: S

6-11. A counter with a repeated sequence: 00, 01, 10.

6-12. $x = 1$; binary sequence is: 1, 8, 4, 2, 9, 12, 6, 11, 5, 10, 13, 14, 15, 7, 3.
$x = 0$; binary sequence is: 0, 8, 12, 14, 7, 11, 13, 6, 3, 9, 4, 10, 5, 2, 1.

6-13.

P.S.		Next state								Output z			
		$xy = 00$		$xy = 01$		$xy = 10$		$xy = 11$		$xy = 00$	$xy = 01$	$xy = 10$	$xy = 11$
A	B	A	B	A	B	A	B	A	B				
0	0	1	0	0	0	1	1	0	1	0	0	0	0
0	1	0	1	0	1	1	0	1	1	1	0	0	0
1	0	1	0	1	0	0	0	1	0	0	0	0	1
1	1	1	0	1	0	1	0	1	0	1	0	0	1

$$A(t + 1) = xB + y'B'A' + yA + x'A; \quad B(t + 1) = xA'B' + x'A'B + yA'B$$

6-14.

Present State	Next State 0 1	Output 0 1
a	f b	0 0
b	d a	0 0
d	g a	1 0
f	f b	1 1
g	g d	0 1

6-15. State: a f b c e d g h g g h a
        Input: 0 1 1 1 0 0 1 0 0 1 1
        Output: 0 1 0 0 0 1 1 1 0 1 0

6-16. State: a f b a b d g d g g d a
        Input: 0 1 1 1 0 0 1 0 0 1 1
        Output: 0 1 0 0 0 1 1 1 0 1 0

6-18.

J	K'	$Q(t + 1)$
0	0	0
0	1	$Q(t)$
1	0	$Q'(t)$
1	1	1

$Q(t)$	$Q(t + 1)$	J	K'
0	0	0	X
0	1	1	X
1	0	X	0
1	1	X	1

6-19.

SD	R	$Q(t + 1)$
0	0	$Q(t)$
0	1	0
1	0	1
1	1	1

$Q(t)$	$Q(t + 1)$	SD	R
0	0	0	X
0	1	1	X
1	0	0	1
1	1	X	0
		1	X

$\}$ either

6-20. (a) $TA = A + B'x$; $TB = A + BC'x + BCx' + B'C'x'$;
        $TC = Ax + Cx + A'B'C'x'$

(b) $SA = A'B'x$; $RA = A$; $SB = A + C'x'$; $RB = BC'x + Cx'$;
$SC = A'B'x' + Ax$; $RC = A'x$

(c) $JA = B'x$, $KA = 1$; $JB = A + C'x'$, $KB = C'x + Cx'$;
$JC = A'B'x' + Ax$, $KC = x$; $y = A'x$

6-21. $(A = 2^3, B = 2^2, C = 2^1, D = 2^0)$; $TA = (D + C + B)x$;
$TB = (D + C)x$; $TC = Dx$; $TD = 0$.

6-22. $JA = x$, $KA = x'$; $JB = Ax'$, $KB = 1$; $JC = Bx + Ax$, $KC = Bx'$.

6-23. $JQ_8 = Q_1Q_2Q_4$ $JQ_4 = Q_1Q_2$ $JQ_2 = Q_8'Q_1$ $JQ_1 = 1$
$KQ_8 = Q_1$ $KQ_4 = Q_1Q_2$ $KQ_2 = Q_1$ $KQ_1 = 1$

6-24. $\begin{bmatrix} 2 & 4 & 2 & 1 \\ A & B & C & D \end{bmatrix}$; $TA = BCD + A'B$; $TB = CD + A'B$; $TC = D + A'B$;
$TD = 1$.

6-25. (a) $JA = B$, $KA = 1$; $JB = A'$, $KB = 1$

(b) $JA = BC$, $JB = C$, $JC = A'$
$KA = 1$, $KB = C$, $KC = 1$

(c) $JA = BC$, $JB = C$, $JC = B' + A'$
$KA = B$, $KB = A + C$, $KC = 1$

6-26. $SA = BC'$ $SB = B'C$ $SC = B'$

$RA = BC$ $RB = AB$ $RC = B$

6-27. $TA = A \oplus B$; $TB = B \oplus C$; $TC = AC + A'B'C'$

6-28. $JA = B'$ $JB = A + C$ $JC = A'B$
$KA = 1$ $KB = 1$ $KC = 1$

6-29. $DA = A'B'C + ACD + AC'D'$ $DC = B$
$DB = A'C + CD' + A'B$ $DD = D'$

6-31. $JA = yC + xy$ $JB = xAC$ $JC = x'B + yAB'$
$KA = x' + y'B'$ $KB = A'C + x'C + yC'$ $KC = A'B' + xB + y'B'$

6-32. (a) $A(t + 1) = AB'C'x' + A'BC'x + A'BCx + AB'C'x + AB'Cx$.
$B(t + 1) = A'BC'x' + A'B'Cx$.
$C(t + 1) = A'B'Cx' + A'BC'x' + A'BCx' + AB'C'x' + AB'Cx'$.
$d(A, B, C, x) = \Sigma(0, 1, 12, 13, 14, 15)$ (don't-care terms).

Chapter 7

7-1. Use an external NAND gate.

7-2. (a) Change inverter associated with CP into a buffer gate, or (b) use flip-flops that trigger on the negative edge.

7-4. $A(t + 1) = AB' + Bx'$; $B(t + 1) = x$.

7-9. $A = 0010, 0001, 1000, 1100$; $Q = 1, 1, 1, 0$.

7-10. $D = x \oplus y \oplus Q; JQ = x'y; KQ = (x' + y)'$

7-13. 200 ns; 5 MHz.

7-14. Ten flip-flops will be complemented.

7-17. $1010 \to 1011 \to 0100$ $1110 \to 1111 \to 0000$
$1100 \to 1101 \longrightarrow$ Self-starting.

7-18. $000 \to 001 \to 010 \to 011 \to 100$
$101 \quad 110 \quad 111$ Not self-starting.

7-21. $JQ_1 = KQ_1 = 1.$
$JQ_2 = KQ_2 = Q_1 Q_8'.$
$JQ_4 = KQ_4 = Q_1 Q_2.$
$JQ_8 = Q_1 Q_2 Q_4; KQ_8 = Q_1.$

7-30. (a) Unused states (in decimal):   2   4   5   6 9 10 11 13
      Next state (in decimal):   9 10   2 11 4 13   5   6
     (b) $2 \to 9 \to 4 \to 8$ 8 is a valid state
        $10 \to 13 \to 6 \to 11 \to 5 \to 0$ 0 is a valid state

7-32. (a) 13, 32
     (b) 32, 768

7-35. (a) 16
     (b) 8, 16
     (c) 16
     (d) $16 + 255k$ where k is the number of 1's in the word to be stored

Chapter 8

8-3. A shift-right register with serial input x and shift control P.

8-5. (a) (1) $B \leftarrow A$; (2) $A \leftarrow B$; (3) $C \leftarrow D$; (4) $BUS \leftarrow B$
     (b) (1) 01000; (2) 10010; (3) 00110

8-7.

	operation	address MUX	data MUX	destination decoder
(a)	write	10	11	—
(b)	read	11	—	10

8-9. A mod-9 counter that counts the binary states from 0 through 8.

8-12. $S: A \leftarrow$ shr A, $B \leftarrow$ shr B, $B_n \leftarrow A_1$, $A_n \leftarrow A_1$.

8-14. PR forms the product of BR and AR by successive additions of the contents of BR a number of times equal to the number in AR. The multiplication starts when S becomes 1 and terminates with $D = 1$.

8-16. (a) 000000

(b) 011000 (24)

(c) 000011 (3)

(d) 100011 (-29)

(e) 001110 (14)

(f) 010001 (17)

(g) 101111 (-17)

(h) 000101 (5)

8-18. (1) (a) Overflow because sum is greater than 127

(b) $C_8 = 1$, $C_9 = 0$

(c) Sign is negative

(d) Overflow because $C_8 \oplus C_9 = 1$

(e) Overflow because of sign reversal

8-23. $(1 - 2^{-26}) \times 2^{255}$ and 2^{-256}.

8-24. $(10^5 - 1) \times 10^{99}$ and 10^{-95}.

8-25.

	coefficient	exponent
(a)	0 111111000000	1 000111
(b)	0 011111100000	1 000010
(c)	0 000111111000	1 000001

8-26. (a) $A \leftarrow A \oplus B$ with $B = 10110100$

(b) $A \leftarrow A \vee B$ with $B = 00100100$ or   11111101

8-27. $A \leftarrow A \wedge \overline{B}$.

8-28. (a) 8

(b) 16

(c) 65,536

(d) 8,388,607

8-31. $q_4 t_3$: $MAR \leftarrow PC$

$q_4 t_4$: $MBR \leftarrow M$, $PC \leftarrow PC + 1$

$q_4 t_5$: $R \leftarrow MBR$, $T \leftarrow 0$

Chapter 9

9-2.   Four selection lines for each.

9-4.   (a) 64×8 RAM

(b) 6

(c) 8

(d) 8 multiplexers of 2×1 each

9-7. (c)

s_1	s_0	Y_i
0	0	B_i'
0	1	B_i
1	0	1
1	1	0

9-8. $s_2 s_1 s_0 C_{in} = 0000\ \ 0001\ \ 0010\ \ \ 0011\ \ \ \ 0100\ \ \ 0101\ \ \ 0110\ \ \ 0111.$

$F = 0000\ \ 0001\ \ \ \ B\ \ \ \ \ B+1\ \ \ \ \ \bar{B}\ \ \ \ \bar{B}+1\ \ \ 1111\ \ \ 0000.$

9-9. (a) $F = B + \bar{A}$ B plus 1's complement of A
 (b) $F = B + \bar{A} + 1$ B plus 2's complement of A
 (c) $F = \overline{A + B} - 1$ 1's complement of $(A + B)$ minus one
 (d) $F = \overline{A + B}$ 1's complement of $(A + B)$
 (e) $F = \bar{A}$ 1's complement of A
 (f) $F = \bar{A} + 1$ 2's complement of A
 (g) $F = \bar{A} - 1$ 1's complement of A minus one
 (h) $F = \bar{A}$ 1's complement of A

9-10. $X_i = A_i;\ Y_i = s' B_i;\ C_{in} = s.$

9-11. $F = $ 2's complement of $(B - A)$ and a borrow occurs if $A < B$.

9-12. $X_i = A_i(s_1' + s_0);\ Y_i = B_i s_1' s_0' + B_i' s_1.$

9-13. $X_i = A_i(s_1' + s_0) + A_i' s_1 s_0';\ Y_i = B_i s_1 + B_i' s_1' s_0.$

9-16. Let $x = s_2 s_1' s_0',\ y = s_2 s_1 s_0'.$

$$X_i = x' A_i + A_i B_i + y B_i;\ Y_i = B_i s_0 + B_i' s_1 y';\ Z_i = s_2' C_i.$$

9-17. Same as Table 9-4 with the OR and AND selection variables interchanged.

9-18. (a) $E = 1$ if $F = $ all 1's
 (b) $C = 1$ if $A > B$
 (c) $A > B$ if $C = 1$ $A \leqslant B$ if $C = 0$
   $A \geqslant B$ if $C = 1$ or $E = 1$ $A = B$ if $E = 1$
   $A < B$ if $C = 0$ and $E = 0$ $A \neq B$ if $E = 0$

9-24. $R5 \leftarrow R1 + R2$ $R6 \leftarrow crc\ R6$
 $R5 \leftarrow crc\ R5$ $R5 \leftarrow R5 + R6$
 $R6 \leftarrow R3 + R4$ $R5 \leftarrow crc\ R5$

9-26. $JA_i = KA_i = B_i K_i' p_{10} + B_i' K_i p_{10};\ K_{i+1} = A_i' B_i + A_i' K_i + B_i K_i.$
 where K_i is input borrow and K_{i+1} is output borrow

9-27. $JA_i = B_i' p_{11} + p_{12} + B_i' p_{13};\ KA_i = p_{11} + B_i p_{12} + B_i' p_{13}.$

9-28. $JA_i = KA_i = E_i;\ E_{i+1} = E_i A_i';\ E_1 = p_{14}.$

Chapter 10

10-4. A negative zero will occur after the computation of $(-A) + (+B)$ provided $A = B$. This can be avoided by clearing A_s if $A = 0$ when $A \geqslant B$.

10-8. $JB_s = KB_s = y$; $JA_s = KA_s = z$; $JE = LC_{out}$; $KE = LC'_{out} + w$.

10-9. $DT_0 = q'_m T_0 + P_z T_3$; $DT_1 = q_m T_0$; $DT_2 = T_1 + P'_z T_3$; $DT_3 = T_2$.

10-12. (a) 0   Same as Table 10-2
        1    $A \leftarrow A + \bar{B} + 1$, $S \leftarrow C_n$, $E \leftarrow C_{n+1}$, go to 3
        2    $A \leftarrow A + B$, $S \leftarrow C_n$, $E \leftarrow C_{n+1}$
        3   If $(E = 1)$ then (go to 6)
        4   If $(S = 1)$ then (go to 7)
        5    $V \leftarrow 0$, go to 0
        6   If $(S = 1)$ then (go to 5)
        7    $V \leftarrow 1$, go to 0

10-13. A microinstruction with 26 zeros.

10-14. 1 $R1 \leftarrow R1$, $C \leftarrow 0$
      2   If $(S = 1)$ then (go to 4)
      3    $R1 \leftarrow \text{crc } R1$, go to 8
      4    $R1 \leftarrow \text{shl } R1$
      5    $R1 \leftarrow R1$
      6   If $(S = 1)$ then (go to 8)
      7    $R1 \leftarrow 0$
      8   Next routine starts here

10-19. $2t(1 + k)$.

10-20. $TG_1 = q_m + T'_0$; $TG_2 = T_1 + P_z T_3$.

10-21. 2's complement of k.

10-22. $(r^n - 1)(r^n - 1) < (r^{2n} - 1)$ for $r \geqslant 2$.

10-23. $JG_1 = q_s T_0 + S' T_2 + T_4 + T_6$; $KG_1 = 1$
       $JG_2 = q_a T_0 + T_1 + E' T_5$; $KG_2 = ST_2 + T_3 + T_7$
       $JG_3 = ST_2$; $KG_3 = ET_5 + T_7$

10-25. T_0: $x = 1$, if $(q_m = 1)$ then (go to T_1) else (go to T_0)
      T_1: $P \leftarrow 0$, go to T_2
      T_2:   If $(A = 0)$ then (go to T_0) else (go to T_3)
      T_3: $P \leftarrow P + B$, $A \leftarrow A - 1$, go to T_2

10-26. (b) $JG_1 = (x + z)T_0 + T_2$; $KG_1 = 1$
          $JG_2 = (y + z)T_0 + T_1$; $KG_2 = T_3$

Chapter 11

11-3. (a) CLE   (b) CLE
         SPA   SHL
         CME   overflow if $E \neq A_{16}$
         SHR